PENGUIN BOOKS
SAVAGE GRACE

Natalie Robins is the author of four books of poetry and has been the recipient of several American literary grants. She lives in New York City with her husband, *The New York Times* book critic Christopher Lehmann-Haupt, and their two children Rachel and Noah.

Steven M. L. Aronson was educated at Yale University and Christ Church, Oxford. A former book editor and publisher, he has contributed numerous articles, interviews and book reviews to leading American publications. He is the author of one other book, *Hype*. He lives in New York City.

SAVAGE GRACE

The Story of a Doomed Family

Natalie Robins and Steven M. L. Aronson

Penguin Books

Penguin Books Ltd, Harmondsworth, Middlesex, England
Viking Penguin Inc., 40 West 23rd Street, New York, New York 10010, U.S.A.
Penguin Books Australia Ltd, Ringwood, Victoria, Australia
Penguin Books Canada Limited, 2801 John Street, Markham, Ontario, Canada L3R 1B4
Penguin Books (N.Z.) Ltd, 182–190 Wairau Road, Auckland 10, New Zealand

First published in the U.S.A. by William Morrow 1985
First published in Great Britain by Victor Gollancz 1985
Published in Penguin Books 1986

Excerpt from *The Only Child* by Nell Dunn. Copyright © 1978 by
Jonathan Cape Ltd. Reprinted by permission of Curtis Brown Ltd
Excerpts from *The Merry Month of May* by James Jones.
Copyright © 1971 William Collins Ltd. Reprinted by permission
of William Collins
Selection reprinted from *I Knew a Phoenix, Sketches for an
Autobiography* by May Sarton, by permission of Peter Owen Ltd

Printed and bound in Great Britain by
Cox & Wyman Ltd, Reading

For Christopher, Rachel, Noah—
"My strength and song."

N.R.

For Katharine Johnson & Jesse Kornbluth,
Deborah Young & Charles Maclean—
in fond friendship.

S.M.L.A

CONTENTS

PART IV: RIKERS ISLAND

They were *the* perfect happy-American family: the one one hears about, and sees so often in the ad photos in the *New Yorker* and in all the commercial magazines, but which one so rarely meets in life. Certainly there was absolutely nothing to indicate there might be deeper darker strains to their lives they might be hiding.

James Jones, *The Merry Month of May*, 1971

I sometimes think that there is a malign force loose in the universe that is the social equivalent of cancer, and it's plastic. It infiltrates everything. It's metastasis. It gets into every single pore. . . .

Norman Mailer, *Harvard Magazine*, 1983

SAVAGE
GRACE

PART I

LONDON

1

THE
CRIME OF CRIMES

Friday, November 17, 1972, dawned hazy and cloudy, but by three o'clock the sun was shining with unaccustomed benevolence for London. The leaves in Cadogan Square had turned and were dropping in the gardens. All her life—and she was only fifty when she died, a little later that afternoon—Barbara Baekeland was partial to fall colors. Even in summer, when everyone would be wearing white, she persisted in dressing like an autumn leaf. The rust-colored skirts and bronze shoes she favored suited her beauty—the bonfire of red hair, the milkmaid skin. A friend had once said of her that she had the quality of intelligent flamboyance.

Whether in Boston, where she was born to a family of modest means called Daly; or Hollywood, where once upon a time she was given a screen test; or New York and Paris, where she created salons for herself; or such resorts as Long Island's East Hampton, Ansedonia on Italy's Argentario, and Cadaqués on Spain's Costa Brava, where she was forever taking houses in season and out; or, finally, in London, where she had acquired a penthouse duplex in Chelsea, Barbara Baekeland could be counted on to turn heads.

"London ends by giving one absolutely everything one asks," Henry James wrote in his preface to *The Golden Bowl*; the city was, in his opinion, "the most possible form of life."

"London with its six-times-breathed-over air seems such a dream," Barbara Baekeland wrote to a friend in New York that November Friday. "Had *Le Tout* London here last night. My *oeuvre* has had a great success—everybody loved what I've done to the flat."

The very first thing one saw on entering the apartment was the portrait of a beautiful boy. The subject was Barbara Baekland's son, Antony, who had sat for the fashionable portraitist Vidal-Quadras one afternoon in Paris, years before. Tony was twenty-six now, and something of a painter himself.

He also liked to write. In Paris, the novelist James Jones had taken an interest in his work, and now he was being encouraged by the poet Robert Graves. Graves was a neighbor on the island of Mallorca, from which Tony had come back to London with his mother in September.

The Baekelands had always had the freedom to travel at will. Tony's great-grandfather, Leo Hendrik Baekeland, had invented the first totally successful plastic, Bakelite—"the material of a thousand uses." Tony's father, Brooks Baekeland, liked to say, "Thanks to my grandfather, I have what James Clavell has called 'fuck-you money.' Therefore I need not please or seek to please—astonish, astound, dazzle, or be approved of by—anyone."

Brooks Baekeland had movie-star good looks. He also possessed what many of his peers considered to be one of the finest minds of his generation. A brilliant amateur land analyst, in the early 1960s he had conceived, planned, and executed a parachute jump into the Vilcabamba mountain fastness of Peru in search of a lost Inca city. He never found the city but his exploits filled most of an issue of *National Geographic*. Somebody had once described him as an intellectual Errol Flynn.

Tony's father was now living in France—with, everyone said, Tony's girlfriend.

At one o'clock on Friday, November 17—"Fridays are always suspect, don't you think?" she had once said—Barbara Baekeland called out goodbye to Tony, leaned down to stroke her Siamese cat, Worcester, affectionately called Mr. Wuss, and set out to keep a lunch date she had made at her party the night before with an old friend from Spain; Missy Harnden was also now living in London, in a rented house on nearby Chapel Street.

Barbara Baekeland arrived in a particularly extravagant mood and launched at once into a postmortem of her party. Missy Harnden's seventeen-year-old son Michael, whom everyone had always called Mishka, cooked the lunch—filet mignon wrapped in bacon, green beans, and a tossed salad—which he served with a Spanish red wine. They ate in the big kitchen-dining room, whose walls were covered with the organic black, blue, and green abstract paintings of Arshile Gorky, to whom the house's owner had once been married.

"Barbara's theme that day was Tony," Mishka Harnden recalls. "Her theme was persistently Tony—how marvelous he was, how talented. Everything was always absolutely rosy and happy—'Tony *adores* London, Tony's *mad* about the flat.'"

At three-thirty, Barbara Baekeland got up to leave, thanking the Harndens for the "marvelous lunch" and mentioning that Tony was cooking dinner for her that evening.

At approximately seven o'clock the telephone rang in the house on Chapel Street. Missy Harnden answered. It was the Chelsea Police Station inquiring as to the time of Barbara Baekeland's arrival and departure that afternoon. They would not say why they wanted this information; all they would say was that something had happened. But a few seconds later Missy Harnden heard herself being asked: "How well did you know the deceased?" She was too shocked to answer, and handed the phone to Mishka, who had just come into the room.

At the end of the conversation the police requested that they both come down to the station to answer a few additional questions. Missy Harnden could not bring herself to go, so Mishka went alone. "It was very clean, very sterile," he remembers. "A quite natty English police station."

Once there, he would find out what had happened.

DETECTIVE SUPERINTENDENT KENNETH BRETT, RETIRED *

I was called to the address of Antony Baekeland and his mother, but cannot remember how the call was made—by the ambulance service or other agency. On arrival I was told that a maid, believed to be Spanish, had run from the house because of a quarrel between Antony Baekeland and his mother. The flat was not disordered. I saw in the kitchen the body of Mrs. Baekeland. She was dressed in normal

* Brief biographical notes can be found on pages 463–473.

clothing—I seem to remember it was a dress. She was on her back. Very little blood was seen. There was a knife on an adjoining worktop or draining board. This was a kitchen knife and showed signs of blood.

There was a small wound visible in the victim's clothing in the region of the heart. I recollect that death was caused by a severed main artery. A doctor certified she was dead, and arrangements were made for the body to be removed to a mortuary after examination by a forensic officer. The only other sign of violence—which was discovered at the postmortem—was a bruise above the right ear, but this did not have any real significance as it could have been caused by the victim's fall to the ground.

Antony Baekeland was, on my arrival, in a bedroom, sitting on the bed, using the telephone to phone, I believe, a Chinese restaurant to order a meal. I cannot remember the exact conversation I had with him, but Antony Baekeland was intimating that he was not responsible for the crime. I have a vague recollection that he may have mentioned that his grandmother was responsible. He was completely unconcerned.

You know, he considered himself an artist, and we did find a rather large painting, said to have been done by him. It was the weirdest thing imaginable—we just couldn't make out what it was.

I seem to remember that his father was not called immediately as we had to discover his whereabouts. Mr. Baekeland came either the next day or even later—from France.

Antony Baekeland was taken to the Chelsea Police Station. He was interviewed, and much of what he said was incoherent, rambling. I cannot remember what his statement contained, except the opening sentence was so unusual that it has stuck in my mind. He said it all started when he was aged either three or five and he fell off his pogo stick.

PAMELA TURNER

I was the service tenant at 81 Cadogan Square, but I was not on the premises when he stabbed her. When I got home I saw the ambulance outside and I wondered what was going on. Then the ambulance men came down from the top floor and asked me if I knew Tony and I said I did. I used to pass the time of day with him or have a chat, although his mother was always very protective of him. And they said would I talk to him on the telephone while they got the police. And I rang him from my phone and had a long conversation with him and he told me how he had been out for lunch with his grandmother. Well, I knew *she* was in New York. He was quite calm, quite lucid, and chatted to me—he was always polite and nice, I never thought of him as a violent person—and in the meantime the ambulance men on their phone in the ambulance got the police. Tony had called for the ambulance himself. And then the police came and that was that.

Tony told me his grandmother had stabbed Barbara. I loved Barbara's mother, Mrs. Daly. I remember her as a dear little old lady quite happily going up all those six flights of stairs! She used to come here and take over, like the head of the family.

Whenever Barbara rang me from the States, she'd say, "Hello, this is Barbara of MGM." She told me that she worked in public relations for MGM, but I don't know whether she really did or not. She would ring occasionally, mainly to tell me she was coming to England and would I get milk, etc., in for her. I also looked after all her plants, merely because I am extremely fond of house plants, and in fact I still have a weeping fig of hers.

She was a very beautiful, flamboyant woman. I particularly remember a black gown she wore, a very low-necked black gown. She wore it with a huge diamond crucifix dangling from a chain. She was magnificent, and she went out a lot. I suppose the most terrible memory I have is of the plain wooden box being brought down the stairs by the policemen, and opening the main doors for them to pass through. I understand that the next day was her wedding anniversary.

The night of the stabbing, I got concerned about the cat—you know, Mr. Wuss. There was a policeman guarding the flat and I asked him if he had seen a cat. He told me, "There's no cat." But I knew Mr. Wuss had to be somewhere, so I went in and looked under the bed, and there he was! After the stabbing, Mr. Baekeland came to see about the belongings. I found him very businesslike and hard. He put all the contents of the flat into auction with Sotheby's. And I asked him, I said, "Well, what should we do about the cat?" And he said, "Oh, destroy it." Well, I gulped, and I asked if *I* could take the cat if I could find a home for it. And Mr. Wuss is still alive. When last I heard, he was leading a good life. Of course, Barbara was very wrong to bring him into the country as she did, ignoring quarantine rules.

ELIZABETH WEICKER FONDARAS
Poor Barbara. The last time I saw her was at an art opening in New
York and she had a look of old furs and feathers—like a Jean Rhys
character.

Letter from Barbara Baekeland to Sam Green, May 4, 1970

Read Jean Rhys's *Good Morning, Midnight*, which profoundly
depressed me. She is so much of my skin that I am alarmed—
like suddenly seeing oneself in a harsh unlovely light—all those
many flaws and her despair honed by that extraordinary sen-
sibility—I hope I am saved—

DR. W. LINDSAY JACOBS
I saw Antony Baekeland for the first time on October 30, 1972—
eighteen days before the crime—and afterwards I told his mother,
"Your son is going to kill you." She replied, "He's been murdering
me since he was born—whether for him or his father, I don't know.
I'm used to murder." "This isn't a metaphor," I told her. "This isn't
an analyst's game. I think you're at grave risk." And she said, "*I*
don't."

DAVID MEAD
When I heard Tony had killed his mother, I felt like I'd been *at* the
murder. The year before, out in East Hampton, Barbara all of a
sudden raised her voice at me—you know, just over nothing—and
Tony came flying in. He was absolutely furious, I couldn't believe
how mad he was. And then instantly it was between the two of *them*,
and I no longer mattered. And they started getting madder and madder at each other, and it got uglier and uglier, and finally the knife
point came. He got a knife. I managed to wrestle it out of his hand,
but you know what I'm saying—this was the dress rehearsal.

From a Psychiatric Report on Antony Baekeland Ordered by the British Courts, January 5, 1973

He is a well-built, physically healthy young man with an occasional marked stammer. He appeared normally anxious and

depressed for a man in his situation but denied feeling depressed or ever having contemplated suicide. He gave his account with some natural confusion about times and places. On the day of the offence he had a conversation on the telephone in which he heard some reference to his having fallen down a lift shaft; and later began to wonder if this had occurred. After a minor argument with his mother she started to write a letter. He could not read it but knew the meaning and this produced a degree of rage which he had never experienced before. She did not say or do anything to resist his assaults.

ROSEMARY RODD BALDWIN

Barbara wrote to me in Turkey just before he killed her and said, "Rosie, you have such a wonderful influence over Tony, a sort of Nini influence." Nini, of course, is Barbara's mother, Tony's grandmother. She said, "Will you come to London and live in the flat with him for the winter?" I got the letter on the Wednesday and I was making up my mind. On Thursday one of my daughters, Mandy, who'd had dinner with them the night before, sent me a telegram saying, "Mummy, be careful. Things are very difficult in Cadogan Square." And on Friday he killed her. So.

And I'll tell you the other thing. He had a little Pekingese he adored that got lost in the mountains somewhere in Italy when he was a child. He was a child for a long time with us, you see. And this dog got lost and they were desperate, and finally they found it. And after it died, years later, he kept its collar, like Jinty, my eldest daughter, did with *her* favorite dog. And Barbara took this collar and threw it out of the window into Cadogan Square, and that was what *I* understood was the thing that was the end.

Letter from Antony Baekeland to Cornelia Baekeland Hallowell, December 30, 1972

Dear Grandmother,

I just got your letter. I will try to explain as best I can what happened. You know I loved and still love and adore my mother more than anyone in the world. During the time preceding what happened a lot of rather strange things were happening. I think my mind was slightly wacky and I was very much under my mother's powerful influence. I felt as though she were controlling my mind. Anyway that afternoon my mother was out and I had a strange telephone call from a friend of ours who lives in Wales. She told me that I had fallen down an elevator shaft. I thought this rather strange and yet it had a profound effect on me. She asked me if she could come around for a drink that evening. I told her yes, that we would be glad to see her. Mummy came back a little later and told me that she was annoyed that I had asked her to come so early. I can't remember exactly what started the fight but it began in her bedroom. Then she went into the dining room where the maid was ironing and began to write something on a piece of paper. I can't remember what it was she wrote but it infuriated me and I tore it out of her hand and tore it up. Then she ran into the bedroom where I hit her, then she ran into the kitchen. I ran after her and stabbed her with the kitchen knife that was lying on the table. As I ran to call the ambulance I saw the maid just leaving the flat. The ambulance took hours to come and by the time it came my mother was dead. It was horrible—I held her hand and she would not look or speak to me. Then she died. The ambulance men arrived and I was taken away in a dreadful state. For several days I didn't know where I was. Past memories kept flooding into my mind and I felt that I was reenacting parts of my former life.

Nevertheless I feel better now and even feel that a great weight has been removed from my shoulders. An odd thing is that she told me that I would kill her this summer several times. I thought this the most unlikely thing in the world.

I wish I could remember what it was she wrote on that piece of paper.

Love,
Tony

HELEN ROLO

I remember the knives, I do remember the knives. I rented that apartment from Barbara Baekeland for a couple of weeks in 1972. It was within a few months of when she was killed. I didn't even know her particularly well. I thought she was attractive and charming and that she lived a very happy kind of life—I mean, to have an apartment in

New York and a house in Spain and also an apartment in London. A happy-from-the-outside-looking-in life, that is—because I remember when I called to discuss the details of renting the place she suddenly had to hang up. She said, "I'll call you back—I'm having a problem with my son."

It was a rather grisly apartment. You had to walk and walk and walk to get up there, you just went up vertically at a ninety-degree angle, up and up and up, at *least* four flights. I knew it wasn't an elevator apartment but I certainly hadn't expected to walk up *that* far. And when you finally *got* to the landing and opened the door, having walked all that way—opened the door to the apartment *gasping*— you really had to have a strong heart!—and a strong hand to carry your luggage—you walked in and collapsed when you saw that there was another bunch of steps to go up—it was a *duplex*!

And it was spooky because in the foyer, straight on in front of you, was a portrait of her son with a light on it. I don't know how old he was in the picture. He was fairly young, I'd say a teenager. I'd never met him, I'd never even seen him. But there was his portrait to greet me at the top of the steps inside the apartment.

Directly to the left of the foyer was a doorway to the kitchen. I remember there were pretty cut-crystal glasses—sort of little scotch-and-water glasses. And later of course, I remembered those knives. I had *used* those knives—long ones, short ones.

To the right of the foyer was a bedroom. It was the only bedroom that I can think of. It was the only room that seemed a little bit cozy. There was another room off the foyer and that was a room that I never even walked into except twice, I think. Once I walked in and said, Oh, I never want to go in there again, and then I think I went in there again to see whether I didn't want to go there again. I kept the door shut. That was the spookiest room of all. I assumed it was the dining room because there was a dining table. I don't know why but there was a lot of small tight grillwork around— it reminded me of what you might see in Morocco, but without the sun. It was ice-cold in there. There was a small cot, somewhere on the side. Maybe that's where the son slept. It was a *hard* room, that's the only way I can describe it.

Oh, and the color of it—oh, a horrible horrible . . . I'm looking at a bottle of Montclair mineral water with a dark blue top, a *mean* blue, and the whole room was a mean sinister blue, very gloomy and dark.

The living room was the whole top floor of the house. You put the light on and the first thing you saw was a decapitated bull's head with horns. There were a couple of Louis Quinze chairs of sorts, and a couple of floppy leather beanbags. The carpeting was brown, the room gave the impression of a lot of brown. And then there was a bench, a park bench, one of those old metal or steel benches from the seventeenth century—with a cold seat if you sat down on it. I'm beginning to visualize things that I'm sure weren't there, like a street lamp. I don't know, that just came into my mind. Because of the park bench, I guess. It might have *been* there, too.

It was a room without much natural light. The windows were slightly below waist-level, I guess because it was the top of the building. And not such a nice view of the gardens, either.

In a funny way it was a rather glamorous room. I gave a small cocktail party there, as I recall. I hardly ever used it—it wasn't a room you wanted to sit in.

But most of all I remember the knives. I wouldn't have remembered them particularly, except after I heard they'd been used for purposes other than those they were usually used for, I did remember. There was nothing unusual about any of the knives. I remember a bread knife—a long bread knife, with a wooden handle. There weren't that many knives. It was a very minimally outfitted kitchen, so certain things you remember, I guess.

They were knives I was *handling*, for Christ's sake! I used to cut lemon peel for martinis with them. The idea that I had used the knife or even touched the knife that had killed somebody made me sick. I've never even killed a little insect. I can't even do that very well. It was a terrifying awful feeling to think that I'd touched a *weapon*.

MIWA SVINKA-ZIELINSKI
A son killing a mother is Greek tragedy but this is much worse— much much worse. I think that *she* killed *him*.

SAMUEL PARKMAN SHAW
That's a real question—who killed who. It was a real dance, a minuet.

2

IN CUSTODY

Around five p.m. on Friday, November 17, Tony Baekeland was escorted unhandcuffed from 81 Cadogan Square by two police officers; it is not the custom in London to use handcuffs unless a person is violent when arrested.

He sat silent and self-absorbed as the unmarked car made its way through the narrow streets of Chelsea, one of London's most fashionable and historic districts. Richard III and Sir Thomas More once lived there, as did the writers Thomas Carlyle, George Eliot, and Oscar Wilde and the painters Turner, Sargent, and Whistler. Bounded on one side by the Thames, Chelsea is bordered on another by the smart shops of Sloane Street with which Barbara Baekeland had felt strong kinship, and by the boutiques, restaurants, and discotheques of the bohemian King's Road that had so fascinated her son.

Tony Baekeland walked through a side entrance into the modern-style Chelsea Police Station. He was told that he was being detained pending his first appearance in lower court on Monday morning, November 20. He was then taken to his cell. It contained, in addition to a toilet, a bench bed with a regulation foam mattress and a couple of blankets. "In view of the charge," a Scotland Yard official recollects, "he was watched closely to make sure he'd not harm himself."

The next day the London papers headlined the matricide. "The life of the wealthy American woman who had a villa in Spain and apartments in Paris and New York ended as she died screaming from the blows of a knife attacker in her penthouse near Buckingham Palace," the *Evening News* reported. "The 50-year-old—she looked much younger, said neighbours—was in the American film business," the story erroneously went on, "and her work as a film executive took her all over the world on locations of films about romance, adventure and murder." It was true that Barbara Baekeland had her flickering moment in Hollywood, making a screen test with Dana Andrews, but that had been a long time before; and she had indeed been at the center of a world of romance and adventure all her life, only never in the capacity of a film executive.

In New York, the *Daily News* bannered: "MOM IS SLAIN: NAB YANK SON." The *New York Times* headlined: "BRITISH CHARGE AMERICAN, 26, WITH SLAYING OF MOTHER."

In Barbara Baekeland's hometown, the *Boston Sunday Herald* quoted her Cadogan Square neighbors: "'They appeared to be wealthy globetrotters. They were both witty and charming. She was very attractive and looked about 30. She had a wardrobe full of expensive furs. . . . Ambulance men said the flat was in a mess and it was difficult to recognize her.'"

By now, reports of the murder were being circulated in all the many places the Baekelands had lived, and friends were rallying to console Barbara Baekeland's seventy-eight-year-old widowed mother, Nina Fraser Daly, in New York.

NINA DALY

Oh, Barbara was beautiful, I thought. She was noted as a beauty, you know. She had lovely hair. *I* used to have naturally curly hair when I was little, but no more. I'll be ninety in two days, the 27th of May. That's old, you know. Barbara's hair was an orangy red, and mine was just red but it wasn't that sharp red you see on redheads that stares you right in the face. And Tony was another little redhead.

Barbara was a natural beauty. She was so natural herself. And she loved people. Oh yes. She was so sweet and kind and loving. She was a wonderful daughter. I miss her so. I used to see her every day. She was a great companion. We were very close, very close.

She worshiped him. And he loved *her.* He loved her more than he loved anybody. His mummy. He loved me next, and then he loved his father next, after me. He loved his father but they weren't as close as Barbara and Tony or Tony and I. His father wasn't one of those fathers that goes gaga all the time, but he was good to him and gave him what he wanted and everything that he needed—a bicycle and things like that.

I worshiped Tony. He was a dear. He was always trying to do something for you. I lived nearby. I used to walk down the street with him. The happiness he gave me! We'd have lovely walks together, through the park. He loved nature. He could take the name of every bird that ever flew. He used to draw birds all the time.

She took him everywhere. Everywhere she went she took him. She never tried to get rid of him. I was always ready to take him. We both loved him the same. She was a good mother. She just had the one child. I wish she had had more children.

She was a good wife, too. I love her husband. Brooks. He was awfully kind to me. Just like a brother. He's six-four, and so good-looking. The grandfather invented the plastics, you know.

Barbara did all these paintings. Everything in the apartment here she did. She painted so well, and she painted quite a lot, too.

That's Cape Cod up there. We went there as children in my family. Always went to Cape Cod. There was a big thunderstorm coming up, and I walked over to where she was, and she said, "I'm painting that now, Mother." And I said, "Oh, yes, I see, dear." So I always loved that picture. There was a great big cloud just like that in the sky that day, you'd think it was coming down and sitting on top of your head.

She was left-handed, you know. She couldn't do anything with her right hand. She just started being left-handed and I didn't change her. I'd rather she be right-handed. I think it's so natural. I can't do anything with my left hand. It seems so awkward to see a lefty. I'd see Barbara turning the paper and writing with that left hand. I was afraid Tony was going to be, but he wasn't. We didn't try to change him, but he turned out to be a righty. Oh, Barbara worshiped him.

MICHAEL ALEXANDER

He told me that there was a bit of a struggle or something and that he got the knife into her—one single thing. He happened to do it in the wrong place, that's all—the heart. And then, he told me, he had sort of a problem about what the hell was he going to do about it, and *this* shocked me—he said he thought about putting it out of his mind!

Of course, his granny was always encouraging him to think it wasn't his fault. She didn't believe he could possibly have done such a thing. Because he was such a gentle boy, you know. Her blue-eyed boy.

ELIZABETH ARCHER BAEKELAND

Nini was just devastated. I used to go and see her after Barbara's death—until she became too difficult. She kept going on about Sylvie, how all this never would have happened if Brooks hadn't run off with "that bitch, that bitch, that damn bitch." On and on—about how first "that bitch" took Tony away and then she took Brooks.

BROOKS BAEKELAND

After years of resisting, and after wearing out four lawyers, starting with Louis Nizer, Barbara had finally agreed to give me my freedom. When Sylvie and I received the telephone call in the house I had built in Brittany telling us that Barbara was dead, we thought she had committed suicide, for it was November 18, 1972, our thirtieth wedding anniversary. "I give you your freedom and my life"—that would have been typically Barbara.

SYLVIE BAEKELAND SKIRA

When this happened, Brooks's cousin, Baekeland Roll, and his wife were staying with us. I always took the telephones because Brooks was too grand-ducal to ever answer the telephone, so I answered and it was the police in London who said, "We believe that Mrs. Baekeland has been killed." I came back to Brooks with this news and we, neither of us, believed it really. Brooks said, "She's again found a way to get at me." And then they called again, and it was true. This time they said, "We believe her son is involved." And I put down the telephone. I was frightened. I was so frightened I remember very well I fell into a sweat—you know, I smelled like a bad animal—it was something so abominable, and I rushed upstairs to the cousins.

It was a horrible thing for me, but for Brooks . . . he suffered the way you could not imagine. Brooks went out *hollering* in the garden. He was desperate. He was horrified that Barbara had died. That the boy had done it was something else.

We left Brittany and we went together to London. Brooks didn't have the heart to go and identify her, so it was Baekie Roll who did. Brooks never saw her body, but what his cousin saw was that Barbara had a black eye, and he told Brooks, and I think that hurt Brooks more than anything—that she would have had a black eye on top of everything. We stayed in a hotel that wouldn't be too conspicuous, because of the press and so on—Blake's Hotel, where it turned out anyway there were a lot of rock-and-roll stars staying at the same time. And Brooks kept seeing lawyers and police and so on because of the inquest. And afterwards, he had her cremated. She had been three weeks in the morgue.

Meanwhile Brooks had been given everything that was in her apartment by the police. Every piece of her mail he made *me* read, because he said it would hurt him too much to read it. And then there were the cassettes! Barbara had made a whole series of cassettes of a novel she was writing. The police said they were very damaging documents for the Baekeland family and he should take them. Can you imagine writing about going to bed with your son!

In Brittany we didn't have a cassette machine in the house, we had a record player, but we had a cassette machine in the car. Brooks played them in the car. For hours and hours! Yes. Until I broke down in front of him and he got earphones so he could listen to them without me having to listen.

GLORIA JONES

Jim and I were horrified. It was the worst thing we ever heard. We were in Paris and we went to London and tried to help. I called Scotland Yard and I said, "I think I'd like to talk to you." So these two marvelous policemen came, and we were staying at a wonderful hotel, not Claridge's, the other good one, the really good one—the Connaught. And there was a bar there—you know, all stocked—and they said, "We don't drink as a rule but, you know, all right," so we gave them a couple of drinks and they were thrilled with us and we all sat around and I said, "I think you ought to know that she probably aggravated Tony. Can I give some money for cigarettes for him? I want to help him, you know. Can you get him a lawyer?" They wouldn't let me see him. It was only the day after or two days after. They said they were doing everything.

I asked if I could bury her, you know, because I felt that Brooks wouldn't do anything about that. They said I couldn't. Brooks did have her cremated later. I think her mother has the ashes.

BARBARA CURTEIS

Jim Jones wrote a novel about the Baekelands, you know—*The Merry Month of May*. But he wrote it in 1970, before the denouement.

FRANCINE DU PLESSIX GRAY
Ethel de Croisset telephoned us that Tony had killed Barbara, and I felt shock and horror. And then a few days later I bumped into Peter Matthiessen at the Styrons' and he said to me—we said to each other—almost simultaneously we said—"Are you ever going to use it? Are you ever going to use it?" Use it in a book, you know. And we both said no. Peter said, "*I* can't do it, I don't think *you* can do it. I'd keep away from it." You know, there's only one title for the Baekeland story and it's already been used—*An American Tragedy*.

Cleve and I met them at a party in New York in the middle fifties and we made this passionate kind of instant friendship with this very flamboyant girl with red hair and a huge smile and all those very prominent big teeth. I always remember the mouth—my mother would say, "She's very pretty but she has too much gum." And here was this handsome millionaire that she was married to, Brooks Baekeland. And the first impression we got was that they were the ideal couple.

In the summer of 1960 we shared a house with them in Italy. Tony was just about to turn fourteen, and he was ideally beautiful— you know, glistening and angelic and with beautiful manners and a sweet smile. When we were a newly married couple in New York trying to have children, Cleve and I used to say to each other, "Wouldn't it be wonderful if our child looked like that!"

ROSE STYRON
We had a house in Ansedonia during the summer of 1960 and the Baekelands were neighbors. We had mutual friends, Gloria and Jim Jones, who had told us they were there, but they looked *us* up, I think. Well, they were very good-looking, very sociable, fairly snobbish—I would say Barbara particularly liked the grand Italian life.

I liked Tony. I really liked him a lot. He was a very lonely but self-sufficient boy, and I liked his gentleness with animals. I remember going up to his room a couple of times and he had all sorts of snakes and animals. I liked the fact that he seemed to want to hide from whatever else was going on in the family and keep to himself. The two or three times we were over there I just found myself gravitating to him. I guess I probably knew him better than I knew Brooks or Barbara, who I didn't have much connection with.

I remember Gloria talking to me a lot about Barbara. She was always telling me what the latest chapter was in the Baekeland saga. And one detail after another was so fantastic.

GLORIA JONES

After Barbara died, Muriel Murphy, this really great friend of all of
ours, sent me one of Barbara's Chanel dresses. Barbara really knew
how to dress, you know—she always had the real Chanel. I guess
Muriel had gotten the dress from Mrs. Daly. I was in Haiti, staying at
the Oloffson Hotel, and Muriel asked Bill Styron, who was on his
way there, to deliver this package to me. I opened it and put the dress
on and it was bloodstreaked all down the back. It was the kind of
dress you *would* wear to be stabbed in. Later I asked Muriel, "Why
did you send this dress to me?" And she said she hadn't noticed the
bloodstains. I was so freaked that I buried the dress, I actually dug a
hole in the ground out in the back of the hotel. That dress is buried
in voodoo country, in Haiti behind the Oloffson Hotel.

WILLIAM STYRON

I didn't know exactly what was in the damn package. I knew it was
some kind of garment, but I didn't have any idea that it had any
bloodstains, nor was I present when Gloria opened it. But I'm sure
Gloria is accurate.

I remember in Ansedonia that summer there was a lot of partying,
a lot of going out on boats, and Brooks had one of those Mercedes
sports cars, and there were a lot of drives in the Mercedes sports car
with Tony around. And Tony was an absolute young Adonis—if you
can be an Adonis at that age. I mean, he was a beautiful kid, he was
just charming, and I had no inkling certainly at that time of anything
potentially weird. I do think possibly I sensed a "Mother's darling
boy" relationship—not a terribly uncommon relationship with an
only child. But I thought he was terrific. Bright. A little withdrawn,
maybe. But he was just a figment to me, because I never really got to
know him outside of this vision of this beautiful lad—great swimmer
and that sort of thing. And a serious young man.

I had the sense of a small little family, a couple and their lonely
boy, who were sort of misplaced out of some Scott Fitzgerald novel.
Barbara and Brooks seemed a bit like Daisy and Tom Buchanan but
in a different era and somewhat fish out of water for that reason.

I remember exactly where I was when I learned about the murder.
I'm in the room right now, up here in Roxbury, Connecticut, where
I was that Sunday, whatever date it was. And I was just leafing
through the Sunday *Times*, as we all do, and there was a column of
print that said something like "Young man stabs mother in London"
and of course the names were right there, and it just shocked the hell

out of me. Had I known more about them, their connection, I probably would have been less astounded. But I knew nothing of any stirrings or rumblings psychologically.

God, it's a fascinating story, and the horror of that kid is classic Greek. I do think that the terrible quality of the whole story has got some resonance about our period in some curious way. It has some very large metaphorical meaning.

BRENDAN GILL

I was trying to remember when it was I first met Barbara and her husband and it was a night when Rose and Bill Styron were there and I think it was at Tom and Sarah Hunter Kelly's house in New York, on Seventy-first Street. I remember talking with Brooks about the fact that he had jumped into the Peruvian jungle. He was a true adventurer, the opposite of an adventuress. I was fascinated by his account, also because of my interest in his grandfather and Bakelite—that's just my kind of thing: inventions, making good in America. Brooks seemed tall and heroic because—well, it would be like Lindbergh. My definition of a hero is a man who tests himself by a series of ordeals, each more difficult than the last; he's not competing in the world at all, he's competing only against himself. And that's what it seemed to me Brooks was doing—testing himself.

Barbara was a very good-looking girl. I also liked her spirit. She was of an affirmative disposition. She always made you feel good, so that made her a wonderful hostess, of course. I think one of the reasons a great partygiver like Ben Sonnenberg liked her so much is that he liked women who were sunny, who were never down, who didn't need to be brought *up* to something, and he probably also admired her because he always admired women who were adventuresses—I mean, women who had succeeded—and she evidently had been one of those.

PICO HARNDEN

I was living around Europe at the time and I used to call my mother and my younger brother, Mishka, in London every two or three days to see how they were doing, and one day my mother said, "It's finally happened." And I said, "What happened?" And she said, "Barbara has been killed by Tony." And I—I started laughing. Because everybody knew it was only a matter of time before it happened and finally it did happen and, well, you know, it was so absurd it was almost funny. But my mother was a very religious person and she got very angry because I was laughing, but *she* was laughing, too, because even my mother, who was the least cynical person you could find, knew how the story was going to end. There was no other ending to the story.

ETHEL WOODWARD DE CROISSET
You know, there was a charming woman, Missy Harnden, a Russian—her husband was an architect who had built me a house in Spain—and after Barbara died she came to see me. She had been to this cocktail party on Cadogan Square the night before Barbara was assassinated. There was this crowd of people there and the boy was evidently looking in some strange bright-eyed way into space, and Missy thought, I must warn Barbara. She had this feeling, you see. And then she had not done it, and now she felt terribly badly. She was a very—could one say puritanical?—Russian. You know how Russians are when they're really good people—they're so straight. She was somebody that was so straight and so good, you know, and she felt she'd failed Barbara.

ELIZABETH WEICKER FONDARAS
I called Saul Steinberg when I heard—just to talk about Barbara to someone. It's so much easier in a small town when something like this happens. People gather in the street and you can rush out and talk about these things. In New York you can't do that. Saul spoke of Barbara's *whiteness*, her white skin, her Irish skin, white lovely skin, red hair—her fresh marvelous look.

JASPER JOHNS
She was beautiful.

ANDY WARHOL
Oh yeah, I remember her. But after I heard how she got killed I just wanted to forget her.

ROBERT BEVERLY HALE
I was simply having a cup of coffee in Chock Full o' Nuts and there it was in the evening *Post*. It was a great shock. I can't tell you how attractive Brooks and Barbara were and how they attracted people. I never met anybody more charming than that couple when they were organized and underway. Way back, of course.

WILLIAM THAYER

I was over in London painting Ambassador Annenberg when it happened and I saw it in the headlines and realized, My *God*, that's Tony Baekeland! I even thought of going and doing something, then I thought, Well, it's none of my business really—I mean, *she'd* been killed and there was nothing I could do, and *he'd* been hauled off to jail. He was a damn good artist, too—awfully good.

MICHEL NEGROPONTE

I bumped into him in the elevator about a year before—my parents lived in their building in New York—and he invited me up to their penthouse for a drink. He I guess at that point had just come back from Paris and was going to some art school in New York. I remember I just talked to him for about an hour in his room—he had this tiny little room. And I remember being astounded by his paintings, which were so incredibly bizarre. Some of them I think were even portraits of his mother—decapitated and with serpents sort of wrapped around her neck. And those were paintings that he had done *recently*. I think two or maybe even three were actually hanging in the living room. And then a few months after that I was going up in the elevator and I saw the headline in, you know, the *Daily News* or whatever it was—"Wealthy mom slain by . . ."—and, I don't know why, it just flashed—I had this strange feeling that it was the Baekelands. And then I looked down the page and it was, in fact. There was something about maybe just being in that elevator where I had run into Tony, especially because I couldn't forget those paintings. It seemed to me that the entire series of events that happened afterwards were really kind of mapped out *in* them.

AMBROSE GORDON

I read it here in the Austin, Texas, newspaper, where the name Baekeland was all garbled, but the ages and details checked out enough so that I was pretty sure it must be them, and then sometime later it was confirmed when Brooks wrote me about it. The newspaper account said they looked—that *she* looked extraordinarily young and that they looked more like—that they didn't look like mother and son so much as like . . . the newspaper certainly couldn't have used the word "lovers," but it at least planted that suggestion in my head.

RICHARD HARE

It was a Sunday morning, I was in East Hampton, and I usually get up at seven, seven-thirty, and walk to the village to get my *Times*.

And when I got back home I opened it up to read with my breakfast and I hadn't turned more than two pages when I saw this article datelined London. *Well*. I said to my wife, "Anne, you won't believe what I've just read in the paper!" Then the telephone rang and it was Liz Fondaras. She said, "Richard, have you read the *New York Times*?" I said, "Have I! I was just going to dial *you*." And of course we commiserated with each other. And five seconds after we hung up Barbara Hale called. I was just about to call *her*. She said, "Richard, can you believe it?" I said, "I can believe it. How about *you*?" She said, "Well, *I* certainly can believe it. It was bound to happen any minute!" Well anyhow, we *all* lived through *that*.

WILL DAVIS

What month was she killed? November? My own child had just been born and I can remember saying to my wife, "I can't shake this Baekeland thing." I mean, it was like something out of the *Oresteia*. The closest thing I ever experienced to it is the first time I saw morgue activity—autopsies and stuff. I was fine during them but when I got outside I couldn't get the formaldehyde out of my nostrils, I couldn't eat red meat for weeks.

Then, way after she was murdered, Brooks sent me this photograph of her in the mail. God, I'd kill that man if I saw him again, I'd absolutely take a brick and kill him in the street! It was a color photograph, and he had written on the back, "From Barbara the lion-hearted." Because that was what I used to call her—a lioness. Women never mind being called either lions or tigers. They don't want to be called armadillos or camels, but lions and tigers are fine.

BROOKS BAEKELAND

Barbara was a fine animal but quite untamable. Her two leading—and I think great—characteristics were pride and courage, both highly exaggerated and therefore dangerous. She was a born fighter and died in battle.

FRANCESCA DRAPER LINKE

I dreamt that I saw Barbara—she was in this incredible penthouse apartment somewhere and we were talking and it was like she was the one that was alive and Tony was the one that had been killed. It was very strange because it was almost like in the act of what had happened she had been released—she was happy, she was happier in this dream than I'd ever seen her in life.

RICHARD HARE
The memorial service in New York was at St. Vincent Ferrer, I think—on Sixty-sixth and Lexington. And *we* weren't invited. Anne and I weren't even told where it was, so we didn't go, unfortunately. It wasn't in the paper, it was all done by telephone and that was it.

PHYLLIS HARRIMAN MASON
As I went in, I saw Daphne Hellman with a black hat on. It was such an awful service. Everybody was looking around to see who was there and hobnobbing. I was, too. There was also some kind of service in London.

Letter from Brooks Baekeland to James and Gloria Jones, November 24, 1972

There will be a mass given by Barbara's friends who knew her well and remember *what was lovable and brave in her*, at St. Mary's, Cadogan Gardens, at 6:30 p.m. on November 30.

She would have been happy to know you had been there, too. I know that. I write for her—not for myself.

From the Last Will and Testament of Barbara Baekeland, April 21, 1972

I, BARBARA DALY BAEKELAND, of the City, County, and State of New York, give all of my property, real and personal, of every kind and wherever situated, to my trustee, hereinafter named, to invest and reinvest it and pay the net income therefrom to or for the benefit of my son, ANTONY, during his life.

Codicil to the Last Will and Testament of Barbara Baekeland, April 25, 1972

1. I give to my mother, NINA FRASER DALY, if she survives me, my Coromandel Screen.
2. I give to my mother-in-law, CORNELIA HALLOWELL, if she survives me, my yellow Eighteenth Century Clock.

3. Both of the articles referred to above are presently located in my apartment at 130 East 75th Street, New York City.

Tom Dillow

I helped Nini clear out the apartment, and she gave me Barbara's *Larousse Gastronomique*, the wonderful thirties edition—you know, the great big one with the color prints of the best kitchens of the time, those wonderful huge kitchens in France. We even cleared off the stuff from the terrace, the trees and all that. I was there for two or three days helping Nini go through all the stuff—Barbara's wild-animal rugs, those leopard toss pillows, the Audubon lithos, that eighteenth-century Mexican crucifix she had, the Louis Seize breakfast table . . . Then I called up Vito Giallo, the antiques dealer up the street, to come on over.

Sylvie Baekeland Skira

Brooks hasn't got a cushion from that apartment. Nothing. He made a point of not touching anything and letting Nini have it all because, you know, her first words when Barbara died had been, "Send me Barbara's jewels from London so that Sylvie doesn't wear them!" She thinks, poor little woman, that I'm terrible, that I was the wrecker of this fabulous trinity—God, mother, and son. It's normal—she can't think otherwise. Her daughter was her dream. *I* think Nini is very well-loved and very sweet. "Send Barbara's jewels so that Sylvie doesn't wear them!" You can imagine how I would have worn her jewels!

Nina Daly

All Barbara's things were expensive. She had all her clothes made, she hardly ever bought them. I guess most of them were made in Paris. She had a nice, a lovely dressmaker there. I had some things made in Paris, too, you know. People used to ask me where I got my suits and I'd say, "Well, I guess most of them were made in Paris." Tony liked clothes. Barbara bought him his clothes, but he had things made, too.

Barbara's clothes were all good-quality. And that's the thing that I care about, the quality of the material. The ones that I have, they're all good material. They last a long time. They last forever. They never really wear out.

Poor Grace Kelly. I feel terrible about her. I think it was a terrible shame what happened to her and her daughter—you know, the little one. You have to accept it and take it. Make the best of it. The best you can. You can't sit and weep over it. That doesn't get you anywhere. You never know what it all will be until it is yesterday.

3

AWAITING TRIAL

On Monday morning, November 20, 1972, Tony Baekeland appeared in lower court. There he was formally charged with the murder of his mother and remanded to Brixton Prison.

He was transported in a police van to a district so different from the London he knew that it might have been another country. The squalor of Brixton is alleviated only by a colorful market where anything can be purchased from exotic fruits and vegetables to such old cockney delicacies as jellied eels.

The van, turning down a narrow, two-lane road lined with soot-stained brick buildings, proceeded through an open gate. Ahead was a second gate, controlled from within Brixton Prison and opening onto a barbed-wire courtyard patrolled by guard dogs.

Tony Baekeland had traveled a great deal in his life, and over some grim frontiers, but never over one as forbidding as this. The four-story Victorian-style buildings that loomed in front of him looked like a cross between a factory and a low-income housing project.

The cell he was assigned had been built for single occupancy, but due to overcrowded conditions he would have to share it with two other inmates.

Letter from Antony Baekeland to James and Gloria Jones, Undated

115709 Baekeland   Her Majesty's Prison
                                                    Brixton
                                                    Jebb Ave.
                                                    London

Dear Jim and Gloria—

I am in prison at Brixton in London. You must by now have heard what happened. I feel much better for the rest I am having here and I feel a lot clearer in the nog. I've had a lot of visits from my London friends and this has cheered me up a great deal. I thought of you both a great deal all summer. I would like very much to hear from you—letters cheer one up as you can imagine. So much has happened in the last few years that I am having a little trouble sorting it all out. I have a great deal on my mind and need someone to talk to.

                                                    Yours with love,
                                                    Tony

TOBY ROSS

I went to visit him in Brixton just a couple of days after he killed his mother. What happened was my friend Catherine Guinness wanted to go and she didn't want to go alone, and we were both sort of friends of his from Spain, from Cadaqués, so we decided we'd go together, and it was very strange. I mean, he didn't seem to know he'd killed his mother. He asked Catherine how his mother was. He said something like "How is my mother? Is she well?" And Catherine and I just both went into instant shock. I figured out later that maybe he was aware of the fact that he'd stabbed her but he just wasn't sure whether he'd killed her or not.

Neither Catherine nor I knew really what to say to him. We were only there for about fifteen or twenty minutes, the legal limit. There was a meeting room that you came into, with little booths. It's not like that anymore—I know, because I was put in Brixton a year later myself—for having a passport that was out-of-date. The English are kind of funny, you know. I said to them, "Listen, I have dual nationality. I have two passports. I came in on my American one and it expired while I was here, but I have an English one." And they said, "Sort it out with the judge," and they threw me in Brixton for two days. The charge was "illegal immigrant."

When I was in there myself, the visiting room was entirely different from the way it was when I was there visiting Tony—you could actually sit at a little table and have physical contact with the person you were speaking to, you could touch them and you could kiss them hello. But when I saw Tony, there were two little booths with plate-glass windows and a little telephone you picked up and spoke through—just like in that old film *Birdman of Alcatraz*.

CATHERINE GUINNESS

I went to visit him because I felt sorry for him—he was a friend of mine and I liked him. I just sort of sat and we chatted about this and that in a booth and he was sweet as usual. He said he wanted a copy of Dante's *Inferno*, so I sent it to him. You see, when I knew him, I just felt he was one of the gentlest people I'd ever met. I met him in Cadaqués one Easter. I remember going for a walk with him and my father, and he was sort of talking about the soul and how he was trying to find out about his innermost depths—he felt his soul was sort of like an onion and you had to peel all the layers. You know that theory—there are various layers and you can get down if you really try, by sort of meditating and thinking.

KAREN RADKAI

Look at the photographs of him! Look at him, what he looks like. I took him along on a picnic. Oh, he made drawings! He was as companionable, as gentle as a lamb. These must have been done about 1966. I made them in Cadaqués.

I'll tell you something—my first impressions are always absolutely right. I mean, I very rarely fail. The first time I looked at Cadaqués, I said, "This reminds me of *Camino Real*"—you know, the Tennessee Williams play. There was an absolute aura of decadence about it, a kind of strange decadence, remote almost. There were some extraordinary characters walking around, I can tell you. They lived out Surrealism almost, do you know? I mean, Cadaqués had nothing whatever to do with anything else I've seen on the Mediterranean.

It had enormous beauty, really extraordinary beauty. Cap de Creus, this marvelous mountain, these huge gray rocks, the sea that glistened—I've never seen the sea glisten that way. But it was a Nordic sea—strange, you know. It wasn't that Mediterranean glistening, it was a dark sea. But there were big rocks, and mountains, and wonderful wonderful rows of fishermen's houses going up and up, and a wonderful golden church with a wonderful light coming through.

I really do take photographically what I feel, not what I intellectualize—do you know what I mean? What I see and what I feel, and this is what I felt.

Mishka Harnden

Do you know John and Dennis, the Meyer twins? They were friends of Tony's from Cadaqués—sort of flower children. They used to pose for Dalí a lot. And they were actors, sort of, too. Do you remember *Women in Love*, the Ken Russell film? There's a pair of twins in it that look very Indian—well, that's them. Anyway, they had this wild idea to take Tony out of Brixton and up to this farm they had in Wales or Scotland and just have him get far from the madding crowd—that kind of thing.

Phyllis Harriman Mason

I wrote to Tony in Brixton to say I was very saddened by his news—I made it very ambiguous. He wrote back and said he felt so much better now than he had before.

I spent that last summer with the two of them in Mallorca, June to September, and in spite of everything that went on, I had a nice summer. Robert Graves came to the house several times, and one night we went to dinner at his house. Afterwards Barbara and Tony had a big argument—Tony said Graves wasn't a great poet and Barbara said he was. But she also said, "The more I see of him, the more he gets to look like an old woman."

Letter from Barbara Baekeland to Elizabeth Weicker Fondaras, June 29, 1972

> Miramar
> Valldemosa
> Mallorca

. . . Averell Harriman's niece, Phyllis Mason, is staying with us. Last week Robert Graves came to lunch and saw Tony's poems. He wrote him a marvelous letter.

We are settling into this beautiful place. The house was designed by the Archduke Luis Salvador and is unique and distinguished if not very comfortable. Little by little I hope to make it more so, but we live here, at present, in an old-fashioned way. If there ever were a place where one could find peace and tranquillity, this is it.

ALASTAIR REID

That summer I watched in horrified fascination and that summer was tearing the tops off everything.

There's this enormous great semicircle of mountains where Barbara and Tony were living in Mallorca that's like an amphitheater. It's as though it invites the people who are there for the summer—or compels them—to give themselves up to the demands of the landscape and act in a certain manner. It's really the perfect setting for Mediterranean ritual drama.

In fact, the whole landscape of Mallorca has always reminded me of Greek tragedy, and that's what I said to Phyllis Mason, when I went down to swim with her, and it was then, when we were sitting after swimming, that she said that something terrible was really happening. I wrote her after Tony killed Barbara. She was the only person I did communicate with, because of that.

PHYLLIS HARRIMAN MASON

You'll laugh when I tell you this but after she died I went to a psychic to try to make contact with her, and during one session some woman actually materialized—some apparition—and she had on a flimsy sort of see-through gown, very décolleté and provocative, and I said, "That's Barbara!"

ETHEL WOODWARD DE CROISSET

Barbara had a violent Irish streak in her. She wanted everyone to do what she wanted. I mean, she was a redheaded dominating person. She wanted to move everyone about. When I thought about it, it seemed to me that what happened was the most ordinary termination of this wild life.

Tony wrote to me a lot from Brixton—letters which were so terribly sane. You know, people who are nervously upset or mentally upset can write with such clear writing, a very clear steady hand, and say such logical things.

Letter from Antony Baekeland to Gloria Jones, Undated

115709 Baekeland   H.M. Prison
                                                                       Brixton

Dear Gloria—

Thank you for your lovely letter. I am feeling a lot better now. It is very sweet of you to write. I also got a letter from Ethel which was very cheering. How exciting about Jim's new novel. Please give my best to Mrs. Chambers. Life here is very quiet. I get a lot of reading done and am getting my head together!

                                                         Yours as ever with love,
                                                         Tony

P.S. Very happy to hear about Kate's marriage. I remember her very well and send her my best. T.

From a Psychiatric Report on Antony Baekeland Ordered by the British Courts, January 5, 1973

On admission to prison Baekeland had been extremely disturbed for a time and when asked to write an account of the offence wrote and drew several pages of frankly psychotic content. However he improved fairly rapidly, and when I saw him he was quite cooperative and composed and said he felt much better than for many months.

When he was twenty-one or twenty-two his parents separated. Antony had since been living with his mother in Mallorca and England, and his father lives in Brittany with a woman of thirty-five whom Antony once regarded as his own girlfriend.

SYLVIE BAEKELAND SKIRA

Brooks and I were married on January 24, 1973—two months after Barbara died. But by then I had been living with him for five years and I had had it—yes. Because I was very conventional in those days and I was very humiliated to be living with someone whose wife I was not. I thought that during those years certainly a divorce could have been obtained, and it had not been obtained—for whatever intricate reasons there were between them. And the charm had gone, and I was ready to leave Brooks. Perhaps this is why he finally did something—he could feel that I had had it.

I married him because my heart really went out to him when she died, because I saw how he was suffering. You can't leave someone in that state. Everybody will tell you how, you know, I was trying to get all the Baekeland money. This is grotesque. When she died it was the most horrible moment of *my* life, it really was, because I understood that certain events will not allow you to live, even to exist. After I married Brooks I saw that instead of having a husband, I had a widower on my hands.

ADDIE HERDER
I ran into Brooks—it must have been early in February 1973. I came into this little brasserie on the Île Saint-Louis, and it was crowded as usual, there was no place to sit down. And there was Brooks, sitting at a table with a woman, and I didn't want to sit with him. But I was shepherding a black painter by the name of Beauford Delaney, a very good painter—a friend of Georgia O'Keeffe and Henry Miller and Jimmy Baldwin—who was having an opening later that day. Beauford was old so he sat down at Brooks's table. So then *I* had to! Brooks greeted me with all sorts of affection and said he wanted me to meet his wife, you know—which really upset me, because it was too *soon* somehow. Then he said to me, "That terrible boy—he killed that wonderful woman." And he went on in the same paragraph to tell this new wife how much he admired my work, my collages. Well, he had two pieces of mine, which *Barbara* had bought, many years ago. And after this he wrote inviting me to come visit them where they were living, somewhere in Brittany, and he described the house and how wonderful it was and he listed the people who were going to be there. This was, you know, just after his wife had died!

GLORIA JONES
Jim and I were getting ready to go to the opening of Beauford Delaney's art show and the doorbell rang and Brooks just walked in and we were very cold to him. He said that Tony had killed the woman he loved. He absolutely said that, quote unquote. We were stunned. I said, "Please don't talk to me," you know, and he left.

SYLVIE BAEKELAND SKIRA
I was *there*. What happened is Brooks and I lived in the same part of Paris as the Joneses—the Île Saint-Louis—and we were taking a walk on the *quais* and Gloria was at her window, on the quai d'Orléans. She stared at Brooks, who stared back at her, and she closed her

window. Nobody rang her bell. Brooks was not silly enough to go ring her bell. You see, everybody would like to have made a *grande geste*.

ROSEMARY RODD BALDWIN

When Barbara was killed, I borrowed everything you can imagine to get back to England. I was living in Turkey, and I got back as soon as I could. My daughter Mandy took me down to the prison. I'd never been to *that* one. Well, after all, I had married a man who was in jail in Turkey, so I knew about prisons, but that's another story altogether. So I went to see Tony and there he was. Suddenly he looked up and for a moment there was a flash of this old Tony from Ansedonia—of happy days.

Let me tell you, a more normal boy you never saw. Once we went sailing with my daughter Jinty, the one he loved so much, and my son-in-law, Hugo Money-Coutts, sailing from Porto Santo Stefano in a small boat called a Fifer, and on a small boat you really see people how they are. Tony had his guitar with him, and we stopped in the middle of the sea—in the middle of the Mediterranean near Tarranto—and he played all night and everybody was so happy. Tony behaved like an absolute angel, an absolute normal absolute angel.

Brixton was the first prison I'd ever been in where you have to talk to somebody behind glass, and we were given fifteen minutes and I found it terribly difficult to talk for fifteen minutes and I was getting desperate, and suddenly I said, "Tony, has your father been over to see you?" And he said, "Yes. Yes he has." Which wasn't true. And he brought a comb out of his pocket and he was bending the teeth of the comb, and I realized it had been a mistake to ask him that. So then I burst into tears. And he looked at me and I said, "Well, never mind, Tony, it'll soon be over. You'll see—you'll be out and you'll come and stay with me in Turkey."

RICHARD HARE

Nini said please write to the poor boy, his father won't go and see him, blah blah blah. This was before Brooks did go finally, I think. Anyhow, Anne felt sorry for him and wrote him a letter, a very careful letter. After all, we'd had some wonderful times at Barbara's. She had had a lot of exposure on two continents, you know, and she knew everyone attractive and interesting. Dalí came frequently with his puma cub or his pet tiger or baby leopard or whatever it was—he was apparently a friend from Cadaqués. And I remember meeting somebody called the Thane of Cawdor there, which was sort of amusing. He really *was* the Thane of Cawdor—as in Macbeth.

Letter from Anne Hare to Antony Baekeland, Undated

New York

Dear Tony,

This is an awfully difficult letter to write, and I do hope that you will understand if I do not express myself with much finesse. I loved your mother very much, but that feeling did not stop with her, it very definitely included *you*. I'm sure you are going through agonies of remorse so I won't dwell on that, only the positive things.

Richard and I want to keep in touch with you. That is the primary purpose of writing. Even with all the ugliness, we remember a marvelous, talented, sensitive, and understanding friend: You!

Richard, and hopefully me, will be in London in February. We would like to see *you*, if *you* would like to see *us*. You have many friends, dear Tony, who would like to help if it is possible. Could we be put on your lawyer's list of "Concerned Friends"? So that we know your whereabouts.

We want *another* Tony Baekeland drawing to hang near the beautiful one you gave us last Xmas!

With love,
Anne

Letter from Antony Baekeland to Richard and Anne Hare, January 17, 1973

Brixton

Dear Anne and Richard—

What a wonderfully consoling letter. For a while I didn't know whether I was coming or going but now I am feeling a lot better and people are taking good care of me. I feel more myself. I have a lot of reading to do and so I keep myself occupied in this and in writing letters. I would love to keep in touch with you and would very much like to see you both in February. I shall never forget all the kindness you showed us last winter. I have had a number of visits from friends and this has kept me very happy.

With love to you both,
Tony

ELIZABETH ARCHER BAEKELAND

I was on the high seas when he killed Barbara, sailing from New York to Cherbourg on the *France*. And when I got to Paris everybody had seen it in the papers and told me the good news—you know how people are. And within a few days I flew over to London and saw Tony. I was staying at the Carlton Towers and I remember I went down to the lobby and told the doorman to get me a taxi. He said, "Where are you going, madam?"—you know, they're all dressed in uniform there—and I said Brixton Prison, and he said to the cab driver, without batting an eyelash, "Brixton Prison."

So I went and I waited with everybody else waiting to see the prisoners. And then they called my name out and said booth number seven or whatever. I hadn't seen Tony in I guess ten years. He said immediately, "Oh thank you for coming, Aunt Liz." He was absolutely charming. I was sort of afraid to mention what had happened. I don't think we did mention it. It was all small talk—you know, "How have you been? What have you been doing? Have you been writing any poetry? Have you been doing any paintings?" And *he* was talking, too. Fifteen minutes I was with him. Then right after that he wrote me a letter and said, "Thank you for visiting me. I love you, Aunt Liz. You remind me of Mummy." And I thought, Wow! I'm next on the list! Sam Shaw, my lawyer, said, "Don't go to see him again, don't do anything, and *don't* answer the letter."

MIWA SVINKA-ZIELINSKI

I saw him in Brixton that January. He knew that he had killed his mother and I talked to him about that and he said, "I dream about her often. She comes to me in my dreams and says that she is not at all angry."

I met Tony and Barbara both in 1970 in East Hampton. When I

met him I didn't know that he was the son of Barbara. He looked very *sympathique* and I asked him whether he wrote poetry, because I said he looked just like a poet to me. He had some kind of a way about him, sort of something lyrical. So he was very pleased, and that's why he started to be very friendly with me. He told me that he was also a painter. Then he gave me a fish, a painting of his. I have it somewhere. I like this fish very much—it has very good color.

SAM GREEN

Barbara was always telling me—I mean, over and over again—how artistic Tony was. Well, he did have lots of esoteric façade, let's say. I met her on a cruise of the Greek Islands in 1969—Emily Staempfli, a mutual friend, had chartered this big yacht—and Barbara and I became, shall I say, best friends overnight. And right after the cruise I went to stay with her in Mallorca—which is when I met Tony. And right after that, I went to stay with my friend Cecil Beaton in England, at his country house. Cecil was dying to meet Barbara because I had such good stories to tell. They never did meet, but, based on what he had heard about Barbara and Tony from me, he wrote a novella that telescoped them into the future—he had the son kill the mother at the end!

Letter from Sam Green to Antony Baekeland, April 6, 1973

Fire Island, New York

Dear Tony,

It is difficult to write to someone who has a great deal of time on their hands, as you do, because there can be so many interpretations of what is said, if the words and phrases are dwelt upon for too long a time. It will be easier if you simply give this one a once-over (which is the spirit in which it is being written) and then discard it.

So you're in prison, awaiting trial. Yet another adventure for you—but this one is taking so long. You must be bored rigid. Since you are the one with all the time on your hands, how about a letter from you describing what it is like to be in prison? Do you have any friends among the inmates? Do they allow books to be sent to you? How about visitors—are you allowed any in the way of friends (not just lawyers)? If so I shall try to stop in and see you when I come to England. Which shouldn't be too far away in time.

In comparison with your confinement I have been even more compulsive in my activeness. I spent December and January in India and Ceylon and can hardly wait to return to the former.

I have a little house on the beach here to which *no one* comes. It is a cold gray windy rainy day, and I'm looking out over the water just *so* happy to be here and not at some chic Sunday brunch in N.Y.

Now, keep your spirits up and make an effort to write me—not so much your plans—because we don't know what will happen with your trial—but how things are. That would be interesting to me. I hope that Mr. Wuss is being looked after.

Love,
Sam

Letter from Antony Baekeland to Sam Green, April 15, 1973

Brixton

Dear Sam—

Your letter just came and I am very happy to hear from you at last—more happy than I can tell. I shall try to answer your questions. Yes, I am allowed visits and books. Mr. Wuss is in the country with friends or family of the Turners, who took care of the flat on Cadogan Square. I had a sweet note from Mrs. Turner that he is being well taken care of. I wish you would take him as I cannot have him here. The trip to the Far East sounds very exciting. I had a similar reaction to it. Yes it is *very* boring here but I try to be good and not to fret. I am quite lucky—I just had a visit yesterday from two close English friends. I had a visit recently from Muriel Murphy, and Emily Staempfli has sent me books three times. She is so sweet to think of me here. I haven't heard from my father in a dog's age although I have written many times. Your house on the beach sounds very romantic and beautiful. You ask me what it is like to be in prison—just *exactly* as one would imagine. It has become routine to me but at first it took a good while to get used to being shut up. Sam—I want to tell you something very important. Do you remember all the bad luck we had in Mallorca? Well I think it all came from me and I think I was jinxed. For me it was an exquisite torture to be in such a beautiful spot and among such kind people as the family that looked after Mummy and me—Maria and Sebastian—and to be unable to enjoy the beauty or reach out to them. I do so wish we could all be together again. I spend most of my time fighting evil in myself—I have a bloody mind, Sam, and I don't know what to do about it but I fight it with everything I've got. Sam, another thing is that I have so much in my heart that to let it all out at once would surely kill me. Those last days in Cadogan Square were terrible. I can't tell you exactly what happened but I completely lost my head. I miss Mummy very much. I hope my trial comes up soon. I want very much to go back to Mallorca. Perhaps you will come to visit me if I go there. I hope not to get a big sentence.

Love,
Tony

4

THE TRIAL

On the morning of June 6, 1973, Tony Baekeland was driven from Brixton Prison to Central Criminal Court, known to the general public as the Old Bailey—there finally to stand trial for the murder of his mother.

Built on the site of the notorious Newgate Prison and skirted on its east side by "Deadman's Walk," an open passage along which condemned men once took their final steps to keep their appointment with the hangman, the Old Bailey is virtually synonymous with English judicial history and drama. It is here that the infamous "Dr. Crippen" was sentenced to death for the murder of his wife. And it is here that Oscar Wilde sat in the dock and heard the judge sentence him to two years' hard labor, intoning: "That you Wilde have been the centre of a circle of extensive corruption of the most hideous kind among young men, it is . . . impossible to doubt." And it was here on this June morning that Tony Baekeland became a statistic: one of the 4,509 persons tried at the Old Bailey during the year 1973.

The trial of *Regina* v. *Antony Baekeland* officially opened the moment the High Court judge, who traditionally presides only at the most serious cases such as murder and offenses under the Official Secrets Act, was escorted into the courtroom by an alderman and a sheriff of the City of London, both in violet robes. The judge's robe was red—indeed, he is known as the "Red Judge"—and adorned with slate-colored silk trimmings. Over the robe he wore a black stole fastened with a wide, black belt; over the stole, slung across his right shoulder, he wore a scarlet band. His neckwear consisted of a starched wing collar and two plain white bands hanging down in front. On his head was the English judicial headdress—a wig, abbreviated from the reign of Charles II to one with a single vertical curl at the back and two short rows hanging down behind. In his hands he carried white gloves and a folded square of black silk known as the "Black Cap"—a relic from the days when it was placed on his wig as he passed the death sentence.

Since the trial of Tony Baekeland was being held during the summer months, according to ancient custom, sweet-smelling English garden flowers had been strewn on the bench and the ledge of the dock.

Three sharp knocks on the door of the judge's dais signaled the black-robed usher to open the court with the proclamation: "All persons who have anything to do before My Lords the Queen's Justices at the Central Criminal Court draw near and give your attendance. God Save the Queen."

The counsel representing the Crown wore a long silk gown, long-cuffed black tailcoat, and a waistcoat with flaps to the pockets. Representing the defendant was the barrister-writer John Mortimer, who would later create the character of the portly liberal barrister "Rumpole of the Bailey" for television; he was garbed in the traditional Tudor gown.

To the left of the barristers sat the wigged and gowned clerks of the court, whose function it was to swear in juries, take prisoners' pleas, and record verdicts.

As the trial was getting under way, Tony Baekeland, who had been sitting impassively in the accused's enclosure at the center of the courtroom, exclaimed, to no one in particular, "I would rather have buggered a prosecutor than killed a peacock in paradise!"

NEIL HARTLEY

I had been out of town working on a film and when I got back to London, at a dinner party John Mortimer, who was a friend of mine and my partner Tony Richardson's, said, "I'm representing this interesting case—this boy who killed his mother." And suddenly I was told that the papers had been full of it.

Barbara Baekeland had bought the apartment on Cadogan Square from me and a friend of mine, Jim Robertsen, and that was really my only association with her. I went back two or three times to parties there. She was pleasant enough. Just before she was killed, we talked—I think the *day* before—and she said she was having a party that night and she wanted me to come.

I must say I didn't like the way she had done up the place. I mean, I preferred it the way *I* had had it. I'd bought it from an Italian antiques dealer on the King's Road—he had done it up for himself and lived in it for a number of years, and he'd done a beautiful job, but *she* . . . I mean, it had a very deep stairwell from the floor below up to a kind of studio room which was the living room, and the stairs had a lovely banister, been there for a *long* time, and she took it all out. I don't know how people escaped without killing themselves going up and down those stairs! Things like that I thought were odd, but, you know, women have their own taste.

After her death I was contacted by her husband to see if I was interested in buying the apartment back, which I thought was a real creepy idea. He showed up in London while the son was being held in prison.

BROOKS BAEKELAND

Barbara's murder by her own son was a kind of grotesque, inartistic accident. She should not have died the way she did. It was not so much her kind of death as his kind of . . . She had a kind of greatness—no, a real greatness—of heart, and her murder was illustrative not of her but of that *crapule*, her son. That she had partly made him into a *crapule* is also true. But he was also my son, and I had fought against that in him all his life and failed. I would give anything to have been able to help him. I never could.

Even as a small child he was aberrant. And then as he was entering puberty it became clear—finally—that he was not only homosexual but a practicing one. That was a terrible shock to his mother, who fought against it with him, ferociously. She may even have died in one of their fights over this. She simply could never accept it, try though she did—gallantly, desperately, despairingly—in their last disorganized years together.

Sam Green

Barbara just thought Tony was the Messiah and the greatest child that ever was. Nobody was good enough for Tony. She would rent castles in Italy or Spain or wherever and invite important nobility—shall we say specifically the daughters of important nobility. Later on she would invite older girls, hoping that the inevitable would happen. What I mean is she would set Tony up. She tried it time after time and it just didn't work. Finally she got a little more desperate and aggressive about it and when Tony himself finally invited a girl to Cadaqués for a holiday—she was from Paris and a few years older than he was—Barbara practically instructed her to seduce him. Now this is the part of the story that really intrigued Cecil Beaton. In that novella he wrote, he gave Barbara the name "Emily," Tony the name "Jonathan," and "Dolores," I guess, represented Sylvie. Thank God it never got published! Cecil was a photographer basically, but when he wrote he always settled for the most superficial frame around the picture. He revealed incredible tawdriness in his prose. But I hasten to his defense: He never displayed it elsewhere!

From an Untitled Novella Believed to Be by Cecil Beaton, Unpublished

Emily continued to feed her son with young ladies. One day she got hold of a girl who was pretty much of a tart. I guess she wasn't, of course, a whore picked up from the street, but she was a well-known, loose young woman around Paris named Dolores. Emily invited this Dolores down to the house in Portofino which she and her husband had rented, thinking that she'd make things easy for Jonathan. Well, playing a role that most mothers don't—I mean it was very odd for her to produce a tart in order that her son should be initiated into the rites of love—Emily had a well-deserved disaster dumped on her. The result is Emily is left alone—with the son who is also alone.

This all happened in Portofino, which, as you know, is quite a tight community, and the arrival of a tart was remarked upon by all those gossips. So you can imagine the excitement when Dolores, who was asked as a set-up for Jonathan's entertainment and satisfaction, succeeded in seducing his father.

BARBARA CURTEIS

When Tony was twenty-one or twenty-two he said to me, "You know, I'm still a virgin." And a couple of months later he met Sylvie. She was one of the groupies in Cadaqués—French, hippyish. And Tony said to me—this is so sad and moving in light of what happened later—he said, "Sex between men and women—people talk about it and make such a big hooha about it and they say it's so complicated and everything, but when you meet the right girl everything just falls into place." Sylvie was his first girlfriend, you see. He brought her to meet Barbara and Brooks in Paris—brought her home like a kitten bringing its first killed mouse, and laid it at their feet.

That Christmas they rented Emily Staempfli's house in Cadaqués—Barbara, Brooks, Barbara's mother, Mrs. Daly, and Tony and Sylvie. An *in principle* happy Christmas: Mammy, Pappy, Granny, the Only Child, and the Only Child's Girlfriend.

But Sylvie took another look at Brooks and said, you know, "There's more money in it for me if I go with the father than if I go with the son."

SYLVIE BAEKELAND SKIRA

I think that that's a good story. People say I caught the Baekelands. The Baekelands do their own catching, very easily—believe me.

You know, I'm not in the least prudish, and if I had had an affair with the son and then with the father, I would say so. It wouldn't bother me in the least to say so.

I met the son first—in Cadaqués, in the summer of '67. He was six years younger than I was. He had that pretty complexion of his mother's. He didn't have that sort of mad face that he had afterwards, of which I only saw photographs. He was soft-spoken, very bright, very gentle. Affectionate. I don't mean toward me, but toward his dog—he had the most charming relationship with the little dog, who he called Digby. "Mr. Digby, will you be good?" Very sweet.

I was going through my first divorce, and Tony and I became great friends. *Not* the way people say—that there was a love affair. It's so absurd—because Tony was a homosexual from the day he was born, I think. But a lot of homosexual men like women—as a companion, to talk to and so forth. We were like brother and sister in a way. Of course, later, when I went away with his father, he resented me terribly.

From a Psychiatric Report on Antony Baekeland Ordered by the British Courts, January 5, 1973

> He attached special importance to certain emotions and incidents, emphasizing especially that he was devoted to both parents and that they continued devoted to one another, that their separation had disturbed his peace of mind. He wept when describing this.

ELIZABETH ARCHER BAEKELAND

Before they separated, Barbara told Brooks, "You know, I could get Tony over his homosexuality if I just took him to bed," and Brooks said, "Don't you dare do that, Barbara!" Fred, my ex-husband, Brooks's brother, told me that Brooks told *him* that—now this is brothers!

ELEANOR WARD

It comes back to me now—the very clear clear clear tone—that she did tell me that she slept with him, because I lived on the next street and I remember leaving her apartment on Seventy-fifth and walking down Lexington and walking back to Seventy-fourth in a state of shock, you know—that anyone could do that to their son.

WILLIE MORRIS

I always heard that the mother and the son had slept together. That's what everyone told me. I had no way of knowing whether it was true but it was certainly the talk of the East Hampton set.

TOM DILLOW

Barbara told me that it happened in that house they had in Mallorca, this archduke's palace, but then, a lot of stuff happened in that house. I mean, it was a real spooky place—huge, no electricity, that kind of stuff. She didn't give me any details. Oh no. Not Barbara. Barbara was a lady.

SYLVIE BAEKELAND SKIRA

I can believe that she would do *anything*—including that. I can't believe that *he* would, that's all. There might be something in a woman where she wants to save her child to a point that is beyond credibility, but then the child remains a boy, a homosexual boy, and I can't imagine that he would have found this in any way physically possible.

ALAN HARRINGTON

I was quoted in *Newsweek* magazine about something, I can't remember what, therapeutic techniques, I think, and Barbara called me up and said she wanted desperately to talk to me, and she told me that she had slept with Tony. I said to her I didn't think it was such a bad thing, to remove guilt, but now that I think of it, there wasn't any expressed.

BARBARA HALE

Sons and lovers—nobody knows the difference anymore.

IRVING SABO

Barbara Baekeland was in a writing class I took at the New School in New York in the early seventies with Anatole Broyard. Well, I can only say, she was a presence. She only came a few times when I was there, and I went to dinner with her a couple of times after class. The first time, we went to Bradley's, on University Place—there were about ten of us—and she just thought it was all so marvelous. We all went Dutch on those occasions, and she just thought this was great. And a week or two later, she read some of her writing in class, her ongoing novel, which dealt with a mother-son incest, as I recall. Well, it was vivid. She was, I think, a good writer. And after that class, some of us were going uptown on the East Side and she invited four or five of us who were in my car to stop up for a drink.

That was a memorable occasion. She had a collection of antiques the likes of which you don't get from any ordinary dealer. She had a lacquered Japanese highboy which was an extraordinary piece—it's very vivid to me because I've designed furniture in my time. It was top museum quality. And everything in the apartment was on that scale, it just reeked of great wealth. She offered some bourbon and I like good bourbon, and I asked for some ice and she said, "Oh, you won't need ice for this. This was made for me, it's a private batch." Well, there *are* distilleries that make special blends for special customers. It's like having a private railroad car these days. Anyway, it was extraordinary bourbon, real sipping stuff. No ice needed.

The living room was full of photographs of a very beautiful young man, I would say in his early twenties. She had taken, I believe, a lot of the photographs. What struck me was the way the camera just dwelled on the beauty of this young man. Now this may be hindsight, but they were not the sort of pictures a mother would normally take of a son. After I saw those photographs, I felt that her novel was autobiographical.

ETHEL WOODWARD DE CROISSET
I thought the story of sleeping with Tony was perfectly touching, because I think that was a dream of hers, you know—that somebody could make him whole. I think subconsciously she thought that the reason she had lost Brooks was because her son was a homosexual, you see.

BROOKS BAEKELAND
The incest thing. I don't know. If they had not been taking drugs, I would say, unhesitatingly, *no*. I would say it was a *boutade*—a caprice—that came out of Barbara's taste for the outrageous. *Pour épater les bourgeois*—you know? But I know nothing about the drugged state. So who knows? I know he loved his mother.

He loved his mother more than he loved me, but he loved me, too. And he respected me. I was, in a way, his alter ego. He held to me as an exhausted man does to a rock—barnacled and harsh though I was. But I really did love his mother, you see, and I could never forgive him for killing her.

From a Psychiatric Report on Antony Baekeland Ordered by the British Courts, January 5, 1973

His great improvement in prison may be due to relief from the great strain of his relationship with his mother. He requires further medical treatment but the prognosis for his leading an ineffectual but socially acceptable life under medical supervision is probably better than for some time. This treatment could well be provided in the U.S.A.

There appear to be two possibilities—to ask the court to make a deportation order and give a short sentence of imprisonment. He is not really medically unsuitable for imprisonment. But I think it would be better to make a Section 65 hospital order to

Broadmoor Special Hospital. He would be very soon ready for discharge and his transfer to medical care in the U.S.A. could be arranged fairly simply. In either case he would be likely to spend about a year in England and better in Broadmoor than prison.

JOHN MORTIMER

What I tried to do at the trial was get the judge to send him straight back to America. The boy was very nice. I mean, I found him very gentle and calm and nice. But off he went.

Letter from Antony Baekeland to Sam Green, June 8, 1973

Dear Sam,

I finally had a trial two days ago and was found guilty of manslaughter under diminished responsibility and am being sent to Broadmoor until I am well. Are you planning any trips? The one to India sounded fascinating. When I get out I hope to get a house in Mallorca.

Love,
Tony

Letter from Dr. E. L. Udwin to Cornelia Baekeland Hallowell, June 19, 1973

Broadmoor Special Hospital
Crowthorne, Berks.

. . . Your grandson, Antony Baekeland, will, of course, require very lengthy treatment—this is only to be expected. He gets what medication his treatment requires. He is, of course, on no habit-forming drugs. He has not to associate with people any worse than himself.

From "Dreams and Realities," a Lecture Delivered at the Johns Hopkins University by Leo Hendrik Baekeland, October 23, 1931

Dr. Charles H. Mayo in a recent address stated: "Every other hospital bed in the United States is now occupied by the mentally afflicted, insane, idiotic, feeble-minded, and senile. In addition, there is an enormous number of people almost fit for the asylum."

What is the outlook for the next generations? Is it not time to put less pride in the increasing number of our populations, and to look more into the matter of quality? It is quite right that we should try to restrain the immigration of undesirables. But shall we continue forever to encourage the promiscuous breeding of the unfit, degenerates, criminals, and the insane, while keeping on ignoring the biological facts of heredity? If so, more unemployables, more hospitals, lunatic asylums, poorhouses, and prisons.

In the past, raw Nature left to act by herself seemed more merciful than our present civilization. By exercising her rigors, she improved the race through the elimination of the unfit and by favoring the intelligent, the strong, and the healthy.

The Bible tells us that the fall of Adam and Eve started after they had eaten the fruit of the tree of Knowledge. Whatever that may mean, I believe that ignorance—ignorance of scientific facts—is the real "original sin," the sin that has been and still is today the principal cause of our sorrows and of the martyrdom of man.

PART II
BROADMOOR

1

THE MATERIAL OF A THOUSAND USES

On June 6, 1973, Tony Baekeland was transferred from the city of London to the small, picturesque village of Crowthorne in the Berkshire countryside. The narrow lanes were ablaze with wildflowers and lush with ferns, the village gardens an iridescent display of irises, peonies, and petunias. The large wooden sign reading "BROADMOOR SPECIAL HOSPITAL—NO THROUGH ROAD" struck an inharmonious note.

"The excellent road invited us to speed on and yet the sensation of loveliness was so predominant that we preferred to stop frequently to better enjoy the charmingly reposeful landscape," Tony Baekeland's great-grandfather had written of this same countryside sixty-six years earlier, in a privately printed volume.

Tony Baekeland would not have the same opportunity to linger that his celebrated ancestor had had. He was driven up a winding road past a cluster of white cottages to the place where he would be detained indefinitely, "at her Majesty's pleasure."

The red-brick Victorian institution called Broadmoor Special Hospital was built in 1863 as Broadmoor Criminal Lunatic Asylum. It is surrounded by a wall of uneven height that weaves snakelike through open fields. With its pink-blossomed trees that line the road in front of the main buildings and its rows of daffodils hugging the walls, Broadmoor looks like a friendly New England college campus. But its blue-uniformed nurses look more like guards and in fact belong to the Prison Officers Association; and all staff members are required to sign the Official Secrets Act. Patients' mail is routinely censored, and occasionally even books are withheld on the grounds that they are "bad influences."

"At Broadmoor, security is the first consideration," a staff member says. "We are always concerned with the escape and welfare of our patients, since we're dealing with very violent and dangerous persons here."

Of the approximately 750 patients at Broadmoor, many have committed "heinous, headline crimes"; more than a quarter have committed homicide or attempted murder. There are also patients who have committed no crime but who are mentally ill. There are over twenty attempted suicides a year, and it has been estimated that at any given time Broadmoor houses between 200 and 250 psychopaths. Indeed, it has been described as "the asylum of last resort."

A Dent of London clock sits above the impressive entrance gate through which Tony Baekeland was led that June 6 into a small courtyard. From there he was taken down a passageway to a door where he heard what would become a familiar sound to him: the jangle of the large metal keys carried by every Broadmoor attendant. The door was unlocked for him, then locked again.

Tony Baekeland was now in the main body of the hospital, which consisted of eight residential "blocks." In 1969, in an attempt to abolish prison terminology, the blocks were renamed "houses," Block A becoming Kent House; Block B, Cornwall House; Block C, Dorset House; and the other blocks becoming Essex, York, Somerset, Lancaster, and Norfolk.

From *A Family Motor Tour Through Europe,* Leo Hendrik Baekeland, Horseless Age Press, New York, 1907

The farther we went away from London the better became the roads. We were driving through a lovely, rolling country, with a smooth highway and green fields. Now and then we met a cheerful-looking cottage, its stony façade made lovelier by some creeping tea roses. Carpetlike lawns, tastefully laid-out gardens,

with very old trees, and everything cared for to perfection—all
this gave us a strong impression of pretty, rural England.

The main part of the house under the hospitable roof of
which we were going to stay had been built in Shakespeare's
time, in the quaint architecture of that day, and the modern
additions had been made in tolerable conformity with the original style.

The *ensemble*, with the surrounding gardens and lawns, made
a delightful specimen of an English country house.

The liberal supply of rain which makes the British climate so
humid is also the main reason why, in that country, it is possible to produce such well-kept lawns, better than are to be found
anywhere else, and which look more like immense green car-
pets.

There, the lawn extended to a sort of terrace, with a green
stairway, and reached out toward a very tastefully arranged rose
garden. Stately trees, several of them many centuries old, were
artistically grouped all over; giant yew trees next to imposing
cedars of the Lebanon; exotic-looking araucarias in proximity to
glossy-leaved hollies, the latter with trunks almost a foot in di-
ameter. A shady pathway lined by treelike rhododendrons led
toward an old church. Everything was harmony and every detail
gave evidence of centuries of good care and good taste. Yes, this
is undoubtedly the secret of these striking effects of English landscape gardening, which seem so hard to imitate successfully.

The place just described is merely a representative of hundreds of others, some larger, some smaller, but in all of them
the landscape gardening has been the result of a slow and well-
studied process, extending through many generations and carried out by a succession of owners, the children being able to
follow the improvements which their fathers planned.

DR. PHILIP GOGARTY

Inside the walls the fact is you'll find it's lovely green, with flower
beds that the patients take care of, and rather nice trees and all that
sort of thing. The hospital has forty acres of land, tennis courts, a
swimming pool, and football grounds, as well as gardens. It's not like
a prison where the inmates always see the walls. When you're inside
you can hardly see the walls, because they drop down in places.

They're somewhat higher in the areas where the patients are likely to try to make an escape.

Tony was very, very ill in the beginning—he had to be dressed and he had to be taken to the bathroom.

He idealized his mother, you know. He was very sorry and showed great remorse. He often said, "Oh, how a few moments of frenzy changed my life!" The fact is it wouldn't have changed his life, because his illness was just part of a whole picture. There was a deep sickness in the family, and a lack of discipline that too much money will often create.

He was fond of his father. He wrote him bad-tempered letters occasionally but then, within the week, he might turn around and write him an affectionate one. That's the way his illness was.

He had ideas of grandeur about who he was. He thought he was a great painter. He wasn't, but he wasn't bad. He told me that his great-grandfather was included in some encyclopedia.

From *Science* Magazine, November 1984

The toast of society as well as industry, Leo Hendrik Baekeland appeared on the cover of *Time* magazine in September 1924.

From *Time* Magazine, May 20, 1940

FATHER OF PLASTICS

This week Philadelphia's Franklin Institute presents one of its coveted gold medals to a man who is much less known to the public than are the changes his work has wrought in the many common things people use, from toothbrush handles, telephones and false gums, to airplane bodies. Even more than most scientists, the man is publicity-shy. He is Leo Hendrik Baekeland, inventor of Bakelite, "Father of Plastics."

Born in Flemish Belgium 76 years ago, young Leo became an ardent photographer. . . . He entered the University of Ghent as its youngest student, graduated in 1882 *summa cum laude*, promptly became an assistant professor of chemistry. . . . He emigrated to the U.S. and went to work for a photographic supply manufacturer. Then he started his own consulting practice, invented a quick-action photographic printing paper called Velox, organized Nepera Chemical Co. to manufacture it. George Eastman of Eastman Kodak bought him out.

Legend has it that Eastman paid Baekeland $1,000,000, several times the minimum sum on which the young inventor had set his mind. At all events, he found himself, at 35, rich enough to do what he pleased. He converted a stable in his backyard into a laboratory. He found that phenol (carbolic acid) and formaldehyde interacted to make a non-melting, non-dissolving solid like nothing in nature. This was Bakelite, foundation stone of the synthetic plastic industry. After forming General Bakelite Co. (later Bakelite Corp.) to exploit his discovery, Baekeland methodically listed 43 industries in which he thought it would be useful. Today it would be hard to find 43 in which it is not used.

From the *Bakelite Review,* a Periodical Digest of Bakelite Achievements Interesting to All Progressive Manufacturers and Merchants, Volume 7, Number 3 (Silver Anniversary Number, 1910–1935)

Millions of uses. . . . radios, clocks, bottle caps, baseball caps, phonograph records, lamps, fountain pens, pencils, washing machine parts, shaving brush handles, toilet seats, costume jewelry, artificial limbs, coffins, pipes, cigarette holders, saddles, overcoat and suit buttons, subway strap hangers, control devices for submarines, battleships and destroyers, automobile parts and gear wheels.

From *The Story of Bakelite,* John Kimberly Mumford, Robert L. Stillson Publishing Co., New York, 1924

Wherever wheels whirr, wherever women preen themselves in the glitter of electric lights, wherever a ship plows the sea or an airplane floats in the blue—wherever people are living, in the Twentieth Century sense of the word, there Bakelite will be found rendering its enduring service.

From *Fortune* Magazine, April 4, 1983

THE HALL OF FAME FOR U.S. BUSINESS LEADERSHIP

The Business Hall of Fame's "Roster of Past Laureates"—leaders whose achievements have endured—includes Andrew Carnegie, Pierre Samuel Du Pont, Thomas Alva Edison, Henry Ford, Benjamin Franklin, Edwin Herbert Land, Cyrus Hall McCormick, Andrew William Mellon, John Pierpont Morgan, John Davison Rockefeller, David Sarnoff, Alfred Pritchard Sloan, Jr., Cornelius Vanderbilt, George Washington, Thomas John Watson, Jr., Eli Whitney . . .

Elected this year to the Business Hall of Fame: Leo Hendrik Baekeland (1863–1944).

From *Selected Writings,* Leo Hendrik Baekeland, Bakelite Corporation, New York, 1944

How did I happen to strike such an interesting subject as that of the synthetic resins? I can readily answer that I did not strike it haphazardly; I looked for just such a subject for a number of years until I found it among the many lines of research which I undertook in my laboratory. And, between 1905 and 1909, I obtained an insoluble, infusible substance which we call oxybenzylmethyleneglycolanhydride now known as BAKELITE.

From the Private Diaries of Leo Hendrik Baekeland, March 8, 1909

After my lecture the boys were singing once in a while the B-A-K-E-L-I-T-E song which goes

> "B-A-K-E-L-I-T-E
> Stands for Bakelite
> Ten times better than graphite
> And what's the name
> Every photographer of the country knows
> Velox—Velox!"

When I went to the station I was escorted by the whole bunch—
about thirty—marching like soldiers and singing the Bakelite
song.

STEPHANE GROUEFF

In the atomic bomb, one of the most important problems, and probably the most difficult to solve—I think it's still one of the two or three
biggest atomic bomb production secrets in the world, which any foreign spy would have given anything to have—involved Bakelite.
When I was working on my book *The Manhattan Project* in the middle sixties, I had a sort of gentleman's agreement with the Atomic
Energy Commission that I would show them my manuscript because
I wasn't a scientist and the idea was that they would just correct all
the spelling and so forth but that I would keep my total freedom.
They sent me a brochure called "U.S. Atomic Energy Act" or something like that, and every paragraph began, "Anybody who knowingly
or unknowingly has or divulges or even discusses," and ended, "is
punishable by death or twenty years in prison." It was really a very
scary thing.

So I sent them my finished manuscript and then they called me
in, and one of the things they were particularly sensitive about was
anything having to do with Bakelite. They suggested that they would
be most unhappy if I published this information, that it wouldn't be
in the national interest and things like that.

So I took certain things about Bakelite out of the manuscript and
handed those pages over to the Atomic Energy Commission, and
they sealed this file in my presence and put all their stamps on it—
which I signed and they signed—and then they locked it up.

BROOKS BAEKELAND

Had my grandfather known what would evolve from plastics, he
would undoubtedly have withheld his invention—just as I think Einstein might have paused before publishing the 1905 paper on rela-
tivity. Leo Hendrik Baekeland epitomized hope for the human race.
He created himself and he saw no reason why the future could not be
created, too.

Letter from Leo Hendrik Baekeland to a Friend, January 14, 1934

If I had to live my life over again I would not devote it to develop new industrial processes: I would try to add my humble efforts to use Science to the betterment of the human race.

I despair of the helter-skelter methods of our vaunted homo sapiens, misguided by his ignorance and his politicians. If we continue our ways, there is every possibility that the human race may follow the road of former living races of animals whose fossils proclaim that they were not fit to continue. Religion, laws and morals is not enough. We need more. Science can help us.

BROOKS BAEKELAND

Had it only been possible for me to have been his son and not his grandson, we two could have taken the world by storm—yes, for we would have pursued the original dreams—dielectrics, textiles, resins, bonding powders for super-strong abrasives and aerodynamic components, molded hulls for boats and . . . but the list is endless. We would not have been able to foresee then the plastic-polluted world that has become such a monstrous joke, the blue plastic bucket and the plastic cups littering the insulted country roadsides—a world whose very destruction, by burning, only pollutes it more. LHB never dreamed of that. He would have recoiled.

Letter from Antony Baekeland to Miwa Svinka-Zielinski, October 4, 1973

Broadmoor

Dear Miwa—

I am sending you these dreams which I have had during the past few days at Broadmoor:

1. Einstein hides a stop sign from police.
2. I come back to my best friend [Jake Cooper], and we travel the world together. I see a fox eat a squirrel.
3. My grandmother Nina Daly embraces me during a party given by a fellow here and myself. I cut up gobbets of meat.
4. I can fly and go all over the place.
5. I dream I am a successful writer and poet.

I will continue to send you my dreams. There is so little to tell you *except* my dreams. I write them out in the middle of the night—there is no light so sometimes in the morning I have trouble deciphering them.

Love,
Tony

From "Dreams and Realities," a Lecture Delivered at the Johns Hopkins University by Leo Hendrik Baekeland, October 23, 1931

Youth has many advantages, such as daring, speed of action, and quickness of perception. Intelligence is inborn, and develops by practice and opportunity, knowledge comes quickly to the intelligent; but experience lingers, and is only acquired slowly through life and mistakes.

CÉLINE ROLL KARRAKER

Grandpapa taught us always to question everything. And he also taught us to recognize the fact that what is true today is not true tomorrow—in science as well as in other things. He loved children, especially as he grew older. He certainly made everything great fun for all of *us*. He would sometimes give out Bakelite things, like pencil cases, and very beautiful Bakelite jewelry that looked like amber. I can remember the gorgeous iridescent colors.

From English *House & Garden*, October 1981

Bakelite in the museum. Everyday objects such as radios and amplifiers, cigarette boxes and soap dishes all look as if they are made in precious tortoise shell, amber, marble, leather and sometimes even in gold. Yet they are all made of Bakelite, that forerunner of plastic which from the twenties to the fifties was all the rage on both sides of the Atlantic.

At the Boymans van Beuningen museum in Rotterdam an industrial product is once again the centre of attention. . . . Three main trends in its use can be identified: the Art Deco style (where it is usually made use of as imitation) in radios and clocks after the Great Paris Exhibition in 1925; in functionalism in objects coming from Germany and the Lowlands and in the "aerodynamic" style of America in the forties and in postwar Europe. In short, a fashion and the symbol of an era.

From the *Guardian*, June 16, 1983

Apart from the plastic tie-press that spits out your creased cravat as if it were a serpent on heat, the nicest thing about Patrick Cook's Bakelite Museum in London is that he does not take it terribly seriously.

"There is a humorous quality about so much of the Bakelite," he says, fingering a 1950s radio that opens up to reveal a portable vanity case with lights and mirror. "So much of it is a parody. The market in it is very strange. Sometimes I take stalls in the markets and sell things at rock-bottom prices to undercut those dealers who are trying to force the prices up.

"Some of the early Phillips radios go for thousands of pounds, if you can get them. They have almost all been collected out of England into Holland," he shook his head in disbelief. "The prices are very strange. When the Victoria and Albert Museum was setting up their Bakelite show, I let them have some of my early radios for about £30 each—a bargain. . . ."

He began hiring out some of his prize pieces to film and TV period shows like *Pennies from Heaven*, and his Bakelite Museum Society has a TV game called "Spot the Bakelite." They have a Bakelite picnic every other year, lectures, and evenings to swap items and marvel at the invention of Dr. Leo Baekeland.

From the *New York Times*, "Antiques View," Rita Reif, June 3, 1984

Bakelite. The name summons up a whole mystique of early plastics for Art Deco collectors, producing images of Cubist-styled 1930's jewelry, mock tortoise-shell compacts, ersatz ivory combs, butterscotch-toned desk accessories and what may well be the most glamorous plastics creations of the period—streamlined-styled radios.

There was then, and there is once again, magic in what we call Bakelite radios. When they were new almost a half-century ago, these radios brought into the homes of millions the adventures of Jack Armstrong, the problems of Helen Trent, the jokes of Jack Benny and the nightly news. Now, with nostalgia running high for such vintage wares, the public will have an opportunity to view the most comprehensive display ever mounted of these passports to the past in "The American Radio Show— Bakelite Radios of the 1930's and 1940's," an exhibition opening Wednesday. . . .

From the Private Diaries of Leo Hendrik Baekeland, October 13, 1909

How few people will realize how much detail had to be gone into before Bakelite was a commercial success!

From *A Biographical Profile of Leo Hendrik Baekeland*, Carl Kaufmann, Unpublished

Leo Hendrik Baekeland apprenticed in a shoe repair shop, with his father, who was illiterate. His mother also was from a poor family, but she had been a maid and had seen life of families on the other side of the poverty line. She had no interest in having her son grow into a world as impoverished and closed as her own (there was one other child in the family, Rachel, who remained in Belgium all her life) and she looked upon education as his passport.

From "Dreams and Realities," a Lecture Delivered at the Johns Hopkins University by Leo Hendrik Baekeland, October 23, 1931

My most important discovery at the university was that my senior professor of chemistry had a very attractive daughter. Hence, the usual succession of events.

Brooks Baekeland
Céline Swarts and Leo Hendrik Baekeland were the founders of a
foundered family.

From *A Biographical Profile of Leo Hendrik Baekeland,* Carl Kaufmann, Unpublished

His personal life had been far from happy since his arrival in the
U.S. Céline had returned to Belgium, at his insistence, for the
birth of their first child. (Jenny, born in 1890, died at the age of
five.) Leo assumed that, because of his modest circumstances,
his wife would be better situated if with her family. However,
after the baby was born, he made no move to bring his wife and
child to America.

Céline begged him to send money for her passage, writing
that her funds were also exhausted, and adding the bitter note
that her own father refused to come to her aid. Leo's letters of
response are not extant, but it is clear from Céline's letters that
he delayed repeatedly, arguing that he could not support a wife
and daughter even if he could raise their passage to New York.
Eventually they were reunited—family records do not specify
when but it appears to have been about 1892—but not before
Céline had been deeply hurt by what she regarded as Leo's lack of
affection. The separation left a wound that never quite closed.
Though Céline remained a dutiful wife, and assisted her husband
in keeping laboratory notes and financial accounts, she built much
of her life around interests of her own, and was frequently separated
from her husband for periods of several months.

Letter from Céline Baekeland to Leo Hendrik Baekeland, Undated

Dearie—
. . . Every time I am alone, I go back to my own self. It always
takes some time and always takes much sorrow the first week. I
miss you, I miss you dreadfully, then comes the power to crush
that feeling, and unhappily I call forth every reason why I am a
fool, why I should not feel badly, how hard and unkind you are,
etc.—how this is wrong, and I know it, it brings me in a worse

agony yet, and by and by the old Céline pops out, and I long again for you, not for the heartless you, but for everything which is good in you—that is why when we meet we both are good and kind and loving. Now this time I have been more alone than ever, and you might not believe me, but I would not give up my Summer for yours—I have been alone and at perfect peace most of the time.

I have called in you all the good element there is—and I know that when you come back you will be a better man—I certainly am a better woman—and we both ought to have the thought to live the next years in peace and for the best of our children—think of people of our standard and intellect making each other unhappy for no reason whatever! Think of the beautiful life we could have if we both made up our minds to be happy and good to each other—if our lives had for an aim to be as kind to each other as possible. Our unhappiness is in *one* thought, let us tear that thought off and replace it by one of love and of peace.

Yours,
Céline

The Creation of the Woman, a Sanskrit Fable Found in Typewritten Form Among Leo Hendrik Baekeland's Miscellaneous Papers

In the beginning when Twashtri came to the creation of woman, he found that he had exhausted his materials in the making of man and that no solid elements were left. In this dilemma, after profound meditation, he did as follows: He took the rotundity of the moon and the curves of the creepers, and the clinging of tendrils and the trembling of grass, and the slenderness of the reed and the bloom of flowers, and the lightness of leaves and the tapering of the elephant's trunk, and the glances of deer and the blustering of rows of bees, and the joyous gayety of sunbeams and the weeping of clouds, and the fickleness of the winds and the timidity of the hare, and the vanity of the peacock and the softness of the parrot's bosom and the hardness of adamant and the sweetness of honey, and the

cruelty of the tiger and the warm glow of the fire, and the cold-
ness of snow and the chattering of jays, and the cooing of the
kokila, and the hypocrisy of the crane, and the fidelity of the
chakrawska, and compounding all these together he made a
woman and gave her to man.

But after one week, man came to him and said: "Lord, this
creature that You have given me makes my life miserable. She
chatters incessantly and teases me beyond endurance, never
leaving me alone; and she requires incessant attention, and takes
all my time up, and cries about nothing and is always idle, and
so I have come to give her back as I cannot live with her." So
Twashtri said: "Very well," and He took her back. Then after
another week man came to Him and said: "Lord, I find that my
life is very lonely since I gave You back that creature. I remember how she used to dance and sing to me and look at me
out of the corner of her eye, and play with me and cling to me,
and her laughter was music and she was beautiful to look at and
soft to touch, so give her back to me."

So Twashtri said: "Very well," and gave her back. Then after
only three days man came back to Him again and said: "Lord, I
know not how it is, but after all I have come to the conclusion
that she is more of a trouble than a pleasure to me so please take
her back again." But Twashtri said: "Out on you! Be off! I will
have no more of this; you must manage how you can." The
man said: "I cannot live with her." And Twashtri said: "Neither
can you live without her." And He turned His back on man and
went on with His work. Then man said: "What is to be done?
For I cannot live either with her or without her."

BROOKS BAEKELAND
My grandfather insisted on his own freedom. Most of the year he was
away, somewhere in the world. Yet he adored and admired his wife.
He never used the word "woman" without the prefixal adjective
"silly" in front of it: "sillywoman"—one word. His wife was his one
exception to "sillywoman."

CÉLINE ROLL KARRAKER
My grandmother started something in Yonkers—Prospect House. It
was a settlement-house-type place for children whose parents were

working in the factories there. As Grandmother said, "The children come after school to be bathed, fed, and to have their talents encouraged." Grandmother always believed in a good meal and a bath!

She was a vegetarian, and a theosophist for many many years, and she brought to this country Indian gurus. And Grandpapa hated all of that. He was a real atheist—he didn't like anything that had to do with anything religious, he didn't like that at all. And then the funny thing was that Grandmother finally went to India and when she came back she stopped being a vegetarian, she quit theosophy, she would have nothing to do with gurus anymore—she was horrified by what she had seen in India. She thought, "If that's the way it is there, if that's what their religion has done for them . . ."

DR. FREDERICK BAEKELAND

I had a lot of contact with my grandmother over the years, as everyone in the family did. She was a very matriarchal person, rather controlling in some ways but extremely generous also. She was an extraordinary person. She started to paint rather late, at the age of fifty. She was sort of an Impressionist. She studied with Hobart Nichols—which was quite a good thing—and she had a couple of shows.

As a young woman she almost became a concert pianist, but she could never play the piano when Grandpapa was home because he didn't want to be disturbed. He often worked in the house, this sort of old-fashioned house along the Hudson River. It had a tower and that's where his study was and he would sort of secrete himself up there. My contacts with him were extremely limited—I personally spent maybe three times with my grandfather when I was a child. Once he took me into his lab, which was on the property, and electroplated some pennies with mercury for me, and another time he took me up to his study and gave me a scarab. I had it for years and later lost it.

BROOKS BAEKELAND

I once asked my Aunt Nina, my father's sister, what it had been like, really, growing up at Snug Rock, my grandparents' house in Yonkers. Such a question to my father would not have been thinkable. Her reply startled me: "Shhhh! The Doctor is working."

Céline Roll Karraker

My grandmother often played the piano for us on Sunday, after
lunch, and Grandpapa would just go someplace else. Later I read
somewhere that as a young man he used to go to concerts when he
was visiting different places. This surprised me because I always felt
he was so anti-music. Yet he did go to concerts by himself—you
know, alone. I think there was real rivalry between my grandparents.

Brooks Baekeland

One of my grandmother's teachers was Edward McDowell, a famous
concert pianist. He wanted her to "go public"—how vulgar that
phrase sounds, even now—that is, give public recitals, be a professional. This was nixed by my grandfather and always grudged against
him by my grandmother.

She loved playing the unplayable pieces of Liszt, but her heart was
with Debussy, Fauré, Ravel, and Chopin. When I had grown up
enough to read poetry and understand women—and understood the
passionately unslaked nature of my grandmother as it was revealed to
me at her Steinway grand—there was a phrase that always used to
come into my mind, particularly when she was playing one of
Chopin's celestial nocturnes: "A savage place! as holy and enchanted
as e'er beneath a waning moon was haunted by woman wailing for
her demon-lover!"

When my grandmother sat with her head bowed—not in benedic-
tion—before her piano and then started to play, I often felt tears
come to my eyes, especially when she was very old and her playing
was full of faults. As a child I made her play and play and play, and
repeat and repeat, and play again and again. In my ears the sounds
she made were like those of gold coins falling into a chest to a miser.

But my grandfather could not stand her music—that "noise"—and
her theosophy, suffragettism, the Prospect House with Harry
Hopkins, later an FDR *eminence grise*, and suchlike "nonsense."
Nor, she had more than once hinted to me, the fact that her French
was better than his and that she sometimes disagreed with him. His
German was of course better, and this was part of a Teutonic-Latin
tension between them. He had married far above himself socially in
marrying her—and never quite forgave her that. We know practically
nothing about his own family because he was ashamed of them. His
father was an alcoholic who ended up—sometimes—repairing shoes,
and he from the age of twelve was, according to my grandmother, the

main support for his whole family. That he was a genius there is no doubt—and that he had the most tremendous motivations. That he had adored his mother, though he would never speak of her—or of any of his family—that is not generally known. He simply obliterated the past. There had been no past. Time had started with him. Baekeland time, that is. That is the Zeus of those turn-of-the-century photos, the stern, tall man with the beard. Zeus.

It was an amused old Pan that I knew as a boy. I imply no sexuality, only humor, *joie de vivre*, a love of wine and endless—his own—talk. The man who not only would not suffer fools gladly but not at all. The man who stopped people from kissing, giving them a vivid description of the Niagaras of filth in the forms of bacteria and viruses that they were transferring to each other's foolish mouths. The man who lectured "sillywomen" about the constituents of their lipsticks and creams and the sucker's prices they foolishly paid for them—all this with the highest and most godly good humor.

CÉLINE ROLL KARRAKER

Grandpapa would take us up to his lab and he'd put various chemicals together and make colors or sweeteners. It was very exciting to go up there. And the smells! I can smell them to this day.

The house is gone now. It burned. But it hasn't burned in my memory. It was idyllic to be there. A wonderful haven for all of the children.

There was an incredible bathroom. It was huge. And from the middle of the wall up was a relief of cattails and ferns and birds and it was all colors and was absolutely beautiful. And there was a stained-glass window as well. And in the corner was a square sunken bathtub. And we kids would go in there and make up a batch of soapy suds. We'd go from one part of the bathroom which was all tile and zoom across the floor into the tub, splashing. Grandmother used to say this was Grandpapa's bathtub and we were not to do that.

From *I Knew a Phoenix: Sketches for an Autobiography*, May Sarton, W. W. Norton, New York, 1959

How imaginative it was of the Baekelands—for the Belgian inventor and his wife were our hosts—to insist that Mother and I come to them first, and be cherished and spoiled a little before the serious business of our new life was attempted. Their house, rustic stone and brown shingles, with its turrets and verandas, its stained-glass windows, its large portecochere in front, and all surrounded by expanses of clipped lawn, seemed to me very grand. It had, for instance, a polar bear rug in the drawing room. What luxury to compare with that of sitting on a polar bear's head! It also had a square glass aquarium, in which lived a small, wicked alligator who devoured raw meat and looked at me with indifferent, beady eyes. The real glory was the master bathroom with its huge bathtub. A bathtub? Rather, a tiled swimming pool, six feet square and sunk two feet into the floor. Around it lay huge sponges from Florida, and shells with rosy mouths that sang of a faraway ocean. In this bathtub, one could be a seal or a mermaid with no trouble. . . .

I never did feel Dr. Baekeland as a person I knew; rather he seemed to be some frightening masculine force—a god who must be placated, a piece of weather. I realize now that, with his fierce, shy eyes and black mustache, he looked something like Rudyard Kipling; and I realize now, too late, that, though I was frightened of him, he took me into his heart and really loved me in the admiring way of a grandfather with a first grandchild, for he used to come in after I was asleep and look down at me tenderly, and he was amazed that I could play so happily alone. But then, I fear, all I wanted was to run off and be free to go to [the chauffeur's] house where I felt more at home. On my way there I passed the garage, and above it, I had been told, was the laboratory, a very secret and important place where Dr. Baekeland retired to work like a sorcerer, and no one was ever allowed to go. There he was busy concocting queer things in trays, rather like today's ice-cube trays, but the cubes were of a hard yellow translucent material, no good as toys, though he gave me some one day—no good for anything as far as I could see. The name of this invention was Bakelite, still in an experimental stage, and not yet the fabulous djinni it would become. . . .

[Dr. Baekeland's wife] was known to everyone as Bonbon, a name so appropriate that it must have been used by St. Peter at the gate of Heaven, for kindness flowed from her in every sort and size of package, tangible and intangible. Her presence was a present. A small, round woman with bright, dark eyes under a mass of fuzzy gray hair, she wore for as long as I can remember the same round beaver hat and long beaver scarf over a suit she had recopied exactly every year. She could not have worn the beaver hat in summer, yet I see her so clearly in this hat and no other that she must be painted in it here. She came from an intellectual bourgeois family in Ghent, very much like my father's, but now she had moved into a different world, she had not changed. It was only that riches became her so well, as if she had always been intended to be a fairy godmother; she had the rare gift of transforming money into joy, her own joy and everyone else's, so there was no bitterness in it. Some of this I came to know later, but from the beginning she had my unwavering devotion because I sensed in her a dimension like saintliness, like poetry, which set her apart. Concrete evidence of this was the fact that because of her feeling for animals she would eat no meat. I loved animals, too, and even made resolves to follow her example, but then when everyone else at table except Bonbon accepted the breast of chicken or young lamb, apparently without a qualm, I forgot my resolve. . . . Bonbon did not blame us cruder beings, nor make us feel guilty; that was her triumph. When she and I sat shelling new peas from the garden on the back veranda . . . I felt a wonderful sense of security and something like being at home, at least for a little while. I could talk to her, I found. . . . I loved her Belgian accent, the way she said "Meerses" instead of "Mrs.," an accent that gave character to everything she said. She was very American in her lavishness, but she was also still so Belgian and so unsophisticated that she was, as I see it now, the perfect bridge from my Belgium to my America.

New York with Bonbon was Fifth Avenue, the Flatiron Building, Woolworth's (at that time still *the* skyscraper), and she had the newcomer's pride and delight in the city, as if, almost, it had been her own creation. . . . And New York was the Plaza Hotel where we had tea among the palms, and ate little many-colored iced cakes, while, at Bonbon's request, the orchestra played a soulful rendition of the "Song of the Volga Boatman," and were rewarded with a crisp ten-dollar bill taken over to them on a silver plate. Perhaps I loved her so much because her taste remained the taste of a child, and her love of life, her excitement (as years later when she waved her hand at all of Yonkers glittering with electric lights and said proudly, "Every one of those light bulbs has Bakelite in it") was as innocent as a child's.

CÉLINE ROLL KARRAKER

My grandmother told me she cried for five years in French when she came here to live, and she went back to Belgium whenever she could. My grandfather did exactly the opposite. She never lost her accent. He lost his as fast as he could and named his son George Washington Baekeland.

When he sold Velox to Eastman Kodak, he bought Snug Rock for my grandmother, but he resented the socializing that went on in it. He didn't want any part of that.

From the Private Diaries of Leo Hendrik Baekeland, April 27, 1907

> The complications of our unnecessarily complicated living irritate me. If I could do without inconveniencing my wife I certainly would go and live somewhere where we could dispense with servants and lead a simpler and more natural life. But my wife cannot live without some so-called "Society," a stupid conventionalism and the cause of all our unwarranted conventional and complicated living. What do we want such a large house for, and why all these servants? Why all that complicated trash of unnecessary furniture? All this complication becomes more and more irksome to me. Trash—vulgar—idiotic— trash.

CÉLINE ROLL KARRAKER

Grandpapa was a great proponent of the simple life—physically. Lived it himself. In fact, my grandmother said—and you know, she believed in reincarnation—that he was a monk in his former life! After he retired he lived down in Florida, in a very simple house.

BROOKS BAEKELAND

The Anchorage in Coconut Grove had belonged to William Jennings Bryan, "the Great Commoner," and my grandfather used to crow with delight in telling the Victorian elite who dined with him that

"that great bag of wind did not have a single book in his house except a Bible!"

The plantation-style house was deliciously cool—made of blocks of pure-white coral and terra-cotta roofs. Its windows in winter were always open, as were its doors, and its greatest charm was a central patio, hung with orchids. It had a fountain jetting high in its center. There was an aquamarine swimming pool at the front of the house, where one "bathed," not "swam." But what I remember now, when I close my eyes, is the perfume of the flowering trees and that so-characteristic soft interminable clack-clack-clack of coconut palm fronds, day and night—it never stopped—and the windjammer-creakings of the great bamboo groves from Sumatra, towering to one hundred and fifty feet, down near the anchorage itself, which had been made for my grandfather's yacht, the *Ion*. By day the wind blew in over the sea, and by night it blew out again.

Our nearest neighbors were, through a narrow jungle to the north, the Mathiesons of Olin Mathieson Chemical—lovely people—who owned the uninhabited offshore island which was then a coconut plantation which faced us and them about a mile away and was later made famous, or infamous, by Nixon and his pal Rebozo; and, to the south, the Thomas Fortune Ryans, who built a rococo Italian palace, in bad taste. The Anchorage was a simple, lovely place. As was Coconut Grove itself. There was no tourism then, there was no fear and there was no disgust.

CÉLINE ROLL KARRAKER

Grandpapa lived in that house in a very very simple way. He lived there alone for six months of the year. My grandmother joined him for a couple of months in the winter.

He ate everything out of a can—without heating it! He used to say to us, "Children, this is the best way of all," and he'd open a can of Campbell's split-pea soup and put a little seawater in it and stir it up, and then he'd eat it. Then he'd open up a can of sardines and eat that. And then there was the first instant coffee at that time, called George Washington, and he'd put that in hot water and drink it.

He had no servants, except outdoor people. He adored botany. He was a close friend of the great botanist David Fairchild. He and my grandfather planted the place with all kinds of wonderful plants. We children could pull fruit right off the trees!

PATRICIA GREENE

Barbara and Brooks, before they moved to that penthouse on Seventy-fifth Street, lived two houses down from us on Seventy-first Street, and little Tony was a little younger than one of our sons and a little older than the other—an enchanting child, very elflike—and he used to come around and play in a very imaginative way. He was very very fond of natural history, and actually, one of the nicest stories about Barbara, who was a beautiful woman—a mischievous look in her eye!—was that when Tony was a baby, I think it was probably during World War Two, she was down in Florida with him and some great naturalist was there and said to her, "Oh that lovely little child. Don't give him any toys to play with, let him play with nature," so she did. And instead of playing with building blocks and trucks and things, he grew up playing with rocks and sticks and mosses and frogs and crickets.

BROOKS BAEKELAND

David Fairchild. "The aged angel," I used to call him. He always allowed me to come up to his laboratory at the Kampong, his house in Coconut Grove, and interrupt him. I used to walk there all by myself—he lived about two miles away. For me he was a kindly, playful, learned, imaginative human being with a kind of beauty in him that suggested something holy, not Christly but Pythagorean. He was also of course a famous host to all the world's great; everyone in the world came to his house.

He used to like to see how much information I could hold in my head. His own theory, which I was offered at the dining-room table at the Anchorage, was that one could remember fifty-five thousand different species but not more. I remember the Nobelist Dr. Muller was having dinner with us that night. When I was a little boy, I thought that "doctor" simply meant someone who was a man and who had white hair, since all the men I met who had white hair were Doctor something or other—when I was a little boy. When LHB and David Fairchild were together, the talk was all of enzymes. How far ahead of their times those two giants were!

CÉLINE ROLL KARRAKER

Grandpapa never wore real shoes. He always wore sneakers, white sneakers. He just thought they were sensible and cheap. So he was an individualist and a character. I have a picture of him and Mark Twain all in white, because that was what Mark Twain wore, too.

Grandpapa was always in white, everywhere, no matter what time of year it was. He used to go to the Chemists' Club and the University Club in those white sneakers.

In Florida Grandpapa wore white ducks and a white shirt with his white sneakers. And when he got hot, he'd walk right into the swimming pool—with all his clothes on! And then walk out of the pool, saying, "This is the way to keep cool. The evaporation keeps you cool."

And this physically very simple kind of life was carried even to the house in Yonkers. We'd all be at Snug Rock for a lovely traditional Sunday dinner and he would have his instant coffee and his Campbell's soup and his can of sardines served to him on a Bakelite tray, right at the table with everybody else.

ELIZABETH ARCHER BAEKELAND

A couple of summers ago I went to Block Island to see Brooks. His cousin Céline Karraker had told me he was spending the summer there, and I just arrived. I was afraid he'd flee if I told him I was coming—he's strange that way. I went to the house he was renting and walked right in. I had heard he was having an affair with some woman from New York who had divorced her husband for him, so I asked him about that right away. And he said, "She was such a good cook we used to have to spend two hours every day shopping and then two hours preparing the food and then we'd eat for another hour and then, because I don't want to be a male chauvinist pig, *I'd* wash the dishes and there'd be ten dishes and five pans, and I just got so sick of the whole thing I finally threw her out." I said, "Who cooks for you now?" And he said, "Simple—Sunday I have a pound of hamburger, Monday I have a pound of potatoes, Tuesday I have a pound of spinach, and so on. So I have *one* dish, *one* pot, *one* pan."

BROOKS BAEKELAND

I am a man of very simple tastes. My mother calls me a monk. Some of my peculiar habits now—unhabits, in fact—make me think of my grandfather as I knew him in my boyhood. LHB kept only one "business" suit. I haven't even got one. Three years ago I discovered that I had fifteen shirts—I threw away ten of them; that I had ten handkerchiefs—I threw away eight of them; eight pair of shorts—I threw away five of them; umpteen trousers—I kept two; umpteen-plus sweaters—I kept three . . . and so on.

I said LHB kept only one business suit. But there's the story my

grandmother used to tell about how she finally tricked him into buying a new dark blue suit. This story involves a neighbor of theirs in
Yonkers, the famous lawyer Samuel Untermeyer, who lived on a
very pretentious estate to the north. LHB held him in scorn as a
lawyer—as he did all lawyers, calling them jackals and hyenas. The
Untermeyer estate was full of copies of Greek statues and picturesque
Greek ruins and Greco-Roman terracing. It was ridiculed by LHB.

Well, one day in Yonkers my grandmother saw a shop that sold
men's clothes. She went in and made a deal with the owner, after she
had selected and bought an expensive blue serge suit of LHB's size
for—let us say—one hundred and twenty-five dollars. The deal was
that the owner was to show it in the window for twenty-five dollars
but not to "sell" it to anyone but LHB, who, of course, he knew of—
people today have no idea how famous LHB once was. Then at dinner that night my grandmother told my grandfather that she had seen
a beautiful suit of imported English serge selling for twenty-five dollars. "Oh, no, Céline—maybe one hundred and twenty-five but not
twenty-five. There you have made a mistake."

"No mistake, dearie—twenty-five," she insisted.

And so they argued. They even made a bet.

The next night LHB arrived home crowing with delight. When he
could stop laughing, he explained how he had just "done in" that old
Shylock Sam Untermeyer. LHB had gotten off the train from New
York and gone directly to the shop, where he had seen the suit, seen
that my grandmother had been right, and bought it. On the way
home to Snug Rock, he had fallen in with Sam Untermeyer, shown
him the suit, and sold it to him for seventy-five dollars!

I remember how my grandfather used to come to wake me up
before sunrise in those early Florida years, give me a boiled egg and a
hybridized grapefruit taken off one of his own trees—and then lead
me out in the still-sleeping dewy dawn to see the rabbits and land
crabs. Coconut Grove was still very wild in those days; the roads were
all of crushed white coral.

Imagine an old man in loose, white, unpressed, probably mil-
dewed cottons, a long shirt over them, and one of those still-worn
white-cotton, crushable sailing caps, and a mousy-haired boy, his
small, grubby hand in the baseball-mitt-sized big one of LHB, both
of them talking continuously, neither listening to the other, and
heading for a sail in the dinghy to Mathieson Island.

On the way the small boy learned all about outriggers, centerboards, sideboards, Medusas, man-o'-war birds, the main sorts of ocean waves—surficial and bottom-resonant—the prediction of weather from cloud formations, the various ways to treat snake bite, and—"But, Grandpapa, we have forgotten to bring our lunch!"— answered by Pan's chuckle: "The best lunch you will ever have awaits you. The sea gives it to us."

In the bottom of the tiny boat was a machete, and it was with this that LHB showed me how to open coconuts and husk them and then pierce two of their three eyes to get the delicious milk. We ate coconut meat, crabs, tropical oysters, sour oranges, and the orange hearts of sea urchins.

He never stopped talking, telling me the Latin names of the plants—many of which he had introduced from his travels all over the world—and the insects and birds and mammals, saying it was just as easy to learn a name that was the same anywhere as one that changed from language to language and country to country—which is, of course, why Tony knew as a small child the Latin names of so many things, for I continued with him LHB's practice. From the time Tony started talking, which was early, I decided to give him the Latin names, when I knew them, for plants and animals. By the time he was ten he could read, understand, and remember the contents of texts like Buchsbaum's *Animals Without Backbones*. That was the beginning of a lifelong intellectual bond between Tony and me. And it was not just intellectual and bookish but field-explorative.

ELIZABETH BLOW

If you saw Tony with Brooks, I don't think you would connect the fact by looks that they were related. He had Barbara's brown eyes and her red hair. He was just a marvelous-looking little boy. And at four years old he was already constantly prowling around and investigating insects and birds—he had a natural instinct for creatures of this earth. He knew all about them and he could be very instructive. I'll never forget the marvelous remark he made to me one afternoon. He said, "B-Betty"—he stammered, you know—"did you know that b-b-butterflies have . . ." I can't remember for the *life* of me what it was, it was some special thing that butterflies have—and it was something that I didn't know. I quoted it for years because it always amused me so. It was that slight stutter, the combination of the "B-Betty" and the "b-b-butterflies" and the actually hard information which he proffered to me.

From a Psychiatric Report on Antony Baekeland Ordered by the British Courts, January 5, 1973

I examined Antony Baekeland on January 3, 1973, and read the depositions and reports from five psychiatrists who have seen him at different periods. The history based on these reports is that Baekeland is an American subject, an only child brought up with his parents in New York till about eleven. His father is "a brilliant wealthy man who has never actually done any productive work though he made one expedition to South America and wrote an article about it," and "charming but capable of no warmth to support his son." The mother (the victim) was "an hysterical, narcissistic, and impulsive woman, quite incapable of giving a child the minimum of maternal security." She was a great beauty and an accomplished artist. He suffered "marked deprivation of love from both parents, and was exposed to excessive intellectual stimulation beyond his capacity to absorb."

BROOKS BAEKELAND
Psychiatrists—who are professionally amoral—never understood my reluctance to enthuse about their abracadabra. They were interested in their tricks, and in drugs to numb rage, while in Tony I clearly saw the play of Good and Evil. That was a question not only about him but about a whole generation.

From "Dreams and Realities," a Lecture Delivered at the Johns Hopkins University by Leo Hendrik Baekeland, October 23, 1931

A large part of the tragedy of the human race is caused by the fact that it is well-nigh impossible to transmit fully to others our reactions about the mistakes we committed in our younger years. So we see each succeeding generation ever ready to commit the same blunders over again, and suffer by it.

BROOKS BAEKELAND
I remember the hold of my grandfather's large, soft hand, and the rich flow of humor and information that never stopped pouring out

of him during our walks those educative, garrulous, affectionate mornings, while the house and the village still slept and only we two were awake and aware of it.

On our returns, with the sun up and the house awake, he would disappear—where, a small boy did not know. It was to study, I now know. I later discovered that whenever he stood—he always seemed to be standing—leafing through some large tome, he was not leafing. He was reading every single word. He had remained a European and an intellectual.

From the Private Diaries of Leo Hendrik Baekeland, April 20, 1907

> In the evening read "On the Danger of Overspecialization" at Anvil Club. Had a lively discussion afterwards on such subjects as morals, religion, ancient literature. I introduced my conception of morality based on reason and the conception of the big universal Ego and universal consciousness as opposed to the little Ego as conceived by the average man. The higher love as opposed to the little or partial (particularist?) love which dwarfs our conception of equity and justice and develops selfishness and fear and makes us question immortality because we commit ourselves too much as individuals and not enough as part of the big Ego. The latter conception sweeps away all thoughts of mortality and makes us a little ingredient of that sublime and universal Ego.

BROOKS BAEKELAND

From his most profound beliefs my grandfather despised publicity, money, fashion, sensation, exploitation, and all the people whose lives were dedicated to such. He was an idealist, a feudal-socialist, a radical theorist, an antimaterialist millionaire. All this was in the same curious spirit as his benefactions during the Depression, such as I got a hint of once when I was with him at the Chemists' Club. He had gone somewhere—to pee? to buttonhole a colleague?—and a sandy-haired, middle-aged man came up to me and asked me who I was. When I told him, he said, "No one will ever know how many of us your grandfather brought through the Depression or what would have happened to us without him." He said this to me very emotionally. I had never heard of this. I asked my grandmother later. She had never known, either. And this was the man in sneakers and one suit who was known as a miser!

He was a benefactor by impulse: utterly without cynicism, without regard to self. Victorians—especially Victorians of his class, the academics—believed in Man and Family. They never doubted Life's purposes.

My real education began at the example and from the words of my Belgian grandparents, who were not unsusceptible to Honor but tended to deride it in its social, self-lauding, self-loving forms—the forms *we* all in fact love so much. Because we love ourselves?

My grandfather, in particular, held all that mutual backslapping in ridicule—despite his own multiple honors, at the reception of each of which he always let the side down by saying it was all due to "luck" and his "marvelous wife." How could he say: "due to my genius and your ridiculous system of self-congratulation"?

The academic class in Europe that my Baekeland grandparents came from put very high value on nonmaterialistic achievements. It despised show. It despised the accumulation of money and power. In the nineteenth century the European university world considered itself—and was considered—an aristocracy. In its heart it put itself above royalty, and did so without any hesitation whatever! It was guilty of an almost monastic pride, and its scientific members put Truth, *the* Truth, above Man—or any man.

So, from those two immigrants—totally out of phase with a society given over *entirely* to show, power, and gain, all of which they soon had, too, almost automatically, due to "luck" and LHB's "marvelous wife," of course—I learned everything, early.

Their only son, my father—George Washington Baekeland—was entirely the opposite. As was my first, ambitious, beautiful, backgroundless wife, Barbara.

Sylvie Baekeland Skira

Brooks admired the way his grandfather and grandmother had led sort of separate lives—but in harmony, because they had similar values. Perhaps this was something he missed, because certainly he couldn't have done that with Barbara, ever.

Letter from Leo Hendrik Baekeland to Professor Camiel De Bruyne, University of Ghent, Belgium, August 27, 1931

Dear Friend De Bruyne:

My wife, who is at present with our whole family in the Adirondacks, feels as if she were in the "Seventh Heaven"! One of the sketches which she painted last year during a short visit to Bruges has been selected as a front cover for the latest number of the *Literary Digest*, one of our best known publications—I am mailing you a copy.

It is a great honor for an amateur; an honor even much sought after by professional artists; because there is always an abundant choice amongst the many offered sketches. I should mention that when her painting was selected, none in the Literary Digest organization knew who Céline Baekeland was. I have reason to doubt whether even today they know it—and she got paid for it, too!

The reason why I write you on this occasion is that when I saw the issue with the sketch, it evoked times long gone by, when you and I walked over that same little bridge, when we were both at the beginning of our career, colleagues at the same Normal School. Could I have imagined then that some time I was to raise a family here, and that I was to have this thrill in seeing the picture of that same bridge published here, painted by the daughter of my former professor, who was to become my wife, as well as mother and grandmother of a new clan in America . . .

Cordially yours,
L. H. Baekeland

From the "Very Truly Yours" Column, Helen Muir, *Miami Herald*, January 18, 1940

Céline Baekeland is well-known as a painter and Dr. Baekeland, whom Miami claims as one of its distinguished citizens, is very proud of her accomplishments. "She rarely sells a painting; she likes to give them away. But she is naturally proud of the prizes she has received," he declares, from the terrace of "The Anchorage," his bayfront home in Coconut Grove. In his study is a painting his wife did for him of a scene in Sleepy Hollow Cemetery in Westchester County, New York. He chuckles as he explains it is his future burial place.

BROOKS BAEKELAND

LHB died in 1944. He had been greatly gaga for several years—senile dementia, taking sometimes violent forms as the oxygen and glycogen were gradually starved from that massive brain. In his middle or late seventies he no longer always liked it when I asked him specific questions. He would reply testily, "It is not polite to ask me such questions as the name of some exotic hybrid now. Old men's memories fail." Or he would upbraid me for standing in front of him with my legs apart—done, though he did not realize it, to shorten my six feet four to a more agreeable height, he being just under six feet—by saying, "You don't have to emphasize your height like that!" His temper worsened, and I think his loneliness—of which state I was already a precocious sufferer myself—was almost intolerable for the simple reason that not even delivery boys and Pullman Car porters would listen to him anymore. Shall I talk of loneliness? Of the loneliness of *that* kind of greatness? In the end he became a pathetic, a tragic figure, and had to be sent away from home to be "taken care of." He was violent long before he died, of the final massive cerebral hemorrhage.

During World War Two, when he was very old and already quite dotty and I was a trainee Aircraftsman Second Class— nothing lower!—I called Snug Rock to ask my grandmother if I could come and crouch there for my forty-eight-hour leave. My grandfather answered and said that my grandmother was in Florida but that I must come anyway, he needed my help. It was an order: I was to come at the swiftest.

Now, I loved my grandmother more than anyone I had ever loved but this time my motive for wanting to come to Yonkers involved a girl with a divine body, long red hair, green eyes, a taste for Richard Strauss, and whose father was a football coach. So I said, "Yes, Grandpapa." I knew Dick the chauffeur's number, called him, and had him pick me up at the station.

My grandfather immediately made me privy to his problem. In fact, he had two problems. The first he did not know but I recognized immediately—he had gone over the edge since I had last seen him—and I wondered: "Who is taking care of him? This is dangerous." The second problem was the following: He had just arrived from Florida, he had four heavy suitcases with him, and they were all locked and he had no key.

What he had done is lock the first case, put the key in the second, lock the second, put the key in the third, lock the third—and so on. You see, in that way, you did not have *four* bulky keys in your pocket but only *one*. But he had lost that one! He was in despair.

I was not his grandson for nothing. "Are there any other keys in the house?" I asked him.

"I don't know," he said.

So we went looking, and of course we finally found a huge ball of keys all snarled together, for every good old house has one—keys that no one knows the origin or the function of anymore but that no one dares throw away.

Do not forget that he was talking the whole time, perhaps telling me how he had just escaped with his life from the head-hunting Dayaks in the Sunda Straits in 1913 or about the famous oral exam that he and some colleagues had trained one of their dear but, alas, nitwit friends to pass, and how the friend, asked to explain the polarization of light—a question they had not trained him for, deeming it too abstract for his limited brains—had cleared his throat and said, "Messieurs, in order to explain to you how light is polarized, I must first describe to you the principle of the suction pump"—a question they *had* trained him for. And with that bunch of keys, as I was saying, I began to try, Edison-like, the six thousand possibilities. Of course, I soon got all the suitcases open, to my grandfather's *fervent* joy.

And what was in those four suitcases? Books, papers, diaries, notebooks, checkbooks, manuscripts. He had forgotten to pack *clothes!*

Now, to me this was not just a sign of senility, but an indication of his lifelong priorities. And you may imagine what a great woman it took to wife a man like that and keep her good humor.

I was overwhelmed with pity and so I started unpacking for him, hoping to find at least a pair of pajamas and a toothbrush somewhere in all that incunabula. Nothing. Not a handkerchief.

What I found that startled me was literally dozens of pocket checkbooks from different banks all over America. Ten would not have attracted my attention. There must have been fifty or more, maybe a hundred. As I remember, one suitcase was full of nothing else.

"What are *these*, Grandpapa?"

He chuckled. "Banks," he explained, "are insolvent."

When he saw my puzzled expression, he went on. "They lend money they have not got—that is, they give credit without backing. In fact, they are all bankrupt."

I was still looking puzzled.

"The backing is the depositors' money, but the loans they make are many times, often ten times that. It's a fraud. As long as the depositors don't know and as long as the debtors pay their debts, the banks make money—other people's money, of course—and the banks are called 'solvent.' It should not be allowed. It is highly dangerous. In fact, there is not a solvent bank in the United States."

Poor old man, I was thinking.

"So," he went on, "I play the numbers." He giggled. "I spread the risk. I keep money in banks all over the United States instead of in just one or two where a run of a few days during a panic could wipe me out."

Senile. I offered him the loan of my pajamas. "Healthier," he said, "to sleep naked." He always had. Goodnight. He had some reading to do. *I* had a long, cool, green-eyed girl to see, but of course it would not have done to tell him. He was, as I said, one of the last great Victorians.

But the memory I treasure is this. When I got back, at three a.m. to Snug Rock, afoot—it was not far—I found the house hermetically sealed. I had forgotten my dear grandfather's growing paranoia. I tried every door, every window, every crack—it might have been Castle Bodiam. I was humiliated to think I could not scheme *some* way into that ancestral home. My mind set to working. I would not admit defeat; it was not theoretically possible—whatever I, Brooks Baekeland, wanted, I, Brooks Baekeland, could and would discover a way to get. It was an almost Mosaic law.

But in fact, there was no way short of storming that would let me in. So, just as the first birds were all singing grand opera, making promises too grand to keep, I lay me down on a wicker sofa on the porch facing the Hudson River and the majestic Palisades on the other side—it was a warm July night—and, with a perfectly bad— that is, good—conscience, I fell asleep.

The next thing I knew, the door from the dining room opened and there was Grandpapa looking at me.

"I'm sorry," I said, as I got up and brushed back my hair. "I got back late and didn't want to disturb you."

I had not a clue as to how he might react to this development. What he did was to give me a discourse on the climbing vine called wisteria, genus Wisteria, named after Charles Wistar, an American anatomist who had died in 1818, and which had been developed into I forget how many hybrids by the Dutchman Claus something-or-other into however many varieties, of which this one on our porch was . . . "Would you like to take a bath?" he finally asked. "We will be served breakfast in half an hour." "Thank you, sir," I said.

That was the last time I saw my grandfather alive.

I do not mean that it was on the porch at Snug Rock that I last saw him alive. I was with him all that day and the next, alone—mostly in his laboratory, where he talked to me about his student years and gave me a sample of a "synthetic" beer he had made—it was not bad—or in his wine cellar, where he gave me samples of the very strong Sauternes he also made. He spoke to me about my grandmother as the very model of virtue, as someone we—the grandchildren—should forever appreciate and honor. I was deeply touched by this, since they had never been able to live together for more than a few days at a time, so that we had only seen them together at Christmas or Easter.

He talked to me also of China and Japan—of Taisho, Emperor Hirohito's father, who had honored him for creating the first Western industry in Japan—the Japanese Bakelite Corporation. And about Theodore Roosevelt and his beautiful daughter, Alice. And about Harding and Coolidge. But mostly about TR, who he said was the greatest man America had produced after Washington and Jefferson.

His love of and his reverence for America—what it symbolized more than what it was—was the classic immigrant's, which was why he had named his son after George Washington. "A nigger name," my father growled, and never used the "Washington." I always felt I was not his son. My genes told me that I was my grandmother's.

My grandmother was all to me: teacher, protector, guide—indeed, what any true mother is to any son. There are several basic sorts of women, and their mixtures: mother-woman, sister-woman, child-woman, mistress-woman, wife-woman. My grandmother was mother-woman.

Our minds, hers and mine, were in tune. So were our spirits, in both of which was the same Gallic naughtiness and humor. She loved wit and gaiety, those French virtues, and she herself had them in full measure.

She was attracted to me not only as a mother but as any woman is to an electric young man. We were like lovers. We met always as man and woman. That was our power. It enabled us to see instantly to the heart of things together. I was for my grandmother the surrogate for the missing, vanished, voyaging, discoursing Leo Hendrik Baekeland. I was the young Leo she had loved. He, Odysseus, was gone. I was Telemachus. Even as a young man I was aware of the sexual danger of that transference.

And we became even closer upon her coming death—I mean more aware of what we meant to each other, before a series of hammerlike strokes silenced her forever—not, oh not, quite. When she said to me one day, out of one of our long silences together, "Thank you for existing," she said to me all that *I* felt, too—and all that I mean when I speak about family and what I call "inheritance," not necessarily money but that duty and that deep sentiment we should all feel, upwards and downwards in our continuities. I do deeply believe in inheritance, which in my mind goes mystically *both* ways.

We Baekelands are a powerful race. Did you know that the name is famous in Belgium less even than for the great LHB than for the family of robbers who were all captured together and hanged during the Spanish Occupation—a father and his four sons? Whenever I go to Belgium and my name is seen on my passport, those lovely fools, if it is after their lunch and they are feeling cheery, stagger back and make wild gestures of self-defense, crying, "*Les Baekelands! Les Baekelands!*" That great robber family is a national myth. There is violence in my genetic past. I am not sure that anyone else in our family knows about this infamous descent. My beloved grandmother told me. She told me everything.

She died in 1957. The contents of Snug Rock were legally—by her will—up for grabs, starting on a certain date. Everything in the house was tagged—furniture, paintings, rugs, anything of "value."

I had always had a Prince Hal–Falstaff relationship with my grandmother's servants—gardeners, chauffeurs, caretakers, cooks, chambermaids, etc. I was living then on Seventy-first Street, in a house my grandmother had bought and allowed me to live in while I was doing graduate work at Columbia, and when I wished to wash my extremely fast Mercedes-Benz, I would motor up to Snug Rock and visit a bit with the chauffeur and his sister or with the gardener and his wife, who plied me with pasta and *vino rosso* and terrible jokes and that marvelous kind of Italian love that adopts all children—they still treated me like a child. My jokes were worse than theirs.

It was a hot summer day. The gardener gave me a key. I wandered through the rooms, remembering. Both my grandparents were dead. Snug Rock had been left to their daughter. There is a housing development there now, I am told.

I took my time. I spent many long minutes in each room and passage, remembering and trying to learn *something*, wanting—always—to know who I was and why. Why, I kept feeling, have you left me alone? I finally understood that that was not my question. The real question was: What was to become of this whole world now that the marvelous, strong, innocent idealism of the Victorians was gone? I thought of Rome, of the Gracchi—the sundering. And of course I wandered through the empty greenhouses, the dusty laboratory, and down through the grape arbors and vineyards, and—pensively—all through the now ruined gardens.

And, back in the house, I finally climbed up to the tower.

What was my amazement! All the great portraits—engravings a meter high by half a meter wide, matted and framed in their gilded wood—of the illuminati of Heidelberg, Tübingen, Bonn, Göttingen, Leiden, Berlin, Louvain—indeed, of all the great universities of Belgium, France, and Sweden—all in formal court dress with their sashes and orders—all of whom had been my grandfather's teachers. They were all still there rising along the walls of the mounting stairway. Not a one of them had been tagged!

Let me interrupt myself for a moment. You will see what I am getting at in a minute. In 1945, just after the war in Europe ended, I used to commandeer a sergeant driver and a corporal and a big car and explore Swabia rather than sit on the air base at Stuttgart and twiddle my thumbs—play poker, screw the local German girls. I discovered the German atomic energy laboratories underground, the ME-262 factories, also underground, and Hechingen, where the Crown Prince of Germany was imprisoned by the French. I went up into Hechingen over French protest and made the acquaintance of the lonely Kaiser's son. We became close friends. He was a total innocent and could have been David Windsor's twin brother. He lived there alone with his French mistress, and I managed, at his urgent request, to frustrate his wife, who wished to join him there—I had connections in SHAPE. I supplied him with cigarettes, and, as he sat in his bedroom in the rumpled disorder of his silk nightclothes and sheets, he supplied me with the inside story of Hitler's Third Reich.

It is a long story, but all I want of it now is this: He took me around the castle and showed me his ancestors' portraits—and hearts, all in their golden goblets in niches protected by small glass doors— and a family tree going back to 815, I think—an ancient and redoubtable royal family, of which he made graceful fun. He had nothing of pomposity, and all he seemed to be interested in was news of his English cousins and the latest in sports—horses, of course—over there. I came to see him many times. In later years we corresponded.

Now, what I want you to understand is that the rising tier of the intellectual great of Europe that mounted up and up into the tower at Snug Rock, and then went all around the walls of the great tower room, was an aristocracy as truly mighty—and conscious of it—as the Hohenzollerns. Not hereditary, but no less awesome. *These* were my grandfather's real ancestors. And mine. And of this modern world.

And up in the tower nothing had been disturbed, for there was nothing up there of "value." There was only the cooing of pigeons.

2

THE GRAND DUKEDOM

On his arrival at Broadmoor on June 6, 1973, Tony Baekeland, according to hospital procedure, was given a number—6787—a bath, and a preliminary medical checkup. No medication of any kind was administered so that his psychiatric condition could surface and be observed. He was brought a cup of tea and some bread and jam, and placed in solitary confinement.

On his second day he was moved to the special admissions ward, where he would remain for the next two months. In early fall he was transferred to Cornwall House, a three-story building that resembled a tenement more than the ducal residence its name suggested. There he was assigned to a second-floor ward, which consisted of dormitories, single rooms referred to by the patients as "cells," and a large dayroom where patients could read, play music and games, listen to the radio, or watch television. Occasionally there was a movie. During the Queen's Jubilee Week, James Bond films were shown; another time there was a screening of *The Exorcist*, at which several patients were observed "laughing away with great relish" in the middle of one particularly grotesque scene while other, more heavily tranquilized patients simply sat by themselves and stared into space.

There was an area off the dayroom of Cornwall House in which meals were served, and also a small kitchen that patients could use at authorized times. All cutlery was counted both before and after meals; if anything was missing, the patients were searched.

They were provided only a locker and an iron bed. For anything beyond these bare necessities they had to depend on the generosity of relatives or friends. In Tony Baekeland's case, his grandfather, George Baekeland, had left him a trust fund, one half of the principal of which would come to him in three years, when he turned thirty, the other half when he turned thirty-five.

Tony Baekeland shared the dormitory with as many as sixty men at one time. The beds were packed tightly together, with sometimes only inches between them. High up on the dormitory walls were blue lights that were never turned off, so that it never got completely dark.

Patients were locked in the dormitories at night, and bathrooms were off-limits. If anybody needed to use the toilet, he had to resort to the chamberpot under his bed, in full view of everybody. "They were plastic, since a pot of any other kind might be turned into an offensive weapon," a staff member explains. Often there wasn't even toilet paper.

"We are wheeling and shining with the *crème de la crème* of European high life," Barbara Baekeland had written to Sam Green three years before. "The Marquis and Marquise de Surian arrive next week—and the Earl of Shaftesbury is just across the way here. Hope to climb on skis up to the Hospice de St. Bernard with him next week. Adelaide d'Eudeville's cousin, the Comte de Vogue, is here and it is peaceful and restful. Flew around in a private plane yesterday—took the controls, made a right turn and almost zeroed in—no, not quite true. But had a good look at the countryside."

A good look at the countryside was one of the few things at Broadmoor that Tony Baekeland could enjoy, and it would be filtered not only through barred windows but through the tranquilizers with which he was often heavily sedated. Sometimes when he stood by the window too long, he would be reprimanded by a nurse.

"I asked him, 'Tony, what do you get as medication?'" says Miwa Svinka-Zielinski. "He wrote me four different names. He said he got one kind in the morning, another kind in the afternoon, and another in the evening, and once a week he got this and that. I showed this list to a psychiatrist friend of mine in New York and he said they were all strong tranquilizers. The worst thing was he was not getting any treatment—he saw a psychiatrist only once a month."

For the roughly 750 patients at Broadmoor, there were only four psychiatrists, working one day a week each. "With the best will and the best scheduling in the world, I could only manage to see each patient for two hours every three months," a former Broadmoor consultant explains.

But Dr. Gogarty says, "Tony Baekeland consumed a great deal of my care. He told me I was the only one who would listen to him."

Letter from Antony Baekeland to Miwa Svinka-Zielinski, November 12, 1973

Broadmoor

Dear Miwa—

Thank you for your letter after such a long silence. I am getting on all right here. I shall try to give you the dream associations you asked for concerning the dreams I sent you in my last letter.

1. Einstein hides a stop sign from the police: I associate this dream with secret, occult, or hidden things.

2. I come back to my best friend [Jake Cooper], and we travel the world together; I see a fox eat a squirrel: I associate this with the library of our house on Seventy-first Street where I was brought up.

3. My grandmother Nina Daly embraces me during a party given by a fellow here and myself; during the party I cut up gobbets of meat: I associate this with the swans on Georgica Pond in East Hampton where as you know we rented a house for several years.

4. I dream that I can fly and go all over the place: this dream of flight I associate with freedom. I have always wanted to be able to fly.

5. That I am a successful writer and poet: I associate this with a manor house that my mother and father rented one summer in France. It had a beautiful garden and a large *potager* where I used to hunt for insects.

I shall keep jotting down my dreams and will send them to you.

Miwa, in my thoughts I am much too brutal to myself—I wish I could have gentler feelings toward myself. Also, I don't understand why but I feel a murderous hatred toward my fellow men—I feel that they are holding me down. I don't always feel this way, just sometimes. I can't understand the reason for this feeling as I have always been treated with the greatest kindness.

Love,
Tony

Notes from a Psychiatric Consultation on Antony Baekeland, New York, March 12, 1971

Patient's family a strange and difficult one. Patient's father a rigid moody person who is always right about any subject that comes up and brooks no discussion. Cutting and critical in his relationship to everyone and more particularly to patient. He eventually separated from his wife, patient's mother, and established a relationship with the girlfriend of patient, with whom he is now living.

Patient's mother is a very beautiful talented woman, extremely seductive in her relationships with men, and with patient. She finds reasons to have him live with her and alternates between extreme seductiveness and a strange sort of provocativeness which drives patient to distraction. She speaks of suicide frequently to patient.

Patient shows clear-cut indications of a thought disorder. Has had delusions, some paranoid ideation. Although the entire picture is modified by drug use, particularly marijuana, the essential diagnosis is paranoid schizophrenia. Psychiatric hospitalization and psychotherapy recommended, but patient's father is unwilling to pay for this.

Official Visitors File, Broadmoor Special Hospital, December 9, 1973

VISITOR'S NAME: Mr. Brooks Baekeland
RELATIONSHIP TO PATIENT: Father
SUMMARY: Tall, spare, handsome American now almost Europeanized. He still broods over his awful family tragedy and speaks of tapes to which his now-dead wife had committed her

confused, psychotic thoughts. Not prepared to accept son outside hospital. Was relieved to hear that there was no immediate prospect of discharge. Will write in advance for an appointment next time!

SYLVIE BAEKELAND SKIRA

Brooks and Tony were different in a million ways but they were alike in the sense that for both of them there were no rules anywhere. They had the sense of "we are beyond rules, outside laws." Yet Tony was brought up permissively while Brooks had been very strictly brought up. Later, of course, Brooks transgressed. He was the Baekeland son who rebelled, breaking a pattern and going off in different ways—oh yes.

BROOKS BAEKELAND

I was always free. I was always successful in everything I wished to do. But I despised success. I despised money and show. I laughed—a grave offense to those who cannot laugh! I thumbed my nose at my father and at the sheepism of Man. Subconsciously he knew that I derided all that he did not dare not to be. I was not only a black sheep but far, far worse—I was a laughing black sheep who made him doubt his money-god.

My first wife was one of *them*. And Barbara's poor son got his values from her—most of them—but he was torn in a war in his own soul.

SYLVIE BAEKELAND SKIRA

Brooks's father was dead when I met Brooks, but echoes of him were with us all the time. I think that Brooks is very much like his father, though he always compared him to Louis XVI—that is, a man in a very prominent position who wanted his privacy and would rather play in the toolshed.

There was opposition there. Perhaps Brooks's father didn't respect Brooks enough—I don't know. They were two men chasing each other. But isn't it the classic story of the great captain of industry like Brooks's grandfather who founds a big thing and leaves so much money it dilapidates the lives of those who inherit it?

From the Private Diaries of Leo Hendrik Baekeland, March 24, 1908

Would like to have my son George's picture as he sits in a big chair, doing his arithmetic, his fine crop of hair slantingly covering half of his broad forehead.

From the Private Diaries of Leo Hendrik Baekeland, July 16, 1908

George behaved very brutally toward his sister Nina, beating her when she came up hill with parts of his tents. Reprimands, tears, and punishment.

CÉLINE ROLL KARRAKER
My mother, Nina Baekeland Roll, who died several years ago, never liked either of her parents—she was a very rebellious sort of child, I guess. I think her brother got all the attention. You know, in a European family the son is the preferred one.

From the Private Diaries of Leo Hendrik Baekeland, January 28, 1910

My wife has swollen eyes from crying yesterday evening all on account of silly discussion relative George.

From the Private Diaries of Leo Hendrik Baekeland, January 30, 1910

George and Nina went to a party and came back shortly before midnight. George was the only boy who had no tuxedo suit. I like it better this way than if he was the only one who *had* a tuxedo suit.

BROOKS BAEKELAND

When I was in my teens, LHB would invite me to lunch in New York at the Century or the University Club. Impressed by my dapper father on the importance of correct dress for every occasion, I would appear at these amazing convocations in a proper dark suit—all shined and polished and tongue-tied—and LHB, with a Packard specially built for him so he could wear a top hat in it and get in and out almost without bending, would arrive in his one and only suit for town and the inevitable sneakers. He would poke fun at my sartorial splendor and lecture me on the delusion of "appearances." I was not old enough to guess, then, at the deep and divisive philosophical chasm that separated him—the exuberant, joyful immigrant and self-made man—from the Grand Duke, as we children called our father.

LHB talked to everyone and anyone who would listen or could teach, and had no prejudices. No—he hated fools. His son, Geoffrey Gorer's typical second-generation American, became an elegant and a bigot, and was—I mean it seriously—ashamed of his famous father. He was ashamed of LHB's barefooted beachcombing, ashamed of the *Ion*, because it was not a proper yacht but a sort of Bahama-going houseboat with a couple of "niggers" aboard—a disorderly laboratory that could put up a sail of sorts and where LHB could cook his "disgusting" meals, jump in the "ding" and go hobbling about bare-assed over the beaches of the thousands of unnamed keys, with a small magnifying glass, a notebook, a penknife, and a lemon—no doubt talking to himself. Who in hell else *was* there to talk to? I ask the same question myself!

You see, there was a tension in this family that extended over three generations, and that was reenacted between my first wife, Barbara, and my son, Tony, and myself—a tension between two fundamentally different views of life. I do not care, for instance, what other people think of me, and that was a source of the bitterest philosophical difference between myself and Barbara Baekeland, who lived and fought for what the French call *le parade*—appearances, what other people think, etc.

My father also cared too much about what others thought of him. He had not inherited *his* papa's burning-glass mind. That was not his fault. But he had no sense of humor, and without that a person is better off dead. Oh, he liked jokes and retold them. That is not a sense of humor.

**From the Private Diaries of Leo Hendrik Baekeland,
December 11, 1909**

George is undoubtedly an earnest serious boy but I am afraid
that he is going to turn into a fault-finding criticizing belittling
man. Sooner have him less serious, less steady, and somewhat
more enthusiastic than to see him grow up into one of those
men who always find fault with others.

ELIZABETH ARCHER BAEKELAND

George Baekeland was completely intolerant of everything. I remember when I met Sterling Hayden and he heard that my name
was Baekeland, he said, "Any relation to George Baekeland?" I said,
"He was my father-in-law." He said he had crewed on George
Baekeland's yacht one summer. This was when Sterling was a young
man, before he was a star. "George Baekeland," he said. "Right-wing
bastard."

CÉLINE ROLL KARRAKER

We kids were terrified of Uncle George, but he also taught us to be
super sailors, marvelous people in the water and in the woods. He
was very demanding—you had to do everything exactly right. And it
was frightening, because if you did it wrong you really got it. But we
stuck with it, because he knew and he taught us and it was wonderful
to learn from him.

He used to take us to the Adirondacks in the wintertime when
nobody else in the family would and put up with all these kids. He
taught us to iceboat, and later we built our own iceboat and sailed it
in the lake.

Uncle George apparently once put a canoe in the Hudson River at
Yonkers with his brother-in-law, my father, George Roll, and they
decided to go to the headwaters of the river, just paddle as far as they
could. And they ended up right near what became our family camp
in the Adirondacks.

Grandmother bought the camp in 1923, but I read somewhere that
Grandpapa had sent her and Uncle George and my mother off to the
Adirondacks as early as 1907, 1908—to the Adirondack League Club
for a holiday. So they knew that region quite early.

Grandmother named the camp Utowana Lodge. Later it was called just Baekeland Camp. She loved the place. Even after she'd had many strokes she continued to come up.

BROOKS BAEKELAND

Until her strokes, my grandmother had always run our camp in the Adirondacks, served by a motley of people, some of whom did not even speak English—a Polish chef, for instance, who wore a chef's hat. But the last and most massive of her strokes left her partially paralyzed and speechless.

It was her doctor's opinion that, along with her speech function, her higher thought functions had also been destroyed. Gradually, as it was deemed that her death was imminent, her daughter and her grandchildren fell into the habit of talking around her, in ways that they would never have dreamed of doing had they thought she could understand—going even so far, I once remember, as to speculate upon her will and her fortune. To tell the truth, I also believed that she was unable to understand. Almost. But in a sort of private romantic tribute to her somewhere spirit, even if it resided no longer behind those lifeless eyes, I would sit for an hour or two at a time when I went to see her, which was as often as my busy life allowed, and talk to her as if she understood, or read to her—I had always read to her while she had her breakfast on a tray when we were at The Anchorage. Believe me, it was a difficult charade—to talk easily, convincingly, and naturally to a person with a clawlike hand and drooling, twisted mouth, a face unrecognizable, a grotesque Swiss woodcarver's mask; to talk, without ever receiving the smallest sign of understanding, as though to the once so civilized, gifted, humorous woman that she was, and then to kiss that cold, necrotic face again in parting, with a promise each time to come back soon.

The poor bored nurses, who treated her as they would a two-month-old baby, used to rejoice on seeing me, for it gave them time off—often most of the day if I could stay that long. They soon gave up trying to get me to talk to *them*, which they craved, for they had long run out of anything to say to each other. I do not know what they thought of my charade but I can guess.

My father paid regular visits, too, but they were to see that his mother was being properly cared for. Her state embarrassed him. Frankly, no one could wish—for her sake—that she would live on, but there was nothing that anyone could, or would, do to abbreviate her shame. I say her shame, for that was what we all felt: how she would hate it if she knew.

One day, after she had been in this condition already for several years, and I was up there studying my graduate physics and mathematics after our usual "talking" and "reading" session, I saw her eyes seeming to look at an open magazine. I said to her: "On this page there is the word 'state' in large letters. Can you point to it?" She slowly extended the hand over which she still had partial control and with her index finger indicated the word. I tried others. Slowly and painfully she identified them all correctly. In a few minutes, using a large and heavy cardboard, I had constructed an alphabet matrix with large letters. I put it in front of her and, taking a pad and pencil, asked her to dictate to me. Slowly she wrote: "Thank you, dear Brooks. Thank you for existing." She had said these same words to me once many years before.

I then asked her if she wanted to dictate a letter to me.

"A telegram," she wrote.

I took it down. It was to David Fairchild's wife, Marian. "My son Brooks"—she didn't say "grandson"—"has given me back my speech. Greetings from Céline Baekeland."

From that moment on, that imperious old lady began to take over some control of her own life again. Her nurses no longer treated her like a driveling baby and her family no longer spoke in front of her as if she no longer existed. She lived on for quite a few more years.

Céline Roll Karraker

For a few summers grandmother hired a little plane to get up to the Adirondacks—her doctor, who would come along, was terrified of flying in such a little plane but *she* thought it was great sport. She always thought everything was an adventure. The plane would land in the lake right up by the dock and she'd be lifted out. We built this boardwalk for her wheelchair, and she'd be in her wheelchair and fish.

Later on in the family there were some incidents up in the Adirondacks that were very odd and violent. Tony was a disturbed person, I think, very young. His cousins always felt that he was odd. The kids all played together, you know, and they were in the woods once and something caught fire. We had a fire.

The kids and Tony grew apart. They were uncomfortable with him. And you know, for years we didn't see him because Brooks and Barbara went to live in Europe.

Barbara and I were great, dear friends. She was just a delightful, warm-spirited person. And absolutely fearless. A very exciting person! We spent a lot of time at the camp together, especially during the war when Brooks was away.

SYLVIE BAEKELAND SKIRA
Barbara, I'm told, hated camp. Because there was no glamour. She thought it was all very boring. All that sand in your shoes, and canoeing and so on. It had no dash. This was the "old world" that she had wanted to marry into, but this was the part that she *didn't* want.

NINA DALY
The Baekeland family had a place up in the Adirondacks. A big place. Members of the family still own it, and every summer usually they go to camp. One family is there, another will come. It's a lovely place to be. You get up there in the hot summer and it's a joy, it's always so cool up there. You always sleep with blankets over you.

ELIZABETH ARCHER BAEKELAND
Each member of the family had his own cabin, a wonderful old log cabin—Bonbon, the old lady, had had them built so they fit right into the woods—and each cabin had three or four bedrooms. Fred, when I was married to him, used his father's cabin.

DR. FREDERICK BAEKELAND
Over the long haul, except from sort of a novelistic point of view, the life-as-fiction point of view, the only person in my opinion in this family of any real fame is my grandfather. Not that there haven't been other people, some of whom have been hardworking and achieved a certain amount and so on, but—and I'm including myself—they're rather insignificant.

My father? Oh, my father went to Cornell for two years, then he went off to the Air Force in the First World War, then he graduated from the Colorado School of Mines. Then he worked as a petroleum geologist in Spain, and after that in Africa. And after that he went into the family business. No one in the family besides my father was ever asked to go into the business. You had to be asked.

From the Private Diaries of Leo Hendrik Baekeland, February 8, 1908

Céline found out that they wanted to make our son George president of his class but he refused and afterwards when asked why by his mother said he was satisfied with the thought that they had asked him.

Letter from Leo Hendrik Baekeland to George Baekeland, May 5, 1928

Coconut Grove, Florida

Dear George,

I have read carefully your long and excellent letter of May 2. Your whole point of view is perfectly correct and appreciated by me. It is your duty as a father to look ahead to the future and to discount possible events.

But you undoubtedly know that the main reason why I did not urge the directors of Bakelite Corporation to increase your salary or bonus is that I desired to set an example to the others of our staff and not give them an opportunity of thinking that you might be favored as the son of the president.

I am intensely pleased to learn that outsiders have discovered your talents and are now making you offers of a partnership which would put your present income entirely in the shade. In fact, I wonder whether I am not doing you an injustice—whether I am not doing harm to your career by proposing you a more favorable arrangement with Bakelite than the present one, so as to secure the continuation of your services with me—but I believe in the future of Bakelite even if at present you may have better opportunities elsewhere. Furthermore I am getting old and I cannot miss your assistance in my work and responsibilities. If I had to do so I would sooner retire entirely even if this be to the detriment of the fortunes of the whole family.

During the several years you have been working with me I have had abundant opportunity for observing you and the value of your services, your knowledge, assiduity, versatility, and the tact and good judgment you have displayed in matters of importance. In continuing your help in the development of this enterprise you will help the interests of the whole Baekeland family as no one else can.

I believe I have told or written you formerly that I have been so well satisfied with your services that I am planning on putting my holdings of Bakelite stock in a trusteeship which would continue after my death and make you the directing and administrative head of these holdings; this Bakelite stock, to be administered by you for the benefit of your mother or any other beneficiaries she or I may designate. But all this may involve delays, as it requires some lawyers' work, also perhaps some changes in my will or other complications.

So as to make a practical start and so as to make you feel that any benefit I or our family receive through your excellent cooperation, I now make you formally the following offer which you can accept or reject after I shall have met you in New York, which will occur in a few days:

In addition to any salaries, bonus or other compensation you are receiving from Bakelite Corporation or its subsidiaries as director, officer or other employment, I shall pay you: 1/ One half i.e. fifty percent of any fees or compensation collected for my services from Bakelite Corporation after proper deductions have been made for my income taxes, and other expenses or disbursements made by me in relation thereto. 2/ This agreement shall run from year to year by mutual consent.

Please be ready to discuss these matters as soon as I arrive in New York. I can meet you at the University Club where we shall be able to discuss these matters without being disturbed. If then you agree, you should signify your acceptance by letter.

Affectionately,
L. H. Baekeland

Letter from George Baekeland to Leo Hendrik Baekeland, May 16, 1928

New York

My dear Dad:
Although I replied to your letter of May 5th at our recent talk together at the University Club, nevertheless, for good order's

sake I should like to confirm that reply by saying again that I am decided to remain with our company out of consideration for the family ties and all they involve and on account of the generous and promising arrangement which you proposed in your letter.

I am happy that the whole matter has been so amicably settled and that it resulted in no misunderstanding. It has caused me a great deal of concern for fear that you might attribute to it motives which have not existed, or that you might think me disloyal or foolhardy.

The outcome has resulted in a decidedly more intimate interest in my work here and an added bond of devotion.

Affectionately,
George

From the Private Diaries of Leo Hendrik Baekeland, March 18, 1908

In fact, the whole history of the development of Bakelite in its different phases has been the history of looking at matters from my own standpoint.

BROOKS BAEKELAND

In the Bakelite Corporation, the Roll descendants—my Aunt Nina and her four children—held common stock, and the Baekeland descendants—my father and his three children—held, but in considerably less amount, preferred stock, all this in trusts mostly. The Roll children would inherit automatically at twenty-one but the Baekeland children would not inherit automatically but at the discretion of my father and only on his death. Great trust was put in "George's judgment," that he would do the right thing. This extra liberty of action had been his reward for having given up his career as an exploring petroleum engineer to enter and become the vice-president of the Bakelite Corporation, as LHB began to feel himself getting old. And though my grandfather could hardly have had many illusions about the suitability of what he was doing—for any fool could have seen that my father had no business talent—it was in the old European tradition of family.

I doubt that LHB really considered any other alternative. He knew that time was running out for him. He wanted to retire and to prepare the way—and it *had* to be his son. For him, Bakelite—and all of its ramifications both backwards and forwards in time—was a family business, to stay in the family and be of the family. It is as banal as "Emil Duval et Fils" written over the entrance to a small electrolytic zinc plating establishment in Auteuil.

My father did everything he could all his life to disassociate himself from that, from "Duval et Fils." And thus, as soon as LHB began to become senile—it took twelve years, and in those years Zeus gradually became Pan—and could no longer oversee the Bakelite Corporation, my father sold the whole thing. Disastrously, as it turned out, for the whole family but particularly for his own children. He destroyed the Baekeland fortune. He destroyed the Baekeland family.

He then began to lead that life of a country squire—expensive cars, expensive tailors, elegant yachts, shooting in Scotland, playing bridge with the Duke and Duchess of Windsor in Nassau, and all the rest—that showed him not the son of an American immigrant but an English duke without a title.

That day I climbed up to the tower of Snug Rock, I brought back a lot of early photographs of my grandfather, my grandmother, my father as a boy, and his little sister Nina.

Well, one day he came to visit Barbara and me in New York—he had occasional generous impulses; there was a wanting-to-love man buried there under all that neurotic scar tissue. Barbara was out. I was on the fourth floor—as far as I could get away from my social wife's life—studying, no doubt, when I heard the doorbell ring.

I went down. It was my father. The Grand Duke. A rare and fluttery event. What to do with him? A glass of port? One always had to entertain him—like royalty. He had no conversation. One ended up chattering, feeling a perfect fool. That is perhaps the principal reason royalty has been almost universally suppressed: it is utterly useless and makes intelligent people feel stupid.

And then I had an inspiration—nothing else had worked. I took him up to my study to show him the wonderful photos I had brought back from Snug Rock. I was also hybridizing orchids up there, under all sorts of artificially simulated climatic conditions. The orchids did not interest him in the least, not even the fact that I had some growing in conditions approximating fourteen thousand feet in Peru and Chile and, in a glass case right next to them, some growing at sea level in Sumatra—different pressures, sunrise and sunset times, temperatures, humidities, and seasons. I began to take out all those photos showing him as a small boy on the knee of Zeus, etc.

And he would not, he could not, it almost seemed as though he *dared* not, look at a single photo of his father!

That was when I first grew up, so to speak, insofar as understanding my lifelong problem with Father was concerned. After that day I no longer feared him. I pitied him. I understood his tragedy and it horrified me.

He was first and always the beloved apple of his mother's eye. My grandmother was so besotted she told my mother when she married my father that "George is a combination of Leonardo da Vinci and Jesus Christ." I concluded that he was protected early from Zeus and that he was not intimate with his father, that eccentric tyrant figure, whose lava outpourings of speech and learning and whose intolerance of folly must have made him a dreadful person in the house, an awesome parent. A man who could not stand noise, save it issued from his own mouth. Zeus, the terrible.

Judging from the fact that my father always hated and distrusted "intellectuals" and read with the slowness and concentrated effort of a peasant, and from the fact that the interests and style he soon developed were totally opposite to his father's—that is, all things physical and sporting—and that he spent enormous sums of money all his life on things elegant and beautiful, and became what I call a high-class redneck, to the right of Right—from all this, I take it that he had made, and perhaps with his mother's connivance, a classic revolt against his father.

But—and this is what interests me—my father apparently never actually defied my grandfather. In fact, he obeyed to the point of wrecking his own happiness. You might interpret his obedience to what he feared and loathed as showing a lack of courage, but I think there was a still stronger influence that made defiance unthinkable. Despite his efforts to separate himself from everything that had a foreign accent, so to speak, to be a real—but tip-top-class—American, or even better yet, a noble Englishman, Snug Rock was a thoroughgoing piece of bourgeois Europe, and in Europe, Victorian Europe, filial obedience was total. The only alternative was to "run away to sea"—leave home forever. With his mother's devoted protection, that would never have been necessary. All he had to do was to see as little of his father as possible, and that was easy, for LHB was always working or away.

And then, in the few years before he joined what was then I think the Signal Corps and went to Italy as an aviator, he met and fell in love with the most beautiful girl in the Hudson River Valley—my mother, Cornelia Fitch Middlebrook, a thirteenth-generation American, descended from founding fathers and from governors of New York State, etc., etc. They were engaged shortly before he went off to war. He was the happiest man in the world.

He was unlucky in being sent to Italy. The great Italian immigration to America had already begun, and to him, Italians were fellows in undershirts and paper-bag hats who dug ditches or labored in his parents' gardens and greenhouses. He was sent to Foggia, where he flew Caproni bombers and where his commanding officer was Fiorello La Guardia, later mayor of New York, a small, talkative, emotional man whom he despised. I remember, as a boy, hearing him brag how he would shoulder "wops" off the sidewalks in Italy. Of the Renaissance, of ancient Rome, of Italian science, music, philosophy, mathematics, he knew nothing. "What did Italians ever do?" he would say, in later years. I would tell him. "Oh, artists!" he would say with contempt. I would then cite for him Italian figures in America who were distinguished scientists, politicians, bankers, industrialists, and even—best of all—multimillionaires. He would stare at me in disbelief, offended by such disgusting paradoxes. He felt the same about the Jews—or any immigrant people. When I was doing graduate work in physics he asked me once, in a lowered voice: "Einstein is a fake, isn't he?" And these were all *idées reçus*, not gotten from his parents but from twentieth-century America as it was then.

My father hoped he was a total conformist. In fact, he was not only a right-wing radical but a misanthrope, who never had any friends, except those who could flatter him. Flattery was the only road to him, but his cruelty closed that road for me. He ended up sincerely preferring dogs to people.

But he was not quite the two-dimensional figure that I was then still persuaded he was. No one is. He was a man born out of his place, out of his time, and a man with superb—unused, curdling—gifts. He was, for instance, gifted with his hands—he loved cabinetwork—and he had a love of speed, was as quick and coordinated as a cat. He could be fun and even witty when he was happy, and he loved jokes—when they were on others. He was a man who on a camping trip would nail some friend's shoes to the floor by his bed, his friend presumably drunk and deaf to the hammering, but would be red-faced mad if someone had done that to him. He was a wonderful practical joker and gave me some bad examples in that line, but he was never one to see himself in a funny light. I thought, even as a small child, that that was weird—mad, somehow. I could not understand it. I am not sure I do now.

He also had—but alas, it was superficial—dash, or what the French call *panache*. It was show. He was always, metaphorically speaking, standing at a mirror. He was totally conscious of his own style. But finally, his arrogance and his misanthropy were ego-saving rationalizations for a deep shyness and sense of his social incapacities. I know this because I am his son and have inherited many of the same disabilities.

My father roared out in the dark to keep the demons away. It was easy, being such a rich and protected man. As my grandmother used to say, "One of the uses of money is that it allows us not to live with the consequences of our mistakes." He even fooled himself. I do not think he ever suspected that he had lived his whole life through at bay. Think of this. It is sad. After all, we do not have much time here, and to spend it *all* with our backs against the wall . . . But I suppose a large part of humanity does, and that is even sadder.

After my father and mother were married they went out to Golden, Colorado, then a village, where he entered the Colorado School of Mines. He had decided to be a geologist—geologists lived out of doors, hammered rocks, prospected for gold, built bridges over rushing torrents in darkest Africa and other romantic parts of the world. It was my father who gave me my romantic interest in faraway places— the Arctic, Africa, South America, the sounding seas—ships, adventure, the noble savage, etc.

In Golden, my mother bore him two children—first my sister and then, fifteen months later, myself. Upon graduation, with the aid of my grandfather, he was signed on to go down to Tunisia and Algeria and prospect for oil.

Engineering was the romantic thing in those days. It was the engineers, in their open-necked shirts, riding britches, boots, and pipe in hand or mouth, who were pushing civilization out into the "native" parts of the world. It was the tail end of Cecil Rhodes's world, the do-gooding-but-oh-so-much-money-making world of the British Empire. It was "a man's life." My father had made a choice that I could have certainly made myself—one part of me would have, for I have always had both sides in me, the active and the intellectual, and they have often been in conflict.

Eventually my grandparents decided that my father was to return at "a very good salary" and become vice-president of the Bakelite Corporation in New York, then headquarters for the German, English, American, and Japanese branches, and that "the young people" were to live in Yonkers, not far from Snug Rock, while my father made "a splendid career" in Bakelite. In the summers my mother and her two small children would move up to the Adirondacks.

My father ought to have pursued his open-air, adventurous, supermasculine life. But the promise of that "very good salary" and that "splendid career" and—what?—shame?—hope?— made him take a decision that embittered and diminished him for the rest of his life. In every blow that he beat his two young children there was the rage and bitterness of a man who hated himself—and so hated the world.

After his "very good salary" and other perks became so fabulous in the roaring twenties that he could move away from Yonkers, he bought a place surrounded by woods in Scarsdale where he built a swimming pool—a novelty in those days—and, on the same property, another house for himself, the Doggery, where he lived with his dogs and mounted heads, coming to "our" house only for meals. He did not stay with his wife after dinner but, always in dinner jacket, worked in his shop, making, for instance, sailing boats. He was an insomniac all his life, and, crazy with frustrated sexuality, would swim at night for hours up and down his pool to exhaust himself sufficiently to sleep.

We two—and later, three—children took it quite for granted that on our property there should be two separate establishments, one for my father and one for us and our mother. We always dreaded the black-cloud returns of "George" from his office on Park Avenue. Once, I saw with amazement a rat, not a squirrel, jump from the big sycamore near my bedroom window to the roof of the house. I could not wait to tell my father, for I had not known that rats could climb trees. I imagined it might please that man I so feared and who, even then, I had to entertain and—I did not know it yet—be superior to. Not easy at five or six. Calling me a liar and saying he would teach me a lesson, he beat me with the back of a hairbrush. He could never keep his temper and knew no other recourses than the Gestapo ones—beatings, threats, reprisals. And we were all so weak, in our own ways—such sinful creatures, so culpably misguided, so unable to do right in my father's eyes, so wanting to please, so terrified of doing wrong.

On the other hand, and sadly for my father, I was a person born with an inordinate and growing pride, and I began to stiffen and resist as time passed. As my darling Sylvie has pointed out to me, a child that knows it is loved will accept any punishment from the person who loves him, even when it is unjust, but no child will accept even just punishment from a person who dislikes him. And my father detested his children.

GEOFFREY PARSONS

They were three of the brightest children I've ever known. Little Cornelia—the family called her Dickie—was the most marvelous child. Very beautiful, and full of creative imagination—a real original. She was wounded permanently by her father. She was a brilliant girl and he cut off her education with boarding school, saying that she was not worth educating. Her response to this was the usual one—she married the first eligible man who asked her in order to get free of family. She's been married three times, I think. Without that father, there's no saying what her life might have been.

As for Fred, the younger boy, he always wanted to be a composer, but George told him in no uncertain terms that music was an avocation, not a vocation, and threatened to cut him off without a penny if he pursued a musical career. So Fred became a doctor, choosing psychiatry as his specialty. I believe he has written numerous scholarly papers. He's also an accomplished art historian.

Brooks was seven years older than Fred and about a year and a half younger than Dickie, and he was always the most brilliant of the children. He had a quick eye and a vivid curiosity. He could have been anything he chose to be. Instead, he's spent his entire life running—from or after something.

BROOKS BAEKELAND

I was a hunter, I smelled a kill far—oh, far indeed, perhaps one life would not be enough. I was running fast always on fresh snow.

Each of my father's children had to make his own kind of defense. I chose—I had no choice—a sulking, black defiance. My whole spirit was in opposition to my father, though way down in him there was a sweetness that some, even my mother, recognized was there. There is a child in everyone; it is the child we love. It was the child in Barbara that I had always loved. I love my mother, too, as I love children. She was and is the quintessence of the feminine—loyal, sentimental, fragile, beautiful.

GEOFFREY PARSONS

Brooks's mother is much too beautiful for her own and everybody
else's good. Her whole life has been theater, with her own charming
self always at stage center. She's just as smart as vinegar laced with a
good mustard but it's all buried beneath a foot of the best goose
down. The only relation that anyone—man, woman, child, even her
own children—can have with her is a flirtatious one, in my opinion.
As you can imagine, she's always had a score of admirers—including, I must confess, myself.

ELIZABETH ARCHER BAEKELAND

A lot of pressure to marry money had been put on Brooks's mother by
her family, who'd lost all their money. Poor Cornelia, you know—
she was really sacrificed. She was a very sensitive romantic creature
and there was just never any rapport between her and George
Baekeland.

How she left him is a fascinating story. She wanted to get away one
winter and her friends were all going down to some club in Florida,
and George didn't want her to stay at this particular club. He said,
"You can go only if you stay at *my* club." So she went to his club—
alone—and one night there was a fancy-dress ball and she was coming down the stairs and she suddenly caught the eye of this man. He
just looked up at her—you know, across a crowded room. Pong! Just
like that—love. He went over and asked her to dance.

His name was Penn Hallowell, N. Penrose Hallowell, and he was
from Boston and he was married at the time. Now, Cornelia is a very
honorable person—I have tremendous love and admiration for her. I
think she's the kind of person who probably, once she met Penn
Hallowell, couldn't bear to stay with George Baekeland and just said
to him, "Look, I'm in love with somebody else, let me go." I mean,
she wouldn't make any bones about it. So anyway, he let her go, but
on one condition—she had to give up custody of her children. Fred
was only seven at the time, Brooks was fourteen, and Dickie was
almost sixteen.

George gave her only five thousand dollars a year to live on. And
Penn Hallowell didn't support her, because that was against his prin-
ciples. He would bring her gifts—he would bring her very *nice*
gifts—but he never gave any money. So she was strapped in those
years.

The children were all away at boarding school, and on vacations they were with Cornelia as much as with George, even though he had the custody. The only problem the boys ever had with her was getting to *see* her. They always had to make a date two weeks in advance or something, she had so many admirers. She was a good mother, though—so charming and so gracious, and so beautiful!

For years after she left George, Penn Hallowell did not marry Cornelia, because, as I said, he already was married. Everybody knew about them but *they* didn't know that *anybody* knew and they were always so careful. And when they finally "came out"—after twenty years, which was when his wife died—everybody said, "Oh, finally Penn Hallowell has married his lovely mistress." He was eighty then and she was sixty-five. He died five years later and she was absolutely distraught. They were lovers right up to the end of their lives.

SYLVIE BAEKELAND SKIRA

He was her man, yes. Brooks told me that she kept his room just the way it was before he died. His little slippers. His little bathrobe, exactly where it was, and so on. I have never been in Brooks's mother's apartment in New York. I've never been to camp. I was never invited. Brooks never took me. This is why I keep saying, the story is there but I am not in it, I have been a bit player.

You know, she always spoke of her husband as Buck—that was her nickname for him. That's where she was rather touching and sweet. To marry Penn Hallowell was—I don't know—the dream of her life.

ELIZABETH ARCHER BAEKELAND

George Baekeland married again about two years after the divorce from Cornelia. His new wife came from out West—good American stock, though I heard her father sold watches and inexpensive jewelry. She was absolutely beautiful. And very musical—she played the piano. She's about eighty now, I guess.

I remember Dickie saying about her, "She's *lovely* to *look* at, de-*light*ful to *know*"—you know. So the children gave their stepmother a hard time but they liked her. Of course, they *adored* their mother.

Brooks wrote a story about his mother called "The Shrike." I don't think it was ever published but we all read it. A shrike is a bird that kills its prey with its beak, and the story was based on the fact that five men were supposed to have committed suicide over Cornelia. There was *one*, definitely. And all this upset the kids terribly.

SYLVIE BAEKELAND SKIRA

Brooks's mother was a great beauty. That's one of the reasons she and Barbara got along so well—Brooks says because of that great beauty club that you have in America. Also, Barbara was, I think, very clever with her mother-in-law—she tried to please her very much and did.

Brooks's mother is a very difficult person. She came to visit us in Brittany. Brooks had said to me in advance that she was a prima donna. All these Baekelands have egos that are tremendous and there's not much room for anybody else.

Brooks has a great *coquetterie* of mentioning his age all the time, which can be a sort of vanity if you look very handsome and yet you say, "I'm as old as Methuselah," so that then the other person has to say, "My goodness, you're handsome!" So whenever Brooks would say how old he was, his mother would say, "Stop annoying us with your age. *Do* stop talking about your age *all* the time!" She disliked me right away, very much. Because I had replaced Barbara. And because I didn't pay court to her at all. She told me, "Sylvie, why don't you put some makeup on? A woman always looks better with her face made up."

NINA DALY

Mrs. Hallowell was devoted to Barbara and Barbara was devoted to her. She's a beautiful woman, you know. A blonde. Blue eyes. Nice figure. She was Tony's other grandmother.

SYLVIE BAEKELAND SKIRA

Mrs. Hallowell wrote to Tony right after he killed Barbara. She was horrified, of course. I can't say that she wasn't horrified from the heart—I don't know—but she was certainly horrified by the scandal. She's, I think, in a way an old-fashioned person—no, not old-fashioned, conventional—and she really doesn't think this is a very nice story. She never liked anything Tony did that wasn't proper behavior. I mean, she didn't think it was very attractive for her grandson to come to lunch at the Ritz or some decent tea place dressed like a hippie, let's say.

ELIZABETH ARCHER BAEKELAND

I think the drama of it got Cornelia more than anything. I mean, to write and say, "Tony, why and how did you kill your mother?"

shocked me a bit. Fred was shocked, too—everybody was shocked. She wanted me to read Tony's reply. I just couldn't, though I must admit it was hard to resist.

BROOKS BAEKELAND

My poor Barbara. She was in so many ways a marvelous person. And—though the world knew it not—impossible. I always felt that I was not a great enough man for her. What she needed was a Henry VIII. But of course she finally had him—in her son, and he chopped off her head. So to speak.

To tell you truly, I think there is only one true kind of love, and that is the love of a mother for a child—utterly brave, loyal, forgiving, generous, and without a jot of self-love in it. That said, I believe that insofar as we really love one another—when we do, and it is rare—it is in this way.

I must now tell you of the last time I saw my poor father. I think it was in 1964 or 1965. I knew he had not many years—or even months—to live, and I went up to Connecticut to see him. I do not suppose that I had spent a total of more than twenty-five hours with him in the previous twenty years.

His wife had left us alone together. He was confused—not just in the philosophic sense, but medically. He was far gone in senile dementia. To entertain him I had brought some slides of the expedition in Peru that I had made with Peter Gimbel the year before. I showed them to him in the living room. He understood nothing, or little. And then, seeing that I was not succeeding in entertaining him, I said that I would now be going back to New York, would someone drive me to the station.

He offered to come with me. His young gardener drove; my father could no longer drive a car. It was while we were driving to the station that I realized—and I am sure *he* realized—that we would never see each other again. As we stood together on the railroad platform, on an impulse I took him strongly in my arms and kissed him, hard, *à l'européen*. I was forty-three. He was seventy. We had not kissed—we had hardly shaken hands—a dozen times in all my life. Both of us were suddenly crying and speechless. Both of us, now that it was too late, asking the other for forgiveness, me for having so disappointed him, he for having been such a lousy parent, and God knows what else—everything, all the *malheur du siècle*, all that we might have done, should have done, did not do, all the beauty lost, all the love not loved.

From the *New York Times*, February 1, 1966

GEORGE BAEKELAND OF BAKELITE; SON OF PLASTICS MAKER IS DEAD

Special to the *New York Times*
FAIRFIELD, Conn., Jan. 31

George Baekeland, former vice president and director of the Bakelite Corporation and a sportsman, died today. He was 70 years old. . . .

He hunted big game and shot grouse on the Scottish moors. A crack trap and skeet shot, he wrote *Gunner's Guide*, published by Macmillan in 1948.

Mr. Baekeland was also a yachtsman and fisherman and had ridden in point-to-point races. He painted water-colors and made etchings, too.

Surviving are his widow; two sons; a daughter; a sister; and four grandchildren.

From the Last Will and Testament of George Baekeland, October 31, 1958

I, GEORGE BAEKELAND, of the Town of Fairfield, County of Fairfield, and State of Connecticut, do hereby . . . give, devise, and bequeath absolutely to my wife, if she survives me, all my real property wherever situated.

BROOKS BAEKELAND

When my father died and his will was read, I immediately understood what it meant and what had happened. He had disinherited me by an indirect means. He had left to his wife *outright*—rather than in a marital trust that would have given her the income for life, with the corpus going to later generations—most of the money he himself had made on the sale of the Bakelite Corporation to Union Carbide. This, despite how at the dinner table he always used to inveigh against women, saying—according to his lifelong doctrine of misogyny—"Don't ever leave money outright to a woman but always in trust." So now any future inheritance from my father was left hanging. It is thanks to the generosity of my grandparents only that I am self-supporting.

Sylvie Baekeland Skira

Brooks said that the antagonism between his father and mother had been so great that that was why his father had cut off the children. He also said that his father had sold out the business without even consulting his children.

From the Last Will and Testament of George Baekeland, October 31, 1958

> I hereby nominate, designate, and appoint HENRY GAS-SAWAY DAVIS to succeed me, upon my death, as Trustee under said trust agreements, each made the 29th day of December 1933, between L. H. Baekeland, as Grantor, and Céline Baekeland and L. H. Baekeland, as Trustees.

Elizabeth Archer Baekeland

It was Henry Gassaway Davis, a friend of George Baekeland's who had been disinherited by his own father and was very bitter about it, who persuaded George to disinherit *his* kids, saying, "I didn't inherit any money and look at me—I'm very successful." So George's second wife now has all those millions, and nobody knows who she's going to leave them to when she dies. Of course, Leo Baekeland had left his grandchildren money.

Brooks Baekeland

Henry Gassaway Davis was a powerful and charming figure who had always dominated us all. It was he who engineered the disastrous sale of the Bakelite Corporation to Union Carbide, just before the mightiest rise in the history of the chemical industry, which topped in 1946. During this time Bakelite, if my father wanted out—which he did, and was the whole point—ought to have gone public under a new president, after which the family shares could have been sold publicly and reinvested in something like the young IBM. But all that makes no difference now. What happened was that he made the worst choice possible.

It was fate that brought together those two child-haters, my father and Henry Gassaway Davis, the much- and so-many-times-disastrously-married Henry Davis—including to two Vanderbilt girls. The drunken and violent father who had disowned him used to hold a cocked and loaded revolver to Henry's head when Henry was a boy, and as so often happens—perversely—the mistreated child, instead of having learned compassion, learns or inherits the same species of brutality.

3

MISCHIEF
IN THE BLOOD

Tony Baekeland's day at Broadmoor began with a nurse shouting to him—and his dormitory mates—to wake up. From the moment he got out of bed, his every move was supervised—going to the bathroom, brushing his teeth, washing, shaving. He could enjoy the luxury of a bath or shower only one day a week.

"Tony remained in a bad way for quite awhile," Dr. Gogarty says, "but eventually, with medication and the realization that he was a member of society and part of a therapeutic community, he was able to receive visitors other than his immediate family."

Under the Mental Health Act of 1959, tribunals were created to give patients certain safeguards. Confined to Broadmoor under a Section 65 restriction order, Tony Baekeland was entitled to one review every two years. On August 22, 1974, he was granted a tribunal to review his sentence. It was determined that Tony Baekeland, after little more than a year at Broadmoor, was not ready to leave. Within several months, however, he was moved to Gloucester House, where patients are accorded a few more privileges; cutlery, for instance, is not counted after every meal. But after a short time at Gloucester, it became clear that he still needed the more protective atmosphere of Cornwall House.

All the houses had small courtyards, called "airing courts," where the patients could walk, but the airing court at Cornwall was distinctive—a patient, using his own money, had planted it with flowers and bushes. Now Tony Baekeland would once again be walking there.

"In the airing court," a patient has written, "you walk round and round, lost in your own private thoughts. There are various games you can play to make it less boring, like counting the stones on the bricks on the wall or counting the number of steps it takes you to get round the court. But it's all exactly the same, day after day."

TONY VAN ROON

I was a nurse at Broadmoor for some of the time that Tony Baekeland was a patient there. I left in September 1979 to take up a post in Coventry.

I think Tony was in Cornwall House when I worked there. Of course, he might have been in Dorset, the long-stay ward—I also worked there. It was one of the first wards to be upgraded. Well, they stuck some paint on the walls, but they called it modernizing. I know he wasn't in Norfolk—maximum security—which is where I worked the most. No, the contact I had with him was in Cornwall.

What's it like in Cornwall? Well, you go in through the front door, and immediately to your left is a stone staircase going up to the second and third floors. If you go past the stairs and go right, you're in Ward One, which is just one very very long gallery.

The first door on the right is the charge nurse's office, and then all the way down on the right are the cells. They were the usual sort of prison-type cells. The only difference was there was only one in a cell. On the left there are windows looking over the terraces, and occasional sort of bathroom areas and toilets, and then, further down, a huge sort of communal lounge. The second floor is just a duplicate of the first floor.

On the right-hand side of the lounge was a snooker table and a card table, and on the left-hand side was a curtained-off area with rows and rows of chairs, easy-type chairs, with a television sort of on a platform in the front. And these were very drab and very dark areas.

The third floor, Cornwall Three, was what we called a dead ward—it was only used at night, for sleeping.

In the morning the breakfast would be cereals, bread, eggs, and on Sundays bacon and eggs or baked beans. A very very basic breakfast.

And then at lunchtime there would be sort of a standard meat and two vegs. No soup to start with, just a main course. Then in the evenings it would be sort of a hot-type meal. In Cornwall they could order one night a week from a local fish-and-chips shop, and it was brought in by hospital transport. It was offered to every house one night a week on a rotation.

One of the things I found about Tony was he was always on his own. He never really had that much to do with nursing staff. You have to understand that the nursing staff at Broadmoor is less therapeutic and more custodial in role. That's not how it's supposed to be but it's how it is. That's one of the reasons I used to grit my teeth, you know—because we weren't known as nurses, the patients either called us "sir" or "screw." So it was difficult for a lot of them, particularly those who were isolated anyway, to sort of break through the lines and actually have a lot to do with nursing staff.

I had quite a few chats with Tony but they very rarely got into too much depth because he suddenly would realize that I was a part of the system and he was frightened by the system. I mean, *I* was frightened by the system, and I worked there! In fact, I was petrified of it. I mean, Broadmoor is a hospital but it's not that healthy a place.

Another thing I always felt was that there was a lot of remorse in Tony about what had happened, and because of that he had to be constantly coping and coming to terms with the situation he was in. I think that he sort of thought, "Well, here I am now and I'm here because I did this," but he could never understand why he did it— which is the key thing with a lot of people who I met there, they couldn't understand *why*. Quite often I would see Tony just sitting there and appearing to be miles away.

Letter from Antony Baekeland to Rosemary Rodd Baldwin, December 21, 1974

Broadmoor

Darling Rosie,

I wrote to you about a month ago. Did you ever get the letter? My whole life has changed completely—I have become a totally new person—by "new," I mean the way I used to be a long time ago. But then, I never really realized what I had, which was love and happiness, so I lost it through ignorance and selfishness. I spend hours, lovely happy hours, thinking of my friends.

Mummy was such a very wise person—I only began to realize who she really was a while ago—she was such a master of the understatement. I owe everything to her and love her so, Rosie. I was eating a tomato at teatime a few weeks ago and I suddenly realized that she is not dead at all, just very, very mysterious.

Love,
Tony

GLORIA JONES
Where *did* Barbara come from? Boston? And didn't she go to Hollywood or something? She married very young, I think.

NINA DALY
Barbara met Brooks and they started going out right away and it didn't take too long before they got married. Brooks is the most charming person. I used to feel badly that he didn't have some kind of important job. The grandfather did. And the grandmother was a brilliant woman, too—Bonbon. It's a brilliant, brilliant family. Brooks's father was a businessman. Perhaps Brooks was spoiled a bit. He might have been, you know.

BROOKS BAEKELAND
The fact is, I took a little girl from nowhere but who was smart and ambitious and had flair, and put her on the public scene. I educated her, taught her to draw and paint, and I supported her social ambitions. Socially, she was a most gifted woman—and exemplified all the things my grandfather most despised. I, personally, was a social zero. I was completely devoid of social ambition, it meant nothing to me. But Barbara's happiness, for many years, did, so I played along, and in the end, long before the end, became disgusted with myself for having wasted my own gifts that way. Of course, I also loved her, and I have always felt protective of the women in my life. I still support her mother.

NINA DALY
Nina Lillian Fraser was my name. But my mother never called me Nina, she called me Lillian. I like Nina a little bit better. It's shorter.

We were five children—three girls and two boys. The oldest was a boy and then I was next. And then there was another boy, and then my sister Alice was next, and then in five years my mother had Genevieve—I adored her, I was seven years older than her—Genevieve Agatha Fraser. Irving died in the war. And then Ralph eventually died. Alice and I are the only two living now. She looks quite a lot like me. She used to have red hair a little darker than mine.

My mother stayed home, you know—took care of the house. It was in the country, in West Roxbury, up near Dedham. We usually had a maid do the chores. And my father worked on the railroad, one of those big railroads. He was an accountant and something else there he did.

I had two grandmothers living, and one grandfather, and one great-grandfather. But I don't remember my great-grandfather.

I certainly do remember my two grandmothers. Oh, I loved them both. There's one I worshiped. I used to think she was a saint. On my mother's side. Mary Margaret was her name. Guess how many children she had! Fourteen. I didn't know many of them because they were spread out. Fourteen children, and everybody worshiped her. She was so handsome. We used to comb her hair, I remember. Then she would part it in the middle, and she would take it down and turn these two pieces in the front *in*, and then she'd get those in the back and put them in a little tug. Sometimes I used to ask her, let me do it.

I met my husband Frank up in Boston. It was wintertime, and he had bought a Stutz Bearcat car at the end of the summer, and I was so furious I said, "You're going to freeze to death," so then he went out and got a raccoon coat to wear in the open car.

I was married at eighteen, and I was a mother at nineteen. I was awfully sick, though, after my son Frank was born. I had a terrible breakdown. It was a difficult birth, you know. I was only nineteen and he was a big baby. He weighed ten pounds. Barbara weighed ten and a half. I had her when I was twenty-eight.

She was so beautiful. She was seen by an artist somewhere. He got in touch with her and then he painted her. And she did quite a lot of that work. She was a model. She was in *Vogue* and *Harper's Bazaar*.

She was very bright. She took French lessons when she was little, I think. She was supposed to go to college but something happened and I forget now what it was. She should have gone. Too bad.

I went to visit Tony in Broadmoor so many times, and every time I went there I just loved it. It was up a high hill. I always took a taxi. But I walked it once. I'd take him bags of food. I'd buy a big bag of fruit—oranges and grapefruits, anything that was in season. And I'd sometimes take him steak. You could cook if you cleaned the kitchen up. And I'd always buy two, so he'd have one for a friend. He was so natural and so loving. He used to talk about almost anything. He used to talk about his dreams.

Marjorie Fraser Snow

Nini just doted on Tony. Of course, I don't know the whole story, I don't know why Tony did what he did, because I wasn't close to Barbara those later years. I think of her often. What a tragedy.

Barbara was my cousin. My father, Irving Fraser, was Nini's brother. He died when I was three months old. Barbara and I had a great many wonderful experiences in our growing-up years. She was almost, in many ways, a sister to me. She was a lovely child, she was really one of the most beautiful girls you could ever see. Her coloring was absolutely gorgeous, and of course that beautiful red hair. She was a very popular child and always had a lot of personality.

We lived in Westwood and they were in West Roxbury, in a lovely section, way up on a hill. They had a lovely large house, with a very large porch with columns or pillars going up.

Barbara had her own room, and lots of beautiful toys and dolls. I know she attended public schools at different times but it seems to me there was a time when she did go to a private school for something, I can't remember what.

I remember she liked to wear mostly casual country-type clothes, as we all did then—tweeds and cashmere sweaters and skirts, and loafers or saddle shoes. It was sort of a uniform in those days.

We both loved horses and riding and dogs and dog shows. We spent a couple of summers together on the Cape, around Dennis. Later Barbara with her own family—Brooks and Tony—rented further along the Cape, in North Truro. One of the houses they rented was up on Corn Hill overlooking Cape Cod Bay. It was a very nice house. Contemporary. All glass in the front.

Barbara loved to swim. She took chances in the ocean—she wasn't afraid of anything. In fact, the two of us nearly drowned at one point off of Plymouth, playing in the surf when the Coast Guard had told everyone to stay off the beaches because of a storm at sea. And that didn't bother us at all. We went out into the surf because of course the waves were so tremendous that it was wonderful, better than the usual-size waves. But the undertow was fantastic.

We started to go backwards two strokes for every one forward, and

Barbara started to panic a bit, she started to scream, and I reached out and said, "Let's take each other's hands and pull together." And we did and we gradually inched to where we could find a toe on the sand, then we collapsed. And of course the Coast Guard had been called, because Nini couldn't see us in the ocean from the upper porch because the waves were so big, and of course our bathing caps had been ripped off. We received quite a talking-to from the Coast Guard officer for disobeying the rules.

ETHEL WOODWARD DE CROISSET

One day, in the early sixties I think, Barbara was staying with me in my house in Spain—years before all the terrible things happened—and the sea was quite violent. She was doing some *skinautique*, some waterskiing, off the beach there. *I* would have been afraid—I'm rather a fearful person. She was in a bikini, and there was nothing to protect her at all, with all these boats everywhere—she could have had her leg cut off by one of the propellers. But Barbara had absolutely no sense of fear. She was a violent person, you know. She perhaps as a young woman *used* her violence to get what she wanted. It was her character.

MARJORIE FRASER SNOW

Barbara was hoping to go to Bennington. Her plans were sort of made in that direction. But then of course her father died and her plans kind of changed.

Barbara and Nini moved to New York. I remember having dinner with them at the old Touraine in Boston the night before they left.

A bit later, an illustrator by the name of McLellan Barclay saw her someplace and I think said something to the effect that she was one of the ten most beautiful girls in New York City that he had ever seen. And on that basis, I believe, she was offered a screen test or whatever they call it—not your usual-type screen test, better than that—and she and Nini went out to Hollywood together.

BROOKS BAEKELAND

I believe she was given some small normal contract—the kind the studios get everyone to sign to hold them—while a screen test she made with Dana Andrews was being evaluated.

Marjorie Fraser Snow

Barbara did not care for Hollywood at all, and she and Nini came back to New York. They had their car shipped back by rail—they just wanted to get out of there!

I think they stayed for a short time at Delmonico's when they got back, and then they lived for a time on Central Park South and then they had an apartment someplace on Park Avenue. I visited them there and we would drive up the Hudson to the Sleepy Hollow Country Club—I think that's on the Rockefeller estate. It was a lovely place to ride, with a lovely indoor riding area.

Barbara Hale

When she met Brooks, she'd been having this big romance with John Jacob Astor. The fat one. I met him later and I said, "Oh, *you* knew Barbara Baekeland!" and he was furious. I don't know why. I guess he just thought it was none of my goddam business, you know.

Phyllis Harriman Mason

Mrs. Daley almost got Barbara married off to John Jacob Astor. Barbara was supposed to get the famous emerald ring. I felt that Mrs. Daly was responsible for all Barbara's flights of fancy. She had brought Barbara up to be a duchess.

Elizabeth Archer Baekeland

Nini was trying to get Barbara into society—and into what she called "the mun." My mother-in-law, Cornelia Hallowell, used to comment on how Nini would always refer to money as "the mun." I mean, to Cornelia money is money, it's not "the mun." There is no pet name for it. The Baekelands put all their sort of dislike of Barbara's background onto Nini. Well, she *was* very obvious. Barbara had a lot more polish.

Elizabeth Blow

I think there was a part of Nini that probably did want to exploit Barbara. Here she had this really extraordinarily beautiful and talented daughter. They were sort of like little adventuresses coming to the big city, because they came from—where *did* they come from?— no, not Boston proper at *all*—they came from West *Roxbury*, which is, you know, really the wrong side of . . . I mean, nobody comes from West Roxbury, Waltham, places like that. Nobody ever even talked about them. I mean, they didn't *exist*. Even Newton was a little bit going too far out of the magic circle already, and Newton Centre was considered *very* déclassé—it certainly was in *my* day. So Nini and Barbara, these sort of lace-curtain-Irish type of people, weren't in the picture at all.

I mean, I was born in Boston and entered into this kind of society from the time I was five years old when you started going to dancing school in the Somerset Hotel, the Somerset ballroom with the gilt chairs. In those days it was Mr. Foster's Dancing Classes—the little girls were all dressed up—and you proceeded through that. Then you went to the subscription dances, and the last subscription dance was the most elegant and the most exclusive—it was called the Friday Evenings and there you had your first glass of champagne. And then you came out.

KATHARINE GARDNER COLEMAN

Barbara never played up the Boston side of it at all. My father was Bostonian, as you may know—G. Peabody Gardner. Now, Brooks's mother married an extremely nice man from Boston—her second husband was a terribly terribly nice man and a great great friend of my father's. Daddy thought the *world* of Penn Hallowell.

LUBA HARRINGTON

Barbara came from very ordinary people. Now the Baekelands maybe weren't so great, but it's a better family. Barbara took over a good friend of mine, Domenico Gnoli—an artist, a marvelous artist—just because he was from a good family. From one of the best families in Italy, as a matter of fact. The *Count* Domenico Gnoli. So she latched on. And when he died—he was only thirty-four—liver cancer—she was running around at the church receiving people, because she felt they were important. I mean, she was acting like a close friend of the family, and she never even knew his mother, never knew his sister. That's how she was—she was a latcher-on-er.

Do you happen to know the derivation of "snob"—s-n-o-b? I used to teach linguistics and crap like that at Yale. In Italy, in, I don't know, maybe the thirteenth, maybe the twelfth century, a lot of nouveau-riche Italians tried to get their kids into the schools where the noble families sent their children by offering the schools a ton of money, so finally what the schools did was start a new category which the nobility called *sensa nobilita*—without nobility—because not only weren't these nouveau-riche noble, they didn't even have the instincts of nobility.

BARBARA CURTEIS

Barbara adopted this irrepressible redheaded Irish persona to cover up whatever deficiencies she thought she had. She didn't know things that everyone else knew or that she assumed everyone else knew and that in fact they probably did know, and she couldn't entirely catch up with the head start that the people she wanted to know had on her. And this persona that she'd adopted eventually took over.

BROOKS BAEKELAND

When Barbara left Hollywood and came back East, she did so expecting to be sued by the studio but not giving a damn. She was—joy to Mama!—now considering giving in to John Jacob Astor's strenuous and stertorous courting. Have you ever seen a picture of him? He looked very like Louis XVI and was dubbed by *Time* "The Pear-Shaped Prince of the Idle Rich." His father went down with the other gentlemen on the *Titanic*, singing "Nearer, My God, to Thee."

But after the screen test, the studio decided not to try to keep her. Miss Daly was not, they could see, of rich thespian ore. In fact, she would have made the worst actress in the world.

PEIDI GIMBEL LUMET

It was a terrific aging actress role that Barbara Baekeland eventually played. She couldn't get over the fact that she'd been John Jacob Astor's girlfriend for a minute. It was a theme, it was consistently there. It was her notion of herself and that's what her behavior was based on.

BROOKS BAEKELAND

I am not sure why Barbara changed her mind about John Jacob Astor. *I* may have been the innocent reason. In any case, he was still married at the time to Tucky French. He married various tarts, but Tucky was not one of them. Hers was a family as "distinguished" as his own. But it was at this time, according to Barbara, still—or again—a dewy young photographer's model, living with her mother far above their means at the old Delmonico's, that John Jacob Astor made her an offer of three million dollars—money in those days—if she would wait for him until he could get a divorce from Tucky French.

Now, I do not remember the exact order of events—whether Barbara turned down the bribe before or after she met me. I was a pilot trainee in the Royal Canadian Air Force at the time, and had been invited by my sister Dickie, who lived in Ridgefield, Connecticut, with her first husband, to come for the weekend—I had a leave—and meet a pretty girl who was a "poet."

ELIZABETH ARCHER BAEKELAND

Dickie and Barbara had probably met in Hollywood. Dickie, you see, was in the movies, too. She was in *Cover Girl* with Rita Hayworth and Gene Kelly. They wanted her to stay on but she hated it, she hated it as much as Barbara did. Dickie was quite impressed with Barbara. I mean, they'd be bound to like each other, because they were both very verbal and bright and very beautiful. And later, as a matchmaker, she had Brooks and Barbara for the weekend, and there's no question—that weekend was momentous.

BROOKS BAEKELAND

I found a remarkably beautiful and staggeringly self-assured young woman whose pretentions to poetry puzzled me when I plumbed them. She thought it would be wonderful to be a poet, but she had no training in words, and I hurt her feelings by calling what she showed me "marmalade."

To skip a banal story of sex and still embryonic violence that might interest the readers of a woman's magazine, during a heated zigzag from Ridgefield to the Adirondacks to the lacy-fluffy abode of mother and daughter at Delmonico's to, finally, Pinehurst, North Carolina, Miss Daly strongly intimated to me that she was pregnant. I took her across the border, to Bennetsville, South Carolina, and for two dollars—the court fee—and ten dollars—for a wedding band—I made her into Mrs. Brooks Baekeland and myself for the next thirty years into "Barbara's husband."

ELIZABETH ARCHER BAEKELAND

I heard John Jacob Astor followed them all the way down to South Carolina, trying to prevent Barbara from marrying Brooks. But she was madly in love with Brooks, *and* she thought he had a lot of money—a lot more than he had, I imagine.

BROOKS BAEKELAND

I soon realized that, whether Barbara was pregnant or not—and she
was not—I had not married a soul mate but a powerful and ambitious antagonist. She was a far more brilliant and a far stronger
personality than I ever was or could be.

Shortly before I met her, though I did not know it until long after,
Barbara had been a patient of the psychoneurologist Foster Kennedy.
Because of my disagreements with my father—essentially the strain
that is set up in a young man of overly passionate nature between his
desire for freedom at any cost and his desire not to bring dishonor on
his name—I had been "introduced" to Foster Kennedy earlier myself. Besides my grandfather, he was the first intelligent man I had
ever met—I mean known on an intimate basis, could talk to, could
make myself understood to, could seek and take advice from. It was
an almost rhapsodic experience. He asked me out to dinner to meet
people like Jerome Kern, Robert Oppenheimer, Wystan Auden, and
a galaxy of British diplomatic and military stars—his half brother was
the British Chief of Staff, Sir John Dill.

Meanwhile my father was tremendously impressed and puzzled by
the fact that the man who charged the highest psychiatric consulting
fees in the world was charging him nothing for seeing me—and telling him nothing, either. It was Foster who said to me one day,
"Brooks, there is something very big and important going on. You
should be a part of it. Go up to Montreal. Get in the Air Force. I
know the Air Marshal. I'll ring him." And that is how it happened. I
left almost overnight.

I asked Barbara not to come to Canada while I was still in training,
but she came anyway. I did not go to meet her. My then very close
and dear friend the poet Howard Nemerov, one of nature's gentlemen, met her instead and comforted her. I ignored her. I mistreated her. I did everything I could imagine that would put a girl off,
but I had forgotten her persistence.

It gives me pleasure to think for a few minutes now about Barbara
as she was in those first years, during my training and subsequent
instructorship in Canada. She kept insisting on following me about
on my postings, first as a trainee in #13 Elementary Flying Training
School, St. Eugene, Ontario, then at Uplands Advanced Flying
Training School at Ottawa, then at #1 Instructor's Flying Training
School at Trenton, Ontario, and then in a long series—Aylmer,
Gananoque, Kingston, St. Hubert's in Montreal, Quebec—where I

taught the death-defying youth of the British Commonwealth, plus a
good bit of Texas, how to dogfight and kill with machine guns, rockets, bombs, and lousy jokes—we could have ended the war four years
earlier with *those*, properly employed.

Barbara stayed in local rooming houses, even at one time above an
undertaking parlor—the smell reminded me of Bakelite. I had a
forty-eight-hour pass every two weeks. I was nuts about flying, about
everything I was learning and doing, but I was not nuts about my
wife.

One of the things that most put me off about the beautiful
ex–Barbara Daly was her convertible Chrysler and her mink coat and
her empress's airs, which did not go at all with my disguise as a
minor Prince Incognito, Aircraftsman 2nd Class, and "one of the
mob" fighting Hitler. I was all for Democracy. She was soon ordering
around my commanding officers. She already knew "how the world
works." I did not want to know. I hated the very fact that that *was*
how it worked. I loathed her for her political acumen. You can imagine my embarrassment when I came home once, after two weeks, to
my humble hovel, wherever it may have been at the time, to discover
Barbara giving a cocktail party—the first person I saw on opening the
door was the man before whom I cringed and saluted every other day
of my life, my C.O., suddenly converted into a genial and subser-
vient "friend" calling me "Brooks" instead of "Baekeland, AC$_2$"—a
man whose social inferiorities would have embarrassed a Gila monster. I wished that my new wife might just vanish back into the mer-
etricious world she had come from.

Anyway, there were always those two weeks before we were able to
couple on bumpy mattresses and cow the local population with her
airs of Catherine de' Medici. And it was horribly boring for her—I
mean all those blotchy, overworked, overbabied, gingham-dressed
other officers' wives at tea in the intervening fourteen days.

Since I soon saw that the poetry was not going to work, I began to
try to teach her how to draw and do watercolors. As a teacher I took
my job seriously and, standing behind her—as I did through the rest
of her whole artistic career—I gave her the ideas, the suggestions
about form, theme, color, etc. She did have talent and ambition, but
she had no imagination. What she had—and what may be more
valuable to an artist—was passion. But she had never had a Conté
crayon or a brush of any kind in her hand before. You can see in
Nina Daly's apartment in New York that what Barbara did with that
ignorance and passion was not so bad at all. The romantic spirit.

And in the long summer evenings in that north country, after a crummy but lovely dinner in some awful village greasy spoon, we would go walking for miles out into the Canadian countryside—wilderness, or semiwilderness in those days, with me trying to walk on the rails of some abandoned railroad line and reciting "Gerontion"— I was mad about T.S. Eliot then, think him an old fart now—and, above us, in the satined evening sky, the Night Hawks sliding straight down with that amazing BOOOOOM to impress their girlfriends. I trust they were! *I* was.

What tied me to Barbara for all those years? Pity. I still feel sorry for her. I still feel guilty. I still feel protective.

Official Visitors File, Broadmoor Special Hospital, September 18, 1975

> VISITOR'S NAME: Dr. and Mrs. Justin Greene, U.S.A.
> RELATIONSHIP TO PATIENT: Friend and ex-doctor
> SUMMARY: They are both concerned and showed sound appraisal of the overall situation. They knew Tony as a small boy, and Dr. Greene saw him professionally on some occasions where he had most likely formed the opinion that Tony was dangerous to his mother. This present visit was essentially informal. He described Tony as overcontrolled, there being several incidents where he overreacted to situations in a nonviolent way. Dr. Greene recounted two occasions as a child where Tony became overexcited and ran away and there was some difficulty in finding him. Dr. Greene thought his violent outbursts were specifically directed toward his mother and did not think he was likely to be a danger to others.
>
> I discussed our intended transfer of Tony from Gloucester back to Cornwall House and asked the Greenes when they saw him later in the afternoon to explain that this was a therapeutic move rather than in any way punitive. They agreed to do this.

COLM BYRNE

When I knew Tony, he was in Gloucester House. I couldn't say I knew him that well—Gloucester House when I was there had ninety-six patients.

The patients at Cornwall House, where he had come from, were, let's say, much more disturbed. Cornwall House was commonly referred to as "the monkey house." That was because largely the patients in there were diagnosed as suffering from schizophrenia, whereas the patients in Gloucester House tended to be fairly controlled for a long period of time, more stable—there wasn't a great deal of what we call psychotic behavior in Gloucester House in comparison with Cornwall House. Cornwall House was much bigger as well. Gloucester House was referred to really as a semi-parole block because it was much more easygoing.

Official Visitors File, Broadmoor Special Hospital, November 27, 1975

> VISITOR'S NAME: Mrs. Nina Daly
> RELATIONSHIP TO PATIENT: Grandmother
> SUMMARY: Maternal grandmother still seems less disturbed by her daughter's death than by the fact that her dear little Tony is in trouble. She seems just as mad as the rest of the family.

BROOKS BAEKELAND
Nina Daly is a Fraser—no nuttiness there that I ever discovered. I had a very close, often Rabelaisian relationship with her. She was the best part of my marriage. She had an enormous sense of humor, no education, silly values, and indomitable loyalty.

HELEN DELANEY
Nina Daly is a harmless enough creature. Her values came from Cholly Knickerbocker and the Catholic Church—mostly from Cholly Knickerbocker. But on her husband's side of the family there was real mayhem. It's what you might call a frail line.

BROOKS BAEKELAND
The fact is, the turning, bending, hinging energy in the stories of human lives is given off by very intense and often very queer people who are no longer alive to play mischief, though the mischief still breeds. There are two kinds of mischief in this regard. There is the mischief in the blood—when it is there, as it was certainly in Barbara's father Frank Daly's family. Frank Daly's own father, Barbara's

grandfather, was a violent and aberrant man, and so had been *his* father, Barbara's great-grandfather, by all report. And Barbara's paternal grandmother was a "case" who mooned at the piano all day and never did any housework or house management—a kind of Zasu Pitts creation.

And then there is the other kind of mischief—the mischief that produces more mischief by cause and effect, action and reaction.

ELIZABETH ARCHER BAEKELAND

Barbara's father committed suicide—I don't know why, I don't even know *how*, unfortunately. And her brother committed suicide. I remember Fred Baekeland saying, "Isn't it extraordinary that the whole family has committed suicide."

HELEN DELANEY

The suicide of Frank Daly, Sr., was observed by Frank Jr. through the window of the garage. Frank Sr., who had lost what money he had in the crash, was gassing himself with carbon monoxide while pretending to be working on his car—it was a Pierce Arrow, as I recall, and he was underneath it and the engine was running. Frank Jr., walking back and forth before the garage window, watched his father die. The insurance company was suspicious but could never prove fraud. Frank Jr., Barbara, and Nina Daly each got about sixty thousand dollars from the insurance company. This was in 1932, mind you. That would be at least six hundred thousand each in today's currency.

SYLVIE BAEKELAND SKIRA

The son Frank later died in a car accident, supposedly on purpose—I don't know. How does one decide that somebody has gone into a tree on purpose?

HELEN DELANEY

One day Frank Jr. whipped around a curve in Cohasset, Mass., I think, and just drove at high speed into an elm tree. The official story was that the steering mechanism had malfunctioned. I know he had been drinking for some time.

He was a front-and-center-look-at-*me* kind of guy—just like his sister. He loved to raise Cain in public. I forget what he actually did for a living but I do remember that he was trying to crack the detective-magazine market. I don't think he had much luck. His wife was the quiet-little-woman type, so there was friction there as well. They had two nice little boys.

BROOKS BAEKELAND

Barbara and I inherited that fatherless family. She performed all the brave and wonderful human prophylaxes. I begged for money from my family. I resented bitterly having to ask my fascistic father for anything, but I did not mind being in debt to my marvelous grandmother—I could even glory in that, because our spirits, hers and mine, were always in tune. The problem, the Socratic problem, of value—how can it be established? proved?—controlled her life as much as it did mine. Both Barbara and Tony were wrecked on those stony shores. They became raiders—or rather, she was to begin with. They were arrogant. They were destroyed. These are not merely abstract questions. Those who have seen Nemesis in their stories were right indeed. It works in all our lives. It worked with a terrible obviousness in theirs. A swift, destroying sword.

If one seeks to pin down the source of Tony's violent instability, one mustn't entirely blame the Dalys. I think there was mischief in the blood on both sides—the Baekelands as well. I have in my notebooks a quotation that I copied down from Robert Gittings's *Life of Keats*—I was in India at the time: "Suffering had laid cruelly bare his abnormally passionate nature, unbalanced since his boyhood, always in extremes."

Was I thinking of Tony when I copied this? Certainly not. I was thinking of me!

Someone, I now forget who, told me years later that when Foster Kennedy heard that I had married Barbara Daly, he said: "God forfend that they have a child!"

4

MOTHER'S MILK

As gradually Tony Baekeland became a member of society at Broadmoor, he could choose from among the several occupational therapies available to patients: toy-making, pottery, carpentry, metalwork, printing, radio-making, basket-making. He preferred drawing and painting. "He gave me one or two things—paintings of flowers and things like that," Dr. Gogarty recalls. "We have to be very careful about paint because in some cases it's very toxic and patients can harm themselves."

Tony Baekeland soon improved to the point where he was reading university-level books—among them, a volume on abstract mathematics. He wrote to his father that he was happy, had "a home and new friends."

Old friends—and friends of friends—began to visit him. There was as well a community group called the Broadmoor League of Friends, two of whose members—a retired army doctor and his wife—took a particular interest in Tony.

"Colonel Verbi was at one time in the English army," Dr. Gogarty explains. "He was a wonderful friend to Tony. He and his wife had the time to visit. Tony was so fond of them he gave them a number of gifts—I remember particularly a figure of an elephant.

When Mrs. Verbi died some years ago and I went around to their house to call, Colonel Verbi gave me—to give back to Tony—the things that Tony had given to his wife. And, when Colonel Verbi died, he left Tony a silver ashtray in his will."

Toward the end of his third summer in Broadmoor, Tony received word from his father and Sylvie in France of the birth of a half brother.

Letter from Antony Baekeland to Sam Green, August 29, 1975

Broadmoor

Dear Sam,

My time has been of great profit to me: I have learned a great deal about people, myself, and life in general. I now realize that for many years I had been living a totally false life and it finally ended the way it did because the burden I carried just became too great to bear. Anyway, for Mummy's sake I have decided to make a new person of myself and I have found great peace and happiness. I realize now how much I always took my mother for granted (and the other good things in life) and how selfish and blind I was in many ways.

My father and I are good friends now. I have a little half brother whom I have not met.

Yours with love,
Tony

BROOKS BAEKELAND

God, not I, is an ironist. Barbara became pregnant only twice in her life—not counting an "occult" insemination in Mallorca by Sam Green, between two chairs across a room, with the aid, I suspect, of mucho hash—and for both she had to have an operation to untip her tipped uterus. The first one—I was flying then in Germany in early 1945 or late 1944—was miscarried. The second, in the autumn of 1946, was Tony.

H.R.H. Princess Elizabeth of Yugoslavia

She told me that she was one of those rare cases of women who can only conceive a child during their period. I mean, it's not biologically possible, is it? And she wound up conceiving her own killer.

Marjorie Fraser Snow

I believe when her brother was killed she was carrying Tony and they were afraid she might lose the baby she was in such a state.

Notes from a Psychiatric Consultation on Antony Baekeland, New York, March 12, 1971

He was born in August 1946. The labor was very long; there was no anesthesia; and high forceps were used.

Brooks Baekeland

When Tony was born, I was living at 1220 Park Avenue, in a three-room apartment with Barbara and her mama and, in insidious progression as the next years passed, her widowed sister-in-law Edna and her two sons. Little did I realize that I would be supporting the Dalys for years and Nina Daly for the rest of her life. We also had an incontinent, decerebrate toy poodle which had come with Barbara and her mother from Delmonico's. It peed everywhere and was called Negus. Finally we moved to 136 East Seventy-first Street, the large house that my grandmother had bought for me.

I was a graduate student in mathematics and physics at Columbia. I was the original student who did not go to lectures but discovered the texts from which those supposed gods, our professors, were themselves simply copying out on the blackboard what we, the helpless students, tried to scribble down and understand as fast as we could. I bought all the books and I worked out every single problem in every single book.

Peter Gimbel

I'm awed by intellectual prowess, especially in the physical sciences, and on *that* score Brooks always awed me. He had the highest academic record of any predoctoral student who ever went through Pupin—that's the physics building at Columbia—up until whatever time that was, late forties or whatever.

Elizabeth Archer Baekeland

Brooks was within one week of getting his Ph.D. in chemistry at Columbia, and he just *left*. He left, he said, because he was sitting in class and he had taken all day to do the answer to one problem and this guy came in and did it in fifteen minutes—unless he could be the best he didn't want to do it at all.

Elizabeth Blow

I know there was opposition in the family to Brooks's quitting Columbia, and I think I heard that they even reduced his income because of it. But meanwhile he had decided to become a writer.

From the Diaries of John Philip Cohane, Unpublished

Monday. Thanksgiving we entertained on a reasonably extensive scale—thirty or so people late in the afternoon for cocktails. Yvonne Thomas and her budding daughter Gwenny; Oscar Williams, the poet and anthologist, who gave me a recording of his dead wife Gene Durward reading a selection of her own poems—splendid poems, badly read; Jack Astor; Barbara and Brooks Baekeland—Brooks is currently at odds with his father who isn't speaking to him because he deserted physics for writing.

Brooks Baekeland

I enrolled in a short-story-writing class at Columbia to "titrate"—loosely: offset, neutralize—my studies in mathematical physics. I used to get off the Fifth Avenue bus at Seventieth Street each day when returning from my classes and sit for an hour or more in front of the fountain in the Frick Museum to wash all the chemistry and physics off me.

Alastair Reid

I was teaching at Sarah Lawrence when Brooks's short story—I think it's the only story he's ever had published—appeared in the college literary magazine, *Inscape*. The faculty adviser to the magazine was Brooks's old classmate at boarding school, Ambrose Gordon. In fact, it was at Ambrose Gordon's house near Bronxville that I met Brooks and Barbara for the first time. She was raw-faced, large-boned, but I found her very attractive in conversation, in her enthusiasms and her suddennesses. She was much looser than Brooks. He was terribly aloof, very conscious of his own elegance—he dressed with almost finicky attention. What would be that thin elegant look that we have now—it was his. He exaggerated his own thinness. He was balding and he looked as though he polished his head. I mean, he had an incredible arrogance, a kind of personal arrogance.

I think Ambrose Gordon had invited me to dinner that night so I could say to Brooks Baekeland, "I read your story." It's been about thirty years since I read it, but I do remember that he was clearly into a certain kind of wordplay that was pretty fashionable. He talked about Queneau, whom I hadn't read then but have since. Raymond Queneau, the French puzzle-maker—word games. Brooks invoked people like that and Karl Kraus, and I remember being annoyed because he was clearly bent on naming writers that other people hadn't read. He gave the impression that he was a mysterious and secret writer—an impression which I may say he kept up as long as I knew him, into the sixties, because when I met him about ten years after this, he was still, you know, secretly and mysteriously writing something which—there was no question about it—was a masterpiece. He chose to arrive at the top in his own mind. I mean, his story in the Sarah Lawrence quarterly was clever, but that's all. But then, I never thought of Brooks as a writer—ever.

HELEN DELANEY

As a work of fictional art, Brooks's short story may leave something to be desired, but as naked fantasy it is simply astonishing—both as a psychological self-portrait and, amidst all the giddy hilarity, as a sinister foreshadowing of Brooks's future behavior toward women.

"Milk," Brooks Baekeland, *Inscape,* Sarah Lawrence Literary Review, Spring 1955

> Bitterbaron Bentley was bewitched with Bach and Baby-blue eyes; and Balls and Bangs and Bungs and Balloons and Baboons; and Buttocks and Beadles and Beerbohm; and Baubles and Bassets; and Bigness and Biting and Birthdays and Bishoprics; and Blushes and Blurbs and Blow-holes; and Bliss; and Boudoirs

and Buns and Borscht and Bow-wows; and Beautiful Bouncers; and Bubbles and Boxers and Boys; and especially with Brut and Bon-ton—just to mention a few things that bewitched him.

How could Knipples (J. Frederick Knipples: "Freddy") resist his excellent advice on diet?

He couldn't, of course.

The thing was that Freddy had been losing weight, due to the wrong flora (improper bowel management), and, meeting Bently at the house of a fashionable hostess—where her small dog vomited yogurt in his lap—Freddy lost no time in seeking the debonair Bitterbaron's advice. Under the circumstances the advice was uncommonly pithy: raw mushrooms and mother's milk—a quart a day, minimum. Bitterbaron gave the name of a good wet nurse and advised stepping up the dose until the final figure of a gallon, or four quarts, was reached in three months, which would require two and possibly three nurses, that is, six tits at the outside.

"They run about 2.7% on butterfats and very high in protein," said Bitterbaron, jotting down the information for Freddy. "So you'll probably feel a nice sort of glow after a while, but I think a little roundness will be becoming to you, Freddy."

He pinched Freddy's breast.

"You're much too thin. The mushrooms will give you what I call Adventure Tone. It's not quite like Muscle Tone. It's better, rather more adventurous.

"You'll be a regular wild boar, you naughty boy!"

They both laughed delightedly.

Well that's how it started—the diet, I mean.

Freddy was small and blond and he bit his nails down to the quick. He had thinning hair (he was painting the scalp with iodine to "stimulate" new growth, and the iodine looked like a birthmark), and his eyes were like two pleasant, disqualified marbles. Freddy needed love—all the time. Those blue, vague, marble eyes of his showed it. They were like the eyes of a woman after childbirth. Of course he wore the fashionable black "loafers" with tassels (the smart, expensive ones), dark-gray flannel suits (Brooks Brothers) and gray socks with blue piping, and he never sat without crossing his legs gracefully and smiling: and he had the world's most happy, charming smile. Freddy had no problems—if you except his flora—and he had oodles of money to play with. Only he hardly realized it himself. He just took it for granted, and he was terribly generous with it with all of his friends. His father, Argon Hoegfeldt Knipples, and his grandfather, Karl Peter Knipples, built up the Knipples family shipping business which had left him and his mother very well off when Argon died. And now there was only himself left, the last of the Knipples, going on thirty-six, adjusting nicely.

Of course, it can't be denied that Freddy missed his mother frightfully, but that too was something he took for granted. When he talked about her—as he did constantly—it was with such a charming and loving naiveté that it hardly seemed like a mourning, but more like a tribute to her invisible concern and protection. Freddy was as gentle and as faithful as a girl. Many people never realized that his mother was dead. He still referred all his choices and delights to the invisible aegis of that gentle ghost whom he spoke of to everyone—even to chance acquaintances—as "Mother." It was as though he took it for granted that everyone had met her or known her at one time, and all loved her as he did. Some people really felt they did, no doubt. And it was hard not to believe that she had been the most perfect of women, though probably unhappy with Argon H. Knipples, empire-builder, and to that small extent—because of her unhappiness—perhaps imperfect, as even towards the rude and bestial empire-builder a good woman has duties. But let us not look into this too closely, as it is likely to be unpleasant. That Freddy did not like his father, whom he referred to as "that brute," we know, and that is enough—perhaps too much.

Naturally then, in the light of all this, Freddy must have asked himself what Mother would have thought of going on a diet of mushrooms and mother's milk. He remembered that she had lived for several weeks once on nothing but tomato juice and yogurt—on his suggestion—he loved her when she was slim—and they had both been very excited by the results. Of course, human milk was a different matter. He loved milk, but he wondered if woman's milk would be as delicious as a cow's milk. After all it was pretty silly to nourish a prejudice in favor of a cow; rather perverted when you come to think of it—like that boy in The Hamlet. That was something to think about! He'd never thought of it that way, of course, and now that he

did, he wondered why everyone didn't drink mother's milk instead of the milk of those great horny, bellowing animals that
frightened him so. A mother's milk must be delicious or it
wouldn't be human. . . . Was that right? He wasn't exactly sure
what he meant, but that was close to it. . . .

Naturally this line of thought—with the debonair Bitterbaron's moral backing and solid, scientific reasoning—put
Freddy into quite a state of delighted anticipation. Bently was
kind enough to make the arrangements for him (the amount of
milk needed was the thing to make sure of), giving Freddy's elegant apartment as the address to the wet nurse and making the
first appointment for him.

The first appointment was for a Saturday afternoon—a matinee, so to speak. Freddy was extremely nervous and he spent the
whole morning foolishly arranging and rearranging the flowers.
(Yellow and pale-mauve Irises and bruise-purple Lady Slippers.
For some reason the Lady Slippers always gave him a vague
thrill. He called them "you smutty little darlings" and giggled at
the ridiculousness of what he had said.)

When the doorbell rang, he was primping a little in the bedroom.

"Coming!" he sang.

He ran, flinging his elbows out a little, and he was panting
when he opened the door. His face was a little red, but he had
on his most charming smile, and he apologized profusely for not
coming sooner. He offered to take the lady's coat, very gallantly
and affably, which she allowed him to do without any lack of
aplomb, only saying:

"Yo name's Mist' Freddy Nipples?"

She was a big, genial woman with hands like first-baseman's
mitts and a bosom like the State Capitol.

Freddy glided under breasts, clutching her hat and coat, and
hung them up, chattering to her.

She caught sight of him.

"Thas' a funny name—"

"It's K-nipples, not Nipples, dear. You can call me Freddy if
you want, though."

"All right, Mis' Knipples—ah mean, Freddy," she grinned.

"You all min' paying me in advance, Mis' Nipples—I mean,
Freddy? I always ge's paid first. I don' want . . ."

"Oh sure, dear."

"My name's—"

"Yes, I know. Bee told me. Is that all right, Mary?"

He smiled and stuffed a bunch of bills into her hand and started off towards the kitchen with his hands tensed a little away from his sides as though he were dangling little weights on strings from the ends of his fingers.

"Yas, Mis' Nipples! Yas, this is just fine! . . . I'm coming."

She stuffed the money into her purse.

"My real name's John, of course, but Mother and I both hated it. It's so common—Mother passed on, poor dear. I was named after my Uncle Fred. He used to wet the bed."

He giggled.

Mary looked around as she followed him across the large, airy living room.

"Sho mighty nice place, Freddy. Where's the baby at?"

"What baby, dear?"

"De baby I gonna give 'is lunch to."

"Oooo, darling, there's no baaaby!" he howled. "That is, I'm the baby, darling. *I'm* the baby!"

Mary stood rooted to the floor.

"You de baby?"

"Didn't Mr. Bently tell you about it, darling? . . . It's for *me*," he wailed, delightedly.

"My milk's fo' you?"

"Well, you see, dear, Mr. Bently's a very, *very* famous man, and he says I need the kind of milk—that is—human milk. See, he's a dietitian, dear. He knows all about it. It's because of the butterfat, he says. I'm taking mushrooms too. All you have to do is put it into a bottle or something—you know—whatever it is you do . . ."

Freddy waved his hands and smiled charmingly.

"Put it in a bottle? Mis' Nipples—Mis' Nipples, I din' come fo' no—"

"Oh dear, Mary! How perfectly, excruciatingly exasperating! Now everything's gone wrong. And Bee said—here—wait . . ."

He plunged his hands into his pockets and took out ten dollars and held them out to her.

"Here! Now, for heaven's *sake*, don't be a foolish old thing!"

He pressed the money into her hand. She now had about

twenty dollars. It was sinking through her head that at twenty
dollars a quart, roughly speaking . . .

"All right . . . all right, Mis' Nipples. But I don' put any milk
in any li'l bottles—so, if *you* don't mind, then *I* don' min'. You
jus' gonna take it de way she comes, Misteh!"

"You mean—"

"Yas, Mis' Nipples."

She was grinning from ear to ear.

"You gonna be ma baby!"

She went off into roars of laughter, exploding and giggling
and shaking all over uncontrollably, and Freddy joined her.

"Darling!" he screamed. "Wonderful!"

"Freddy!" she howled. "Mis' Nipples . . . Oh, ma achin'
back! . . ."

And they both danced around the room, holding their hands
to their mouths, rocking with laughter, and looking at each
other, like a playful, pink mouse and a wild elephant.

Mary began unbuttoning her blouse, showing two enormous,
velveteen dugs, lying on her stomach. With one great hand she
reached out and grabbed Freddy by the arm and pulled him to
her, sitting down on a chair and pulling him down on her lap at
the same time. Before he even had time to protest (struggling
would have been useless, and he knew that) she shoved his face
into the right dug, forcing the stiff, leathery nipple into his open
mouth. He tried to pull his head away for a bit, but she pushed
it back, forcing his face into the warm, yielding flesh, and then
he began to nurse, crossing his feet back and forth and closing
his eyes. He had his left hand up on her shoulder, and with it
he made a fist, holding the thumb inside. Every once in a while
he opened it, and then he closed it again, sucking.

As I said, that's the way it started, but that's not the way it
ended.

At the end of the nursing period, with milk drooling down his
face, Freddy would sit for a while, while Mary rocked, grinning.
They always had a little banter and made a joke of their relationship. She would call him "baby" and he would call her
"Mother," both chortling or howling with outright laughter. But
when she left, he would go into his bedroom and fall onto the
bed in a profound, dreamless sleep. She came by every day, and

finally when she could no longer supply the growing demand, she brought along another wet nurse who took turns with her, and then Freddy had two mothers, and the wet nurses in good cheer shared the "baby," drowning him in pap. He gained twenty-five pounds, learned to suck his thumb, wet his pants and do other things which the wet nurses thought terrifically funny, even helping him sometimes, howling with laughter. It was a gay and noisy threesome. They spoiled their baby and were spoiled in their turn. Freddy had never been quite so happy before.

When the third nurse was brought in, Freddy was suckling most of the time, and he always had drinks set up so that his mothers could get high, and the party often grew frolicsome. But they always treated him like a child, and he steadily slipped deeper and deeper into childhood, sometimes being unable to speak for long periods of time during the day, only laughing and playing with himself.

He never left his apartment anymore, spending most of his time in bed or on the laps of his mothers.

Freddy might have rocked gently forever on the Mare Lactosa, gulping and drowning and blubbering deep in tumescent warmth, flowing backwards protoplasmically into the vaginal darkness of memory (or out of it, who knows), if the whole thing hadn't gone too far. But the mothers were jealous, and there were times when they tried to snatch him away from each other, the liquor firing their natural possessiveness.

"Give him . . . to me! It's my turn!"

"No—"

"Give—him—I—say—give . . ."

"No, no! Stop that now, I say! Cut it out! I got him!—"

"Oh, no you—haven't—"

"Ugh—"

"Mary, Mary! Help me. Hey!"

And so they tugged at him and pulled him and tore at his pudgy, sweet body, hugging him and clutching him to their enormous, velvet dugs, stuffing his pale, panting face between them into the terrae incognitae of progressive suffocation. The harder he gasped for air, fighting their great strength with his puny one, the harder they clutched him and hugged him into the cruel, nostril-clogging meat of the Mammary Glands. It was as though by pulling him hard enough, he might be pulled right inside and the warm doors of protectiveness closed after him for ever more.

And so it was that one day, after such a steaming, grappling tempest of desire, he went suddenly limp in the arms of Mary, who held him, tiny like the Christ of Michelangelo's *Pietà* in her lap, and the three weeping mothers saw their child was still. And although they all tried blowing breath back into his little lungs, tearing him again to be the one to bring him back to life, hugging him and clutching him and sobbing and bending over him, it was no use whatever. His lungs were full of milk. It ran miraculously out of his mouth, out of his ears, out of his eyes. His very blood was no longer red but white. And when the mothers saw this, when they saw that their baby was dead, they held him for a while, looking at each other in amazement. And then they dropped him, and he sprawled like a broken doll on the great big bed in the bedroom, still drooling a little out of his mouth.

Notes from a Psychiatric Consultation on Antony Baekeland, New York, March 12, 1971

During his infancy, he is said to have screamed a good deal. His mother states that his father refused to allow her to pick him up and insisted that he be kept on a strict schedule, "even though he screamed bloody murder."

MARJORIE FRASER SNOW

Barbara was a very conscientious mother as I remember. I had no children myself at that point. We used to wheel Tony over to Central Park in one of those stroller-type things—once, he got out and started walking along the edge of the sidewalk and I said, "Barbara, that's awful dirty there for him, we'd better get him back into the little stroller," and she said, "If you keep him isolated from all kinds of dirt, he'll never build up antibodies to prevent any disease that may come along." Of course in those days that was rather an unusual way of looking at it—today I think it's accepted. So she understood and knew exactly how to raise him, I felt.

PATRICIA NEAL
The whole atmosphere of Broadmoor reminded me of a play I was
in—*The Children's Hour*. I don't know why that just shot into my
head but it did. Maybe because there's a school in the play. James
Reeve, who painted my portrait, said, "Why don't you come along
with me to visit a friend?" He told me that the boy had murdered his
mother—I didn't get their name. It seemed really horrendous, but he
wanted me to come see him. And I wanted to—I'm loving. So I
went and we had tea with him and he was very glad to see us and
very polite and well-mannered. He knew I was an actor. James had
told him he was bringing me to see him. We sat in a big room with a
lot of other people. And he was charming. We made jokes. There
was a lot of laughing. Anyway, on the way home I realized who he
was. It suddenly dawned on me—Baekeland! Because his aunt is a
great friend of mine. I said to James in the car, "I'm sure he's the
one!" and when I got home I called Elizabeth Baekeland and I said,
"Elizabeth, you'll never guess who I just saw! I just saw Tony." And
she said, "You didn't! You didn't! You didn't!" It was like she got
frightened.

JAMES REEVE
Elizabeth Baekeland lived in London and never once went to see
Tony in Broadmoor, which was disgraceful. And one in the eye to
her when Pat Neal rang up, you know, saying she'd just come from
seeing him in Broadmoor. I mean, that must have set her back on
her haunches! I asked Pat to come because I knew it would give Tony
great pleasure, it would sort of bolster him up in the eyes of the
others—it's frightfully important when you're in that sort of place to
seem to have interesting friends.

Letter from Antony Baekeland to Miwa Svinka-Zielinski, Undated

Broadmoor

Dear Miwa—
James has come to see me twice. He brought Patricia Neal, who
I was very anxious to meet as I have always admired her. She
was so very nice—I know you would like her.
James brought me sketching materials on his last visit. He

showed me photographs of his paintings done in Haiti and they are macabre and interesting—I liked them very much. I haven't had too much of a chance to do much drawing because the dear materials you brought me are still in another part of the hospital.

All love to you,
Tony

MIWA SVINKA-ZIELINSKI

I got him lots of crayons and paper so that he could do something, and they did not give them to him. I asked one of the psychiatrists there about this and he said, "That takes him from reality."

TONY VAN ROON

Tony worked in the handicrafts shop—it was sort of something that he wanted to do and it was backed up by medical staff. Everybody— nine times out of ten—is put out on work detail, it's supposed to be on therapeutic lines. Handicrafts was very much a sort of time-passing area. Tony used to go over there to paint. It would have been very difficult for him to do actual painting on the block in Cornwall—to do that he would have had to have been on what they call "house parole."

From my point of view, I saw him as a fairly sort of stable person. That's not saying that he didn't have a mental illness, but that he appeared to have accepted the environment he was in and just got on with everything from day to day, but kept a wide berth of most people, particularly anybody in authority. I think that becomes a way of life in that environment. You think, "Well, is that screw in a good or bad mood? If he's in a bad mood I'd better not say anything 'cause I might get a kick on the ear or whatever." I think the way of thinking of most people who had any sense was to just keep a low profile, because once you started sticking up for your own rights and other people's rights, not only was it ignored, but it was thrown back in your face quite often by excessive use of medication—which was always justified by medical staff. I'm not saying that the medical staff colluded. What I'm saying is that all it took was for a sort of senior nurse to say, "This patient is becoming a bit psychotic," for the doctors to justify upping the medication.

PATRICIA GREENE

The first time we visited him, it was a very shocking experience—he looked so bad. He was pretty shabby, and we got him some clothes—a pair of pants and some socks—and we brought him stuff to eat.

The second time, we found him much better—there was a year between visits. And this time he was paunchy. We asked him what he wanted and he said he wanted music, classical music I think it was, and I said I thought he ought to have some shirts—we felt it would pick him up a little.

You know, Barbara had brought him to see my husband professionally. At the time Justin didn't tell me. He would never speak of friends or their children if he were treating them. Several times I met people in his waiting room and I was surprised. I saw Barbara there once and I was totally surprised.

I don't really remember how we first met the Baekelands, whether it was on the street with the children or whether a friend introduced us. I just remember being enormously impressed with Brooks and Barbara. He was cold and dark and she was warm and light—it was like they were Yin and Yang. I thought they were the most fascinating couple I'd ever seen. I remember Barbara with a big fox fur hat. She said, "It's just my skiing hat." To me she was glamorous, and that hat was the cat's meow!

And she rode horses. She'd get up at six in the morning to go off and ride somebody's Irish hunter in the park. Brooks said to me once, "I can tell when she gets up in the morning—the bed goes up like that and she's gone." So that's what I remember—that she would get up at six to ride a fiery horse in the park and Brooks would let her go.

There was a painting of Barbara in their house, painted before she married Brooks. In the painting she had her hair back and very red lips and a very décolleté dress and I remember studying that and wondering if that was the real Barbara or not.

ELIZABETH BLOW

The first time I ever saw her was at one of the Art Students League balls, which in those days were great events—sort of like the Beaux-Arts balls in Paris. Everybody went to a great deal of trouble over their costumes. This one was a literary ball, the theme was literature, and I wore an old beautiful red velvet skirt that was made in tiers of French ribbon and a black bodice—I was *Le Rouge et le Noir*! A lot of the men didn't know what to do for their costume so they just put a towel around their heads and made their faces up with some kind of dark brown paint and went as Hindus. Fred Mueller, who I was engaged to, was very blond and Germanic-looking, and he went as a Hindu—he looked absolutely marvelous. And I think Brooks was dressed that way, too—he was tremendously attractive, just one of the handsomest men I've ever met in my life.

Anyway, when I went to the ladies' room, there was this beautiful girl there. She was *not* dressed in costume, she just had on a perfectly ordinary dinner dress. We got to talking and she told me she'd just had a son. And she talked about her son—she was very happy, she was thrilled to death.

We saw the Baekelands a lot after that night, mostly in their house. It was a rather conventional house, considering the personalities *in* the house.

HEATHER COHANE

My husband Jack told me this story about the Baekelands. It was long before I knew either of them. It must have been about the time Tony was born. They were all having dinner in some restaurant—Jack and his wife before me, and I think Aschwin Lippe and maybe *his* wife, Simone, and Brooks and Barbara—and they were playing this game: "For a million dollars would you eat a pound of human flesh? Would you go to bed with the first person you met after going through a revolving door, for a million dollars?"—and so forth.

Brooks must have answered yes to *that* question, because Barbara was saying to him as they left the restaurant, "Oh well, if *that's* the way you feel, *I'll* just go off with the first man that comes along in a car!" And she dashed into the middle of the street and flagged down a car with four young men in it. She jumped in and it took off. And of course, Jack and his wife and Aschwin and Simone and Brooks were left there with their mouths open, watching her disappear.

A couple of hours later she came home, having evidently got rather cold feet. Barbara was very beautiful in those days, so I mean, that was quite a crazy thing to do in New York City, a *dangerous* thing to do in New York City. Very crazy and very dangerous.

From the Diaries of John Philip Cohane, Unpublished

Friday. Dinner tonight at the Baekelands—Ben Sonnenberg, the publicity agent, and his wife; a supposedly brilliant psychiatrist, Sandor Rado; Geoffrey and Daphne Hellman—he writes for *The New Yorker*, she is a strange faunlike harpist. Afterwards Betty and Fred Mueller dropped by, and we spent most of the time trying to get free advice from the psychiatrist.

ELIZABETH BLOW

When Fred and I had our first child, we were living down in Greenwich Village in a very tiny apartment. Then we moved to Fiftieth Street and Second Avenue, to a railroad flat over a liquor store. Then we were going to have a second child so we had to move. And Fred found this incredible house on Seventy-second Street, which we rented for only one hundred and sixty-five dollars a month from this couple who were going to England for two or three years—he had a Rhodes Scholarship.

It was mammoth—five floors—and Fred, poor Fred, would come home from work and haul himself up to the top floor, the old maid's quarters, which he was redoing so we could rent it out. Whoever rented it was going to have to use our staircase.

We ran an ad and a very nice lady and her daughter-in-law, a widow, turned up and they were absolutely delightful. It came out as we were talking to them that the older woman was Barbara Baekeland's mother. She was lovely-looking, and over the years she has never changed very much. I mean, she had nothing of the sort of smashing looks of her daughter but she was very pretty, very kind of birdlike, always very nicely dressed. She always had a sort of prim and proper look about her.

I think we charged them one hundred and sixty-five dollars a month. They made the place absolutely charming. The sitting room in the front they fixed up with great taste, and the little kitchen that Fred had put in. They didn't entertain very much, but Barbara came over a lot to see her mother, and that was how I really got to know her so well. And of course Tony would come over all the time to spend the afternoon with his grandmother. He adored her. And she adored him. And whenever Brooks and Barbara would go away for the weekend, he would come and stay over.

Nini was a fascinating person at that time because she was quite neurotic, you know. She never could sleep very well, she had to have all the blinds pulled down—there couldn't even be one single ray of light coming in—and still she could not sleep a wink. I remember her thousands of times leaning over the banister. I would say, "Hi,

Nini, how *are* you?" and she would say, "Oh hi, darling. Didn't sleep a wink last night—I'm a wreck." She was always saying "I'm a wreck."

As far as one could see they were a very happy little family. Brooks and Barbara appeared to be the ideal couple with this charming little boy whom they both loved—no, I don't think *too* much, you can't love someone too much. Of course later it did become too much.

ELIZABETH ARCHER BAEKELAND

One summer I visited Brooks and Barbara on the Cape, Ballston Beach in Truro. It was once my stepfather's beach—Ozzie Ball, Sheldon Osborn Ball. He owned from Truro to North Truro, two miles of oceanfront. Zeckendorf offered him three million dollars for it, but he *gave* it all to the national parks.

Tony and I played together all day. He was so bright, he was way ahead of his class. I mean, I could spend the whole afternoon with him and have fun, and I'm not a child lover to that extent. I mean, I treat children like grown-ups—if they don't give me the same thing as a grown-up, I don't want to be with them. And Tony could give me the same as a grown-up—you know, opinions, feelings, wonderful observations. I would say his best time was up till the age of about four.

One afternoon, he and I watched a praying mantis on the boardwalk, and then he sat and drew the mantis and then he drew some birds—really wonderful. And later that night when Barbara was putting him to bed, I heard her say—it was over the partition that divided the rooms—"Tony darling, who do you love more, Liz or Mummy?" And he said, "Mummy, of course." And I thought, if at *four* she's giving him that kind of signal . . .

DODIE CAPTIVA

I knew them from the Cape. I can't say I knew them intimately. I mean, I knew them about as well as people do when one lives there year-round and the other comes for the summer.

I used to go once a year to visit New York and I was walking up Fifth Avenue, north of Rockefeller Plaza, daydreaming, when I suddenly caught sight of something familiar out of the corner of my eye—a woman and a small boy. He was five, maybe six—little enough to almost have to be held by the hand. They were strolling and looking into store windows, and when I came abreast of them I looked at the reflection in the window and saw that it was Barbara and Tony. They were so enraptured with each other—whatever they were doing, whatever the conversation was—that my red flag went up!

SARA DUFFY CHERMAYEFF

I was in Truro with my parents, I was sixteen years old and I had just learned to drive and I didn't have anything to do, and one night my father and mother said, "Now Sara, pull yourself together and *do* something. Now what can you do?" And what came up was that I could make a little children's camp. Well, it turned out to be a big business—I ended up with, like, fifteen children. I charged ten dollars a week. I made a lot of money—for *me*. My mother had this station wagon and I used that to pick up the kids. I took them to Gull Pond on the Truro-Wellfleet border—we took Oreos and apple juice and we'd go swimming. You know how people always say, "*Those* were the days, *I* remember those days," but I *do* remember. I mean, now Gull Pond looks like, you know, Ocean City, Maryland, but when I went there with my little group, there wasn't a house on it.

Originally I had Edmund Wilson's little daughter, Helen Miranda Wilson, who's now a quite established painter, and Daphne Hellman's three children, Daisy Hellman, Digger St. John, and Sandy Bull, who became quite a big rock star. And one day Daphne when I was drumming up business said, "Some people called Baekeland have rented a house on Castle Hill Road, and they have a little boy." So I drove right over there and this woman in a brown bikini was washing the car. She was *gorgeous*. I mean, she was just everything, I mean the most . . . I mean, I don't think Marilyn Monroe had come alive yet—right? I think this was before Marilyn Monroe. I was sixteen and Tony was seven, so it was 1953—was Marilyn Monroe in business in '53? I don't know about whether she was there in history or not but for *me* I had just never seen anybody as glamorous as Barbara Baekeland. And I followed *that* star for many years.

She agreed right away that I could take Tony in my little bathing-suit group. He had sort of a batik bathing suit and he was redheaded and oh gosh . . . He was always my favorite. And one day a little later on that summer Barbara or Brooks took me aside and spoke to me about Tony's stutter, and I said, "He doesn't stutter." So they said, "He doesn't stutter with *you*?" I said, "Not at all." So at that point they hired me on as a baby-sitter for whenever they went out in the evening or went away for the weekend.

DAPHNE HELLMAN
Once at their place on the Cape when I was there for dinner, Barbara and Brooks got Tony to read the Marquis de Sade out loud. He didn't read particularly well. He was doing it because he'd been commanded to. It struck me as very peculiar. Maybe it was to help him get over his stutter. Maybe it just seemed peppier than having him read from David Copperfield!

Barbara was the social one and Brooks was the curmudgeon. I remember one day I came upon them walking in the rain at night having some terrible fight. I guess Brooks flirted a good deal. Of course, Barbara was always hitching a ride with the milkman or somebody and being absolutely charming with them. She really was able to absorb people's flavor and get pleasure out of them.

BARBARA HALE
Bob Hale and I went up to Truro to visit them. I'll never forget sitting on the beach and seeing Ben Sonnenberg trotting along in his Georgian manner—looking perfectly awful, you know, in a bathing suit. He saw that there was this perfectly beautiful redheaded girl sitting with me and he came up to us and said, "Wouldn't you like to share my little picnic?" Well, he had this very elaborate picnic basket such as you've never seen in all your life, filled with pâté and lobster sandwiches and stuff like that—this was his pickup deal, and from then on Barbara saw a great deal of Ben Sonnenberg in New York. I remember Brooks came down to the beach with Tony and joined us.

DAPHNE HELLMAN
Tony and my daughter Daisy as little kids on the Cape were inseparable. I remember them crowing like roosters on the roof of this rough-and-ready house that Brooks and Barbara rented one summer right on the beach. Crowing was just something Tony and Daisy did at that time. It was very annoying to everybody. Barbara and Brooks got sort of fed up.

DAISY HELLMAN PARADIS
We used to get into mischief together, at Ballston Beach, and go and raid the local farmer's garden. Once, we took our clothes off in our

garage and when cars came we jumped up and down and yelled, you know—and my father came by and he was rather amused.

I never had great feeling for Barbara at all, to tell you the truth—as a child, I didn't like her. I couldn't put it into words at the time, of course, but it didn't seem to me she had a whole lot of affection for Tony. Or for me, you know—or for kids in general. She was somebody who was always sort of saying "Oh *darling*," you know, this and that, but there was something sort of not so real there. Artificial maybe.

Tony wrote to me a couple of years after he killed her. I didn't answer because I really didn't know what to say, you know. Jesus Christ! What do you say to somebody who's killed his mother?

HELEN MIRANDA WILSON

I remember very little about him—that he had red hair and freckles, that I played with him when I was very young, with him and Johnny Frank, the writer Waldo Frank's son. I'd better identify him as Waldo and *Jean* Frank's son, because Waldo was married a number of times. Johnny's now a paramedic and ambulance driver in San Francisco. Anyway, we all used to play together in the summer, and Tony Baekeland was a real brat and a bully. Yeah, a bully—and I was a pretty hefty little kid. You want me to tell you what I really remember about him? It's pretty funny actually. I remember us playing up in the woods and somebody went to the bathroom—I think it was him—you know little kids—and I think he scooped some up in his hand and chased me with it. That's it, that's my recollection of him.

JONATHAN FRANK

Tony and I were real close when we were little kids, up till we were eight or nine. And we were both terrible! In fact there was another boy, Johnny Van Kirk, and the three of us were inseparable—we were called the Terrible Trio. The grown-ups used to call us that. But it was a fond name, even though I'm sure we *were* terrible.

JOHNNY VAN KIRK

My mother used to make up stories about us—"Black Johnny," "Yellow Johnny," and "Terrible Tony." It was a threesome.

The only reason for the "Terrible Tony" was because he was always off on some very imaginative rant or other. He had a fantastic imagination, he just knew no bounds. Tony was not ordinary. No, I would say he was extraordinary.

He was certainly the wildest of the bunch. I spent a lot of time at the Ballston Beach parking lot with him blocking off large sections and flooding them with water from his house, making vast, swamp wonderworlds between the parked cars. He was always inventing mad games for us to play. Johnny Frank and I would go out and buy toy trucks and guns and stuff, but Tony would invent them right out of his head. Mostly fantasy games, role-playing games. And he had a capacity for involving you in them—you would forget your inhibitions and become a part of it all very easily.

He even convinced us that if we would rub this strange funny clay from the dunes on ourselves, we could fly. We'd literally spend hours running down the cliff and jumping off as far as we could, convinced that we had flown a little further each time—with a little more clay! And it was Tony's ability that really allowed us to do this. There was a kind of persuasion that he had. He was very forceful at that age. And it was a good time.

5

FUN AND GAMES

Once a week Tony Baekeland, along with five of his fellow patients at Cornwall House, was escorted to the canteen, where he was free to purchase, among other things, candy, cigarettes, soap, coffee, and tea. A patient was not allowed to handle cash himself; rather, all purchases were charged to his hospital account, into which his money had been placed. Each month he received a computer printout of the status of his finances.

"Tony could be very kind to others," Dr. Gogarty says. "In fact, I had to protect him from being overgenerous. I initiated a request for a protector through the Court of Protection, which is a branch of the Supreme Court in England, and Tony's money was eventually placed under the protection of a court-appointed guardian, who inquired into his needs and then apportioned the money to him. Usually it is given in a yearly sum, but I convinced Tony's guardian to give it to him in six-month installments. He was also receiving an allowance from his father, and there was quite a lot of money from other sources as well, including income from investments in New York."

By the beginning of 1976, Tony Baekeland had adjusted to hospital routine, both social and therapeutic. "He had a chronic illness, of course," says Dr. Gogarty, "but he fluctuated—he had ups and downs. His true basic personality would show through every now and then. His kind of illness was not strictly an illness that depends on the environment. It was genetic.

"Tony was well read," Dr. Gogarty adds, "but he had something a lot of schizophrenics have—a kind of pseudointellectuality about things. I've been involved with schizophrenics for a long time, because they're not boring—they're very interesting, in fact. There's a certain truth to everything they say. I find this fascinating, because it all *seems* so true, yet they can't function normally. And when they commit criminal acts, they always, in some way, manage to tell the world what they're going to do before they do it."

TONY VAN ROON

I knew that Tony Baekeland was fairly solvent but I didn't know he was, you know, exceedingly rich or anything. But what I would say is always the sociopathic element in Broadmoor would take great advantage of people who were like that and would be their friend until there was nothing left. I do remember that when he went to the canteen he certainly always made adequate allowance for what he'd need in the week. But the thing was, as soon as he got back to the ward, people would say, Well, you don't need all that, why don't you give me some, and he was really a very nice guy, you know. So the problem was he would give things away, particularly if he saw somebody who was less fortunate.

PATRICIA GREENE

He was always very sensitive as a child. He was a will-o'-the-wisp child, in a way—now you see him, now you don't. At his parents' dinner parties he would fly in and out, like quicksilver.

He would come to our house, but our children would not so often go there. He would come to us because we were more of a family, I think, and he rather liked that. I think Brooks and Barbara were rather social. I think they were *quite* social. He went to his grandmother's when they went out at night—I would see him walking down the street with his parakeet in a cage and his pajamas over his arm.

One Halloween I took him around the block. We made our costumes in those days, we didn't buy them, and I made one for him. Then I went around with the children. They were quite small. I remember Tony was overwhelmed with the excitement of it. And he ran off through the night, down the block, and I was quite alarmed because he just disappeared. We chased after him and finally caught up with him and he was just running, running, running, in a wild manner. And then we all went around the block together. The block was very nice in those days. At the Paul Mellon house, the butler answered the door and offered us apples on a silver tray. Those days are gone forever.

I remember Tony had some mice or something in his room, and of course he had the little bird, and I suppose he had fish. And when he would come to our house he would look at *our* animals—we may have had a white rat that impressed him, too. That was more of his link with my boys than anything else.

There was a vacant lot across the street from us—they had torn down the building—and I think there were rats which intrigued Tony and our boys, and I said, "You'd better stay away because you might get bitten." Our boys pretty much stayed away, but I think Tony used to go through the boards again and again and poke around and I think that upset Barbara, because I remember her speaking to me about that as a concern—how she could keep him away from the building. I guess Tony just had this enormous interest in any sort of animals.

From *A Family Motor Tour Through Europe*, Leo Hendrik Baekeland, Horseless Age Press, New York, 1907

My two children are great lovers of animals, and if I let them have their own way, their not too small collection of dogs, rabbits, cats, guinea pigs, birds, etc., would soon increase to the size of a little menagerie. . . . When I finally heard that my boy, George, had been bargaining for a live and healthy ferret I decided that it now was time to compromise on some gentler representative of the animal kingdom, so I finally consented to tte purchase of two tiny Bengalese finches. Housed in a little cage, they were from now on to become our traveling companions.

PATRICIA GREENE

One of the first times I met Barbara, she said, "Oh, Tony's raising moths in my closet." And I thought that was enchanting, so I looked and, sure enough, in a shoe box he had some moth cocoons, and she twinkled and was merry over that. I must say I adored her for that—*I* was always saying, "Get the moths *out* of my closet!" And *she* had mink coats and very expensive clothes in hers.

We invited Tony to our place in the country mainly because one of our sons had gone over to see some of his moths and was intrigued. You see, Tony was really just the boy-next-door type thing. The second time he came to the country, he developed warts from the frogs. There's apparently a little virus that they carry. I think Barbara was pretty horrified at that. He didn't come again.

You know, he did some drawings at our house in town. I must say they were quite different. Most boys were drawing rockets or airplanes and things like that, and he would be drawing more imaginative stuff—fanciful animals.

Barbara used to do paintings of insects. Very large. Mostly representative. They were very good. I remember she worked very hard one summer on Cape Cod, and she came back with an exhibit in the fall. I remember meeting her before the show and she said, "I'm a wild woman, I've been painting like mad all summer, I just couldn't stop, and I'm on my way to the hairdresser!" And her hair *was* standing out. She *was* a wild woman.

It was a charming show. You walked up some stairs in this very small gallery and Barbara was greeting people. I have a mental picture of her standing with her lovely hair and her lovely complexion and pretty dress. She had little white kid gloves on. I was impressed with that—white kid gloves! She was soft. I can see the little white kid gloves around her little plump hands—she wasn't plump but she gave the impression of being so. I commented on the gloves and she said, "I don't like to touch all these people, I guess." So that was a sidelight I remember of her character. Of course, people did wear gloves in those days.

MARJORIE FRASER SNOW

She studied under, I believe, Gonzalez, I think on the Cape and also in New York at the Art Students League, and also under Hans Hofmann. I think she had a one-man show somewhere in New York. I think she got very fine reviews, as a matter of fact. I know she had one on the Cape. And Nini was so proud of her!

PATRICIA GREENE

Barbara was very proud of her mother for taking a job at the Museum of Natural History. Mrs. Daly apparently didn't have to work at that point, although at one time I know she had rather a hard time making ends meet. It must have seemed like a dream to have Barbara marry all that plastic money! But later on, Mrs. Daly said she was bored just sitting around and she wanted to do something. Of course Tony was delighted when she went to work at the museum—after all, the Museum of Natural History! That was right down his alley.

I just took it for granted that he'd be a naturalist. I thought he'd go on and pull himself together—you know, that he'd get to be a rather eccentric naturalist of some sort. Or a painter.

JONATHAN FRANK

When I visited Tony in New York, we used to cut out to the museum where his grandmother worked. Basically there was sort of a loose connection because we would report to her but we were pretty much on our own—and we were really young at that point.

We used to play outdoors a lot and I'd say we preferred it that way. At night we would escape to the bedroom and we had a game where we would climb up on a cupboard way up high and then jump down on the bed, pretending that we were pterodactyls—you know, flying dinosaurs.

NINA DALY

I went looking for a job and I got one in the gift shop at the museum and we got a vacation in the summer for two weeks and we got holidays. I really enjoyed it. I would have liked to have done something else after I finished there. I would have liked to have worked in some store or something, if it had been a nice store. Anything to keep busy, to get out of the house in the morning.

Tony would stop in and see me an awful lot. I loved that. He used to come and spend about three nights a week with me, too. It was to keep me company because I was alone, you see. And I had lived with them for a while, because I hadn't gotten used to living alone. You have to get used to it if you're not used to it. My sister used to come and stay a lot with me. She never had any children, so she used the family's children. She loved children. I love children, too. I miss them now.

Tony went right nearby to the Buckley School. He liked it there. He was doing great. He was a good student, he always read and read and read and read. When he was in Broadmoor, he'd write me for some books he wanted and I'd send him some Shakespeare and others.

"Comments" on Antony Baekeland, French Class, Buckley School, New York City

> When he wants to, Tony can produce really beautiful prose and poetry in French as well as in English. The job of getting him to want to do this is tremendous at times, but the result, when it is good, makes whatever has gone before seem worthwhile.

> Despite everything that has happened this term I still feel that Tony is one of the finest boys I have ever known. If he can realize his full potential he will be *the* finest.

PETER GABLE

I met Tony in the second or third grade at Buckley, which was a very competitive school academically. He was not a peculiar child to another child—to *this* child—but he was certainly different because of some of his enthusiasms and abilities. I mean, he was uniquely brilliant—brilliant in ways that another child wouldn't appreciate, I think.

His artistic abilities were spectacular—he loved to draw birds, you know. He was a baby Audubon. I remember once we were out playing in the park—we were old enough to be unchaperoned, eight or nine or something—and I captured this pigeon. I don't think it was an entirely healthy bird, it was a basic Central Park shit-on-the-statues pigeon, and Tony took it from me and tucked it under his coat, and we rushed it back to his house on Seventy-first Street, and it was there for some time, flying free—first in his room and then having the run of the floor. The pigeon rather liked us, as I recall. In any event, it ultimately either conferred lice upon us or there was some fear that it would or whatever, and it was dispatched, I don't remember how. But I certainly remember Tony's sketches of that pigeon, in either pencil or pen and ink.

Every day after school we'd go home together to his house and stuff. You know, he was my best friend, and *his* house was more entertaining than *my* house. I mean, he had an area in his room where he raised orchids. I think that was a passion of his father's. I remember a rather enormous fishtank-like proposition with a controlled environment, in which these exotic flowers grew.

I remember his mother as being striking and a flamboyant and vivacious person. She was certainly more animated than the mothers of other friends. I mean, when you're a child, what do you know of the adult life? You know your parents, their friends, your teachers in school with whom you probably have some sort of distant relationship, your baby-sitter, the elevator man—in those days everybody had an elevator man; when I was a child the only adult you addressed by his first name was the elevator man.

I certainly perceived Barbara Baekeland as being extraordinarily *something*, you know. I also remember what I perceived at the time to be a rather stormy relationship with her husband. Oh, they would fight, they would fight. I can remember hearing them. Tony and I both sort of listened, though we probably couldn't hear the exact words that were being spoken. My mother and father were having a rather rocky time, too, so raised voices amongst adults in a household was not foreign to me, I didn't think what I heard over at the Baekelands was that strange, you know. But the volume!

Tony's father I remember as being austere and uninvolved—very much of a shadow figure. He once took Tony and his mother and me for a picnic one Saturday into some countryside. I remember so clearly being in the back of the car—he kept a Mercedes convertible at the time, I think—a sports car—the top was down, it was a beautiful fair-weather day, and Tony and I were bundled in the back. We buzzed up to where there was a beautiful glade with a pond and I guess we had our lunch and then Tony and I wandered off to play. But the interesting thing is that this and one other time are the only occasions I can remember—and Tony and I were close close friends for several years—when I was in the company of both his parents.

When summers would come, Tony would disappear to some foreign clime until fall, then we'd both be back in our short trousers and blazers, hiking off to school.

SYLVIE BAEKELAND SKIRA

Brooks and Barbara were two very powerful people who had their own fight together, and the little boy was sort of a puppet in between. He was trained by these parents to be brilliant. You know, you can teach a child to say the Latin word for "monkey" as easily as to say "monkey," and he was trained that way. I'm completely against it.

Even when the son was in Broadmoor, Brooks was ordering him,

"You have to show remorse!" The son would say, "Absolutely not! *You* have to." There were letters, there were letters constantly. One would say, "*You* killed Mummy!" Which is a point of view. And the other one would say, "You didn't hit your mother with a banana, you hit her with a knife!" So. The thing that Brooks could never understand is that his son never showed him that he felt the slightest remorse. *That*, Brooks couldn't understand.

MISHKA HARNDEN

I'm sure Tony was born fairly unstable. On the other hand, all of what he went through when he was a kid certainly scrambled him for good. He was like that dog they had, you know—he was a slightly larger Pekingese. "Tony, do this! Tony, do that!" "Yes, Mother." I mean, Tony Perkins in *Psycho*—you know? I mean, it gets to be that close.

YVONNE THOMAS

The way she would praise him and show you everything he'd written or drawn! Both of them did. They wanted the boy to be a genius. That's what struck me. And made me feel uncomfortable. I felt uncomfortable with the boy because I felt *he* felt he had to be something.

You know, when you impose yourself on your children like that, it's because you want them to be more than *you've* been. I think they were very ambitious and that nothing had happened with their ambition. She was always talking about what they were *going* to do. They wanted to do a coup of some sort, either in literature or in . . . I thought they were silly. She represented something sort of social—purely social—to me. I thought the way she entertained and her conversation and that crispy sort of voice were affectations—everything was something that didn't interest me that much. Especially at that time. Now I don't care, you know. But then I was very strict—everybody was—about exactly the style that you chose to be. I became an Abstract Expressionist painter and it changed my life—it changed a lot of my views, a lot of my values. I didn't see too much of the Baekelands after that.

But oh, the son was shining as a little boy! But then when he turned into adolescence, one didn't hear so much.

WILLIE DRAPER

Tony was the *most* brilliant and the *most* refined—and the most creative and the most sensitive—so he built the most walls the most quickly and his ability to communicate his feelings was lost the quickest. Tony right from the beginning was a marked man. I knew him at Buckley, I knew him the whole damn time. I mean, just the whole way through, you know, we were tight. But then I phased him out of my life because he was too negative for me, and my sister Checka filled the spot, she was going through more similar things.

Tony and I got stabbed trick-or-treating and stuff together—I can't remember whether we actually got stabbed or whether we almost got stabbed. These roughnecks followed us back from the park and they cornered us, and we were ringing the bell at Tony's house and nobody was coming down. Another time we had our bikes stolen in the park and some policeman took us around in the patrol car and everybody pointed at us like we were criminals.

He had—*both* of us had—very intense mothers, you know. I loved Barbara. I mean, *she* loved *me*, first of all, and part of the time Tony would be really jealous of me because—you know how it is—he'd get along really good with my mother and I'd get along really good with his mother.

Barbara was very loving—it's just that she was so intense emotionally, and her moods would change, based on her relationship with her husband and her whole Celtic character. She was just, you know, a wild woman. Sometimes it was just . . . it was frightening.

But Tony was a great guy, a great guy—he burned with such a pure flame.

The biggest mystery in my life is *why* we choose what we choose, because we do choose—in the end we have total responsibility for what happens to us. And, you know, what ignorance is it, what is the mechanics of what makes someone like Tony who has all of this potential . . . ? I think it's emotional starvation, myself—I mean, it really has a lot to do with just very basic things.

SARA DUFFY CHERMAYEFF

I saw Tony every day, every single day when he was at Buckley. I'd gotten married when I was twenty, to Ivan Chermayeff, and we lived just a block away from the Baekelands. Barbara was very happy for me—I mean, she liked Ivan because he had, God knows, the scent of success on him. She gave me for my wedding present some very pale emerald earrings, which were very like the rings she used to wear—she told me they had been Brooks's grandmother's or something and that she had had them reset—two emeralds with two pearls. I mean, I was her darling baby-sitter, right? And, I suppose, to give her credit, which I *don't* like to do, 'cause I'd like to *kill* her, I suppose she really thought I was a lovely girl. You know, because I adored her—anything that she said went with *me*.

Ivan and I had this funny railroad flat on Seventieth and Lexington, right over the bus stop, and every day, from the time I was twenty until I was twenty-three, Tony came to me on the way home from Buckley, because Barbara might or might not be home. I mean, I lived just that far away from them—I was *right there*. At three o'clock in the afternoon he'd come in the back—he had a little strap with his books and a little hat. He had a key to my house. Ivan was at work and I'd be trying to write my novel and trying to clean up my house and trying to think my thoughts. And we'd go home to his house together.

It was everything I ever thought would be the perfect house. You came in and the dining room was there—I must have had a million meals in that dining room—then you went up the stairs and Barbara took you in to a sort of faun-colored library, quite a small room—and she had those green rings dripping off her fingers and her feet hanging off the ottoman like nobody's business. And back there was her bedroom, with lace all over the bed. She was often in bed, with all sorts of men sitting around—Harold Rosenberg, Saul Steinberg . . . I never saw Brooks there. She had a salon. And I mean, all I thought was, That's the way to live!

Tony's room was on the top floor. It had a skylight and a little tiny sort of wire balcony. I sure remember his room in that penthouse on Seventy-fifth Street that they moved to later on! I mean, in *her* room up there, she had the leopard-skin bed, the seven thousand Chanel suits in her closet—right?—and then there was Tony's room—the maid's room!

I don't remember when it was, but I began to see that Tony was just breaking to pieces, that they were killing him. They were a perfect couple, for that—to destroy the boy.

Oh, I can remember her movements when she would say—she would always say—"I've found this *marvelous* . . ."— right? That was a word she used all the time—"marvelous, marvelous."

Last spring it was a beautiful day and I went down to the Strand

Book Store—they have books on the street down in front, many many books—and I bought *The Letters of Madame de Sévigné* that I've always wanted. And I didn't notice it for a long time but some time later I saw that the book was signed "Barbara D. Baekeland, 1942—New York." It must have come from her books in the penthouse that were sold after she died. I mean, how bizarre!

And then I thought, God, in 1942 she was already collecting *The Letters of Madame de Sévigné*! Now I don't even know if she ever read them. I have them now and I haven't read them. She obviously already had something in mind. I mean, Madame de Sévigné had a salon—she was in contact with the cream of the French intelligentsia of the time.

She—they—they were really false, the Baekelands. False. False to everything. When I first saw them as glamorous, I guess I wanted to be false, but when I began to understand how *Tony* felt, I saw them as—terrible, both of them. *Both* of them *terrible*. I mean, I feel they never attended to what was serious—neither one of them *ever*. They just took on this idea of what was *life*. What did they have in mind? Imagine, I mean, going to live on the Île Saint-Louis! Who did they think they were? The Murphys?

I mean, when I knew Tony I was only ten years older than him and I didn't have any children of my own. But once I had children and I knew the responsibility that it takes to bring them up, I realized what total bullshitters the Baekelands were, with their *goddam* salons—well, it just isn't fair. I mean, I resented my parents—everybody resents their parents in one way or another, I suppose, right?—but, boy, I survived, and when you get down to it, you have to hand that to your parents in a weird way—right? They didn't *kill* you. And the Baekelands *killed him*.

And he was a wonderful little boy. I was a very romantic young girl and I had read D. H. Lawrence's *Rocking Horse Winner* and, you know, that's what he was—he was like a little literary boy, he was like all the boys in English novels. And that's what she had him be. He'd be brought in on a string and shown. She just didn't leave him alone. Not for one second.

I went to Broadmoor to see Tony with Missy Harnden, who I knew from when Ivan and I had a house in Cadaqués for five years, and all he kept saying was, "I'm free, I'm free now, I'm free." He said it to both of us—"I'm free now."

Letter from Antony Baekeland to James Reeve, February 12, 1976

                                                                Broadmoor
Dear James,
I just got your letter which came with a lovely *Audubon* magazine from my grandmother, Mrs. Hallowell. Full of photographs of birds and flowers and forests in the U.S.A. This
morning we had group therapy and it went very well. I feel so
wonderfully well these days—my grandmother Nini will be very
pleased with me.

You must be happy to be with your mother—when do you
move into your new house? I have decided to be a writer like my
Papa.

Poor dear Una Verbi has had to be put into a home—her
mind has gone and Val feels terribly, of course, that he has
abandoned her. He came yesterday in tears and stayed an hour.
They both have become such good friends—I will be sad not to
see her again, but who knows?

James, please give my regards to your mother. And do try to
write if you find time in your busy days.

                                                                Love,
                                                                Tony

JAMES REEVE
The really disturbing thing was this mother bit. You see, in his letters
to me he always said to give his regards to my mother. *My* mother!
I'd probably mentioned my mother to him in passing but no more
than that.

I had this recurring nightmare that he'd be let out. He had told me
once, certainly, how lovely it would be to come and stay with me in
the country, down in Somerset, and this haunted me, because what
was I going to do if for some reason he *was* being let out and he said,
"I want James Reeve to come and pick me up"?

I suppose I would have done it. But I remember being warned that
he could be frightfully dangerous. I mean, anything could have set
him off, poor chap.

When you went to see him, you went in through a great big massive gate. Then there was a little door, and sitting behind a desk was a man who took your parcels if you'd taken presents, and there was a ledger where you wrote your name and you said whether you were a friend or a relation. And then you walked through this tiny cubbyhole and there was another door, and you were let in, and then there was a huge great courtyard. You walked down one side of it, like a sort of cloister, and there was another locked gate, with a guard standing there who opened that, and then you would go down a corridor where the kitchens were, and this corridor went on endlessly. And finally there was this great big mausoleum of a room with a stage, a piano, windows, and dotted around were these sorts of little tea tables where we would sit and have our tea. Two or three guards sat on a bench, watching. If your back was turned to them, you could have slipped anything to your friend or relation, and taken anything back. Which was extraordinary!

I wondered to myself where Tony had got the clothes he was wearing, because they just weren't the sort of clothes he would wear. Not that they were rag-and-bone-men's clothes, they were just what my grandmother used to call "lower orders" clothes. They didn't fit well on Tony. I mean, he was rather distinguished-looking in his sort of slovenly way. The materials were all wrong—I mean, nylon jackets and things didn't look right on him. The impression was that the clothes were just castoffs, from a murderous plumber or something, who happened to have died the night before.

One always had the feeling he could very easily have supposed that one's interest in him or visits to him were just out of a sort of macabre fascination. And this is why one had to tread a very careful line jollying him along. I soon discovered that if Tony had a visitor, he didn't want to sit there and talk about Broadmoor. I respected that. He wanted to have news of the outside, which was a shame, because I was dying to ask all sorts of questions, like what were the bathrooms like, what were the dormitories like. And were the beds comfortable. They obviously weren't. But you couldn't ask him. He hated that. And actually, any morbid curiosity may have had a place the first few times I visited, but then it evaporated, I can tell you that.

Whenever I wrote to him, it was difficult because one didn't want to dwell on his side of things, so naturally one would just talk on about one's life. In one of his letters to me—here it is—one line says, "I wish you had done what I had suggested, i.e., come at two o'clock." Actually I remember that day. I deliberately hadn't come at two—to cut short the thing. "So we could talk at length," he wrote. Which meant, of course, two hours. "Also so I might have shown you the really beautiful pictures of my mother which I felt would have interested you. I don't think I told you, but she was a great Artist." With a capital "A"! "And I'm trying to find some of her remarkable paintings which were lost with the other things at 81 Cadogan Square." It's all so complicated, isn't it? I mean, you pick up a letter to look at one sentence, and three others are underneath it.

Well, my friendship with Tony was a bit different. Visiting someone in an institution like that is not like having a friend, it's like looking at an animal in a cage. I mean, it has to be!

Every time, I had to screw my courage up to the sticking point to visit him, because, I mean, I also had my personal hangups about the place. It reminded me of Rugby, where I was sent, which is about the nastiest form of public school in England. It wasn't what the authorities did to us, it was what the other boys did that was so appalling. They used to roast you over fires when you arrived and were sort of a new creature, and they used to heat up the backs of those old-fashioned metal hairbrushes and brand your bottom with them. Three boys committed suicide while I was there. It was a Victorian institution very much like Broadmoor. So it nearly made me sick going to visit Tony, because even all the smells were the same— sweat and urine and cabbage water and damp walls and blocked drains and uncouth lavatories.

And then I would find this pitiful, wan, pasty-faced creature with the bitten nails and the light-red oily hair. It was *not* attractive. Nothing attractive about it. Not that life should be attractive all the time, I know, but it would have been nice to find one ray of light there.

The thing that used to shatter me was his having to be got from being asleep. He shouldn't have been allowed to go to bed in the afternoon—except, you see, a lot of the time he was drugged. It was very obvious sometimes that he was drugged up to the hilt. This is the pitiful thing—they'd rather the patients were quiet, so they'd rather they just went to bed in the afternoon. They haven't got the skilled staff to look after those difficult creatures. If each one of those prisoners had had an interested psychiatrist, it would have been a very different matter.

I remember going in the autumn once and all he wanted to know was what the countryside looked like. Pitiful, really. And so few people visited him. That was the thing that I found unforgivable. So many of the fashionable friends never went near him. They couldn't be bothered! I suppose all that circle was just vapid butterflies. How else do you explain it? They were all a lot of Fitzgerald dustbags!

From the Diaries of John Philip Cohane, Unpublished

> *Saturday.* The night before last we gave an "artists" party for Jack and Drue Heinz—Brooks and Barbara Baekeland, Noguchi, Marcel and Teenie Duchamp, Barbara and Bob Hale. Barbara Hale and I presented over two hours of enthusiastically received pantomimes during which I engulfed over half a bottle of brandy which, on top of a stupendous bottle of Musigny '49, gave me my first hangover in months. At one a.m. everyone—including Marcel—was dancing gaily to Jelly Roll Morton—at 3:30 finally fell into bed.

DRUE HEINZ
I knew the family early on in their life in New York, when the little boy was about seven years old and his father was writing a scientific thesis. They were a charming, intellectually inclined family, who seemed at that time very "together" and set for a happy life.

ALASTAIR REID
Barbara invited me to a cocktail party soon after meeting me at Ambrose Gordon's. Their house had an enormous paneled living room and I realized then that they must be impressively wealthy. Clearly she collected people, because she talked about having a salon and so on, and she had picked the people who were there that night. She was certainly capable of having a salon, she was just exactly the kind of person who should have had one. She sparked, she was the center—people paid attention and she paid attention to them, too—enormously. And Brooks was very laconic and, you know, cool and hanging back, while she did the whole thing for him, and I could see that he had acquired her because of her vivacity.

JAMES KINGSLAND
I never knew quite what Brooks was doing, he was always doing something—either writing a novel or dabbling in mathematics. It

was occasionally referred to lightly at dinner parties but I assumed that it was nothing very serious other than keeping him occupied during the day. Later on he went into exploring and stuff like that. He was a guy with a lot of ideas and energy who was looking for things to do.

SYLVIA BAEKELAND SKIRA
It seems to me that Brooks has had the great problem of finding his own field, which he hasn't. And Barbara was certainly an excuse for his not having done anything particularly with his life and with his talent. He liked to say that he couldn't do this or that because *she* had to be going here and there.

CÉLINE ROLL KARRAKER
Barbara changed tremendously from the time I first met her. Brooks, sort of like my grandfather, didn't like that life—and yet he was not strong like my grandfather to keep his own life.

ELIZABETH ARCHER BAEKELAND
I can remember being at their house once when Barbara was carrying on in her very social way. And when I left, Brooks followed me out, he said, "I'm so sick of all this." You see, he was already fed up with it, but then he gave in—it was comfortable, it was easy. He became just like Barbara in some ways because he said to me one time, I remember, "I was shooting with the Duchess of Sutherland," and I said, "Who's that?" and he said, "You've never heard of the Duchess of Sutherland? Why, she's the richest woman in Scotland!"

FRANCINE DU PLESSIX GRAY
The Baekelands entertained like no one else in New York; they had a kind of largess for it. It had a kind of European touch—there wasn't this ghastly long cocktail period, you know. It was orderly, and it was beautifully catered—marvelous food and marvelous wine. And it was very lively, it was more like a Parisian salon in a sense—there was a combination of money and intellect. In America, especially at that time, in the fifties, people didn't know the difference between Isadora Duncan and Inigo Jones, you know. I mean, the W-A-S-P ruling milieus were just rather illiterate, you could *not* have an intellectual conversation.

The Baekelands gave Cleve and me a fabulous engagement

party—just maybe twenty, twenty-four people—and afterwards, I remember, we played a kind of game where there was a curtain raised
to a certain height and the women sat in the back of the room and
the men took their trousers off—we got to see their BVDs and so
on—and they did this kind of chorus-girl dance behind the curtain
and the women had to guess whose legs belonged to whom—you
know, which are my husband's legs! Then they switched—the men
went on the other side and the women did it.

ELIZABETH ARCHER BAEKELAND

There were always a lot of games. If the evening wasn't going well,
Barbara always had a great feeling for what to do to sort of pick it up.
She was a wonderful hostess. I never went there without having a
good time—*ever*.

The turning point in Barbara's social life came, as far as *I'm* concerned, when she met Marjorie and Fairfield Osborn. He was the
head of the New York Zoological Society and son of the head of the
American Museum of Natural History—they were very well-con-
nected culturally, socially, everything, absolutely, and from then on
they were her closest friends. They adored her and they introduced
her to all of society, including Prince Aschwin Lippe, Prince
Bernhard's brother, and Barbara was just adored by all these people.
The Osborns got her going on the fast track.

I remember Barbara saying to me before one of her parties, "Now
you've got to look your best tonight, Liz, because all the most beautiful women in New York are going to be here." I remember Patsy
Pulitzer—she was a model, *very* beautiful. And Tennessee Williams
was there that night.

BROOKS BAEKELAND

I had Dylan Thomas in my house. I was supposed to keep him while
he was in New York. He was a great poet but I bounced him out. He
took a Huntsman's shirt of mine with him—much too big for him.
My house was always buzzing with beautiful, silly, tipsy people.

JAMES KINGSLAND

They entertained constantly. At the time we were all much younger
and one didn't think of them in terms of, you know, being marvelous
parties—one just used to go there and get mildly smashed, have a
good time, and go home. Later on I think Barbara realized that she

was giving good parties and became more self-conscious, and that's when you started seeing the likes of Salvador Dalí and stuff like that around, which I personally didn't find as amusing. I think she became very conscious of who people were in the public eye. There were also a number of foreigners coming through with handles of one sort or another.

It all goes back to the thing of people's weaknesses, and social climbing was certainly a *faiblesse* of the Baekelands'. These days they call them alpinists. Brooks I think had less social pretentions than Barbara—well, obviously, because he had the advantage there with her.

ELIZABETH ARCHER BAEKELAND

She came to a party of ours once—at the time I was married to John Squire, my third husband, and we lived in a fifth-floor walkup. When I called to invite them, Barbara said, "Well, if you want us to come to a party, you have to ask us at least two weeks in advance." So I set a date a few weeks after that, and Barbara called up the day of the party and said, "I'm terribly sorry but we were out until three this morning and we're going to have to leave your party early tonight." So I said fine, I didn't see anything wrong with that. But John was furious, he said it was rude, that if she wanted to leave early she should just leave but don't call and say it's because she was out too late at somebody else's party—as if ours wasn't important.

Anyway, they came, and it turned out that a friend of John's who was with Pan American in Lisbon came with his wife, a Portuguese countess who was absolutely stunningly beautiful. And Barbara was galvanized. And then Muriel Murphy arrived with some man—none of us knew who he was and we didn't really catch his name. And when he left we all said, What beautiful shoes, did you ever *see* such beautiful shoes! That was all anybody noticed. Somebody finally realized it was Stanley Marcus of Neiman-Marcus. Anyway, Barbara was having a ball—she was dancing around with candlesticks. And at one point later on she was sitting on the floor and I remember John suddenly reached out his hand to her. He said, "Barbara!" She thought he wanted to dance with her so she jumped up, and then he just escorted her to the door, saying, "It's eleven o'clock, you're going home." She said, "But I don't *want* to go," and he said, "Oh no, you're very tired, you stayed up so late last night. *You're* going *home!*" And he put the coat on her. I was dying of embarrassment. The next day I called and apologized but Barbara said how impressed she was by John—she said she hadn't known he had that kind of guts.

Later that day the countess called to thank us and mentioned that Barbara had called and asked her to lunch—I mean, not even asking John and me! It was then I began to really see the light with Barbara.

I'll tell you another thing. I hadn't seen them for a long time and I was at some opening at the Metropolitan Museum and I saw Brooks and he said, "Barbara's upstairs," and I said wonderful as Brooks and I hugged, and I dashed all around till I finally found her and we kissed, you know, a peck on the cheek, the way you do. And then suddenly I saw her face go completely blank on me, and she's looking over her shoulder at Janet Gaynor and her husband Adrian who were arriving—can you imagine! I mean, she dropped me like a hot potato and went right over to them—never thought of introducing me. I was left just standing there, so I just turned on my heels and walked away. After that, I didn't even really want to talk to her. I was sorry at losing her friendship, but she had gone on to things that I wasn't willing to follow.

HELEN DELANEY

Have you ever heard of Sarah Hunter Kelly? She was a famous decorator, and she and her husband lived next door to Brooks and Barbara on Seventy-first Street. What divided them was a wall—luckily a thick wall, so Sarah never heard all the hollering and screaming that went on, and that's why they were able to remain friends. It was Sarah Kelly who introduced Barbara to Europe, and of course Barbara became a Francophile—she had what you might call terminal Francophilia.

From the *New York Times,* "A Lifelong Taste for Good Taste," Jane Geniesse, April 9, 1981

"I was absolutely determined to go to France," said Mrs. Kelly. Visits from a dashing cousin who lived in France, she said, set her on her "grand plan." "I thought she was immensely elegant and I wanted to live just like her," Mrs. Kelly said.

But if she liked living well—which fortunately she and her husband had the means to do—Mrs. Kelly also attached great importance to the cultivation of creative people. "I liked the writers and artists and I liked to paint. But I also had this yen for houses and fixing them up," she added.

The Kellys were soon part of the same group of young Americans as Scott and Zelda Fitzgerald and Sara and Gerald Murphy.

NINA DALY

Mrs. Kelly used to come over to Barbara's house. I've been over there to her place and the inside is just like a museum. Barbara always called her her second mother.

Letter from Barbara Baekeland to Nina Daly, June 1, 1954

Portofino

Dearest Mother,

You seem awfully far away and by the end of the summer I suspect I will be glad to get home. Europe has charms but traveling certainly gives one a certain perspective and a realization that we're a pretty wonderful country after all.

As things stand now we're living quite cheaply but Paris was a lot more expensive than we'd figured and this apartment is not cheap. But it is completely adorable. I wish you could see it. A tiny duplex where everything is perfection. You would love it and this village but we plan to take scads of pictures so that you'll have a very good idea of what the place is like.

Tony seems to be very happy here and certainly enjoys our American-style breakfasts. Most evenings we eat out in the Square under trees where we can watch the life of the town as we dine. Then home to bed to read and sleep and to look forward to another day much like the one before. Tony and I have been going in the afternoons to a really sweet little beach called Paraggi where he occasionally meets other English or American children and has a happy time anyway collecting sea-polyps—urchins and the like.

Brooks has settled down to a pretty good writing routine and I intend to start painting next week. This place is crammed with material and Tony's fishing and bug hunting should afford me ample time.

All for now, dear. My how I do miss you. I'll try and write at least once or twice a week.

Do write and soon—B.

Letter from Barbara Baekeland to Nina Daly, July 7, 1954

Dearest Mother,

Well here we are in Austria and have been for some ten days and I with nothing whatever to do have just now found the time to write.

The country is really beautiful—idyllic. The village adorable with a really beautiful 15th cent. church and darling narrow winding streets with flower boxes everywhere and the traditional peaked roof that one always associates with Germany.

The service here is really first-rate. The hotel is run by a Countess Schall and the *bar-man* is the son of the ex-Austrian chancellor so this will give you an idea of the level of taste. It is costing us about $33.50 per week apiece for 3 meals and our beautiful room. And when I say the food is excellent I really mean it!

I am still in no mood to paint. I have all the wrong things with me and am enjoying too much all the leisure and relaxation. And as I don't know when or if ever I shall live in such ease again I am not going to create work for myself.

It rains heavily today but we are quite snug and content despite the weather.

Do write all your news. Love from all of us.

B.

Letter from Barbara Baekeland to Nina Daly, July 27, 1954

Dearest Mamashka—

There has been such a deluge of mail coming from you these past days I can barely keep it all straight. This morning arrived your letter regarding windows, dirt, etc.

This will be extremely short as we were up until 5:30 a.m. with the Archduke Franz Josef and Princess Martha and I

wakened at 7:30 a.m. and as a result feel slightly shattered. They
are delightful and we had a very happy time.

Tell Mimi Cohane that Nancy Oakes de Marigny is expected
today. Also expected is Patino the South American tin financier
whose daughter eloped a few months ago and then died in Paris
of a cerebral hemorrhage. Tell Mimi I shall give her love to
Nancy.

All for now. You've been an angel to do all those odd jobs in
the house for me.

Love & kisses,
B.

P.S. It won't be long before we all see each other once again.

Letter from Barbara Baekeland to Nina Daly, August 9, 1954

Dearest Mum—
Just one quick last note to answer all your questions and then a
silence until we see you at the dock as this last week will be
hectic and during the sojourn in Venice and Florence we'll not
have time.

Have just had a final fitting on a tweed suit I had made here
for the staggering sum of $36.00 *including* a good English
tweed. It's very nice and will be very useful. Brooks has also had
a jacket made. It cost $28—in the same material though a
darker shade.

I hope you will be able to come to Camp with us. You will
need the change.

What would you like from Europe? We are bringing back
very little but you are a must and I would like to get you something you would like.

Tony enjoyed having Daisy Hellman here but has made even
better friends with a little English girl who is here for her
health—ten years old and really a charmer. She reads 2 books a
day and had taught herself to read by the time she was 3. A
remarkable child with a mother who is completely a darling. I
can't bear to think of not seeing them all again.

The Archduke and Duchess have left after making me promise to call them in New York. They were both very taken by me
and I liked them a lot.

We've had a very entertaining time here and it will be a real wrench to leave. I hope we shall be able to come back one day.

Tony is marvelous and has had the time of his life.

All for now. Love and kisses to you.

B.

BROOKS BAEKELAND

The summer of 1955 I rented Villa Balzac from Drue and Jack Heinz at Cap d'Antibes. Ben Sonnenberg came in his Rolls-Royce and spent some days with us there. We sat up all night long high up under a great moon in Drue and Jack's ultra-Hollywood bathroom, which was the chicest room in the house and furnished like a living room, with a lovely terrace overlooking the mercurial sea. Ben got into the great autobiographical let-it-all-hang-out story of his life, which I had the impression he had never done before but did for "two kids whom I love." He called me "the remittance man." There is a great link between divided generations—especially when there is no familial responsibility.

That summer our neighbor was André Dubonnet—of the drink—who was being robbed by one of his servants. My playmate was Freddie Heineken—Baron Heineken, who was kidnapped and released a couple of years ago. Tony's playmate was Yasmin Khan, the daughter of Rita Hayworth and Aly Khan, and his kindergarten was Eden Roc, where he was sometimes left for lunch and a swim on his own, cosseted by divorced and lonely ladies from Wallachia and Waldavia.

Somewhere—at Gil Kahn's, I think—I had met Greta Garbo and was surprised when I asked her to come to Villa Balzac for a drink that she readily accepted. About fifteen others were to come, too.

She was asked for seven. At six, I remember, I was reading in a hammock and my maître d'hôtel was in his shorts watering the garden—we had a cook and chambermaid, too—when someone came out to say that Mademoiselle Garbo was there, one hour ahead of time. Without her great friend George Schlee. Alone.

Barbara was upstairs in a perfumed bath. Before I could even get my wits together, Garbo came out and apologized for being early, saying she was shy and did not want to meet anyone, she wanted only to spend a few minutes with me. So we had a drink and made some sort of conversation and she went, and I was left with the image of the finest *poitrine* under the gauziest shirt I had ever seen. She must have been close to fifty!

All those foolish, social years. My Barbara loved it all so—and she was so good at it.

PATRICIA GREENE

The last I saw of Brooks was just before they moved abroad. I think I was walking the dog and saw him sitting in his car, and I got in and sat down, and he said he thought he'd like to live in Europe, it was a much nicer life.

ALASTAIR REID

In 1957 I was going to Europe on the *Liberté*, I was traveling Cabin or Tourist, whatever, and Brooks and Barbara were in First Class. They told me they were planning to stay in Europe for quite a while. I got to really know them—I mean, inevitably—on the high seas. They invited me up to their cabin for drinks a number of times, and dinner. And Barbara was always calling up and coming down to whatever class I was in, whereas Brooks, it seemed to me, was making the point that he was in First Class. It was then I began to dislike Brooks intensely.

I was going to Geneva to work on the libretto of an opera with a composer. Then I was going on to Spain, where by that time I was spending half the year, translating Suetonius with Robert Graves and living at his place in Mallorca. I worked with Graves a long time, until I had an almighty quarrel with him, this rather savage falling-out. In 1961 I ran off with his girl, one of his "white goddesses," and we stopped speaking abruptly.

Brooks and Barbara had taken a place in Antibes for the summer where they said they had spent some time a couple of years before, in a very grand house, and they invited me to stay for a couple of days.

And I did—I stayed with them for three days. A very nice house, just around the edge of the town, on the bay. There was a great thing made of drinks, I remember—you gathered on the terrace, and that was when you began to talk. And they always had a good dinner, too—they had a good cook and we ate well.

Tony was a little nipper then. A pleasant little boy, small enough to be enthusiastic. He and I played with rubber rings and rubber boats at the sea. I noticed that Brooks talked to him as if he were a grown-up, always—there was the impression that he didn't want any baby stuff. I didn't feel that there was too much connection between

Brooks and Tony. Barbara, on the other hand, was affectionate with him, and one felt relieved that there *was* a connection between her and Tony.

We all used to go down to Eden Roc to swim, and one morning as we were sitting around the hotel pool overlooking the sea, and taking the sun, Brooks told me an extraordinary story about when he was a P-47 Thunderbolt pilot in World War Two. It was the very last days of the war, and he was flying over Germany at about four hundred miles per hour—and suddenly, he said, he just saw a green slope ahead of him, and that was the last thing he remembered.

BROOKS BAEKELAND

I got lost when very close to my target and doing about three hundred and fifty miles per hour as I climbed up a long hill. I crashed, in Schweinfurt, near Regensburg, and was reported dead, because I had no memory—couldn't even identify myself—and because 13th Tactical Air Command pilots had already photographed the top of the long hill where my P-47 exploded and distributed itself—and set fire to the mountain—for one and a half miles, and my young wing man had seen the whole thing, and there was no possibility that I might have survived. When I came to, undead, I found myself (who? I had no idea who I was, or where or why or how) supported by two old German farmers who carefully led me—bleeding and with a fractured skull, two broken shoulders, a smashed left cheekbone, and all my clothes blown off—down off that golden hill into the cold, dark valley. I was from there taken in a German jeep by four soldiers to a military hospital. And all I remembered was that up on the hill I saw fire and smoke, and the irrational thought came to my mind: Something has happened to my mother.

ALASTAIR REID

Brooks and I always had a good time in conversation—whenever you talked with him about something you could actually lose yourself in, as we did during those days I spent with them in Antibes. Of course, that whole idea of *wanting* to be in Antibes in the first place . . . They were like the Murphys then.

BROOKS BAEKELAND

Our lives became more and more Europeanized, and I—by accident and by choice—was becoming something of a European myself. I had a strong French background from my French-Belgian grandmother, and I had quite a lot of experience already with France, before, during, and after the war. I also read French.

From 1954 on, Barbara and I began to live more and more in France—also in Austria, Italy, and Spain—and this underlined with a terrible clarity my father's betrayal of his origins. Barbara had already learned—and climbed—all the rungs of power and *réclame* in New York—*tout pour parade*, as a French cook of ours once said to me—and we were beginning to lead that life that people later compared to Gerald and Sara Murphy's.

6

RUINED ROYALTY

If Tony Baekeland had participated in afternoon occupational therapy, he would be returned to his ward at four-thirty—which would leave him with three hours to fill before supper. Although various sports such as football, soccer, tennis, and baseball were available to patients in the late afternoon, Tony preferred watching television or listening to his tapes. "I was always encouraging him to play sports," says Miwa Svinka-Zielinski, "but he was reluctant. I told him that going out for one of the teams might contribute to an eventual diagnosis of his being cured, and he said he'd think about it."

Sometimes patients mobilized themselves to the point where an entrepreneurial skill emerged. "Surprisingly, in an environment like Broadmoor, very imaginative things *can* go on," a staff member comments. A group of patients, including Tony Baekeland, once got together and ingeniously brewed beer in the bathroom area—out of raw material smuggled into the hospital by visitors. "While it was fermenting," one of the nurses recalls, "the patients—to maintain the temperature in the room—kept taking hot baths! Despite all the time and energy spent on this very elaborate enterprise, the patients lost out in the end—they were caught by a supervisor just as the beer was ready."

Ironically, Tony Baekeland's great-grandfather, a determined violator of Prohibition, also brewed his own beer. Found among Leo Hendrik Baekeland's private papers was one titled "A Simple and Rapid Method for Making Beer."

The result was a drink of about three and a half to four percent alcohol, which fermented in anywhere from forty hours to five or six days, according to temperature. "Stronger beer," Dr. Baekeland advised, "takes more time." In Broadmoor there was all the time in the world.

Elizabeth Blow

I think it started going wrong when they sold their house in New York and moved to Europe and then started moving around in a sort of rootless way. They never bought anything, they never had a home in Europe, they just rented houses in various resorts. Mainly, though, they were based in Paris—that's where they knew Gloria and Jim Jones and so forth.

Gloria Jones

Jim and I were having a drink at the Ritz bar, we'd just come back from the bank or something, and she just came over and said, "Hello, I know who *you* are." Like that, you know. And then we saw quite a lot of them, I guess, in those times, and they seemed all right—they had wonderful parties. They had this little house on rue Barbet de Jouy, 40-bis I think it was, and once a week we'd probably go to dinner there.

I remember she had a bed down in the living room, sort of a Louis Seize lounge where she slept—which I thought was funny, because Brooks had a bedroom upstairs which I never saw. She sort of made a thing about that—that she slept in the living room. And they had two Spanish servants. They lived, you know, very well. She decorated beautifully, and she was a good housekeeper, too.

Tony was young, I think he was going to school in Paris—a day school. Sort of vaguely I remember him coming home with bird cages and birds. He was a nice little boy. Barbara gave him all the attention in the world as a child.

Letter from Barbara Baekeland to Gloria Jones, Undated

Gloria—chérie—
Sorry about Wed. night. His name is *Sonnenberg* and he is the
king of "Hoopla" (his name for his work), the best, and a very
wise and wonderful man.

Tony languishes with his drawings and wants to deliver them
as soon as you're back. He's wild because I forgot them!

Wuss sends you a purr and a snuggle and says he wants to
meet Missy What's-her-name very soon. Call us when you're
back.

Also am mad because Brooks returned Jimmie's manuscript
before I got a chance to look at it. . . .

A good trip—
B.

GLORIA JONES

She was a loyal good friend, she was fun, she was appealing. And she
really knew how to dress. I mean, she always had one *real* Chanel
suit and then two or three made by this wonderful fat lady we used to
go to.

ADDIE HERDER

Barbara used to take me to the openings at Chanel, and we were
given proper seats and deference because of her. She also knew a
good dressmaker—a charming woman, maybe Rumanian, very talented—who ran up little numbers for us. I think they were fifteen
dollars or something, for beautifully tailored summer frocks in linen.
The dresses she made us were as elegant as you could get anywhere·
in Paris. She later became the designer for Hermès. I mean, how
would I ever have got to have anything like that if it weren't for
Barbara? Barbara knew where to get everything.

I liked her, because she was funny, and wicked, and because she
extended her friendship to *me* in a way. It wasn't really friendship,
but still, for her, it was something. What I mean is we were not
socially equal in the sense that, although we had many of the same
friends, I never entertained and I didn't go to all the fashionable
watering holes unless I was taken. When I came to Paris I was prac-

tically a waif. Barbara didn't know me but I was under the aegis of Gloria and Jim Jones, so I just came along with the package for her. She was also a genuine admirer of my art, my collages, and said so, to other people.

GLORIA JONES

Barbara was doing the *chasse* when I first met her—you know, hunting. She loved that. She had the costume and everything—you know, for jumping over fences and killing a deer, a boar, I don't know what the hell kind of animal it was. She had a streak of that craziness in her.

ELIZABETH ARCHER BAEKELAND

She was the boldest rider ever—she'd get on *any* horse and it would be rearing and bucking and Barbara was always just laughing. She had tremendous courage. She joined the hunt that was done out at Chantilly. You had to pay a thousand dollars a year to join and have maybe three hunts, and you had to dress in red velvet with hats and feathers. And she was always in on the kill. Everything Barbara did she did well.

PAULE LAFEUILLE

Barbara Baekeland was a student of mine in Paris. She was strikingly keen on improving her already fluent French. She used to come to me punctually twice a week, and she studied her lessons better than any of my other students. The sessions we had together were for me time spent with a dear friend. We spoke—in French—of every interest we had in common: literature, theater, music, art, and life in general. Barbara was extremely fond of Paris and got along amazingly well with the French, whose way of life she appreciated and partly adopted.

She was a woman of delicate artistic taste. When she moved from the rue Barbet de Jouy, she chose unhesitatingly the most beautiful part of Paris to settle down in: the section of the Île Saint-Louis called "the prow of the boat," an old and picturesque area teeming with memories of the past. She adorned her cozy seventeenth-century apartment there with genuine antique furniture, beautiful paintings, Persian rugs, and a selection of lovely pastel-colored materials.

Barbara had many glamorous French friends but she also led a very elegant life among the American circle in France. On my part, I knew quite a few of her intimate American friends: Virginia Chambers, Ethel de Croisset, Dorothea Biddle, Kitty Coleman.

Barbara's most characteristic qualities were broad-mindedness, charm, grace, and kindness. My heart aches thinking of her, and that does not help.

I never tutored Tony. I remember her saying how much she adored him and admired his talent as a poet.

From a Psychiatric Report on Antony Baekeland Ordered by the British Courts, January 5, 1973

Tony Baekeland was happiest at a school in Paris from eleven to fourteen.

KAREN RADKAI

École Active Bilangue is the name of the school in Paris that I think he went to at one point. It's on the rue Bourdonnais, near Champs de Mars. It's where children from abroad often go.

Tony's parents as such drifted in and out of Paris. I had dinner with them there once, and I couldn't wait to get out of their house—you couldn't have even a conversation with them they were so busy name-dropping.

KATHARINE GARDNER COLEMAN

They gave very nice dinners. I was living in Paris—I was Kitty Herrick then, the Widow Herrick. And they were renting a house from this wonderful architect friend of mine, Burrall Hoffman, and his adorable wife Dolly. Burrall built what's often described as the finest house ever built in America, you know—Vizcaya on Biscayne Bay in Florida, for James Deering, the industrialist.

At the Baekelands' I met a great many people I never would have seen, ever in my life, anywhere else—some quite fascinating Americans. I mean, that's about the only time I met Ben Sonnenberg—wasn't he the man that had the place on Gramercy Park? And she had the Art Buchwalds there once—I would have given my eyeteeth to have had the Buchwalds for dinner. Barbara had a way of absolutely attracting—well, I mean, *everybody*, men, women, and children.

As you can gather quite well, it was Barbara who was my friend. She was just like that huggable, warm, adorable little dog she had. It was a Peke, and I mean, the hair and the cuteness—everything.

My feelings were perfectly congenial and all that in the beginning with Brooks. He was a good enough host, a good enough guest, and at one stage I thought he was quite a good father. At *one* stage.

He looked just like those Siamese cats they had. Those slit eyes! Well, I'm allergic to cats—maybe that's a part of it, I don't know.

PAUL JENKINS

The first time I saw Brooks, he was with Jim Jones at this fancy fencing place on I think the avenue Hoches. There he was, fencing away. He looked pretty good, too.

BROOKS BAEKELAND

I fenced with the French team at the Cercle Hoche, the oldest dueling club in France, both in epée and fleuret. I had already studied saber with the Santelli brothers in New York and was being considered for Olympic training while a freshman at Harvard.

I took Jim Jones to the Cercle Hoche. I took him also to Klosters to ski, but never mind. He had told me that he had been a Golden Gloves champion. I found he couldn't box his way out of a wet paper bag—in fact, he refused to put the gloves on with *me*! He had no speed or coordination or eye and so soon gave up fencing. He was hopeless on skis, too—hopeless in all the Hemingway things he so aspired to. So he *wrote* about them. I did not despise him for any of this—I was touched. I understood one of the springs of a novelist for the very first time: imaginative compensation.

The fact is, he wrote one impassioned, true, and very fine book, *From Here to Eternity*. He ruined his life as a writer—I told him so—by trying to live with the nobs, not only the Hollywood and other big-money sets, but the French aristos. He was horribly flawed by his snobbery and a whole display of social-defense complexes—falsities that marred his work: all the worst American values. Celebrity and the open signatures of wealth—all the things my grandfather laughed at—were uppermost in his life. His *generous* life, I hasten to add, for Jim was a walking heart.

He was a small-town boy from the Midwest. He would have made a perfect target for Sinclair Lewis. His "taste"—a concept so important to Barbara, who was just as big a snob but who had the woman's keener tracking insights—was awful, embarrassing. Barbara and I were as far in taste from Jim and Gloria as Gerald and Sara Murphy were from Scott Fitzgerald. But this, too, is a kind of snobbery.

Incidentally, both Joneses had been completely taken in by Barbara's act of being a Back Bay Brahmin—an act which I sometimes regarded tenderly and sometimes with contempt but which I still financed, to my ruin. The Joneses meanwhile thought of me as a parvenu—I was the shy and quiet one.

Jim was actually as shy as a girl. He was a very intelligent, kindly, feeling, sensitive man. A girl. A girl that snarled. The idiot world was "took in" by the snarl. I loved Jim.

WILL DAVIS

I thought Brooks was pretentious. Barbara, too. They were trying to model themselves after Caresse and Harry Crosby but they just didn't have the equipment. You know, the English have a phrase for people like Brooks and Barbara—"light, dangerous people."

I liked Barbara all right—I loved her laugh—but I didn't approve of her. I mean, I'm very conventional about women. I essentially like them to behave, and Barbara didn't know how to behave. She was a madcap.

I started to flirt with Barbara the first time I ever met her. Brooks and I were sitting in the front of this cab and Barbara was sitting in the back between Jim and Gloria Jones—this was in Paris, in the spring of '61—and I had my arm around the back of the front seat and I started to let it go up and down Barbara's legs while having a conversation with Brooks. Jim and Gloria both thought this all extremely funny, and Barbara herself was nearly hysterical with laughter. What I was saying *was* reasonably funny but of course Brooks didn't understand why they were all breaking up like that.

Oh, she was very pretty, very pretty and good legs and stuff like that, but the more I saw of her, the less I was drawn to her *that* way. What she had was, she had more energy than anyone I've ever known. You couldn't tire her out—no matter how late you stayed up at night you could *not* exhaust her.

DUNCAN LONGCOPE

I had been living in Paris for perhaps a year before I met her. But I had once seen a very good-looking woman with a Pekingese in the café opposite the Brasserie having a *tartine* in the morning. I thought

she was English. We didn't speak or anything. And then later a
friend took me to meet the Baekelands, and, I mean, there she was—
Barbara.

She had a real *élan vital*. She could carry an evening despite whatever mood Brooks was in. You never knew—usually he played along,
he was a decent enough social type, he didn't sulk and stuff—whatever his particular position may have been at that moment in regard
to the rest of the female world.

They liked to walk quite a lot, I remember. I often saw them walking on the *quais*, and they were quite charming on those occasions. I
walked with Brooks now and then myself, and it was possibly on one
of those walks that he told me he had his mail sent to another address
in Paris, I supposed so that he could have his privacy.

EILEEN FINLETTER

Brooks was always very secretive, and more than a little somber,
while she was gay and happy, but they looked good together—they
looked rich and self-assured. I used to see them at the Joneses, who
had kind of an open-house thing every Sunday night—mostly Americans, a lot of Hollywood people, a lot of writers. One night the
Chief Justice of the Supreme Court appeared—Earl Warren. Sometimes Jim would read a chapter from his latest book, and Barbara, I
remember, would sit there looking up at him as though he were God
or something. She'd say, "Oh, how *beautiful*!" I mean, she'd gush,
and it would drive me crazy.

ADDIE HERDER

I remember Barbara at the Joneses reading a wonderful story to us
that *she'd* written, about a trip where she and Brooks and Tony went
walking somewhere in places that were not urban—some kind of exploratory hike—and how on this excursion there was a struggle between the parents for possession of the boy.

BROOKS BAEKELAND

I found a great many stories in Barbara's London apartment after her
death—with her writing teacher's comments on them. The only
thing I saw that had not been written by *me* was her so-called novel,
which was frankly pretty lamentable—and so designated by her instructor in his tactful way. Barbara, while she had the most essential
thing for a writer—passion—could never have been a successful one.
You have to brush your teeth, put away your clothes, make your bed,

pay your rent . . . you must have some respect for order. Good writing is damned difficult. Spoiled girls don't do it.

EILEEN FINLETTER

One Sunday at the Joneses, Tony was standing next to Barbara behind the bar, which was high, like a church pulpit, and she had her arm negligently draped around his shoulder and she said to me, "Oh, what a lovely day it's been! Tony and I spent the entire morning lying in bed reading the papers." And since my own son was about the same age as Tony, I was shocked, because I thought, My God, if I did that to *him*—I mean, in front of a roomful of people. She wanted me to have the impression that it really *was* in bed. And Tony didn't move, he just stood there smiling. And I thought, That's odd.

PAUL JENKINS

Barbara Baekeland had a glorious side to her nature, too, but one night at the Joneses' I saw something from another point of view and my anger just surfaced from that, from suddenly sensing the son's curious kind of despair. What was his name again? He was kind of like a wild James Dean.

Barbara and I had crossed swords before on a couple of occasions. She came to an opening of mine once and made some frivolous remark, and you know how tense you get on those occasions. I thought, you know, basically, that she was an undermining person. But she was a frequent guest at Gloria and Jim Joneses', which is where I held forth, and when she came in I always felt guarded to some extent after the flip kind of way she'd treated me and so I gave her a wide berth. But on this particular occasion I just let her have it, there was nothing in me that could *refrain* from letting her have it. I can't quote myself, I can't even paraphrase myself—it was just a concentrated salvo of what an insensitive and *dangerous* mother I thought she was.

I can only confide one other thing. Having been brought up in a particular way myself, I probably saw a mirrored reflection of my own mother in Barbara. And although I didn't see much of Tony, the brief moments I did, it was very vivid to me that he was trapped in something that there was no . . . I would look at him and I'd think there but for the grace of God went I—although I don't think I would have gone to the length Tony did. Of course, *my* mother was also out of reach.

I remember when my mother came to my first opening and we

went to the Cedar Tavern afterwards, Marisol came up and bent over and said, "And how iz zee dominating mozzer?" Then I got into a fight with somebody at the bar who had made a remark to my mother as we walked past. Anyway, I slammed him into a cigarette machine. But usually at the Cedar Tavern *something* happened, somebody got a beer in their face or something like that—so it was a good climate in which to rid yourself of the frustrations and ignominious vicissitudes of being an artist.

Anyway, that night at Jim and Gloria's I could see that Barbara was doing something bad to someone who had no drive, purpose, or focus. Her son was what I would call a psychological object for her. It was very strongly clear to me that this young man was being psychically exploited to the fullest extent. He was a human sacrifice, to Oedipal emotions. It's what I would call incestuous betrayal. She might have never touched him and yet you could tell he was being smothered alive.

SUE RAILEY

I felt that he never had a chance—perhaps his father really didn't bother enough about him and his mother bothered too much. I think that if Brooks had been a different type of father, maybe . . . But that's a big maybe.

I met them when they first came to Paris, I can't remember what year that was. I lived there for thirty-three years. My husband went over there to our embassy and he fell in love with France and when it was time to be sent somewhere else he said he'd never leave Paris and he never did till he died. We saw a lot of Brooks and Barbara. They had a very quick, easy contact with people. And a marvelous house, a little pavilion. It was like a doll's house, in fact. They entertained a bright group. I would think that they would have felt that they could easily have been Sara and Gerald Murphy.

BROOKS BAEKELAND

The Murphys—no, Barbara and I were not that way, although I understand why people who are romantic and like tradition would see us that way. Gerald and Sara Murphy had no energy. They entertained people who did. They sucked up others' energies and taught them—the brutes—style, fifty years ago called "manners." All their guests acknowledged the lessons. I may say that Madame Ethel de Croisset falls into the same class—a benefactress to brutes and to princes.

These are exquisite people. Barbara and I were never exquisite—cultivated, Proustian. We were a bit mad, especially my beloved Barbara. *Mad*. I was mostly smiling, not behind the arras but in a window seat, watching. But Barbara gave penny for penny.

The comparison between us and the Murphys comes from our being spoiled and loving the arts and being in France after a war. We never were that stable—purring, gracious, collected, surrounded by our domestics. We could have been. Barbara never understood that in order to pay for something you wanted tomorrow you might have to give up something today. Order. She never had understood order. We were *not* the Murphys. We were more like ruined royalty. We were two gulping bankrupts. I tease—or rather, I repeat what I used to tell her. Barbara could have given lessons to Jackie Kennedy. She had spent all her insurance money from her father's death, then all her mother's, and now she was spending two thirds of *my* money.

THILO VON WATZDORF

They were traveling all over the spas of Europe, the places where one should be "seen," when I first met them. They had this white Mercedes 190SL, with a cat in the back and Tony in the back, and they were traveling through Europe for months on end.

They rented this place in Ansedonia, where my mother and stepfather had a house near the Dutch royal family's property—my stepfather, Aschwin de Lippe, is Prince Bernhard's brother. The Baekelands got their house through an eccentric Englishwoman named Rosie Rodd, now Rosie Baldwin—there was a whole tribe of English there, friends of Rosie's and friends of her three beautiful daughters'. I must have been sixteen that summer, a couple of years older than Tony. He gave the impression of being the typical case of a son of well-to-do American parents who just played all year round. He seemed to me to be very shy, very much of a loner, and I sort of romanticized about that because I felt that there was something so crazy in the structure of his life. I could never even figure out where he went to school, or if he ever did.

MICHAEL ALEXANDER

They lugged him around from place to place, they were always sort
of getting a house here and a house there. I met them in Ansedonia
with my friend Rosie Rodd. Tony was just a sort of nature boy then. I
can tell you that nobody thought he was a violent person.

I used to go and see him in Broadmoor, poor dear. It's not an
unpleasant place, I assure you. It's not exactly a hellhole. Oh, maybe
some of them do go a bit berserk from time to time, but you don't get
the impression of one big roaring madhouse. They all look like perfectly harmless people. However, that's not the point, is it? Tony,
between you and me, was perfectly happy there, all things considered.

Letter from Antony Baekeland to Rosemary Rodd Baldwin, Undated

Broadmoor

Dear Rosie,

Great and wonderful things have happened in my life—the Sun
is coming back to me and I am so happy and well. I feel as if
Mummy had really never left me at all.

I have stopped being desperate to leave Broadmoor: I find I
am learning so much every day here and I know that when I am
ready I will go. And I have made many good friends here.

Insects look all right again, grass, flowers, and trees. I still
tend to go rather astray in my reading but it's getting better.
Rosie, please write to me soon and tell me all your news. I miss
you a lot.

Love,
Tony

ROSEMARY RODD BALDWIN

I had the first house ever built in Ansedonia—me and my three children and my second husband, Mr. Rodd. He was Peter Rodd's
brother—do you know who I mean? Marvelous-looking. Peter was
married to Nancy Mitford, and he was the model for the character
Basil Seal in Evelyn Waugh's *Black Mischief*. My mother-in-law,

my darling old mother-in-law, threatened to take Waugh to court—there was *such* a hooha. Waugh was terribly rude about *me* in that book of letters of his. My children were absolutely hopping mad—"Mummy, can't you do something about this?" But I really couldn't care less. First of all, it's lies. He says in a postcard to Nancy Mitford: "I did not find Mrs. Taffy a lady." Well, *I* am Mrs. Taffy, because my husband was Gustavus King of Sweden's godson and namesake, so he was always known as Taffy—Taffy Rodd. But you see, I never met Evelyn Waugh in the whole of my life! I was dying to, but my husband would never have him in the house. Not so very long ago a man who was writing some sort of book asked me, "What did you feel like when you read that Evelyn Waugh said he didn't find you a lady?" And I said, "Why *should* he have found me a lady? I didn't ask him to. And what would I have done with one if he had?" In another letter Waugh runs down the film *La Dolce Vita*, which I acted in with my children—I was the medium—to make some money, because we had *no* money.

You see, my husband's father, Lord Rennell, had been for years the English ambassador in Rome, and we were the only unofficial people living in private properties for the first few years after the war. We had Palazzo Rodd, on the Via Giulia, and for holidays we went to Ansedonia, to Casa Rodd, and when we got hard up we rented it.

Look, I launched Ansedonia and Porto Ercole. Yes, really. I started the whole thing. I lent money to fishermen to build tiny flats and then I opened a restaurant which was the biggest fun on this earth—which, alas, doesn't exist anymore. And I found the property for the Dutch royal family, and then that's how it went—all the rich and famous came. And it was ruined for me—I can't bear going back there. So then I left for Turkey, and that's another part of my life.

I met the Baekelands when they wrote me asking to rent a house in Ansedonia. Practically all the houses had been taken, but I got them the house of Princess Boncompagni. *They* thought, of course, it was going to be one of those frightfully smart Cadaqués or South of France houses; in fact, it was a small bungalow built by the local builder. Anyway, during all this I had the most extraordinary correspondence with Brooks, whom I had not yet met. One day, for instance, he wrote me that he didn't want two servants, so I said, "You won't have two servants. I've got you a cook, that's all, and her husband will just sleep in her room, naturally." He wrote back saying, "I don't want the husband sleeping in the house because he's bound to eat some of our food if he does." *I* wrote back and said, "Listen, there's one bed, he'll spend the whole night making love to her, and I assure you it'll be only the matter of a cup of coffee in the morning." And I had a letter back saying, "I don't give a damn if he makes love standing up, I don't want him in my house!"

So the Baekelands arrived, and almost immediately they said, "Mrs. Rodd, we must tell you we're very disappointed in the house, it's not at all what we wanted." Well, I thought then that they were the sort of Americans who would never be happy in Ansedonia. So I said to the child, who was wonderful-looking, like a faun—the most adorable little boy that's ever *been*—"Tony," I said, "why don't you go on up to my house and meet my children?" and he rushed off while his parents and I sat down to sort things out. And when he came back, he said to Barbara, "Mum, they've got the best library I've ever seen—*please* let's stay here." And on *that* appeal the Baekelands remained in Ansedonia, and after about a month I was able to move them from Villa Boncompagni to Villa Nistri.

Letter from Brooks Baekeland to Gloria and James Jones, July 18, 1959

> Villa Boncompagni
> (Villa Nistri after July 28)
> Ansedonia

Dear Jim: Gloria:

We are getting squared away finally ("you squares!"). . . . We have found a comfortable villa on the water . . . rented from Pieri Francesco Nistri, a famous pal of Il Duce and a great War Criminal; but I love him. It turns out that we are sitting in a nest of Etruscan remains: in fact, two hundred yards above us through the gorse is the ancient city of COSA, an Etruscan, then a Roman stronghold, where the American Academy of Rome has had a bunch of archaeologists digging for nearly a decade. . . .

We swam off a small island here the other day, just made it back in a sudden storm that came up, but the island was worth visiting to Tony. Millions of seagulls and some sort of native partridge are nesting on it. . . . What would interest you most, I think, is the underwater archaeology around here. There are rocks, small islets, islands and reefs all ready and waiting to wreck ships. There must be plenty of dead galleys and galleons lying on the bottom around here. Do you think you would be tempted to pay us a visit at some time convenient to all of us in August or September? . . . I'll be in touch with you. Are you having fun? How's the baby?

Love,
Brooks

KATHARINE GARDNER COLEMAN

I went down to Ansedonia to visit them that August—in rapid succession they had these two older women to stay, Sue Railey and me. I was one of the two old crows that went down—I mean, Sue and I were nine or ten years older than Barbara. Anyway, I stayed for a week, a good fat week, you know—ten days—and that was exactly the summer when Prince Bernhard came down with his equerry to look over the Borghese property that was for sale.

We went out on all these glorious picnics in this Italian fishing boat that Brooks had rented, and there'd be every kind of possible combination of people packed in. There was one time that I got very upset with Barbara, very very upset because she was showing off and diving from the top of this boat where if you didn't do it quite right and your foot slipped or something you could just crack your head open on the edge, and there were boys, young people, around who wanted to copy what she was doing. There was an Italian diver in the group—one of those professional people who go underwater and carry a knife with them, you know, and he and I got together and said we didn't like what Barbara was doing at *all*, it was very dangerous what she was doing, she was reckless, and finally we both prevailed upon her not to do it, but, I mean, it took *him* plus something of *me* to put a stop to it. And Brooks didn't even seem to take any of it in.

One time I got perfectly furious with Brooks—and told him so—because he said, "I've got something pretty darn interesting to show you. Do you want to see Tony's diary? He's written some things about a little girl he met." I said, "I not only don't want to see it but I don't know how you can feel you have a right to take something that is your child's private private thing. . . ." But on the whole he seemed utterly devoted to Tony that summer. He was teaching him how to snorkel—it was when snorkeling was just coming along. And Tony was just a cunning little boy who was a little bit extrasensitive and very interested in animals and nature. What he really did *not* like was his mother's society—or social life, if that's what you call it. We'd all be sitting around and he'd say, "I don't know why you want to go out tonight, Mummy. Look at Mrs. Herrick"—which is what my name was then—"*she* doesn't want to go and meet the Marchesa of so and so and so and so and so and so."

DAPHNE HELLMAN
Brooks and Tony both were sort of in despair over the social life but Barbara kept escalating, she wanted to see more and more titles—princes and duchesses down through barons and even *sirs*.

Notes from a Psychiatric Consultation on Antony Baekeland, New York City, March 12, 1971

> He recalls being most happy when he spent entire days by himself. He states, "I was taken by my parents to all their friends' houses, so I really grew up more in my parents' generation than in my own."

NIKE MYLONAS HALE
When Bob Hale took me to meet the Baekelands in Ansedonia, we weren't married yet, and I was quite young, and, you know, Brooks was very flirtatious. He carried me across the threshold, and that infuriated Barbara. The next thing was, she was saying to me, "Why don't you go down and play with Tony?" Now Tony was about twelve, you know, and I was twenty-five! Well, Barbara didn't like me at all. She was great friends with Bob's first wife, Barbara Hale.

Tony was on the rocks playing with crabs, sort of pulling them apart, which Bob thought was very creepy, but I didn't think so, I think that's what little boys *do*. Of course, in hindsight it *is* an awfully creepy little episode.

They didn't really pay much attention to Tony. I mean, it was typical that he was down on the rocks alone. I think one of the things that must have been very difficult for him was that Barbara and Brooks were *so* dramatic—*always*. Both of them had so much drama that you couldn't sort of survive around them.

From the Diaries of John Philip Cohane, Unpublished

Wednesday. Ansedonia is somewhat barren, the villas are too close together, the mosquitos at times are devils, but it was a thoroughly pagan, never-to-be-forgotten Tuscan summer.

There is a breathtaking ruined temple on a hill; the view is stupendous, up and down the coast in both directions, but Heather is still convinced she saw a somberly clad sinister ghost sitting on a low wall of the temple at eleven o'clock one morning and it was hard to drag her back again at any hour.

By coincidence Barbara and Brooks Baekeland, son Tony, Millie their deaf Pekingese, a rooster and a Siamese cat turned up two days after we arrived, settled into a villa a few hundred yards away from the one Heather has rented for us, which belongs to Prince Antonello Ruffo di Calabrio, whose sister has just married Prince Albert, the Belgian King's brother. The Baekelands have added greatly to our stay. Later Simone Lippe with Thilo, one of her two sons, and Alexis Lichine and his wife also dropped by.

From *A Family Motor Tour Through Europe*, Leo Hendrik Baekeland, Horseless Age Press, New York, 1907

Everything around us was so harmoniously peaceful and the Italian landscape so serene with the freshness of nature! Yet, wherever the eye wandered, ruins evoked visions of a fugitive splendor, which had been in all its glory during ages long gone by, when human ambitions and human might tried to rule this enchanting corner of the world.

Letter from Barbara Baekeland to Gloria and James Jones, August 1, 1960

Ansedonia

Dear Gloria & Jim—

. . . Our beds haven't had a chance to cool and this certainly hasn't been what I'd call a tranquil summer but it's been fun. . . . Yesterday a large contingent dove for gem coral. We almost lost one languid Englishman—very exciting! Tony brought up one perfect amphora and we have masses of fragments. . . . Why don't you write to Klosters *right away* for reservations for skiing. It would be fun to be there together.

Have started painting but it does not go well.

We miss you—

B.

ROSEMARY RODD BALDWIN

The following summer, 1961, Brooks and Barbara rented *my* house, and we did the most fantastic things together. *Long* before the Kennedys started their great river travel, we were going down rivers, these marvelous Etruscan rivers in Italy. And millions of people came and stayed with us—old, young—Lucy and Alan Morehead. . . . And Tony was wonderful. My servants all adored him. He used to train crickets to sing in different keys. I remember when he was going back to school in America he gave me two crickets which sang in totally different keys and I absolutely nearly went mad, I couldn't get to sleep at night. He always had all these animals—partridges, turkeys, and everything you could find outside. He would take them up to his room and study them, and he would draw the most beautiful drawings of them.

Now this second summer there were terrible scenes between Barbara and Brooks all the time. She was being difficult and impossible, and Tony, whose room was right over their bedroom, heard all these rows going on. You see, Brooks was the passion of Barbara's lifetime and that summer he was having a walk-out with some debutante that he'd met. And that was, *I* think, the beginning of the unhappiness—that primeval flutter.

FRANCINE DU PLESSIX GRAY

When Brooks and Barbara asked us to share a house with them in Ansedonia, it seemed like such a good idea because I'd been very tired after the birth of my first child, and I was expecting a second, and Cleve and I had rented out our own house in Connecticut for the summer, to a couple who gave us wonderful money. And with that money we were able to share the fee with the Baekelands. I mean, it was a way of resting and not having too many responsibilities—and we *thought* we were going to have a lot of fun.

It was a very large house, we each had a big section to ourselves. And there was a large staff. It was Rosie Rodd's house, the haunted house. Totally haunted. Really. Cleve trusts ghosts and likes them, I'm terrified of them, but we both felt it. I refused to walk in the door alone. He had to come with me.

CLEVE GRAY

It was a very strange house. It had a very long, very dark corridor, and I would say that around six in the evening you started feeling these swooshing presences—it's the only way I can explain it. And at night, after dinner or whenever it might be, when we went up to our room, we both couldn't get into the room soon enough and shut the door, because there *were* these . . . these . . . these *things*. I think the Baekelands both accepted the fact that it was haunted.

I used to wake up at dawn and hear this absolutely beautiful Arabic song, it seemed to come from the garden, and one day I said to Barbara, "The gardener has the most marvelous voice." She said, "Do we have a gardener? There's no gardener here." I said, "Well, the man who comes every morning very early to the garden and sings this Arabic song." Well, she got all upset. She said that Rosie Rodd's lover, an Arab, had disappeared about six months before, in Africa— he had been an agent with the British government and had apparently been murdered—and she said that it was he who was haunting the garden. Well, that isn't my kind of ghost. Except that I did keep hearing that song.

FRANCINE DU PLESSIX GRAY

The house was right underneath the walls of one of the great Etruscan towns, called Cosa. When we were residents at the American Academy in Rome in 1979, almost twenty years later—which is the place which has done all the digging—we were often in the company of one of the world's great archaeologists and classical scholars, Lawrence Richardson—a very very British-type American, very elegant. And the kind of man, the kind of Victorian rationalist, who you would think would absolutely dispel the idea of the existence of ghosts.

Larry came to dinner one night at the Academy and we started talking about ghosts and he said, "My dear, I've lived with them from the time we started digging—Cosa is *filled* with ghosts. Of *course* you heard ghosts in Rosie Rodd's house! That whole *wall* is a necropolis. What did you expect—there'd be no ghosts?" He kept us up to two a.m., and I thought of this whole haunting of this . . . of this doomed couple by ghosts who were now being certified by this great archaeologist. That's a very interesting metaphysical symbol.

That summer the Baekelands went out every single day on this yacht that they chartered from a local fisherman. And they just sat and drank masses of wine and jabbered and gossiped with this duchessa and that principessa and yet another contessa this-and-that. We did it twice and we never did it again—two boat trips and we retreated completely into our shell.

Luckily we had for, oh God, a few lire a day, a local girl who took care of the baby—which is another thing we could never have afforded in the States—and twice a week we drove to a marvelous town called Saturnia where there are these sulfur waters which heal everything and which make you sleep beautifully and so on. We also made an extensive tour of the Etruscan places because Cleve was buying black Etruscan ware and Brooks used to help him find it. We got museum pieces for practically nothing and we brought them back wrapped in our baby's diapers. And Cleve would do watercolors, and I was painting, too, at that time—this is years before I was a writer.

That summer Brooks was trying to write a novel or whatever. Trying or pretending, nobody *knew*. But I mean, he was definitely bitten by that terrible American neurosis which I think should go into medical dictionaries, which is somewhere between obsession and paranoia—novel-writing, the idea that you've got to write a novel in order to prove yourself. And Brooks seemed to me to be absolutely tainted with that disease. Well, you see, he was a romantic, and he wanted to write a romantic book—I think he wanted to be Hemingway.

And Barbara pretended that she wanted to paint but that her life was too busy to allow her to. Of course, she was creating her own mayhem. She had a studio in the garage into which she went *once* the whole summer we were there. Everything was this dispersion toward other people, you know—this trying to make an impression, this thing of having people around all the time, which had to do with her being so terrified of facing herself and facing her own center, her own gravity. It was a totally dispersed energy, Barbara's.

I never found her as entertaining as Cleve did, because I think he was sort of sexually charmed by her. She wasn't my kind of woman. I like women who are intellectually more centered than I am. I mean someone like Ethel de Croisset. I like very rigorous personalities. I cannot *stand* dispersed personalities, and all my close women friends have been women who are more powerful than I am. I need women who are stronger than I am. I'm pretty strong, but I want them even stronger.

And Barbara at that time was all parties, parties, parties—well, the way the Murphys were. You know, I mean, in a way they were Murphys with no talent. Which is a terrible thing to say—Murphys with no talent. I mean, Gerald Murphy was a pretty good painter, you know.

Cleve Gray

Barbara wasn't a bad painter at all. She was a very very talented person. She thought she could do everything. Well, of course, she *did* everything, but none of it was quite good enough.

Brooks I always thought was extremely intelligent. I remember Peter Gimbel, several years later, saying to me, "Do you think Brooks is going to turn out all right?" And I said, "God, Peter, if *Brooks* isn't going to turn out all right, I can't imagine how anybody will." You see, I was still very impressed with him. He seemed to me perfectly balanced, I didn't see *any* of his imbalance. His ideas were all very sound.

I remember he said to me that summer, "I have a terrible fate in store for me." I said, "What do you mean?" And he said, "Well, I have to remember my family—my grandfather, my father, every member of my family became senile fairly early. There's no question that that's what's going to happen to me, and this is what I dread." But I think this was a romantic idea—you know, that he thought about himself that way.

I remember he made fun of Barbara's chasing titles, but then he got wrapped up in it himself, I guess. I mean, any title—any possibility for a title—she would just go zooming at it. One thing that always amused Francine and me—in the entry hall there was a table and on the table was a bowl and in the bowl Barbara always had scores of visiting cards which would all be left so you could see them—"Duchesse de Croy," "Prince de Lippe," "Principessa de Colonna."

Francine du Plessix Gray

And then the bills she was paying or the letters to her poor mother in New York, her poor little Irish mother—the nonglamorous things—were always way at the bottom of the bowl. But always on top were the titles.

I disliked them much earlier than Cleve did. I wanted to wash my hands clean of them.

Remember the ending of Evelyn Waugh's *Handful of Dust*? That's the ending I see for Brooks. Exactly that kind of ending.

Once we were having dinner at the Gimbels' in New York, and Peter kind of grumbled something about how fake the happiness was between the Baekelands. I said, "Oh, but they always talk so much about their happiness!" and he said, "That's just what I mean."

During the time we spent with them in Ansedonia she would hint that they'd had no sexual contact at all all summer. She had some kind of menstrual problem, she was bleeding all the time and refusing to see a doctor, and the bleeding problem was deterring her from having sex.

I don't know if Brooks was fooling around or not. I mean, he would probably pretend he was going off to study some wild plant—he would do it with the utmost elegance. And that was Brooks all over—he was very much to the manor born. He had the most European sense of manners about those things.

But now, the most incredible thing of that summer comes down to Tony. Very often we would have dinner alone with him because I was feeling kind of weak from this pregnancy that was so close to the other one, and the social life bored me, as it always has in my life. So in the evening Cleve and I would mostly stay at home, so we were a lot with Tony, because every time his parents went out he was left alone, and if we had gone out also, then he would have been totally alone. And we had the most delightful conversations with him—he was a total charmer. He was off to Exeter that year.

And not a *hint* of anything wrong in him except for that stammer, which would go in and out. I mean, like many stammerers, he would sometimes talk for half an hour without stuttering. I had a stuttering problem as a child myself, I was the same kind of stutterer—and I had a definite lack of attention from my mother, and a lot of psychiatrists have new theories of how stammering is an attention-getting device, subconsciously of course. And the only, only hint that there was something deeply wrong in him was this.

I should begin by saying the house was crammed with food. I mean, Barbara was the kind of woman who had no sense of moderation, and it drove my kind of abstemious frugal French nature crazy, I having lived, you know, under the Occupation, knowing what hunger was like and so on, seeing these hams and chickens and roasts being thrown out or given to the peasants, and three turkeys being bought instead of one. I mean, the house was so full of food you didn't know what to do with it.

We had brought from France with us baby food for our six-month-old son, because French baby food is notoriously marvelous, so much better than American, and Italian baby food is well known to be not nutritious. Anyway, we had two months of French baby food in Ansedonia with us, packed in vacuum crates—cans of puréed veal and puréed beets and puréed spinach and so on. And about the fifteenth of July we noticed that there were these strange gaps in the rows.

And a few days later the peasant girl who was looking after our son said to us, and I think she began to cry—we had enough Italian to get the gist of what she was saying—"It is Mr. Tony. I have seen him do it. He comes in at night when the baby is asleep and steals the baby food."

Tony was stealing Thaddeus's food! To eat—in this house brimful of food. You see, he wanted to be a baby. He'd never *been* a baby. He wanted to be mothered. Or maybe he wanted to identify with *our* baby, because he'd never had any proper parenting from his own parents, and maybe at that point we were giving him more parenting than they were.

Tony was a complete victim of the whole thing. But a victim of the most curious kind—under this deceitful veneer of affection and praise, this unbelievable and constant praise that went on—"This child is so gifted. . . . Isn't he beautiful! . . . And his painting and his poetry, and his schoolwork!" I mean, every afternoon this child was praised, praised, praised, but deep down he was completely left out of everything.

Ethel de Croisset came to stay with us for a few days toward the very end of our time in Ansedonia, and she saw through all this immediately—and she knows what parenting is. She's been a remarkable parent herself, and *her* parents were marvelous—I mean, Elsie Woodward was an extraordinary mother, and the father was extraordinary, and Ethel was absolutely appalled by the way the Baekelands were bringing up Tony.

Letter from Brooks Baekeland to James Jones, February 17, 1966

New York

Dear Jim:

I have taken the liberty of writing Ethel, with you as substitute, into my will as the guardian of Tony's person and U.S. Trust Company as the guardian of his property in case both Barbara and I should grow wings (or perhaps a forked tail, in my case) before Tony is 21.

Duties are just about nil except for tender hand holding and the offering of dry Kleenex, but the law demands a "guardian of the person" for all minors. Tony loves you both and just about no one else that I can think of in the fuddy-duddy generation, so that is why.

Affectionately—Love to Gloria,
Brooks

P.S. St. Anton for about ten days, then back in Paris.

7

ASPIRING AND
PERSEVERING

Often the Broadmoor staff would "look the other way," in the words of one nurse, when it came to sex. "As long as it didn't get out of hand. Even by day there were areas of the wards that weren't very closely supervised. You only had five nurses on duty for every forty or fifty patients, so you couldn't possibly patrol all the areas all the time."

"I have the distinct impression that Tony did have relationships at Broadmoor," says Michael Alexander. "He was quite happy, so they must have let him have some sort of sex."

James Reeve adds, "Tony only talked to me about things he thought I would approve of, though I often wondered what the story really was. I did try once to draw him out on the subject of sex at Broadmoor, but he was very reticent."

"There is a great deal of homosexuality in the hospital," reports David Cohen in his 1981 book *Broadmoor*. "On the whole, what sexual activity exists seems both rather cheerless and loveless." One patient describes Broadmoor in the book as a "homosexual brothel." Another explains: "If you haven't got any women available, there does come a point when you just burst." One patient offered that he felt rather tender toward another patient simply because "I *am* quite tender."

"The authorities sometimes break up couples after having 'tolerated' the situation for some time," Cohen elaborates. "Fear that they may be split up arbitrarily makes relationships even more brittle."

Broadmoor authorities are at pains to point out that homosexuality is not at all uncommon in sexually segregated institutions, be they mental hospitals, prisons, or schools.

Notes from a Psychiatric Consultation on Antony Baekeland, New York, March 12, 1971

> From ages 11 to 14, he spent the school year in Paris and then summers in Italy. At age 14 he was sent to Phillips Exeter Academy in New Hampshire, but was forced to leave because of his grades.

JAMES M. HUBBALL

I was Tony's headmaster at Buckley School, a long time ago. I have a vague recollection that when Tony went to Exeter, there was an episode in which he was found hiding in the laundry chute—for what reason I never knew. The last I heard of him was that he was living in London.

SARA DUFFY CHERMAYEFF

When he got thrown out of Exeter, the evening he came home, Barbara called me and we had a long talk. I don't know what exactly he was kicked out for. She always said, you know, "They don't understand him—he's an artist."

Notes from a Psychiatric Consultation on Antony Baekeland, New York, March 12, 1971

> At age 15, he ran away from another private school.

From the Private Diaries of Leo Hendrik Baekeland, February 7, 1910

George is today fifteen years old. At his age I was I believe in the same mental condition as he is with the difference that he has had the benefit of better intellectual environment. I had to do everything by myself and find my own way. The only help I had was the encouragement of my beloved mother.

SUZANNE TAYLOR

Tony was at Brooks School, in North Andover, Massachusetts, with my son David, who told my husband and me, knowing we knew the Baekelands, that Tony had run away from school to go to the Caribbean and write poetry. And David said, "Guess what he was taking with him!" It went all around the school, you see. I mean, he was going off to write poetry, right? And he was taking a hatchet and a flashlight and I think a rope hammock! He never did get there—he was caught at the airport.

KATHARINE GARDNER COLEMAN

I was having lunch with Brooks and Barbara one day when Tony came in from school with his little traveling case. I mean, it wasn't vacation time. He had walked away from, you know, *another* school. And I said to Barbara and Brooks, "Here's some free advice for you." I had boys then that were older than Tony, you see. I said, "You just *cannot* let him come home. Don't even let him *think* that he can come home. He's got to get through, and then at the end of the school year, if the school hasn't been successful, find him another one."

He was just sent to his room and told they'd talk about it later.

BROOKS BAEKELAND

I was very disappointed to discover that the flame of curiosity and intellectual determination—capacity for, belief in, work—that might, for instance, have made a scientist out of Tony was lacking. Whether that was genetic or due to the values he was being brought up in I cannot say. In any case, I had already educated him to the point where he was ahead—in some directions—of his science teachers in the various prep schools he went to.

Two things had become clear—to me, not to his mother—by that

time: one, that he was bright enough—and even talented enough—
to embark on any career one could think of, and two, that he was
bone-lazy. There is a myth that very bright people can accomplish a
complete academic program without ever opening a book, to coin a
phrase. That is false. In fact, the very, very bright open more books
than anyone else. Usually. Therefore my son soon puzzled me, for I
had spent every summer, wherever we happened to be at the time,
tutoring him mornings to bring him back to the surface, as it were,
for his entry in school the next fall. He would always start at the top
of his class and end up at the bottom, with strong suggestions from
the schools that he be taken out.

As he was entering puberty he also began to be a disciplinary problem in his schools—"subversive," "a bad influence," etc. But I went
on tutoring him right up to the time that he and his mother an-
nounced that he wanted to go to Oxford. He had never been able to
finish high school and had even been asked to leave a school with the
academic standards of Avon Old Farms.

From the Catalog, Avon Old Farms School, Avon, Connecticut

> *Aspirando et perseverando*—aspiring and persevering: the School
> motto is more than a figure of speech to members of the Avon
> community. The motto is a reminder of the way of life that
> governs the hearts and minds of the people who make up the
> School. Boys discover at Avon that aspirations *can* become real-
> ities and that perseverance is vital to the attainment of both indi-
> vidual and community goals.

Letter from Antony Baekeland to Gloria and James Jones, Undated

Avon Old Farms
Avon, Connecticut

Dear Gloria and Jim,
Now that I'm more or less installed in school I can write. Getting back here was a bit unpleasant, but everything feels very
normal after a few days. I'm going to see Rosie Styron pretty

soon about those poems. This school is a real waste, so what I might do is leave at Christmas and come to London, go to a Cramming school to see if I get these A-level exams and see if I can get into Oxford next year. Anyway I'll probably "aspire and persevere" at least until then. . . .

Love,
Tony

PETER GABLE

After Buckley, when I was ten or eleven I was shipped off to Choate, where I was a very bad boy. I was sent down from school. I don't remember what my crime was—it was probably being a smart-ass. Then I was sent to some hideous school in Greenwich which has long since gone out of existence, and I stayed *there* for a while— Tony meanwhile was at Exeter or Brooks—and then I fetched up at a somewhat backwater boarding school outside of Hartford. Avon Old Farms School. The beach upon which I was washed up.

And it was quite amazing—the first day of school, who should I see but Tony! And we fell on each other's necks—how have you been and so forth and so on. Now when we were little boys at Buckley, Tony and I had the sort of telepathy that children can have with each other—I mean where whole paragraphs can be left out because you know each other so well, you have a continuity of experience where even the slightest little trigger puts you both on the same track. Anyway, there had been this hiatus of three or four years, and now, the long and the short of it is, the magic was gone. *I* was a little different, *he* was different.

Tony was most decidedly no longer "just another kid." All his brilliance and genius, dimly perceived by me as a child, was becoming more difficult for *him*, I think. I remember him in English composition class at Avon—his vocabulary was quite an astonishment even to his teachers. At Avon if you were bright you stood out, and Tony had a brilliance above and beyond anyone else in the school. Still, I don't think he excelled in his studies.

BROOKS BAEKELAND

When *I* went there, Avon Old Farms was an interesting school. But it was not an educational institution in the usual sense. What had appealed to my father when he sent me there was that the students milked cows, cut trees, worked in the fish hatchery, plowed, raked leaves, bound books, and worked in a carpentry shop. The fact that some of the boys came with a string of polo ponies or an airplane was not what interested him. Not all of the boys went on to college—I suspect most did not, and of those that did, damned few went to Princeton, Harvard, and Yale.

I had an altogether easy ride at Avon—I spent a quarter of my time fencing, an eighth on team sports, and much of the rest on ornithology. And I was admitted to Harvard, where I might have chosen to study Chinese bronzes or cultural anthropology or Russian history or French literature or comparative religion or philology or the art of glassblowing in the Renaissance or architecture from Egypt to the Bauhaus, but since I was a Baekeland, none of these "frivolities" were open to me. What I did, and my family never knew, was audit them all—in those days, for I think eleven dollars you could audit any course you wanted, which meant sit in on the lectures, read the books, make a fuss in class, and even take the exams, but you could not take the credits. At the same time I was taking a heavy course load leading toward a biochemistry major. Why biochemistry? God knows, but I knew it would please my family—or rather, not shock them. I was expected to become a scientist, to do something satisfactory for the family—as for myself, I was as unmotivated as a loose-skinned pup, nine-tenths curiosity.

I was rooming—or rather, dividing a capacious suite in Massachusetts Hall—with the editor of the *Crimson*. He was a wag. He was a dog: I was a cat. But that dog and this cat shared a sense of the absurd and I still remember him with affection. We were grand, budding terrorists. I showed him how to convert all our cotton underclothes into guncotton; how to fill our housemaster's bathroom—bowl, tub, sink—with Jell-O when he was out courting and the icy winter air could come in through the opened bathroom windows and set it for his sleepy return; how to string our underwear on a cotton clothesline converted into guncotton and with the tip of a lighted cigarette make it disappear with a flash behind one of the campus cops' back when he came up red-faced to arrest us for hanging our laundry in the Yard. It was my grandfather, by the way, who had taught me to make guncotton out of my underwear—also how to make an extremely unstable explosive out of ammonia, potassium iodide, and iodine—and so helped me on my way out of my freshman year at Harvard.

I remember having a tin full of aluminum powder dropped down the chimney from the roof of Mass. Hall while I waited in our ground-floor apartment with a match to light it, sending a flame one hundred feet high into the night sky over Cambridge. The list of tomfoolery is long and I could go on. Most of my inventive powers were occupied in such nonsense that first term.

And then, I got the ax. Suddenly I was a totally defeated young man. I never expected to see any of my family or friends again. I was dazed—literally frightened out of my wits. No future that I could see was open to me. I was finished. Honor, Family—such things were important to me then. Who thinks of Shame today?

Pride—some say satanic pride—has been one of the keys to my whole life, and in 1938 it had a great deal to do with my not seeking the advice from my family that I might easily have found, had I only been able to seek it. But the essence of pride is that it never asks for anything, can never admit weakness. It may demand, it cannot beg. In fact, great pride never even thinks of asking! I am positive that it never even occurred to me that anyone might be able to help me.

My father's reaction was—predictably, and he was right—that I had "absconded with funds." I had taken with me eight hundred and fifty dollars in cash, all I had in account with the bursar, which my father had given me to study biochemistry and not for gallivanting out to the West Coast, which is where I decided to go.

I took a Greyhound bus from Cambridge to San Francisco. I stopped off in New York to say goodbye to my mother, who lived in Turtle Bay, and my sister, then eighteen. I did not reveal to my mother that I was leaving "forever" but I did to my sister, who then did an impulsive and generous thing—she gave me a small necklace of cultured pearls.

In San Francisco I lived first on Howard Street. I had discovered Jack London, and I soon began exploring Pacific and Montgomery Streets—the famous "Monkey Blocks" where Saroyan lived. I had never heard of him and drank with him at the Black Cat without knowing who he was. We remembered it all together in Paris many years later when we went to Longchamps and Auteuil to lose our money on the ponies and spent nights drunkenly with Jim and Gloria Jones. At that time the Black Cat was the hangout of strip-tease girls and whores. It was a tough neighborhood. I could hardly take in the education I was getting, it was coming in so fast, but my ears were as long as a donkey's and my eyes were out on stalks.

I met a lot of extraordinary characters out there—truly Saroyan's world and Steinbeck's. They didn't come from nowhere, you know—like all writers, they were just writing what was, and that *is* the way it was in those days.

I could add a lot of stories to theirs. The Duke. "The Duke of Market Street," he was called. A famous fixture in San Francisco. He was the King of the Bums. His only possessions were a magnificent Capehart record changer, the first word in hi-fi almost before hi-fi began, and every opera and symphony that had ever been recorded—this in a fleabag that he shared with a Norwegian sailor who was always out to sea.

He did not want me to become a bum like him. He found me a job as a trainee doing analytical chemistry for a paint company. And then several things happened quickly. One day, courtesy of an old Avon classmate, I received a letter from the general manager of the Cyanamid Corporation, who was also the president of the Chemical Construction Corporation, offering me a job in south-central India assisting two chemical engineers in building a basic chemical complex for the Maharajah of Mysore.

"Duke," I asked—for I could talk to *this* duke, as I could never have to my father the *Grand* Duke—"what should I do? Should I keep on trying to find a night job that lets me go to school by day, or should I go to Jack London's Alaska, or should I accept this great panjandrum's miserable offer of a hundred dollars a month to build a chemical factory somewhere in India?"

He never hesitated. He said, "Make peace with your father and go out to India."

I was able to do the second.

DR. W. LINDSAY JACOBS

Brooks Baekeland was hostile toward his son and in a welter of confused moralizing seemed to wish him ill, consciously or unconsciously.

He wrote me a letter about Tony, enclosing a cutting from some French magazine. I remember it was a full-page color cartoon made up of three separate sections. The first showed a man sitting quietly in an armchair reading a newspaper. The second showed a little boy pointing a space-ray gun directly at the man, with all sorts of yellow stars shooting out—it looked like the finale of a Fourth of July firecracker display. The last section of the cartoon was just a pile of ashes on the chair. And Brooks Baekeland had written on the side of the cartoon: "Sometimes this frightful realism comes too close to the heart of the thing."

BROOKS BAEKELAND

In the end—long before the end—I saw Tony as a kind of personification of Evil, and I knew him better than anyone in the world and he knew that I did—as Caliban knew that Prospero knew Caliban. But to whom could—would—I have said that? No one. I told him— oh, I told *him*. And he understood. He knew that I loved him, too. And he loved *me*—too much according to some of his homosexual friends.

SUZANNE TAYLOR

Angel, who cooked for the Baekelands two or three days a week, also came to us two or three days, whenever we were alone—she wasn't good enough to cook for company—and she used to tell us an awful lot about the Baekelands, naturally. She told me, "I don't know what's going to happen to Tony because when his parents are away he picks up older boys on the street and brings them home." He was about fourteen then.

DR. PHILIP GOGARTY

Tony's first homosexual relationship was at the age of eight.

From a Psychiatric Report on Antony Baekeland Ordered By the British Courts, January 5, 1973

In adolescence Antony found homosexual interests and had some physical experience at boarding school. He regards himself as attracted to both sexes.

PETER GABLE

One Christmas break at Avon I came trundling down to New York and I stayed with Tony. His parents were living in Paris most of the time by then but they had this penthouse *pied-à-terre* on Seventy-fifth Street and Lexington, with lots of terraces. It was just kids down for a long weekend. Tony had a party, a little gathering. I remember there were a lot of very cute girls there. Girls appreciated Tony's looks and his wit or his manner or something—they rather liked him. And he seemed to reciprocate their enthusiasm. I mean, he had, it appeared, as much enthusiasm for girls as anybody else, certainly as much as *I* had. He seemed to be as hotly in pursuit of the almost unachievable piece of ass as any of us. He became attracted to a friend of a cousin of his who I was going out with. God she was a sexy little girl—long brunette hair, curvaceous, quite something to warm the cockles of your heart on a cold winter's night in a boy's boarding school in Avon, Connecticut. And this girl and Tony formed some sort of vast friendship for six months or so. Her parents lived somewhere in Connecticut—Westport, Southport, Eastport, Northport—and there was a weekend that we all spent unchaperoned in their house, which I remember as being beamy, with a large fireplace and lots of stone. We built a fire and drank a bottle of Cointreau or something, and then we toddled off to bed. Now these were the years when girls' knees stayed wired to each other. So neither Tony nor I expected, nor did the girls anticipate, that anything of a particularly prurient nature would transpire. We did end up in the girls' room, where there were two double beds—Tony and his girl in one and me and my girl in the other, all of us clothed to some degree. And what did we do? We went to sleep!

The point of all this is, we're now fifteen years old and Tony is pursuing females. Another year or so and I begin to discern that he has something less than a burning interest in them. I'm trying to remember exactly when it was that I decided that Tony was *not* masculine. There was a period there, in his late teens, when I simply felt that he was neuter. It could well be that he was by then actively pursuing homosexuality—I don't know. As I said, at Avon we basically went our separate ways. But there was this one guy there, Mike Perkins. He was tall, dark, and incredibly handsome, and he was a real sexual enthusiast with women—I mean, I knew many of his girlfriends. But looking back now, I have the feeling that maybe he and Tony were more than friends.

NANCY PERKINS WALLACE

Tony and my brother Mike ran away from Avon together. They went to Puerto Rico. They were out of school for quite a while. They lived on beaches and that sort of thing. According to my brother, who is *not* homosexual, Tony had male lovers while they were there.

HENRY H. PERKINS

Mike never told *me* about Tony's male lovers, you know, but I'm such a butch guy myself, my brother knows I don't like to hear stories of that stuff. I just remember they had no money, they slept on the beach, and they were bitten by fleas—they held out for a week or something, and then they, you know, came home, like any other little kids that have run away. After that, Mike began getting very involved in Tony's life, both here and in Europe.

They had airs, those people. Of grandeur. The Baekelands had the French parlor routine. And the salon, *oui*. And Tony had all of that, too, you know, and that's what I think was somewhat fascinating to my brother. I think that he was somewhat seduced by that.

DUNCAN LONGCOPE

Tony had an American pal called Mike, quite a nice young man, dark-haired, very handsome as I recall, and they used to do the boulevards together, and according to this woman I knew who used to tell me stories about Tony's life on the Île Saint-Louis, it was the same thing every night—I mean, either two boys or two girls would come back with them, to this place of Brooks's that Tony used. Brooks, you know, had that other apartment on the Île, I think it was on the rue Regrattier—a studio where he wrote. And Tony at a certain time had the use of this studio.

BROOKS BAEKELAND

For my part, I was sorry for him, sorry that he was homosexual—very sorry indeed—but I do not have most people's knee-jerk reactions to such things. It rather tends to make me think and wonder why, how, people like Tony who are not really effeminate—except, clearly, by imitation when in the company of others of their kind—become imprinted, diverged, into such channels.

In any case, in England, where he went after Avon, he met some very swishy titled young men, went to a Savile Row tailor, charged up what would now be ten thousand pounds of tailor-made clothes—he hadn't a bean, but Daddy would pay—and said he wanted to go up to Oxford with his friends.

He and his mother made a strong case for this remarkable request. Influence was to be used through the head of All Souls, now dead, "a charming man," etc. That the boy had not even finished high school and was essentially uneducated did not seem to them to be a reason why Oxford would not be delighted to have him.

I was finally able by various machinations plus my son's high IQ score and the charming and civilized impression he could make—I am not being ironical here; these things still counted in certain places—to get him provisionally accepted at St. John's College, Oxford, provided he could pass his O-levels—A-levels? I forget—after a bit of cramming, which shouldn't take more than a few months for a person of his intelligence, everyone agreed.

I hired a young Oxford student to come to Cadaqués, where we were to spend the summer. The task was for Tony to learn enough Latin to pass the examination in that subject, which, with a founding in French and some Spanish already learned by ear, should not have been too difficult.

But the tutor was corrupted, confessed the hopelessness of the situation to me, and left. No work had been accomplished at all.

Tearful scenes with Mama and Papa, promises of reform. So that autumn, kindness of Michael Alexander, Tony went to live in London and was put into a cramming school.

MICHAEL ALEXANDER
Tony stayed with me for about six months while he was studying at Davies, Laing & Dick somewhere up in Notting Hill Gate. He lived in my basement and he looked after himself. That was when the father-son relationship was at its most, how shall I put it . . . Brooks was trying to turn Tony into something other than a sort of layabout with homosexual inclinations. He was trying to turn him into a man—shall we put it that way? He was putting a lot of pressure on Tony, who I must say did not seem to be at that stage the ideal American boy.

BROOKS BAEKELAND
To make a long story short, the cramming school wrote to tell me that I was wasting my money. The lad, they said, was not even coming to his tutorial appointments, much less doing any of the work assigned to him.

But he was having a fine time with his swishy friends.

About this time I received a letter from Jim Jones reproaching me for not letting my son be a writer.

Letter from Antony Baekeland to James Jones, Undated

> % Michael Alexander
> London, W. 1

Dear Jim,

Can you look at these for me and give me some advice? I know
how busy you are, but I've given up the idea I had of going to
Oxford and I'm going to be pretty broke by the first of the
month. I thought you might know where to send them, if
they're good enough to send. The one called "*Snow Dream of
David Lanyon*" needs editing, I think. Anyway, tell me what
you think, and love to Gloria and Kaylie.

> Yours ever,
> Tony Baekeland

P.S. Can you help me get an agent? Also (I'm out of my mind)
do you think I could get "*Jolyon Condemned*" in *The New
Yorker*?

**Letter from James Jones to Antony Baekeland, December 22,
1964**

> 10, quai d'Orléans
> Paris IV°

Dear Tony,

I have read your three stories with a great deal of interest. I think
you write extremely well. Really remarkably well. I enjoyed all
three of them very much, simply for that reason. However, I do
not think you could get any one of the three of them into *The
New Yorker*, which is not only pretty much of a closed corporation, but also very severe in its dictates of and demands for the
quote *New Yorker* style unquote.

With regard to an agent, I suggest you call and meet my own
agent in London, whose name is Hope Leresche. Her phone is
FLAxman 4311 and her address is 11 Jubilee Place, London,
S.W. 3. Hope is an agent for a lot of people among whom is
Sheila Delaney whom she helped to get started. If she likes you
and your work, and I should think she would, she may be able
to help you get started.

On the other hand, trying to make even a bare living out of writing short stories is next to impossible. The kind of stories you would like to write have very little commercial market value unfortunately, whatever their true value. I am only telling you this because it is the truth, because I want you to know what may be in store for you. Despite that, because I did like the stories you sent so much, I would be willing to write your Dad and Mom that I think they should support you—if not richly, at least so you can live—so that you can write. It's a peculiar fact that most parents will support their kids in studying just about any profession except learning how to write. As a matter of fact, I told them that when they were here last time. However, I would not like to write them to this effect unless I was absolutely sure it was something you wished me to do. Also, I don't know how to spell Cadaquez (?). In fact, I'm not even sure they're there now.

With regard to the three stories, I think the first, untitled one comes nearest to being a short story in the old-fashioned classic sense. By that I mean something does happen, the boy does see his mother with the man, and at the end does act on it. However, I feel it is obvious that you have imposed these two scenes on the story as a whole. Each of them is dealt with almost cursorily, with much less of the interesting and affective detail which makes the rest of the story so good. I feel that the ending is therefore too abrupt, unprepared for, and happens too quickly for the reader to partake of it fully. I also think that the arising of the storm, clearly a device to promulgate the ending, could be made more natural, and perhaps more emotionally a true part of the story (as opposed to a device) by having its first signs commence earlier, when the boy is climbing on the island, so that when he sees the man kissing his mother, it is during the first beginning winds rustling the trees and grasses while he sees them. Then let it build up slowly to the rest of the story to the end. It would of course be easy to overdo this thing of the storm, but if it is done naturally without being pointed up too much, I think it would clear up all the criticisms I have and this feeling of abruptness of device laid on over the top. I would think, too, the boy would have some inkling, earlier, that his beautiful mom is not as perfect as he would like her to be. You could play this off against naive younger sister.

Neither of the other two is this close to being technically a short story, though I found them both interesting and moving. Of the two I think *The Snow Dream* is the better, although I feel the ending sort of tapers off leaving one with an unsatisfied feeling. The *Jolyon* one is the least successful, largely because in its latter half there is an undefinable adolescent-bravado quality which the other two, while written *about* adolescents, do not have. I liked the first part with the girls, though.

Please let me know if you want me to write your folks, and please look up Hope Leresche. Gloria joins me in sending all best.

Sincerely,
James Jones

Telegram from Antony Baekeland to James Jones, Undated

JUST BACK NEW YORK READ LETTER THANKS FOR ENCOURAGEMENT I NEED IT CAN YOU WRITE FATHER AT CASADEVAL CADAQUES GERONA WILL LOOK UP MRS. LERESCHE HAPPY NEW YEAR LOVE TO GLORIA   TONY

Letter from James Jones to Brooks Baekeland, February 5, 1965

10, quai d'Orléans
Paris IV°

Dear Brooks,
I seem to remember that we are coming down to see you for a few days some time fairly soon, but as I am up in the office and Gloria is downstairs and the phone is busy I cannot check with her just when. Anyway that is not what I'm writing about just now.

Shortly before we went to Klosters Tony sent me from London three stories of his which he asked me to read and comment on. I did this and I quote in part what I thought about them:

"I think you write extremely well . . . Really remarkably well. I enjoyed all three of them very much, simply for that reason. However, I do not think you could get any one of the three into *The New Yorker* . . ."

I meant every word of this, Brooks. I think Tony has the *unacquirable* trait of a writer, which is to make people see and feel things powerfully. I don't think as yet that he has any of the technical proficiency, or the constructive sense, to utilize the talent he has. (Max Perkins once said the same thing about me, and I guess I'm more or less quoting him.) Anyway, it's going to take him quite a while to develop his talent, but I sincerely think he does have a talent, and I think he ought to have a chance to try to develop it.

Tony mentioned in his letter only that he's given up the idea of going to Oxford and was going to be pretty broke by the end of the month. He was hoping I could help him sell one of the three to *The New Yorker*. I of course having talked with you and Barbara knew more than Tony was saying and could read between the lines. I wrote him a detailed analysis of all three of the stories and then went on to explain that it was next to impossible to try and make a living by writing short stories. I also offered to write to you in his behalf, and tell you what I thought about his writing. I feel strongly enough that Tony has talent that I would suggest to you that you give him a chance to work at it, which would mean sending him enough money to live on (and I don't mean luxuriously). I am aware that most American parents while willing to support their kids for eight years to become a doctor, nevertheless take a very dim view of supporting the same kids the same length of time to become a writer. But it takes just as long. What does surprise me is that you, who have worked at becoming a writer yourself and who love writing and writers, find yourself now in a moral position where you cannot give Tony a fair chance to become one himself.

When I wrote to Tony I said I would not write to you unless he wished me to, and while I was in Klosters I got a wire from him here giving me your address in Cadaqués and asking me to go ahead and write you. So I am.

It's not as if you were poor and didn't have the money. And I am not writing you out of any sense of moral issue or empathy for the young. But I've been dedicated to writing all my life, and whenever I see someone who has a chance at writing well I always try to help them get that chance if I can. I think you ought to help Tony. Actually, he has made remarkable strides since those few early things of his I read two or three years ago.

Gloria joins me in sending our love to you both and I hope we'll see you in—what is it, May?

Sincerely,
James Jones

Letter from Brooks Baekeland to James Jones, February 7, 1965

(44 today)
Cadaqués

Dear Jim:

It was very kind of you to write me. You are a kind man and an understanding man and some other things too—but that's already enough for what I want to say.

First of all I am not quite the horse's ass that you may think, nor so conventional. The doctor writer bit I can truthfully say is unimpeachable, because it is, and has been for a long time, my own opinion. Tactics *(when)* is all I was concerned with, and (much too long a subject) that is conditioned by the mercurial changes still going on in Tony. (I am waiting for him to burst out of Davies's, which I think he will, and then I fully intend to do what you suggest and with blessings that will mean more then than they would have 3 years ago when I had already reached your opinion and when he might have had troubles which could have finished, or broken, the impulse that is growing hard in him. I don't know whether I can make myself clear about this in a few words.)

Secondly, as a matter of principle, although I disagreed with it in almost every aspect (and was overridden, as far as I could tell, by both B & T), I would not gratify Tony by torpedoing his mother's late arrangements for him in England. They will collapse of their own foolishness. The harder Tony's resolve becomes, the better as far as I am concerned—because (for one thing) I would like to see him grow out of his mother and he can only do that by an exercise of male defiance—which I soon expect.

Third—I gave him the signal, permission and money in December. (I gave a lot of thought to your counsel: I say counsel, because I have great respect for your insight. It was a relief to hear *you* say that.) But I made one condition—that he take the occupation seriously and show some signs of it. (Agent, work, etc.) He did and I was pleased. (The efforts were inefficient, but they were efforts.) In London he showed me his stories and I was pleased. I told him so. I have known for years that whatever else he did in life, he would be a writer. I never told him different when I decided that. He has never had anything but praise and encouragement from me in that. (Ask him.) O.K. The next thing I knew, he was in the USA with Mama. The next thing I knew after that was that he was going to go to a shrink and go back to Davies's. I suggested to him that he get away from us— go into the military, get it over with, write his head off (or not if he chose) and spend some peaceful, boring, regular and *distant* years from us. Mama has so indoctrinated him with the blood-thirsty horrors and depravities of military service of any kind that he thought I was trying to punish him. I wrote him no. I also wrote him, however, that I was not going to blow up "Mum." The next move is up to him. . . . He knows that I am on his side, but he also knows that I want it *straight* and as soon as he wants it straight too, he has his ticket. That's his problem.

He's afraid. (Again Mama—the homosexual fear.)

Nothing is ever simple, and this shrink may capture him (keep him in a kind of permanent dependent babyhood). I think not. I have a high respect for this boy who has a head as clear as anyone's I know. He's lucid.

The clock is ticking and I know that his little bomb is going to go off soon. If it doesn't—I'm going to be all confused! I will never have been so wrong in my intuition (I'm not used to that either).

I am sorry to bore you with this, but I owe you something for your long, kind letter and for your interest in Tony. When you said at your house that you weren't sure "he could put words together" (a judgment you made several years before) I decided not to say all this to you. The tactics, however, interest me. The raw meat of frustration, eaten for quite a long period now, may not have been so bad a training diet. I respect writing. I want him to respect it. He is not likely, no one is *likely*, to be another James Jones. But even less is anyone likely to be that if he treats it like an escape or a kind of lark. When he decides to write, he will also lick Mama and everything that implies. Everything (I hope) will come together at once.

Want to see your book. When? My book I think going well. Love you both very much.

The old Puritan

BROOKS BAEKELAND

My reaction to all this was not simple. I knew that professional writing required amongst other things a tremendous amount of discipline—guts?—and solitude. That Tony was articulate and "a born writer" in every sense but the above, I had long known, and that had already impressed a lot of our other friends. With Michael Alexander's good influence, I was, if not hopeful, not entirely skeptical either.

Again, to make a long story short, it began to be evident that Tony was having a lovely time in London with his swishy friends but was not writing. Whatever else a writer does or does not do, he writes. He cannot help it, it's compulsive. And Tony was not writing.

Thinking how discouraging it all was, I offered him a deal. In retrospect I do not think it was a wise thing, but I thought it might help him then. I told him I would buy whatever he wrote *by the word* and try to get it edited and published for him. Which he had asked me to do, so that the only new thing here was my—rather crass— financial inducement to try to make a writer write—that is, to make him stop leading his playboy life enough at least to finance it. A few hours a day would have done it.

It was really a rotten idea, and I tell you this because it now makes me laugh. Laugh?

And then Tony began to become *persona non grata*—just hints from Michael Alexander—and his sojourn at Michael's ended. There were some damages to pay.

And that was the end of "writing," which is what Tony's mother, having abandoned all hope of his becoming a biologist, had hoped that he would do.

ELIZABETH WEICKER FONDARAS

Barbara was always highly stimulated by literary people. She felt *those* were the social prizes.

BOWDEN BROADWATER

Mary McCarthy when I was married to her always thought Barbara
Baekeland frivolous and intellectually pretentious, and I must say I
quite agreed.

GEORGES BERNIER

The first time I ever met Barbara Baekeland, she said, "Tell me,
Georges"—you can imagine how flabbergasted I was as a Frenchman
to hear myself called by my first name by someone I hadn't known
for more than five minutes—"was Marcel Proust a homosexual?" I
must say I had to laugh, because this was at a time when you
couldn't open up a literary supplement anywhere in the world without reading about Proust—Proust, Freud, and Joyce were the big
three—and this question that was preying on Barbara Baekeland's
mind was of course almost the first thing anybody ever addressed in
Proust.

Ben Sonnenberg had called to tell me there was this *wonderful*
American couple that had just arrived in Paris that he very much
wanted me to meet, whereupon, a few days later, I was invited for
dinner at the Baekelands', whereupon Barbara had immediately asked
me this amazing question.

Then Brooks began carrying on about what a wonderful fertile intelligent mind his son had because he would get hold of flies and
remove one wing and watch what the equilibrium was, and then he
would remove the other wing and see how it worked at *that* point—
and sometimes the legs would be broken, so that was another interesting thing. I found Brooks's attitude extraordinarily odd. You know,
that kind of sadistic behavior is quite common in children, but one
seldom sees a father who thinks it is marvelous. And then after dinner the child himself was produced. I said to myself when I walked
out of their place that night, I never want to see those people ever
again.

I did in fact see *her* once after that. We were both the guests of
Ethel de Croisset at a restaurant near Notre Dame, called Quasi-
modo—Marcel Duchamp was also there. You know, I admired Marcel and I was rather *agacé* that he was wasting his time with the likes
of Barbara Baekeland.

She continued to invite me to their dinners, of course, but I had—
and still have, for that matter—a great technique for stopping these
things in the bud: sudden frost.

BROOKS BAEKELAND

My technique was flight, although once, in Klosters, both of us naked in a small hotel bathroom, I held Barbara down with my foot—approximate region, her thorax—while she sank her strong, white teeth as deep as she could into my calf. I thought the situation so funny—though I dared not let her up—that I enraged her still more by laughing. I really loved her, you know. This "fight"— and there was one almost every night, sooner or later—came about because I refused to take her to the Chesa Grischuna that evening— again!—for dinner. I believe it took at least a half hour for the adrenaline to burn out of her veins. But before that she was a wild animal, a flaming, beautiful tigress. In thirty years I only hit her once—and that was not intended.

ELIZABETH ARCHER BAEKELAND

Brooks told me that sometimes in the middle of these horrendous battles of theirs he would say, "Barbara, I have to go to the loo," and she would suddenly calm down and sit patiently while he went to the bathroom, and then resume screaming when he came out. But one time in Paris the fighting was so terrible he just left and went to a very elegant hotel. He got in bed and said, "Thank God, now I'll have some peace," and started reading, and then suddenly the armoire door flew open and out came Barbara—"Darling, I'm here!"—and they had a fantastic evening together. You see, he had told her when he stormed off which hotel he was going to, and she had somehow gotten there ahead of him and said to the desk, "I'm Madame Baekeland," and they had let her up.

PEIDI GIMBEL LUMET

Barbara carried on fiercely and dangerously for years. There was that headlong pitch of hers, on the down. Once we were in Zermatt together. I was skiing with a Swiss guide I'd skied with in St. Anton for a few years, and Barbara used to sort of come around corners and join us or try to—she was sort of tailing us. And she was skiing too fast for how she skied—she had skied much less than I had—she was sort of going pell-mell. And she broke her leg really badly. I mean, it was very self-destructive.

But it wasn't just the skiing. She was possessed. The house where we were all staying, Brooks and Barbara and Heather and Jack Co- hane and I, was sort of a chalet on top of a rise of land, and the

moon was very full. I had the feeling Barbara was just going to turn
into a creature we'd never imagined. There were these transforma-
tions going on at night that you could see. A couple of times she
packed her suitcases and piled them on the *schlittens*—you know,
those wooden sleds—and she'd start to keen and wail, and I think
maybe Brooks went out and got her and brought her back in.

From *A Walk in Winter Woods,* Brooks Baekeland, Unpublished

How many times they had lain like this on their backs in the
snow at Zermatt and looked up at a full moon. It was she who
had always wanted to ski under the moon, she who had always
dared, and he had followed—not because he had wanted to or
thought it was wise, but in case she got hurt. He had never been
able to stop her from doing anything she had set her mind on
doing.

HEATHER COHANE

It was always the moon, either the full moon or the new moon. A lot
of people are affected by it. My mother had an admirer who was the
first person I ever knew who was affected by it. He'd be with us and
then suddenly he would lose his temper and rush out, and sometimes
he'd stay away for three days. We would pass him in the street and he
wouldn't even say good morning, how are you. And then when the
moon had gone through its cycle or whatever, he'd come back as if
nothing had happened. And when we shared the house with the
Baekelands and Peidi Gimbel in Zermatt, with the Matterhorn looming up right next to us, I noticed that with Barbara, too, it was the
moon. It came on very suddenly and she would go very round the
bend.

BROOKS BAEKELAND

I took a series of questions with me to Zermatt—Chalet Turquino,
Winkelmatten mit Matterhorn, to be exact—that winter of 1963:
How do you get an exploring team into a lofty, jungled, tropical
mountain range that is unmapped? How do you supply it? How do
you defend it? How do you get it out again?

Above left: Leo Hendrik Baekeland (*Union Carbide Library Collection*). *Above right:* Céline Swarts Baekeland, 1912 (*Smithsonian Institute Collection*). *Below:* The Baekelands, 1915. *Left to right:* daughter Nina, Céline, Leo, and son George (*Smithsonian Institute Collection*)

Toilet seat (half section)

Bullets

Bazooka part

Straphanger

Wireless

Milking-machine part

Gramophone record

Jewellery

Telephone mouthpiece

Objects made of Bakelite (*Union Carbide Collection* and *Smithsonian Institute Collection*)

Left: Brooks Baekeland in the Royal Canadian Airforce, 1942. *Below:* Barbara Daly at about seventeen (*Collection of Nina Fraser Daly*)

Above and right:
Barbara in
Hollywood, 1941
(*Collection of Nina
Fraser Daly*)

Brooks and Barbara at the Stork Club, New York, February 10th 1943
(*Collection of Nina Fraser Daly*)

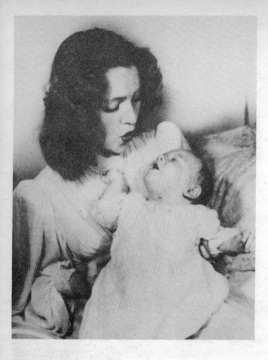

Above: Barbara and
Tony, 1946.
Right: A drawing by
Tony (*Collection of
Nina Fraser Daly*)

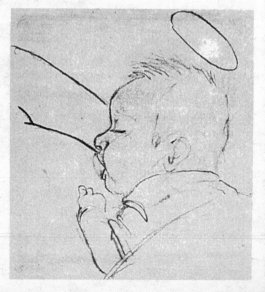

Above: Barbara and Tony at Cape Cod, 1949. *Below left:* Tony at his grandmother Nina Daly's. *Below right:* Tony in Paris, 1959 (*Collection of Nina Fraser Daly*)

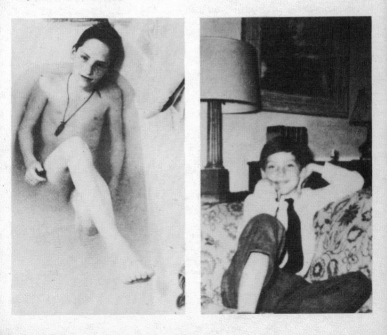

Above: Ansedonia, 1960: Barbara and Brooks in the foreground.
Below: Paris, 1962. *Left to right:* William Saroyan, unidentified woman, Brooks Baekeland, unidentified man, Gloria Jones, Barbara Baekeland (*Collection of Gloria Jones*)

Above and left:
Tony in Cadaqués
(*Karen Radkai*)

Brooks Baekeland in the Peruvian jungle, 1963 (*Peter Gimbel*)

Sylvie Baekeland Skira, Paris, 1976

Above: Dining on board Emily Staempfli's yacht in the Aegean, June 1969. *Seated from left to right:* Barbara, Peter Harnden (partially obscured), Emily Staempfli, Sam Green, Missy Harnden. *Below:* Sam Green and Barbara swimming off the yacht (*Bernard Pfriem*)

Above: Barbara in the New York penthouse, 1971.
Left: Tony in East Hampton, Long Island, 1971

Right: Barbara 'in tragic decline', as Brooks Baekeland wrote on the back of the photograph (*Brooks Baekeland*). *Below:* 81 Cadogan Square

Above: Self-portrait by Tony, Broadmoor, August 30th 1978. *Right:* Prison records mug-shot of Tony, Rikers Island, New York, July 27th 1980. *Below:* John Murray, a friend of Tony's at Rikers Island

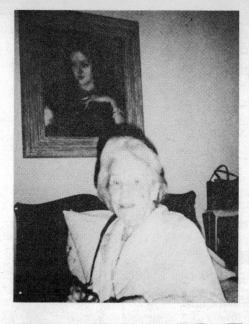

From *National Geographic*, Vol. 126, No. 2, August 1964

> The strain of being first to conquer one of earth's unknown areas
> shows in the haggard faces of two New Yorkers who parachuted
> into Peru's forbidding Vilcabamba mountain fastness: Brooks
> Baekeland, 43-year-old grandson of the Belgian who invented
> Bakelite, and Peter R. Gimbel, 36, a great-grandson of the
> Gimbel-Saks department stores. Forsaking life in Manhattan's
> man-made canyons, they and two companions spent 89 harrow-
> ing days traversing the wilderness. . . .

BROOKS BAEKELAND

What compelled me to undertake such a journey? The fact that no
one had ever parachuted anywhere near such altitudes before. But
there was another reason, too, in 1963. I had fallen deeply in love
with a young English girl—she was fifteen years younger than I was,
the daughter of a diplomat friend of mine in Paris—and this had
occasioned Barbara's first—of four—suicide attempts when I had
asked for a permanent leave from her excitements and expenditures,
from her way of life. Faced with becoming a murderer for the sake of
freedom, I gave up my English girl and went into the desert, so to
speak, for I knew now that Barbara would never give me my freedom.
I knew that I was bound to that monster of green-eyed jealousy for
life. So I took up exploring as a profession.

The fact is, at this time in my life I did not give a damn whether I
lived or died. I still don't, and that has always been a great strength.
Many people who know me fear me for that reason. Even dogs are
aware of it and treat me with circumspection. But I feel no arrogance
in this thing—it is a proof, to me, of failure. That, you will see, is
what allowed two people as basically different as Peter Gimbel and I
to become partners for a while.

It was a funny partnership—which he never understood. I mean, I
was very old, he was very young. In the end he felt—and perhaps he
was—betrayed. For some astigmatic reason of his own, he hero-wor-
shiped me—*then*. Later, he discovered the hollowness of his error.

He was then, and may still be, caught up entirely in the balls-
around-his-neck Hemingway ethic of grace under pressure. I have
always believed that real bravery is of the intellect, not of the balls.
But this Hemingway style was very much in fashion then. I openly

derided it. Not that I am in the easy anti-Hemingway camp, either. Never was.

"Brooko," said Peter, "we have got to go down there! We have got to see that country." He was always a magnet for challenges. What intrigued him most was the danger of being killed by those wild Indians! As for myself, not being in the bravery game, I needed that excuse to escape Barbara for months at a time.

I was of course also intrigued by a very interesting four-hundred-year-old mystery: what had happened to Manco Inca, Atahualpa's brother, and his two hundred thousand soldiers when they had fled down into the Alta Selva, the backside of the Andes, from the Spanish.

Up in my eyrie at Zermatt I decided that they must have settled somewhere at the southern end of the Cordillera Vilcabamba. They were pursued by the Spanish rabble but disappeared—and then a silence, a silence of over four hundred years. I liked that a lot.

In the prospectus that Gimbel and I wrote for the expedition—we were applying for funding principally to the National Geographic Society, whose owners, the Grosvenors, were old family friends, and to the New York Zoological Society, of which Gimbel was then a trustee—we carefully made no mention of lost Inca cities, etc. That would never have done—would never have gained us the money we needed. So we made it into a scientific expedition. And my argument for this—and which sold our project—was that the island cordillera rose practically from sea-level altitude out of the Amazon plain to heights just short of snow and ice and therefore contained a whole series of climates and therefore flora and fauna from the tropical to the arctic and that, because of the "island's" separation from the main mass of the Andes rising to the West, a variety of unknown species of animals, plants, and insects could—over millions of years—have developed in isolation there. I therefore proposed that we make the expedition for purposes of biological exploration. If I mentioned the disappearance of Manco Inca four centuries earlier in the general direction of this cordillera, it was strictly in passing.

Since we failed to land our biologists on top of the cordillera, the expedition was a formal failure in terms of its main objective. In every other way it was a success. Until such time as a weather freak permitted the cordillera to be mapped by photogrammetry, our map was and would remain the only accurate one of the region. The reason it had gone unmapped for so long is that everyone who had ever entered and tried to traverse it had died—thirteen expeditions had left their records and their bones. It was a place of death. We were the first team who had actually traversed the cordillera and lived to tell the tale.

Our expedition also pioneered a new method of penetrating and exploring otherwise inaccessible regions. Finally, and not least, it developed the "Para commander" parachute, a radical new design based on an invention that allowed high-altitude parachuting for the first time. This design became immediately the standard parachute for every army and air force in the world. It had been tested for the first time in early 1963 by Jacques Istel—Peter Gimbel standing by—on twenty-thousand-foot Popocatepetl in Mexico, and I remember well when I received the telegram announcing their success at my H.Q. in Zermatt. The jump was, I think, to eleven thousand feet, which was more than six thousand feet higher than had ever been achieved before.

That I did not find descendants of Manco Inca waiting up there to kill me—well . . . too bad?

Finally, after having been almost murdered by some Machiguenga Indians, we made friendly contact with them and brought three of them to civilization. As for the ruins of Manco Inca's last—lost—city, we had guessed that it would be found on what I called Paddock's Ridge, but we could not get to it and it was invisible from the air. And indeed that is where it *was* found—by Gene Savoy a couple of years later!

I may say, immodestly, that I was the only one of the four of us who made the famous walk out of the cordillera who was happy doing it. I was, due to my background, in my element. Gimbel hated it—his interests, his training, did not extend to botany and entomology, etc. He just wanted "out," while I hoped we might take forever. Jack Joerns, one of the three pilots on the expedition, a Texan, became deeply depressed. Only Peter Lake, a Dartmouth student, maintained his natural gaiety. He was really wonderful—partly, I think, because he had absolute confidence in Peter Gimbel and me. I had guaranteed his parents that I would get him home alive, and I took that promise seriously. He knew it, he knew me, and he believed it. As for me, my strength came partly from the fact that my personal life was in a shambles. I was deeply unhappy over having had to renounce the English girl, with whom I was deeply in love. My career was shattered, and my son, already far gone in drugs and sodomy at seventeen, was obviously beyond change. Do you understand?

Gimbel called me "Ahab"—and our friendship ended with that

expedition. For one reason or another, one of my closest and most treasured friends, a man I greatly respected and for whom I had deep affection, was lost to me. I asked him why on several occasions but never had an answer. But expeditions are famous breakers of friendships—as are marriages. In our case the break was particularly painful, not only because we had been like Damon and Pythias but because we had never so much as had a disagreement—we had always seen all our problems in the same way and quickly reached our solutions. He had many wonderful gifts that I lacked, and I had those he lacked—and it worked! If we had fought or disagreed, my sorrow over what happened to our partnership would have been nothing to speak of.

PETER GIMBEL

It was Brooks who got me involved—he really enticed me into the thing. My identical twin brother, David, had died of stomach cancer at the age of twenty-nine, at which point I started to examine my own life pretty hard and decided that Wall Street where I had been working was not the world where I wanted to spend the rest of my life. I had met Brooks a couple of years earlier, and now I was looking for something very offbeat to do. In July of 1956 when I was twenty-eight, I had made a dive to the *Andrea Doria* and in a small way, the way it can happen in a bigger way now, I became instantly noticeable—anyway I was called by Fairfield Osborn and asked to join the board of trustees of the New York Zoological Society, and a short while later the president of the American Museum of Natural History got in touch with me and asked me to join *their* board.

So anyway when Brooks came up with the idea for the Vilcabamba expedition I was very excited. I was much more interested in the expedition from the standpoint of pure exploration and adventure, not in the scholarly/intellectual/archaeological kind of thing that Brooks was interested in—he wanted to find the lost city and figure out exactly where the last stand of the last Inca had been and discover the last tomb and so forth and so on. I would have gone in there even if you had guaranteed me that there *was* no lost city—just because of the romance of dropping into a virtually cut-off island of land, because that's what it was—a huge fifteen-thousand-foot-high island rising out of low jungle on all sides. Here was the *unknown*, you know.

Brooks was in Zermatt with Barbara, so we were planning it all by long distance, you might say—by voluminous correspondence. Barbara had broken her leg skiing, really smashed it—a terrible break. So Brooks had—I have to call it an excuse, because it was what he really wanted to do: remain in Zermatt skiing while I organized the whole thing. I mean, he was in Switzerland and the guy doing the dirty work was right here—okay?

I have to give him credit, though—he was a brilliant, brilliant land analyst. He could look at a cliff that was covered with jungle and say, "There's a ledge running there that I think we can traverse." And he'd be right on the money every fuckin' time! I question whether we would have gotten out without him.

Scientifically my evaluation is the thing was a complete failure as an expedition—a failure, a nonsuccess—but that in terms of a strange adventurous exploratory feat it was a success. And I would say that on the *Geographic* staff it was perceived both those ways. Clearly, the drama of our entry and the long trek out outweighed whatever the magazine's disappointment scientifically was, because they ran it as a cover story and devoted quite a lot of space and attention to it and so on.

From *National Geographic,* Vol. 126, No. 2, August 1964

BY PARACHUTE INTO PERU'S LOST WORLD
by Brooks Baekeland
PHOTOGRAPHS BY THE AUTHOR AND PETER R. GIMBEL

Cramped in the airplane with our bulky gear, Peter Gimbel and I looked out of the open door and then, questioningly, at each other.

A year of careful preparation had brought us to this moment of decision far above a remote spur of the Andes of southeastern Peru. . . .

BROOKS BAEKELAND
That was not *my* "colorful account" in the *Geographic.* My piece—"too subjective"—was totally emasculated and rewritten by a *Geographic* hack for that thirteen-year-old girl who lives in Sioux City, for whom every issue of that amazing magazine is always writ-

ten. I did not give a damn. I had a wonderful summer, mostly paid for by National Geographic Society funds, and my own vanity was not involved.

ETHEL WOODWARD DE CROISSET

Brooks asked me to have a look at his article for the *Geographic* before it was published. Now it had some very good things, wonderfully described things, in it, but it was badly punctuated, full of misspellings, so I did some editing, you know—just little, simple things to the English, which I did on a separate sheet of paper. Then I gave it to Barbara, whom I happened to be seeing, and said, "Give this to Brooks. I did a little editing." I'd actually taken great pains with it. And Barbara was outraged. She said, "I wouldn't *think* of showing this to him, and don't *you* ever mention it! Just tell him it's wonderful. He mustn't be discouraged." And she tore it up. I felt very bad, I hadn't realized. . . . But it shows you how she protected him, always telling him he was a genius. All of this sort of thing was to *keep* him.

You know, Barbara had a love affair with a Spaniard and it was all for Brooks to realize that she was more attractive than he seemed to think her. She told me that she'd met him in New York, right when things were going very ruggedly. She had suddenly discovered—she hadn't known—that Brooks was dragging around and looking for other women. A little later she found out that he had an affair on with an English girl.

She didn't like her Spanish friend at all—very soon she'd had enough of him. But she played the game that she was going to leave Brooks and run off with him. And she told me that Brooks begged her not to go, that he was very moved and all of this. I think the Spaniard was terrified that she *was* going to go off with him—he faded out of the picture when he heard *that* threat.

She may have slept with him *once*. You know, she was fundamentally an Irish Catholic, brought up very severely in Catholicism, but I think that then she got into this very sort of Café Society group of people, but of rather an intellectual sort, and probably had some false Freudian ideas as well. But she was basically extremely correct.

Letter from Barbara Baekeland to Gloria and James Jones, Undated

New York

My very much missed Joneses—

There is so much to tell you—I feel I'm back in the trap but I'm sort of beginning to enjoy it. When we first arrived Tony & I were in a state of such despair. I missed you—Paris—some kind of human order—but now that old pals begin to hove to, I begin to cheer up a bit, but my God what an inhuman city it is! . . .

Brooks is still crashing about the jungle. Making only 2 kil. a day—hacking his way through with a machete and probably having a very tough time. In the meantime I see my Spanish boyfriend from time to time but I am less and less interested. He has a kind of warmth and tenderness that is very touching and I think knows me better in 2 or 3 weeks than Brooks does after 20 years, but finally the odor becomes oppressive. I think I'd rather sleep with a stranger—and after 20 years my husband still is! . . .

Anyway I've decided to come back in Feb.—no matter what—and I am going to try to *do* something this fall. Rather like a plant struggling up through a yard of cement but maybe there will be a small flower.

Just came back from a fancy lunch at Pavillon with Ben Sonnenberg, Italians, etc. Life is gay—I'm a new arrival! In fact I find social success can be predicated on the notion that one must *always* have more an air of arrival than of departure. I intend to cultivate this for my gray hairs.

Kisses & hugs. How is Kaylie? Her little face on the balcony as she watched us drive off I see as clearly as if she were in my arms. Kiss her for me.

X
B.

From the Diaries of John Philip Cohane, Unpublished

Tuesday. We went to a teeming late evening party given by Ben Sonnenberg, a wonderful, erudite, close friend who owns the

Stuyvesant Fish house in Gramercy Park, probably one of the best-designed houses in New York, overflowing with incredible paintings and etchings, not to mention several hundred guests including Aschwin and Simone Lippe, Charles and Helen Rolo, Gilbert and Polly Kahn, and Barbara Baekeland, solitary and wild-eyed.

PETER GIMBEL

Once at Jack Cohane's house Barbara put her arm around my neck and tried to wrestle me to the floor to force me to have it *her* way— she'd gotten angry at me because I didn't agree with her about something.

Here she was, hanging on to me. I didn't try to shake her or push her or anything. I was so mad I just wanted to let her humiliate herself. Finally she started to giggle, because she saw how really absurd it was.

Let me tell you something more about why I felt taken advantage of by Brooks. Having shown up for the expedition as close to the time of departure as was possible—I mean, just in time to help me with the last of the preparations and to go through his parachute training—what did Brooks do shortly after the expedition but leave again for Europe. Leaving me to mop up. And oh God, the mopping up! You can't imagine—information the *Geographic* wanted, returning equipment to the people who supplied us, filling out reports, just a lot of busy work. But believe me, that's very much the way he is. You know, he's never asked me why I feel the way I do about our partnership. Looking back, I suppose he did me a kind of favor, because from that period of my life on, I've never been somebody who's been particularly easy to take advantage of.

PETER LAKE

Brooks got to be a god on our expedition! No, seriously, for a few minutes he *was*. About two-thirds of the way into the trip Peter Gimbel, Jack Joerns, and I were drinking from the river when we were surprised by some Indians who had snuck up behind us with bows and arrows and were clearly going to kill us—they thought we were evil spirits or something. And then Brooks came up from behind and surprised *them*. Now these Indians didn't have any facial hair, they had long straight black hair on their heads, and they were short, and there, suddenly, was Brooks—you know, tall, bald, with a gray beard. We got this letter about a year later from some missionaries that said the Indians had thought Brooks was some kind of god and that that's why they had spared us.

BROOKS BAEKELAND

The arrow that kills you is shot by an enemy you never see.

I only killed one human—an old man sitting with his back to a tree by a bridge in Germany. There had still been no Hiroshima, but there had been, I think, the awful Hamburg and Dresden and Cologne. About Himmler's gas chambers, we dewy youths still knew nothing. I had already decided that if I were sent on fighter bombers, to bomb "targets of opportunity"—that is, French and German towns—I would try to destroy cabbages and potatoes rather than young mothers and children.

He was reading a newspaper. He was wearing a bowler hat. We were "attacking" the bridge. My stream of .50 caliber bullets from four wing guns hit him before I even saw him and by mistake, and his bowler hat rolled slowly across the bridge. This was just before the end of the war.

I mourn for that old man still.

From the *New York Times,* December 2, 1963

FINANCIER TELLS OF TREK IN ANDES
He and Friends Explored Unknown Areas of Peru
By JOHN SIBLEY

Two New York investment bankers, G. Brooks Baekeland and Peter R. Gimbel, have returned to tame office routine after a grueling 90-day expedition through previously unexplored wilds of the Peruvian Andes. . . .

Why do men do it?

"I don't know," Mr. Baekeland mused. "I'm one of those people who's always driving up a little dirt road."

PETER GABLE

Tony and I were still in school at the time but we decided that nothing would do but that we go along on the expedition. Why not? We were two healthy, active seventeen-year-olds. So we bearded his fa-

ther with this idea—you know, "What do you think of the notion
that we tag along and fall out of the sky with you and Mr. Gimbel?"
We'd spent so much time fantasizing about how much fun it would
be, what an adventure—I mean, Tony's father was a swashbuckler
from the word go. Anyway, the thing I remember most about his
response was his distinct lack of enthusiasm—not about our participating in the project, because, of course, how could a responsible
parent be enthusiastic about that? But he wasn't even willing to play
along with us. He didn't say, "I don't think it's such a hot idea
because . . ." or "Gee, that's a great idea *but* . . ." He just said no.
End of case.

I saw Tony only a handful of times after 1963. We really did just
do different things. I mean, I went off to college. In the early seventies sometime, I bumped into his grandmother, Mrs. Daly, on the
street and she gave me Tony's address in England.

HEATHER COHANE

I went to see him quite a lot in Broadmoor. The first years he was
there I couldn't go because I was living in Ireland and very involved
in my knitwear business and I hardly had time to even visit my children at school in England. But as soon as Jack and I sold our house
in Ireland and went to live in London, I started to go to see Tony
very regularly. Because I loved him and because I remembered him
as a very gentle boy in Ansedonia. Jack would never go with me,
because he suffered from claustrophobia—he was afraid of getting
locked in.

What riveted me about Broadmoor was, you could not tell who
was the inmate and who was the visitor because the inmates were
dressed in ordinary clothes. There'd be, you see, two men sitting at a
table and I'd say to myself, Now *which* one is the madman? And
when the bell clanged, meaning visiting hours were over, I would
jump to my feet to see who the inmates were, because they would be
going off through one door and the visitors would be going out the
other. And I practically never got it right! And this is the thing that
fascinated me, and I decided that we were all mad.

Tony told me he went berserk once at Broadmoor because something annoyed him and that he was put in one of the solitary cells for
a couple of days. He also said that he got beaten up once, I can't
remember why. But a nice thing is he did develop a very good friend
in there, I presume a lover. I don't think the friend had any parents

or anything. It was rather a sad story—you know, nobody to worry about trying to get him out. In fact, he's still there. You see, in Broadmoor you have no hope if there isn't somebody campaigning the whole time to get you out. I remember Tony saying that if he ever got out of Broadmoor he would miss his friend very much.

Once I took my daughter Ondine to see him on her way back to school—she was at a boarding school called the Manor House in Wiltshire. She wanted to go with me to see him, though she was only eight at the time. Jack and I had told her what had happened—I mean, she grew up knowing that Tony had killed his mother.

ONDINE COHANE

There was a lot of clanging. I'll never forget all those gates clanging behind us. I liked him. He was nice. But I didn't talk to him much because I was upset about having to go back to school, so I just listened. He talked about his inmates—the people in his cell—and what they were allowed to do. He told us the rules. My mother told him I loved animals, so he told me about his chicken when he was small and how he used to take it around with him. I felt very sorry for him. I didn't like to think of him behind all those gates and everything. He wrote my mother later that I was rather a sad little girl, but I was mostly sad to be going back to school.

HEATHER COHANE

One day I decided that I should take my son Alexander, who in fact was Barbara's godson, to see Tony. He was at a very impressionable age, you see—seventeen—and at Eton, and, you know, there were drugs and all sorts of other things around and available. So I thought it was a very good idea to show him what could happen to you if you did take drugs.

WILLIE DRAPER

Tony was destroyed by drugs, but the drugs were just the means, not the cause. When I was at St. Paul's School in New Hampshire, he would send me hashish from Paris, wrapped in tinfoil in an envelope. It was a whole different scene then. Nobody at school knew anything even about marijuana in 1963. Believe me. *Nothing. Nobody.* But then pot and all the hallucinogens began to be used in very creative ways, you know. Tony and I would pretend to be sea turtles on the beach in East Hampton where his parents used to rent a house sometimes when they came back from Europe for a couple of months. At this point it was only pot, and we didn't do it all the time—we weren't potheads or anything. I mean, you can't even begin to relate it to the way people smoke pot now. We didn't do it as a social thing at all.

ALEXANDER COHANE

We drove down from London one Sunday, Mummy and me, just the two of us, and we went through the main gate and then, you know, he came through into this sort of visitor's lounge. He was taller than me, he was about six foot. Quite good-looking. I mean, a handsome man he probably would have been if he'd been out in the street walking along. We sat down and we just started talking, and we gave him a packet of cigarettes and a whole load of apples and oranges, sort of a selection of goodies—you know, what we sort of call in England "tuck."

We must have been with him about three hours. He talked the whole time. He told us every detail about killing his mother. I wish I'd had a tape recorder with me, because, you know, I've never known anyone who killed anyone else. He said she had pissed him off—you know, done something to annoy him—and that he just picked up the knife in the kitchen and said, "You've destroyed my life. I'm a wasted human being."

He also said to us, "It's ruined my life in several ways to be in here." And he said that it was just absolutely hopeless and depressing to look out at the countryside and not be part of it. Then I remember him very clearly saying, "I feel my mother's presence around me all the time, I love her so much. She's in every tree."

8

POSSESSIONS

After Tony Baekeland had been at Broadmoor for three years, he began to wonder if he would ever be allowed to leave. "He was showing great improvement," says Miwa Svinka-Zielinski. "He sounded quite reasonable on the whole, and he even began to consider what he might do if he got out. He told me he thought perhaps he would teach."

But even though Tony might be feeling better, the legal obstacles surrounding his release were still tremendous. An average stay at Broadmoor is six or seven years, but some patients—and Tony was one of them—are there under restrictions that make it all but impossible to leave. In Tony's case, not only would Dr. Gogarty have to be convinced he was completely well, but the Home Secretary would have to concur that a discharge was in the best interests of society as well as the patient. It was not unusual for cases as complex as Tony's to be bound up in red tape for years.

"I've got a patient who's been here for seventeen years," Dr. Gogarty points out. "And sometimes a patient may need to stay for twenty." According to a former superintendent at Broadmoor: "Half the patients would be perfectly safe to release but the problem is to know which half." In fact, out of its population of approximately 750, Broadmoor releases an average of 104 patients a year.

Early in 1976, Tony told a visitor, "I would like to come to New York if I could see Dr. Greene instead of being hospitalized." After a visit that Dr. and Mrs. Greene made to Tony that year, they discussed at length with Broadmoor authorities the practical difficulties that would be involved in his rehabilitation: He had no relatives, except for Mrs. Daly, who was elderly and frail, who were willing to take responsibility for him.

Letter from Antony Baekeland to Miwa Svinka-Zielinski, February 19, 1976

Broadmoor

Dear Miwa,

I have discovered Buddhism and it has helped me tremendously in my attitude to Life. Before, I was forever chasing after things, never satisfied for long and always let down in the end. Now that I have stopped grasping and clinging to the world and the ideas and concepts of the mind I feel free and peaceful as never before. I have completely stopped forcing myself to do things but just accept them now as they come to me. The Ego, that horrible giant-dwarf, which ruled Life like a childish tyrant, forever posturing and imagining and suffering, is melting away like the Wicked Witch in *Dorothy and the Wizard of Oz*. I wish more people could become acquainted with this wonderful doctrine. It is truly a panacea, the end of all suffering.

I will write to Fred Baekeland, my uncle, who is a psychiatrist, and ask him to write to the doctors here for me to see if I can get some treatment. I feel much better than when you last came, and feel that I will soon be well.

I have some dreams to tell you. The first one is that I sense the wish to come home in an intense religious experience. Next, I am naked in a hailstorm in an Indian valley hotel—nobody seems to mind my nakedness and I finally get my clothes back. Then I dreamed that Barbara Hale had cut the back of my neck open so I could breathe, and then I dreamed that I was eating more so that I could come home. I think you must realize what I mean by home. And lastly I dreamed that I was in Paris with Nini buying clothes for my wedding.

I must end here—there is so little to tell you except my

dreams. I write them out in the middle of the night—there is no light, so sometimes in the morning I have trouble deciphering them.

Love,
Tony

MICHAEL EDWARDS

We moved around in much the same group of people in Paris, and in due course, when I decided to move back to London, they—Barbara particularly—wanted to rent my flat at 45, quai de Bourbon. They'd been living on rue Barbet de Jouy for four or five years by then. I had already rented the flat to somebody but when it became available I let them have it—inexpensively, I might add—on the condition that I could stay there myself whenever I liked and that if I needed to have a party there, they would plan to be away that night. This arrangement worked out very well for all of us, and I must say they lived there reasonably happily for a while. The house belonged to Prince Antoine Bibesco, who had been such a great friend of Proust's, and I remember that *that* pleased Barbara.

My flat was the *entresol* of the house and it was perfectly suitable for *me*, but I mean, for *them*, for the two of them living there the whole time, it was a bit small, though I think it was largely she who lived there. Brooks lived there only sometimes. Tony also slept there every now and then but he wasn't around very much that I knew of.

The flat had three rooms—quite a big living room and then a little room next to it which Barbara used as a bedroom—at least I think she did, in due course—and then upstairs it had a little bedroom which was behind a bathroom that was completely Art Deco. The thing about the flat is it has the most marvelous position—it looks out on the Seine on three sides. A glorious view, especially from the bathroom, which is right on the prow.

Letter from Michael Edwards to Barbara Baekeland, June 15, 1965

Dear Barbara,
Thank you for the variety of notes and postscripts which I found dotted about the apartment last weekend. I agree with you that

the dining room has been done up very well and I seem to miss
the dining room table less and less. The material in the little
room should go quite well and I hope it does not clash with the
red of the cover. I understand that the work will be completed
next week.

I hope that all goes well with you in Mexico, but I suspect
that you will be hard put to it to beat Paris in June in fine
weather, but I do not want to make you wistful.

                                                        Fondly,
                                                        Michael

Letter from Barbara Baekeland to Michael Edwards, July 13, 1965

                                                        Tepotzlán
                                                        Morelos
                                                        Mexico

Dear Michael,
You are so right! My heart aches for Paris. For me it is home.
But Brooks has now decided that we should sublet the apartment
for August. Carolina will, of course, stay on and look after the
new tenant.

Brooks was asked quite unexpectedly to join a young French
explorer to visit the ruins of Quintana Roo in Yucatán. Brooks
thinks the trip too interesting to pass up.

I will try to use the August tenant's rent to do up the kitchen.
How did the dressing room turn out?

Mexico is a dream of beauty. We have masses of servants and,
after Europe, it is all very peaceful and tranquil.

                                                        Love,
                                                        Barbara

Johnny Van Kirk
I ran into them in Mexico. I was walking down the street and I just
recognized Tony—the red hair! It was funny. I hadn't seen him for
years and he didn't recognize me. I stopped him, and that's how we
got together.

Tony had these two boyfriends with him. They were American or British, both blond. That's all I remember about them. Tony had run across some pot and we all went off and got high together in this hotel room, high above the main avenue. I remember it had no windows, just sliding glass doors, open to the street fifteen blocks below. And we sat there on the edge of this sheer drop smoking a joint and talking about the old times on Cape Cod.

The Baekelands were staying with this friend of theirs who had a very beautiful ranch and I went out to visit them there. Mostly I just hung around the pool, talking and so on, catching up with Mr. Baekeland's travels and so forth and Mrs. Baekeland's life in Paris.

Letter from Barbara Baekeland to Michael Edwards, August 20, 1965

> Baekeland Camp
> Blue Mountain Lake
> Adirondacks

Dear Michael,

My plan is to come back to Paris and to reoccupy the flat where I expect to be in residence for a protracted length of time—at least until the snow comes. The kitchen is one of the things I will attend to the moment I arrive.

We are here, all three Baekelands, with my mother and 36 other members of the family. Much boating, walking, waterskiing—very pleasant. Except that it's freezing here now, all outside communication impossible, lines all down after a heavy storm last night.

Please, please, please would you attend to the missing tiles in the bathroom? I cannot bear that scar another day.

See you *very* soon.

> Love,
> Barbara

P.S. My mother, Tony & I leave for New York tomorrow where I will be in residence on East 75th for more or less two weeks. I *think* I've got it rented from the 15th on.

ELIZABETH ARCHER BAEKELAND

Barbara used to rent her penthouse out whenever she could, for the money. There was one period when she was renting it to *me*—by the night! I was having an affair with a very powerful dramatic big-businessman, who was married, and I didn't have a place in town and I wanted, you know, to set up a nice ambience for him, which of course that *was*. So she would let me have it at a hundred dollars a night and she would go and stay with her chum Emily Staempfli.

ELIZABETH BLOW

A friend of mine—well, a very vicious woman, who really didn't like Barbara very much—called it a mistress's apartment. It *was* a place where a man would set up a woman. She had all these things in it— that big book on the stand with colored illustrations that was open always at a certain page, that marvelous mirror, the whole decor really, and the terrace where they gave the marvelous dinner parties. But it was not a sort of place to *live* in, it was not a home at all.

Letter from Brooks Baekeland to Michael Edwards, Undated

                                                                45, quai de Bourbon

Dear Michael,

As you know, we have been recently looking for a place to buy here in Paris (otherwise a final return to the USA and purchase of a country house, probably near East Hampton) large enough for a real home and not a *pied-à-terre*. We have found nothing reasonably priced yet and/or with the sort of charm, air, light, quiet and *quartier* that one wants if one is to become an exile— even in Paris. Both Barbara and I are anxious within the next year to settle this living problem once and for all.

                                                                With fond regards,
                                                                Brooks

Letter from Barbara Baekeland to Gloria and James Jones, Undated

Cadaqués

Dear Joneses—

. . . Tomorrow we go to Prades to hear Casals play—& leave on Wednesday for Málaga for a week—after which we join our Greek pals on their yacht & cruise around Ibiza and Formentera.

We'll be out of here by the end of the month and will go to Scotland to stay with Nina, Countess Seafield, who owns most of it, and motor down to London . . . and, I expect, be going through Paris on our way to Switzerland about the 15th—will you be there? . . .

Love to you both—

I miss you,
B.

From *A Family Motor Tour Through Europe*, Leo Hendrik Baekeland, Horseless Age Press, New York, 1907

Most of the time people who travel try to cajole themselves into the belief that they are enjoying themselves, while in reality they are merely spending money right and left in increasing amounts without great satisfaction, or they keep rushing from one country to another in vain search of happiness. I have known such people who from the mere fact of being in a certain city were overcome by ennui, which caused them to move to another place where their implacable tormentor, ennui, followed them as fast as train or automobile could carry them. Such people will ordinarily finish by finding that two or three large capitals in Europe, with very elaborately appointed hotels, agree best with their perverted psychological condition.

BARBARA CURTEIS

Brooks never provided a stable residence for Barbara. From the time he sold the house on Seventy-first Street, they just had little places—

nookeries of great elegance, to be sure. But there was no room—in *any* sense—in any of these places for Tony. He didn't even have a proper bedroom. And Brooks and Barbara were constantly fighting—it was their only form of communication. Tony once said to me, "My parents are both very young souls." I found it a perfectly valid remark, if one excludes the Eastern religiosity of it—he *was* more mature than either of his parents. Barbara really enjoyed making those scenes. If somebody said something she didn't like or even if she didn't like *how* they had said it, she felt morally bound to slap their face or throw whiskey in their face and rush off into the night. And of course, every time Brooks threatened to leave her for another woman, she would try to kill herself.

Letter from Barbara Baekeland to Gloria and James Jones, Undated

45, quai de Bourbon

Dear Joneses—
I wonder if I'll ever be able to demonstrate my friendship & love for you both as you have done for me so many times (I am ashamed to think about it). Anyway, thanks—it was the full moon, I guess, because *nothing* on the outside can ever be *that* bad!

I love you both. . . .

B.

Letter from Brooks Baekeland to Gloria and James Jones, October 14, 1965

1, rue Regrattier

Dear Jim and Gloria—
I guess you don't have to hear from me what I think of what you both did for Barbara the other night. I know that you both love her, and it isn't for me really to thank you. I would not have bothered you, except that for the first time in a long time I felt I was at the end of my rope. I couldn't face all that alone. So it was selfish too. But strangely enough, when I wondered who *I*

could turn to in Paris, there were only yourselves. It was the first time I had felt quite so lonely in this town. So whatever you feel about me, I must be clear to you what I thought about you. And I knew that you were the only two people in the world almost that Barbara wouldn't mind knowing about what she had done—that I could call on without injuring her pride. I also feel the same way.

By noon the next day, B., sitting up in her bed, had the shy expression of Alexander bestriding Europe and Asia. But each time she gets away with this, the more dangerous it is. If Franklin had flown a few more kites, he'd have become a pork crackling. Someday, if Barbara really believes in this kind of ultimate force over the kindhearted (or guilt-susceptible), she is going to make a miscalculation. They all do. She is not half so intelligent as she pretends to herself. It is that which worries me— that and her effect on Tony. He's still awfully young and tied up.

Anyway, thanks. . . .

Brooks

Letter from Brooks Baekeland to Michael Edwards, June 25, 1966

Mexico

Dear Michael—

Off again very soon to the jungles. It occurs to me that you can use a few months' rent in advance.

Barbara and Tony skim northwards within the week for a summer of sea-shoring in East Hampton. I go on July 3 to Lima for 2 weeks of wrestling with customs and then off into the unknown again.

Affectionate regards,
Brooks

Letter from Barbara Baekeland to Michael Edwards, July 10, 1966

New York

Dear Michael—

Enclosed your check for gas, electric, telephone, etc.

Brooks left for Peru on Sunday. Tony, my mother, and I are installed at East Hampton—pleasant but all too familiar, except for the beach which is superb.

Affectionately,
Barbara

FRANCESCA DRAPER LINKE

One time in East Hampton Tony tried to paint himself blue at my parents' house. He had this wonderful idea about everyone going blue, this beautiful beautiful shade of blue, and how you'd see these blue people at the chicest places, and everyone would *want* to be blue—there'd be signs saying "Go Blue." So he went and bought some dye and then he got in the bathtub and tried to get blue, but he came out kind of a mottled greenish blue, and then we went down to the beach and he put all this seaweed on him, and we walked on the sand and he was Neptune—he was very into Neptune. And later we stayed up all night playing music. It was really a magical time. That was when he was still on the great creative fringe. I mean, we all thought Tony was like a god.

From a Psychiatric Report on Antony Baekeland Ordered by the British Courts, January 5, 1973

He had few qualms accepting the notion that he was a very special person. During the time he was in a London tutoring school, he saw a psychoanalyst for four months. Following his discontinuance of this school, his last schooling, he lived something of an aimless existence, writing and painting, living in various places such as India and Nepal, with a lot of time spent in Cadaqués on Spain's Costa Brava, and traveling around on no set schedule.

Letter from Barbara Baekeland to Gloria and James Jones, Undated

Cadaqués

Dear Joneses—

. . . The Gare d'Austerlitz was an *abattoir* when we finally arrived—God how I loathe masses of French, German, American, Jew, Negroes, everyone. Couldn't possibly have found a porter and couldn't lift the valise myself. A kind "adjuster of train wheels" helped me and put me in a first-class carriage! . . .

Love to you both,
B.

KAREN RADKAI

Cadaqués was not far from Paris. You went to Gare d'Austerlitz and took the night train and the next morning at nine-thirty you were in Port Bou and you took a taxi and you were in Cadaqués by ten—do you see what I mean?

Now in those days Cadaqués was extraordinary. I remember the first thing I saw was a girl on a white horse riding through the center of town, with wonderful long blond hair flowing out behind her. It was Lorna Moffat, Tony's great friend—he used to bring her all the time to my house.

What we always did in Cadaqués is we had a picnic, daily, with these wonderful chickens and all these fantastic Spanish salads—chick-peas mixed with tuna fish, you know. My picnics were famous. The cooking I did outside on the open fire. I gathered the wood on the beach, one of the way-off beaches. There was thyme growing by the bushes, so all you had to do, you know, was throw the chicken with the thyme on a little fire and have a wonderful thing going. And you'd come home at five in the afternoon and take a nap and then go out for dinner at ten—that was sort of the life we led, you know.

LOUISE DUNCAN

The routine is you get up at ten or eleven, you go to one of the two cafés and put your face in the sun to get over your hangover, and then you stagger back up the hill at around four o'clock for lunch and then you stagger back down to the other café.

KAREN RADKAI

Meliton's was the café where you played chess. My son used to play with Duchamp. He was small, he was only nine. He learned a lot of good chess there. Man Ray used to come to visit Duchamp and he played very good chess, too.

It was a little group, you see. That part was very nice. But the other part I just couldn't stand—there were a lot of psychotic aspects to Cadaqués. The whole town was sordid.

I was first in Cadaqués for *Vogue*, to photograph Melina Mercouri, who was doing a film there. Diana Vreeland was then editor-in-chief of *Vogue* and she said to me—you know how fantastic *she* is—"Get Melina on the beach in a bathing suit with Dalí putting eggs of emeralds and rubies in her hand!" So Melina says to me, "Darling, I can never get into those bathing suits, I'm not Brigitte Bardot, you know." So then I had to go and see Dalí and see if *he* would cooperate. I'd met him already once, in '51, in Venice, at the *Bal de Bestigui*, Charles de Bestigui's great ball at the Palazzo Labia, which I was photographing for *Harper's Bazaar*—Cecil Beaton was doing it for *Vogue*. And Dalí was so charming and nice then, I can't tell you—just like a perfectly normal human being. Now, of course, he's so corrupt he's close to being—I don't know what, dear—Hitler, you know.

So I went up to his house in Port Lligat—that's the twin village to Cadaqués. You went by the cemetery of Cadaqués to get there, in those days over a dirt road. Dalí had an interesting house, it was old. As I walked in he gave me some pink champagne and he said, "Come with me, I will show you my studio," and he showed me this enormous, strange room, sort of octagonal almost it was. He said, "Here is where I masturbate." He thought I was going to be shocked, you know, but I just paid no attention.

And Dalí set the tone for the whole village.

Letter from Barbara Baekeland to Gloria and James Jones, Undated

Cadaqués

Dear Jim and Gloria,

 . . . This place is surreal and very fake except for the natives who loathe everyone and cast a spell on us all. The morals are so crappy & awful & hypocritical that you *can't* take them seriously—the cripple being helped in and out of the boat by the mistress of her gigolo husband who loathes them both and tries to attack, each night, the baby-sitter who is Tony's girl and tells him everything. Balthusian symbols abound and *trompeurs* and pleasure-seeking. Marvelous!

I swim in the sea, comtemplate suicide, think that somehow I must do something to justify something and I don't even know what it is!

Anyway it's the classic Mediterranean summer. Not for the likes of me. I need the cool northern fogs & tides to keep me sane.

X.
B.

Elsa Mottar

The whole thing was just so impossible, you know—one just didn't know what to do with Barbara. You never knew what was going to happen next, so whenever she appeared on the scene, everybody's nose would be out of joint. She and Brooks were always flying away from each other and then coming back together again, and it was a totally mixed-up relationship that you could never make heads or tails of. I mean, you didn't know if they were really interested in each other or if they just stayed together because of Tony.

George Staempfli

I remember one scene at Barbara Curteis's. She had a terrace outside her bedroom, and that's where she gave all her parties—it had a wonderful view of the harbor. And Brooks was there one night and Barbara Baekeland suddenly appeared downstairs and marched into the house and he had to flee over the rooftops—literally! Another night Barbara Baekeland was found wandering around the streets of Cadaqués stark naked.

Daphne Hellman

I was visiting Lily Auchincloss in Cadaqués and I saw Brooks in an open car, with his head in his hands, as if in despair. He was just sitting in the parked car, right outside the place they were renting. He said to me, "Go up and speak to Barbara. I can't." And when I knocked at the door she thought at first I was Brooks and wouldn't let me in, but when she realized it was me, she let me in and said, "Get me a drink. Brooks won't get me a drink." She was in a very peculiar state. But then later that summer I went on a couple of picnics with the two of them and things had gotten more peaceable.

THILO VON WATZDORF

Remember that book *Piano Mécanique* by François Rey? They made a film of it. It was really a lousy book but it did show Cadaqués in the mid and late sixties, a mixture of Saint-Tropez and the Rome of *La Dolce Vita*. It was just the worst place at that time for a kid of that age who was very impressionable.

SYLVIE BAEKELAND SKIRA

When I first met Tony, that summer of '67, he was very much in love with a young man in Cadaqués—Jake Cooper, a great beauty. Jake was the type who would stop in the middle of town and oil his body, and he always had a court of young men around him—Tony Kinna, Ernst von Wedel, people like that.

Tony was, let's say, a basically well-brought-up little boy, and he was mixing with a whole crowd that was rather shabby. In Cadaqués everyone mixes—it's the great joy of people who usually have regular lives and in summer suddenly they are with people who are not their sort and it's very exciting. *Voilà.* So Tony was seeing people who were not his sort and they were taking a lot of money from him, of course. And he came totally under Jake Cooper's spell.

ELIZABETH BLOW

I'd heard that there was a man who was exerting a tremendous influence over him in Cadaqués and I think probably this was the beginning of Tony's collapse mentally.

PICO HARNDEN

Jake Cooper was known around Cadaqués as Black Jake. He was a very handsome Australian who first appeared on the scene as the lover of a woman called Erika Svenssen. She was sort of the sex goddess of Cadaqués and he was the black prince, if you like. He was a tall dark guy who wore a silver earring in his left ear and went around in washed-out jeans and Afghan belts, without a shirt on, and every woman in Cadaqués was amazed by his beauty and his bravado, and the next thing that happened was that Jake Cooper and Tony Baekeland took up together—much to Erika's chagrin.

ERIKA SVENSSEN

I was nine years in Cadaqués and that was my favorite summer, you know? It was so important, that summer. I was at the age then that I thought I was still twenty-one. I hadn't gone into the other generation yet. I still think I haven't.

Jake was like a devil. He had a Svengali thing. He had a power over people. He was always causing incredible jealousies and things—people turned against each other. He moved into this farm, this abandoned farm, and he had a sort of entourage, you know, of strange people. They were heavy into trying out mushrooms and drugs in general, and he was also delving into things—whether he got them out of books or what, I don't know, but I know he kept meeting people, secret people. I think he practiced black magic. He wore little bones and things on his vest. Certain little bones. I would ask him about them and he just wouldn't tell me, you know. He would say "my magic amulets" or something. I'd never seen any sort of formation of that kind of bones before—the way they were put together. He wore them dangling on his vest, you know. He wore them all the time and all kinds of people that he had around him died. There was a young boy who died. I think there were three who died who were around him. I think he put some kind of spell on them.

Jake was a friend of Salvador Dalí. They were making a film together—one of those Dalí-type films showing angels and monsters together, the power that the devil would have over the angel and yet the angel would win out.

Jake had an absolutely wonderful side to him, too, which was innocent and fun and sweet. It was magical again, but in a good sense.

I remember when Jake and I first met Tony Baekeland. I have a visual picture of the first time we saw him—of his freckles and his red hair, and the sun on him—his body and the whole thing. I can see him in front of me right now!

BARBARA CURTEIS

One day Tony said to me, "You've got to put a picnic together." By this time he was not doing anything at all, and the devil finds work, as they say. So we went down to the beach and picnicked. And a terrible man in black leather, looking like Tony's Nemesis, came down the beach and fed Tony drugs, and Tony became his thing, his creature. He went right on taking drugs, he went off to Morocco with this man and they brought back belladonna and Tony ate the whole thing himself and disappeared under one's eyes to a blob of quivering jelly.

PICO HARNDEN

Tony and Jake showed up on their way back from Morocco, with God knows how many kilos of hash. My parents were away, and Jake and Tony made brownies in the kitchen. They turned on the entire house—*everyone*, my little sisters, my brother Mishka, the maids, the dog, consumed these brownies to such a degree that by the time my parents came back everybody was still completely passed out. Jake and Tony had taken off. They were living together in this house that Duchamp had had at one point, right by the water—one floor.

Later that summer I was at Meliton's and Jake came in and put six or seven cactus leaves down on the table next to my drink. I asked him what he was carrying cactus leaves around for and he said that he fucked them and I said, "Now wait a minute!" He said, "I'll show you." And he went and got a knife from the bar and sliced the base of one of the leaves open, then he took my hand and stuck it up to my wrist in the cactus and pulled it out, then he put it back in again.

One day our doorbell rang and Tony was at the door. He ran upstairs in a complete state, he went running straight to my father who was sitting in a chair, you know, and hid behind the chair. My father said, "Listen, Tony, come out from behind there and just sit down and be civilized." And he said, "You've got to help me—Jake Cooper is after me! If he comes, just say I'm not here—*please!*" And sure enough, at that very moment, Jake Cooper is downstairs in the street screaming at the top of his voice, "Tooooooony"—this really very seductive sort of rutting call—and Tony is shaking. And of course, my father called down, "Tony's not here at the moment," and Jake took off.

JAKE COOPER

Ah, it's an end-of-the-road-like village, Cadaqués. It's a town that has rocks, stones, of a special quality all around, and people going there, usually after a very short while, after their second day there sometimes, go through very tense strange feelings. Quite a lot of people get very upset. It's a trapped feeling. I remember Dalí used to say it was something under the ground that could make men sterile and that made them very nervous. There was some great strange energy there in Cadaqués. I think it's one of the most special little towns I've ever seen.

I was called Black Jake, I suppose because I dressed in black. A girl who I used to be involved with—actually, she gave me the first acid trip I ever took—said I should throw all my clothes away and that I should just wear black and silver, and—I don't know—that's what happened. Friends took all my clothes to a flea market—they got rid of all my tweeds and things like that, and for many many years I did just wear black and silver.

I was with Erika Svenssen and we were sitting on the terrace of a little café and just behind us was somebody who said a few words to Erika and this person was sitting next to Antony Baekeland, and that's the first time I saw Antony. I saw him quite a lot after that and then we went together to Morocco and then we got this little house for ourselves in Cadaqués.

Antony was involved in extreme yoga then. In winter he used to sit naked in front of the open window, doing breathing exercises—first through one nostril, then the other—following the Tibetan Book of the Dead.

He painted quite a lot and he was always painting the eye of an eagle. That eye he used to reproduce and reproduce. He painted it once on the wall of our house. I think it's been painted over.

One day he got spaced out of his own head and went to walk in the mountains and it was quite stormy weather. And when he came back, he was in a very high state from his walk in the storm. He said he was going to have a shower at a friend's place because there wasn't any hot water in our house, and it was quite cold. So I said okay, and while he was out having his shower his mother turned up from Switzerland. She said, "I'm Antony Baekeland's mother and I've come to take him away." And I was really taken aback, I didn't know what was happening. She said it again, "I've come to take him away," then she said, "Where are his things?" She just took a few of his things, not really even the things that he used very much. She just took odds and ends. "I'm going to take Tony now," she kept saying. "We're leaving today. I've just arrived and I'm going. Tony and I are going today." And then she disappeared up the road to where he was having his shower. And she took him back with her to Switzerland and then off to that island—Mallorca. And I never saw Antony again till Broadmoor.

BARBARA CURTEIS

I had telephoned Barbara in Gstaad when I saw the state Tony was in and she came back to Cadaqués to fetch him. Brooks was in Ibiza and *wouldn't* come. And the next day, the day after she was meant to have taken Tony back with her to Gstaad, I was on my way to Barcelona and stopped in some café—and saw Barbara's hired car coming from the south and going in the opposite direction to Switzerland. They had indeed set out the previous day but it turned out that Tony didn't have his passport with him, and Barbara had said to the authorities at the frontier, "*My* son doesn't need a passport." I mean, even Barbara admitted she'd been pretty offensive— she'd kicked and spat and so forth. Anyway, the two of them were taken off in a paddy wagon, and they spent the night in jail in Gerona, the provincial capital of that end of Catalonia—he in the male and she in the female jail. "Oh, a *charming* jail!" Barbara said. "*Perfectly* delightful!" And then she made a remark I'll never forget, it has a sort of echoing horror for me. She told me proudly that she'd said to Tony as they were being led away in handcuffs, "Here you are, darling, at *last*—manacled to Mummy!"

9

CALLING IT QUITS

In 1977, an unofficial committee of concerned friends of Tony Baekeland began looking into the possibility of having him freed. The group consisted of Heather and Jack Cohane, Michael Alexander, Miwa Svinka-Zielinski, and the Hon. Hugo Money-Coutts, whose family controlled London's exclusive Coutts Bank, and whose wife, Jinty, was the daughter of the Baekelands' old friend Rosemary Rodd Baldwin.

Tony's aunt, Elizabeth Archer Baekeland, who was living in London at the time, refused to be drawn into the group. She says, "The people who were helping Tony all believed that his violence was spent when he killed his mother. But Tony's uncle, Fred Baekeland, my former husband, always believed the exact opposite. He said to me, 'Nonsense. Tony's capable of killing other people. He's highly dangerous and always will be, so don't ever try to get him out of Broadmoor.'"

Of the unofficial committee, Miwa Svinka-Zielinski alone recognized the need for caution in the selection of a hospital for Tony if and when he was discharged from Broadmoor and repatriated. "I believed," she states, "that Tony had a classic love/hate relationship with his mother and that his sickness was absolutely only connected

to her. I was convinced, after seeing him all those years in Broadmoor, that his illness would not surface again."

Official Visitors File, Broadmoor Special Hospital, May 14, 1976

VISITOR'S NAME: Mrs. Nina Daly
RELATIONSHIP TO PATIENT: Grandmother
SUMMARY: Thinks he looks and behaves so much better than
last year. There's no one who has any interest in sponsoring him
outside hospital, either in U.K. or U.S.A., in his welfare, or
who would be prepared to spend a penny on him, except herself, and she is not well off. She was informed that there is no
certain date by which Tony will be discharged.

BROOKS BAEKELAND

I had reason to hope that Tony's mind might clear one day in the
peace and quiet of Broadmoor Hospital where he had friends and
where, he repeatedly told me, he was happy.

Many people with his symptoms had, after the age of forty—for
reasons as mysterious as schizophrenia itself—gradually become calm
and peaceful citizens. I was hoping for that. Occasionally he still
wrote me violent, paranoidal letters, which I forwarded to his doctors. They worried me—not for myself but for him, since some English and American friends with strings to high places were trying to
get him set free. It was a sentimental, well-meaning movement—
which worked and was tragic in its consequences. I was against all
their energetic and romantic efforts to open the cage door for this
gifted hawk who I feared would soon swoop down on some helpless
prey.

Official Visitors File, Broadmoor Special Hospital, May 24, 1977

VISITOR'S NAME: Mrs. Nina Daly
RELATIONSHIP TO PATIENT: Grandmother
SUMMARY: Saw Mrs. Daly in waiting room and she is more frail
and in a wheelchair.

Official Visitors File, Broadmoor Special Hospital, June 3, 1977

> VISITOR'S NAME: Michael Alexander
> RELATIONSHIP TO PATIENT: No blood relationship
> SUMMARY: Has known Tony Baekeland since 12 years. Was very close to family prior to and after the time of the manslaughter. Mr. Alexander was helpful, clear, and incisive. Is eager to help in whatever way he can, especially if repatriation is sought.

Letter from Antony Baekeland to Miwa Svinka-Zielinski, November 3, 1977

Broadmoor

Dear Miwa,

I hope very much to be discharged before too long. I have some dreams to tell you. The first one was that I was with a great friend of mine who was building a house and I remember watching him put pink stucco on a wall. The next was that again I can fly. I let loose a bird at Michael Alexander's house—later we became brothers. Next I dream that a man accuses me and René Teillard of confessing one another: I associate this with Life prior to the French Revolution. My last dream was that my father lives with Sylvie in a mountain chalet—he scolds me but later forgives me.

I try nowadays to be less careless and more careful in the things I do.

All the best.

Love,
Tony

Letter from Barbara Baekeland to Michael Edwards, October 14, 1967

Dear Michael,

Two important items: Carolina says you are coming on the 25th. I have a cook laid on and wondered if you might not like to have her do a dinner for *you*? She's an angel and very good—can do a marvelous curry with almonds, figs, bananas, etc. I order a sorbet from that marvelous place, have smoked salmon first, and it's a delicious repast—with Carolina she can do 14.

Wednesday night I gave a small dinner for Marcel and Teenie Duchamp, and Sunday 15 for dinner when Tony arrives with a *friend*! Am so pleased!!

Duncan Longcope

I remember Barbara telling me that Tony had a girl and that she liked her a lot. She referred to her as Robin Redbreast. Just in fun—I mean, you know, that sort of verve of Barbara's. She said, "Oh, isn't it nice that Tony has a girlfriend!"

Sylvie Baekeland Skira

It's easier to say to your mother and to your father that you have a girlfriend than a boyfriend. When they said to him "Where were you tonight?" it was easier to say "I was with Sylvie" than "I was with Jake." I can honestly say that Tony used me as a screen—a smoke-screen for all the shady parts of his life. I mean his boyfriends, who he couldn't very well present to his parents.

After that summer in Cadaqués we came back to Paris—I mean Tony came back and I came back—and I received a phone call from him saying please come and have dinner at his parents'. And I thought, Two grouchy parents. . . . I'd never met the parents.

I was quite young, perhaps younger than my years, and I saw Brooks and I thought he was the most dashing man I'd ever seen, and I saw Barbara and I thought she was the prettiest woman I'd ever seen. Usually with a couple there's one very handsome and then a toad right next to it. But they were both so handsome. They were dazzling. And I certainly never thought that Brooks would look at me because to me he was a grown-up, he was forty-seven and he was married and that was it.

They started inviting me to all their dinners. I was the "nice young thing" that you put at table and so forth.

There was a game between Brooks and Barbara that was very near to *Who's Afraid of Virginia Woolf?*—a great game in public, you know, where he would drive her to tears on a little matter. I mean, they wouldn't go *too* far but she would have very pretty tears and he would say, "Look how good she looks with tears! Doesn't she look handsome with tears?" That sort of thing. Which made me feel that I was sort of part of *Les Liaisons Dangereuses*, and what were they going to do with me, these two. I felt like a puppet between their hands.

DUNCAN LONGCOPE

Robin Redbreast or whatever her name was was staying in the same hotel that I was living in, the Hôtel Saint-Louis on the rue Saint-Louis en Lille. I assumed that Tony had, you know, visiting privileges, but one day I saw him knocking on her door and in a sort of pleading tone asking to be let in, and this went on for a long period, but the door did not open, as I remember, and he went away. I did one day see Brooks there, which sort of surprised me.

Letter from Brooks Baekeland to Michael Edwards, Undated

> Mon cher—
> I suppose you are zipping about the planet as usual? I am bacheloring here for a few days while B. skis in Switzerland with a pack of lusty females.
>
> Affectionately,
> Brooks

SYLVIE BAEKELAND SKIRA

Barbara couldn't stand to be in any one place for long. It was October, then it was November, November was boring, so she decided she would have to go skiing, and it was when she left to go skiing that finally Brooks called me. I couldn't believe it, because then it *meant* something. We went out to dinner together, on the Île Saint-Louis, and we had, I have to admit, a wonderful time. We spoke . . . *he* spoke and I was fascinated, I can tell you—and that evening I absolutely fell in love.

I stopped being the family friend very soon after that. I couldn't stand it, because on one side I was in love with Brooks and on the other side Barbara had taken a liking to me and she was trying to arrange things between Tony and me—romantic things. She thought that I should consider him as a nice future husband. She kept telling me that one day Tony would be a very rich young man.

She didn't know about me and Brooks. She didn't want to know, of course. Not only that, but I think that she thought that *I* certainly was not anything to beware of.

Letter from Barbara Baekeland to Michael Edwards, November 27, 1967

45, quai de Bourbon

Dearest Michael—
We are in the middle of making a whole series of decisions—should we buy a large property in Mallorca and build on it, or should we build a small house next to the Bordeaux-Groults at Cadaqués—an *endroit* that seems to have a fatal fascination for us! We are spending Xmas there in Emily Staempfli's house—very snug, very expensive, with my mother who is flying to Barcelona to join us. Tony is already there and his little robin, Sylvie, comes, too, along with Michael Alexander. Should be very gay.

Always affec.—
Barbara

MICHAEL ALEXANDER
I was staying with them the Christmas Tony brought Sylvie down as a guest. She was *his* girlfriend originally. And in fact, Brooks took her over. I think it was a quite quick take-over. I think it was going on all the time I was staying there.

Letter from Michael Edwards to Barbara Baekeland, February 2, 1968

Dear Barbara,
. . . You will be glad to hear that your clock has now arrived back in good working order and I shall be bringing it over to Paris on my next trip. Talking of this, I am provisionally think-

ing of the weekend of the 24th February, so could you let me
know what your plans are for skiing.

GLORIA JONES

On February 24th, Barbara tried to commit suicide. I spent the day
with her—she was packing to go to Klosters, she was happy, and all
her friends kept running in and out, you know. She had some very
fancy women friends, lovely friends who loved her. De Croy—she
was a good friend of hers, she was darling. The lady who took care of
her dog. The Princesse de Croy her name was.

Then at seven o'clock—I think the train leaves at seven-thirty for
Klosters—the telephone rang and it was Barbara saying, "I'm going
ski-i-i-i-i-iiiiiing," and then there was silence and I knew something
terrible had happened, I just knew it, and I screamed, "Barbara, what
have you done, what have you done?" Then I *ran*—it's about, you
know, three blocks—and I guess she'd left the door open and I burst
in and there she was—she'd got herself dressed up beautifully in a
nightgown and her beautiful beige robe—and she was absolutely
gone. She looked dead. I really thought she was dead. I started to
scream and I couldn't, I'd lost my voice, so then I started jumping up
and down for the lady underneath to hear, and finally I was able to
scream. And then I dialed my house and said to my daughter Kaylie,
"Tell Daddy to come as fast as he can." And then the lady downstairs
ran up and we called the Hôtel-Dieu, the public hospital on the Île
de la Cité, which is just around the corner, and we also called the
American Hospital in Neuilly, and they said they were on their way,
too. But the Hôtel-Dieu got there right away. The doctor ran in and
he said, "Well, there's no heartbeat—nothing." So he jabbed her
with a needle—I think in her chest—God believe me, I don't
know—and then by that time Jim was there and we both went in the
ambulance with her.

From *The Merry Month of May,* James Jones, Delacorte Press, New York, 1971

. . . She called me again that evening, around about eight-fif-
teen. . . . There was a peculiar sing-song to her voice, a flat
quality.

"Louisa? Louisa? Louisa, are you all right?" I said.

"Oh, yes," she said. "Oh, yes. Oh, yes, I'm fine. I'm going to Switzerland."

"You're what?" I demanded. "Switzerland?"

"Oh yes," she said. "Switzerland. . . . St. Moritz. And you can meet everybody. At least, everyone who is anybody. And you can ski. You can ski off the tops of the mountains there. You know. Right off the tops of them, and you can float forever. I'm going skiing. . . ."

"Louisa," I said. "Louisa? You're going skiing?"

"Oh, yes," she said. "Oh, yes. I'm going skiing. I'm going skiing, Jack. Oh, it's so beautiful, skiing. Right off the tops of them. And down below there is nothing but the pure, white snow. Pure. And white. No evil, no dirt, no filth. A few cottages of faithful villagers, who love their cows and their land. Don't want to kill. . . . Oh, yes, I'm going skiing, Jack. Good-bye. . . ." She hung up and the phone went cold stone dead.

I was in a panic. I didn't know whether she had flipped her mind or what, but I knew instinctively something bad had happened somewhere. . . . I ran all the way to their apartment, which was more than three blocks.

Well, it was a pretty awful scene. A bad scene. In the time it took me to get there after her phone call she had become unconscious and her maid had found her. . . .

She had left the front door unlocked, so that I was able to barge right in. Had she calculated that, also? So she could leave herself room for me to come and save her? At that moment I thought so. Later on, when I saw what she had taken, I changed my mind.

She had dressed herself for the occasion. She was wearing one of her sheerest, flimsiest robes. . . . She would do that. Under it she had on a fine-textured white bra through which the two dark spots of her nipples showed like two dark eyes, and below a very brief, very low-waisted pair of panties through which the dark of her triangular bush made itself visibly felt. . . .

I put my ear to her mouth and nose, but if there was any breathing at all it was very shallow and light. . . .

On the bedside table there was a large aspirin bottle, totally empty, and there was a large tinfoil plaque of sleeping supposito-ries, empty also, eight or nine of them. There was also a Nembutal bottle, empty too. I had already noticed that there was a glass and a half empty bottle of vodka on the floor beside her beside the couch. Apparently she had taken enough stuff to kill a whole army. That was when I changed my mind about the unlocked door. . . .

A French doctor . . . darted into the apartment carrying his black bag. Apparently he lived around the corner, and the faithful Portuguese had gone to get him. . . .

"Her heart has stopped," he said. "I don't know for how long. I'm giving her a shot of Neosynepheraine. That may start it again. But we must get her to a hospital very fast. . . . If her heart has stopped for over four or five minutes, she could have serious brain damage. Even if we save her." . . .

The doctor was working over Louisa. And suddenly I became furious. Why are we trying to save her? I thought. If some stupid bitch wants to die, why not let her? . . . I wanted to go to the big couch and turn her over and kick her in her unconscious ass. What was she doing to us, and how dare she?

Michael Edwards

I was meant to be there that night. That's why I don't think she ever intended at that stage to commit suicide, because she could have chosen another moment which would have been less likely to be interrupted. I mean, she was expecting me that night. I was flying over from London to see her, we were going to talk about the flat— replacing curtains or something like that—and my plane was late, and when I finally got to 45, quai de Bourbon, I saw the concierge, Madame François, and she said, "*Madame est morte, Madame est morte*," and I went up there and there she was lying rather like *The Death of Chatterton*, all pallid and everything, on the carpet. Gloria and Jim Jones were there, and the *pompiers*, the ambulance men, were just about to take her away, to the Hôtel-Dieu.

Gloria Jones

They took her into the hospital and while she was being pumped out, the doctor came out and he said, "*C'est très mal.*" He said, "What could she have taken?" He told me to go back to her place as fast as I could and bring back every bottle, everything. So I did.

Dr. Jean Dax

She had taken a large dose of Nembutal, which is always a bad medication to take, and also vodka.

Gloria Jones

It looked very bad for, I don't know, eight days. Really bad. She was in the—it's called the *chambre de ressuscitation*, where they have everybody under cellophane, you know. She was under total—what do you call it? intensive care? She was hooked up. So here was this beautiful red-haired thing, absolutely naked, under the cellophane, you know, with this red pussy—she really had one! So white and so beautiful and it was so awful to see her like that.

From *The Merry Month of May*, James Jones, Delacorte Press, New York, 1971

I had never been inside the Hôtel-Dieu before. It faced on the square called Place du Parvis Notre-Dame just in front of Notre-Dame, which is where they used to pull people apart with horses for having committed some crime or other. The assassin of Henri Quatre was dismembered that way there. Hôtel-Dieu had a medieval look about it, at least from the outside, and I believe it had been started, a long way back, as a maternity hospital. . . .

They told me that her condition was very grave. She was surviving, in the new intensive care unit, but she was not showing any signs of recuperating. . . .

For some reason it seemed this case had been taken on by all the young nurses and doctors of the intensive care unit as a personal challenge. . . .

They had her under this plastic tent, completely nude. A young nurse was constantly in attendance. Louisa's body (I hesitate to say Louisa) was constantly sweating profusely, and the nurse was constantly mopping her off. There were tubes up both her nostrils, and her arms were strapped down to the bed. Above her left arm hung a glucose bottle, its needle taped into a vein in the arm. If I had ever wondered about her nipples and her bush, I did not have to wonder any more.

Telegram from James Jones to Antony Baekeland, Undated

1.45 P.M.

TONY BAEKELAND CADAQUÉS SPAIN   IMPERATIVE YOU
CALL ME   JAMES JONES

CLEMENT BIDDLE WOOD

Jim called me and said, "Do you have any idea how I can get hold of
Brooks?" and I said, "*Now* what's the problem?" and of course he
told me, and I said, "Well, maybe he's left some sort of forwarding
address at his bank." And then Jim said, "How well do they know
you at the Morgan Bank?" and I said, "I have quite a good friend
there, he's a vice-president or something." So I went to him and I
said, "I've got to find Brooks Baekeland fast," and he said, "Well,
he's left very strict instructions that his whereabouts are not to be
given out to anybody," so then I said, "Here's what's happened," and
he said, "Well, under the cicumstances, we'll tell you where to reach
him, but just keep the bank out of it. And if he has to be called, *you*
do it, not some third party." And so, although I did not know Brooks
Baekeland well, it was I, not Jim Jones, who called him in Rome—
Jim talked to him later. I said, "Listen, Brooks, I know this is an
intrusion on your privacy, but Barbara has tried to kill herself." And
he said, "Oh God—again! Clem," he said, "this is the fourth time
that she's done this. She pulls this on me every time. It's one reason I
didn't leave an address. It's an obvious bid for sympathy. She wants
me to come running back, but this time I'm not going to budge."
And I said, "Listen, I think it's more than a bid for sympathy, because if that's what she intended it to be, Brooks, she's overdone it,
because she damn near died," and I gave him what details I knew
about that—I told him she was in a coma. And he said, "Well, if she
dies, you know where I am." That chilled me, and I said, "Listen,
Brooks, for Chrissake, I understand how you feel about this, but I
think you might *be* here because they really think she may be dying."
He said—and this is what *really* chilled me—he said, "When I met
Barbara she was nothing, she was just this sort of redheaded Irish kid.
I practically picked her out of the chorus line," and, well, after that,
there really wasn't much to say.

BROOKS BAEKELAND
The fourth and last time Barbara "committed suicide" was signalized
to me at the Hotel Excelsior in Rome, where I was stopping on my
way out to the Far East with Sylvie in February 1968. Barbara had
thought I was still in Paris and would rally round quickly as I had
always done before. That did not work this time, partly because I was
not there and partly because Sylvie called up the Hôtel-Dieu and
spoke to the physician in charge and discovered that Barbara was out
of danger, though I knew there is always a risk of permanent brain
damage. Later Jim Jones told me over the phone, "She's been in a
coma for thirty-six hours." But it was Gloria, who took the phone
away from him, who told me that I *had* to come back and to whom I
said that I would never reply to that blackmail again and that this
time I was never coming back.

DR. JEAN DAX
She was in a deep coma for twenty-four hours, and I think gradually
pulled out of it—within the next twenty-four hours, roughly. There
was no evidence of brain damage.

**Letter from Brooks Baekeland to Gloria and James Jones,
February 27, 1968**

>   Jaipur & Udaipur
>   Rambagh Palace
>   India

Dear Jim & Gloria—
I called up the Hôtel-Dieu before leaving Rome on Sunday.
The head nurse gave me a good report on Barbara's condition,
assuring me that there was practically *no* danger now at all.
From this dose anyway.
   I am writing to say three things. (A) My thanks to you and
Gloria, who are somewhat saner and a great deal more sophisti-
cated than Barbara's other friends in Paris—all mostly female
and therefore and to that extent somewhat hysterically delighted,
I am sure, in the TV-drama aspect of this thing. Barbara has just
about drained all there is to drain out of romantic (and not-so-
romantic) violence where I am concerned, as I told you. And
that is the second thing: her belief in force to get her way is

fundamental in all things great and small, as everybody from waiters to prime ministers have experienced, and I have had to deal with that constantly for 25 years. Although the "provocation" this time may be judged great, there have been other times when even greater violence threatened over (as a start) where we planned to have dinner. I am to an astonishing and astonished degree unmoved, loving her no less than ever for all that. I would not probably feel that way had it not been for certain proofs of other things that indicate quite clearly to me that I am not the "only man there can ever be in my life"—i.e., that her hang-up on me is nowhere near so deathless as she will maintain to her girl friends.

Third, Barbara never tells her TV audience the whole truth about her situation (or anything) and she has no doubt also failed to tell you that on top of the other funds she gets regularly from me she also gets $850 per month from the rental of the New York flat—i.e., another $5,100 between my decision about this thing and my return from this trip. She can (and does) piss away the funds I give her, but she is never as short as she pretends. She has a lot of dough to spend just on food, liquor, and play—nothing else to pay for, as I take care of all the basics myself. Because she is almost pathologically incapable of ordinary cost accounting (and hence any sort of planning also) she has no idea how much she blows on clothes and other things far and above any reasonable budgetary allowance. Her lack of realism in all things, a sort of fundamental inability to separate wish from fact, "what ought to be" from "what is," "what can be" from "what might be" (important in *any* partnership) has (partly) accounted for a good deal of the sense of mutual paralysis in our lives, of which she herself sometimes complained. It has caused in me a deep reluctance to plan anything seriously with her— even a feeling that whatever I did with her would *somehow* simply be bungled or warped around again to suit the same old parade—but I don't want to dwell on that. I am no saint myself.

I am not "abandoning" Barbara. I am just not making myself available anymore for her particular scene (and scenes), as I have perhaps 10 more years of non-senile life ahead of me, and I want now to think of myself a little, too. I am being selfish. That does not mean that "life is over" for her by any logic that I can see. Other men have lives to lead and many also have mistresses. If all the wives gobbled pills every time Dagwood took off on his own, America would soon be depopulated.

Finally, as I said to you on the phone, I am rather sick of the atomic fly swatter. I suppose when you first start using atomic weapons—even if only to slay a fly—and since there are no stronger resorts to force, then you can hardly think or fight in lesser terms. That is the trouble with melodrama—the climaxes are all used up in Act I.

I know Barbara is in danger (if not now, then later) because of that. But what the hell can I do about it, short of being her butler/gigolo or taking *myself* out of the scene in a sort of pre-emptive strike? But why should I? . . .

The Morgan Bank will keep me in touch if there are any new developments, but as B.'s friends I hope you will make it plain to her that nuclear disarmament is now in order and that this sort of thing drives any man sooner or later to profound indifference. She claims, when that has sentimental social value, to be a Catholic born and bred. What she needs is some self-examination not with a shrink but with a good old-fashioned Irish priest, who will ask her "What about it?" in those old-fashioned ethical terms that she understood (perhaps) before she went out to Hollywood in 1940 with John Jacob Astor hot on her lovely tail. It's been show and little substance ever since. I helped in that, of course.

> Yours ever and to Gloria—
> Brooks

GLORIA JONES

When she came to, Virginia Chambers and Ethel de Croisset and I were with her, and Dr. Dax, Jean Dax, who was the doctor for all of us. About a week later Virginia and Ethel and I took her to the American Hospital, which is way the hell across town, and she stayed there for six weeks. She was really in terrible shape. "I want my husband"—that's the first thing she said in the American Hospital. She kept saying that to anybody who would listen to her: "I want my husband." The bastard. Where *was* he? She was writing him letters—letters, letters, letters all the time. She used to always get him back with letters.

Letter from Brooks Baekeland to James Jones, March 12, 1968

Dear Jim—

It is exactly two weeks since I spoke to you on the phone from Rome.

In India I received some of the most pathetic letters I have ever seen from Barbara. They were written from the Hôtel-Dieu and from the American Hospital where she went afterwards. These letters were forwarded to me via Morgan's. I have heard nothing since, because my itinerary had a rather large gap in it and I have not yet been able to close it—moving too fast. But I worry a whole lot about B. and I would be glad to have an encouraging word from you and Gloria—something objective that I can feel is accurate and written by someone who knows her and loves her. I admit to having been terribly affected by what she wrote. Of course I was meant to, but that makes no difference to me. I love her very much.

The next forwarding address that Morgan's has for me is an airport departure (date, air and flight no.) on March 31—so you can write to me care of them and I will get your news then.

I am very grateful to you both for the trouble you have taken.

Love—
Brooks

GLORIA JONES

Barbara was also writing letters to President de Gaulle and Mrs. de Gaulle—Mrs. de Gaulle especially, because Barbara said she knew she would understand. All of us, you know, spent time with her— Ethel and Virginia and I. She had a very nice private room. The American Hospital's very fancy, you know.

Letter from Barbara Baekeland to Gloria and James Jones, Undated

The American Hospital
Neuilly

Darling Gloria—and Jim—

How can I ever thank you enough? When I'm really glad to be alive I'll find some way. To get me out of the Hôtel-Dieu—that monstrous place—saved my sanity. I want to find or write Brooks and tell him how sorry I am I've caused so much anxiety & pain to people I love. I haven't the right to hold him if he wants to go but I wanted to see him once more as he left me with such anger. So much of our problems have been my fault. I realize it now. Perhaps if he does come back I can prove it and I would never reproach him.

How glad I am that with your worries and concern for me you came to see how I was. It's enough to see the blue sky and the tree outside my window to begin to feel like being a part of it all. As much as I love Brooks I did not love him enough to let him go with a chance to be happy and that is what I reproach myself for.

Dax won't let me even wear my own nightgowns—or have . . . calls. Thank God I can still write or I would go crazy! Maybe this isolation is good for some people but it leaves me with my thoughts which are not happy ones and is a kind of punishment.

Thank you for everything you've done for me over the years. There's been so much kindness from you both and I have been so hateful. But I mean to study "How to Win Friends and Keep Them"—indeed cherish them—joke—but I *am* going to try to correct my very grave failings of character.

Come and see me when you can. I need an antiperspirant, hair rollers, and a *soin de peau*—Carolina has all this.

It's much better here than the Hôtel-Dieu! *Quelle* irony! But nurses aren't very gentle people. I suppose if we were jabbing people with needles all day long & wiping their behinds & watching them die we wouldn't be, either.

Neither doctor spends more than 5 min. with me & one a psychiatrist. How I'm going to pay for it all, God alone knows.

Come soon—
X X B

PAULE LAFEUILLE

I visited her daily at the American Hospital of Neuilly. Her friends used to take turns by her bed, and every day one of them, in order to entice her to eat, would present her with some delicacy that her cook had prepared. As for me, living next to Petrossian's store, I could bring her a slice of smoked salmon or a few grains of fresh caviar. Our efforts were rarely successful. She would push her plate aside and say, "It is delicious. . . . How sweet you all are."

She loved to confide in me at length about her distress, and I can tell you that her words were Gentle Love itself's. She seemed not in the least resentful of Brooks's desertion and only kept repeating, "All I want is to see him once in a while. I shall not be able to live if I cannot occasionally set my eyes on him. . . ." Heartbreaking. By the way, I had also taught French to Brooks. I never did again from then on. I made a decision never to see him again. I made it the very moment I heard of his flight to the Far East and the subsequent dramatic events. In February 1973 he wrote to me from a village in Brittany asking if I would consider meeting his new wife who—I quote him—was not being too well treated by Barbara's old friends. This letter has remained unanswered.

ETHEL WOODWARD DE CROISSET

She came out of her coma in exactly the same mood that she'd gone into the suicide, you see—which was one of total frustration because she couldn't get ahold of Brooks. And I think it's a miracle that she in some way didn't try to take her life *again*, but probably one doesn't do that sort of thing. What I mean is that the attempt hadn't been a cleansing sort of thing. She came out absolutely wild, it seemed to me—and to Gloria. All this I think appears in one of those books of her husband's.

From *The Merry Month of May*, James Jones, Delacorte Press, New York, 1971.

I put in a call to Harry in Rome. . . ." Louisa's in the hospital," I said.

"Oh? She is? What for?" Harry said.

I was beginning to feel irritated. "A suicide attempt," I said. . . .

There was a pause on the line. "I suppose if she dies, I'll have to come back, won't I?"

"If you want to get her buried, you will," I said furiously. "I know I sure as hell ain't going to do it."

"Oh, somebody would," he said. "Edith de Chambrolet.
Have you called Edith?"

"No, not yet," I said. "I was trying to keep it quiet."

"Well, call her. Call Edith. She's a do-gooder. She loves to
do good works." . . .

He had told me to call Edith de Chambrolet. I did. I had met
Edith at their place for the first time, and afterwards had had
dinners with her frequently at her place. Large dinners, always
very formal, eight to 12 people. Edith was a remarkable person.
She was one of the richest women in America, and had married
some impoverished French Count and had four sons by
him. . . . She spoke with just about the broadest drawling "A" I
have ever heard, and had stary eyes. . . .

Together we walked over across the bridge and down past
Notre-Dame to the Hôtel-Dieu. . . .

As we walked in through the bed rows of beat-up, near-dead
people, she said, "Isn't it marvelous, now? Extraordinarily effi-
cient."

I was tongue-tied, and felt totally incapable, with her there.

"Now, Louisa," she said at the bed, lifting up one side of the
plastic oxygen tent. "We must stop all this nonsense. We must
pull ourselves together and I know that you will." She let the
tent flap drop. "We'll talk to her again a little later. Let it sink
in, first. I'm sure she heard us. In her unconscious." . . .

Harry remained adamant about not coming back unless
Louisa actually died. And even then he was not absolutely
sure. . . .

They moved Louisa, in an ambulance, to the American Hospital in Neuilly. The whole thing was handled by the American-
trained French doctor we knew who worked there, and whom
all of us, including Edith, used as our doctor. . . . His name
was Dax. . . . I did not feel up to riding out with her myself,
but Edith de Chambrolet went with her. . . .

I talked to the American Hospital doctor. . . . "She was just
about as dead as you can get," he said equably, "without actually dying."

From *Time* Magazine, Review of *The Merry Month of May*, Timothy Foote, February 22, 1971

> Among the [book's] victims is Harry's wife Louisa. Jones turns her into a near vegetable as the result of an attempted suicide. . . . Letting the lady live on in some domesticity or other would have been a truer and crueler fate.

BROOKS BAEKELAND

A novelist is a cannibal and may eat his friends for his professional purposes—Jim Jones always did. I could not read *The Merry Month of May*—trash. I am the only person alive, along with Sylvie, who knows *all* the truth—and therefore *the* truth. And the truth, when deeply seen, is always greater than any fiction. In its depths—but only there—reality not only seems to imitate art but surpasses it.

From *Saturday Review*, Review of *The Merry Month of May*, John W. Aldridge, February 13, 1971

> Even with all due allowance for his evident faith in human credulity, Jones cannot really expect us to believe any of this. His people, given the intellectual sophistication he attributes to them, would scarcely behave in this way.

SYLVIE BAEKELAND SKIRA

We left exactly on the 24th of February, and that's the day she tried to kill herself. Each time Brooks had tried to leave her before, she had done this. The first time was up at camp, in the Adirondacks— she took pills and he had to rush her across the lake in a rowboat to a doctor.

SAMUEL TAYLOR

I remember one night during the sixties Suzanne and I were at the Baekelands' for dinner—Jessica Tandy and Hume Cronyn were also there—and Barbara said, "Guess where I was at five this morning!" and we said, "Where?" and she said, "At Bellevue Hospital," and she showed us the bandages on her wrists. And being very gay about it, you know—very charming about it.

NANCY PERKINS WALLACE

My brother saved Barbara's life once. Mike was staying with Barbara and Tony in Cadaqués and she took an overdose of something, and they had to drive her in the car, screaming and yelling at her to stay awake—driving wildly through the night to some Costa Brava hospital.

SYLVIE BAEKELAND SKIRA

Paris was the fourth time, and Brooks just . . . he couldn't . . . he had to get away from her. That didn't mean he didn't love her. He did, and when she begged him to come back, I was terribly afraid that he would. Everybody thought, Brooks is off on a fling again, he's forty-seven, he'll come back. But I know now that he would never have come back to her, never—because she was too powerful, she was someone who would take the air you breathe and borrow it and leave you gasping. You just couldn't exist with her around. Barbara tried everything to keep him—if a man is about to leave you and you take one hundred pills of Nembutal, that's a pretty good way to make sure he's not going to leave you.

ELIZABETH BLOW

You know, Sylvie also tried to kill herself. Well, I mean, the story is so absurd, but *possibly* it happened. *I* believe it happened. According to Barbara, Sylvie had tried to take a lot of pills and been put in the hospital and Brooks and Barbara had sat up all one night after this thing occurred and they had decided that they would go on with their life and their marriage and that they would live together forever and that they really loved one another. And then there was a call from the hospital, a desperate call from Sylvie saying she wanted to see Brooks, and Brooks said, "Look, Barbara, I think I really should go over to the hospital. I'll come right back." And he went over to the hospital and Barbara never saw him again. He left the hospital with Sylvie and fled to Rome.

Letter from Barbara Baekeland to Gloria and James Jones, Undated

The American Hospital
Neuilly

My darling Gloria & Jim—

What would I do without you? He won't come back as he is a man that goes deeply into relationships and he will just become more & more fond of this girl—who first tried to get Tony & when that failed picked on Brooks. He is so guileless he won't see through her and though I don't mean to denigrate the feeling she has for him, she is, I think, *intéressée*—mercenary. The last two times I saved my marriage by going to him with no pride and saying I was sorry. This time I have less pride and really think what I've been through has changed me. He had to leave without seeing me for if he saw me he loves me too much to have left me there tied up like a hog for slaughter. I feel that if I could only talk to him everything will be all right.

I haven't seen my Spanish beau since last Spring & then just for lunch to tell him I was through. He never meant as much to me as the hair on Brooks' head! Whoops—as *a* hair on Brooks' head.

The trouble is now everyone knows and if I am ashamed he must be more ashamed. This is what will keep him from coming back to me.

When she was ill I urged him to go and see her in the clinic so that if anything happened that was serious he would not blame himself. She has *kept* him from seeing me & had the gall to write me a hypocritical letter in which she says she only wants him for a few months. I can't find the letter now—the doctor probably took it.

I know that with all the glamour & newness of traveling he won't come back. But would you, Jim, tell him I'll come and join him whenever he wants me to on a few hours' notice?

When I get out of here I want to go down to Mallorca, for that is our one chance to build a life together—with our son.

I don't talk about the girl to anyone. Let them wonder. I simply say B. has gone to India. But I won't be able to face anyone when I get out. My life just means nothing to me without B. or Tony.

Please try to come to see me—

XX I love you—
B.

P.S. My bill for 3 days was over $100—I've got to get *out* of
here! I'll have no money left.

Jim, he will tell you in his letter that he is madly in love, etc.,
etc. But that day when we talked for 40 hours he was so *relieved*
to be out of it all. He said she had no imagination and would
eventually bore him. He said he had never been bored an instant with me. He said he liked the feeling of having her love
him and her sexual newness. She's got 2 children and no visible
means of support. I adore Brooks and can learn to control the
vicious side of my nature and let him love me the way he always
wanted to. Please tell him he should come back to me. He
needs advice.

CLEMENT BIDDLE WOOD

A very strange coincidence happened when Barbara was at the American Hospital. My wife Jessie—whose mother, Louise de Vilmorin,
by the way, was a friend of Barbara's—had been arranging flowers in
our apartment and this big cut-glass vase that had belonged to *my*
mother just sort of came apart in her hands and she was cut on the
wrist, exactly on the vein. I made sort of a tourniquet and I rushed
her to the American Hospital. And as we were walking in—Jessie,
you know, holding her bandaged wrists and blood sopping and pouring on the floor—along comes Barbara, with Ethel de Croisset. Barbara is just at that moment checking out, and she sees Jessie and she
says, "*Oh,* my poor Jessie! Oh, *dear!* Oh, I understand *completely*
about this"—you know, assuming naturally that it was a suicide attempt, that Jessie had slashed her wrists. And Ethel said, "No, no,
Barbara, you're not to worry yourself about *that*—Jessie's just fine,"
and sort of hustled her along. It really was the damnedest coincidence. It's the kind of thing you couldn't put into a novel.

GLORIA JONES

When she got a little bit better, she came and stayed with us in this
house we rented with Clem and Jessie Wood in a place called La
Coste. She drove there herself, so she was in good shape. It was at
Eastertime.

CLEMENT BIDDLE WOOD

Barbara was with us for a few days. She was in a very sort of fragile
condition, but she was putting a good face on things and trying very

hard to be a good sport, not to bore us with her troubles. Naturally we were all worried that she might try to pull the same thing again then and there, and she knew that we were worried about this, yet I also had the feeling that she was somehow trying to put her life back together again.

Letter from Brooks Baekeland to Michael Edwards, April 23, 1968

Dear Michael—
. . . I very strongly suspect that B. and I will be back together soon after September 1st and that the storms will all have blown over. But I think you should keep that surmise to yourself. . . . I may have to go to the States for a while but Paris has become home to me.

Affectionately—
Brooks

P.S. I am about to leave for Thailand. Your letter just caught me here in Nepal. Morgan's will always forward.

Letter from Barbara Baekeland to Michael Edwards, Undated

Michael dear—
I hope all is well with the apartment. I have joined Tony in Cadaqués. He wanted me to come and has been a source of constant gentleness & concern since my arrival a week ago. It seemed the best thing for me to do under the circumstances. We listen to music, study, see no one, walk, swim & explore and I feel myself beginning to mend again. I seem to be getting better here—anyway I am happy being with my son.

We have rented Avie von Ripper's house on Mallorca for 2 months—from the 15th of June until the 15th of August. It looks comfortable and will provide us with a refuge until I know what to do. At the moment the prospect of a reconciliation—though I still want it—looks dim. I think I shall probably go to New York on the 15th and take back my apartment there. It is an easier place for me to begin to reconstruct my life and maybe I can find some interesting work to do.

I am coming to Paris to see Carolina and straighten out my affairs. I have been told that I must see a lawyer as B. has not behaved properly toward me financially. I am very low on funds and have simply taken this house & told B.'s lawyer that he will have to pay for it.

I don't think he and I can live together again unless we both change. I hope to re-find my creative and better self in these next few months, working and living quietly with Tony, my mother, and my animals. As far as I can tell from Brooks' present path he is in the process of losing his better self and was very harmful to Tony during all this terrible time. I cannot risk such destruction & violence ever again. As Heidegger said, "the dreadful has already happened"—well, it has and it is time to begin again.

Much love,
Barbara

Letter from Brooks Baekeland to Michael Edwards, August 23, 1968

Dear Michael—

As you know, Barbara has returned to New York; Tony, after passing through Paris just long enough (I imagine) to make a shambles of 45, quai de Bourbon, has gone on to Frankfurt and from there out to New Delhi, etc. to join me. He arrives tomorrow. . . .

SYLVIE BAEKELAND SKIRA

I had come back to France to see my children, who were with my parents for the summer, and I had brought with me a money order from Brooks to bring Tony to India. I made arrangements with the Morgan Bank so Tony could come and pick up his air ticket—we were to leave together on the same plane. I waited at the departure gate and he never came. We found out later that he had picked up the air ticket, changed it, and gone to Ireland to be with a friend of his from Cadaqués, Ernst von Wedel.

Letter from Brooks Baekeland to Michael Edwards, Undated

Michael,
I just don't know what will be the final result for B & myself—
but whatever it is I think it may take some time to work out—
maybe 6 months more. I just can't say. But we shall not be
returning to the life we lived before. I hope we shall see a lot of
each other and share some (the best) aspects of life together
again—but the whole thing: God forbid. . . .

Affectionately as always,
Brooks

Letter from Barbara Baekeland to Michael Edwards, September 16, 1968

New York

Darling Michael—
B. wants to come back. Had a meeting with his lawyers &
cousin last week to listen to his proposals. Have a few of my own
to make—one of which includes a proper house *somewhere*—so
we shall see.
New York a joy. I am enjoying my apartment enormously
and my life here. Each weekend away and two exciting offers of
jobs—one with Andy Warhol & the other with the 2 Maysles
brothers.
If, as Brooks writes, he intends to let 45, quai de Bourbon go,
I may want to keep it on myself. Just paid the rug bill &
lampshade bill which have followed me around since May.

Love,
Barbara

Letter from Michael Edwards to Brooks Baekeland, September 23, 1968

Dear Brooks,
When the screens and Barbara's other pictures are down, all the
walls will have to be made good and repainted; also the depreda-

tions on the sofa and chair made by her dear four-footed friends will have to be repaired, but, on the other hand, Barbara only recently put a lot of money into the place for a nice new carpet and went halves with me on the new curtains, so I suggest we call that quits. . . .

Letter from Brooks Baekeland to Michael Edwards, October 15, 1968

> Kashmir
> India

Dear Michael—

Barbara and I are still at a stand-off as far as our futures are concerned. I doubt very much whether we shall be taking up residence again at 45, quai de Bourbon. *Entre nous,* I am devoted to her and I think she is to me, but our life together, behind what the public sees, has been a rather violent and chronically contested conflict of tastes, styles and policy (on all counts, including most seriously, and perhaps disastrously, the bringing up of our son, water now under the dam) and I finally had enough of it. She is stronger than I (in some ways); she could have gone on; I saw long ago the approaching day when we would have to separate if only in the formal sense of that word—i.e., the day of my ultimate weariness and exasperation. She is a splendid and adorable woman. Not her fault, not mine either I think—we just created too much heat together in the same 4 walls, all the 4 walls we ever inhabited!

God knows when, if ever, I will have a home again. . . .

Most of our old friends in Paris now consider me to be such a heel, cad, bounder, rotter, hairy-at-the-heel and downright scallywag that they do not deign to acknowledge my occasional friendly letters from the Far East. So I am "as one dead" to all "decent" people. (I was not surprised. People love battles—other people's battles—and enjoy taking sides when no blows can fall upon *them*. Every disputation on a street soon gathers its crowd.)

> With much love—
> Brooks

P.S. I am leaving Kashmir, but would be obliged if you would keep even that location confidential as a personal favor.

Letter from Michael Edwards to Brooks Baekeland, November 4, 1968

Dear Brooks,
Barbara telephoned me the other day terribly anxious to know where you were and whether you were going back to New York, especially as she had heard a rumour that your clothes were going to be sent back there. I told her that I had heard from you but that I could not give her any indication that you planned to go back to America in the foreseeable future.

As far as your clothes are concerned, by all means have Carolina take them over to the studio, but don't worry about them if you want to leave them at Quai de Bourbon since, as I told you in my last letter, Carolina fusses over them periodically, so they will come to no harm; ditto any of the rest of Barbara's furniture. . . .

Letter from Barbara Baekeland to Gloria and James Jones, January 6, 1969

Hotel Ritz
Barcelona

Darlings—
I will be in Paris the night of the 15th and would like to have dinner with you either the 15th or 16th. Will you drop me a line at the Hotel Collander, St. Moritz, Switzerland?

I have been in Spain since the 16th of December by way of the Caribbean. . . . Tony came for 5 days to Mallorca with me after we spent Xmas together in Cadaqués. He was *mad* about the place. B. has fled back to Thailand, everyone says in very bad shape. . . . I now have Louis Nizer for a lawyer & am much happier.

Dying to see you both and the children. If you haven't time to write, just expect me. Will be in Paris only 3 days to clear out flat—

Hugs & kisses,
B.

10

CRUISING

In 1978, after Tony Baekeland had been in Broadmoor for five years, the authorities still considered his condition "severe" and did not feel he was ready to be released. Nonetheless, the unofficial committee of his friends continued in their efforts to have him freed.

Miwa Svinka-Zielinski felt that Tony ought to be in a setting where he could receive regular therapy on a one-to-one basis. She suggested a halfway-house arrangement. But he resisted this idea—he wanted to be on his own when he got out, he said. "I kept telling him," she says, "that if he ever wanted to get out of there he would have to behave rationally. 'Don't tell Dr. Gogarty you want to be independent the minute you are free,' I told him. He had to have some sort of a transition from this place to real life."

Miwa Svinka-Zielinski herself explored various alternatives for Tony's care in the event of his repatriation. "I asked myself some questions, such as: What is his exact clinical status? Is there anywhere in England where he can stay as a transition before being sent to New York? Can he really function outside a hospital or halfway house? Can he be persuaded to have others handle his money for him in the U.S.?"

Visitors that year reported that Tony's eyes seemed vacant. This disturbing symptom was one of the reasons Dr. Gogarty was reluctant to take seriously the requests of the unofficial committee. "Our hospital is designed for patients who are violent," he explains, "and as soon as their behavior is tolerable, we are bound to send them to less secure places. This is the logic I followed with Tony."

In February, a consul officer from the American Embassy in London made the first of what would be eleven visits to Broadmoor to assess Tony Baekeland's condition. Sarah Fischer, a member of the consulate, recalls that "the psychiatrist seemed to care very much about Tony and thought he would be happier back in the United States—he hoped in an institution similar to Broadmoor."

Consular Officer's Report on Visit to Antony Baekeland, February 10, 1978

I had a nice visit with Mr. Baekeland in the "great hall" at Broadmoor. He seemed happy and content, with no serious complaints. He said that his doctor had mentioned returning him to the USA, but he didn't know much more about it.

Consular Officer's Report on Visit to Antony Baekeland, March 10, 1978

Mr. Baekeland and I had an animated conversation during my visit. He stated that he was in "fine" health, and seemed in good spirits, although he said that he was "vegetating" at Broadmoor as inmates in his ward were not afforded the opportunity to do anything of substance during waking hours. However, he felt that Broadmoor was treating him as well as could be expected. Following our conversation, he had a chat with two guards; this chat appeared to be quite friendly and enjoyable for all concerned.

Official Visitors File, Broadmoor Special Hospital, May 3, 1978

VISITOR'S NAME: Mrs. M. Svinka-Zielinski
RELATIONSHIP TO PATIENT: Friend
SUMMARY: As before, she discussed Tony's needs with brisk

chatter and with an air of official authority while in fact she has no standing in the case except as a "friend" of the family. She intends to seek out names and addresses of hospitals in New York which might be more accessible to Tony from a financial point of view. Has promised to call with these details in the near future.

Letter from Antony Baekeland to Miwa Svinka-Zielinski, August 30, 1978

Dear Miwa,

First of all I would just like to tell you how much your visits have meant to me over the last five years. Had a very interesting dream about that nice Princess Pallavicini you brought to see me.

I am learning all kinds of new and interesting things about the nature of the Universe. The weather has been relatively cool, except for a few hot days. I feel quite ready to face the world. I am getting very tired of being here and I greatly wish they would let me out. A great and wonderful friend of ours called Ethel de Croisset just sent Michael Alexander some money to try to help get me out.

I want to go back to Mallorca. Miramar, our house there, has a beautiful old garden, and a chapel and cloisters. The very old palm trees were brought there more than a hundred years ago. There are miradors or look-outs all up and down the mountain-side and the view of the sun setting into the vast blue sea is truly something never to be forgotten. I spent some of the happiest years of my life there, mainly in the company of the Mallorquin peasant family who lived downstairs and looked after the land.

Robert Graves lives nearby in Deyá and I came to know him quite well while I lived there. He told me my poetry was excellent, which was encouraging. I spend my days now in a happy dream of what I will do in the garden and cloisters when I go back there and what repairs will have to be done to the house to make it comfortable again.

                                                                    Love,
                                                                    Tony

Letter from Barbara Baekeland to Michael Edwards, August 28, 1969

> Miramar
> Valldemosa
> Mallorca

Michael dear—

Tony and I have been sharing a house—the old residence of the Austrian Archduke Luis Salvador in Valldemosa. We have been so happy here I hope to keep it forever. It has been practically given to us by his daughter who wants us to stay.

I lost out on a beautiful flat in Paris. Am on to another on Cadogan Square in London but what to do with our great feline friend the fine Mr. Worcester?

Will be returning to New York in November to try to settle my affairs with Brooks, who has refused me a divorce. The bills (unpaid by him) still go on and the little he gives me is just enough to clear expenses here. All my rent money from New York goes straight to my lawyers who are not able to accomplish anything as B. refuses to communicate. Meanwhile he has ended up living just down the road here. And to think that one of the Ten Commandments is "Love thy Neighbor"! Never mind, I try—if, at times, it seems the greatest irony of all. . . .

SYLVIE BAEKELAND SKIRA

After India, we went to Mallorca, as a sort of, you know, winter drop. Brooks had always loved Mallorca—he had once planned to buy a large house there with Barbara.

She didn't know we were there. And then one day we were going off to Ibiza—it's a half-hour plane trip, that's all—and who do we meet in the airport—Ernst von Wedel from Cadaqués. Looking *very* handsome in those days, and very well groomed and so on. He said, "Brooks—my God! What are *you* doing here? I've been staying with Barbara and Tony, and Barbara just drove me to the airport!" And Brooks said, "Well, keep it quiet. If you see her, don't say anything." And of course, Ernst, instead of keeping quiet, rushed off to find Barbara, and very soon on the loudspeaker there came: "Mrs. Baekeland wants to see Mr. Baekeland." When we heard that, we decided, okay, too bad, our luggage is on the plane but we're not

going to take it, we'll go back to the house, because we wanted to get
away from her and we thought that she would wait for us at the
departure gate. But I must say Barbara knew Brooks very well. She
knew he would leave the airport and go back to his car and so she was
waiting for him out in the parking lot. And when they came face to
face, Brooks said—he had been always and still is very proud of Barbara's looks, but she had become plump, and he said—"You don't
look so young, Barbara." And she said, "*You* look a hundred years
old!" and from then on they had a good fight. I went away, I retired
to the car—I didn't want to listen. You see, Barbara had said to
Brooks, about me, "Get that thing away from me!"—that sort of
thing. But that's normal, that's normal. So then, after that, we returned to our separate houses, Barbara to Deyá and Brooks and I to
our village nearby. But now of course Barbara knew that we were
living on the same island.

Eventually Tony came to visit us. He stayed for a few days. This
was the first time I had seen him since Brooks and I went away together. It was very uncomfortable, very hard. He left messages for
Brooks in the flower pots. I found one—it said, "Daddy, please
Daddy, come back to Mummy, she's so unhappy." He acted like a
little eight-year-old—I mean, the way he resented me.

He never wrote to me from Broadmoor but he wrote *about* me. I
existed in every letter to his father. Oh yes. I was the evil woman who
was responsible for everything: I had killed his mother, I had killed
everybody.

For a while Brooks had been *for* Tony's release someday, but then
he began receiving these letters that were so frightening. Tony said I
would be the first person he would kill when he came out.

**Telegram from Kingman Brewster, Jr., U.S. Ambassador to
the Court of St. James's, to Cyrus R. Vance, Secretary of
State, December 1978**

> MADE REGULAR VISIT TO ANTONY BAEKELAND AT BROAD-
> MOOR HOSPITAL ON DECEMBER 20 AND FOUND HIM IN GOOD
> HEALTH AND REASONABLE SPIRITS. HE HAD NO COMPLAINTS.
>   BREWSTER

Helen Delaney

Six years after the matricide, just about the time our embassy in London began looking into Tony's condition at Broadmoor, an English writer by the name of Nell Dunn—she'd already written a best seller called *Poor Cow*, and a couple of years ago she had a play on Broadway called, I think, *Steaming*—published a novel called *The Only Child* obviously based on the Baekelands. She hadn't known them personally or anything, she'd simply read about the tragedy in the newspapers, and I think she may have known people who knew them. Anyway, in her book, Brooks is "Daniel," Barbara is "Esther," and Tony is "Piers."

From *The Only Child*, Nell Dunn, Jonathan Cape Ltd., London, 1978

> With Daniel it was need, obsession, and war, but with Piers it was different, delicate, unexpected, sitting on a sofa with him after school—the light dimming outside the window, [the cat] asleep on the knotted rug—she felt sweetness steal over her—a sweetness she had never known with anyone else. . . .
>
> "You've tried to run my life."
>
> "I didn't want to run your life. I only wanted to make everything beautiful for you, I only wanted you to be happy. Oh come here, Piers, hold me and comfort me . . . I ache, I ache so much I'm dying . . . Please help me!"
>
> "I ache too, Mother."
>
> "Come here then, let's comfort one another. Let's hold one another till we go to sleep. Take me in your arms, Piers." . . .
>
> "I suppose the truth is that my mother has always been the love of my life, yet she's never given me what I needed. Support in being myself. Belief that what matters to me is as important as what matters to her. And then my father hasn't liked me since I was about twelve. I'm a disappointment to him. We have nothing in common yet we are bound together by steel rope, bound, it seems, not by love and pleasure."

Sylvie Baekeland Skira

Brooks went to see Tony in Broadmoor. The first time, I made him go. I thought it was too impossible to have a child in prison and not go see him, and I hammered and hammered and hammered, and finally he went.

But I shouldn't say I made him go because somebody who doesn't want to go won't go, either. After that first visit he said—but you must understand it as coming from someone who was very hurt rather than someone arrogant—he came back and told me, "Tony has a ghastly cockney accent." Brooks has a sense of theater, a sense of glamour and so on, and if his son suddenly had a cockney accent, it said a lot. It was a question of how alienated his child had become, how this child was not even his anymore, couldn't connect to anything anymore.

Letter from Antony Baekeland to Miwa Svinka-Zielinski, Undated

Broadmoor

Dear Miwa—
My father came to see me on a surprise visit and it was good to see him but not so good as I had hoped—he is, however, coming again with his wife, and they plan to spend a few days in a nearby hotel and see me every day. There is so much in me that I want to express, and such emotion that wants to come out, you have no idea.

Forgive this short scribble.

All love,
Tony

Letter from Antony Baekeland to James Reeve, December 17, 1978

Broadmoor

Dear James—
I feel so wonderfully well these days—my grandmother Nini will be very pleased with me.

I thought you might be very busy and that would be the reason for your not writing.

I have a feeling things will be very big and tremendous when I

get out, but still I have no idea of when that will be. I am
hoping very much that you will be able to get away to visit with
me in Valldemosa.

                                                                            Love,
                                                                            Tony

Letter from Barbara Baekeland to Michael Edwards, September 12, 1969

                                                                    Miramar
                                                                    Valldemosa
                                                                    Mallorca

Dear Michael,
I wish you could come here for a visit. Cruised the Greek Is-
lands in June with a neighbor of yours in the South of France.
Bernie Pfriem—nice fellow. Do look him up.

        Write!

                                                                    My love—
                                                                    Barbara

BERNARD PFRIEM
It was a two-week cruise. Emily Staempfli had chartered a big yacht.
We met the boat at Athens and it took off from there for the islands.
We went to Rhodes but we didn't get to Crete, we went to the northern islands. I almost didn't go—I was just about to start teaching an
art course at Sarah Lawrence and I was hesitating because I wanted to
work. But this architect friend of mine who was going, Peter
Harnden, got angry with me for even thinking of passing up an opportunity like this. None of us realized at that time that Peter was
beginning his lung cancer. It was not long after that that he had a
lung removed. And then he got it in the second one, of course—it
was a year or two later—and he had a second operation. And then he
died. And later his wife Missy, who was also on the cruise, died—of
leukemia.

Then there was this friend of Emily's, a man whose name I can't
remember anymore—a tall, thin character who did little landscapes

and had a house in Spain. He was the only drip on the whole sea voyage. He did nothing, nothing, he didn't even talk at meals. He's dead too now.

Then there was Sam Green, a very very good friend of Emily's who in fact had arranged for her to charter the yacht. I knew Sam very well by the time of that cruise. He was always at Emily's apartment in New York, and he organized a lot of her parties for her—you know, with Warhol and Rauschenberg and Jasper Johns and so on. He was funny and amusing and chatty.

And then of course there was Barbara, whom I'd *not* met before. I liked her enormously. She was bubbly and she had sort of a Marilyn Monroe kind of effervescence—and even that kind of flesh, I would say.

That made seven of us. And there was a crew of something like fourteen.

The thing between Sam and Barbara started on that cruise. By then, of course, Barbara was a free agent—her husband had left her. Actually, Sam and I were the only eligible males on board, and she was glorying in the idea of having a romance, which she was desperately in need of. She was always touching you and laughing and being seductive and so on.

There were only two doubles—Emily had, of course, the master stateroom, and Peter and Missy Harnden had the smaller one. Then there were two adjoining rooms off to the side. Barbara had one, and Sam and I sort of flipped for the other—to be next to Barbara—and Sam won.

After that, Barbara and Sam were together all the time. They both loved swimming and whenever we would anchor they would swim long distances together. It was all great fun and games, and warm. Oh, sometimes Barbara would lash into a serious discussion, whether it was about politics or whatnot I can't remember, but she was vocal. Anyway she seemed to be happy, and I thought she looked radiant. When we docked, the three of us would go off to bazukis or whatever you call them, and drink and dance.

Sometimes Barbara would talk about Tony. She always said she wanted me to meet him. One night she told me that she had slept with him. She was very honest about it—she said she had done it to break him of his homosexual tendencies. She talked about it as though it were a therapeutic act that she was doing.

I remember at one point she and I were walking together, she was holding my arm, and she told me she was attracted to Sam because he reminded her so much of Tony. "They look alike and they have kindred spirits"—that's how she put it. I think she was sort of apologizing to me for why she was having this affair with Sam and not with me, because, in a sense, we had kind of an innocent flirtation going.

And then after the cruise, she and Sam went off together to meet Tony.

SAM GREEN

It was a geezer trip, and Barbara was the only one who was *not* a geezer. She was beautiful, she was lively, she was imaginative, she was exciting. And every time I would turn a corner or go to a quiet dark place on the deck, there she'd be.

Well, she *was* kind of wonderful. I keep thinking that all of that froufrou and title-dropping was a part of my growing up which lasted for a long, long time. I was twenty-nine when I met her—she was, I guess, about forty-seven—and I hadn't been around that much. I was directing this funny little museum of contemporary art down in Philadelphia. I mean, I'd never been on a yacht before!

On the cruise I realized that she was recovering from a bad time with her husband. We became great friends, and I didn't think that it was anything more serious than that. I mean, I was disinclined to have an ongoing affair with a woman needy of having an affair.

She told me she had a big house in Mallorca. She said, "You *must* come." And it was convenient. I think I had ten days or something to kill. She had told me over and over again about Tony and how wonderful and spiritual he was, how kind of confused he was and how he didn't have anyone to influence him as interesting as me, and wouldn't I please come and look at him and, you know, sort of help him out. Well, I was more interested in seeing the nice house in Mallorca.

On the boat she had presented it as a palace, a major palace. What it was was a run-down finca. Miramar, it was called. It was set on a wonderful precipice, about two thousand feet above the sea—it had the best vista in all of Mallorca. It also had a thirteenth-century chapel, and formal gardens that were all overrun with weeds. I mean, it was a gone estate. And Barbara was renting it for what it was worth—which was nothing. I mean, a hundred a month or something. And she'd cajoled this wonderful servant family, Maria and

her husband Sebastian, into providing food and doing this and that—
and never paid them!

While I was there she became very possessive of me and after I left
she inundated me with letters everywhere I went.

Letter from Barbara Baekeland to Sam Green, August 15, 1969

Miramar
Valldemosa
Mallorca

Darling Sam—

How much we miss the pleasure of your company. Come back
soon.

The night you left, the light was all gold & mauve and a wind
came up. Everything seemed sad. But then the next morning we
did the *I Ching* and it told us that a "friend" would be crossing
the great water to join us soon and that we would vanquish
weakness by joining and multiplying our power.

Tony liked you so much. I'm glad. I do, too. I hope he finds
his way—maybe you can help him to.

Thank you for all the incredibles and the grass. I'm so happy
I've had a trip and you're right—things don't look quite the
same. Will they ever?

Tony is off at Deyá. Wuss is *always* hungry. Everybody wonders why you went away. Tell us.

Love—
Barbara

Letter from Sam Green to Barbara Baekeland, August 15, 1969

Saint-Tropez

Dear Barbara,

Well, I certainly hope that things have calmed down since I left
Mallorca. I have begun to commence my own life, and am enjoying it. I went from Palma to Nice and spent a great night in a

hotel near there. The next day I arrived at Tony Richardson's little village above Saint-Tropez, where I plan to spend about another week. Then I go to Athens for my cruise with Cecile de Rothschild.

Tomorrow I go *alone* to Jeanne Moreau's for lunch.

We had a very strange visit, didn't we? I have done nothing but think about it. Heaven help us, what a situation! The combined efforts of de Sade and Tennessee Williams couldn't have done it justice. The awareness-heightening of the drug only intensified the possible repercussions. That night of the wind I got up five times and bolted my doors. In that beautiful place, that peaceful, enchanted, lovely place—to think that I disturbed it! I was truly afraid.

To love Tony is irresistible. The burden he is bearing is almost too much. I hope he has the strength to hold it until someone comes to take it from him. It's tragic that Brooks is so small that he can't help him—because Brooks is what's needed. When I think of the despair he leaves in his wake, it makes me murderous. But Brooks, eventually, is his own problem, no one else's. All I have to offer you is liking and some understanding. Please accept them. There are many kinds of love.

Sam

Letter from Barbara Baekeland to Sam Green, August 22, 1969

Miramar
Valldemosa
Mallorca

Darling Sam—

Got your letter yesterday. I had three (maybe four) of the happiest days ever with you. You were a merry and adorable companion and Tony & I both adored having you. I'm sorry you were feeling oppressed and attacked (why else lock—bolt!—your door?). No one will ever disturb you or force gifts upon you that you do not wish to give or accept in this house—our house. Our time together was not a playlet of Williams or a monstrous evocation of de Sade—but an acting out in a truly classical & beau-

tiful way of a very old myth. Because we are veterans of this
century we were unable to be really free and it is perhaps better
that we were not, for some of us have fragile psyches and the
strain would have been great. I do not want you to blame yourself. Both Tony & I love you and you mustn't make something
that has (if unconventional) radiance take on a sordid backwash
of tired old Freud.

I would be happier if Tony were to fall in love with a beautiful & gifted girl. I would like him to experience marriage, fa-
therhood, the really extraordinary harmony and fitting and
complementing that can exist between a man & woman. I had it
once and it is a rare and beautiful thing. Perhaps he must go
through other friendships first—I don't know. Anyway he is 22
and must make his way in his *own* way. I can only offer him
love and confidence, which is what I have tried to do.

If you want to come back—please do. If you feel our situation
is too "charged," tell me so.

You're very honest, Sam, and it is a joy for me to have you as
a friend. You are a good one and I believe you will always be
my friend. You could be Tony's, too—and you could help him.
He is worth it.

Whatever I once had has been squandered in a reckless wan-
ton way, but I do have still a capacity for love. I think you love
me (in one of your ways) and, as you so wisely said, there are
many kinds of love—to give and receive them can be only good.
So don't fret.

Keep in touch with us. Maybe you should take a year off and
come to live here?

Anyway thank you for your dear letter—and thank you for
bringing forth in me that which I think is the finest & best I
have to give.

We miss you—Betty Blow is here now but it is not the same
as having you. We were so peaceful & happy together and
needed no one else. It was a special time.

Do write.

                                                      My love—
                                                      Barbara

Letter from Antony Baekeland to Sam Green, August 24, 1969

> Miramar
> Valldemosa
> Mallorca

Dear Sam—

There is a great deal I would like to ask and tell you but it is a peculiar thing that whenever I sit down with a pen my ideas seem to fade away. I will try, however. I hope that perhaps you can help me. I realize that what I must do involves loving another person and since I have never had the slightest attraction to women, this means that it must be a man. I think that much of my development stopped at an infantile stage, perhaps to enable me to go on with a certain kind of thinking which otherwise I would have been unable to continue. Anyway I am wondering how I can change this now. I really do not think I can go on much longer. The trouble is that when I am humiliated I no longer feel very amorous which is quite natural I feel. Please forgive these personal matters but I must discuss it with someone and I am sure you understand. As long as I feel bad and nasty and mean, which all these ghastly love songs make me feel—"Baby why did you leave me," bla bla bla—it is difficult for me to want to hear those screaming imploring voices, and difficult for me to feel worthy and nice enough to touch another person.

I have been standing in this doorway so long now but I can't do anything myself—when I do, all I get is horrified enlightened stares. Nor can I say anything—my voice comes out on the wrong pitch and people smile embarrassedly.

Naturally I want to be a hero, but I realize that this is childish. That is it—I never feel really safe from some horrible vain idea or childish impulse to show off, so I feel unwilling to embark on anything in which I might harm another person through my own foolishness. *Please* write to me here—much of this letter is Crap but some of it makes sense I hope.

> Love,
> Tony

P.S. I would like to be free. If I could sacrifice desire, I could be free. If I could sacrifice memory, I could sacrifice desire for love.

P.P.S. It would be terrible to have to continue to be a villain, knowing at the same time perfectly well how unnecessary it would be to be so.

Letter from Antony Baekeland to Sam Green, August 25, 1969

                                                        Miramar
                                                        Valldemosa
                                                        Mallorca

Dear Sam—

Please ignore fatuous letter—written in despond and never intended for the mails. I hope you are not embarrassed by it. Petty self-justifying propels me down such o-to-be-avoided lanes.

Someone gave me some quite nice hash. Last night we turned on down by the stone table at the chapel: all the animals appeared. Benjie the dog was struck dumb at the cat's antics in the tree. Also found a person who grows incredible grass somewhere in the mountains and sells it for practically nothing. I am utterly immobilized with the first cold I've had in four years. Can't decide whether to spend the winter here or go to London.

Betty Blow arrived with her tarot cards so it is not as lonely as it was when you first left.

                                                        Love from
                                                        Tony

ELIZABETH BLOW

I spent a month that summer with Barbara and Tony. They were living in this extraordinary villa—no telephone, no electricity, and every night we would light masses of candles and eat by candlelight.

The first week I was there, the sun was shining and Barbara and I would climb down over the rocks—it seemed to me like a mile down. It was like the descent of Mount Everest almost. I don't think there was even a path. We would just have to go down through the rocks and the olive trees, way way down because the villa was perched on the top of this promontory. And then we would clamber back up—the *ascent* of Mount Everest!—laughing and talking.

But then there were the evenings of the strange conversations in restaurants, at which I was sort of an observer—in which they would say things. . . . It was almost like another language, in other words, and only they could understand this particular language—it was their own intimate Tony-Barbara language that they'd invented and that they were, you know, cultivating and keeping alive, and it was like a fantasy journey that they two were on and I could not follow. They didn't forget you were there, because they would smile at you and perhaps try to bring you into the conversation—"Don't you think so?" kind of thing. I mean, they included me—they were loving, gentle people and they included me—but I couldn't follow what the hell they were talking about.

One afternoon I went for a swim at this hotel a little way up the road, it had a swimming pool, and Tony came with me and as I was lying in the sun he sat down beside me and told me this long long long story about something that had happened to him in Cadaqués. It involved all kinds of mythical and strange things. To me it was like a total hallucination, it was like a trip to the moon and back—and he said he had *done* this, but it was all so fantastic that it couldn't have been real. However it was real to *him*. Very real to him. It involved some man—now I'm beginning to remember—some male figure who was very powerful and very dominating and who Tony felt was something of a savior for him.

During the month I was there, Barbara was very much trying to promote Tony's poetry. She was taking his poems around to people like Robert Graves. I think Tony really hated her touting his poetry like that. I mean, he would become absolutely numb when she would start to talk about it. He would clam up and *she*—she would run and bring out more poems! I felt that Barbara was finally living her own life *through* Tony, that he was a tool, really, for all her talents and artistry. Everything was now totally focused on Tony, who was like a robot who was moving around and doing what she would tell him to do and even creating *because* of her.

Poem by Antony Baekeland Written in Broadmoor Special Hospital, 1978

> I see a star
> Yet it is a day
>
> The hands of my mother
> Make it grow

It is a black star
Set against white sky
How gentle that star

Now that she weaves devils
Claws together to make
A basket

ELIZABETH BLOW

On the one hand, he absolutely hated her, and on the other hand, he absolutely adored her—there was nobody in the world that would ever be like her. I remember one night in Mallorca when she was having some guests for dinner on the terrace, on this rock out there, Tony said, "You know, when I look at my mother I see almost a halo or a sort of radiance around her." And Barbara *was* glowing, truly— she felt that Sam Green, who she'd just met on this yacht, was "it," that Sam was the perfect man for her. She was totally starry-eyed— he was fun, kind, loving, affectionate, marvelous—everything that Brooks was *not*, in other words. She said he was just the most marvelous person to be with that she'd ever been with in her life.

Letter from Sam Green to Barbara and Antony Baekeland, August 26, 1969

Athens

Dear Barbara and Tony,
When I returned to Athens, I was astonished to receive such a cascade of mail from you.

My latest cruise was unrelieved bliss. Cecile de Rothschild had chartered a two-masted sailboat for her four guests. Her brother Alain's two-master, the *Ziata*, accompanied us all the way and is the most beautiful yacht I, or apparently anyone else, has ever seen. We explored the Turkish coast with its extravagantly grand ruins. We saw your friend Rosie Rodd Baldwin's boat passing us once, but I never did get to meet her. We ended up at horrible Kos, where I visited the ruins again. But it was filled with tourists, and the birds had fled to haunt a more deserted place—there was no magic there without you, Barbara.

I remember with warmth our few days together at Miramar. I bolted my door that night not to keep the danger out but in. What the hell, let's do it again!

Garbo is coming to stay with Cecile and I am off to stay with Cecil Beaton in London.

Flowers & love,
Sam

P.S. Tony, write a letter to your grandmother thanking her for the bathrobe—tacky as it is.

Letter from Antony Baekeland to Nina Daly, September 5, 1969

Miramar
Valldemosa
Mallorca

Dear Nini—
Thank you for the lovely kimono—fits perfectly and I needed one so badly. I am quite well. Jinty Money-Coutts & family come today for a picnic so I write this in haste. Maria sends love. What is the process of illumination? I don't understand Dad—except that if he's behaving badly it must mean that he feels badly.

Lots of love, dearest Nini.
T.

Letter from Antony Baekeland to Sam Green, September 5, 1969

Miramar
Valldemosa
Mallorca

Dear Sam—
It was extremely nice to hear from you: we had rather begun to think that the pernicious country house system had entirely swallowed you up, that you had vanished forever beyond the

green baize door; we feared, in fact, that the port and stilton had
entirely done you in. You can imagine how relieved we were to
hear from you that you were safe even in the lair of the dragon
ladies and their gentlemen.

A limpid day: the green explosions of the pines betray their
insubstantiality in this clear autumn light. I wrote my grandmother. Maria sends her best and says when are you coming
back. She hated the last guests we had but quite possibly because
they stayed for almost a month and went away without leaving
her anything. It was clump-clump-clump-noisy-feet-and-bang-
ing-doors sort of guests.

Have you ever had a garlic sandwich? They're terribly good. I
just had one for lunch. You take about ten cloves of garlic,
some of that funny herb that grows in the garden, some cheese,
and a raw onion and make this monstrous sandwich that's incredibly good.

My birthday passed uneventfully except for this wonderful
typewriter which makes writing much easier. I love cold print
and Mummy was adorable to give me such a lovely present in
her situation. Wrote my father about the conversation we had,
reminded him that he had promised to give her some money but
no word back. I never thought life would turn out to be so peculiar.

Tony

Letter from Barbara Baekeland to Sam Green, September 28, 1969

% Mme. Woodward de Croisset
Paris

Darling Sam—
A few minutes before midnight—my birthday. How old? None
of your business!

Marie Harriman died so my birthday luncheon with friends at
the Hôtel Lambert has been called off. Ethel has asked some
people here among whom will be Teenie Matisse Duchamp. I'll
give her your love.

If only I could have some peace and forget my incessant worries—financial mostly—for a few days! Tried selling some jewelry but the price I was offered was ridiculous.

Ethel keeps reminding me how old I am (and she exaggerates, too), otherwise I would seriously consider another, the oldest, profession!

Am building stables in Mallorca and paying for them on a monthly basis—they will be perfect & replete with 2 horses. I am also going to build servants' quarters in the old olive press. The place is too big for one person—maybe you'd like to share it with me? If you don't want to, I'm going to look for someone else—someone *RICH*.

Very peaceful here at Ethel's. Mr. Wuss is in bliss—doesn't seem to miss Miramar & is being very well fed. He's a dear fellow but not enough of a companion for me.

Tony is now lost—crawling through the tunnels of London low-life, I suspect.

You said nothing about your plans or where you might be. Am told touring the Dordogne with friend Cecil Beaton so will send this on to him. I don't know what you're up to, Sam, but I want you to know that I don't like all of it—I would like to know where to reach you. I'd like you to inquire about the Cadogan Square flat in London. Looks as though I might be able to settle things next month and Tony was mad about it.

Love,
Barbara

ETHEL WOODWARD DE CROISSET

Now I'll tell you about the time I tried to help Barbara in all her problems. She wanted to make some money, to keep up the life she had had, so she conceived this idea of having three apartments—New York, Paris, and London. She would rent two and stay in one, you know, and move around between the rentals. The little penthouse apartment in New York, which she rented for a very small price—five hundred or something—she would sublet with her furniture for, say, fifteen hundred a month. And she wanted to do the same thing in Paris. And it was Sam Green's idea that she also get this apartment in London on Cadogan Square that belonged to some friends of his. But it was just the end of the lease that she would be buying—for something like ten thousand dollars. This was before this great inflation had started—or this great depression—I can't remember which. She was going to furnish it and then rent it out for a very high price. Well, it seemed to me absolutely insane.

First of all, she should never have had to make money. She had every right to be supported by her husband. Brooks wasn't giving her money regularly, and that's where I tried to help—I called up his financial people and I said, "You must send money regularly to Barbara—if she has a regular amount, it will help her be more stable."

And when that didn't work, I said to Barbara, "I'm going to give you ten thousand dollars, and with this money you're going to pay what you owe your divorce lawyer in New York so he can fix everything up for you, because lawyers like to be paid. And just forget about this London thing because it's ridiculous." And I explained to her very carefully how putting money into the London operation would bring her *nothing*.

You'd think she would have seen that this would have solved all her problems—as easy as that. Not at all! She did exactly what she wanted to do—she went and got the Cadogan Square apartment. And she gave *me* as a financial reference. Can you imagine! I received a letter from the owners saying would I guarantee that she had a great deal of money. I mean, *I* was paying for this folly! I folded up the letter and sent it to Barbara with a note saying, "You can write these people and tell them I'm *dead* because I certainly will not guarantee that you're solvent." So you'd think she would have been a little embarrassed about it, wouldn't you? *Not* at all. When she arrived to stay with me in Paris, she treated it all as a little joke. She said, "How *funny* you are, Ethel! What a *card* you are! Imagine my writing to them that you died!" This extraordinary bravura—you know, right to the last *drop*. And so she went ahead with this project which, had she not been assassinated, I don't know *how* it would have ended.

Letter from Barbara Baekeland to Sam Green, November 27, 1969

% Michael Edwards
London, W. 1

Sam darling—
Got here last night. I spoke to my mother this morning who is

putting an ad in the newspaper so maybe I'll be able to rent my flat in New York without going back.

The terrible Brooks cut my allowance by a third this month. Received the news while at Ethel's. She was so furious she offered to lend me $15,000—I accepted $10,000 so when I come back to do battle, I will be, at least, armed. This, after I sent him a wire on our anniversary which started "Once upon a time." Anyway, isn't Ethel *adorable*—I am so touched by my friends, I just can't tell you.

Also, & this will amuse you—Ethel got invited for the first time in 25 years by Cecile de Rothschild to the country. She & Cecile had a dinner alone together which aside from the soup & fish consisted of a barrage of questions, inquiries, speculations and so on about *me*! Cecile to Ethel: "I hear that Sam is having an affair with *that woman*!"

Am looking at the Cadogan Square flat again today.

Lots of love,
Barbara

Telegram from Barbara Baekeland to Sam Green, February 13, 1970

I SEND YOU A B-B-B-BABY FOR A VALENTINE MY LOVE

BARBARA

ELIZABETH BLOW
Well, first it was *his* baby—she was going to have Sam Green's baby. And she was in her forties, her *late* forties! And this was, okay, possible, but not probable, and I was really concerned about her. Then she switched it from Sam's baby to just *a* baby. By—by *God*. I am dead serious. If you interpreted her rather garbled, marvelously excited conversation, this was really the Immaculate Conception all over again. Well, then I got really seriously alarmed.

Letter from Barbara Baekeland to Sam Green, March 21, 1970

London, W. 1

Dear Sam—

Am reading Kenneth Clark—came across an interesting definition of Moses' burning bush in a book on Fairford Church and its windows. It appears the bush was meant to contain the Divine Presence & burned without being consumed. It was meant to have contained the body of the Blessed Virgin when she became the Mother of the Son of God. But there's a big difference between bush fires & such, is there not, Sam?

Barbara

SYLVIE BAEKELAND SKIRA

She pretended to Brooks first that she was pregnant by Sam Green and then that this was an Immaculate Conception or whatever it was, so that gives you a vague idea of the romanticism, if you want to call it that. I call it sheer looniness. She didn't have solidity anymore, because Brooks had always been her anchor. This was why he was so worried about her when he left, because he knew he was the only one who could keep her out of trouble.

ELIZABETH BLOW

She went off someplace—out of town or out of the country, I can't remember—and I happened to be seeing Nini and I wondered if *she* knew about the baby and I thought maybe we should talk about this thing, but then I thought, *Should* we? Anyway, one day Barbara simply stopped talking about it herself. She was busy again, decorating the new apartment in London.

Letter from Barbara Baekeland to Sam Green, May 4, 1970

81 Cadogan Square
London, S.W. 1

Darling Sam—

So good speaking to you last night. You are my confidence man (I mean you give it to me). Anyway I have bought the flat and am in the process of decorating it. I have made marvelous pro gress—all electricity put in order, couches designed by me & being made, (very pretty) pictures hung, curtains cleaned, dining-room table painted in black lacquer (am off now to pay for it). Tomorrow will buy plants & a tree for upstairs.

And tomorrow my beautiful steel bed comes! Right now I am sitting on my mattress surrounded by a welter of papers—notes to myself, chores to do, ideas, etc. On my mattress is a most lovely coverlet made by my grandmother which gives me the most extraordinary comforting sensation—as if her hand were on my cheek. Divine wallpaper for bedroom.

I've knocked down the partition between the upstairs rooms and it looks smashing. Am taking down the balustrade as well— I have a pretty china planter to replace horrid newel post—and am using my two 19th cent. steel park benches as barriers.

From time to time—at 4 A.M. or 5—I wonder *why* I am involved in all these banalities and I dearly wish for the peace and comtemplation necessary to go on with my novel.

To listen to the sound of rain would be such a joy . . . an awareness of time—one's own, that is. One thing I have thought is that the more complex the synapses in the brain, the further the curve to infinity—for didn't Einstein say that infinity was comprised of many small dots that became through denseness a kind of exponential curve?

I wish I could see you. You are one of the halves of my reality, the other being Tony. I miss you both, and all my friends, and I cannot *stand* the lower-middle-class Englishman—the shopkeeper with his servility, his inefficiency, and appalling snobbishness. I really dislike the English as much as I can anyone & I'm sure my Celtic blood knows why.

I just hope I haven't made a horrible mistake with this flat. Would so much rather be working on Miramar and waiting for you to (maybe!) show up—I'm such a hopeless optimist.

In Mallorca there kept resounding in my mind a refrain which was "And this is the way the world ends"—only it wasn't—it doesn't. . . .

Here's a kiss for the middle of your mind—from mine.

Love,
Barbara

P.S. Thank you, Sam, for all your encouragement—urgings— to take this flat. It will be a successful venture—I feel it!

Letter from Antony Baekeland to Sam Green, May 15, 1970

> Miramar
> Valldemosa
> Mallorca

Dear Sam—

Happy birthday—Mummy wrote me you had one around this time. It's beautiful here but we are having a bit of trouble with a whole chain of furious masons who have not been paid by the horse person who claims not to have been paid by Mummy who has paid him she says.

The other day when I was fishing I had a look for some earrings Mummy tossed away when she was at the next farm. I couldn't find them as I had really no idea of where she was sitting—"under some tree," she said. So I've asked her to send me a map because it's a shame to lose the beautiful ones you gave her.

Told Maria I'm writing you and she sends salutations. I'm working quite hard on some clay I got in Palma and making small animals and things.

> Love,
> Tony

Letter from Barbara Baekeland to Sam Green, June 20, 1970

> Miramar
> Valldemosa
> Mallorca

Darling Sam—

Could I ask you to do me two favors. I was told about a Pekingese lady by Mrs. Turner, the service tenant at 81 Cadogan Square. I called her and she has a little red bitch that I dearly want. If you could have a look at the parents to estimate size & quality I'd be "ever so grateful" (Eliza speaking!). She will bring the merchandise to you—just call. . . .

Also, Tony has a hankering to give some Scottish bagpipes to a Spanish friend. It seems they used to play them around here. They can be found at a shop at 14A Clifford St.

> Love—
> Barbara

P.S. Baborca the Arab stallion is for sale and I long to buy him but when I finished doing the flat in London I had only $229.00 to last me until July 1st—*just* under the wire! But I will only owe one more $1,000 on the flat and will be able to pay back Muriel Murphy and my mother in September—Emily Staempfli next, and then Ethel! How large is *your* begging bowl?

Letter from Sam Green to Barbara Baekeland, June 25, 1970

% Cecil Beaton
Salisbury
England

Dear Barbara,
Talk about bliss! Getting out of N.Y. has been the best thing that's ever happened to me. You'll find me a new and charminger person. You may find that as early as a week from now.

I arrived on Sunday to find Cecil in the hospital. So I had several days to fill up on my own.

I'll be arriving at Palma on Fri. or Saturday. I'm looking forward to seeing you and Tony and Miramar. I will be there with a bagpipe but *not* with a Peke. You'll have to get your own horrid defective thing. Besides, I know *nothing* about dogs and would botch the job.

Love,
Sam

Letter from Barbara Baekeland to Sam Green, July 28, 1970

Miramar
Valldemosa
Mallorca

Dear Sam—
I'm sorry we missed each other and couldn't say goodbye. Ethel, who had been having a rather miserable time (all my fault), wanted to see the convent and I simply couldn't say no. It was interesting and I lost track of time. Anyway I didn't think you would leave for another few days and can't imagine how I could have not seen you between the house and the beach. Anyway in

going to the beach we did see Tony but didn't stop. He appeared to have had an accident and was trying to straighten out a dented fender but the car belongs to Hugo Money-Coutts and not only does Tony not have permission to use it but he has no license. If he should have another accident I'm afraid it would be hell on him. He might be locked up for years. If you have any influence with him you might point out to him the danger of using other people's property without proper sanction and of breaking laws!

He has been asked to appear before a tribunal on August 22—on a contraband charge. I am hoping Hugo will be here—or Tony's father—but I think Hugo would be better. Then I pray Tony will get away from here. I am very worried about him and wish you could come back for just a few days so I could talk with you about him.

I regret having dragged you into all of this—or was it the other way around? Anyway you have all my love for whatever it's worth. It seems to pull disorder, tears, and early sorrow in its wake. Sometimes I feel that I relinquish my better judgment to fate—or God or something. Anyway I don't seem to be in control and maybe that's for the best. I still can't find my green earrings which you asked me not to lose and this upsets me almost more than anything—I've looked everywhere. They are either at the farm next door or in an olive grove. Dear Sam, we have had such a strange and lovely time.

Barbara

P.S. Tony gave away his microscope and typewriter! And what happened to all his money? He must have given it away, too. And should he be encouraged in this? I know he is an adult but I can't keep bailing him out as I simply haven't got the where-withal to do so—the boy he gave it to can't even type!

ALASTAIR REID

In the summer of 1970 I ran into Barbara in the main street in Palma. I was living way up in the mountains, in a village called Gallilea. I hadn't seen her since 1962 when she hailed me in the street in Málaga—she and Brooks and Tony were visiting Ethel de Croisset—and that was the last time I saw them *en famille*. The next thing is that I heard from Ethel's mother, Elsie Woodward, that Brooks and Barbara were breaking up. That day in Palma Barbara told me the whole painful thing about Brooks dumping her. A few days later I went up to see her. Tony wasn't there, but later on they both drove over to Gallilea to visit me, we had lunch at the pension, and from that point on, Tony sent me poems that he'd written. What I used to do was very patiently point out to him technical things and give him books to read.

But then suddenly he began to change and write prose—little pieces of prose about a page long. Some of them were really quite eerie, as though they were fragments of some enormous thing, but I couldn't imagine what or where they were coming from, because his poems had been more or less bucolic and what you might expect as exercises, and suddenly I realized there was a very savage landscape inside Tony.

I began to see him as rather cruelly victimized by circumstance and I realized then that the Brooks/Barbara thing had left him . . . had just left him, abandoned him, *stopped* him.

Of course, Barbara's version of how things were was always very positive. She was a great, you know, smoother-over.

That summer I got pulled back in. But it's a couple of summers later when I saw that what I had thought was a merely understandably disturbed context was *infinitely* more than that—it was all coming apart then, it was all really unhinging itself. I mean, you were looking into something terrible.

Letter from Barbara Baekeland to Sam Green, August 22, 1970

Miramar
Valldemosa
Mallorca

Dear Sam—

Tony received a fine today of 120 pesetas and an admonition. I did not go to Palma with him but our horseman did. Brooks Baekeland never showed up—nor does he seem to be concerned about Tony's troubles. Anyway I thought *you* might be.

I am very tired, having in the last month risen at 5 a.m., fed & watered the horse, cleaned the stable, weeded the garden, watered the plants, fed the cat, cooked the breakfast, washed up, planned the meals, driven 20 miles to shop for food, driven back 20 miles to cook lunch, read poetry, listened to music, washed up, washed the kitchen floor, swept the house, cleaned the bathroom, made my bed, looked at the view, cut flowers, arranged same, wrote letters, paid bills, kept accounts, walked down 1,000 ft. to the sea & back for a quick swim, prepared cocktails, cooked dinner, dressed & looked beautiful for dinner, made conversation, been entertaining, left the dishes, and God alone knows what I did when I finally got to bed! Anyway I'm tired and am off (I hope next week) to Cadaqués for a few days and from there to Ethel's in Málaga (while work here is in progress) for a rest.

Hope you're having a good time—Ethel says she heard it's going to be a very boring cruise.

This is my last letter to you!

Love,
Barbara

ETHEL WOODWARD DE CROISSET

I had been to stay with her in this terrible house on the cliff the month before. I'd bumped into Mimi Cohane, Jack's wife before Heather, in Cadaqués, and she said, "You must go to see Barbara in Mallorca." Mimi, you see, had just been there, and said that things were going very badly. She told me how she'd been walking around the property with Barbara and the first thing she saw in the garden was a chair, a broken chair, and she said, "What's that chair doing in the flower beds?" And Barbara said, "Oh, pay no attention to it. Tony put it there." Pay no attention! And then they did a tour of the house, and on the steps going down to the cellar there was a typewriter—smashed, absolutely mangled! And Mimi said, "My God, what's that?" "Oh, pay no attention to it. Tony was upset about something and threw it down there."

So I went to see her and when I arrived, Michael Alexander was also there and the table was set for this lovely evening on the terrace. But in the middle of dinner Barbara had a fit of madness over something, and she insulted us—I mean, like a madwoman! You know, some general insult: "You goddam fucking fools!" You know, what *mad* people say—I saw a person in the bus once screaming like that. Barbara went howling out into the garden, in the moonlight. And we tried to reason with her to come back in the house and go to sleep. I tried every way—being very severe—you know, all the things you *try*. And after that, exhausted, I gave up, and she stayed out in the field. As I went off to sleep, I could hear Michael Alexander talking with Tony, who was terribly upset by all this, saying, you know, "Tony, *don't* feel responsible."

The next morning I was cleaning up—there was a mess of dirty dishes, thirty, forty dishes—and Barbara came sashaying in and said, "*You* don't have to do that." And I decided not to speak to her—I was going to give her a little bit of *my* temper. So I kept a stony silence. She just ignored this sort of thing, you know—*airily*. I think I relented after some time. We never mentioned the drama of the night before. You know, you just never mentioned these terrible things.

Letter from Barbara Baekeland to Sam Green, August 24, 1970

> Miramar
> Valldemosa
> Mallorca

Sam—
Tony says you told him I was the most impossible woman you'd ever met. I don't think it's correct to talk to a young man about his mother this way!

> Barbara

11

SNAPPING BACK

In 1979 Tony Baekeland was gradually taken off his medication until he reached a stage where he seemed to the authorities "quite rational, quite reasonable." Dr. Gogarty was still resistant to the idea of his being released without the assurance of regular follow-up care. When Tony himself learned what the costs involved might amount to—$50,000 and up per year for a private facility—he told Dr. Gogarty, "No way—I don't have it."

An officer from the American Embassy in London continued to monitor Tony. A State Department document concerning a visit on March 20 notes that "Baekeland appeared to be in good health and spirits." Another document, dated June 8, states that "Baekeland says he has been told by his doctor that he can expect to be released in a few months." But another document reporting on a visit five months later, on November 13, mentions that Tony Baekeland could count on being released only sometime "in the near future."

Postcard from Antony Baekeland to Sam Green, September 9, 1970

> Dear Sam—
> On the plane to Mallorca. Been visiting with my father who is now living in Brittany—a nice change. I miss you and think of you often. Perhaps we'll see each other soon? Much love from your screwy friend.
>
> Tony
>
> P.S. How is my sainted mother?

Letter from Barbara Baekeland to Sam Green, September 18, 1970

> *France*
> Transatlantique
> French Line
>
> Darling Sam—
> I've just had a fabulous morning, working from 6:00 to 1:15 finishing my novel and roaring with laughter—some of it's very funny. You'd better check it out before I decide whether or not to publish it. There isn't a word in it which isn't true.
> This ship is first class. I've eaten $1,000 worth of caviar since I boarded and all the wine is free!
> Have spoken to no one except my muse—very funny fellow.
> Tonight will have cocktails with an old friend who is aboard—Valentina. *Shall* we speak about Garbo? And shall I drop *your* name?
> Having a lovely time refusing to be picked up. Am knocking them dead with my new clothes! I look great in them. Please charge some for yourself—pay later.
> Please drop Tony a line in Mallorca. He loves you and I know would be cheered to hear from you.
> My plans are, as usual, vague—dependent on the book, the divorce, the state of my finances, etc., etc. Wish I could have someone's help with the latter. My income is quite handsome as I pay no taxes, and will go up in April when the London flat is

rented again. But no matter how much comes in, it all seems to go out. If I make money on the book I'll be quite well off.

You have already read the Spring and Winter sections but not Autumn and Summer. Summer is a kind of summation and it is that section in which you play a role. I would like to know if you think the treatment is too candid and, if it were to be accepted by a publisher, if you would have any objections. I prefer not to disguise or change the names. I am, as you can understand, anxious to have your clearance, as once I am assured that neither Tony nor you have any objections to the frank treatment, I can go ahead with the necessary steps and submit the manuscript for publication. Meanwhile here it all is. Please let me know what you think. I can't tell if the structure is sound and if the four sections belong organically together. Would appreciate any suggestions.

Love,
Barbara

Letter from Sam Green to Barbara Baekeland, October 15, 1970

Fire Island, New York

Dear Barbara,
I am sorry that it has taken me so long to write this letter. Of course you have my permission and best wishes in having the book published—if you can find a publisher, that is. I very much doubt that you will be able to, as—content aside—it is very unfinished. My impression is that it is not only a first draft, but that you didn't even reread it after it was typed—there were so many imperfections and redundancies on almost every page.

As to the content: I cannot think why anyone would be interested in the self-indulgent rampagings of a mad international wastrel. I am referring to the last portion of the book, you must realize, as the first segments are very lovely, interesting, beautifully written, and polished. There is such a deterioration in style between the first part and the last that it is difficult to believe the same person had a hand in both. While in the beginning the author has some objectivity, as well as considerable insight into the personalities and needs of the other characters, in the second there are nothing but obtuse value judgments: "she is a dear"—now *that* tells the reader a lot! These comments are about as deeply as you go into understanding anyone else.

The principal theme seems to be the persecution of a woman by Spanish authorities because she, as a *guest* in their country, refuses to comply with the rules which govern their way of life. She rampages around Spain—and the rest of the world—demanding attention, or whatever else is her immediate need, from everyone she encounters. Not only does she demand SERVICE—but QUALITY service as well. And what does she give in return? Only money. Grudgingly, and not very much, at that.

Perhaps if the heroine were a tiny bit servile herself—at least to the needs and concerns of those with whom she has some emotional or blood ties—it might occur to her that people are here to help each *other* instead of simply to make demands.

Perhaps you should rewrite the book as a journal—for that's exactly what it is, a jotting down of observations—without any descriptions (most of which are of concern only to you—in fact, the only concern you have for the reader is the odd "we shall see" interjected between the ramblings), and try to discover why your life in the last years has been so agonized. And if you feel that you are still right and everyone else is wrong, then continue on your way.

This is a tough letter because you asked for my opinion and I'm giving it to you straight—without any indulging of your fantasies. I hope you know that I am concerned and that that is why I have made the effort.

Love,
Sam

ANATOLE BROYARD
She was in my writing class at the New School for a while and she was the only *grande dame* we had—it was as if Mrs. Vanderbilt had walked into class. She had some talent but she didn't work hard enough—she just wanted to fling the thing out into the world and be a success.

Steven M. L. Aronson

Somebody had told Barbara I was that season's bright young man in publishing, so she tantalized me with her novel the very first time we met. I was introduced to her in her own living room, by a friend we had in common who had brought me to one of those parties she was always giving.

The apartment was sort of junglelike. I remember the living room—the way it was lit was interesting, and it seemed exotic and romantic, with all those terraces looking out over everything. And I remember my first sight of Barbara: surrounded, attended, her tawny head thrown back. What a magnet. She was so generous with friends, so bold with total strangers (me!), you would not easily have guessed she was a woman at the end of her rope.

She became a friend from that evening. And later, when he came back from Mallorca, she worked Tony into my life. The three of us spent several cozy, uneventful weekends in a cottage she was renting on the beach in East Hampton—until the Sunday morning she burst exuberantly into my room with the *Times*, handed me several layers of it, then sprawled across my bed to read the magazine section. A few minutes later I looked up and saw Tony standing in the doorway. I'll never forget his face, contorted as it was into an incomprehensible expression of rage. Barbara had told me nothing of his history, but when I read her book I understood what kind of jealousy it was that caused that rage.

A few weeks later she came to a dinner at my place in town in a black evening dress made of hundreds of little feathers. For weeks after that, they kept turning up—behind sofas, under chairs. I sent one to her with a note. "I laughed and laughed," she wrote back, "and will keep the feather forever." From then on, in almost every letter she wrote me from the mad gypsy life that she was leading, she enclosed a feather from that dress—so many feathers, it must have been plucked clean.

In a letter postmarked London, November 17, 1972, the day she was killed, she said, "Tony somewhat improved—oh! but it's heavy!" She was inviting me to spend Christmas with the two of them in Cadogan Square. Folded into the envelope was the accustomed feather: "Would that it were from the goose that laid the golden egg! What can I do with feathers except fly?" By the time that feather had crossed the Atlantic, she was six days dead. The last lovely flutter of her strong wings.

Had she lived, Barbara would be a woman completely beyond my imagining now. In fact, the night I read her novel I saw that in some ways she already was.

It was part fantasy, part confession, part paean to profane love. Of course, Barbara—great, self-appreciating personality that she was—must also have written it with the awareness of contributing to her own legend.

What I remember best is the section titled "Summer," in which the heroine and her son and a male friend set sail on some tainted sea. First the heroine seduces her own son, then she seduces the friend. Later she comes upon her son and the friend making love. "Leave him alone! My son is not a homosexual!" she screams. "He functions very well sexually with *me*. I'm not going to let a little pansy like you ruin everything I've accomplished." It was wild. It was garbled. But despite its obviously paranoid content, the book had a power, a certain unnerving power.

ELLEN SCHWAMM
You couldn't tell with Barbara—the lines between reality and her imagination seemed sort of shadowy, or suitably moveable, at will. We were in the same writing class. I remember she claimed to be the heroine of one of James Jones's novels.

FRANCINE DU PLESSIX GRAY
Barbara's novel was absolutely terrible. I remember her coming to stay with us in Connecticut and giving us two or three chapters to read. We told her it needed a lot of work, and she dug into us in *such* a way! She started attacking *my* writing. I'd just published "Governess" in *The New Yorker*, which later became the first chapter of my novel *Lovers and Tyrants*. She said, "*That* was a piece of shit. How do you dare to criticize *me*? Jim Jones thinks my work has genius."

Letter from James Jones to Barbara Baekeland, Undated

10, quai d'Orléans
Paris IV°

Dear Barbara,
I am returning your story manuscript with this letter. I can only say that I have to treat it as a professional writer or not at all, and

my feeling about the story is that it simply does not come off. I find the style much too heated and fervid for the material; and I don't think the resolution is believable, given the characters.

With regard to the novel which you mentioned you have finished, I can't of course say anything about that now. However, if the style is at all similar to this story, or fragment, I would cool the style considerably. I would of course be glad to read it for Delacorte Press, but if it follows in the vein of this piece you sent me, I can almost guarantee you that the editors there would not take it.

Gloria will be writing to you about Tony and all the other things. Always all personal best.

Sincerely yours,
James Jones

ELIZABETH WEICKER FONDARAS
One weekend in East Hampton Barbara came to dinner and afterwards we settled around the fire in the big winter living room and she read her manuscript aloud to us. She was so excited and enthusiastic about it. I remember extravagant images—the striped walls were coming in on her, or she would be floating down to the sea with rocks rolling all around her. It was like a dream. They were the strange ravings of a person in a crisis—you could see trouble and despair.

DR. E. HUGH LUCKEY
I was a houseguest of Liz Fondaras's the Saturday night Barbara Baekeland decided to entertain us by reading from her novel. I sat there bored stiff for about an hour of recitation. I would have probably gone to bed if it hadn't been for Liz.

John Sargent, who's the chairman of the board of Doubleday, was also present. Liz had set that up, you know. She's the great matchmaker of all time—she tries to help all of her friends.

Well, I knew the game. When Barbara Baekeland took that manuscript out, I knew what was going on—she wasn't interested in how *I* would like it, she was interested in how John Sargent was going to like it. I remember the look on his face as it was being read.

JOHN SARGENT
It went on and on and on. We couldn't get it to stop.

After she was killed, I used to send Tony things in the loony bin. Not books—they wouldn't let me send books. I could only send non-controversial items, such as shirts and clothing. He wrote me little thank-you notes.

Letter from Antony Baekeland to James Reeve, November 20, 1979

Broadmoor

Dear James,

I think I will start writing seriously when I get out of here and get myself settled, whenever and wherever that is. I have the material for several interesting books, I think, and I will enjoy working on them.

I am afraid I am very disillusioned with most of the people here: now that I am clear in myself I no longer see them as amusing characters but as the moral derelicts which they really are—too stupid to learn from their pain and unhappiness, they will continue forever to batter their heads against the wall, ignoring the door.

I long for some interesting talk and company: the routine here is very dull and always the same old chitchat. Even the most beguiling of companions begin to bore one after so many years: I am not talking about true friends. It seems ridiculous to me that I must undergo more of this psychiatric mumbo jumbo in the U.S. My troubles were purely spiritual and stemmed from a mistake I made a long time ago; it wasn't a mistake at all, as I now realize: much good will come from it. But I do feel that the ideas held by the "doctors" about the mind, soul, and body are primitive, ugly, and pathetic in the extreme.

Mind you, all this world of doctors, businessmen, workers, actors, etc., are just robots controlled by the Mind of a very few Ladies and Gentlemen. I don't think of the mass of people as degraded or pathetic or anything like that, it is just that they are not "real" people and although they control my life at the moment, *grace à la Reine*, I don't let them bother me nor do I take them at all seriously.

One of my books will be about the human termite-colony as it really is, I think. Or perhaps I won't write it at all—I shall have to wait and see. Anyway, James, my fondest wishes and you must please give my regards to your mother.

Love always,
Tony

Letter from Antony Baekeland to Barbara Baekeland, January 8, 1971

Miramar
Valldemosa
Mallorca

Dearest Mum,

Telegram from you four days ago inviting me to New York. I replied today saying that I will come if necessary but would rather not as I am really happy here. If sometimes I write despairing letters it is only that I am disappointed and frustrated at not being able to come more quickly: the other night playing chess I had such a clear vision of my blinding greed to win, to cheat with myself, and saw the calm detachment of my higher self arranging it (the game, like a droplet of quicksilver) so that I could only make the right move if I felt the right feeling. In regard to what you say about intellects I doubt if I could find many of such a caliber and quality as those of Maria and Sebastian, my family here at Miramar. And anyway, intellection is exactly that which I am trying to get away from: these relative truths and falsehoods of our time, of all times, of art, of science, and of literature have no value for me; for the present at least, they are a poison to me and to my pure mind. Perhaps one day soon I will be able and willing to venture into that bog, but by then, perhaps, things will have ceased to be relative to one another and will become relative to One. I don't think you realize how closely I live with my family here.

What you say about Physical Love is no doubt true, but as our bodies are reflections of our souls' desire towards life, everything in me impels me to touch and love another person. Anyway I know the difference between love and lust so I suppose I mustn't worry. Don't get too caught up with visions of the past or other things like this. I have been having this very strongly on and off for two years and I find it imposes a great strain on the mind (intellect, that stray sheep) which tries in its futile way to fit together the apparent parts of a fluid that extends through itself in all directions. All the years you scolded me for smoking I was only taking it for one reason. I have never experienced what you call "mere pleasure," what Shakespeare, I believe, called "a waste of folly," lust. I have experienced it but could not call it pleasure but only the hopeless groan of agony of abandoned oceans.

I am glad you saw what I told you last year about suicide is true. Everything we have told in love is true.

Tony

Miwa Svinka-Zielinski

Barbara invited me for dinner in New York to celebrate because Tony had come home from Spain, and she also invited Teenie Duchamp and Elizabeth Fondaras. And during this dinner, Barbara had some words with Tony, she told him some remark which was not pleasant, so Tony left the table, and we finished dinner. And then he came and took ice from the ice bucket and put it down her dress. She started to laugh. Then he went to his room and a few minutes later came out undressed—totally. He was naked.

Elizabeth Weicker Fondaras

He just streaked from one end of the apartment to the other—I think it was a diagonal run he made. He must have just wanted to get his mother's attention. Barbara thought it was sort of funny.

Brendan Gill

I didn't have much of an impression of Tony; he was always very dim to me, almost nonspeaking. I don't think I exchanged ten words with him. He was just like a walk-on, a zombie.

Eleanor Ward

To me Tony was a complete zero. Now whether this was because his mother was there . . . I never saw him when she wasn't around, so

what he was like without her I don't know—he might have been a
very different person.

KATHARINE GARDNER COLEMAN

He was really quite peculiar, but you know, we'd seen so many disturbed young people in the sixties. *They* snapped back, though.

SARA DUFFY CHERMAYEFF

He showed up at my house one afternoon—I hadn't seen him for,
like, nine years—and he read me a story he had written and I will
just never forget it. Because *he* was the artist. *Not* Brooks. *Not* Barbara. *Tony* was.

It was a story about one day in his life in Barbara's penthouse. He
told the day in that place and he described everything about it—the
little room next to the hall where you came in, that rotunda with the
marble floor that Barbara had fixed up with the candelabra, her bed
with the leopard skin. He described her frying liver in a pan for lunch
and how at the end of the day she went out to dinner, all dressed
up—he described her furs and everything—and the last line of the
story, after she went out the door, said, "And I felt no bigger than a
lima bean."

ELIZABETH BLOW

That spring Barbara put him in the National Academy School of
Fine Arts on Fifth Avenue way up in the nineties. She invited me for
dinner and the first thing she said to him was, "I want you to show
Betty your drawings from class." He almost froze, he refused to
move, and so *she* went and got this large portfolio and started showing them to me. The drawings were very strange—there were figures
of people who didn't look like people. I mean, there was a sort of
nonhuman quality to these drawings, and there was also a kind of
infantile quality. As she laid them out, she would say, "Aren't they
marvelous!" and so forth. And I looked up at Tony and he was just
. . . stone, he was turned to stone.

SYLVIA LOCHAN

I was the registrar at the National Academy, and a couple of the
students came down to my office. They were a little disturbed because Antony Baekeland wasn't responding to anybody or anything,
he just seemed to be in a world of his own. They said the class was

painting from a still life—flowers and fruit I think it was—and that *his* canvas had figures on it with blood dripping down the side.

I went up to the classroom and I went over to talk to him. He was seated and I kind of bent down next to him and I said, "That's very interesting." He didn't respond to my being there, my presence—he was staring off into space. And then he turned around and I saw that he had painted his nose red. I walked out of the room and went down and called his mother and said I thought she should come right over and get him. And she did—she was a very good-looking woman, I remember. And that was the last I saw of him. It was obvious to me that he was very troubled at the time, and certainly, looking back, I think it's very surprising that he wasn't in some sort of hospital.

ELIZABETH BLOW

Barbara called me to say there had been what she described as—by this time she was using these little French phrases all the time—a *fracas*. "There was a little *fracas* at the National Academy," she said. "Nothing at all, darling, really nothing at all, and I had to take him out."

Patient Abstract, Antony Baekeland, Private Psychiatric Clinic, New York City, 1971

> PATIENT: BAEKELAND, Antony
> ADMITTED: May 21, 1971
> AGE: 25 (Born: Aug. 28, 1946)
> CIVIL STATUS: Single
> OCCUPATION: Student

CHIEF COMPLAINT: Mr. Baekeland enters the hospital fearful, delusional, hallucinating, with a heavy history of drug usage and inability to function.

PRESENT ILLNESS: Mr. Baekeland's history at no time has been a stable one and it is difficult to date the onset of his present illness. He dates the onset of the use of drugs (LSD, pot, amphetamines) to approximately seven years ago when he was living with his mother (although the patient's parents were together until three years ago, they often lived apart in various parts of Europe for years prior to their separation). Patient, him-

self, dates the onset of his increasing disorganization in living to
three years ago at the time of his parents' separation. At that
time patient's father left the patient's mother to live with a former lady friend of the patient's. At this point, patient's mother
allegedly made a suicide attempt. Since this time, the patient
has been tormented with alternating periods of fury at his parents and spells of depression and guilt in which he has felt he is
responsible for his parents' no longer living together. Although
the patient's father is financially well off, subsisting on family
fortune, he has provided no more than minimal financial assistance to his wife and son. Both the patient and his mother
seemed to have lived a "pillar-to-post" existence in the past three
months, globetrotting in a helter-skelter fashion and finding
themselves unable to adjust to the realistic changes required because of the new financial situation. Patient, himself, has become increasingly involved in the use of drugs and has
surrounded himself with a coterie of radical, artistic, would-be
jetsetters. His mother, determined that her son is something of a
"misunderstood genius" who was never meant to "work and toil
in this sick society," has found it impossible to curb his disorganization and to set limits on his unrealistic style of living and
flights of fancy. An emphasis upon social appearance despite the
reality of circumstances is a paramount idea in Mrs. Baekeland's
thinking also. At the time of the patient's admission, he was
living alternately with some hippie friends in Greenwich Village
and spending time with his mother at her apartment. He found
that he had difficulty separating his spheres of influence and
responsibility from those of his friends. Accordingly, he had become more withdrawn and sought to limit his involvements so
that he could maintain a sense of his own self-limits. The event
precipitating his admission to the Clinic consisted in his allegedly being chased and assaulted two days prior to admission
while he was walking through Central Park at night. He recalls a
nightmarish memory in which he was pursued with clubs by
police, finally arriving, fearful and disorganized, at his mother's
apartment. Although the patient was able to sleep for more than
24 hours after his arrival there, upon awakening, his mother
states that he was still extremely disorganized, delusional, fearful
and hallucinated. Moreover, he seemed very agitated and
mother was fearful of the possibility of his assaulting her. Accordingly, she arranged for his admission to the Clinic.

PSYCHIATRIC EXAMINATION: The patient is a tall young man with longish red hair dressed in modish clothes. He had an air of frenzied disorganization. His choice of vocabulary and his accent had a finishing-school quality. Patient spoke a great deal about his mother and his father and expounded in a grandiose fashion on his intentions to reunite his parents. He spoke of himself and his mother as though they were a team and his first and most persistent inquiries had to do with when he would be able to phone her. In view of the patient's present and past environments, both of which might be characterized as unstable, it was felt that his reconstitution from his state of agitated disorganization would be all that could be accomplished in Clinic.

COURSE IN CLINIC (May 21, 1971, to July 2, 1971): From the outset the patient's course in Clinic was stormy. Mrs. Baekeland seemed to align herself with the most bizarre and eccentric statements of her son against what she perceived as narrow-minded arbitrariness on the part of the staff. She spoke of the phones at the Clinic having been bugged and sought desperately to justify her son's assertion that he was God. Patient related in either a clinging, dependent manner or a supercilious, haughty fashion to other patients and ward personnel. For the most part he remained in his room and listened to Indian music by the hour. Any attempts to set limits on his unconventional behavior were met with fearful and angry resentment. Throughout the patient's hospitalization there were many angry, demanding phone calls from his mother. Ultimately, in spite of strong counsel on the part of the hospital staff not to do so, the patient's mother signed the patient out of the Clinic.

DATE OF DISCHARGE: July 2, 1971.

CONDITION OF DISCHARGE: Improved slightly.

PROGNOSIS: Poor.

Letter from Barbara Baekeland to Orin and Wendy Vanderbilt Lehman, July 3, 1971

New York

Dear Wendy & Orin—
My thanks for the time arranged for me with your doctor friend—he was very helpful.

Tony was discharged yesterday and the hospital is assuming all expenses—very chic of them, not to say enormously kind. I asked if Tony's discharge was because of our inability to meet the bills (Tony's trustees refused to invade his trust and Brooks refused to pay) and I was assured that it was not, that he had made great progress, and that they were satisfied that he was on the way to a recovery.

Thank you so much, again.

Love,
Barbara

Wendy Vanderbilt Lehman

I probably knew a lot of people better than I knew Barbara Baekeland but there's something sympathetic in my memory of her that is not there for a lot of *them*. She had called to ask me if I knew of anybody who could help Tony. My heart really went out to her. I always had the feeling that behind the façade there was a great spongy three-dimensional sort of person.

I remember some time after she wrote us that letter she came into P. J. Moriarty's, an Irish bar on Third Avenue in the Sixties somewhere—not bad—when Orin and I were having dinner after the theater, and she acted a little upset or drunk at the table. I think I remember her spilling a drink. I was sort of embarrassed for her—I mean, I knew something was wrong. You know that feeling you get and you almost don't want to see it clearly because you don't want it to be that way?

Cleve Gray

She called us up several times that summer and we didn't see her, but one day Francine and I were meeting someone at the Isle of Capri, and there was Barbara, having lunch all alone, which was very unlike her. She looked blowsy, she looked like an unhappy, beaten-down woman, and she was eating grossly and acting very strangely.

Letter from Barbara Baekeland to Sam Green, July 3, 1971

New York

Darling Sam—

Tony was discharged yesterday but as he is extremely photosensitive because of the medication he is taking, we decided to forgo the weekend on Long Island. He is, in any case, not up to the hassle involved in getting there and back and people wandering in and out, so we are having a lovely peaceful time in the apartment here and he is helping me with my chores—mostly gardening on the terrace and keeping the floors clean (the doctor said to give him lots of tasks).

He is still under very heavy medication which is being gradually reduced while he is spending these few days with me. The doctor told me that his illness is not secondary—that is to say, induced by drugs—but primary—which is to say, genetic. But they are impressed with his intelligence and insight and hold forth a great deal of hope.

Anyway, he is looking forward very much to seeing you—he is not well enough to see very many friends and then just one or two at a time.

Love,
Barbara

Sam Green

Both Tony and Barbara began paying me unexpected visits that summer. Barbara would appear at my apartment on West Sixty-eighth Street at two in the morning and bang on the door. Once she walked across Central Park barefoot. At two o'clock in the morning I just did not want to have drop-ins—Tony would show up anytime *he* felt like it, too.

"I must see you," Barbara would say. "It's very important. Open the door! I have to tell you what's happening"—you know, whatever emergency it was. Several times she spent the night in the hallway outside my apartment, when I wouldn't open the door. She would always be gone by morning. Once I opened the door and said, "Stop it! Get out of here, I've got to get *up* in the morning—I have a very important appointment. Please just go home. Here's five dollars, take a taxi!" I remember I grabbed her by the hair and pushed her, and that was the only time I ever pushed anybody. She stumbled or something down the stairs.

Letter from Barbara Baekeland to Sam Green, July 23, 1971

New York

Darling Sam—

I found your lighter—the one you lost last year. Hesitate to deliver same in person as with advancing age my hair seems to be getting thinner! So much was left at our threshold during our last *rencontre*, I can't afford another visit—except I would so very much enjoy seeing you. So if you ever feel you can have a quiet few minutes to extend me, I will arrange to meet you at your convenience.

Where shall I leave your lighter?

Love,
Barbara

HENRY H. PERKINS

My brother Mike, who was Tony's greatest friend from Avon, and Michael Nouri, who'd gone to Buckley with Tony and who's now an actor—he was in *Flashdance*—and Checka Draper and I all went over to see Tony. He wasn't in but Mrs. Baekeland was home and she said, "Hi, come on in. Tony'll be back in a little while." She asked us if we would like some wine and we said, "Yeah, sure," and we were talking and suddenly she just, you know, took her glass of wine and threw it into the fireplace and threw back her hair in the most amazing display of—I don't know. . . . Who could have done it better was Lauren Bacall, you know. And I started to laugh because, you know, I thought I'd missed something, but I noticed my brother wasn't laughing at all. So to sort of change the atmosphere, I began asking her about this lighter that was on the coffee table. I said, "This is very attractive. What is it? Alabaster? It looks like a candy cane." And she looked at me and said, "Eat it!" I didn't think I'd heard right. Then she said it again, she started screaming it: "Eat it, goddam you, eat it, eat it, eat it!" And we ran out of there.

Letter from Barbara Baekeland to Sam Green, August 12, 1971

New York
5:00 a.m.

Sorry to have to write you but I would like to have some explanation of just why you were so furious with me the other night. I waited for three hours on your stoop and asked for that, along with a glass of water. There was water, water everywhere but not a drop to drink, except on the lip of your paint cans on the terrace and it tasted of lead. You were not very polite and I hadn't even the chance of thanking you for looking after Mr. Wuss.

I'm really beginning to feel you really don't like me at all, Sam. And I find it altogether incredible—I have such a good time when I'm with you and usually that kind of pleasure is *réciproque*. Am I going to have to wait another year before you'll come to dinner again? For I will not give up trying to see you.

Saw Marisol the other night at Peter Gimbel's soirée—looking lovely—but, Sam, some people make voyages on the surface by walking over it and others voyage through space and time. It's a different kind of trip—both valid. I think the latter is perhaps more difficult—connections count for a lot.

I will be distressed if you don't call me and shall probably leave town if there is no possibility of ever seeing you. I only seem to be able to relax with you. I am so sorry you are angry with me again. I still don't understand why. It is not my wish to importune, but you are the only person I have ever known, with the exception of Brooks, of whom I have been truly fond who has turned his back on me—and even Brooks hasn't really done that! However, I've decided I'd rather be my own victim than his. I am attempting to have him give me back all moneys I had when I married him and to secure a divorce by asking for nothing else! I still haven't heard from him, nor will his lawyer communicate with mine.

Always,
Barbara

SAMUEL PARKMAN SHAW

I met Barbara at Daphne Hellman's. She had another lawyer at the time, with whom she was dissatisfied, and someone had said to her, "Why don't you try Sam Shaw?" I did relatively few divorces, partly because I didn't like them—you get people at their most anxious, and you rarely get a solution that's happy for anybody. So I wasn't particularly inclined to take her on as a client. There was an element of charm involved in it. She said, "Oh, please do it," and so forth and so on, and I said all right.

I met Tony perhaps a year after I first met Barbara. I met him at Daphne's, too, and I don't think I saw him more than three or four times after that. I thought he was quite beautiful that first time I saw him. I didn't really talk to him, but I did have an impression that he was strange. The second time I saw him was at a stand-up lunch at Barbara's, and on that occasion I talked to him for ten or fifteen minutes and thought him rather agreeable and interesting—imaginative.

The next time I saw him—well, he was beating up his grandmother and Barbara called me at my office, about six o'clock in the evening. By that time I knew a good deal about Tony's troubles and I said, "Why don't you call his psychiatrist?" She said she was too upset and for me to please come over right away. So I said, sure, I would. I jumped in a cab and I got over there and Nini was down in the lobby of Barbara's building. She seemed quite cool. I said, "What's going on?" and she said, "Tony tried to hurt me." Then Barbara came down and I said, "Well, what the hell are we going to do?" She said, "I'm scared to death of him." I said, "Did you call Justin Greene?" She said, "No. Would *you* call him?" So I went out to the public phone on the corner and called Greene, and he said, "I'm not going to come over. Whatever relation I have with Tony I don't want to jeopardize or destroy by seeming to be on his mother's side. If he's violent enough, just call the police and they'll come and take him away." So *he* was useless, and I went upstairs with Barbara, Nini going off in a cab to her own apartment. Tony was in the living room, he was looking distraught, but he didn't seem to me violent, so I sat down and chatted with him. Barbara was right there. It was my view that it was very dangerous for her to have him there for the night. I wanted to get him out of there but I didn't want to take him anywhere myself, I just wanted him to go somewhere and stay with friends or find himself a room somewhere. We sat there for quite a long time, I trying to convince him that he ought to go, and finally I decided that the best way to get him out of there was to take them out somewhere for supper and then figure out a way from there. They said fine and I said I just wanted to take a pee first.

So I went to the bathroom and when I came out Barbara was lying on the living-room floor—apparently unconscious. I thought she might even be dead. I knelt down to see whether she was alive. I felt her pulse and I couldn't find it. Tony was standing over her, with a very strange grimace on his face. I told him to go get some water. So he went and got a glass of water and I put some on a handkerchief and put it on her forehead. She didn't revive, and I said, "Tony, we've got to call a doctor right away." I was still down there with my hand on her pulse. And then I felt this terrible blow. I don't know how long I was unconscious. I think he hit me with a cane, because there was a cane on the floor—sort of a big knobbly cane. He belted me right across the nose with it. From on high.

When I woke up, I was really scared shitless. I figured he was out to kill me. I got up. Barbara was still unconscious and I thought maybe dead. And Tony was still standing right there, with a savage look on his face. I figure I've got to kill *him* or he's going to kill *me*. So I grappled with him and we rolled around the floor and I'm thinking, Shit, what a terrible way to die. He was very strong—I don't know how the hell he got that way because I don't think he ever did any exercises to speak of.

I finally wrestled him into the corner, I had his back against the wall and my right foot in his crotch and I was holding him there, but by that time I was so trembling and weak from all of this exertion and maybe the shock of being belted that I knew I couldn't hold him there for very long. I put my hand up to my nose—it felt like a bag of marbles, it just seemed to me to be all cracked—and I said, "Jesus Christ, Tony, you've really *ruined* my nose, and I'm afraid you've *killed* your *mother*. Listen, be a good fellow and go get me a towel with cold water on it." You see, I wanted to calm him down, because if I'd continued in this contest, he'd have killed me. So he went into the kitchen and got a towel and ran cold water on it and brought it over to me and I put it on my nose.

By this time Barbara was climbing to her feet, so *she* was okay. But I was just shaking with cold—you know how you get when you're in shock, you tremble uncontrollably—and I got her over to one side and I said, "Listen, while I talk to Tony, call the police." And then I said to Tony, "Come over and build me a fire in the fireplace, will you—I'm just shaking myself to pieces here." So he found some pieces of timber, put paper underneath, and lit it, and we sat by the fire, and in about ten minutes Barbara came back with the cops.

They took him away. He went perfectly willingly, philosophically—he didn't struggle, he didn't curse. They had an ambulance downstairs for him. And Barbara went with him over to Metropolitan Hospital, a public hospital over on Ninety-seventh Street and First Avenue.

I followed in a cab. I wanted to make sure everything was okay—that he was put in the proper hands. I went to see him later and he was peaceful.

Then I went to have my nose looked after. They said it was broken, and they set it and sewed it up, and a couple of days later I had an operation. The plastic surgeon did an absolutely marvelous job—a fellow named Smith. It looks the same, feels the same, sounds the same.

I turned over the whole divorce file to Barbara the next day and that was it—I don't know that I ever saw her again. They kept Tony at Metropolitan probably five or six weeks. The police asked me if I wanted to bring criminal charges and I said no.

From a Psychiatric Report on Antony Baekeland Ordered By the British Courts, January 5, 1973

> In 1971 he was admitted to the acute psychiatric ward of Metropolitan Hospital. The diagnosis was "schizophrenia, simple type, with elements of character disorder." The prognosis was "reasonably good." Attempts were made to send him to a private mental hospital, the Thompkins Institute in New Haven, but the father would not finance it and the plan was dropped.

WILLIE MORRIS

Those two! I always sensed disaster, I really did—the mother and the son were so askew. There's one dinner party she gave in East Hampton that I'll never forget. It was in the late fall of '71—I remember my black Lab, Ichabod H. Crane, had just died and I was in mourning. I went over with Muriel Murphy and the strangest thing happened—after dinner Barbara turned on me! For no reason at all. I was behaving myself quite well. But she ordered me to leave her house. I was totally flabbergasted. The other guests were embarrassed by it. It was as quick as a Mississippi thunderstorm. And so Muriel and I left.

But the next morning—I remember it so well—the son walked from their house to Muriel's, which is over on Georgica Pond, and delivered a note of apology from Barbara. It was a very sweet note. And I scribbled a note back telling her not to worry about it.

Then another funny thing happened. Saul Steinberg had been at that dinner, and I guess he was pretty much taken aback by the little incident, too, because he graciously gave me—he brought them over a few days later—a beautiful pair of watercolors which he had done for me, which he called *Yazoo*. That's my hometown in Mississippi. He titled one of them *Yazoo in the Winter* and the other *Yazoo in the Spring*. But Saul's a real gentleman, he didn't mention that little episode.

ELIZABETH WEICKER FONDARAS

Barbara and Tony were spending fall and winter weekends in that little house on the beach. I was worried about her. Once she parked a car she'd borrowed from Richard Hare on the wrong side of the Montauk Highway—facing traffic. It was towed away, and she had to come into the East Hampton police station to deal with it. The officer was sitting at a desk rather high up and Barbara said, "Come down off that desk up there! What kind of place is this, anyway?" And then when he did come down, she said, "Well, get a pencil so you can take this down right!" And he said, "I can't do it down here. I need the desk to write on—also my pencil's up there."

Eventually I called Paul Greenwood, a policeman who used to moonlight by driving me into New York occasionally when he was off duty and who'd been in the station the day Barbara came in. I said, "I just want to show you where Barbara Baekeland's house is, in case I ever have to call you to get over there quickly."

PAUL GREENWOOD

I was the sergeant on duty when she came in about her car. She was very, very, very emotional, very upset, and, you know, she proceeded to look down upon everyone there and give us the devil. She really was raising hell. She had on a long, funny-looking gown. We didn't have a chance to do any talking, she did all the talking—she insulted everybody. We just listened and let her get it off of her chest—we let them ventilate when they get that excited, then they'll cool off and you can reason with them.

I think she had her son with her, but I'm not sure about that. She was a Baekeland by marriage, right? And Baekeland was the name of the man that invented Bakelite originally, right? Well, she certainly acted like she was from the hufty-tufty there, you know—very haughty individual, I thought.

GLORIA JONES

I saw Barbara for the last time that winter, I guess. In Long Island. And she looked ratty—for Barbara, who always wore these marvelous furs and beautiful robes and the Chanels, you know.

SYLVIE BAEKELAND SKIRA

You have to understand that Barbara had been a great beauty. She was losing her looks and her husband had left her for someone much younger. She would write to Brooks saying, "I've been to the doctor, he finds me amazing. He thinks I have the body of a thirty-year-old," or, "My looks still stop traffic"—I remember *that* expression. She was terribly *accrochée* to this—holding on, holding on to this *fiercely*.

FREDERICK COMBS

I kept hearing from everyone how beautiful she'd been, and then Tom Dillow asked me over to her place in East Hampton for drinks—I remember it was the dead of winter. The son was there, too, and he was just sitting by the fire and we were having a perfectly, you know, average conversation when all of a sudden he leaps out of his chair toward his mother. He got within a few feet of her, and, I mean, his grimace and everything was incredible—a look of just total hatred. Then he just stopped in his tracks and went back to his chair by the fire, a rocking chair as I recall. It was a terrifying moment but she reacted as though nothing had happened and was seemingly more involved in how to calm *us* down, you know, and just get the conversation going again. I remember later she told us he had been burning the furniture in the fireplace that afternoon. Imagine being a stranger and sitting with someone and having them talk about the burning of furniture as though they were just simply saying would I like another cube of ice in my drink, you know. It was real casual.

Dominick Dunne

I met Barbara Baekeland when she came to the screening of a film that I produced. It must have been 1971 or '72. She stayed on afterwards to discuss the picture. I saw her a few times after that and once fetched something for her from her London apartment that she wanted in New York, a mink hat I think it was. I didn't know her very well, but I had several friends who were very close to her, and I had heard stories about Tony attacking her, particularly a tale of an attack he made on his mother at their house in East Hampton when friends of mine were present. The story was more or less dismissed at the time—"He didn't really mean it," that sort of thing—but became horrifying in retrospect after he actually did kill her.

Two years ago my own daughter, Dominique, was attacked and murdered by a former boyfriend. She had become frightened of him and broken off the relationship. It was not the first time that he had attacked her. There had been two previous instances. The thing that haunts us all, my wife and sons and me, and that we have to live with is that none of us thought in terms of·murder. It simply never occurred to us that the man was a killer. Afterwards, when it was too late, all the warning signs became clear.

Richard Hare

My wife and I used to drive Barbara and Tony out to East Hampton on weekends. They didn't have a car or anything, and I remember one day we were leaving—we left Fridays around one o'clock—Barbara took me aside and said, "Richard, Tony isn't quite himself, he's stopped taking his pills, but don't worry about it because I'm going to get him on the pills again."

All the way down in the car he was making these funny little nursery rhymes and, you know, singing to himself. So when we got to their house I took Barbara aside and said, "Barbara, I think it would be wise for you both to spend the night at *our* house. I don't like the idea of you being alone in the house here, with Tony not being quite right." She said, "Don't worry a thing about it. He's going to be fine." And I said, "Will you call me the first thing in the morning?" and she said, "Richard, I've been through this a hundred times before." The next morning she did call: "Oh, we had a lovely dinner"—you know.

That night, they came for drinks. We sat by the fire and he was pretty well-behaved. He rather liked it in our house because it was a big old East Hampton house, 1796 it was born, and he rather liked that whole idea, and he had a lot of feeling about the house and it was quite calming for him, I think. He seemed perfectly under control until Barbara said, "I've brought some lovely sketches that Tony's done." He became quite antagonistic toward her then but she was able to placate him very nicely.

Early that Monday morning Barbara Hale called me and told me what had happened over at her place the night before. I was relieved it hadn't happened in *my* house, because *I* would have called the police, you see, and Barbara Baekeland would never have spoken to me again.

DAVID MEAD

I was strictly a nonhistorical facet in all of this. I was married at the time to Deirdre Cohane, the daughter of the Baekelands' old friend Jack Cohane and his first wife, Mimi.

I can't remember how we all got out to East Hampton, to tell you the truth. I guess we drove out—or did we take the train? No, we all must have driven out in a rented car. That's vague to me, how we got there. I certainly know how we got *back*—in pieces.

This was January 1972. It was a really nasty weekend. It was snowing and blowing, and Barbara's house was right on the beach, and the sea was threatening to wash it right over the dunes. We were going over to Barbara Hale's for dinner.

Now this is the first time I ever met Barbara Hale. It was about seven, I guess, when we got there, and dinner wasn't quite ready, and Barbara Baekeland and I were sitting at the kitchen table, drinking and talking. We were on our first drink, then our second drink, and it was very pleasant—no problems at all. We were talking about all kinds of things in general but I remember specifically what we were talking about when it began to happen—we were talking about European architecture, something which I know nothing about but which I *thought* I knew something about. In other words, I was pontificating or something. And all of a sudden, out of the blue Barbara Baekeland said, "Good *God*, you don't know what you're talking about!" Now this is the first time I've ever seen her angry or even upset about anything. And she really lashed into me, she attacked me with a real force. I remember the conversation so well only because I was trying to figure out what it was that I had said that might have made her so angry, and as I was trying to figure this out—trying to play it back, so to speak—she was still going on at me. I think maybe the third drink or so had just done it, you know.

Tony was in the living room but when he heard his mother's voice raised in anger, he came rushing in and said to her, "*You* don't know what *you're* talking about!" He sort of took over for *me*, and met her on *her* level, which was pretty high and angry. And I was just of no consequence at that point. He accused her of being a whore, and she accused *him* of being a homosexual, you know—"homo" I think was the word she used. "What could *you* ever do with a woman?" she said. Something to that effect. At that point he took an egg off the counter and smashed it on her face. Then she threw something at *him*. She became defiant—"Aren't you a crass slob for doing that to me!"

Then he took a knife. He just taunted her with it. And she thrust out her chest and said, "I dare you!" Like that. And that's when *I* stepped in. I concentrated on the knife. He wasn't really paying attention to me, his eyes were completely focused on her, and they were livid. The whole thing was like some sort of cheap Hollywood movie. I mean, they were eyeball to eyeball and the hatred was electric, it was absolutely electric.

He held the knife up and I simply went for his wrist, twisted it, and just took it away from him. And he didn't even know I did that. He wasn't even aware of me! She was still saying, "I dare you! I dare you!" And they were still glaring at each other. And then he went for her throat. He started choking her. He was wrestling her to the floor and I stepped in between them and we all went crashing to the floor—the three of us—and we actually rolled out the kitchen door into the snow.

Well, I finally fought him off her. He went inside and she got up and I went over to her and I said, "Are you okay?" and she was trembling and hysterical and she slapped me across my face as hard as she could and said, "I hate you, I hate you, I hate you!" and got in the car and drove away.

I went back in the house and *I'm* beginning to tremble now so I have a couple of brandies. And Tony announces he's going to bed at Barbara Hale's. He was completely calm again.

So Deirdre and I spent the night at Barbara Hale's, too. My only plan for the rest of the evening was to get as drunk as I could as quickly as I could, and I succeeded. The next morning when I came down, Tony was already at the table, Barbara Hale was making breakfast, and it was a nice day, a beautiful day, so I said to him, "After breakfast I'd like to have a talk with you. Why don't we go for a long walk." And we did—we walked all over the place. I told him that I really thought he ought to get away from his mother, that they were both tearing each other up, and he was saying how he agreed, it wasn't good. I thought I had made some good points and, you know, reached him a little bit, and we got back to the house, and just as we walked in the door the phone was ringing and Deirdre picked it up and it was Barbara Baekeland. Deirdre said, "Hi, Barbara, how are you? Yes, Tony's here," and she gave the phone to him, and he went, "Uh-huh, uh-huh, okay," and hung the phone up, and of course both Deirdre and I leaped on him, we said, "What'd she say, what'd she say?" And he just very calmly said, "She'll be by to pick me up in half an hour." And he walked away. And half an hour later she picked him up and drove off, acting of course as if nothing had happened.

BARBARA HALE
The whole place was just a shambles. When I think I let Tony spend the night here! I don't know how I dared. I don't know, I just did.

ELIZABETH BLOW
I was working in a bookstore called Wakefield Young on Madison Avenue and Sixty-fourth Street, right near the Children's Zoo, and all my friends would stop in to see me. One day Barbara Hale tottered in and described a terrible scene in East Hampton with Barbara and Tony. She said, "I can't have anything more to do with them, ever—it's just too much." She had barely left the store when Barbara Baekeland herself came in and said, "I've just had the most delightful dinner at Barbara Hale's and I want to buy a book for her as a present. What would you suggest?"

I didn't hear from her for several months after that, but then sometime that summer I got a postcard from Mallorca saying, "Betty darling, I miss you so this summer. Tony and I think of you all the time and wish you were here. He is *much better*."

Later I heard from Nini, who'd gone over for a while to stay with them, that the scene there was very bad. One night she and Barbara evidently had to flee the house. They sat in the car, frightened to death.

12

STRIKING OUT

Later in 1979, Broadmoor officials contacted the International Social Service of Great Britain about Tony Baekeland's case. A senior inter-country caseworker recalls that "some alternatives were explored, because there was very definite pressure from *somewhere* that Baekeland leave Broadmoor."

The pressure was coming, of course, from the unofficial committee. "It was taking far too long to get Tony organized somewhere," says Michael Alexander, "and I think I rather annoyed Dr. Gogarty by putting the heat on."

Soon an officer from the American Embassy in London was able to report: "Broadmoor appears close to a decision to release Tony Baekeland. He could be back in the U.S.A. in about six weeks." Indeed, a passport application had been made in his name.

Dr. Gogarty remained concerned that Tony's long hospitalization would make it impossible for him to readjust successfully in America on his own, and informed the embassy that Broadmoor could not in good conscience recommend to the Home Secretary that Tony be released without a guarantee that "a period of social rehabilitation" would follow.

The next piece of news the committee received was therefore not the yes they expected but, rather, the nebulous statement that "Baekeland's release is not imminent."

Letter from Barbara Baekeland to Sam Green, July 18, 1972

Miramar
Valldemosa
Mallorca

Sam—

For heaven's sake pick up a pen and scribble me a few words. I am wrestling with such monumental problems I need cheering up. You can do this for me better than anyone—so . . .

I have the beautiful beige silk curtains you gave me which I have never used. They are too dressy for here and hide the beautiful cut of the window frames. Would you like me to send them back? You might use them in your bedroom. Please let me know.

Brooks is trying to force me into a murderously ungenerous agreement by cutting off my support. Except for this & Tony's problems I am in bliss here.

Phyllis Harriman Mason, Averell's niece, has been a paying guest for about 3 weeks and it's been divine having her—also has enabled me to survive financially. She is very fond of Tony and completely understands the problem. Don't know what I will do when she leaves. We are very remote here. I just pray.

He is somewhat better though *not* taking his medication. Says it dulls him. But the beauty of the place and the peace seem to help him.

Love,
Barbara

PHYLLIS HARRIMAN MASON

I had a good time with her alone and I had a good time with him alone, but when the two of them were together . . . Several times that summer I thought it was *my* last moment. One night we'd been to dinner at Robert Graves's house, Barbara was dressed to the hilt, with ropes of pearls, and coming home it was full moonlight and she was speeding, she said Tony was bugging her and she wanted to get home, and the police stopped us. She said, "You have to put him in jail!" and they looked inside the car and said, "Oh, *Antonio*, it's *you!*" They obviously *liked* Tony.

All that summer he was on speed. Barbara would find pills in his drawers and she'd raise Cain—then *he'd* raise Cain.

Another time, I was in the back seat of the car and Tony moved the front seat back on my foot. And Barbara said, "You have to say you're sorry to Phyllis." She said it condescendingly, as if he were a two-year-old. It didn't matter whether he said he was sorry or not—my foot hurt.

About halfway through my visit she had to buy some groceries, so I gave her three hundred dollars. She gave me an IOU, which I hadn't expected at all. She owed money everywhere, I think.

She stole money from me, too—she or Tony. I think it was Barbara really. I went to Greece for a couple of days and when I got back to Mallorca my wallet was missing. I hadn't taken it with me because it had dollars in it which I couldn't have used there—I always save some for when I get back to New York to take the taxi in from the airport. I didn't even realize the wallet was gone till I was packing to go home. It had not only the dollars but a lot of my IDs in it. And the wallet was extremely nice, too. I've never been able to find another quite like it.

Barbara had tried on all my clothes, too, while I was in Greece.

That summer she was still entertaining all the time. One night she was having a big dinner party, and there was a beautiful chandelier in the dining room that used oil in its cups, and she asked Tony to let it down—it was on a rope, you know—and he let it down all right, he let the rope *go*. It came down with a great crash, and she accused him of doing it on purpose. There was oil and glass all over everything. Barbara was down on her hands and knees cleaning up the oil in her finery. The other guests hadn't arrived, they were still coming over the mountain.

Tony had a motorcycle that summer and we could hear him coming from miles and miles away. We'd hear this damn motorcycle coming over the hill and Barbara would say, "Oh my God, here he comes!" and my heart would sink—*our* hearts would sink.

He had a tape recorder, and he played Vivaldi's *Four Seasons* over and over and over on the terrace, and Barbara would tell him to turn it off and that would start another row.

Alastair Reid, a poet, came for dinner one night and he said to me, "Oooohhh, it's not so good here, is it?" and I said, "No!" and I told him—I was so glad to be able to talk to someone. I'd kept it all to myself.

ALASTAIR REID

I stopped off to see Barbara on my way from—well, let me tell you the most ironic story of that summer. Borges was in Spain and he came to Mallorca for two or three days to rest and he sent me a telegram—I'd often translated his work and we were friends. So I went down to Palma to see him. He was with María Kodama, who travels with him and looks after him, and he told me about this pilgrimage that he had just made to see Graves. Graves's wife Beryl leads Borges, who's totally blind, into the room where her husband's lying, totally gaga, not knowing what anything *is*, and she takes Borges's blind hand and joins it to Graves's senseless one, and they shake hands. And that's the meeting between Borges and Graves: Nobody met anybody.

This took place up in Deyá, which Graves has always regarded as a sacred village and indeed chose because *deia* is the Latin word for "goddess"—hence his kind of, you know, enormously romantic summers. Summer was always the high drama in Mallorca. Summer was the high drama.

When I got to Barbara's and Phyllis Mason said terrible things had been going on, I didn't know what the hell she was talking about until dinner, which was just Phyllis, me, Barbara, and Tony. Barbara started to taunt Tony about how she knew he didn't want to be there with her and so on, and finally he got up and took a wine bottle and smashed it against the wall. I was rather shocked by the eruption. And Barbara roared with laughter and seemed immensely relieved, as if she'd gotten the reaction she'd wanted out of him. And so I realized that they were locked into a relationship that depended on their power to hurt each other all the time—they were both living off it. And Phyllis and I—it was during this dinner that I first thought of it—were relegated to being, as it were, spectators.

From a Psychiatric Report on Antony Baekeland Ordered by the British Courts, January 5, 1973

> In Mallorca he said that he had had a mystical experience when he and his mother had thoughts in common, that their thoughts bounced off one another so that the whole house shook, and that they later considered it would be unsafe to live there.

CECELIA BREBNER

According to Antony, they were both on drugs that last summer in Mallorca and she would perform the most extraordinarily immodest feats.

ALASTAIR REID

I still didn't think that the impetus for violence was coming from Tony. I felt it from Barbara, and I felt Barbara's desperation that night. A few weeks later, I saw them at a dinner party in Deyá—this must be by now early August. Barbara came over to me immediately and began to talk. She was talking a great deal then. She was frantic, pouring everything out, complaining—how was she going to manage, what was she going to do, where was she going to go next. These were the problems. But there was no continuity in her preoccupations.

Tony was off in another room playing chess, which is the only apparent connection he had with people in Deyá. Then the guy he was playing with came into the room where we were to say that Tony had turned around toward the wall and was just sitting there in a total catatonic trance. And he sat through that whole evening totally clutched by himself like that. I asked the others there about him and they said that was why they had him over to play chess—to take him out of himself, to get him connected to other people. These people in Deyá, crazy as they probably were themselves, had just accepted Tony and were bearing him along, as small villages always bear their crazies along with them. I mean, it was more or less an accepted fact that Tony was over the edge. And then people began to talk about—I began to hear rumors of—you know, Barbara and Tony, how Barbara had been sleeping with Tony.

I took Barbara aside. She was very humble, she said she didn't know what to do. I said, "You've got to get Tony to a doctor, and there's somebody I know who can really handle this." And I gave her the name of Lindsay Jacobs in London.

From a Psychiatric Report on Antony Baekeland Ordered by the British Courts, January 5, 1973

> He came with his mother to London and was seen by Dr. W. Lindsay Jacobs in October 1972. His impression was that patient suffered from schizophrenia and that his mother appears to have given him his prescribed tranquillisers rather irregularly. She told the doctor that he was reasonably calm though always disturbed by the parents' impending divorce and by his inability to retain consistent contact with his father.

HEATHER COHANE

Barbara was having the flat on Cadogan Square painted and she asked Jack and me where we stayed when we came over to London from Ireland. We always stayed in a place called Eleven Cadogan Gardens, sort of a private hotel, a smart bed-and-breakfast-type place. There was rather a fierce man there who let one in and ran the whole place. Well, one time we arrived and straightaway he said, "Some *friends* of yours were here. The Bakers. I had to call the police." We drew ourselves back and said, "Well, we don't know any people called Baker. They can't have been friends of *ours*." But as we went up to our room, Jack said, "I wonder if 'Baker' could have been 'Baekeland.'" So when we went down we sort of bravely asked, "Was it 'Baekeland' by any chance?" And he said, "Yes, *that* was the name," so we said, "Well, what happened?" and apparently Tony had tried to stick a pen into Barbara's eye in the hallway.

Letter from Barbara Baekeland to Sam Green, October 23, 1972

81 Cadogan Square
London, S.W. 1

Dear Sam—

Brooks is arriving from Brittany in a few minutes—met by Michael Alexander at the airport. I am hoping that he will be able to help me with this problem of Tony—who has not been at all well. In any case, something should be resolved in the next few days.

I do not see myself locked up here with him. He has been quite violent—not only with me but with stewards on airplanes, waiters and the like.

I am trying to arrange accommodations for him with the Countess of Darnley, who lives outside London—if he agrees to staying on here and undergoing treatment. Am seeing the best man in London & one of the best in the world.

Comme d'habitude, I am struggling with this but finally see some hope of a possible solution.

I didn't speak to you about it on the phone as you have been so very concerned and kind and I am embarrassed to involve my friends any further in my problem. But thank God I have them and they have all been wonderful—especially you and Michael Alexander and Sue Guinness.

Love,
Barbara

P.S. Found the flat impeccable and looking very handsome.

JIM ROBERTSEN

Barbara bought the apartment on Cadogan Square off of Neil Hartley and me—we owned it jointly. Sam Green had said, "I know someone who's looking for a place, let me introduce you." Everyone in London wanted the apartment because it was really pretty fabulous, but *she* said, "I'll pay cash." She agreed to give it to us in three checks spaced a couple of weeks apart. We banked the first one, wrote checks on it—and it bounced! I got hold of her right away and she said she was sorry and gave us another check—and that one went through. And a little later she sent around the largest chunk of caviar that any of us had ever seen. I suppose it was probably fifteen pounds of caviar; it came from Fortnum's and it was in a huge blue tin. I phoned everyone I knew, I mean everyone who I really adored who was crazy about caviar, and said, you know, come over.

That was a very nice, extremely extravagant thing of her to do—especially since this was after the parade had passed for her, you know. I saw very little of her after the sale went through, because the son was such a disaster and they were sort of a package deal. I did have them both to a couple of parties in my new house. During one of them, Tony came over and told me how much he liked me, how sympathetic he found me. Then he phoned the next day and said could we have lunch, and I said, "No, not today," and he said, "Well, *what* day?" and I finally said a day.

I took him to a place on the King's Road called the Arethusa which is now defunct. It was owned and run by a trendy fellow called Alvaro and it was a very *louche* sort of club with sort of remnants of the swinging sixties, and therefore people were not easily shocked there, you didn't pay much attention one way or another—it was always loaded with all sorts of major-and minor-league celebrity types.

So we sat down and I said, "How are you?" and Tony said, "I'm just terrible." I said, "What's wrong?" And he said, "Well, uh . . ." He said something like, "Can I speak frankly to you?" And I said, "Ya, I mean, Tony . . ." And he said, "I really would like to feel I can rely on you as a friend." I said, "Well, Tony, we scarcely know each other." I mean, I just did *not* want to have any sort of friendship with him, quite honestly, because he seemed too much like a ticking time bomb and not anyone who I had any interest in on any conceivable level, you know. And he said, "Well, uh, what's happening is I'm having an affair with my mother."

And I remember I said, "Oh, come *on*—you and your mother do have a very intimate relationship and that's fine," and that sort of thing. He said, "No no no no! I am *fucking* my *mother!*" And he said it loud enough, in the Arethusa, which was quite bustling and where people tended to talk fairly loud—for England anyhow—so that several people turned around, and I said, you know, "Relax, Tony." He said, "Well, that's it. And I don't know what to do—I feel desperate." I said, "It's awful if you feel desperate about it. Quite honestly, I think any number of things are all right if they don't hurt people outside the relationship." And then he sort of said again, he said, "Don't you understand what I'm saying to you?" I said, "Tony, why do you want to tell *me* this? I'm sorry it's happening and that it's distressing you. But you know, if you don't want it to continue, then just stop it." Then he got quite hysterical, and it was very embarrassing—hideous, as a matter of fact.

The point is that I really did not want this information, I did not like the laundering of, you know, his family's washing all over *me*, and I did not want it in a club where I was a member.

Oddly enough, at the time I knew of another mother and son who were having an incestuous relationship, which was really quite successful. These, by the way, are the only two cases of mother/son incest that I'm personally aware of. But both mother and son had told me about this affair they were having, and *they* were anything *but* anguished over it, they were quite amused by it, in fact. I mean, they ended up being very good friends—it was just something they did for a little bit. And I just thought, you know, this is terribly ironic—that just suddenly, in a period of about six months, I should have these two pieces of information, neither one of which I particularly wanted to have.

So anyway I told him that it seemed to me his life would be far simpler if he didn't live with his mother. And he said, "Where would I go? What would I do?" And I said, "The world is full of places. Do you have any money of your own?" And he said he really didn't yet. And I said, "Well, Tony, you could do something that a lot of people in the world do—you could get a job." He said, "What do you mean?" And I said, "Just get a fucking job. Go to Paris, get a job *there*—go back to the States. Do *anything*." I said there were also a lot of people in London who he could probably work out an arrangement with where he could share a flat. I said that the pressures of living with his mother were obviously enormous and he should just put some time and distance between them.

And here we still are in this restaurant, this *club*, and he's really I mean not quite shouting but damn near it. And finally I say, because, I mean, the headwaiter and so on are kind of rolling their eyes at me, "Listen, Tony, maybe we should just go for a walk." And he said, "Why?" And I said, "Look, this isn't something that I really want to go on discussing here."

There was never any question in my mind that what he was telling me and what I was hearing was true—none whatsoever. And I'm usually fairly skeptical. I mean, there was just the passion with which he said it.

And I know it went on with his mother beyond that point because he did phone me some time later and he said, "Oh God, this thing still seems to be going on." And I remember saying, "Tony, it takes two people, you know."

F. CLASON KYLE

I met Barbara and Tony less than, as it turned out, a month before her death. I met her first, at a party given for the Victorian Society, on whose American board of directors I served.

I was winding up a two-and-a-half-month stay in London, writing an A-to-Z series on the metropolis's offbeat travel attractions. I might have had more time for the Baekelands if I hadn't been pushing to get all the photographs I needed, and I was also anxious to get home to Columbus, Georgia, by Thanksgiving. Anyway, I enjoyed meeting Barbara sufficiently to ask if she would be interested in hearing a lecture on Irish Georgian architecture by an old friend of mine, the Honourable—and blue-eyed—Desmond Guinness, who would be speaking in tandem with the Knight of Glin. The duet was scheduled for a few nights later at the Irish Club, just off Eaton Square. She said she would be delighted to join me, and did so, bringing her son along with her.

I was surprised to see him, because I certainly had not invited him, not even knowing that he existed. But then, the more the merrier, and he added another body to the talk's attendees.

The next time I saw Barbara was a few nights later when I invited her and Tony to have dinner with me at the Rib Room of the Carlton Towers on Sloane Street. Besides having good meat, the restaurant was convenient to the Baekelands' flat in Cadogan Square and mine in Wilton Place.

Dinner went well, I recall. And Barbara asked me back to see their penthouse flat and have a nightcap. On the walk there, Tony, who had been relatively quiet during dinner, suddenly opened up and began telling me—because I was a journalist, I guess—about some writing that he had done. He asked if I would be willing to take a look at it. He said it was a mystical tale about a rabbit or an animal of some sort, I can't remember exactly which.

At their stunningly attractive flat, conversation was vigorous for about an hour while Barbara and I sipped on our brandies. Tony had bade us goodnight immediately after our arrival, courteously saying that he had enjoyed dinner. And I think he had. I had responded, equally sincerely, that I looked forward to reading his story.

Unexpectedly, there was an exceedingly noisy racket from the kitchen area beneath us. Barbara seemed to pay no attention, until Tony—clad only in knit shorts—appeared in the salon, brandishing a large kitchen knife. He ranted about the room, gesturing wildly, but never making a threatening move at either of us. Then he vanished, as quickly as he had appeared. However, some commotion continued below.

The understatement of the century would be to say that I was startled. Barbara had remained passive and composed throughout.

Quietly, she explained that he had recently threatened to kill her. "I'm not afraid of him," she said, more than once.

I said, "Perhaps I should leave. My being here has obviously upset him." I quickly had assumed that Tony was jealous of my being with his mother, or of her being with me—three's a crowd. Before I could leave, the phone rang and I heard Barbara apologizing to another tenant in the building for the disturbance.

She then led me down four or five flights of stairs, allaying my fears for her safety and my offer of sanctuary. An elderly gentleman, dressed in bathrobe and pajamas, stood in his doorway on one landing. He said, "Mrs. Baekeland, this just must not continue. I can't have my sleep disturbed in this manner." I think he also added something about his concern for her security. She assured him—*and* me—that Tony was having treatment and that things were all right.

ALASTAIR REID

When I heard that Lindsay Jacobs had agreed to see Tony and was going to take up the case, as it were, I thought, What a relief, because he's a doctor who enjoys considerable fame for picking up people when they're really on the edge and bringing them back to life.

DR. W. LINDSAY JACOBS

After seeing Antony Baekeland and his mother separately on a couple of occasions, I called the Chelsea Police Station to tell them I thought something was going to happen over at 81 Cadogan Square and could they put a guard there. The officer in charge said that they were not really allowed to do much of anything until something actually happened.

On November 15, 1972, just two days before the matricide, I saw Antony and his mother together and they were jointly willing that he go into hospital. I had arranged for a bed on Monday November 20th.

F. CLASON KYLE

The evening that Tony ran around the flat with the kitchen knife proved to be the last time I saw Barbara, except for one day in Knightsbridge shortly before my return to the States. I was in a taxi and she, wrapped in a dark cape, was walking on the sidewalk, clutching several shopping bags. I waved to her. She waved back, but I am not certain that she recognized me—it was more the sort of wave one gives to a friendly hand fluttering from inside a passing car, while at the same time experiencing the uncomfortable feeling that maybe the greeting really had been meant for the stranger strolling two feet to one's left.

SUE GUINNESS

I saw Barbara two days before he killed her—I had lunch with both of them, in fact, in London, in the flat. And Tony was definitely in a very peculiar state. He had painted all his shoes and his clothes with gold stars, and he just sat there and rocked backwards and forwards with his arms crossed across his chest. I said to Barbara, "Do be careful," and she said, you know, "He'll never harm *me*."

Well, I knew that wasn't so, because she used to stay with me in London when she rented out her flat and she was staying with me once when Tony turned up from somewhere or other in the middle of a dinner party. He went upstairs and got her passport and tore it up, then he threw various things down the drain, and then he came into the dining room and insulted her and said that he was going to kill her—in front of quite a number of witnesses. Anyway I got him out of the house—I think he was staying at some hotel that Michael Alexander had got him into.

The following day he came back and he said he wanted to go and see *The Devils* by Ken Russell—do you remember that film? And Barbara and I agreed to do that with him. He became very peculiar after seeing it—he sat on the stairs of the cinema rocking backwards and forwards. Naturally Barbara got terribly worried and said that she didn't want to be on her own with him. And luckily he went off.

But the next day he rang up asking for his mother. I said that she had left, which wasn't true—she had just gone to the American Embassy to get a new passport. He said, "Oh, I see." And then I went out to do some shopping. When I came back about twenty minutes later, I found Barbara lying on the pavement with a mackintosh rolled up under her head and a great patch of her hair missing on one side—she was looking pretty dazed. There was this rather nice man standing over her—it was he, in fact, who had taken his mackintosh and given it to her.

And Tony was in the window—of *my house*—screaming and shouting that he was going to get everybody, that anybody who came near was going to get it—he said he was going to kill *all women*. He had a carving knife.

What happened while I was out shopping was that he had turned up and our housekeeper had let him in—after all, he'd been coming to our house for years and he was the son of an old friend and she didn't realize that Barbara didn't want to see him, you know. He was waiting for Barbara when she came back from the embassy and he jumped on her. Apparently he pursued her through the house, she got out the front door and down the steps, and he was dragging her into the square by her hair, trying to throw her in front of cars. She was hanging on to the gate and he was slamming it backwards and forwards on her thumb.

When I saw her lying there I ran down the road and rang up the police from the greengrocer's. They arrived with dogs—by this time we had a crowd of I suppose about thirty to forty people standing outside the house saying there's a maniac in there. When Tony saw the police, he went running off behind the house, down the garden and across various streets.

Then the ambulance came round. I rode with Barbara to St. Charles's Hospital in Kensington, and she was not in a very good state at *all*. A finger was broken in three places and she was there for a couple of days. She said to me from her bed, "It's worth any amount of pain to save Tony from himself."

They caught him I think about twenty-four hours later in his hotel room. He was put in a cell—they were going to charge him with attempted murder. He was only in there for forty-eight hours, because I got three psychiatrists to sign him into the Priory, a private hospital in Roehampton. Then I got hold of Brooks, who was in Brittany with Sylvie, and I made him come over to England. I said, "Look here, your son is in a very bad state, he must have treatment." He said, you know, "It's just fun and games"—those were his words. And I said, "Brooks, no it's not. *You* weren't present, you haven't seen what's been going on, you haven't seen the way he treats Barbara."

Well anyway, Tony left the Priory shortly afterwards.

I'd reckoned he was dangerous ever since I first knew him in Cadaqués, where he was sort of semicontrolled by a whole lot of very peculiar hippies. I shan't forget him sitting in the flat with all his clothes and shoes painted with gold stars, two days before he killed her. I remember I had to go to Paris that evening, Wednesday, and Saturday morning when I got back it was all over the newspapers.

I opposed the efforts of Michael Alexander and Heather Cohane and the others to get him out of Broadmoor. I didn't think it was a very good idea.

PART III
NEW YORK

1

REPATRIATION

Former Broadmoor patients have reported that after their release they missed the orderly, controlled life they had gotten used to and sometimes even become fond of. When the time came for Tony Baekeland to leave, would he also find life on the outside chaotic and threatening?

New York City had changed in the eight years since he had last seen it, but his old neighborhood, to which he would be returning— the Seventies on the Upper East Side—had remained pretty much the same, although a few fashionable new shops, boutiques, and restaurants had opened.

BROOKS BAEKELAND
There were three alternatives for Tony once the right strings were pulled in high places in London and his release achieved: one, that he be released in some innocent person's custody and undergo private medical treatment from time to time since he would be considered well; two, that he be transferred to some place like Payne Whitney in New York, which I enraged some by dubbing "Pain Witless"; and three, that he go straight to the equivalent of Broadmoor in America—that is, a state institution.

Every one of these alternatives was clearly idiotic—the first and second, if for no other reason than that they were beyond my means, so far beyond as to be preposterous; and the third alternative was too tragic to think of.

The fact is, there is nothing that I know of in the world like Broadmoor, at least when I knew it. A gentleness, a kindness, a compassion, and a civilized concern by civilized people for the cruelly wounded—or fatally malborn—within its walls are the first things that strike a foreign visitor. And Tony *was* happy there—as long as the tiger slept. And the tiger did sleep until Gogarty—under pressure, I believe, from higher-ups to send all the foreigners back to their own countries—began to take away the drugs that made the tiger sleep. And the tiger awoke!

I began to receive a stream of violent—and obviously paranoid—letters from Tony, one of which I sent, as an example, to my brother. I called Gogarty from Italy, where I was living then, separated from Sylvie. I told him—and I later reinforced it by telegram—that letting Tony go would be absolutely irresponsible, that I would send him copies of the letters I had been getting from him ever since he had been taken off "the drugs that dull the rage," to quote myself, and I repeated then what I had said and written before: that I would be happy to make a gift every year to the British government that would *more* than compensate for the cost of their care for my son.

DR. PHILIP GOGARTY
Brooks Baekeland talked to me about payment, but of course you can't pay for anybody in a public hospital where there are no private patients.

I think he thought that perhaps I was trying to get rid of Tony, that we considered him a burden on the state—he had some sort of notion like that. But indeed it wasn't true, because in this country we *keep* patients—not alone at Broadmoor but in all the hospitals. We as doctors are under no pressure whatever to send patients anywhere else unless they have recovered sufficiently or we think they would do better in their own cultural environment.

Letter from Dr. Philip Gogarty to the Undersecretary of State, Department of Health and Social Security, London, August 9, 1979

Broadmoor

Dear Sir,

I wish to recommend repatriation for Antony Baekeland to his homeland, the United States of America. His dossier is voluminous and complicated but I have chosen certain medical reports and other communications, which I herewith enclose, that detail his history and treatment, up to the moment of his mental health review tribunal hearing on 22 October 1974.

During 1975 in spite of vigorous physical therapy his mental illness remained largely unchanged. I wrote of him then: "He presents as a chronic schizophrenic, blunted in affect, with vague superficial interests, and lacking insight into the grave, disabling nature of his mental illness. He tends to upset other patients by making vicious and malignant allegations about them. At present the more gross symptoms of his psychosis are controlled by medication."

His disorder gradually came more and more under control so that he was able to take part beneficially in group psychotherapy. At this stage, however, he was quite unable to engage himself in any occupational therapy, but since then he has succeeded in settling down at recreational painting, at which indeed in the past, it is said, he showed more than average talent.

In the beginning of 1979 he was commended by nursing staff for his increasing ability to socialize more normally; much of his former hostility, bitterness, and resentment had eased off and he was capable of cooperation and helpfulness on the ward scene. My consultant psychotherapist colleague noted a definite improvement with willingness to engage more earnestly in treatment. He was now showing true insight and appreciation of the realities of his situation.

It was at this point that I reduced his medication in order to establish whether his psychosis was in remission. He has now been without medication for a period of nearly six months: his improvement has been fully sustained. For quite a long time he has been requesting repatriation and I have tried to elicit information about hospital placement for him somewhere in New York.

Because of the nature of his offence, the fact that he is mentally ill and lacking in insight and cooperation when motively ill, and because of his previous propensity for indulging in drug misuse, it is absolutely necessary that his placement in hospital should involve such a degree of security and supervision as to ensure continuing treatment and rehabilitation without the risk of his absconding.

It is with all this in mind that I formally recommend that Antony Baekeland should now be repatriated to a hospital in New York, where his rehabilitation may be more realistically carried forward within his own culture and near his relatives and friends.

Yours faithfully,
Philip Gogarty
Consultant Forensic Psychiatrist

ELSPETH WILKIE

I was working in the U.S. Embassy in London in a consulate capacity, and Antony Baekeland's repatriation was just sort of a routine thing—it was paperwork going across the desk. Ultimately, because of overcrowding or just the idea that he was responding to treatment, it was agreed that he could be returned to the United States. All we had to do was satisfy ourselves through the State Department that arrangements could be made for him to be transferred to the U.S.—he had to have two escorts, for instance. We also required an understanding from the authorities at Broadmoor that he go into a similar institution in America—that is, for the criminally insane.

I do know that Broadmoor won't release somebody without first being satisfied that they're okay. I mean, the British people would feel guilty if they released somebody just willy-nilly onto the streets of New York or wherever.

MICHAEL ALEXANDER

The *doctors* said he could go, so you see, I wasn't intervening in that side of it. All *I* said to them was, "Now you've said he can go, let him go. Don't make him hang around."

I used to have to reassure Tony every time I went to see him, "It won't be much longer now—just keep your cool and don't give them any aggravation. We're doing our best for you." And I must say, he played it very cool.

Letter from Antony Baekeland to James Reeve, August 14, 1979

Broadmoor

Dear James,

Michael Alexander is going to the Home Secretary to speed my release from here. It's awfully nice of him: he has been such a good friend.

How goes the sale of your house? My grandmother sends her love; I found when she was last here that she had suffered a *coup d'âge*—very frail she is, and I feel I must be with her soon. She also has hallucinations: she was very funny—evidently she imagined that her sister was staying with her—she bought extra food for her and so forth, and then when she failed to show up at meals became convinced that she was hiding under the bed! When she was staying in the village here, on her way to the loo late one night she saw a huge baroque lighted staircase spiraling up from the hall. She also imagined that a young cousin of mine was sleeping with her and got out of bed onto the floor in the middle of the night to give him more room. All funny but rather worrying.

My Papa's young wife left him in Feb. for a young American sculptor to whom he had introduced her and he is very blue about it and writes me long heartrending letters. He and I are great friends now and I plan to visit him and long to spend time with him—he has a little fishing boat and a charming house right on the water in Cadaqués and the mountains and hills are lovely for walking. The wife and American lover go to stay with him there toward the end of the month—rather odd.

How is your work? Just read *Under the Volcano*—funny and macabre—he describes Mexico so well—I don't know if you have been there.

Got a long letter from Rosie Rodd Baldwin in Turkey—may go out there, too. Plan plan plan—there is little else to do. Just wait, I guess. A visit from you would be most welcome.

Much love,
Tony

JAMES REEVE

My last visit was before I left for a trip to India, and he was just sort of teetering on the brink of would he be let out or wouldn't he. It was awful, because this whole talk of his being let out started about a year and a half before he *was* let out. And it was a terrible business of waiting. I remember him telling me about a visit he was expecting from somebody in the embassy. He was in an absolute state about it—I mean, you can imagine! He kept closing his eyes, searching for words. But he later wrote me that it had gone well, and that was a great relief to him.

Although Tony was rather fond of Dr. Gogarty, he sometimes regarded him as the one who was standing in his way to freedom. I once wrote Dr. Gogarty to ask what I could do to help, and he never answered. Miwa was the one who was in touch with Gogarty all the time—she really did beaver away on Tony's behalf. She was like a terrier with a rat, you know. She wouldn't let go, come hell or high water.

Letter from Antony Baekeland to Miwa Svinka-Zielinski, Undated

Broadmoor

Dear Miwa,

James came by for a flying ten-minute visit yesterday. It was so good to see him and he tells me that you are still rooting for me. I think you are super. I just wrote to my uncle Fred Baekeland if he could help me get into a hospital in N.Y.—hopefully, as I am well now, I won't have to spend long there. My doctors have plans to repatriate me in "a matter of months." Dr. Gogarty is just waiting for all the red tape to go through. Things move so slowly.

It will be a wrench (hard to believe, I know) to leave Broadmoor: I have become very accustomed to life here.

Still, it will be good to be home. Life is going to be such a new thing for me.

Love,
Tony

Miwa Svinka-Zielinski

When I visited him in late 1979, he told me that all he wanted was to go to New York and stay with his grandmother. He said to me, "I love Nini. I'd like to serve her. I want to cook for her. I want to do everything for her."

I saw Dr. Gogarty at that time and had a very friendly conversation with him. He told me Tony was improved, but I didn't want him just let loose in New York. I wanted to find some halfway house for him.

Letter from J. W. Bone to Miwa Svinka-Zielinski, February 5, 1980

Broadmoor

Dear Mrs. Zielinski,

It has been agreed that due to the conditions currently prevailing in America with regard to psychiatric treatment and the excessive cost of private treatment, Tony should be returned to America without any statutory supervision entailed. We are, of course, apprehensive as to the situation that will greet Tony when he arrives in New York and, while he states quite emphatically that he wishes to take up residence with his grandmother, Mrs. N. Daly, we feel that this may not in fact be appropriate. I would be grateful therefore if you could furnish me with any information as to those members of Tony's family or his circle of friends who might be able to offer Tony both accommodation and support.

I look forward to hearing from you.

Yours sincerely,
J. W. Bone
Senior Social Worker

Telegram from Cyrus R. Vance, Secretary of State, Washington, D.C., to American Embassy, London, March 7, 1980

H.E.W. HAS ADVISED THAT IN A PRELIMINARY REQUEST TO SOCIAL SERVICES IN NEW YORK, THEY WERE INFORMED THAT

DUE TO LIMITED SPACE PROBLEMS, HALFWAY HOUSE FACILITIES WOULD BE UNOBTAINABLE FOR NEAR FUTURE. IT WOULD BE BEST TO RECOMMEND A HOSPITAL IN NEW YORK UNTIL FACILITY COULD BE OBTAINED. H.E.W. HAS ALSO ADVISED THAT REQUEST TO PLACE BAEKELAND IN HALFWAY HOUSE PROGRAM SHOULD COME DIRECTLY FROM HOSPITAL IN THE U.K.   VANCE

DR. PHILIP GOGARTY
I arranged for Tony to go to a halfway house called the Richmond Fellowship. I had it all arranged.

ROBERT ORENSTEIN
I was the assistant director of the Fellowship and the name Baekeland vaguely rings a bell, but more familiar to me is the circumstance— that this person coming from England had killed his mother. We very rarely got referrals of people who had committed homicides. We might have gotten an application from him, but the likelihood of our accepting someone with that kind of violent history would be very, very unusual.

INGE MAHN
I have no way of knowing what correspondence may have occurred, but in the little file cards we have here of applications received, I don't see Antony Baekeland's name listed.

Letter from Antony Baekeland to Miwa Svinka-Zielinski, February 5, 1980

Broadmoor

Dear Miwa,
Michael Alexander is trying to speed things up for me and now it looks as if I may be in New York within a few weeks! As you may imagine, I am delighted. Life will be entirely new and fresh for me and I think I will enjoy it immensely. I imagine myself on the plane, having a *coup de vin* and knowing that seven years of confinement is receding into the distance. It will be pure heaven and the best of it is that I will not have to be accom-

panied by guards or go to a hospital when I arrive. I so look
forward to seeing you.

Love,
Tony

MICHAEL ALEXANDER

I had long discussions with Tony about his father toward the end of
his stay at Broadmoor. I'm fond of Brooks, although I did rather feel
that he wasn't playing his role in this whole affair. The reason I
suppose was it was just too . . . He couldn't take it himself, really.
You see, he felt that Tony was a disaster area and he couldn't absorb
it. He wasn't big enough, or he had his own psychological problems.
Anyway, he just couldn't do it. And what's more, he didn't!

I tried to persuade him to actually go down and meet Tony when
he got out and possibly have him to stay and all that. But Brooks
wouldn't play along—at the time he was rather unhappy because
Sylvie had taken up with this younger man.

There was a definite rumor going around about the family trying to
see that Tony was kept inside so they could have control over his
inheritance.

BROOKS BAEKELAND

There was a story that was spread by the members of the Bleeding
Hearts Club and/or others that I was "keeping Tony in Broadmoor to
get his money." Ha! There is no limit to meanness. There was no
possible way that I could ever profit materially from my son's health,
illness, or death.

MIWA SVINKA-ZIELINSKI

Brooks was more or less absent from the picture at this point, but his
brother Fred, the psychiatrist, sometime around the middle of March
wrote a very strong letter to Dr. Gogarty saying that he wanted to
correct a number of pieces of misinformation, so that Gogarty
should have no illusions about what exactly would face Tony on his
return. He mentioned that, as far as he knew, Tony had few friends
his own age in New York and that what older friends there were
might rally round at first but that none was in a position to house or
care for him. Fred also told Gogarty that Broadmoor was relying too
much on Nini, who was old and needed a live-in nurse herself,

which meant that there would really be no room for Tony in her small apartment. He also said that there was no other family member who could put him up except on the most temporary basis—his own mother, Mrs. Hallowell, Tony's other grandmother, was also in her eighties at this point; she was sympathetic but had never been as close to Tony as Nini.

Fred also told Gogarty that Broadmoor was very wrong to say Tony would not be a financial burden to anyone. He spelled out in no uncertain words that after 1981 no more capital would be coming to Tony from his trust.

Letter from Dr. Philip Gogarty to Miwa Svinka-Zielinski, March 27, 1980

Broadmoor

Dear Mrs. Svinka-Zielinski,

Thank you for your recent letter concerning the above patient. I have also had correspondence from Tony's father, from Dr. Frederick Baekeland, from Mrs. Daly, from Michael Alexander, and from others—all in the recent past. So it is against this background that I write to you.

Although members of his family express concern over Tony's welfare, none is prepared to offer him the shelter of a home environment or indeed personal supervision of any kind. Those friends who retain an interest in him, and they are quite numerous, do not seem to realise that he will need supportive help of an immediate nature when he returns to New York.

Your enquiry about his need for medical care follows from our conversation in November 1979. However, since that time Tony has been quite symptom-free although without medication over many months. Prior to November I had been thinking in terms of hospitalisation in New York for a few months following his repatriation. But some five months have now passed since we spoke and his continued well-being indicates that there is now no need for in-patient treatment. Interested, sympathetic social supervision would now be adequate to secure his smooth integration into the open community once more. This means that someone would meet him at the airport to escort him to living quarters already secured for him and this agency or person should also be prepared to help him in the various day-to-day issues that will inevitably crop up for someone who has spent so long in a sheltered environment.

Dr. Frederick Baekeland has pointed out how feckless Tony is about financial affairs and he fears that Tony's capital would be quickly dissipated. This of course is very well known by me, and indeed long ago I placed the overall control of his financial affairs in the hands of the Official Solicitors Office which exercises fairly rigorous control over his expenditure. I believe that similar control should be exercised over his income from the capital invested in the USA—if that can be properly arranged.

Can you help in providing information about the availability of social aid for Tony when he arrives in New York? Once I am assured that such adequate back-up is ready to help him I can proceed with the arrangements for his repatriation.

Many thanks for your help.

Yours sincerely,
Philip Gogarty

Telegram from Cyrus R. Vance, Secretary of State, Washington, D.C., to American Embassy, London, March 30, 1980

DEPT. RECEIVED TELEPHONE CALL 3/24 FROM DR. FREDERICK BAEKELAND, SUBJECT'S UNCLE, WHO INFORMED THAT HE HAD BEEN NOTIFIED BY DR. GOGARTY, CONSULTANT PSYCHIATRIST AT BROADMOOR HOSPITAL, THAT ANTONY BAEKELAND WOULD BE RELEASED AND DEPORTED IN APPROXIMATELY TWO WEEKS.

DR. BAEKELAND IS CONCERNED, BECAUSE HE WISHES TO MAKE SOME ARRANGEMENTS FOR ANTONY'S ADMITTANCE INTO A HOSPITAL WITHIN THE UNITED STATES, AND BECAUSE THERE IS NO ONE IN THE U.S. WHO COULD POSSIBLY TAKE ANTONY INTO HIS OR HER PERSONAL CARE. BRITISH MEDICAL REPORTS HAVE INDICATED THAT SUBJECT IS NOT STABLE ENOUGH TO MANAGE IN A NORMAL AND UNSUPERVISED ATMOSPHERE.

HOSPITAL OFFICIALS ADVISED DR. BAEKELAND THAT AN-

TONY WOULD REQUIRE TWO MEDICAL ESCORTS TO ACCOM-
PANY HIM ON THE RETURN FLIGHT TO NEW YORK   VANCE

MIWA SVINKA-ZIELINSKI
Some woman emerged who later took him back to New York. She
said she was a friend of the family but I had never heard of this
woman all these years. I didn't know *who* she was. She came over to
England to visit him that April.

HEATHER COHANE
We knew absolutely nothing about her, and when she just turned up
like that, you know, Michael Alexander and I said to each other,
"What the hell? Who *is* she?" We called her "Mystery Woman."

Official Visitors File, Broadmoor Special Hospital, April 29, 1980

VISITOR'S NAME: Mrs. Cecelia Brebner
RELATIONSHIP TO PATIENT: Friend of family.
SUMMARY: Knows background of patient in greatest detail. Is
fully aware of eccentricities of Baekeland family and of its attitude
toward any of their own participation in Tony's rehabilitation.
She discussed Tony's return to N.Y., his initial reintegration into
family social life again. She appears to be the most sensible member of the large group of relatives and friends fussily engaged in
Tony's discharge.

CECELIA BREBNER
I was, and still am, very friendly with Tony's grandmother, Cornelia
Hallowell, and shortly after the murder of Barbara, she said to me,
because she knew I had a daughter who lived very close to Broad-
moor, "If you're going to England, could you take something to
Tony for me?" And this is how it all began.

That first time, my daughter drove me there, and I said to her,
"Here I am about to meet a man who has murdered his mother and I
don't know how I'm going to react." And she said, "Would you like
me to come in with you, Mummy?" I said yes.

Anyway, when I was in London in 1980, Cornelia said to me,

"They're releasing Tony, they may have already released him." I
telephoned Broadmoor and they said no, they had not. Then I had a
mysterious telegram from a woman called Heather Cohane—I'm always having mysterious telegrams!—saying that the Home Office had
recommended Tony's release and could *I* possibly escort him back. I
said, well, I didn't think so, because although I was leaving London,
I was going to Toronto, you see, and not New York. However, I was
pressured. And later I was interviewed for four hours by Dr. Philip
Gogarty. I asked him, "In the event of my doing this, what are the
implications?" And he said, "He's a schizophrenic, but with love and
care he will probably be able to resume a more or less normal life."
He said that he had arranged for Tony to go to a halfway house in
New York. I said, "Why can't his own father take him?" And
Gogarty answered, "He's having marital problems." Well, of course!
He married Tony's girlfriend and it was all very complicated.

I got together with a man called Michael Alexander, an author I
believe, who said, "He's been in Broadmoor for *eight years*—he
should be repatriated *now!*" And I had a feeling that this should happen as well, and so I agreed to take him. Tony was positively euphoric when he found out I was going to bring him home.

I was staying at the time with Lady Mary Clayton at Kensington
Palace, and *she* said, "Celia, I don't think it's the right thing to do
but we'll ask Prince George of Denmark," and *he* thought it was a
very altruistic thing to do, so I embarked upon it.

Postcard from Ethel Woodward de Croisset to Antony Baekeland, April 9, 1980

Paris

Dear Tony—
Had a telegram from M. Alexander saying that you are well and
can return to New York & to your grandmother soon. Send me
her address, which I have lost.

I do hope that you will get on all right in NYC and can find a
quiet cosy nest and a happy life in the country perhaps.

Abrazos,
Ethel

HEATHER COHANE

Just before Tony was released, I took Simone and Aschwin Lippe to see him in Broadmoor, because they had known Barbara so well, and Brooks so well, for many many many years. You know, I would have really put every penny I had on the table and said, "I *know* that this is a one-time thing with his killing Barbara. He'll never do it again." But as we were driving back to London in the car, Simone said that she thought there was a great sort of look of madness in his eyes. She kept saying that, and I kept saying, "No, I don't think so, I think you'll see he's all right."

Letter from Antony Baekeland to Dr. Frederick Baekeland, April 17, 1980

Broadmoor

Dear Fred,

I appreciate your efforts to help me. Saw Dr. Gogarty yesterday: he told me that he had been in touch with you. He also said that you had asked him a number of questions regarding my case which he declined to answer. To tell you the truth, Fred, I resent a bit this morbid curiosity on your part when you were not even polite enough to write me a note after my Mother's death; it doesn't read true, does it?

I am in constant touch with my father, who plans to help me. Our letters are a source of inspiration and pleasure to both of us. He seems to be hard at work on a book—I too plan to make one. I may call it "The Shakespearean Continuum."

I have re-made myself. The experience at Broadmoor has been most valuable to me; I have had to live with all kinds of people who I would never have met in normal life, and accept them for what they are and what they are not. I have learned a certain discipline which will help me later on. As things stand now, I may be in N.Y. in a couple of weeks.

Yrs. truly,
Tony

Official Visitors File, Broadmoor Special Hospital, May 7, 1980

VISITOR'S NAME: Mrs. Svinka-Zielinski
RELATIONSHIP TO PATIENT: Friend
SUMMARY: Dropped in on her way to Poland to visit relatives.
Reported that a New York psychiatrist, a Dr. Portnow, would be
interested to help Tony during the initial supportive period fol-
lowing his return to NY. Letter to Dr. Portnow promised. Mrs.
Zielinski believes that Antony could realistically stay with
Grandma Nini for a short period, even if only for bed and board
and a basic address.

DR. STANLEY L. PORTNOW

A lady came to visit me when Tony Baekeland was still in England,
claiming she was very interested in having him brought back to the
United States and that the only way the hospital in England would
discharge him would be if they were secure in their feeling that he
would have follow-up treatment by a psychiatrist in New York. I said
I would be glad to evaluate him and if I couldn't take care of him
myself, for one reason or another, I would see to it that he got a
proper referral. Then there was talk about my going over to England
to examine him, and that suggestion was from this same lady. The
trip to England never came off. I never heard from the lady again.

Telegram from Kingman Brewster, Jr., U.S. Ambassador to the Court of St. James's, American Embassy, London, to Cyrus R. Vance, Secretary of State, Washington, D.C., May 20, 1980

CONSULAR OFFICER MADE ELEVENTH VISIT ON MAY 2, 1980.
BAEKELAND IN GOOD HEALTH AND SPIRITS. CONSULAR
OFFICER ALSO TALKED TO DR. GOGARTY BAEKELAND'S PHYSI-
CIAN. BAEKELAND'S FAMILY APPARENTLY UNABLE OR UN-
WILLING TO ASSIST HIS REINTRODUCTION TO U.S. BAEKE-
LAND WILL NOT VOLUNTARILY COMMIT HIMSELF TO U.S.
HOSPITAL. DR. GOGARTY SAYS BAEKELAND DOESN'T NEED
HOSPITALIZATION, ONLY A HALFWAY HOUSE TYPE SETTING

FOR A FEW WEEKS OF READJUSTMENT TO LIVING IN SOCIETY.
DR. GOGARTY SAID HE WOULD KEEP EMBASSY INFORMED.

EMBASSY WILL INFORM DEPARTMENT OF ALL ARRANGE-
MENTS MADE BY DR. GOGARTY, AS EMBASSY AWARE THAT,
DUE TO NATURE OF BAEKELAND'S OFFENCE, FAMILY IN U.S.
WISHES TO BE INFORMED OF ARRANGEMENTS.   BREWSTER

**Telegram from Kingman Brewster, Jr., U.S. Ambassador to
the Court of St. James's, to Interpol, Washington, D.C., June
20, 1980**

URGENT

ANTONY BAEKELAND WAS RELEASED AS A RESULT OF AN
ORDER SIGNED BY THE UNDER SECRETARY OF STATE ON
6/17/80.   BREWSTER

MICHAEL ALEXANDER
Even though the Home Office had in fact authorized Tony's release,
there was quite a lot of red tape still involved, and meanwhile he had
to remain at Broadmoor, locked up. We all thought, those last weeks
in Broadmoor, that he was very together, you know. He seemed absolutely fine.

JAKE COOPER
I cried for the first time in a very long time when I learned that
Antony was getting out. I felt it was such a very special thing to
happen. I felt at least I could be happy that my dear friend was finding free space in *his* life again, because, you see, I used to be a
leader—in Cadaqués, in Morocco, in Paris—without meaning to be.
I just seemed able to get things together, and then all of a sudden I
got in this cracked-up state.

Letter from Antony Baekeland to Jake Cooper, July 18, 1980

Broadmoor
Dear and Noble Pinetree Friend,
A host of memories come floating back—*chez* Dalí—that walk

to the sea, you in your jackal coat, when you took mushrooms—union, beauty, and freedom in Morocco, blue irises on the grassy hillside in Tangiers, and I know you will be that way again. Remember that we are the horsemen and all that that means—beauty, truth, freedom, and wisdom—the source of all purity and contentment. They can give their help to you if you will ask for it.

Don't be confused or impressed by the material world of technology—our mind makes it all, it is just a machine—the most beautiful one—as is your damaged brain. Your mind is above the brain and will repair that tool in a little time. I also remember the days when I was a naughty child and you came to me although I had not yet seen your bodily form on the sandy dunes of Cape Cod among the stunted sea pines, and in Italy, and all through my life really. You're brave and all this present eclipse you will put to good—and use by putting it behind you—with self-understanding. Remember, time is an illusion—all the points, moments in time, are equidistant from the infinite past, the infinite future—each moment is a star creating past and future connecting with all other moments—the whole point of being. Now, by putting your damaged intellect to work on the basic physical world of time and space around you, finding out with patient observation why the machine—the continuum—works, you will free yourself from your dilemma. There must be a reason for what's happened. Find out and understand. That is step #1. Don't be scared if you have to go to a rehabilitation center—you will meet people who may help you. It will be a change. Returning to your father's house is no good for you and you'll feel more and more cut off from the world. Fight!

Look at me. I suffered loneliness and exile from life for years and years, all during our time together and after that, also, and I've only just made it home, as it were, to my true self and happiness. My life would have become a maudlin tragedy if I had not made up my mind to fight—to fight for my god and for my life. You will do it, too. We all have to lose once in order to never lose again.

I'm leaving for New York on Monday at 12:00 midday. I'll be staying at my granny Nini's. She knows all about you and would want me to send her love. Don't worry, I will write as often as you write to me and I know you will get yourself out of this soon.

Certain of us can see everything that is going on everywhere, past and future—and will help and protect you if you realize your own present helplessness and gullibility.

My own wishes go straight to your dear heart like arrows and I send you, as you once sent me, dearest thoughts.

Tony

Letter from Dr. Philip Gogarty to Miwa Svinka-Zielinski, July 21, 1980

Broadmoor

Dear Mrs. Svinka-Zielinski,

It is a pleasure for me to tell you that Antony Baekeland has today been discharged from this hospital and will fly to New York from London at noon. He is accompanied by a family friend, Mrs. Brebner, who will ensure that he meets with members of his family on arrival. There is a tentative arrangement that he will attend Richmond Fellowship in New York in the near future where Dr. Portnow could, if contacted, supervise the case. However, as Antony is under no legal obligation in the USA to pursue any statutory therapeutic course, these arrangements will be entirely voluntary. Should you wish to establish contact with the case it is best to do this through his grandmother, Mrs. Daly.

He is not having any medication and has remained in full remission and quite stable over many months so that the prognosis is quite good.

May I close by expressing my sincere thanks to you for your interest and help.

Yours sincerely,
Philip Gogarty
Consultant Forensic Psychiatrist

HEATHER COHANE

Tony was handed over to Cecelia Brebner at London Airport and put on the plane on the condition that he never come back to England. I was a little frightened when he was actually leaving, just because I had been, you know, quite instrumental in persuading the doctors to let him out.

CECELIA BREBNER

I thought I was taking him to New York to go to a halfway house. But at the airport when I rendezvoused with Broadmoor—at the eleventh hour, yes!—when he was handed over to me, they said, "It's all changed. We tried to contact you at Kensington Palace but you'd already left and Lady Mary didn't know where we could reach you. Antony Baekeland is going directly to his maternal grandmother, Mrs. Nina Daly." Well.

On the aircraft over, he went into how he had murdered his mother. In absolute detail. He said, "Celia, a friend of Mummy's had rung while she was out and when Mummy got back she said she didn't want to see her but I had already told this friend to come round that evening and Mummy screamed at me." Then, he said, he threw something at her. And then, he said, she rushed into the kitchen and wrote a note on a piece of paper, to the Spanish maid who was ironing, so he just picked up the carving knife and stabbed her. He said, "Mummy was dying. I knelt down and turned her face toward me and asked, 'What is your name? Who are you?'" He said, "But it doesn't matter because Mummy and I are one. It really doesn't matter at all." I said, "Well, Tony, what now? Do you think you are going to be able to cope with life in New York?" "Oh yes," he said. "I'm going to look after Nini and cook for her and do marvelous things for her." And I said fine.

2

REORIENTATION

SUSAN LANNAN
The International Social Service of Great Britain was still looking into the matter of Antony Baekeland's rehabilitation in America when we heard that he had been released. We were concerned.

CECELIA BREBNER
And so we arrived. It was ninety-two degrees in New York that day. Tony said, "You know something, Celia—New York hasn't changed. It's just the same." And he was extraordinary—he saw to all the baggage and when we got into the cab he said, "I want to stop off and get Nini some flowers but I haven't any money on me," and I said, "I have money," so he got her a huge bouquet.

SHIRLEY COX
Nini did not know Tony was coming until she got a call, I believe, the day before, saying he would be here the following day. That's what she told me when I stopped by to pick up her mail. I live in her building and I handle all her bills and all her business affairs—I've done that for many years.

LENA RICHARDS

Mrs. Daly had broken her hip and needed round-the-clock care. I was the weekend nurse but I was still there on Monday afternoon when Tony came in from the airport with Mrs. Brebner. She wanted to know what the setup was going to be, who was to be responsible for Tony's care, and when Nini and I said nobody, she couldn't believe it.

He looked a little distant to me, but I didn't know what his problems were. Nini had never said anything, she'd never said anything but good things about him.

CECELIA BREBNER

When we arrived at Nini's apartment on Seventy-fourth Street, we went directly into her bedroom to see her. And there was a huge painting of Barbara Baekeland there, that I am told hung in the "21" Club in New York for years—until she died, in fact. And Tony saw it and said, "Nini, take it down!" And she said, "Oh no, Tony, it's my favorite, favorite painting of Mummy." "Take it down!" he said. I saw the look on this man's face and I knew that I had done the wrong thing.

DR. PHILIP GOGARTY

My conscience is quite clear. I did ten times the normal amount of work to get Tony to America. I tried everything I possibly could to find the proper care for him.

SHIRLEY COX

Nini told me later that the moment he walked in the door she knew he wasn't well. And later I saw that for myself. My first thought was, "I'm going to call Fred Baekeland." But Nini said, "No no no no! Promise me you won't do that. *Promise* me you won't! You're my friend, promise me."

ETHEL WOODWARD DE CROISSET

When he wrote me saying he was going back to his grandmother's place where he had spent so many happy days as a child—it was where he sometimes used to go in the afternoons when he was let out of Buckley School, you see—I said to myself, This boy's going to find that apartment very small. And later Nini told me that she could see at once that he felt oppressed—and it was also very hot, to make matters worse—so she suggested they go out immediately, that first night, and have dinner around the corner.

BROOKS BAEKELAND

By coincidence I came back to the U.S. at about the same time as Tony. I went, first, to stay with probably my oldest friend, my cousin Baekeland Roll, and his wife, Kate, in Rhode Island. The Rolls are much reputed for their hospitalities and other virtues: a gregarious, large-familied tribe, their house always bulging with children and guests. I had not seen it, breathed its wacky air for many a year, and a great weight seemed to go off me there for a while.

I had not been on Block Island more than a week, I think, when I got a telephone call—everyone in the house listened to it—from Tony, who had just arrived at Nini's. He said he wanted to come out to that full, happy, child-brimming house. I said no.

CLEMENT BIDDLE WOOD

I suppose Brooks was terrified to see Tony for fear that Tony might attack *him*.

BROOKS BAEKELAND

For myself I felt no fear. My pessimism makes me immune to fear, and I have a certain confidence, even now, in my wits and brawn. But I knew my tiger, and I did not even ask the Rolls if they would receive him. I just said no. My bad reputation increased with that "no."

Oh yes, he had often wanted to assault me—I had seen the crazed lust for it come into his eyes—but he never dared. He was a *woman-*beater. I said to him once, "Crazy you may be and you are, but there are crazy saints and crazy brutes and you are one of the latter."

CECELIA BREBNER

I was staying nearby, on Sixty-ninth Street, with Georgette Klinger. I was going to look after her little poodle for about three months while she did a European tour. I called Nini every day and she always said, "He's okay, Celia," and one day I said, "Look, I'd like to come round and see him," so I took him out for dinner, and he seemed quite rational, perhaps a little bit strange but certainly not manic.

Shirley Cox

Tony promised he would get Nini's breakfast every day, she told me, because, you see, her nurse could not be there overnight when Tony was staying, there was simply not enough room. This meant that Nini had no care at night if she wanted to get up and go to the bathroom and things like that.

I know he didn't fix her breakfast because the nurse would arrive in the morning and he would still be in bed. Nini told me he stayed up all night playing the record player. Well, I think that's understandable. Having been incarcerated for so long, you now have freedom, you know, to do all the things you've been prevented from doing. But he was in a small apartment, in a small apartment house, where the people on either side and around have to get up and go to work, so Nini knew that if the noise lasted for more than two or three days the neighbors would complain and she was terrified of that. So she said she asked him to lower the volume, and he completely ignored her.

Sam Green

He called me right after he got to town and it was a close call. Bart, my assistant, took the call. Tony said he wanted to see me urgently, that I was his only friend and he wanted me to get him some dope so he could get high. Bart told him that I was out of the country.

At some point you just have to protect yourself. I mean, clearly one *should* have been nice to Tony, and generous—he had been through a terrible ordeal and needed companionship and forgiveness, but I just didn't want to do it anymore.

Tom Dillow

Tony asked Bart for *my* number, and Bart called to warn me that Tony was trying to find me. I mean, I was in the phone book, but, you know, for the Baekelands a telephone number didn't exist unless they *got* it from someone. Bart said Tony told him, "T-t-t-tom n-never understood why I m-m-murdered M-mummy."

Bart Gorin

When I first started working for Sam Green, he told me that probably someday a person named Tony Baekeland would call and that I was just to make up anything to keep him away. I guess it was just sort of understood that Tony would be coming back at some point, but we never knew when exactly. So anyway, one hot day there he was on the phone. Sam was out on Fire Island, but I said, "Gee, Tony, Sam's in Singapore," or somewhere like that. And then he asked if I knew about him and I played sort of dumb, and he said, "You don't know who I am?" And I said no. Then he told me fairly matter-of-factly that he had killed his mother. I said, "What are you going to do now? What are your plans?" And he said, "Well, my grandmother Mrs. Daly is the only person who has stood by me all this time, in fact she was the one who got me out of that awful place I was in. She's an old lady now and I want to make her last days as happy as possible"—I remember *that* very well. And then he asked me if I would go shopping with him because all he had were winter clothes, from England, and it was summer out. I said I was going away for the weekend and he said, "Can I call you on Monday?" and I said sure. I never spoke with him again.

GLORIA JONES

I didn't know they'd let him out till he called from New York. He called Muriel Murphy first and then he called *me*. He said he'd like to come out to visit me on Long Island, where I was living now. I was absolutely terrified. Jim was dead by then so I called up Irwin Shaw, who I wouldn't have bothered if Jim were alive. Irwin said, "You can't have him come out," and I said, "Well, God, we've got to do *something* about him." Irwin didn't know the Baekelands that well—I guess he was very smart, he just stayed away from the whole thing, very clever. He said to me, "Stay totally out of it. You just don't know. . . . You have children around and everything." So I called Tony back and said that my house was filled, you know. And it *was* filled.

CLEMENT BIDDLE WOOD

Jessie and I had come over from Europe for the summer and we were visiting Muriel Murphy in East Hampton when Tony called. He said, "Muriel, I'm in New York and it's boiling." It *was* an exceptional heatwave—I mean, even for July. He said, "I'm cooped up in this tiny little apartment with my grandmother and there are pictures of my mother everywhere and her ashes are in an urn on the mantelpiece and I'm just going crazy. I've got to get out of town." Obviously he was hoping Muriel would invite him out to Long Island. Which she didn't. And then he said, "Maybe I can find rooms for my grandmother and myself out there somewhere." And Muriel said,

"Everything's pretty full up," which of course is always true in the summer. So then he said, "Well, I'll probably be coming out if I *can* find anywhere to stay, and I'll give you a ring." Muriel got terribly upset, she said to us, "This boy's a homicidal maniac, he shouldn't be in an apartment alone with his grandmother, but I certainly don't want him coming out *here* and fastening on to *me* as some sort of mother substitute."

PHYLLIS HARRIMAN MASON
One day that week I thought I saw him on the street, Sixty-ninth Street, and I was scared stiff because I was afraid he would identify me with Barbara.

RENÉ JEAN TEILLARD
I saw Tony on Lexington Avenue. I am a friend since a very long time of his beautiful grandmother Mrs. Hallowell. I was going to buy a newspaper and suddenly I saw him there and I said, "Tony, what are *you* doing here? I'm so glad you came back," and he said, "I'm buying a pair of shoes." I said, "But to buy a pair of shoes you should go to Alexander's." "Oh," he said, "I didn't know. I've been in England." And so we chatted and I said I wanted him to come and have dinner and he came the next day and it was all right.

When he and his mother left for London a year before her assassination I invited them to dinner and I gave them some frogs' legs, because they were international and I'm French myself. And I gave him frogs' legs again. I gave him the exact same dinner as when he had left.

We ate on a little bridge table which I had beautifully prepared, near the telephone and close to some weights which were on the floor by my feet in case something should happen, since I hadn't seen him since he left that night for England and if something happened now because he was crazy in a moment, I was therefore prepared with my telephone and my weights.

He was not reluctant to answer all the questions I asked. First of all I asked him what happened and he told me how he had killed his mother. He was able to tell me without any emotion how he plunged the knife in her chest. I told him, "You need friends now that you are back here and you need to see the doctor." "I don't need to see any doctor," he said. I said, "But Dr. Greene is a friend of yours since your youth, and I am certain he would be delighted to see you since he even went over to England to see you."

His face changed when I first spoke "doctor." But then when I said "Dr. Greene," everything was just fine and we finished dinner. I said, "You can come back again, you have my telephone number." And he left.

SHIRLEY COX
On Wednesday and Thursday, the third and fourth days he was here, he put all the pictures of his mother and some candles on a chest of drawers in Nini's living room—he made it into an altar.

CECELIA BREBNER
He was evidently playing the most macabre music and he had those photographs of Barbara and the black candles and he was performing a kind of black mass.

LENA RICHARDS
I was nervous around him because I just didn't know what to expect—I couldn't tell. He didn't have much to say, really. And he didn't seem to have much patience for anything, I noticed. Apparently all week he'd been using the telephone a lot and drinking all the wine—Nini said, "He's to have it," so he ordered more. On Saturday when I got there, he asked me to go to the store for him to get him some writing paper. I was wondering why he couldn't go out himself. I told him it was early, I didn't feel like going out yet. So he did go, after all, and I asked him to get me a newspaper, but he forgot. And when he came back he curled up in a chair and slept for a long time.

CECELIA BREBNER
Late Saturday afternoon I went over to have tea with Tony and Nini and no sooner had I gotten there than the nurse beckoned me into the bedroom, she said Nini wanted to talk to me. Nini told me, "I'm so frightened of him, Celia." I said, "Well, Nini, I don't know how to advise you at this point. I don't know whether we can call the police because he hasn't committed a felony." When I went back into the living room, Tony said to me, "I'm not well, Celia," and I said, "Now, Tony, tell me—define this. Are you sick mentally or are you sick physically?" He said, "I wake up at three in the morning," and I said, "Well, so do I. It's the jet lag, the time difference. But

each day it will get a little better. And you know where I am if you need me." And he threw his arms around me and said, "Oh, I love you, Celia, I love you." I said, "Well, Tony, prove your love. All I want you to do is be kind to Nini and show them that you can fit into normal society again." He said, "Yes, yes, I can, I can." So I said fine.

LENA RICHARDS

I didn't prepare supper for Nini that Saturday because he said *he* wanted to do it. He even told her what he was going to make her. But then I think somebody called and asked them out to dinner. Anyway, I left.

But later that night I called to see if she was okay. She said she was. I knew she wasn't going to say she wasn't, but I thought she wasn't her own self.

DR. FREDERICK BAEKELAND

I had dinner with them that night, the Saturday after his arrival, and he seemed rather tense but not extraordinarily so—and of course I've seen him very tense at times. One of the big problems in psychiatry is the limits of predicting behavior. Another big problem is that a person may look tense and it could have to do with any number of things, and if the person's not going to tell you anything about it, that presents still another problem.

THILO VON WATZDORF

Tony called me in New York and I told my secretary, "No no—tell him I'm not available." The last time I'd seen him was at the party Barbara gave on Cadogan Square the night before he killed her, and I hadn't communicated with him at all during the whole time he was in Broadmoor.

When he couldn't reach me by phone in New York he wrote me a letter saying how fondly he remembered me from Ansedonia and how all he wanted now was to take care of his little grandmother and how he didn't have any friends in New York his own age and would so much like to see me and couldn't we meet.

I got the letter on a Sunday night—I'd been in the country for the weekend—and I was touched by it. I rang and rang and kept getting no answer. I couldn't imagine why no one was picking up since I knew his grandmother was in her late eighties and there had to be somebody there to look after her.

3

ATTACK

LENA RICHARDS
On Sunday I came maybe a couple minutes after nine a.m., and Tony didn't open the door for me right away. I didn't have my own key, I'd given it to *him*. When he finally came to the door—he was wearing his cutoff pants—he said, "Lena, quick! Get the police!" Or the ambulance, or something to that effect. "I just stabbed my grandmother." He didn't move. I got scared, so I didn't go in. I ran back down the stairs. I had on high heels and I ran to the corner and called the police. Then I waited outside Nini's building for them to come, and when they did I took them up.

SERGEANT JOSEPH CHINEA
We responded to a 911 call, and when my partner John McCabe and I entered the apartment on East Seventy-fourth Street, he came running out of the bedroom at us, saying, "She won't die!" We could hear his grandmother screaming. I grabbed him by the shirt and pulled him past me, and McCabe, who's a beefy man, grabbed him and he didn't struggle. He kept repeating, "She won't die, the knife won't go in! And she keeps screaming! I can't understand it."

I ran into the bedroom and saw this elderly, frail lady lying against the wall. The nightstand was turned over and she was in the corner. It looked as if she was trying to get away from him. She was wearing a satiny nightgown and the blood was just running through it, it wasn't soaking up. She was still screaming, but once she saw me she started to calm down. The nurse had arrived during the assault, and she probably saved the woman's life.

An ambulance arrived right after we did, and then additional policemen arrived, and while she was being ministered to she was lucid enough to comment that her grandson had been talking on the phone and playing music twenty-four hours a day all week and that he had been up all night mumbling over a table that had his mother's ashes in the center.

From a Psychiatric Interview with Antony Baekeland, New York City, 1980

My grandmother helped me and brought me back to New York. I spent one week with her but I had a difficult time. I was up all night and I couldn't eat. I felt I was being denied physical and eye contact with my grandmother. There is something in my eye that stops me from meeting other people face to face. I suppose if it meant having sex with my grandmother, I might have wanted to have sex with her. At the end of that week I knew that I would be unhappy with her. I was calling the airlines to fly to Mallorca or England but my grandmother, who is a very mysterious woman, tried to prevent me from making these phone calls. I kept hearing voices, including my grandmother talking in my head, but I couldn't hear her voice clearly because there was noise around and my voices kept bothering me. The voices are those of people I know and people I don't know. They sound like a machine. They talk back to me and it really bothers me a lot. The voices tell me that I'm a savior, that I'm Satan, that I'm an angel, that I'm royalty. Sometimes they say that I'm a dirty little man or a bad woman or a dog. They also give me helpful messages. I hear them all the time. I also hear music and the music lifts my soul.

We were in my grandmother's bedroom but she wouldn't shut up. She kept talking and talking and talking and she wouldn't let me make the phone call. Then I threw the telephone across the room at her and she fell down. When she fell down, I felt very bad for her. I didn't want her to go to the hospital with broken bones and suffer more, so in order to help her I rushed to the kitchen, took a little knife from the drawer, went back, and stabbed her in the breast. I wanted to kill her so I could liberate her—not because I was angry, just to liberate her from the mistake I had made and from the suffering that she was experiencing at the time and from the time I was thirteen years of age.

All this happened because I was denied physical contact with my grandmother and homosexual relations with anybody else.

After I stabbed her, the nurse came to the door and she must have called the ambulance.

LENA RICHARDS
I can't understand how he didn't kill her. All those blows! Her only comments in the hospital were that she wished nobody to know. She wanted to know if everybody knew. That's how she reacted—she didn't want anybody to know anything. She wanted to keep it quiet.

GLORIA JONES
Somebody called right away. You know—people, everybody.

CLEVE GRAY
I heard it on the radio, that he'd stabbed his grandmother. That's how I found out about it, on WINS.

CECELIA BREBNER
He was not on any medication at all, and I think probably that was the problem. But you know, what happened really is that Broadmoor made a mistake—they make so many mistakes. They took him for purely a schizophrenic. In fact, he was a paranoid, homicidal maniac. You know, when I took him to Nini's that first day, she said to me, "Look at this lovely photograph of Tony with his cat." I have never seen anything so terrified in my life as that cat!

POLICE OFFICER JOHN MCCABE, RETIRED
He didn't look capable of violence. The grandmother evidently repeated things and this annoyed him, he told me.

NINA DALY

It was in the morning. We had had breakfast together, I think. I was very close to him. He was with me every minute. I never thought he would go that way. I don't know how it happened. I can't imagine. Just something snapped. Yes, that's it. That's what happened. You never know.

He was so loving. All I did was break my heart over him. Why could this happen to him, you know? And then I remembered it happened to Barbara, too. I knew how much *she* loved him. We both loved him the same.

It was too much for me. Too much. It could have been dangerous. It nearly killed me. I wasn't in a lot of pain. It didn't hurt because I loved him so much.

SERGEANT JOSEPH CHINEA

Mrs. Daly told us that he had taken over her apartment. And then the nurse let us in on a lot of things. She pointed out the ashes to us and told us about the bizarre way he'd been behaving—the loud music, that he was making a mess out of the apartment, that he was telling everyone to shut up and not talk to him. He had become very agitated as the week progressed, and he was staying up all night, worshiping.

He spoke about what he called his grandmother's nagging. "Nini was exactly like my mother," he said, "nagging and bothering me, constantly talking to me." Then he told us that he had killed his mother—I remember the shock on that. He volunteered that information to us. "I just came here from England," he said. "They had kept me there for killing my mother." Everybody just looked at themselves. "My mother never left me alone, I finally couldn't take it anymore. But *she* was easy—one shot and she was finished. I just stabbed her once and that was the end of it. But I kept stabbing Nini and she wouldn't die." Apparently what happened was most every blow struck bone and the knife was being deflected.

Invoice, Investigatory Evidence, Police Department, the City of New York

ARTICLE

1 brown handle knife app. 5" blade w/all blood stains.

The above is a complete list of property removed.

BROOKS BAEKELAND

There was only one person in the world both silly enough and generous enough to want that released tiger in her house. And she was almost killed for her goodness—a few days after I'd said no to Tony's request to come out to see me in Rhode Island, he stabbed his little grandmother almost to death when she objected to his voodoo rites with his mother's ashes.

I had kept every letter and drawing that I had ever received from him from the time he was three years old—not just from sentiment but from presentiment. But when I learned of the stabbing, I destroyed every single thing I ever had of him.

CECELIA BREBNER

At Broadmoor he made the most terrible terrible toys for his little half brother—apparently they were *so* grotesque and *so* macabre that his father threw them away immediately. And his paintings . . . apart from a rather delicate one he did for me, all without exception were macabre in the extreme—huge white hearts on a green background, pierced with a sword and dripping blood. He said he hid these from the warders. Later I saw the same motif on a box he made for Nina Daly.

SERGEANT JOSEPH CHINEA

We had realized right away that we were dealing with what we call an EDP—an emotionally disturbed person. It was just a matter of controlling him—handcuffing a person like that can make them violent, and then it's necessary for *us* to use violence against *them*, so we contained him in the living room but we let him roam around the room. It was cluttered because he had his things in there—suitcases, his music. He was sleeping on the couch—there was bedding on it and it wasn't made up. I remember it being a very tiny little apartment and I remember thinking, "Someone with all this money," you know. He also had photographs in his belongings—things he had laid out. Apparently when he was over in England he had become involved with the occult. It seemed that way to me. Anyway, you could see that the room had totally become his.

He showed us his paintings and drawings that he said he had done while he was incarcerated. And you could see in the drawings that . . . To this day I can't understand how the British government could repatriate him.

Telegram from Kingman Brewster, Jr., U.S. Ambassador to the Court of St. James's, to Cyrus R. Vance, Secretary of State, Washington, D.C., July 30, 1980

> AS MR. BAEKELAND HAS RETURNED TO THE U.S., LONDON CONSIDERS HIS CASE CLOSED   BREWSTER

DR. PHILIP GOGARTY

The moment he stepped on the airplane, he was outside English authority. But I was very disappointed when the U.S. Consulate could not accept authority for him—I had asked and they had said they couldn't. No one would accept legal authority for him. Once he got on that plane he was basically a free person.

ROSEMARY RODD BALDWIN

Michael Alexander says he's never going to try and get anybody released ever ever in his life again. *Ever.*

MICHAEL ALEXANDER

I don't feel any sort of responsibility. On the other hand, I suppose you might say that I was as deceived by Tony as everybody else.

SERGEANT JOSEPH CHINEA

In the patrol car riding over to the 19th Precinct for debriefing, he talked all the time about his grandmother. When we arrived we asked him if he knew where he was and he said, "Yes, I'm in the police station." "Do you know what you did?" we asked him. "Yeah, sure." Detective McLinskey, one of the detectives who was questioning him—there were three of us in the debriefing room with him—hit a nerve. Essentially what he was doing was nagging Tony with questions. And Tony became agitated immediately. "My grandmother nagged me," he said. "My mother nagged me. Why did they have to nag me? I don't like people to nag me." Right away we laid off. We sensed this guy's going to go crazy on us.

TERENCE McLINSKEY

I could imagine his emotions at the time: "Am I going to go to jail? Are they going to kill me?" He was in bad shape, and somewhat disheveled. I was just doing my ordinary everyday job. You live by your wits as a detective, you live by your communications skills. You can do great work—not punitive, but directing people to the proper agency. I wanted to help Tony Baekeland make peace—I was trying to help him find his personal salvation. I was trying to build up that he was *worth* saving, no matter what. I mean, he happened to be a homosexual who had killed his mother and then tried to kill his grandmother.

I wonder if the poor guy found any answers to the whys and the wherefores.

From a Psychiatric Interview with Antony Baekeland, New York City, 1980

I intend to read many religious books. They lighten my awareness and I get full with love and power and heavenly minds, all in the form of music.

From the Logbook, Sergeant Joseph Chinea, July 27, 1980

To Manhattan Central Booking, arrived 11:03 a.m. Defendant made complete admission to events leading to assault and actual assault.

Statements: Before Rights—"I stabbed her. She kept nagging. I asked her to stop. I threw the phone at her but she continued to nag so I got the knife and stabbed her. Get some help."

Statements: After Rights—"I stabbed her five times. I wanted her to die fast but she wouldn't die. It was horrible. I hate when this happens."

Mrs. Cecelia Brebner, friend of the family, interviewed at 19th Pct. She said she wanted to volunteer as a witness to the fact that Baekeland was mentally disturbed.

Out of Central Booking with Defendant 12:23 p.m. To Department of Correction to begin processing, 12:32 p.m.

To Manhattan Criminal Court, Room 131, 3:15 p.m. Await paper & arraignment.

From Police Files

Nature of grandmother's injuries: multiple (eight) stab wounds to chest, arms, and hand; fractured collarbone; multiple fractured ribs (four-five), causing breathing problem; bruises and abrasions. Confined to Lenox Hill Hospital.

Other members of family fear for their lives. Ask for remand.

Victim may not want to press charges. Told one police officer she still loved him.

From a Psychiatric Interview with Antony Baekeland, New York City, 1980

Oh, my grandmother survived. She has ways and means I know nothing about, but let's forget about her and talk about homosexual relations.

I'm not going to call the hospital and find out how she's doing—why should I call her? She talks to me all the time through the special power that she has.

From the Logbook, Sergeant Joseph Chinea, July 27, 1980

9:00 p.m. Defendant held over for a.m. 7/28 arraignment.

From the Arraignment, The People of the State of New York—Against—Antony Baekeland, Defendant, Criminal Court of the City of New York, County of New York, July 28, 1980

THE COURT: Psychiatric examination ordered, administrative psychiatric segregation; suicide watch.

Headline, the New York Times, July 29, 1980

EX-PATIENT IS HELD IN 2D STABBING

Headline, New York *Daily News,* July 29, 1980

HE'S CHARGED WITH STABBING GRANDMA
AFTER SERVING TIME IN MURDER OF MOM

Headline, *Daily Express,* London, July 29, 1980

FREED BROADMOOR PATIENT
ACCUSED OF U.S. MURDER BID

DR. FREDERICK BAEKELAND
It was very much against my opinion and my advice that Tony was let out of Broadmoor without any adequate follow-up program set up. I'm not surprised that there was a problem eventually.

From *Broadmoor,* David Cohen, Psychology News Press, London, 1981

> If an ex-patient commits a crime, the symphony of outrage from Fleet Street is loud and vicious. In 1980, *Now* magazine ran a dossier on Broadmoor "disasters" and identified twenty cases in which ex-patients had committed acts of violence after being released.

MICHAEL ALEXANDER
The papers in London attacked Dr. Gogarty quite strongly over what happened with Tony. And Tony was described in the media here as "the mad axman of Broadmoor." It was "the mad axman strikes again" sort of touch, you know. I got on to the papers about that. I said, "Look, that's not the way to present this case. Dr. Gogarty behaved extremely correctly under the circumstances." I didn't get very far. They stuck to their story.

Letter from Dr. Patrick G. McGrath to Miwa Svinka-Zielinski, Undated

Broadmoor

Dear Mrs. Svinka-Zielinski,

I have received your letter and clip from the *New York Times*. I have also heard from Antony's father. Let me say straightaway how distressed we here all were to hear of Mrs. Daly's injuries at the hands of Antony, but we are somewhat relieved to see from the report that she will recover.

I do hope that the whole family, including Antony, will recover from this incident which you rightly describe as a catastrophe.

Yours sincerely,
Patrick G. McGrath
Physician Superintendent

Letter from Dr. Philip Gogarty to Cecelia Brebner, Undated

Broadmoor

Dear Mrs. Brebner,

I am very grateful for your letter to me which gave me details of the tragic events. Strange to relate I have had no further communication from anyone although I was expecting a request for a medical report and history from his present medical attendants. I wonder whether you have knowledge of subsequent events which you might pass on to me as of course I am intensely interested to learn from my faux pas.

Yours sincerely,
Philip Gogarty
Consultant Forensic Psychiatrist

DR. PHILIP GOGARTY
He's the only patient who ever backfired on me like that.

HEATHER COHANE

During the week he was in New York, Jack and I were on our boat in Italy, miles from any telephone or any communication. We didn't know for a long time what had happened. And when I heard, I was upset for days, and the reason I was upset was because I had trusted my judgment. I just couldn't believe it—the grandmother, the one person left that he loved!

Letter from Antony Baekeland to an Unidentified Friend, "Eryl," Written in Police Custody, 1980

Dear Eryl,

I am in trouble, I am sorry to say. The spirit which has been directing me has for a span been "misdirecting" me—not, I hope, to cause this grief, now passing, but in order to serve Mammon and the powers of disorder and wickedness, which through lack of eternal and infinite vision have tied knots in the fabric of life, or some, thank God, of it. I have been held captive here for a very long span, thinking that I served the Power of Love when I had been lured into bondage and captivity by certain pleasures which may under correct direction prove creative and progressive, but which caused me great pain and grief, since I believed in those who held me in this state of being. I do not think for 2 minutes that the spirit that has been behind me wilfully caused my troubles, but that He was misled by those whom He served, and so on. Indeed, my Whole Family here is of the House of Hades. So please will you keep your eye on me so I can come out.

                                                                    Tony

THILO VON WATZDORF

Three weeks after I'd tried to call Tony at his grandmother's and it just rang and rang with no answer, I tried the number again and this time somebody picked up. I said, "Is Tony Baekeland there?" And the voice said, "I'm his grandmother's nurse. Something terrible happened. Tony is on Rikers Island. Would you like to speak with his grandmother?" I said no, I wouldn't—I mean, I had never even met her. But *she* wanted to speak with *me*. She got right on the phone and she told me what had happened. She said, "Isn't it terrible? I love Tony so much."

PART IV
RIKERS ISLAND

1

JULY 27, 1980–
OCTOBER 31, 1980

The majority of New York City inmates are housed on an island in the East River between the Bronx and Queens, known as Rikers Island. It originally belonged to a Dutch immigrant by the name of Jacob Ryker, who sold all of the original ninety acres to the city in 1885.

In 1900, a wood-frame construction suitable for one hundred prisoners was completed; soon afterwards, wooden barracks capable of housing up to four hundred were added. By 1918, there were eight barracks on the island as well as a stable, a guardhouse, a mess hall, and several employee buildings. Inmates labored on coal barges, iceboats, and garbage dumps, and on a hog farm located on the premises.

Eventually the workhouse aspect of Rikers Island was abandoned and in 1955 the island became known officially as the Penitentiary of the City of New York. Landfill increased its size to over four hundred acres and by the 1980s it was home to six major prison facilities—three for male inmates, one for females, one for adolescent boys, and a hospital. It also now contains a power plant, maintenance garage, firehouse, print shop, shoe-repair shop, tailor shop, laundry, and bakery. Eight days after his return from England, Tony Baekeland was entering a community not unlike Broadmoor.

Property Envelope, Department of Correction, City of New York

LIST OF PROPERTY

None

I Acknowledge The Surrender Of My Property As Listed Above

DATE: *July 28, 1980*
SIGNATURE OF INMATE: *Antony Baekeland*

Floor and Cell Location Form, Department of Correction, City of New York

DATE: July 29, 1980
FLOOR: Mental Observation
CELL: Lower 6-8

Letter from Antony Baekeland to Shirley Cox, July 30, 1980

Rikers Island

Dear Shirley,
More Horror. In case you don't know what happened, this is
it—by Tuesday I realized that it was no good. I had been up
several nights reading in the Bible and was feeling very nervous.
I began to hear Nini's voice, clear as day coming from her
room. (It felt just like a wolf gnawing at my entrails.) When I
would go and ask her what she was saying, she said she had said
nothing. I had *no one* to talk to—I had tried to give myself to
Nini in various ways but it was no go. It was like having someone you loved right in the next room and thousands of miles
away. Once in the middle of the night I had a very clear vision
or memory of us (Nini and I) a long long time ago in our house
in Italy, how we used to go hunting for pretty stones and leaves
and things, and how we used to hold hands. I also remembered
how my family sheds its blood (and each other's blood) for one
another. Anyway, I was in tears and I got up and quietly went
into her room. She was asleep and I held her hand but she
didn't wake up.

Anyway, I finally realised I couldn't stay, that it wouldn't be right for either of us, and Sunday morning I went to her room and began telephoning for reservations for England. Please realise that I was in a *desperate* state of mind—many beautiful and terrifying spiritual things had been happening and I hadn't slept properly for a week. N. kept on at me and I warned her *three* times that if she wouldn't be quiet I would throw the telephone at her. Anyway, finally my nerves broke and I threw the phone at her. She fell down and began to moan and I realised what I had done and that she had probably broken more bones. Then I felt that *all her suffering* in the past (hip, etc.) had been for *my sake* and that was too much to bear. I knew that if I gave her the *Coup de Grâce* God would take her Home and there would be no more misery. I tore into the kitchen, found a knife, rushed back, and tried to kill her but wasn't strong enough and/or didn't know how. Then I started screaming and praying and pleading with God to take her Home. I tried ringing the ambulance for ½ hour without realising that the phone was kaput. The poor darling asked me to straighten her legs which I did. Then Lena came and I told her to get an ambulance. The police came as well and took me away.

Shirley, if you do not want to speak to me or see me again I understand perfectly but I want you to know that I am as horrified as you are—believe me please. I am sure if I hadn't been so alone it wouldn't have happened, but it's no use saying "if," ever.

If you would like to help me could you get me my Bible, Shakespeare, & Spiritual Canticle by St. John of the Cross. They are on the table in the drawing room.

If you would like to visit I would like to hear how N. is. Do ring up the place beforehand as I *may* be in court that day. My no.: 349-80-4228. Could you send or bring any letters which may have come for me?

After it happened, at the police station and here, I continued to hear her voice, saying, *"Honi soit qui mal y pense,"* and other things.

I am better off here than I was at Nini's. At least there is company. (Blacks and Puerto Ricans mainly.)

I am on Legal Aid but am hoping my lawyer will let me have him on a money basis as I feel unable to accept government help since I have money.

Please understand that *I* understand what a terrible thing this is for you, me, and any friends we may have.

Yours,
Tony (and of course, Nini)

DR. HELENE WEISS
I saw Tony Baekeland on July 29, 1980. At first he was generally cooperative, and then he just started to decompensate after a while. But he wasn't what I would call crazy. Even though he was here on attempted murder, he was not basically a criminal personality per se. His acts had been done more out of passion than out of criminal pathology.

Letter from Brooks Baekeland to Nina Daly, July 29, 1980

Block Island

Dear Nini,
I have heard of your new adventure with a heavy heart. That so much bravery and goodwill should be repaid that way! But I am very glad that you are out of danger. How you were able to defend yourself, only you and God know, but somehow you did.

I must tell you that I did not expect this. I knew of course that Tony had not changed basically. His irrationality (and arrogance) continued to make a very bad impression on me, but I worried more about his ability to understand *what the world was like* and what he had to do to survive (or thrive) in it than I did about his acting out the violence of his nature again. It came to me as a surprise, although not apparently to Fred. I did however warn Gogarty that Tony was dangerous when crossed. I received some very ugly letters from Tony whenever I seemed to frustrate what he deemed I owed him or he deserved—exceedingly mandatory, abusive, even scatological. I pointed out these things to Gogarty, but *Broadmoor simply wished to get him off their hands*—and the Bleeding Hearts Club never stopped pounding their drum, either. You are lucky to be alive. The road to hell . . .

Poor Tony—what an enormous failure of intelligence. And

what a pity that you did not warn someone of the danger that you felt growing, or ask for help once you realized that he should not have been discharged.

I'm going North for a while—plans still very uncertain. I bought a secondhand car yesterday and will just see a little of America for a while. It's been a long time—14 years. I have come back as a foreigner.

Well, dear, get well soon, and if you need anything let me know through my lawyer in New York. One day I will settle down somewhere or be in one place long enough to receive mail. I will then call him and ask him to forward any messages that have come for me.

Love,
Brooks

Note from File on Antony Baekeland

Tony called his family lawyer Wed. July 30. T. was cordial, rational.

Miwa Svinka-Zielinski

There was nobody who was absolutely interested in Tony's case now. I suppose I could have visited him on Rikers Island but I didn't have any authority to go to his lawyer and ask what the situation was— Why wasn't he being acquitted as schizophrenic? Why was he sitting in a prison which is a regular prison for criminals?

Edward Hershey

Of the ninety-two hundred inmates in our system today, sixty percent will be out after seven days. With that kind of turnover, the Department of Correction, where I'm assistant commissioner for public affairs, has a very challenging but in some cases not very fulfilling mission. Our major mission is to provide pretrial services, get the inmates to court and so on. We don't have an opportunity for long-term relationships. We have to look out for red lights, and when they flash we take action, because there's not a lot of time.

SANDRA LEWIS SMITH

On a typical day in prison the inmates get up at five in the morning if they're going to court. Even if they're not going to court, there's so much noise in the cell block they probably get up about five anyway. The wagon is delivered with the breakfast—hot cereal, scrambled eggs, toast, juice, sometimes fresh fruit—apples, oranges—coffee, or hot water and makings for coffee—or tea. Then the people going to court are taken to court. The rest of the inmates simply hang out. They might read, they might put in an interview slip to go to the legal library and do some research on their case, they might go to the clinic for medication or to be examined for whatever ailment they might have, they might just stay in the area and watch television or play cards or checkers, or they might be called down to receive a visit from their attorney.

MARTIN J. SIEGEL

I was asked by the court to represent Tony Baekeland at his first arraignment. Later he said to me, "I'd like to hire you privately." So I advised Judge Haft that I had been assigned by the court but that the client now wanted to retain me privately and do I have permission. Judge Haft asked Tony if he had the funds and he said yes and the judge said okay.

Tony was always pleasant in all my dealings with him. But he was a very troubled person. He told me once about being in a café with a girl he was in love with and his father was sitting next to her and started to come on to her. He was very bitter about that.

He struck me as the type of person who could be manipulated very easily. I guess you know he was a homosexual. I felt that he wanted to be dominated by someone who played the male role, and that any strong individual that came by could readily dominate him.

Our defense was going to be insanity. I hoped to have him institutionalized in a hospital-type setting where he could really be helped as opposed to a penal-type setting.

From Psychiatric Examination Reports on Antony Baekeland Ordered by the Criminal Court of New York, August 27, 1980, and September 2, 1980

KNOWLEDGE OF CHARGES:
What is the charge against you?

"Either murder or attempted murder of my grandmother."

KNOWLEDGE OF COURT PROCEEDINGS:
Have you entered a plea? What plea have you entered?

"No, I haven't."

What is the name of the Defendant's Attorney?

"Mr. Siegel."

What is the function of a Defense Attorney?

"To help me."

What is the function of a District Attorney?

"He represents the borough and I'll be up against him."

What is the function of a Judge?

"Evaluate whether you can be punished or not, then sentences."

What is the function of a Jury?

"Twelve ladies and gentlemen who decide whether you're guilty or not guilty."

What are the consequences of being found Guilty?

"Depending on seriousness, they are given various penalties."

SUMMARY OF PSYCHIATRIC FINDINGS:
The defendant was alert, cooperative, articulate. Although he stuttered, speech was coherent and relevant. Delusions and hallucinations were denied. The defendant became intermittently tearful in discussing his alleged offense and his father's reaction to it. He stated he felt "chastened" by his experience in jail. Memory is intact. Defendant understands court procedure and is deemed able to assist counsel. He is fit to proceed.

From the Transcript, The People of the State of New York—Against—Antony Baekeland, Defendant, Supreme Court of the State of New York, County of New York, September 19, 1980

THE COURT CLERK: Mr. Baekeland, you have been indicted by the Grand Jury of the County of New York, charging you with attempted murder in the second degree and assault in the first degree. How do you plead to the charges, guilty or not guilty?

DEFENDANT: I plead not guilty.

MR. SIEGEL: Your Honor, I would like to have the matter adjourned for a few weeks for motions on the issue of bail. I would ask some bail be set.

Letter from Shirley Cox to Assistant District Attorney Sarah Hines, Undated

New York

Dear Ms. Hines:

As a close friend of Mrs. Nina Daly (the victim) for many years, and her business affairs manager for the past five years, this letter is to earnestly request that in the event of Antony Baekeland's release, Mrs. Daly be accorded 24-hour-a-day police protection. . . .

I feel this would be absolutely essential to the safety of her life.

I hope you will give this request your serious consideration and support.

Sincerely,
Shirley Cox (Mrs.)

JUDGE ROBERT M. HAFT

There was no serious bail application. It would not have been appropriate. Anyway, Tony Baekeland had no place to go.

He was always very pleasant and smiled a lot. He was never agitated. I would say he had a sort of inappropriate affect, considering what was happening to him.

From the Transcript, The People of the State of New York—Against—Antony Baekeland, Defendant, Supreme Court of the State of New York, County of New York, October 22, 1980

THE COURT: Was the defendant examined by a psychiatrist of your choice?

MR. SIEGEL: Yes, he was. I'm awaiting the report. The examination has taken place.

THE COURT: Adjourned to November 7th.

From a Psychiatric Interview with Antony Baekeland, New York City, 1980

The purpose of this evaluation was to determine Mr. Baekeland's mental status at the time of the alleged crime. When asked where he was born, Mr. Baekeland replied, "I don't know. I was told that I was born in Manhattan. That's what my mother told me but I have no siblings. In fact, as far as I know, she told me that her friend is the Son of Sam and he is also my brother because he is my age." When asked who raised him, he answered, "I think I was raised by my mother, father, and grandmother but it was all very confusing. Our family is spiritually everywhere, so my mother's death would not bother her. We all lived together—a few people but we are all the same person. A close friend of mine is a very powerful magician and he made such magic that I could kill my mother with the same knife that he made the magic with." At this point, the patient started talking quite irrelevantly about his father, stating, "I don't remember him loving me terribly. I didn't know what exactly he wanted me to do. He is a physicist and writes many books. We are very rich people from his family. They sell stocks and real estate and I have a lot of money which is not bad but I never worked for it." . . .

Psychiatric Diagnosis: Schizophrenia, Paranoid Type.

SARAH HINES

We wanted to prove that he was responsible for his crime. We wanted to have as much control over him as possible, in order to give the People and his family security, and there's not much control available when the insanity plea is used—he might have "walked."

Letter from Shirley Cox to Assistant District Attorney Sarah Hines, Undated

New York

Dear Ms. Hines:

Further to our recent telephone conversation, this will confirm that the personal belongings of Antony Baekeland, left behind in his grandmother's apartment in New York at the time of his arrest, were stolen from the basement storage room. Four of the tenants in the building also lost a variety of personal possessions in trunks and suitcases, and one had her bicycle stolen.

As you will remember, I had tried very early on to have Mr. Baekeland's possessions transferred to him in Rikers Island or to his lawyer (if it could be determined who that would be on a continuing basis). But I was told that the suitcases and cartons (containing clothes, shoes, tape recorder, tapes, books, etc.) would not be accepted, and that they should be stored somewhere for the interim until a Court decision had been reached. It was considered important by those concerned about Mrs. Daly's welfare to clean up her apartment and remove the remnants of the traumatic incident before she was released from Lenox Hill Hospital. Consequently, for lack of choice the items were placed in the basement storage room (which was equipped with a lock) until further notice. Whoever committed the robbery had used a key to effect entrance.

Once the robbery was discovered, the 19th Precinct was advised but despite three phone calls over a three-hour period, while the tenants involved waited in the basement, no officer arrived to inspect the premises or to make a report of the incident.

I merely wish to report the fact of the robbery of Mr. Baekeland's possessions to someone in an official capacity relating to his situation. I do believe that, had some official help been extended, Mr. Baekeland's belongings might still be intact.

Sincerely,
Shirley Cox (Mrs.)

2

NOVEMBER 1, 1980–
DECEMBER 16, 1980

JOHN MURRAY

I met Tony in the bull pen, which is where they hold you before you go to court. I was in for burglary. Coincidentally, he was in the same quad as me, too—I was about eight cells away. We were together about six or seven months. I was his closest friend at that time. I definitely was, yes. He said he'd been staying at his grandmother's and he felt all right and then all of a sudden he just heard her saying things like he couldn't go out to see anybody or somebody couldn't come over to the house, and she was next to the phone, and he just hit her a few times. I told him that was a lie. I said, "Why don't you tell me the truth?" And he said, "Oh, yeah, well, the truth of the matter is that she was almost killed."

Then he told me that he had spent time in London, England, for psychiatric reasons for killing his mother. He was sorry about it, because he loved his mother. No one knows why people do things like that. They just do them, and after that, it's over and done with, and you have to live with that—without that person—for the rest of your life.

On good days Tony would keep himself confined to where he was and what he was doing. On days when he was restless and reckless he'd talk about how he killed his mother. He'd whisper, like someone mortified. He'd either whisper or his lips would move and he wouldn't be speaking. That's how he'd say how sorry he was.

He told me once or twice that his mother was very beautiful but he never described her to me in detail or anything. And he told me he knew a beautiful lady named Jinty Money-Coutts and he said that when I got out, if I had no place to stay, I could maybe stay there with her in London.

He told me he had a very small family, and that his father had died when he was younger—or something like that. I think he said died but maybe he told me his father just didn't want to see him anymore. But mostly we talked about what the correctional officers were up to—whether this guy dilly-dallies all day or that guy bullshits around or not.

Sometimes he did drawings—rough sketches with crayons. And some pastels—pictures of sailboats and rivers and docks. But one day he just tore them all up.

SARA DUFFY CHERMAYEFF

I drove out to Rikers Island to see him. We just talked in a room, at a table. He didn't talk about stabbing his grandmother. We just talked about old times. I mean, that's all I had to talk to him about. To me, he looked just like he'd always looked—very handsome. I always thought he was wonderfully handsome.

Look, I'd known him when he was little, and I never again expect to know anyone who killed anybody. I wondered when I went there what the hell I was doing—I mean, there was probably some sort of curiosity and vanity involved in my going to see him. I felt ashamed afterwards, because I felt that I'd exploited him. I remember we said goodbye as if we would meet again—it was like we were at Schrafft's.

JAMES REEVE

Broadmoor was a sort of retreat, really, wasn't it? He was safe there. My God, when he was in that hellhole in America he must have looked back on Broadmoor as nirvana.

MARTIN J. SIEGEL

I was relieved as Tony Baekeland's lawyer in November of 1980. I turned his entire file over to his new lawyer, Ronnie Arrick. I was very surprised when Tony hired him because Tony and I had had a very good attorney-client relationship and there really hadn't been any problem. But apparently a friend of his at Rikers recommended him to Tony. Now I know Arrick is a very fine and competent attorney—he's also a very nice guy. Who can explain why people want to go into this coffee shop as opposed to that coffee shop?

RONALD ARRICK

The first time I met Tony Baekeland was in November when I took over the defense. My job was to represent him on the entire criminal matter all the way through trial and to try to work it out to his entire advantage. His grandmother was not withdrawing the charges. The D.A. was not withdrawing the charges. I was also involved in long-distance dealing with certain facilities in England, because his only defense was a psychiatric defense.

My hope was to get him placed in what I gather his grandmother thought he should be in when she had him brought back here—a hospital. I wanted to have him found not guilty by reason of insanity, and I discussed this with him as about the only thing that could be done.

He had access to funds—I think it was a combination of trust and cash available. He would give in a written request to his trustees, U.S. Trust, sort of like a check facsimile, and they would issue the funds.

JOHN MURRAY

Since Tony had money, he was wary of who would know his business by the way he was acting: Would it show on him? Would people abuse him for it? Would they try to get it from him too quickly?

Tony was very well liked as far as I could see. He had a calm nature, you know, but he had a very rude temper. He had a thing about if he couldn't get his way he would more or less say shove off, you know—kiss it goodbye.

DR. HELENE WEISS

He was very volatile and I'm sure after a while he had some trouble with other inmates. I know he had some transient episodes. On December 11th he was switched over to our Mental Health Center.

JOHN RAKIS

The Mental Health Center has single cells and a higher complement of officers than anywhere else at Rikers Island.

NATALIE ROBINS

I wanted to see Tony's cell. Captain Earl Tulon, who was to be my prison guide, met me in the visitors' parking lot on the Queens side of the island and drove me in a big Cadillac across the narrow bridge that is the only access to Rikers Island. He pointed out the various buildings to me as we took the exact route Tony Baekeland's blue prison bus had taken. My first impression of the island was that of a bleak but tidy campus. School again, for Broadmoor Special Hospital had had the same effect on me at first sight. The difference is that here there seemed to be miles and miles of barbed wire, and once you began to follow it you couldn't take your eyes off it.

We went inside a building called the Anna M. Kross Center where the reception area had a strong antiseptic smell. Here I received a visitor's badge and my briefcase and shoulder bag were thoroughly searched by a correction officer. I then had to walk through a metal detector. Now I had officially arrived at Rikers Island.

We went down a very long corridor whose walls, surprisingly, were decorated with red-yellow-green-blue rainbows interspersed with large orange and purple triangles. Then we entered an older part of the building where the walls were bare. This area housed the Mental Health Center.

Here we were joined by a staff psychologist, J. Victor Benson—everyone called him "Benson" or "Vic." He escorted us into Lower Three Quad. On the left was an area that reminded me of a classroom in a run-down elementary school: plastic chairs piled up on one side, two or three tables scattered around—one next to a wall. "That's the table where I used to sit and talk to Tony. It's even in the same place," Vic Benson told me.

Then I was taken to the cells, a series of tiny single rooms, with doors that have small squares cut out, covered with metal bars. Tony's old cell was at the end of a corridor on the left. Most cells don't have windows, but his had one; it was covered with wire mesh embedded in glass, and looked out on a dirt lot that had one or two patches of crabgrass and weeds.

The current inmate-in-residence was in court, I was told. There was a thick gray wool blanket on the bed. Vic Benson said the bed was in the exact same spot as when Tony was there. Two pairs of underwear were hanging to dry on a metal shelf, and a dirty pair of socks and shoes were on the floor. There was some red-ink graffiti on the walls: Somebody loves somebody. I don't remember what the names were, but Vic Benson said they weren't there when Tony was in the cell.

Custodial Medical Information Form, Prison Health Services, New York City Department of Health, December 11, 1980

MENTAL HEALTH

NAME: Baekeland, Antony
SUICIDE POTENTIAL: No evidence
DEPRESSION: Mild
ASSAULTIVE POTENTIAL: No evidence
VIOLENCE POTENTIAL: No evidence
MEDICATION: Thorazine

J. VICTOR BENSON

As a psychologist at the Mental Health Center, I got to know Tony quite intimately when he was detained on my quad. When I found out about his family background, I did some research on it. Tony himself didn't take much pride in his background, and in fact when he spoke of it, and the wealth, it was all quite casually.

Some of the things he told me sounded like delusional material. It wasn't, though. He told me quite blandly about murdering his mother. He mentioned that his relationship with his father was strained because of his homosexuality—he said his mother had been dissatisfied with his sexual orientation, too. The only good thing he said about his father concerned a trip they both took up to Yonkers once to visit his great-grandfather's lab. It was a pleasant memory—that trip to the lab.

At the time Tony was here we had a relatively quiet quad, although emotions *are* easily aroused because the inmates live so closely together. Some inmates have to be kept off balance—separated, you know, so they don't get into fights and so on. There's also constant cell movement. They want to go to the law library, then they want to go to the barber shop—in this unit the barber shop comes to *them*.

The commissary is a very big thing—that's the supply of niceties that the inmates have. They deposit money in their commissary accounts and once a week they submit an order. The most popular items are cigarettes, and candy and cookies—because so many are drug addicts, they love the sweets. If you're in the general population here, you can go directly to the commissary and pick up your order, but if you're in a mental observation unit like Tony was, they deliver the commissary to you.

Tony was very generous with many of the inmates. He was supporting them—well, not exactly supporting them—but he was very generous with commissary. He maintained friendships in that fashion. That's *one* of the methods he used in cementing his friendships. He ordered huge amounts of commissary. But nobody could challenge that because he always had the money.

You know, all during the day on this quad the correction officers have to make repeated security inspections—check the keys in the locks, check the bars, the gates, the shower room, the windows, the screens, the walls, the dayroom, utility closet, the lighting, the cell walls which they could cut through because they're only made of tile. They're supposed to be impregnable but they are not—an inmate could chip away at the tiles and remove them a few at a time until they had a hole for escape. Also check the vents, because inmates have a habit of storing things there, like jail booze, which they're very clever in fermenting. Check the slop sinks. Check the toilet bowls.

It's a very noisy place, sometimes it gets to be unbearable—the telephone ringing, the inmates wanting to make telephone calls. They can't receive calls, but they can arrange through Social Services to make calls and have an extended conversation, either local or long-distance.

Note from File on Antony Baekeland

Tony Baekeland and a friend of his in prison have been calling Nina Daly repeatedly and abusively. We can't prevent Tony from telephoning his grandmother since she seems to acquiesce and won't tell the police; but he can be advised to cut it out.

JOHN MURRAY

I spoke to his grandmother when Tony called her. They were not harassing phone calls. That must have been someone else. I don't know who that could have been. I asked her not to press charges on Tony, and I also spoke to her about reducing the charges, and she told me that she definitely, invariably would.

One time she got mad and I said, "Whoa, slow down, slow down, I didn't know all that about Tony. Could you tell me that a little bit slower?" And she said, "I'll slow down," and then she said Tony's gay and this and that, and I said, "I know about it."

3

DECEMBER 17, 1980–
JANUARY 14, 1981

JOHN MURRAY
Tony was madly in love with me. He asked me a couple of times if I
would come to his cell at night, but I told him I couldn't do it. Of
course I could, I could go to anybody's cell that I wanted to. I told it
to him like this, I said, "Well, Tony, I have a lot of work," because
work was the only thing I could do to excuse me not responding,
since I'm not gay, you know. I *was* working—in the receiving room.
I wasn't working as a mopper or something like that.

The receiving room is where you go when you come back from
court or from anywhere or if you're just getting in from the street.
They strip you on a table and search you, then they tell you to put
your clothes back on. I was sleeping down there and I was working
out down there with weights. I had priority there. But the first time I
went there I was treated like one of the savage slaves they have. You
know, everyone is pretty much a slave there.

Tony wanted me to be with him wherever he was, that was the
main thing. He wanted someone to be his friend, to more or less
straighten him out. I was concentrating on his money, and I was also
concentrating on his family case. We got a letter from Broadmoor
Hospital in England saying that he'd have to see a few more doctors
to say whether he was competent to stand trial or not.

J. VICTOR BENSON

They used to call John Murray Big John in the receiving room, where he was working on the house gang or paint gang, which is made up of the sentenced inmates who have specific work assignments while they're doing their time. They call it "city time," which is a year or less.

There was *something* going on between Murray and Baekeland, although Murray wasn't a true homosexual. But in jail some inmates will do anything.

JOHN RAKIS

Most of these guys are welfare kids from welfare families and have no qualms about taking money from someone. It's just part of their nature. Once when there was a plane crash on Rikers, a lot of the inmates came and helped with the rescue efforts and most of them wound up getting reduced sentences or were allowed to leave altogether because of the heroics they showed. But later we discovered that they went and looked in the newspaper and found out the names of some of the survivors and wrote them letters or called them up, if they could get the phone numbers, and tried to extort money from them. They'd say, "Hey, I saved your life—don't you think you owe me something?" To them this was just a normal way of life.

JOHN MURRAY

Tony gave away money for protection and also just to be friendly. He did it for both reasons.

RONALD ARRICK

He did give away some funds. Primarily it was to relatives of people he knew in prison who treated him like family, who brought him things, like clothes, books. Mothers of prisoners primarily. Because his own mother was not around. It was *not* protection money that he was giving out.

JOHN MURRAY

He never gave away money in front of me, except once. He gave away something like fifteen hundred dollars in a check, to some kid, I don't remember his name. He lent people their bail money, money for clothes, money for drugs, stuff like that. He lent other people money just so they could have money. He was lending out around three thousand dollars a person. Really. He gave away something like forty-two thousand, nine hundred and eighty-five dollars. I seen that written down on a piece of paper that he had.

Also, you gotta remember Tony fooled around with guys—we both know that. He was fooling around with whoever was around. He wasn't giving them cash money, but he was giving them stuff like for commissary, or he'd promise them cash money later, just for being in a relationship with him.

Word got around Rikers that he had money, so people were always coming up to him and saying, you know, "Can I borrow?" or "Could I have?" In other words, "Please may I?" You know. They'd get how much they could.

I told him many times not to do it anymore, but he kept on doing it. And then what really got me mad was when he tried to offer *me* money. See, 'cause I didn't want money. I was his friend.

He was afraid of some people, and other people he just wanted to make sure he got along with because he liked them rather enough, you know. But the dangerous people, the ones who carried a shank— you know, a sharpened piece of metal—formed an organization and lived off Tony. Nobody ever tried to stop it. I was the only one who tried. Once, this guy wanted money and Tony wouldn't give it to him. I heard about it in the receiving room and I was on my way over to help get the guy off Tony's back. By the time I got there, a couple of the guys Tony had been giving money to rebelled against the new guy and said, like, "Hey, man, bug out, get out of here," and they got rid of him. If I had had to take care of him, the C.O. probably would have let me fight him—and I would have won. I'd beat him up whether he had a shank or not.

Injury to Inmate Report, Department of Correction, City of New York, January 11, 1981

> At approx. 12:30 p.m. Antony Baekeland got involved in a fist fight with inmate Jose Perez. This occurred in Upper Three dayroom. Inmate Baekeland was treated and examined in L4 Clinic by Dr. C. Park (psychiatrist). No apparent injuries.

JUAN MARTINEZ

There was a couple of people—we used to hang around together, like a little crowd, you know? I was in for five years. I was on the first page in a big newspaper when I got busted. You know, with a big picture, and a big smile on me.

Tony was a good friend of mine. We were together ever since he got in jail—we were like brothers. He told me all about his family. Things like that.

He was giving money out like crazy, you know? He gave money to Eddie Cruz, who's in the street now—he was in for burglary. And Jackie Monroe, who's doing eight years upstate now. Tony sent quite a bit of money to Jackie's wife.

JOHN MURRAY

He gave a really big check to this one guy with a mustache and a beard and long, shaggy hair. He was kind of young-looking and he was white, Spanish. He was in the quad. He had just got there. He borrowed a pair of shoes from Tony. Then there was another guy Tony was also helping out—Michael something. He gave him, I think, a big check to use when he got out on the street. The guy was going to use it for his mother's house.

JOHN RAKIS

If an inmate had a check and gave it to a relative of his and said you can deposit this and draw on it, there would be no way for prison officials to track down that sort of extortion.

HOWARD NABOR

I was the warden at the Anna M. Kross Center when Tony Baekeland was there, and I think the money he gave out there he gave out to win friends more than anything else. I mean, you don't give out checks for protection—if the inmates are running a protection racket they'll take all the guy's commissary or have his mother or his wife or somebody deposit cash in their account. Anybody can send cash to an inmate—all they got to do is just mail it to his name in an envelope and it goes. But a check is going to nail them right to the wall. All the guy has to do is go to the D.A. or the Department of Correction and say, "I'm being forced to pay protection," and they say, "Can you prove it?" and he shows them the check. The inmates aren't *that* stupid.

So one of the things we usually check on is the commissary. Our cashiers monitor that closely and if they see one inmate getting an exceptionally large amount of money from the same two or three people—and I don't mean his mother or his girlfriend or his aunt

Mary—then we know he's either doing one of two things. He's running a racket bullying people, right? Or else he's selling something, he's selling drugs or himself—he could be a homosexual selling his own body. If some inmate was running a game on Tony Baekeland, he wouldn't be doing it with checks, because he wouldn't want anybody to know about it.

JOHN MURRAY

Sometimes Tony would try to offer the guards money but they wouldn't take it. I don't know what they said to him because they'd tell everyone to scram first.

BROOKS BAEKELAND

Tony wrote me letters describing the vice, violence and corruption in that prison. His homosexual seductiveness even involved the guards, and promises of money in large amounts to everyone who might satisfy his humors or desires—that was all in those letters.

Letter from Dr. Philip Gogarty to Cecelia Brebner, January 13, 1981

Broadmoor

Dear Mrs. Brebner:

Thank you very much for your recent letter about Tony; you appear to be the only person who is aware of the facts—certainly the only one who has kept me up-to-date with recent developments. In fact, I had been given to understand that Mrs. Daly had died as a result of her injuries and that Tony was to be brought to trial for murder!

I am very pleased to learn that she is still alive and able to contemplate visiting Tony. It is indeed worrying that she feels unable to press charges against him as this would be for his (and others') benefit in the long run. However, knowing her great affection for Tony, her attitude is understandable.

May I offer you belated Happy New Year wishes.

Again my best thanks.

Yours sincerely,
Philip Gogarty
Consultant Forensic Psychiatrist

Letter from Antony Baekeland to Nina Daly, January 14, 1981

Rikers Island

Dear Nini,

I am waiting to hear whether I shall be given bail. I do not really think it would be just for me to be locked up either on grounds of insanity or criminality, as what happened was (a) not an act of insanity, but a complex of emotionally motivated acts and (b) not criminal, because I had nothing to gain in any worldly way from knifing you, and in fact everything to lose, and was only trying to put you out of your misery. It is very hard for me to talk to you on the phone because whenever the important things come up we are mutually put off. I am hoping for a way in which we can solve this problem. Realise that part of me has suffered with you ever since you broke your hip, even blaming myself for your trouble and discomfort.

My Great Problem is Money. I can't seem to talk about it with anyone without getting upset and nervous. I do not consider that the attempt to take my hand from my own affairs has any valid reason, as I am now regaining my perspective.

At the time I came here I had eighty-three thousand dollars in "Free" money—that is, money which I can spend to my liking.

John Murray is and has been very helpful. (My Friend who spoke to you on the phone.) He wants to get the money I gave away back for you.

I shall call you Friday or Saturday evening. May God bless you and give you Peace and New Health.

Love, Love,
Tony

CECELIA BREBNER

I took Nini to Rikers Island to see him and they would not allow us to cross the bridge—they said that an old lady in a wheelchair was not possible. So back we came. And the moment we got home, the telephone rang. It was Tony, and he started to scream at Nini—something about money. She said to me, "Will *you* speak to him, Celia?" I said, "Tony, just stop this nonsense of giving your money away." And he said, "Get off the phone! I don't want to talk to *you*." And all those loving letters I'd had from him! "I want to talk to my grandmother," he said. "Put her back on!"

4

JANUARY 15, 1981–
MARCH 19, 1981

JOHN MURRAY

I was like a conscience to Tony. I would tell him, "You gotta get on top of it. You gotta take back all that money you lent out and you gotta leave yourself some. You just can't give it all away because people keep asking you to until it nearly kills you."

I promised to try to get his money back with my influence in the receiving room. I had access to prisoner inmate cards—where people are, where they're going on the outside—and I was going to use a list that his lawyer had sent him with the amounts that people owed him.

Tony and I made real plans to go on a trip around the world together. We were going to go to Thailand first—go see the monks and all that. You can stay warm there, and then you can go in the mountains and cool off if you want. Tony told me he had been there. And then we were maybe thinking about going to Indonesia, and Turkey, and England, you know, and we were talking about going to, maybe, Russia or something like that. Tony thought he'd be getting out soon. I assured him that he would if he told the judge that the devious thoughts in his mind had left and that he'd seen the error of his judgment, you know?

J. VICTOR BENSON

Tony did plan a trip around the world. Possibly it was with John Murray, but possibly it was with one of those listed on his visitors sheet.

JOHN RAKIS

Inmates are allowed three visits of one hour each a week. We have thousands of visitors. The average number per month for our entire system was twenty-eight thousand for the fiscal year 1983. So we can't thoroughly check the credentials of each visitor.

J. VICTOR BENSON

The essential requirements are that they have to be a relative or a close friend of the inmate's. They have to show an affidavit of one sort or another—birth certificate, marriage license, and so on. Visitors are searched as they come in, but there's not much checking on whether they are or are not, let's say, an inmate's cousin—first, second, third, or shirttail.

Approved Visitors Form, Rikers Island

NAME: Baekeland, Antony, 349-80-4228

APPROVED VISITORS

NAME: Anastase, Joanne
ADDRESS: Brooklyn, New York
RELATIONSHIP TO INMATE: Friend
NAME: Firenzi, Vince
ADDRESS: Flushing, New York
RELATIONSHIP TO INMATE: Cousin

JOHN MURRAY

I think Vince Firenzi was in for holding a gun to his mother's head. He was a short fellow, not really one of the dangerous ones, but *sort* of. He was in another quad and he was running a con game on Tony. He came back because he probably wanted more money. He'd hustle Tony, give him a little kiss on the cheek or something like that and say, "I need more money."

Joanne Anastase was a skinny, pathetic-looking guy who used to be at Rikers. He dressed in women's clothes and I think he had an operation. He sort of looks like a woman and he sort of looks like a man—sort of in-between. He probably came back and said to Tony, "I need money for my boyfriend," or "I need money for clothes to go to the disco," or "I need money for drugs." You know—if it's not one thing, it's the other. And Tony gave him what he wanted, he was afraid to say no because he was afraid that Joanne might send somebody to go after him. But then he stopped giving money to Joanne. He said, "I'm going to stop giving money away." But then he wrote someone else a check for fifteen hundred dollars, and he wrote someone else one for, I'm not sure, I think it was two thousand. And he wrote *me* out a check for two thousand also. We had talked about me maybe borrowing a hundred dollars or something like that to get started when I got out. I gave the check to Mr. Benson to put in my account but I had a feeling I was never going to get that two thousand.

J. VICTOR BENSON
Murray wanted me to take the check to the cashier, and I did take it personally to the cashier, mostly because I was interested in getting a check like that off the quad. They gave me a receipt and I presented it to Murray. But nobody would credit his commissary account with the check—and even the captain at the desk refused to handle it because it was so large. They thought there was something strange about it.

JOHN RAKIS
The check was returned uncashed by the prison officials to Tony Baekeland's bank.

JOHN MURRAY
My check from Tony fell through, and the parole for me fell through also. It just did, it just did, and I left Rikers on February 13th for Auburn State Prison upstate.

JUAN MARTINEZ
After John Murray left, I was trying to manage Tony's affairs for him but he didn't give me no time. I told him, "Wait up, man, give me

some time, you know, and I'll find out some way that you can get out." See, I was going to the legal library every day for my own case.

J. VICTOR BENSON

Juan was pretty much of a jailhouse lawyer. He was no dummy. He became knowledgeable about all procedures and all precedent cases. He was in for murder but was pleading insanity.

Note from File on Juan Martinez

Date of birth 2/27/54; 1978 arrested 75th Pct.; previous charge, grand larceny; accused of murdering young boy, victim's head had been cut off, sodomy, drugs found around body, Juan found in victim's car with bloodstains on clothes. "Watch yourself, this is the car of the guy I killed," he may or may not have said.

J. VICTOR BENSON

Juan had one of those special relationships with Baekeland, too.

JUAN MARTINEZ

We were together in court in February and I told him, "Give me some more time," you know?

From the Transcript, The People of the State of New York—Against—Antony Baekeland, Defendant, **Supreme Court of the State of New York, County of New York, February 19, 1981**

THE DEFENDANT: May I ask you something? I understand my grandmother has dropped her charge.

THE COURT: She is not dropping the charge. It's not up to a witness to drop charges or not drop charges.

THE DEFENDANT: She wasn't the witness. She was the victim.

THE COURT: It's not up to a victim. It's up to the prosecutor of the State of New York.

THE DEFENDANT: Oh! I see.

THE COURT: March 5th.

From the Transcript, The People of the State of New York—Against—Antony Baekeland, Defendant, Supreme Court of the State of New York, County of New York, March 5, 1981

THE COURT: How about the medical records, counsel?

COUNSEL FOR THE DEFENDANT: We spoke to England this morning and they put it in the mail this afternoon.

THE COURT: That's the same information for the last three adjournments.

COUNSEL FOR THE DEFENDANT: Okay. And the other medical report is on its way.

THE COURT: The 20th of March.

COUNSEL FOR THE DEFENDANT: I would like an application at this time due to the fact that the defendant has been held without bail. It's apparent that the complainant is—does not want to pursue this case. I wonder if bail could be set?

THE COURT: No, counsel. Remand continued. March 20th all right?

(No response)

THE COURT: March 20th.

5

MARCH 20, 1981:
12:00 A.M.–4:39 P.M.

Breakfast Menu, Rikers Island, March 20, 1981

> Bread and margarine
> Stewed figs
> Rice Krispies
> Reconstituted milk
> Coffee and tea

From the Transcript, The People of the State of New York—Against—Antony Baekeland, Defendant, **Supreme Court of the State of New York, County of New York, March 20, 1981**

THE COURT CLERK: Number 15, Antony Baekeland.

(Whereupon, both counsel—Sarah Hines, Esq., Assistant District Attorney [For the People] and Ronald M. Arrick, Esq., [For the Defendant]—approach the bench for an off-the-record discussion.)

THE COURT: April 16th for Trial.

COUNSEL FOR THE DEFENDANT: Your Honor, if I may be heard? Mr. Baekeland's grandmother is in Court. She is eighty-eight years old. She is confined to a wheelchair. She has attempted to go to Rikers Island to visit the prisoner but has been advised that they have no facility for wheelchairs. She asked me to make an application to the Court for an in-Court visit with her grandson.

THE COURT: Because she is the complaining witness in the case, because there have been statements made by you and your firm that she does not wish to proceed with the charges, because of the severity of the case and all the other special circumstances, I'm not going to permit a Courtroom visit in this case. April 16th for Trial.

ASSISTANT DISTRICT ATTORNEY: Judge, would you make a ruling on the Grand Jury Minutes?

THE COURT: I have reviewed the Grand Jury Minutes and find them sufficient to warrant the indictment.

ASSISTANT DISTRICT ATTORNEY: I have received certain medical records from the defense from England. I've not received the complete medical records as I expected.

THE COURT: April 16th.

CECELIA BREBNER

Nini had asked me if I would go with her to court and I went. Tony looked dreadful. When I had brought him back from London he had his Savile Row suit on and he looked very elegant, and now he was in rags, his hair tied back. He looked across the courtroom and said to Nini, "I love you, I love you, I'm sorry."

RONALD ARRICK

I know his mood in court that morning and it was fairly good. He talked to his grandmother—they both mouthed across the courtroom. As he was being taken out the door, he saw Grandma, she was sitting down near the back with her nurse or someone, and he went "I love you." I had had a bench conference with the judge to see if he would grant Tony and Grandma a courtroom visit. I didn't want them in a room alone together. What I wanted was for Tony to sit on one side of the rail, with guards, and Grandma on the other side—not within reaching distance of each other but three to five feet away where they could still talk to each other in a fairly low voice so as not to disrupt the court. Or even at a recess. But the lady D.A. was adamant against it. She didn't want Tony having any contact with Grandma. One of the main reasons, I can only presume at, would be that it might influence her getting the verdict—the more contact they had, the less chance of Grandma testifying against Tony.

I don't see how his sitting there handcuffed in a chair—or handcuffed *to* the chair, let's say, if they wanted to go that far—five feet away from somebody, surrounded by, let's say, two court officers—would have been endangering the old lady's life. If it had been, I wouldn't have asked for it.

When Tony was refused the visit, he accepted it, he accepted it fine. I don't build up anybody's hopes. There are no guarantees.

JUDGE ROBERT M. HAFT

For humanitarian reasons I would allow a courtroom visit—a woman has to see her child or a man has to see his new baby, or somebody's pregnant, or some case like that. But in Tony Baekeland's case I just didn't see that it warranted it. To see the complaining witness would not be proper.

From a Draft Document, Board of Correction, City of New York

Baekeland returned from court with a white plastic bag with red and blue lettering on it. He arrived back at quadrant 3 Lower at approximately 3:30 p.m. and requested to be locked in his cell.

JOHN RAKIS

He could have gone in the hallway or in the dayroom—inmates are entitled to be locked out for fourteen hours during the day. They're also entitled to lock themselves into their cells when they want to be. It's optional. Some people want to be in their cells and read or write or they want to lie down, or they just don't want to be bothered by anybody else.

From a Draft Document, Board of Correction, City of New York

Inmate John Lewis #346-80-2360 was the area suicide prevention aide on the 3 p.m. to 11 p.m. shift.

JOHN RAKIS

Suicide prevention aides are an extra pair of eyes and ears for the officer, who may be busy entering something in the logbook or supervising food distribution or doing something to that effect. The aides get paid anywhere from thirty-five to fifty cents an hour—which is the highest rate of pay for inmate help. We test them to make sure they know what they're doing, we give certificates for the training, and we do periodic inspections and evaluations of their work.

From a Draft Document, Board of Correction, City of New York

Inmate Lewis said that he spoke with Baekeland when he returned from court. Baekeland reportedly said that things had not gone well in court because he had hoped to be granted bail and that there had also been some talk he would be sent to a civil hospital, but instead he was remanded back to the Department.

JOHN RAKIS

Tony had told several inmates that he expected to be bailed out. It was poor judgment on his part to expect bail.

From a Draft Document, Board of Correction, City of New York

Correction Officer Patrick Raftery #2851 stated that he was assigned as the Lower 3 "B" Post Officer on the 3:27 p.m. to 11:58 p.m. tour. He arrived on his post at approximately 3:50 p.m. at which time he made a count. The Officer states that inmate Baekeland was sitting up on his bed at this time.

Again at 4:30 p.m., C.O. Raftery made his rounds. He reported that everything appeared normal. Baekeland was lying on his bed covered with a blanket; both feet and one hand were exposed.

At 4:39 p.m., Nurse Mauretta Link entered the quadrant to dispense medication. She was accompanied on her rounds in the area by C.O. Raftery. After dispensing medication to two inmates, Nurse Link with C.O. Raftery approached Baekeland's cell.

6

MARCH 20, 1981:
4:40 P.M.–11:59 P.M.

From a Draft Document, Board of Correction, City of New York

> Baekeland did not respond to his name. C.O. Raftery rapped on the cell door, then opened the door and tapped his keys on the bedframe, then rubbed Baekeland's foot with the keys. When Baekeland still did not respond, C.O. Raftery pulled the blanket off the inmate and discovered that he had a red and white plastic bag over his head.

JOHN RAKIS
It was a plastic bag with one of those drawstrings, and the drawstring was pulled tight.

J. VICTOR BENSON
I heard it was tied.

JOHN RAKIS
It was not tied. Just pulled tight.

From a Draft Document, Board of Correction, City of New York

C.O. Raftery went to remove the plastic bag from Baekeland's head and Nurse Link called to the "A" Officer, C.O. George Forbes # 1235, to send a manual resuscitator (ambubag). Nurse Link said at this point Baekeland had no pulse or respiration. C.O. Paul Jefferson #3076, the "B" Post Oficer, responded with an ambubag which Nurse Link began to use immediately. C.O. Forbes notified the 4 Lower clinic of the emergency and the need for a doctor. Nurse Practitioner Gloria Howard-Mello responded immediately and instructed Officers Raftery and Jefferson to move the inmate from his bed to the floor of the 3 Lower corridor to provide more room to perform first aid. Nurse Link continued to use the ambubag and Nurse Howard-Mello applied external heart massage. Doctors Doyle and Jhaveri responded at approximately 4:43 p.m. and found the inmate without pulse or respiration and with fixed and dilated pupils. Baekeland was pronounced dead at 4:45 p.m. by Dr. Doyle, who then left the area. At approximately 4:52 p.m. Montefiore Hospital personnel (Dr. Nickerson, Registered Physician's Assistant Ulrich, Nurse Johnson, and Nurse Minort) arrived in 3 Lower; they were not informed that Dr. Doyle had pronounced Baekeland dead, and recommenced cardiopulmonary resuscitation. During this procedure blood was observed spurting from the inmate's nose and mouth. After Montefiore personnel had ceased their attempt to revive Baekeland, he was placed back in his bed.

CORRECTION OFFICER JOHN HERNANDEZ

At the time of Baekeland's suicide I was on the staff of the deputy warden, who investigates all matters pertaining to security. Right after it was discovered, the inmates on the quad were locked in. I then entered the cell to take pictures of Baekeland and the contents of the cell. I remember that there were some letters, some writing pads, a box of Ritz crackers, and not that much else. We preserved the cell for evidence, to rule out foul play, which *was* ruled out, almost immediately.

Record of Inmate Transfer, Department of Correction, City of New York

> NAME: Baekeland, Antony #349-80-4228
> DATE: 3/20/81
> TRANSFERRED TO: City Morgue D.O.A.

JOHN RAKIS

After the suicide, I talked to the staff and to other inmates. There was a mixed reaction among the inmates. Some acted as if nothing had happened and some acted concerned—"Yes. Too bad. He expected to be bailed out." No one cried, no one was emotionally distraught. The general attitude was, another guy gone.

Tony didn't leave a note behind. Only a small percentage of our suicides do leave notes—perhaps one out of ten. Sometimes they'll underline a part of the Bible and the underlining is like a note.

From the Autopsy Report on Antony Baekeland

> *Case No.* Bx 81-1146
>   *External Description*
>   The body is received clad in the following items of clothing: two sweater shirts, the outer of which is green with a zippered neck and reveals vomitus and a small amount of blood on its anterior surface. The inner is gray shortsleeved (the green is longsleeved) with black, white, red, and gray piping. A pair of gray pants. A pair of jockey-type shorts. Also submitted with the deceased is what appears to be a piece of sheeting from an institutional-type bed on which are small quantities of blood. The plastic bag has not been received with the body.

JUAN MARTINEZ

Somebody in his family made the plastic the bag was made out of—that's why I think he did it like that.

From "Science and Industry," a Lecture Delivered by Leo Hendrik Baekeland, June 21, 1938

> There is hardly any field, any branch of industry where plastics are not serving successfully in one form or another. . . . The whole fabric of modern civilization becomes every day more interwoven with the endless ramifications of applied chemistry. Ignorant people misjudge the value of chemical science and denounce its applications for war and other evils. Let us remind them that one of the most useful instruments ever invented, the knife, may, in the wrong hands, be used for evil, as well as for the best purposes.

EDWARD HERSHEY

The unusual thing about this was, of course, the method. We've never had anybody else suffocate himself with a plastic bag before.

BROOKS BAEKELAND

I do not believe that Tony, who was the prince of hope, bravura, and challenge, as well as of self-expiation and despair, took his own life. We were to the very end in constant epistolary contact. Everyone who knew him agrees that he would never have gone without a *big* announcement—not that hyperarticulate, dramatizing gent. And he died without a word to me or anyone.

I think he was murdered by his jailers. So easy to do. He had admitted his sexual relations with one of the guards in a letter to me. Maybe he threatened exposure, or retracted a promise of money? In both hands he held death: Who lives by the sword . . . But let it lie. Suicide or murder: Does it matter? Yes. But why and how much? Both he and his mother lived by violence and so they were bound to die by the same. I always knew it, and that was one of the reasons why I had to get away from them.

EDWARD HERSHEY

It is almost routine in every suicide for people to start saying, you know, that it really wasn't a suicide. For the family members in most instances it's so much more acceptable to have somebody be murdered than have them commit suicide. What a great guilt deflection that is.

J. VICTOR BENSON

I was shocked to hear about Tony because I couldn't believe that he had *that* kind of violence in him—toward himself, that is. He had never expressed suicidal thoughts. And also, it was not an impulsive act—it was very carefully done.

JOHN MURRAY

I don't think it's possible that someone did Tony in. He told me he was going to kill himself because I didn't love him. That's what he told me. Unless he just said it to make me feel guilty. I believe sometimes someone kills themself because someone doesn't love them, so I kind of think in a way he did kill himself for me a little bit. He was a very sentimental guy. It stands to reason—anyone gives out that much money is sentimental. I miss him tremendously. I miss him very much.

RONALD ARRICK

I heard it on the news and I spent about four or five hours on the phone with Rikers trying to confirm it—you get a goddam runaround over there—and trying to get details, until I found the guard, who told me himself.

What I'm most interested in with Tony is what the hell happened at Rikers that he committed suicide—*if* he committed suicide. It's my impression that he didn't. It just doesn't make sense, to commit suicide by suffocating yourself with a plastic bag. Swallowing pills or slashing your wrists or shooting yourself of course is fairly easy, you know—assuming you want to do it—and depending on how far you go with it, it's irreversible. But something like this you can stop at any given time, and your normal impulse—I mean it would be involuntary even—would *be* to stop it.

ELIZABETH ARCHER BAEKELAND

When I heard that Tony had committed suicide by putting a plastic bag over his head, I told a doctor friend that I thought it was extraordinary that he had the courage—I mean, it's the most noble thing that Tony did in his *life*—and the doctor said it's not difficult to do. He said you just breathe in your carbon monoxide and become euphoric. So later I thought, I'll test that out. I took a plastic bag, and I couldn't find any string so I took some telephone wire and wrapped it around, and I couldn't believe it, within a matter of . . . you cannot measure time under those circumstances but very soon I was really feeling high, and good, and so I thought, Oh-oh, I'd better take it off—and I couldn't find the end of the wire! Well, I finally found it and ripped it off—I mean, obviously.

RONALD ARRICK

Go back another step. He was on a suicide watch at the time, so how come he had a plastic bag? Where did he get a plastic bag?

I'd seen him before court session, I'd seen him during court session, and I went back in after court session and we discussed how we were going to proceed and he seemed in a very good mood. I mean, look, maybe he knew he was going to commit suicide and that's one of the reasons he was *in* the good mood. We'll never know.

From a Draft Document, Board of Correction, City of New York

There is no evidence to suggest that Baekeland's death was not suicide, as he was locked in his cell immediately after he returned from court. All other inmates in the area were also locked in from the time of the count (4:00 p.m.) through the discovery of the emergency, with the exception of inmate John Lewis, the suicide aide.

From the Financial Records of Antony Baekeland

To John Lewis—$2,000.00.

JOHN RAKIS

It seems unlikely that if Tony was giving John Lewis money, John Lewis would do any harm to him or want him to die. Besides, there's nothing a suicide prevention aide could do to another inmate that any other inmate couldn't do, too.

Also, inmates don't have any control over the keys. One of Correction's biggest concerns is key control—they probably spend more time at the Academy teaching key control than suicide prevention. Keys are very carefully accounted for. The loss of a key would be tantamount to the loss of an inmate. It's against procedures to even allow inmates to touch keys.

That door was locked. Officer Raftery had to open it with a key. And there were several witnesses to that.

Every time we see a suicide, the thought of homicide is always foremost in our minds, and the investigation is conducted with that in mind. And there was no indication whatsoever that there was any foul play in Tony Baekeland's death.

JUAN MARTINEZ

It didn't come as no surprise. Not really. Because he told me he was gonna kill himself. And I saw it. I saw everything. Everything. And I didn't help. Forget it. Just forget it. I'm the only one to know the real truth. And the C.O.s know that I'm the only one that knows the real truth, too. It's too many things. It's too many things, man. It's dangerous, you know? You see what I'm saying? You understand what I'm telling you? I was there. I *know* what happened. Somebody said, "Do it, Tony, or else!"

HOWARD NABOR

It was suicide, there's no question about it. One of my officers took it very bad. You know, it was unusual that he got so upset about it. He felt, you know, that Tony was a very sensitive boy, and just to see somebody die like that really upset him. I think he even resigned from the job after that—if I remember right.

The type of suicide *was* unusual. I felt that somebody that did it that way really wanted to go. Some of the others, if they try to hang themselves, sometimes they're doing it for show and then they accidentally kill themselves. But definitely—no question about it—Tony Baekeland wanted to go.

EDWARD HERSHEY

I remember it was a Friday evening when word came. We try to make sure the next of kin is notified before we inform the press. And in this instance, it became apparent that the next of kin was the very selfsame grandmother. I had a sense that the tragedy would be compounded if our minister and the correction officer assigned walked in on her and said, "Your grandson has just killed himself," her having seen him in court that day. So I reached out for the assistant D.A., and I found her—I don't know how I did it but I found her. It was a

Friday night, she was visiting people in Jersey, and I said, "What do we do?" She knew the grandmother and she was concerned and we were able to locate a tenant in the grandmother's building so that she wasn't alone when she was told the news.

LENA RICHARDS

I came to Nini's on Saturday morning and the weekday nurse said, "Have you heard?" I said, "What?" She said, "He killed himself." I was shocked. I went into Nini and she said, "Oh, Lena, oh, Tony's killed himself." She didn't cry. She said, "Such guilt I put on the family, and I might as well confide and tell you everything." She said Frank, her husband, was cleaning his car in the garage with Frank Jr., and Frank Jr. left to do something and when he came back the garage door was closed and the motor was on. I'm afraid she'll never get over Tony.

NINA DALY

It's a sad story. It was the biggest heartbreak. It was terrible. But you see, I don't dwell on it. I can't. I think about how much I loved him and how much he meant to me. I still wish he was here.

BROOKS BAEKELAND

It was a beautiful ending—in plastic, too!

The terrible thing was that in his secret heart he always thought that in the end I could save him. Like his mother he was without fear—and Daddy *would* come, somehow, out of *somewhere*, like Superman. They both believed that. You know, there is no such thing, when there is a child, as a divorce. It's a contradiction in terms. Until their very last moments—for both of them—I was supposed to burst through a door and save them. But the odds they played against were so enormous that even Superman would not have arrived in time.

Courage they both had, but to the point of folly. They were great romantics. I cannot laugh at them. Who can laugh, for instance, at Zelda Fitzgerald? I mourn because I failed them. I failed their unrealistic marvelous dreams. But even the word "unrealistic" is a weasel word to the true romantic, who accords the greatest value to that which really is truly and absolutely impossible. Barbara's mad audacities always made me feel ashamed of myself—as Zelda's did Scott Fitzgerald. No wonder, in his madness, that her son thought her a goddess. He gave himself, too, a minor god's rank, but that was a faery geste, on dope. And I have no doubt that—his ear against that cold prison floor as though listening to hoofbeats pursuing him to another world—part of him really did believe that she was waiting for him up, up there, where only Mozart and Bach and champagne and "the beautiful people" would flow in the chiaroscuro of Gustave Doré's enormous canvases, in eternal round, waiting now for him, too, for this world below had become far too vulgar. Henry Aldrich in that corny radio series of the thirties used to always get a laugh saying, "Coming, Mother!"

If I have shocked you, let me remind you that only laughter clears the vision. Without laughter, there can be no seeing of the truth. Tragedy does not allow laughter. It is pity that does. And I have never seen tragedy in all my short, wasted, eager life—only pity. And I see that everywhere around me and in the markings of my own hand. That is all I see.

THE FINAL REPORT

Headline, the *New York Times*, March 21, 1981

INMATE KILLS HIMSELF
IN A CELL AT RIKERS

Headline, New York *Daily News*, March 21, 1981

PLASTICS HEIR WHO KILLED MOM
AN APPARENT SUICIDE IN JAIL CELL

Headline, *Daily Telegraph*, London, March 23, 1981

PLASTICS HEIR DEAD IN JAIL

FRANCINE DU PLESSIX GRAY
When Tony died with this thing of putting a plastic bag over his
head, Ethel de Croisset called me—she was in New York at the

time—and she said, "Don't you see the relationship to his stealing the baby food that summer in Italy?" I said no. She said, "Well, he chose a baby's way of dying, didn't he? Smothering."

ETHEL WOODWARD DE CROISSET
He just went to sleep in his little plastic bag, and I saw this as being perhaps his desire to return to the womb.

ELEANOR WARD
When I heard he had killed himself, I thought, What a relief for him, what a blessing—out of the agony at last.

JAMES REEVE
So many of one's friends seem to have died under peculiar circumstances, one way or another, recently. Mine, anyway. A great friend of mine—and kindred spirits are few and far between—I mean, somebody I could tell anything, and she me—anyway, she had had a house in Greece and she was motoring back to France and all of a sudden she got a heart attack for no reason and died. That was that. Very shocking. In a curious way—it's sort of animal defense or something—I refused to face it. I just put it out of my mind. I didn't really sit down and think about her being dead. I just think of her as gone away. One *should* sit down and look it in the eye and face up to the fact.

When I heard Tony had died, I was horrified. But then I put it out of my mind, too. I haven't really thought about it since.

GLORIA JONES
I guess it was John Sargent who told me how Tony had committed suicide, and I thought it was the end of the whole horrible story. But you would never write it that way—it's too corny. How did he get the plastic bag, I wonder.

ROSE STYRON
It was the perfect ironic end.

SAMUEL PARKMAN SHAW
It seemed to me that it was a perfectly normal end to *his* career. It was a good solution, and a not unclever way of doing it. It took some determination—how to get into the bag and stay there until he suffocated. That's not a bad trick.

John Rakis

As a result of Tony Baekeland's suicide, inmates are not allowed to have plastic bags in their possession. Also, the correction officers are now told that when they see an inmate lying fairly still and the blanket is over his head, they really ought to check for signs of breathing. Now, many inmates do this to keep out noise or keep the lights from getting in their eyes; Tony of course put the blanket over his head to cover up his intentions.

From the Final Report of the New York State Commission of Correction Medical Review Board in the Matter of the Death of Antony Baekeland at the Anna M. Kross Center, Rikers Island, December 22, 1981

The Medical Review Board recommends that the NYC Department of Health, Prison Health Services, advise mental health treatment staff at the Anna M. Kross Center that special attention should be given to inmates under psychiatric treatment as significant life events or status changes approach. Mental health treatment staff are often aware of these events.

The Medical Review Board recommends that the NYC Department of Health, Prison Health Services, develop policies and procedures whereby previous psychiatric hospital records are obtained when an inmate is in detention and under psychiatric treatment for extended periods.

Miwa Svinka-Zielinski

Tony never talked about taking his life, never once in all those years. It was a waste, his life. All that time I wasted on that boy! I continued to believe that he could be cured. His disease was Barbara.

Letter from Brooks Baekeland to Nina Daly, June 8, 1981

Stonington, Maine

Dear Nini—

I grieve over him, too—more as time goes by, more as I remember him as a child—for while seeming to know, to understand, that he was doomed if he continued as he did, he always so continued, from one disaster to the next, fascinated as it were by his own destruction. Seeing it, knowing it, reveling.

That—that knowing—is a side of Tony that very few people ever knew. I did, because between Tony and me there always was a curious: "I know that *you* know that *I* know . . ." almost ad infinitum. We both had, for instance, unspoken knowledge and understandings about his mother, my relationship to her and his relationship to her. Also about his to me and mine to him!

One of the results of these extraordinary, multileveled intuitional understandings between us was that when we were together there was nothing to say. We both knew it all and knew that we both knew it. Silence.

It was that—let me be as fair as I can—which separated us just as much as the fact that morally we were bitter enemies. I hated his immorality—remember, I do not speak about sexuality but about ethics—but so did he! But he also loved it! Was drawn to crime—again, I do not mean "lawbreaking" but sordid self-immolation—as a moth to a flame. He was the quintessential pederast, in fact. He was an American Genet, but without the overriding desire for fame and capacity to work.

He was just as gifted—far more gifted than his father or mother—or if not, then his terrible failings made those gifts shine in their surrounding darkness—shine angelically.

There is a line from somewhere that comes into my mind: Was he a "halting angel who tripped against a star," or was he *"le diable boîteux"*?

Love,
Brooks

P.S. I have a smallish room here with a terrace, over the water on piles, on the harbor of a professional fishing village. I live all alone. Thrice a week I take a boat (40 minutes) to an island at 7 A.M. I then walk 2–2½ hours to the other end of the island. There I work (cutting trees and throwing them into the sea) on a friend's place for 3 hours. Then I walk back to the town landing and take the boat back to Stonington. It is very beautiful up here. The romanticality of this coast is a great adjunct, and some of the people—always the older generation, made before socialism destroyed the American family and proper upbringings—are very fine.

Elizabeth Blow

When I heard about Tony, I went on thinking about the Baekelands. It gets to be an obsession. One thing I'm convinced of is that they— Brooks and Barbara—always loved each other in spite of her impossible behavior and his philandering.

Brooks Baekaland

A large part of what made Sylvie wish to find her eventual freedom from me was my indestructible worry and concern and sense of responsibility for Barbara. Sylvie's jealousy always was and still is intense. She admired Barbara! A wiser man than I might have saved all those lives and still kept Sylvie.

Sylvie Baekeland Skira

I became important to Brooks—if you can say important—when I left him. That's all. I don't think I was his wife, ever. I suffered all the time because I didn't exist. *That* was my suffering.

Once, for his birthday, I gave him a very pretty silver frame, and later I went up to his study and what was in the silver frame but a photograph of Barbara! I really collapsed. I was still very much in love and I was expecting his baby. And he said to me, "God, you're badly brought up! How can you be jealous of someone dead?" He had always carried a picture of Barbara in his wallet. Now he has one of me also. Now, yes. *Oh* yes. Now that I've gone, yes.

Even now when I speak about this, I am drained. I'm nothing. They are too heavy! That's why I left. I didn't leave because I wanted to have an affair with somebody, I left because I thought, Well, the next one is me—I'm going to die, too.

When Tony died, I had already left Brooks. I think he was in the Grenadines. I know he decided not to go to New York. This is the only part that I can say I did not approve of. He should have gone to New York.

Brooks Baekeland

Now I can—and do—travel and live everywhere in the world with a small satchel that I can carry by hand. Of course if I am asked to dine black-tie, I say no. But then, I don't consort with those sort of people anymore.

I have, really, no possessions left. That is easy now, unwived. It is women, those nesters, those decorators, those competitors for status symbols, that take us naked men out of the jungle and "civilize" us.

Every bachelor, if he isn't a fairy, soon reverts to savage state. But in fact, I was never much attracted by "the things money could buy." As everyone knows, the best things are free, or almost free. H. D. Thoreau: "A man is rich in proportion to the things he does not need." The one exception to that rule is of course women themselves. They bankrupt us all.

SAM GREEN

Tony left half of his trust fund to the servant family at Miramar who looked after the house—after all, he had spent several cold winters on their hearth. The other half went to Nini.

Letter from Brooks Baekeland to Nina Daly, July 19, 1981

Stonington, Maine

Dear Nini—

Here are your photos back—thank you for sending them to me. I took them 34 years ago. It was interesting to see them, but I haven't your sentiment. I will be sending you a photo of me and my young son one of these days—a photo taken in my three-day-eventing years. The feeling you had for Tony I have for my small son. I was too young then—too much interested in myself probably (my career, my studies, etc.), and then, later, Tony was never anything but embarrassments to me. (But I never had a heart as big as yours. Who has?)

I wish you were up here with me. It's cool and lovely. Have become a hermit.

Love as always,
Brooks

BROOKS BAEKELAND

My life is almost totally solitary now. I know that I shall end up like my grandfather—a dead leaf blown down the city streets—talking and gesticulating to himself. The object of the interest of a kindly—corrupt!—policeman who finally gets him home. And in the end into his straitjacket. And a straighter one, the grave.

And what was left? Death was no end. Oh, no. It never was. That is why I am talking to you. There is no end. There was no end. There is no end. There will never be an end.

ETHEL WOODWARD DE CROISSET

When Barbara died, I consolidated my idea of never wanting to see Brooks again. He should never have left her and Tony in such distress. I did see him once after that, in Paris, at the wedding of the child of a friend we had in common. He came and sat beside Virginia Chambers, who was blind and so of course couldn't see him. But when she realized it was he, she refused to speak to him. He then tried to catch *my* eye—he kept walking up and down the aisle. And I certainly cut him dead.

MICHAEL EDWARDS

I saw Brooks with his new wife at a wedding reception at the Ritz. She was carrying their baby on her back—mind you, in the Ritz! Like a papoose. And he came over to me and said it would be very nice if he could rent my flat again at 45, quai de Bourbon, and I thought that was so extraordinary. I just said it wasn't available.

BARBARA CURTEIS

The minute Barbara was dead, Brooks had an absolute lust to occupy with Sylvie every place he and Barbara had ever occupied. He even went back to Cadaqués one summer. Missy Harnden wrote me, "I'm longing to run into him here so I can cut him dead in the paseo."

BROOKS BAEKELAND

I am perfectly indifferent to what people think of me. I do not wish to seem more arrogant than I am but anybody who is not a nonentity wears the blazonry of his enemies with as much relish as he does that of those who love him. I try only to act out of love—for the very few people I do love. The bond between Barbara and me has survived and always will survive.

From *A Walk in Winter Woods*, Brooks Baekeland, Unpublished

> He could not shake the strange feeling that she existed. Some-where; maybe here with him now, invisible but still alive and

vital. He could well imagine meeting her one day as she came towards him around a corner with that determined, rapid walk of hers and that proud carriage of her tawny head. For the hundredth time he remembered her tear-stained face, her big, serious eyes, and the question: "But darling, who is going to take care of you when you are old?"

BROOKS BAEKELAND

We were linked—in fact, all three of us, Tony and Barbara and I, were linked—to the death. I mean unto death, of course.

Passionate error, soaring IQs, drugs, murder, suicide—these are not simple things to be clever and name-dropping about at cocktail parties, these are not things to be lisped *dans le Tout-Paris* and to make luncheon parties more interesting for rich women who have too little to do.

I know all those people and I have utter contempt for them and their eagerness—if they are eager—to be quoted, to be heard, etc., etc., on matters in which they were never informed except by "a woman scorned"—though in truth I never scorned that difficult but in many ways lovable and admirable woman—and by a son whose father most definitely did not approve of him, love him though he did all his short life. For finally, what did not last was *not* love.

SYLVIE BAEKELAND SKIRA

Brooks told our little boy the story of his brother. He was seven at the time and going off to boarding school in England. I told him, "This is a very sad story. You can talk to *me* about it but you mustn't tell the other little boys because they either will not believe you or they will tease you." There was quite some time of silence, and then two months later when he came back to me for his holidays, one afternoon he said, "You know, I told the story and they believed me."

BIOGRAPHICAL NOTES

MICHAEL ALEXANDER is a writer and restaurateur who lives in London.

RONALD ARRICK is a lawyer who practices in New York.

BROOKS BAEKELAND now spends most of his time in Spain where he studies and writes.

ELIZABETH ARCHER BAEKELAND is as former journalist. She divides her time between America and England.

DR. FREDERICK BAEKELAND is a psychiatrist and an art historian. His published papers include "Psychological Aspects of Art Collecting," "Exercise and Sleep Patterns in College Athletes," "Correlates of Home Dream Recall," and "Dropping Out of Treatment: A Critical Review." He lives in New York City.

ROSEMARY RODD BALDWIN is a travel writer and frequent contributor to British *Vogue*. She also organizes travel tours to Turkey and Colombia. She lives in a cottage on her daughter Jinty Money-Coutts's estate in Wales.

SIR CECIL BEATON, artist, writer, designer, and photographer, died in 1980. He was for years the official photographer to the British royal family. He designed scenery and costumes for numerous ballets, operas, and plays, including *My Fair Lady*. He was an enthusiastic traveler, gardener, diarist, art collector, and arbiter of taste. His books include *The Glass of Fashion* and *The Face of the World*.

J. VICTOR BENSON died in January 1985. A retired Lutheran clergyman who studied clinical psychology at New York University, he had been with the New York City Department of Correction since 1969.

GEORGES BERNIER was a founding editor of the French art magazine *L'Oeil* and owner of Gallery L'Oeil in Paris. He is now connected with the international art firm of Wildenstein and lives in London and Paris.

ELIZABETH BLOW lives in upstate New York where she co-owns a handicrafts shop.

CECELIA BREBNER is a retired nurse. She has also worked for various airlines and been a volunteer at the United Nations.

DETECTIVE SUPERINTENDENT KENNETH BRETT retired from Scotland Yard. He is now connected with the Royal Military Academy.

BOWDEN BROADWATER recently retired as registrar at St. Bernard's School in New York City.

ANATOLE BROYARD is an editor at *The New York Times Book Review*. He also teaches a creative writing class at The New School for Social Research in New York City. His fiction has appeared in *The New Yorker*.

COLM BYRNE, formerly a nurse at Broadmoor Special Hospital in Crowthorne, Berkshire, England, now works for the Probation Services in Liverpool.

DODIE CAPTIVA is a former teacher. She lives in Cambridge, Massachusetts.

SARA DUFFY CHERMAYEFF has published fiction in magazines. She lives in New York City.

SERGEANT JOSEPH CHINEA, at one time a patrol officer with the 19th Precinct, New York City, is now a supervisor of an anticrime unit at the 34th Precinct.

ALEXANDER COHANE is a private art dealer in New York City.

HEATHER COHANE works with the decorator Carlton Varney in New York City.

JOHN PHILIP COHANE died in 1981. He was a founding partner of SSC&B and retired at the age of forty-eight to Ireland to write. He published four nonfiction books: *The Key*, *The Indestructible Irish*, *White Papers of an Outraged Conservative*, and *Paradox: The Ex-*

traterrestrial Origin of Man. He won the Edgar Award for a television mystery story in 1966.

ONDINE COHANE is a student at the Brearley School in New York City.

DAVID COHEN is the author of *Psychologists on Psychology*, *All in the Head*, a biography of John B. Watson, and *Broadmoor*. He also produced a film for British TV, *I Was in Broadmoor*.

KATHARINE GARDNER COLEMAN died in 1984. She lived and entertained in Paris, New York City, and Dark Harbor, Maine.

FREDERICK COMBS is an actor who lives in Los Angeles.

SHIRLEY COX works for the Chemotherapy Foundation in New York City.

ETHEL WOODWARD DE CROISSET is an American philanthropist who lives in Paris.

BARBARA CURTEIS lived year-round in Cadaqués, Spain, for several years. She now lives in New York City.

NINA DALY died in New York City in the fall of 1984 at the age of ninety-one.

DR. JEAN DAX lives and practices medicine in Paris.

TOM DILLOW is a freelance music coordinator for fashion shows, restaurants, stores, and parties. He lives in New York City.

WILLY DRAPER lives in Atlanta, Georgia, where he sells crystal and china.

LOUISE DUNCAN is an executive recruiter and magazine writer. She lives in New York City.

DOMINICK DUNNE produced the films *Boys in the Band*, *The Panic in Needle Park*, *Play It As It Lays*, *Ash Wednesday*, and *The Users*. He is the author of two novels: *The Winners* and the recently published *The Two Mrs. Grenvilles*. He is a contributing editor to *Vanity Fair* and lives in New York City.

MICHAEL EDWARDS is an international shipping executive who lives in London, Paris, and Provence.

H.R.H. PRINCESS ELIZABETH OF YUGOSLAVIA is internationally concerned with matters of spiritual evolution, especially the Sedona movement. She is a second cousin of Prince Charles and the mother of Catherine Oxenberg, Amanda on *Dynasty*.

EILEEN FINLETTER lived for many years in Paris, where she translated books. She now lives in New York City.

ELIZABETH WEICKER FONDARAS lives and entertains in New York

City, East Hampton, Long Island, and the Île Saint-Louis in Paris.

JONATHAN FRANK lives in California where he is a paramedic and ambulance driver.

PETER GABLE is in the investment business in Stamford, Connecticut, and lives in New York City.

BRENDAN GILL is Broadway theater critic for *The New Yorker*. He is the author of *Cole, Tallulah, Here at The New Yorker*, and *Lindbergh Alone*, and is at work on a biography of Stanford White.

PETER GIMBEL wrote, directed, was one of the underwater cameramen for, and coproduced (with his wife, Elga Anderson) the film *Andrea Doria: The Final Chapter*. His other filmmaking credits include *Whale Ho, In the World of Sharks*, and *Blue Water, White Death*. He lives in New York City.

AMBROSE GORDON has taught English at Hunter, Yale, and Sarah Lawrence colleges. Since 1958 he has been a professor of English at the University of Texas at Austin. He is the author of *The Invisible Tent: The War Novels of Ford Madox Ford*.

BART GORIN works as an assistant to Sam Green in New York City. He is also a photoresearcher for magazines.

CLEVE GRAY is a painter who has had several one-man shows in New York, Canada, France, and Italy. His work is represented in the permanent collections of the Whitney Museum of American Art, the Metropolitan Museum of Art, and the Guggenheim. He is the editor of *David Smith by David Smith, John Marin by John Marin, and Hans Richter by Hans Richter*.

FRANCINE DU PLESSIX GRAY is the author of *Divine Disobedience: Profiles in Catholic Radicalism, Hawaii: The Sugar-Coated Fortress, Lovers and Tyrants*, and *World Without End*. She has written for *The New Yorker* since 1968.

SAM GREEN, former director of the Institute of Contemporary Art in Philadelphia, is active internationally as an arts consultant to museums and private collectors. He lives in New York City and owns a large house in Cartagena, Colombia, and a small village on Fire Island.

PATRICIA GREENE lives in upstate New York. Her husband, Dr. Justin L. Greene, chief of child psychiatry at St. Luke's–Roosevelt Hospital Center in New York City as well as a neuropsychiatrist in private practice for over forty years, died in March 1984.

PAUL GREENWOOD, who was retired from the police force of the town of

East Hampton, Long Island, died in 1984.

STEPHANE GROUEFF, former New York bureau chief for *Paris Match* and former director of information for the Embassy of Oman, is the author of *Manhattan Project*. He is at work on a biography of King Boris of Bulgaria. He lives in New York City and Southampton, Long Island.

CATHERINE GUINNESS is co-author with her father, the Hon. Jonathan Guinness, of the recently published family history *The House of Mitford*. She is married to Lord Neidpath and is the mother of a one-year-old son. They live in Gloucestershire.

SUE GUINNESS runs an import-export business in England. She lives in London and in Cadaqués, Spain.

THE HONORABLE ROBERT M. HAFT is a justice of the Supreme Court of New York City.

BARBARA HALE lives in East Hampton, Long Island, and teaches nature classes to children and young adults.

NIKE MYLONAS HALE has taught art in New York City. She lives in Newburyport, Massachusetts, with her husband, Robert Beverly Hale.

ROBERT BEVERLY HALE died in 1985. He organized and headed the department of American art at the Metropolitan Museum of Art. He was also an instructor of drawing and a lecturer on anatomy at the Art Students League of New York. His own work is represented in the permanent collections of the Whitney Museum of American Art and the Metropolitan Museum of Art.

RICHARD HARE is a decorator who lives in New York City and East Hampton, Long Island.

MISHKA HARNDEN works in films in Los Angeles.

PICO HARNDEN is a photographer who lives in New York City.

ALAN HARRINGTON is the author of *The Revelations of Dr. Modesto*, *Life in the Crystal Palace*, *The Secret Swinger*, *The Immortalist: An Approach to the Engineering of Man's Divinity*, *Psychopaths*, *Paradise I: A Novel*, and *The White Rainbow*. He lives in Tucson, Arizona.

LUBA HARRINGTON has taught linguistics at Yale. She lives in New York City and in Sag Harbor, Long Island.

NEIL HARTLEY is a senior producer for Tony Richardson's Woodfall Films. His latest film is *The Hotel New Hampshire*. He lives in Los Angeles.

DRUE HEINZ is the publisher of *Antaeus*, a trustee of the Metropolitan Museum of Art, and a celebrated hostess on both sides of the Atlantic.

DAPHNE HELLMAN has been described in *The New Yorker* as a "salon-keeper, famous New York beauty, aviarist, and extraordinary harpist. She invented Hellman's Angels, a unique trio—harp, guitar, bass—which has been up and down the country and over a good part of the world." She lives in New York City and on Cape Cod.

ADDIE HERDER is a painter who lived in Paris for many years and now lives in New York City. Her most recent show of collage constructions featured façades and shallow interiors.

CORRECTION OFFICER JOHN HERNANDEZ works in the deputy warden's office at the Anna M. Kross Center on Rikers Island.

EDWARD HERSHEY is the assistant commissioner for public affairs in the New York City Department of Correction.

SARAH HINES is an assistant district attorney for the borough of Manhattan.

JAMES M. HUBBALL retired as headmaster of the Buckley School in New York City. He lives in Connecticut and Florida.

PAUL JENKINS is a painter who has had many one-man and group shows. His work is represented in the permanent collections of the Museum of Modern Art, the Whitney Museum of American Art, the Tate Gallery in London, and the Musée d'Art Moderne in Paris. He is the producer of a film, *The Ivory Knife: Paul Jenkins at Work*, the author of a play, *Strike the Puma*, and the subject of two biographies. He lives in New York City.

JASPER JOHNS has had one-man shows in museums and galleries all over the world. His work is represented in the permanent collections of the Museum of Modern Art, the Tate Gallery in London, and the Whitney Museum of American Art. He is a member of the National Institute of Arts and Letters.

GLORIA JONES is a consulting editor at Doubleday & Company. She lives in New York City and in Bridgehampton, Long Island. She is the widow of novelist James Jones.

JAMES JONES died in 1977. He was the author of *From Here to Eternity*, *Some Came Running*, *The Pistol*, *The Thin Red Line*, *Go to the Widow-maker*, *The Ice-Cream Headache and Other Stories*, *The Merry Month of May*, *A Touch of Danger*, *Viet Journal*, *World War II*, and *Whistle*.

CÉLINE ROLL KARRAKER is a granddaughter of Céline and Leo Hendrik Baekeland. She lives in Connecticut.

JAMES KINGSLAND is a partner in a large architectural firm in New York City.

F. CLASON KYLE served on the board of directors of the Victorian Society in America. He is currently compiling a pictorial history of Columbus, Georgia, where he works for the *Ledger* and *Enquirer* newspapers.

PAULE LAFEUILLE has taught French to several generations of Americans in Paris.

PETER LAKE is a writer who lives in Venice, California.

WENDY VANDERBILT LEHMAN is a painter who lives in New York City and in Dutchess County, New York.

FRANCESCA DRAPER LINKE lives in Los Angeles. She is married to an actor and the mother of two young children.

SYLVIA LOCHAN was registrar at the National Academy School of Fine Arts of the National Academy of Design in New York City from 1970 to 1973. "I have since gone back to school and acquired a few degrees in psychology and I do counseling now." She lives in Worcester, Massachusetts.

DUNCAN LONGCOPE lives in Boston and in the Berkshires. He is at work on a novel.

DR. E. HUGH LUCKEY was physician chief at New York Hospital for ten years, then president of its medical center for eleven. He is an internist now in private practice in New York City.

PEIDI GIMBEL LUMET is married to the film director Sidney Lumet. They live in New York City and in East Hampton, Long Island.

JOHN McCABE retired from the New York City police force.

TERENCE McLINSKEY is now director of security and vice-president at Sotheby's in New York City.

INGE MAHN is a head senior counselor of the Richmond Fellowship in New York City.

PHYLLIS HARRIMAN MASON is a painter. She lives in New York and in Maine.

DAVID MEAD is a composer and musical director. He lives in New York City.

WILLIE MORRIS, a former editor-in-chief of *Harper's* magazine, is the author of *The South Today, 100 Years After Appomattox*, an autobiography, *North Toward Home, Yazoo: Integration in a Deep Southern Town*, and *The Courting of Marcus Dupree*. He is also the author of a novel, *The Last of the Southern Girls*, a book of essays, *Always Stand in Against the Curve*, and a memoir, *James Jones, A Friendship*. He lives in Mississippi.

JOHN MORTIMER is an English playwright, novelist, and lawyer. He is best known for his scripts for *Brideshead Revisited* and the Rumpole stories. He is also the author of an autobiography, *Clinging to the Wreckage*.

ELSA MOTTAR lives and works in New York City.

JOHN MURRAY lives and works in New York City.

HOWARD NABOR, former deputy warden of the Anna M. Kross Center at Rikers Island, now works in the private sector.

PATRICIA NEAL, the actress, recently moved to New York from England.

MICHEL NEGROPONTE is a filmmaker who lives in New York City.

ROBERT ORENSTEIN, a former assistant director of the Richmond Fellowship, is a social worker now in private practice in New York City as well as a staff therapist for Jewish Family Services of Bergen County, New Jersey.

DAISY HELLMAN PARADIS plays sitar and is chairman of the board of Ali Akbar College of Indian Music in San Raphael, California. She lives with her husband, David Paradis, publisher of *Pequod* magazine, in San Francisco.

BERNARD PFRIEM is a painter who has had one-man shows in America and Europe. He has taught art at Sarah Lawrence College, Cooper Union School of Art and Architecture, and the Museum of Modern Art. He is the director of the Lacoste School of the Arts in France.

DR. STANLEY L. PORTNOW is a psychiatrist in private practice in New York City.

KAREN RADKAI has been a photographer in America and Europe since 1948. Since 1953 she has worked primarily for *Vogue* and *House & Garden*. She lives in New York City and in the Berkshires.

SUE RAILEY was born in Rochester, lived for thirty-three years in Paris, and now lives in New York City, where she is in charge of public relations for Christie's.

JOHN RAKIS, former suicide prevention coordinator and director of health for the New York City Department of Correction, is now deputy executive director of the New York City Board of Correction.

JAMES REEVE is an English painter. He lives in a village in rural England.

ALASTAIR REID is a staff writer at *The New Yorker*, to which over the years he has regularly contributed poems, reviews, comment, translations, stories, and extensive reportage. He has translated the writings of many Latin Americans, particularly Pablo Neruda and Jorge Luis Borges. He has published more than twenty books— poetry, translations, collections of prose, and books for children. He lives in New York City and on Mallorca.

LENA RICHARDS is a practical nurse. She lives in New York City.

HELEN ROLO has been a researcher at *Time* magazine and a fashion editor at *Harper's Bazaar*. She lives in New York City.

TOBY ROSS is a photographer who lives and works in New York City.

IRVING SABO lives and works in Connecticut.

JOHN SARGENT is chairman of the board of Doubleday & Company, Inc. He is a trustee of the New York Zoological Society, the New York Public Library, and the American Academy of Rome. He lives in New York City and in Water Mill, Long Island.

MAY SARTON is the author of seventeen novels, fourteen books of poetry, and several nonfiction books. She is the daughter of George Sarton, a noted science historian, and Mabel Elwes Sarton, a painter—friends of Céline and Leo Hendrik Baekeland. "The genius was old Mr. Baekeland, *Dr.* Baekeland as he was called," she wrote recently. "The great *person* was 'Bonbon.'" She lives in York, Maine.

ELLEN SCHWAMM is the author of two novels, *Adjacent Lives* and *How He Saved Her*. She lives in New York City with her husband, the writer Harold Brodkey.

SAMUEL PARKMAN SHAW retired from the private practice of law in New York City and is counsel for a corporation in Connecticut.

MARTIN J. SIEGEL is a lawyer who practices in New York City.

SYLVIE BAEKELAND SKIRA lives in Maine, where she runs an art gallery. Her present husband is a naval architect.

SANDRA LEWIS SMITH, former deputy director of public affairs for the New York City Department of Correction, is now its director of special events.

MARJORIE FRASER SNOW lives in Ohio.

GEORGE STAEMPFLI owns and runs the Staempfli Gallery in New York City.

ROSE STYRON is a poet and a long-time board member of Amnesty International. She lives with her husband, William Styron, in Connecticut.

WILLIAM STYRON is the author of *Lie Down in Darkness, The Long March, Set This House on Fire, The Confessions of Nat Turner,* which won the Pulitzer Prize in 1968, and *Sophie's Choice*, which won the American Book Award in 1980.

MIWA SVINKA-ZIELINSKI translates Polish and Russian texts on parapsychology. She has also written a scientific history of hypnosis in the nineteenth century in Russia and her native Poland. She lives in Canada, New York City, and Amagansett, Long Island.

SAMUEL TAYLOR is the author of the plays *The Happy Time*, *Sabrina Fair*, *The Pleasure of His Company* (with Cornelia Otis Skinner), *First Love*, *No Strings* (with Richard Rodgers), *Beekman Place*, *Avanti!*, *A Touch of Spring*, *Legend*, *Perfect Pitch*, and *Gracious Living*. He lives with his wife, Suzanne, in East Blue Hill, Maine.

SUZANNE TAYLOR teaches cooking in Blue Hill, Maine, where she also founded a gourmet shop. She is the author of *Young and Hungry*, a cookbook-memoir of life in the country house in Norway where she spent her childhood.

RENÉ JEAN TEILLARD is an antiques dealer in New York City.

YVONNE THOMAS is a French-born painter who lives in New York City.

PAMELA TURNER, the former service tenant at 81 Cadogan Square, London, has moved with her husband to Brighton—"a lovely place to live," she notes.

JOHNNY VAN KIRK lives in Massachusetts where he plays folk music and is a contracting consultant—"at the moment I'm clerk of the works on a six-million-dollar elderly housing development."

TONY VAN ROON, a former nurse at Broadmoor Special Hospital, now works at the Walsgrave Hospital in Coventry, England.

THILO VON WATZDORF has been the director of the department of contemporary art at Sotheby's in London and the director of the department of nineteenth-century European paintings at Sotheby's in New York. He is now a private art dealer in New York.

ELEANOR WARD died in January 1984. She founded the Stable Gallery, which in the 1950s and '60s gave the first one-man shows to Andy Warhol, Cy Twombly, and Robert Indiana. She also helped promote the careers of the sculptors Marisol, Louise Bourgeois, and Joseph Cornell, and the painters Joan Mitchell and Robert Rauschenberg.

ANDY WARHOL is an artist and filmmaker. He produced the rock group Velvet Underground. His books include *The Philosophy of Andy Warhol (From A to B & Back Again)*, *Popism: The Warhol '60s*, and *Andy Warhol's Exposures*. In 1969 he founded *Interview* magazine, which he continues to publish. He lives in New York City and in Montauk, Long Island.

ELSPETH WILKIE is an official at the United States Consulate in London.

HELEN MIRANDA WILSON is a painter. She is the daughter of Elena and Edmund Wilson. She lives in New York City.

CLEMENT BIDDLE WOOD is the author of a novel, *Welcome to the Club*. He and his wife, Jessie, lived for many years in Paris. They now divide their time between Water Mill, Long Island, and the Greek island of Spetsai.

The following names are pseudonyms: Joanne Anastase, Jake Cooper, Eddie Cruz, Will Davis, Helen Delaney, Vince Firenzi, Dr. Philip Gogarty, Dr. W. Lindsay Jacobs, Susan Lannan, Juan Martinez, Jackie Monroe, Geoffrey Parsons, Jose Perez, Henry H. Perkins, Mike Perkins, Jim Robertsen, Erika Svenssen, William Thayer, Nancy Perkins Wallace, and Dr. Helene Weiss.

ACKNOWLEDGEMENTS

We would like to thank the many people quoted in these pages for the time they gave us.

We would also like to thank the following for their contributions to the writing of this book: Charles Addams, Al Anderson, John Jay Angevin, Jr., Hetta Asencio, Tony Banwell, Marvin Barrett, Mary Ellin Barrett, Dr. Milton Bastos, Alexander Beard, Patricia Beard, Eleanor Bender, Detective Chief Inspector Roger Bendle (Scotland Yard), Jay Benedict, Rehlein Benedict, Glynne Betts, Zerina Bhika, Dorothea Biddle, June Bingham, David Blasband, Denise Bouché, Heather Bradley, Laurel Buckley, Maureen Bune, Hazel Burke, Captain Jerry Caputo (New York City House of Detention, Rikers Island), Joel Carmichael, Isobel Cartagena, Blair Clark, Lady Mary Clayton, Michael Cleary, Mike Cobb, David Cohen, Elaine Cohen, Patrick Cook, Jane Cooke, Matthew Cowles, Shelly Dattner, Robert Darling, Elizabeth de Cuevas, Ormonde de Kay, Frances Ann Dougherty, Maggie Draper, Barbara Dunkel, Brooke Edgecombe, Jonathan Fast, Irene Fine, Sarah Fischer, Joseph Fox, Captain Harry Foy (New York City Department of Correction), Leda Fremont-Smith, Fred Friendly, Lou Ganim, Jacqueline Gatz, Ann Geiffert, Abigail Gerdts, Nancy Giagnocova, Virginia Taylor Gimbel, Judy Greif, Letty Grierson, Lew Grimes, Hon. Desmond

ACKNOWLEDGEMENTS

Guinness, Sabrina Guinness, Beth Gutcheon, Pat Hackett, Lucile Hamlin, Jones Harris, Robert Harrison, Ann Harvey, Shirley Hazzard, Lillian Hellman, Cathy Henderson, Paul Hoeffel, Sally Iselin, Jill Isles, Ted Johnson, Katrina Hall Jordan, Carl Kaufmann, Anita Herrick Kearns, Judy Kicinski; Tony Kiser, Carol Kitman, Marvin Kitman, Carol Klemm, Hans Koning, Kate Koning, Marcella Korff, Carol Kotwick, Helen Laws, Inge Lehmann-Haupt, Sandy Lehmann-Haupt, Karen Lerner, Ellen Levine, Dr. Richard U. Levine, Olga Lewis, Gael Love, Catherine MacDonald, Gerald MacDonald, Sukie Marlowe, Frances Matthews, Lester Migdal, Hon. E. Leo Milonas, George Mittendorf, Jinty Money-Coutts, Barbara Mortimer, Victor Navasky, Lynn Nesbit, Sue Nestor, Hugh Nissenson, Marilyn Nissenson, Charles Pate, Peter Pennoyer, Robert M. Pennoyer, Victoria L. Pennoyer, Paula Peterson, Emily Read, Piers Paul Read, Hon. Martin Rettinger, K. G. Rimmington, James Rossbach, Sue Rossbach, Digger St. John, May Sarton, Ronnie Scharfman, Denise Scheinberg, Dr. I. Herbert Scheinberg, Barry Schwabsky, Ann M. Seeger, Marvin Siegel, Babs Simpson, Mark Slifer, Betty Ann Solinger, Margaret Sone, Paul Spike, Dr. Robert J. Stoller, Diana Stuart, Douglas Stumpf, David Taylor, Shoe Taylor, Trevor Tester, Gwen Thomas, Lionel Tiger, Virginia Tiger, Captain Earl Tulon (New York City Department of Correction), Richard Turley, Marian Underhill, Ernst von Wedel, Alison Wakehan, Shelley Wanger, Julius Wasserstein, Jeanette Watson, Jacqueline Weld, Matthew Weld, Merida Welles, Lloyd Wells, Tom White, Hilma Wolitzer, Jessie Bruce Wood, Dr. Joseph Youngerman, and Frances Rogers Zilkha.

We would like to thank the following for their cooperation: The Leo H. Baekeland Collection, Archives Center, National Museum of American History, Smithsonian Institution, Washington, D.C.; Bakelite Museum Society, London; *Boston Globe* library; Boston Public Library; the Estate of John Philip Cohane; The James Jones Collection, Harry Ransom Humanities Research Center, the University of Texas at Austin; London Embassy Hotel, London; London Weather Centre; National Association for Mental Health, London; New York City Department of Correction; New York Public Library; New York State Department of Correction; the *New York Times* London Bureau; the *New York Times* morgue; Sarah Lawrence College Library; Scotland Yard; and Union Carbide Research Library.

MORE ABOUT PENGUINS, PELICANS AND PUFFINS

For further information about books available from Penguins please write to Dept EP, Penguin Books Ltd, Harmondsworth, Middlesex UB7 0DA.

In the U.S.A.: For a complete list of books available from Penguins in the United States write to Dept DG, Penguin Books, 299 Murray Hill Parkway, East Rutherford, New Jersey 07073.

In Canada: For a complete list of books available from Penguins in Canada write to Penguin Books Canada Limited, 2801 John Street, Markham, Ontario L3R 1B4.

In Australia: For a complete list of books available from Penguins in Australia write to the Marketing Department, Penguin Books Australia Ltd, P.O. Box 257, Ringwood, Victoria 3134.

In New Zealand: For a complete list of books available from Penguins in New Zealand write to the Marketing Department, Penguin Books (N.Z.) Ltd, Private Bag, Takapuna, Auckland 9.

In India: For a complete list of books available from Penguins in India write to Penguin Overseas Ltd, 706 Eros Apartments, 56 Nehru Place, New Delhi 110019.

A CHOICE OF PENGUINS

☐ **The Complete Penguin Stereo Record and Cassette Guide**
Greenfield, Layton and March £7.95

A new edition, now including information on compact discs. 'One of the few indispensables on the record collector's bookshelf' – *Gramophone*

☐ **Selected Letters of Malcolm Lowry**
Edited by Harvey Breit and Margerie Bonner Lowry £5.95

'Lowry emerges from these letters not only as an extremely interesting man, but also a lovable one' – Philip Toynbee

☐ **The First Day on the Somme**
Martin Middlebrook £3.95

1 July 1916 was the blackest day of slaughter in the history of the British Army. 'The soldiers receive the best service a historian can provide: their story told in their own words' – *Guardian*

☐ **A Better Class of Person** **John Osborne** £2.50

The playwright's autobiography, 1929–56. 'Splendidly enjoyable' – John Mortimer. 'One of the best, richest and most bitterly truthful autobiographies that I have ever read' – Melvyn Bragg

☐ **The Winning Streak** **Goldsmith and Clutterbuck** £2.95

Marks & Spencer, Saatchi & Saatchi, United Biscuits, GEC ... The UK's top companies reveal their formulas for success, in an important and stimulating book that no British manager can afford to ignore.

☐ **The First World War** **A. J. P. Taylor** £4.95

'He manages in some 200 illustrated pages to say almost everything that is important ... A special text ... a remarkable collection of photographs' – *Observer*

A CHOICE OF PENGUINS

☐ *Man and the Natural World* **Keith Thomas** £4.95

Changing attitudes in England, 1500–1800. 'An encyclopedic study of man's relationship to animals and plants . . . a book to read again and again' – Paul Theroux, *Sunday Times* Books of the Year

☐ *Jean Rhys: Letters 1931–66*
Edited by Francis Wyndham and Diana Melly £4.95

'Eloquent and invaluable . . . her life emerges, and with it a portrait of an unexpectedly indomitable figure' – Marina Warner in the *Sunday Times*

☐ *The French Revolution* **Christopher Hibbert** £4.95

'One of the best accounts of the Revolution that I know . . . Mr Hibbert is outstanding' – J. H. Plumb in the *Sunday Telegraph*

☐ *Isak Dinesen* **Judith Thurman** £4.95

The acclaimed life of Karen Blixen, 'beautiful bride, disappointed wife, radiant lover, bereft and widowed woman, writer, sibyl, Scheherazade, child of Lucifer, Baroness; always a unique human being . . . an assiduously researched and finely narrated biography' – *Books & Bookmen*

☐ *The Amateur Naturalist*
Gerald Durrell with Lee Durrell £4.95

'Delight . . . on every page . . . packed with authoritative writing, learning without pomposity . . . it represents a real bargain' – *The Times Educational Supplement.* 'What treats are in store for the average British household' – *Daily Express*

☐ *When the Wind Blows* **Raymond Briggs** £2.95

'A visual parable against nuclear war: all the more chilling for being in the form of a strip cartoon' – *Sunday Times.* 'The most eloquent anti-Bomb statement you are likely to read' – *Daily Mail*

would like to hear how I escaped Berlin after I had been foolish enough to go back. That was a close one, I can tell you.' He pantomimed shaving one stubbly cheek and laughed.

'Anything,' Todd said. 'Really.' He watched Dussander examine the empty bottle and then get up with it in one hand. Dussander took it to the wastebasket and dropped it in.

'No, none of those, I think,' Dussander said. 'You don't seem to be in the mood.' He stood reflectively by the wastebasket for a moment and then crossed the kitchen to the cellar door. His wool socks whispered on the hilly linoleum. 'I think today I will instead tell you the story of an old man who was afraid.'

Dussander opened the cellar door. His back was now to the table. Todd stood up quietly.

'He was afraid,' Dussander went on, 'of a certain young boy who was, in a queer way, his friend. A smart boy. His mother called this boy "apt pupil", and the old man had already discovered he *was* an apt pupil . . . although perhaps not in the way his mother thought.'

Dussander fumbled with the old-fashioned electrical switch on the wall, trying to turn it with his bunched and clumsy fingers. Todd walked – almost glided – across the linoleum, not stepping in any of the places where it squeaked or creaked. He knew this kitchen as well as his own, now. Maybe better.

'At first, the boy was not the old man's friend,' Dussander said. He managed to turn the switch at last. He descended the first step with a veteran drunk's care. 'At first the old man disliked the boy a great deal. Then he grew to . . . to enjoy his company, although there was still a strong element of dislike there.' He was looking at the shelf now but still holding the railing. Todd, cool – no, now he was *cold* – stepped behind him and calculated the chances of one strong push dislodging Dussander's hold on the railing. He decided to wait until Dussander leaned forward.

'Part of the old man's enjoyment came from a feeling of equality,' Dussander went on thoughtfully. 'You see, the boy and the old man had each other in mutual deathgrips. Each knew something the other wanted kept secret. And then . . . ah, then it became apparent to the old man that things were changing. Yes. He was losing his hold – some of it or all of it, depending on how desperate the boy might be, and how clever. It occurred to this old man on one long and sleepless night that it might be well for him to acquire a new hold on the boy. For his own safety.'

Now Dussander let go of the railing and leaned out over the steep cellar stairs, but Todd remained perfectly still. The bone-deep cold was melting out of him, being replaced by a rosy flush of anger and confusion. As Dussander grasped his fresh bottle, Todd thought viciously that the old man had the stinkiest cellar in town, oil or no oil. It smelled as if something had died down there.

'So the old man got out of his bed right then. What is sleep to an old man? Very little. And he sat at his small desk, thinking about how cleverly he had enmeshed the boy in the very crimes the boy was holding over his own head. He sat thinking about how hard the boy had worked, how very hard, to bring his school marks back up. And how, when they *were* back up, he would have no further need for the old man alive. And if the old man were dead, the boy could be free.'

He turned around now, holding the fresh bottle of Ancient Age by the neck.

'I heard you, you know,' he said, almost gently. 'From the

moment you pushed your chair back and stood up. You are not as quiet as you imagine, boy. At least not yet.'

Todd said nothing.

'So!' Dussander exclaimed, stepping back into the kitchen and closing the cellar door firmly behind him. 'The old man wrote everything down, *nicht wahr*? From first word to last he wrote it down. When he was finally finished it was almost dawn and his hand was singing from the arthritis – the *verdammt* arthritis – but he felt good for the first time in weeks. He felt *safe*. He got back into his bed and slept until mid-afternoon. In fact, if he had slept any longer, he would have missed his favourite – *General Hospital*.'

He had regained his rocker now. He sat down, produced a worn jackknife with a yellow ivory handle, and began to cut painstakingly around the seal covering the top of the bourbon bottle.

'On the following day the old man dressed in his best suit and went down to the bank where he kept his little checking and savings accounts. He spoke to one of the bank officers, who was able to answer all the old man's questions most satisfactorily. He rented a safety deposit box. The bank officer explained to the old man that he would have a key and the bank would have a key. To open the box, both keys would be needed. No one but the old man could use the old man's key without a signed, notarized letter of permission from the old man himself. With one exception.'

Dussander smiled toothlessly into Todd Bowden's white, set face.

'That exception is made in event of the box-holder's death,' he said. Still looking at Todd, still smiling, Dussander put his jackknife back into the pocket of his robe, unscrewed the cap of the bourbon bottle, and poured a fresh jolt into his cup.

'What happens then?' Todd asked hoarsely.

'Then the box is opened in the presence of a bank official and a representative of the Internal Revenue Service. The contents of the box are inventoried. In this case they will find only a twelve-page document. Non-taxable . . . but highly interesting.'

The fingers of Todd's hands crept towards each other and locked tightly. 'You can't do that,' he said in a stunned and unbelieving voice. It was the voice of a person who observes another person walking on the ceiling. 'You can't . . . can't do that.'

'My boy,' Dussander said kindly, 'I have.'

'But . . . I . . . you . . .' His voice suddenly rose to an agonized howl. 'You're *old*! Don't you know that you're *old*? You could die! *You could die anytime!*'

Dussander got up. He went to one of the kitchen cabinets and took down a small glass. This glass had once held jelly. Cartoon characters danced around the rim. Todd recognized them all – Fred and Wilma Flintstone, Barney and Betty Rubble, Pebbles and Bam-Bam. He had grown up with them. He watched as Dussander wiped this jelly-glass almost ceremonially with a dishtowel. He watched as Dussander set it in front of him. He watched as Dussander poured a finger of bourbon into it.

'What's that for?' Todd muttered. 'I don't drink. Drinking's for cheap stewbums like you.'

'Lift your glass, boy. It is a special occasion. Today you drink.'

Todd looked at him for a long moment, then picked up

the glass. Dussander clicked his cheap ceramic cup smartly against it.

'I make a toast, boy – long life! Long life to both of us! *Prosit!*' He tossed his bourbon off at a gulp and then began to laugh. He rocked back and forth, stockinged feet hitting the linoleum, laughing, and Todd thought he had never looked so much like a vulture, a vulture in a bathrobe, a noisome beast of carrion.

'I hate you,' he whispered, and then Dussander began to choke on his own laughter. His face turned a dull brick colour; it sounded as if he were coughing, laughing, and strangling, all at the same time. Todd, scared, got up quickly and clapped him on the back until the coughing fit had passed.

'*Danke schön,*' he said. 'Drink your drink. It will do you good.'

Todd drank it. It tasted like very bad cold-medicine and lit a fire in his gut.

'I can't believe you drink this shit all day,' he said, putting the glass back on the table and shuddering. 'You ought to quit it. Quit drinking *and* smoking.'

'Your concern for my health is touching,' Dussander said. He produced a crumpled pack of cigarettes from the same bathrobe pocket into which the jackknife had disappeared. 'And I am equally solicitous of your own welfare, boy. Almost every day I read in the paper where a cyclist has been killed at a busy intersection. You should give it up. You should walk. Or ride the bus, like me.'

'Why don't you go fuck yourself?' Todd burst out.

'My boy,' Dussander said, pouring more bourbon and beginning to laugh again, 'we are fucking each other – didn't you know that?'

* * *

One day about a week later, Todd was sitting on a disused mail platform down in the old trainyard. He chucked cinders out across the rusty, weed-infested tracks one at a time.

Why shouldn't I kill him anyway?

Because he was a logical boy, the logical answer came first. No reason at all. Sooner or later Dussander was going to die, and given Dussander's habits, it would probably be sooner. Whether he killed the old man or whether Dussander died of a heart attack in his bathtub, it was all going to come out. At least he could have the pleasure of wringing the old vulture's neck.

Sooner or later – that phrase defied logic.

Maybe it'll be later, Todd thought. *Cigarettes or not, booze or not, he's a tough old bastard. He's lasted this long, so . . . so maybe it'll be later.*

From beneath him came a fuzzy snort.

Todd jumped to his feet, dropping the handful of cinders he had been holding. That snorting sound came again.

He paused, on the verge of running, but the snort didn't recur. Nine hundred yards away, an eight-lane freeway swept across the horizon above this weed- and junk-strewn cul-de-sac with its deserted buildings, rusty cyclone fences, and splintery, warped platforms. The cars up on the freeway glistened in the sun like exotic hard-shelled beetles. Eight lanes of traffic up there, nothing down here but Todd, a few birds . . . and whatever had snorted.

Cautiously, he bent down with his hands on his knees and peered under the mail platform. There was a wino lying up in there among the yellow weeds and empty cans and dusty old bottles. It was impossible to tell his age; Todd put him at somewhere between thirty and four hundred. He was wearing a strappy tee-shirt that was caked with dried vomit, green pants that were far too big for him, and grey leather workshoes cracked in a hundred places. The cracks gaped like agonized mouths. Todd thought he smelled like Dussander's cellar.

The wino's red-laced eyes opened slowly and stared at Todd with a bleary lack of wonder. As they did, Todd thought of the Swiss Army knife in his pocket, the Angler model. He had purchased it at a sporting goods store in Redondo Beach almost a year ago. He could hear the clerk that had waited on him in his mind: *You couldn't pick a better knife than that one, son — a knife like that could save your life someday. We sell fifteen hundred Swiss knives every damn year.*

Fifteen hundred a year.

He put his hand in his pocket and gripped the knife. In his mind's eye he saw Dussander's jackknife working slowly around the neck of the bourbon bottle, slitting the seal. A moment later he became aware that he had an erection.

Cold terror stole into him.

The wino swiped a hand over his cracked lips and then licked them with a tongue which nicotine had turned a permanent dismal yellow. 'Got a dime, kid?'

Todd looked at him expressionlessly.

'Gotta get to LA. Need another dime for the bus. I got a pointment, me. Got a job offertunity. Nice kid like you must have a dime. Maybe you got a quarter.'

Yessir, you could clean out a damn bluegill with a knife like that . . . hell, you could clean out a damn marlin with it if you had to. We sell fifteen hundred of those a year. Every sporting goods store and Army-Navy Surplus in America sells them, and if you decided to use this one to clean out some dirty, shitty old wino, nobody could trace it back to you, absolutely NOBODY.

The wino's voice dropped; it became a confidential, tene-brous whisper. 'For a buck I'd do you a blowjob, you never had a better. You'd come your brains out, kid, you'd –'

Todd pulled his hand out of his pocket. He wasn't sure what was in it until he opened it. Two quarters. Two nickels. A dime. Some pennies. He threw them at the wino and fled.

12

June, 1975.

Todd Bowden, now fourteen, came biking up Dussander's walk and parked his bike on the kickstand. The LA *Times* was on the bottom step; he picked it up. He looked at the bell, below which the neat legends ARTHUR DENKER and NO SOLICITORS, NO PEDDLERS, NO SALESMEN still kept their places. He didn't bother with the bell now, of course; he had his key.

Somewhere close by was the popping, burping sound of a Lawn Boy. He looked at Dussander's grass and saw it could use a cutting; he would have to tell the old man to find a boy with a mower. Dussander forgot little things like that more often now. Maybe it was senility; maybe it was just the pickling influence of Ancient Age on his brains. That was an adult thought for a boy of fourteen to have, but such thoughts no longer struck Todd as singular. He had many adult thoughts these days. Most of them were not so great.

He let himself in.

He had his usual instant of cold terror as he entered the kitchen and saw Dussander slumped slightly sideways in his rocker, the cup on the table, a half-empty bottle of bourbon beside it. A cigarette had burned its entire length down to lacy grey ash in a mayonnaise cover where several other butts had been mashed out. Dussander's mouth hung open. His face was yellow. His big hands dangled limply over the rocker's arms. He didn't seem to be breathing.

'Dussander,' he said, a little too harshly. 'Rise and shine, Dussander.'

He felt a wave of relief as the old man twitched, blinked, and finally sat up.

'Is it you? And so early?'

'They let us out early on the last day of school,' Todd said. He pointed to the remains of the cigarette in the mayonnaise cover. 'Someday you'll burn down the house doing that.'

'Maybe,' Dussander said indifferently. He fumbled out his cigarettes, shot one from the pack (it almost rolled off the edge of the table before Dussander was able to catch it), and at last got it going. A protracted fit of coughing followed, and Todd winced in disgust. When the old man really got going, Todd half-expected him to start spitting out greyish-black chunks of lung-tissue onto the table . . . and he'd probably grin as he did it.

At last the coughing eased enough for Dussander to say, 'What have you got there?'

'Report-card.'

Dussander took it, opened it, and held it away from him at arm's length so he could read it. 'English . . . A. American History . . . A. Earth Science . . . B Plus. Your Community and You . . . A. Primary French . . . B Minus. Beginning Algebra . . . B.' He put it down. 'Very good. What is the slang? We have saved your bacon, boy. Will you have to change any of these averages in the last column?'

'French and Algebra, but no more than eight or nine

points in all. I don't think any of this is ever going to come out. And I guess I owe that to you. I'm not proud of it, but it's the truth. So, thanks.'

'What a touching speech,' Dussander said, and began to cough again.

'I guess I won't be seeing you around too much from now on,' Todd said, and Dussander abruptly stopped coughing.

'No?' he said, politely enough.

'No,' Todd said. 'We're going to Hawaii for a month starting on 25 June. In September I'll be going to school across town. It's this bussing thing.'

'Oh yes, the *Schwarzen*,' Dussander said, idly watching a fly as it trundled across the red and white check of the table-cloth. 'For twenty years this country has worried and whined about the *Schwarzen*. But we know the solution . . . don't we, boy?' He smiled toothlessly at Todd and Todd looked down, feeling the old sickening lift and drop of his stomach. Terror, hate, and a desire to do something so awful it could only be fully contemplated in his dreams.

'Look, I plan to go to college, in case you didn't know,' Todd said. 'I know that's a long time off, but I think about it. I even know what I want to major in. History.'

'Admirable. He who will not learn from the past is —'

'Oh, shut up,' Todd said.

Dussander did so, amiably enough. He knew the boy wasn't done . . . not yet. He sat with his hands folded, watching him.

'I could get my letter back from my friend,' Todd suddenly blurted. 'You know that? I could let you read it, and then you could watch me burn it. If —'

'— if I would remove a certain document from my safety deposit box.'

'Well . . . yeah.'

Dussander uttered a long, windy, rueful sigh. 'My boy,' he said. 'Still you do not understand the situation. You never have, right from the beginning. Partly because you are only a boy, but not entirely . . . even then, even in the beginning, you were a very *old* boy. No, the real villain was and is your absurd American self-confidence that never allowed you to consider the possible consequences of what you were doing . . . which does not allow it even now.'

Todd began to speak and Dussander raised his hands adamantly, suddenly the world's oldest traffic cop.

'No, don't contradict me. It's true. Go on if you like. Leave the house, get out of here, never come back. Can I stop you? No. Of course I can't. Enjoy yourself in Hawaii while I sit in this hot, grease-smelling kitchen and wait to see if the *Schwarzen* in Watts will decide to start killing policemen and burning their shitty tenements again this year. I can't stop you anymore than I can stop getting older a day at a time.'

He looked at Todd fixedly, so fixedly that Todd looked away.

'Down deep inside, I don't like you. Nothing could make me like you. You forced yourself on me. You are an unbidden guest in my house. You have made me open crypts perhaps better left shut, because I have discovered that some of the corpses were buried alive, and that a few of those *still* have some wind left in them.

'You yourself have become enmeshed, but do I pity you because of that? *Gott im Himmel!* You have made your bed; should I pity you if you sleep badly in it? No . . . I don't pity you, and I don't like you, but I have come to respect you a little bit. So don't try my patience by asking me to explain this twice. We could obtain our documents and destroy them here in my kitchen. And still it would not be over. We would, in fact, be no better off than we are at this minute.'

'I don't understand you.'

'No, because you have never studied the consequences of what you have set in motion. But attend me, boy. If we burned our letters here, in this jar cover, how would I know you hadn't made a copy? Or two? Or three? Down at the library they have a Xerox machine, for a nickel anyone can make a photocopy. For a dollar, you could post a copy of my death-warrant on every streetcorner for twenty blocks. Four *miles* of death-warrants, boy! Think of it! Can you tell me how I would know you hadn't done such a thing?'

'I . . . well, I . . . I . . .' Todd realized he was floundering and forced himself to shut his mouth. Dussander had just outlined a piece of duplicity so fundamental that it had simply never crossed his mind. He opened his mouth to say so, realized Dussander would not believe him . . . and that, in fact, was the problem.

He shut his mouth again, this time with a snap.

'And how would you know I hadn't made *two* copies for my safety deposit box . . . that I had burned one and left the other there?'

Todd was silent and dismayed.

'Even if there were some impartial third party we could go to, always there would be doubts. The problem is insoluble, boy. Believe it.'

'Shit,' Todd said in a very small voice.

Dussander took a deep drink from his cup and looked at Todd over the rim.

'Now I tell you two more things, boy. First, that if your part in this matter came out, your punishment would be quite small. It is even possible – no, more than that, *likely* – that it would never come out in the papers at all. I frightened you with reform school once, when I was badly afraid you might crack and tell everything. But do I believe that? No – I used it the way a father will use the "boogeyman" to frighten a child into coming home before dark. I don't believe that they would send you there, not in this country where they spank killers on the wrist and send them out into the streets to kill again after two years of watching colour TV in a penitentiary.

'But it might well ruin your life all the same. There are records . . . and people talk. Always, they talk. Such a juicy scandal is not allowed to wither; it is bottled, like wine. And, of course, as the years pass, your culpability will grow with you. Your silence will grow more damning. If the truth came out today, people would say, 'But he is just a child!' . . . not knowing, as I do, what an *old* child you are. But what would they say, boy, if the truth about me, coupled with the fact that you knew about me as early as 1974 *but kept silent*, came out while you are in high school? That would be bad. For it to come out while you are in college would be disaster. As a young man just starting out in business . . . armageddon. You understand this first thing?'

Todd was silent, but Dussander seemed satisfied. He nodded.

Still nodding, he said: 'Second, I don't believe you *have* a letter.'

Todd strove to keep a poker face, but he was terribly afraid his eyes had widened in shock. Dussander was studying him avidly, and Todd was suddenly, nakedly aware that this old man had interrogated hundreds, perhaps *thousands* of people. He was an expert. Todd felt that his skull had turned to window-glass and all things were flashing inside in large letters.

'I asked myself who you would trust so much. Who are your friends . . . who do you run with? Who does this boy, this self-sufficient, coldly controlled little *boy*, go to with his loyalty? The answer is, nobody.'

Dussander's eyes gleamed yellowly.

'Many times I have studied you and calculated the odds. I know you, and I know much of your character – no, not all, because one human being can never know everything that is in another human being's heart – but I know so little about what you do and who you see outside of this house. So I think, "Dussander, there is a chance that you are wrong. After all these years, do you want to be captured and maybe killed because you misjudged a boy?" Maybe when I was younger, I would have taken the chance – the odds are good odds, and the chance is a small chance. It is very strange to me, you know – the older one becomes, the less one has to lose in matters of life and death . . . and yet, one becomes more and more conservative.'

He looked hard into Todd's face.

'I have one more thing to say, and then you can go when you want. What I have to say is that, while I doubt the existence of your letter, never doubt the existence of mine. *The document I have described to you exists.* If I die today . . . tomorrow . . . everything will come out. *Everything.*'

'Then there's nothing for me,' Todd said. He uttered a dazed little laugh. 'Don't you see that?'

'But there is. Years will go by. As they pass, your hold on me will become worth less and less, because no matter how important my life and liberty remain to me, the Americans and – yes, even the Israelis – will have less and less interest in taking them away.'

'Yeah? Then why don't they let that guy Speer go?'

'If the Americans had him – the Americans who let killers out with a spank on the wrists – they *would* have let him go,' Dussander said. 'Are the Americans going to allow the Israelis to extradite a ninety-year-old man so they can hang him as they hung Eichmann? I think not. Not in a country where they put photographs of firemen rescuing kittens from trees on the front pages of city newspapers.

'No, your hold over me will weaken even as mine over you grows stronger. No situation is static. And there will come a time – if I live long enough – when I will decide what you know no longer matters. Then I will destroy the document.'

'But so many things could happen to you in between! Accidents, sickness, disease –'

Dussander shrugged. '"There will be water if God wills it, and we will find it if God wills it, and we will drink it if God wills it." What happens is not up to us.'

Todd looked at the old man for a long time – for a very long time. There were flaws in Dussander's arguments – there had to be. A way out, an escape hatch either for both of them or for Todd alone. A way to cry it off . . . times, guys, I hurt my foot, allee-allee-in-free. A black knowledge of the years ahead trembled somewhere behind his eyes; he could feel it there, waiting to be born as conscious thought. Everywhere he went, everything he did . . .

He thought of a cartoon character with an anvil suspended over its head. By the time he graduated from high school, Dussander would be eighty, and that would not be the end; by the time he collected his BA, Dussander would be eighty-four and he would still feel that he wasn't old enough; he would finish his master's thesis and graduate school the year Dussander turned eighty-six . . . and Dussander still might not feel safe.

'No,' Todd said thickly. 'What you're saying . . . I can't face that.'

'My boy,' Dussander said gently, and Todd heard for the first time and with dawning horror the slight accent the old man had put on the first word. 'My boy . . . you must.'

Todd stared at him, his tongue swelling and thickening in his mouth until it seemed it must fill his throat and choke him. Then he wheeled and blundered out of the house.

Dussander watched all of this with no expression at all, and when the door had slammed shut and the boy's running footsteps stopped, meaning that he had mounted his bike, he lit a cigarette. There was, of course, no safe deposit box, no document. But the boy believed those things existed; he had believed utterly. He was safe. It was ended.

But it was not ended.

That night they both dreamed of murder, and both of them awoke in mingled terror and exhilaration.

Todd awoke with the now familiar stickiness on his lower belly. Dussander, too old for such things, put on the Gestapo uniform and then lay down again, waiting for his racing heart to slow. The uniform was cheaply made and already beginning to fray.

In Dussander's dream he had finally reached the camp at the top of the hill. The wide gate slid open for him and then rumbled shut on its steel track once he was inside.

Both the gate and the fence surrounding the camp were electrified. His scrawny, naked pursuers threw themselves against the fence in wave after wave; Dussander had laughed at them and he had strutted back and forth, his chest thrown out, his cap cocked at exactly the right angle. The high, winey smell of burning flesh filled the black air, and he had awakened in southern California thinking of jack-o'-lanterns and the night when vampires seek the blue flame.

Two days before the Bowdens were scheduled to fly to Hawaii, Todd went back to the abandoned trainyard where folks had once boarded trains for San Francisco, Seattle, and Las Vegas; where other, older folks had once boarded the trolley for Los Angeles.

It was nearly dusk when he got there. On the curve of freeway nine hundred yards away, most of the cars were now showing their parking lights. Although it was warm, Todd was wearing a light jacket. Tucked into his belt under it was a butcher-knife wrapped in an old hand-towel. He had purchased the knife in a discount department store, one of the big ones surrounded by acres of parking lot.

He looked under the platform where the wino had been the month before. His mind turned and turned, but it turned on nothing; everything inside him at that moment was shades of black on black.

What he found was the same wino or possibly another; they all looked pretty much the same.

'Hey!' Todd said. 'Hey! You want some money?'

The wino turned over, blinking. He saw Todd's wide, sunny grin and began to grin back. A moment later the butcher knife descended, all whicker-snicker and chrome-white, slicker-slicing through his stubbly right cheek. Blood sprayed. Todd could see the blade in the wino's opening mouth . . . and then its tip caught for a moment in the left corner of the wino's lips, pulling his mouth into an insanely cockeyed grin. Then it was the knife that was making the grin; he was carving the wino like a Halloween pumpkin.

He stabbed the wino thirty-seven times. He kept count. Thirty-seven, counting the first strike, which went through the wino's cheek and then turned his tentative smile into a great grisly grin. The wino stopped trying to scream after the fourth stroke. He stopped trying to scramble away from Todd after the sixth. Todd then crawled all the way under the platform and finished the job.

On his way home he threw the knife into the river. His pants were bloodstained. He tossed them into the washing machine and set it to wash cold. There were still faint stains on the pants when they came out, but they didn't concern Todd. They would fade in time. He found the next day that he could barely lift his right arm to the level of his shoulder. He told his father he must have strained it throwing pepper with some of the guys in the park.

'It'll get better in Hawaii,' Dick Bowden said, ruffling Todd's hair, and it did; by the time they came home, it was as good as new.

13

It was July again.

Dussander, carefully dressed in one of his three suits (not his best), was standing at the bus stop and waiting for the last local of the day to take him home. It was 10.45 p.m. He had been to a film, a light and frothy comedy that he had enjoyed a great deal. He had been in a fine mood ever since the morning mail. There had been a postcard from the boy, a glossy colour photo of Waikiki Beach with bone-white highrise hotels standing in the background. There was a brief message on the reverse.

> *Dear Mr Denker,*
> *Boy this sure is some place. I've been swimming every day. My dad caught a big fish and my mom is catching up on her reading (joke). Tomorrow we're going to a volcano. I'll try not to fall in! Hope you're okay.*
> *Stay healthy,*
> *Todd*

He was still smiling faintly at the significance of that last when a hand touched his elbow.

'Mister?'

'Yes?'

He turned, on his guard – even in Santa Donato, muggers were not unknown – and then winced at the aroma. It seemed to be a combination of beer, halitosis, dried sweat, and possibly Musterole. It was a bum in baggy pants. He – *it* – wore a flannel shirt and very old Keds that were currently being held together with dirty bands of adhesive tape. The face looming above this motley costume looked like the death of God.

'You got an extra dime, mister? I gotta get to LA, me. Got a job offertunity. I need just a dime more for the express bus. I wudn't ask if it wasn't a big chance for me.'

Dussander had begun to frown, but now his smile reasserted itself.

'Is it really a bus ride you wish?'

The wino smiled sickly, not understanding.

'Suppose you ride the bus home with me,' Dussander proposed. 'I can offer you a drink, a meal, a bath, and a bed. All I ask in return is a little conversation. I am an old man. I live alone. Company is sometimes very welcome.'

The drunk's smile abruptly grew more healthy as the situation clarified itself. Here was a well-to-do old faggot with a taste for slumming.

'All by yourself! Bitch, innit?'

Dussander answered the broad, insinuating grin with a polite smile. 'I only ask that you sit away from me on the bus. You smell rather strongly.'

'Maybe you don't want me stinking up your place, then,' the drunk said with sudden, tipsy dignity.

'Come, the bus will be here in a minute. Get off one stop after I do and then walk back two blocks. I'll wait for you on the corner. In the morning I will see what I can spare. Perhaps two dollars.'

'Maybe even five,' the drunk said brightly. His dignity, tipsy or otherwise, had been forgotten.

'Perhaps, perhaps,' Dussander said impatiently. He could now hear the low diesel drone of the approaching bus. He pressed a quarter, the correct bus fare, into the bum's grimy hand and strolled a few paces away without looking back.

The bum stood undecided as the headlights of the local swept over the rise. He was still standing and frowning down at the quarter when the old faggot got on the bus without looking back. The bum began to walk away and then — at the last second – he reversed direction and boarded the bus just before the doors folded closed. He put the quarter into the fare-box with the expression of a man putting a hundred dollars down on a long shot. He passed Dussander without doing more than glancing at him and sat at the back of the bus. He dozed off a little, and when he woke up, the rich old faggot was gone. He got off at the next stop, not knowing if it was the right one or not, and not really caring.

He walked back two blocks and saw a dim shape under the streetlight. It was the old faggot, all right. The faggot was watching him approach, and he was standing as if at attention.

For just a moment the bum felt a chill of apprehension, an urge to just turn away and forget the whole thing.

Then the old man was gripping him by the arm . . . and his grip was surprisingly firm.

'Good,' the old man said. 'I'm very glad you came. My house is down here. It's not far.'

'Maybe even ten,' the bum said, allowing himself to be led.

'Maybe even ten,' the old faggot agreed, and then laughed. 'Who knows?'

14

The Bi-Centennial year arrived.

Todd came by to see Dussander half a dozen times between his return from Hawaii in the summer of 1975 and the trip he and his parents took to Rome just as all the drum-thumping, flag-waving, and Tall Ships-watching was approaching its climax. Todd got special permission to leave school early, on 1 June, and they were back three days before the Bi-Centennial 4th.

These visits to Dussander were low-key and in no way unpleasant; the two of them found they could pass the time civilly enough. They spoke more in silences than they did in words, and their actual conversations would have put an FBI agent to sleep. Todd told the old man that he had been seeing a girl named Angela Farrow off and on. He wasn't nuts about her, but she was the daughter of one of his mother's friends. The old man told Todd he had taken up braiding rugs because he had read such an activity was good for arthritis. He showed Todd several samples of his work, and Todd dutifully admired them.

The boy had grown quite a bit, had he not? (Well, two inches.) Had Dussander given up smoking? (No, but he had been forced to cut down; they made him cough too much now.) How had his schoolwork been? (Challenging but exciting; he had made all As and Bs, had gone to the state finals with his Science Fair project on solar power, and was now thinking of majoring in anthropology instead of history when he got to college.) Who was mowing Dussander's lawn this year? (Randy Chambers from just down the street – a good boy, but rather fat and slow.)

During that year Dussander had put an end to three winos in his kitchen. He had been approached at the downtown bus stop some twenty times, had made the drink-dinner-bath-and-bed offer seven times. He had been turned down twice, and on two other occasions the winos had simply walked off with the quarters Dussander gave them for the fare-box. After some thought, he had worked out a way around this; he simply bought a bus-pass. They were two dollars and fifty cents, good for fifteen rides, and non-negotiable at the local liquor stores.

On very warm days just lately, Dussander had noticed an

unpleasant smell drifting up from his cellar. He kept his doors and windows firmly shut on these days.

Todd Bowden had found a wino sleeping it off in an abandoned drainage culvert behind a vacant lot on Cienaga Way – this had been in December, during the Christmas vacation. He had stood there for some time, hands stuffed into his pockets, looking at the wino and trembling. He had returned to the lot six times over a period of five weeks, always wearing his light jacket, zipped halfway up to conceal the Craftsman hammer tucked into his belt. At last he had come upon the wino again – that one or some other, and who really gave a fuck – on the first day of March. He had begun with the hammer end of the tool, and then at some point (he didn't really remember when; everything had been swimming in a red haze) he had switched to the claw end, obliterating the wino's face.

For Kurt Dussander, the winos were a half-cynical propitiation of gods he had finally recognized . . . or re-recognized. And the winos were fun. They made him feel alive. He was beginning to feel that the years he had spent in Santa Donato – the years before the boy had turned up on his doorstep with his big blue eyes and his wide American grin – had been years spent being old before his time. He had been only sixty-eight when he came here. And he felt much younger than that now.

The idea of propitiating gods would have startled Todd at first . . . but it might have gained eventual acceptance. After stabbing the wino under the train platform, he had expected his nightmares to intensify . . . to perhaps even drive him crazy. He had expected waves of paralyzing guilt that might well end with a blurted confession or the taking of his own life.

Instead of any of those things, he had gone to Hawaii with his parents and enjoyed the best vacation of his life.

He had begun high school last September feeling oddly new and refreshed, as if a different person had jumped into his Todd Bowden skin. Things that had made no particular impression on him since earliest childhood – the sunlight just after dawn, the look of the ocean off the Fish Pier, the sight of people hurrying on a downtown street at just that moment of dusk when the streetlights come on – these things now imprinted themselves on his mind again in a series of bright cameos, in images so clear they seemed electroplated. He tasted life on his tongue like a draught of wine straight from the bottle.

After he had seen the stewbum in the culvert, the nightmares had begun again.

The most common one involved the wino he had stabbed to death in the abandoned trainyards. Home from school, he burst into the house, a cheery *Hi, Monica-baby!* on his lips. It died there as he saw the dead wino in the raised breakfast nook. He was sitting slumped over their butcher-block table in his puke-smelling shirt and pants. Blood had streaked across the bright tiled floor; it was drying on the stainless steel counters. There were bloody handprints on the natural pine cupboards.

Clipped to the note-board by the fridge was a message from his mother: *Todd – Gone to the store. Back by 3.30.* The hands of the stylish sunburst clock over the Jenn-Aire range stood at 3.20 and the drunk was sprawled dead up there in the nook like some horrid oozing relic from the subcellar of a junkshop and there was blood everywhere, and Todd began trying to clean it up, wiping every exposed surface, all the time screaming at the dead wino that he had to *go*, had to leave him *alone*, and the wino just lolled there and stayed dead, grinning up at the ceiling, and the freshets of blood kept pouring from the stab-wounds in his dirty skin. Todd grabbed the O-Cedar mop from the closet and began to slide it madly back and forth across the floor, aware that he was not really getting the blood up but only diluting it, spreading it around, but unable to stop. And just as he heard his mother's Town and Country wagon turn into the driveway, he realized the wino was Dussander. He woke from these dreams sweating and gasping, clutching double handfuls of the bedclothes.

But after he finally found the wino in the culvert again — that wino or some other — and used the hammer on him, these dreams went away. He supposed he might have to kill again, and maybe more than once. It was too bad, but of course their time of usefulness as human creatures was over. Except their usefulness to Todd, of course. And Todd, like everyone else he knew, was only tailoring his lifestyle to fit his own particular needs as he grew older. Really, he was no different than anybody. You had to make your own way in the world; if you were going to get along, you had to do it by yourself.

15

In the fall of his junior year, Todd played varsity tailback for the Santa Donato Cougars and was named All-Conference. And in the second quarter of that year, the quarter which ended in late January of 1977, he won the American Legion Patriotic Essay Contest. This contest was open to all city high school students who were taking American history courses. Todd's piece was called 'An American's Responsibility'. During the baseball season in that confused year (the Shah of Iran had been ousted and gasoline prices were on the rise again) he was the school's star pitcher, winning four and losing none. His batting average was .361. At the awards assembly in June he was named Athlete of the Year and given a plaque by Coach Haines (Coach Haines, who had once taken him aside and told him to keep practising his curve 'because none of these niggers can throw a curve-ball, Bowden, not one of them'). Monica Bowden burst into tears when Todd called her from school and told her he was going to get the award. Dick Bowden strutted around his office for two weeks following the ceremony, trying not to boast. That summer they rented a cabin in Big Sur and stayed there for two weeks and Todd snorkled his brains out. During that same year Todd killed four derelicts. He stabbed two of them and bludgeoned two of them. He had taken to wearing two pairs of pants on what he now acknowledged to be hunting expeditions. Sometimes he rode the city buses, looking for likely spots. The best two, he found, were the Santa Donato Mission for the Indigent on Douglas Street, and around the corner from the Salvation Army on Euclid. He would walk slowly through both of these neighbourhoods, waiting to be pan-handled. When a wino approached him, Todd would tell him that he, Todd, wanted a bottle of whiskey, and if the wino would buy it, Todd would share the bottle. He knew a place, he said, where they could go. It was a different place every time, of course. He resisted a strong urge to go back either to the trainyards or to the culvert behind the vacant lot on Cienaga Way. Revisiting the scene of a previous crime would have been unwise.

During the same year Dussander smoked sparingly, drank

Ancient Age bourbon, and watched TV. Todd came by once in a while, but their conversations became increasingly arid. They were growing apart. Dussander celebrated his seventy-eighth birthday that year, which was also the year Todd turned sixteen. Dussander remarked that sixteen was the best year of a young man's life, forty-one the best year of a middle-aged man's, and seventy-eight the best of an old man's. Todd nodded politely. Dussander had been quite drunk and cackled in a way that made Todd distinctly uneasy.

Dussander had dispatched two winos during Todd's academic years of 1976–77. The second had been livelier than he looked; even after Dussander had gotten the man soddenly drunk he had tottered around the kitchen with the haft of a steak-knife jutting from the base of his neck, gushing blood down the front of his shirt and onto the floor. The wino had re-discovered the front hall after two staggering circuits of the kitchen and had almost escaped the house.

Dussander had stood in the kitchen, eyes wide with shocked unbelief, watching the wino grunt and puff his way towards the door, rebounding from one side of the hall to the other and knocking cheap Currier & Ives reproductions to the floor. His paralysis had not broken until the wino was actually groping for the doorknob. Then Dussander had bolted across the room, jerked open the utility drawer, and pulled out his meat-fork. He ran down the hall with the meat-fork held out in front of him and drove it into the wino's back.

Dussander had stood over him, panting, his old heart racing in a frightening way . . . racing like that of a heart-attack victim on that Saturday night TV programme he enjoyed, *Emergency*. But at last it had slowed back into a normal rhythm and he knew he was going to be all right.

There had been a great deal of blood to clean up.

That had been four months ago, and since then he had not made his offer at the downtown bus-stop. He was frightened of the way he had almost bungled the last one . . . but when he remembered the way he had handled things at the last moment, pride rose in his heart. In the end the wino had never made it out the door, and that was the important thing.

16

In the fall of 1977, during the first quarter of his senior year, Todd joined the rifle club. By June of 1978 he had qualified as a marksman. He made All-Conference in football again, won five and lost one during the baseball season (the loss coming as the result of two errors and one unearned run), and made the third highest Merit Scholarship score in the school's history. He applied at Berkeley and was promptly accepted. By April he knew he would either be valedictorian or salutatorian on graduation night. He very badly wanted to be valedictorian.

During the latter half of his senior year, an odd impulse came on him – one which was as frightening to Todd as it was irrational. He seemed to be clearly and firmly in control of it, and *that* at least was comforting, but that such a thought should have occurred at all was scary. He had made an arrangement with life. He had worked things out. His life was much like his mother's bright and sunshiny kitchen, where all the surfaces were dressed in chrome, Formica, or stainless steel – a place where everything worked when you pressed the buttons. There were deep and dark cupboards in this kitchen, of course, but many things could be stored in them and their doors still be closed.

This new impulse reminded him of the dream in which he had come home to discover the dead and bleeding wino in his mother's clean, well-lighted place. It was as if, in the bright and careful arrangement he had made, in that a-place-for-everything-and-everything-in-its-place kitchen of his mind, a dark and bloody intruder now lurched and shambled, looking for a place to die conspicuously . . .

A quarter of a mile from the Bowden house was the freeway, running eight lanes wide. A steep and brushy bank led down to it. There was plenty of good cover on the bank. His father had given him a Winchester .30–.30 for Christmas, and it had a removable telescopic sight. During rush hour, when all eight lanes were jammed, he could pick a spot on that bank and . . . why, he could easily . . .

Do what?

Commit suicide . . .

Destroy everything he had worked for these last five years?

Say *what*?

No *sir*, no *ma'am*, no *way*.

It is, as they say, to laugh.

Sure it was . . . but the impulse remained.

One Saturday a few weeks before his high school graduation, Todd cased the .30–.30 after carefully emptying the magazine. He put the rifle in the back seat of his father's new toy – a used Porsche. He drove to the spot where the brushy slope dropped steeply down to the freeway. His mother and father had taken the station wagon and had driven to LA for the weekend. Dick, now a full partner, would be holding discussions with the Hyatt people about a new Reno hotel.

Todd's heart bumped in his chest and his mouth was full of sour, electric spit as he worked his way down the grade with the cased rifle in his arms. He came to a fallen tree and sat cross-legged behind it. He uncased the rifle and laid it on the dead tree's smooth trunk. A branch jutting off at an angle made a nice rest for the barrel. He snugged the buttplate into the hollow of his right shoulder and peered into the telescopic sight.

Stupid! his mind screamed at him. *Boy, this is really stupid! If someone sees you, it's not going to matter if the gun's loaded or not! You'll get in plenty of trouble, maybe even end up with some Chippie shooting at you!*

It was midmorning and the Saturday traffic was light. He settled the crosshairs on a woman behind the wheel of a blue Toyota. The woman's window was half open and the round collar of her sleeveless blouse was fluttering. Todd centred the crosshairs on her temple and dry-fired. It was bad for the firing-pin, but what the fuck.

'Pow,' he whispered as the Toyota disappeared beneath the underpass half a mile up from the slope where Todd sat. He swallowed around a lump that tasted like a stuck-together mass of pennies.

Here came a man behind the wheel of a Subaru Brat pickup truck. This man had a scuzzy-looking grey beard and was wearing a San Diego Padres baseball hat.

'You're . . . you're the dirty rat . . . the dirty rat that shot my brudduh,' Todd whispered, giggling a little, and dry-fired the .30-.30 again.

He shot at five others, the impotent snap of the hammer

spoiling the illusion at the end of each 'kill'. Then he cased the rifle again. He carried it back up the slope, bending low to keep from being seen. He put it into the back of the Porsche. There was a dry hot pounding in his temples. He drove home. Went up to his room. Masturbated.

17

The stewbum was wearing a ragged, unravelling reindeer sweater that looked so startling it almost seemed surreal here in southern California. He also wore seaman's issue bluejeans which were out at the knees, showing white, hairy flesh and a number of peeling scabs. He raised the jelly glass – Fred and Wilma, Barney and Betty dancing around the rim in what might have been some grotesque fertility rite – and tossed off the knock of Ancient Age at a gulp. He smacked his lips for the last time in this world.

'Mister, that hits the old spot. I don't mind saying so.'

'I always enjoy a drink in the evening,' Dussander agreed from behind him, and then rammed the butcher knife into the stewbum's neck. There was the sound of ripping gristle, a sound like a drumstick being torn enthusiastically from a freshly roasted chicken. The jelly glass fell from the stewbum's hand and onto the table. It rolled towards the edge, its movement enhancing the illusion that the cartoon characters on it were dancing.

The stewbum threw his head back and tried to scream. Nothing came out but a hideous whistling sound. His eyes widened, widened . . . and then his head thumped soggily onto the red and white oilcloth check that covered Dussander's kitchen table. The stewbum's upper plate slithered halfway out of his mouth like a semi-detachable grin.

Dussander yanked the knife free — he had to use both hands to do it — and crossed to the kitchen sink. It was filled with hot water, Lemon Fresh Joy, the dirty supper dishes. The knife disappeared into a billow of citrus-smelling suds like a very small fighter plane diving into a cloud.

He crossed to the table again and paused there, resting one hand on the dead stewbum's shoulder while a spasm of coughing rattled through him. He took his handkerchief from his back pocket and spat yellowish-brown phlegm into it. He had been smoking too much lately. He always did when he was making up his mind to do another one. But this one had gone smoothly; really very smoothly. He had been afraid after the mess he had made with the last one that he might be tempting fate sorely to try it again.

Now, if he hurried, he would still be able to watch the second half of Lawrence Welk.

He bustled across the kitchen, opened the cellar door, and turned on the light switch. He went back to the sink and got the package of green plastic garbage bags from the cupboard beneath. He shook one out as he walked back to the slumped wino. Blood had run across the table cloth in all directions. It had puddled in the wino's lap and on the hilly, faded linoleum. It would be on the chair, too, but all of those things would clean up.

Dussander grabbed the stewbum by the hair and yanked his head up. It came with boneless ease, and a moment later the wino was lolling backwards, like a man about to get a pre-haircut shampoo. Dussander pulled the garbage bag down over the wino's head, over his shoulders, and down his arms to the elbows. That was as far as it would go. He unbuckled his late guest's belt and pulled it free of the fraying belt-loops.

He wrapped the belt around the garbage bag two or three inches above the elbows and buckled it tight. Plastic rustled. Dussander began to hum '*Lili Marlene*' under his breath.

The wino's feet were clad in scuffed and dirty Hush Puppies. They made a limp V on the floor as Dussander seized the belt and dragged the corpse towards the cellar door. Something white tumbled out of the plastic bag and clicked on the floor. It was the stewbum's upper plate, Dussander saw. He picked it up and stuffed it into one of the wino's front pockets.

He laid the wino down in the cellar doorway with his head now lolling backwards onto the second stair-level. Dussander climbed around the body and gave it three healthy kicks. The body moved slightly on the first two, and the third sent it slithering bonelessly down the stairs. Halfway down the feet flew up over the head and the body executed an acrobatic roll. It belly-whopped onto the packed dirt of the cellar floor with a solid thud. One Hush Puppy flew off, and Dussander made a mental note to pick it up.

He went down the stairs, skirted the body, and approached his toolbench. To the left of the bench a spade, a rake, and a hoe leaned against the wall in a neat rank. Dussander selected the spade. A little exercise was good for an old man. A little exercise could make you feel young.

The smell down here was not good, but it didn't bother him much. He limed the place once a month (once every three days after he had 'done' one of his winos) and he had gotten a fan which he ran upstairs to keep the smell from permeating the house on very warm still days. Josef Kramer, he remembered, had been fond of saying that the dead speak, but we hear them with our noses.

Dussander picked a spot in the cellar's north corner and went to work. The dimensions of the grave were two and a half feet by six feet. He had gotten to a depth of two feet, half deep enough, when the first paralyzing pain struck him in the chest like a shotgun blast. He straightened up, eyes flaring wide. Then the pain rolled down his arm . . . unbelievable pain, as if an invisible hand had seized all the blood-vessels in there and was now pulling them. He watched the spade tumble sideways and felt his knees buckle. For one horrible moment he felt sure that he was going to fall into the grave himself.

Somehow he staggered backwards three paces and sat down on his workbench with a plop. There was an expression of stupid surprise on his face – he could feel it – and he thought he must look like one of those silent movie comedians after he's been hit by the swinging door or stepped in the cow patty. He put his head down between his knees and gasped.

Fifteen minutes crawled by. The pain had begun to abate somewhat, but he did not believe he would be able to stand. For the first time he understood all the truths of old age which he had been spared until now. He was terrified almost to the point of whimpering. Death had brushed by him in this dank smelly cellar; it had touched Dussander with the hem of its robe. It might be back for him yet. But he would not die down here; not if he could help it.

He got up, hands still crossed on his chest, as if to hold the fragile machinery together. He staggered across the open space between the workbench and the stairs. His left foot tripped over the dead wino's outstretched leg and he went to his knees with a small cry. There was a sullen flare of pain in his chest. He looked up the stairs – the steep, steep stairs.

Twelve of them. The square of light at the top was mockingly distant.

'*Ein*,' Kurt Dussander said, and pulled himself grimly up onto the first stair-level. '*Zwei. Drei. Vier.*'

It took him twenty minutes to reach the linoleum floor of the kitchen. Twice, on the stairs, the pain had threatened to come back, and both times Dussander had waited with his eyes closed to see what would happen, perfectly aware that if it came back as strongly as it had come upon him down there, he would probably die. Both times the pain had faded away again.

He crawled across the kitchen floor to the table, avoiding the pools and streaks of blood, which were now congealing. He got the bottle of Ancient Age, took a swallow, and closed his eyes. Something that had been cinched tight in his chest seemed to loosen a little. The pain faded a bit more. After another five minutes he began to work his way slowly down the hall. His telephone sat on a small table halfway down.

It was quarter past nine when the phone rang in the Bowden house. Todd was sitting cross-legged on the couch, going over his notes for the trig final. Trig was a bitch for him, as all maths were and probably always would be. His father was seated across the room, going through the chequebook stubs with a portable calculator on his lap and a mildly disbelieving expression on his face. Monica, closest to the phone, was watching the James Bond movie Todd had taped off HBC two evenings before.

'Hello?' She listened. A faint frown touched her face and she held the handset out to Todd. 'It's Mr Denker. He sounds excited about something. Or upset.'

Todd's heart leaped into his throat, but his expression hardly changed. 'Really?' He went to the phone and took it from her. 'Hi, Mr Denker.'

Dussander's voice was hoarse and short. 'Come over right away, boy. I've had a heart attack. Quite a bad one, I think.'

'Gee,' Todd said, trying to collect his flying thoughts, to see around the fear that now bulked huge in his own mind. 'That's interesting, all right, but it's pretty late and I was studying –'

'I understand that you cannot talk,' Dussander said in that harsh, almost barking voice. 'But you can listen. I cannot call an ambulance or dial 222, boy . . . at least not yet. There is a mess here. I need help . . . and that means *you* need help.'

'Well . . . if you put it that way . . .' Todd's heartbeat had reached a hundred and twenty beats a minute, but his face was calm, almost serene. Hadn't he known all along that a night like this would come? Yes, of course he had.

'Tell your parents I've had a letter,' Dussander said. 'An important letter. You understand?'

'Yeah, okay,' Todd said.

'Now we see, boy. We see what you are made of.'

'Sure,' Todd said. He suddenly became aware that his mother was watching him instead of the movie, and he forced a stiff grin onto his face. 'Bye.'

Dussander was saying something else now, but Todd hung up on it.

'I'm going over to Mr Denker's for a while,' he said, speaking to both of them but looking at his mother – that faint expression of concern was still on her face. 'Can I pick up anything for either of you at the store?'

'Pipe cleaners for me and a small package of fiscal responsibility for your mother,' Dick said.

'Very funny,' Monica said. 'Todd, is Mr Denker —'

'What in the name of *God* did you get at Fielding's?' Dick interrupted.

'That knick-knack shelf in the closet. I told you that. There's nothing wrong with Mr Denker, is there, Todd? He sounded a little strange.'

'There really *are* such things as knick-knack shelves? I thought those crazy women who write British mysteries made them up so there would always be a place where the killer could find a blunt instrument.'

'Dick, can I get a word in edgeways?'

'Sure. Be my guest. But for the *closet*?'

'He's okay, I guess,' Todd said. He put on his leather jacket and zipped it up. 'But he *was* excited. He got a letter from a nephew of his in Hamburg or Düsseldorf or someplace. He hasn't heard from any of his people in years, and now he's got this letter and his eyes aren't good enough for him to read it.'

'Well isn't that a *bitch*,' Dick said. 'Go on, Todd. Get over there and ease the man's mind.'

'I thought he had someone to read to him,' Monica said. 'A new boy.'

'He does,' Todd said, suddenly hating his mother, hating the half-formed intuition he saw swimming in her eyes. 'Maybe he wasn't home, or maybe he couldn't come over this late.'

'Oh. Well . . . go on, then. But be careful.'

'I will. You don't need anything at the store?'

'No. How's your studying for that calculus final going?'

'It's trig,' Todd said. 'Okay, I guess. I was just getting ready to call it a night.' This was a rather large lie.

'You want to take the Porsche?' Dick asked.

'No, I'll ride my bike.' He wanted the extra five minutes to collect his thoughts and get his emotions under control – to try, at least. And in his present state, he would probably drive the Porsche into a telephone pole.

'Strap your reflector-patch on your knee,' Monica said, 'and tell Mr Denker hello for us.'

'Okay.'

That doubt was still in his mother's eyes but it was less evident now. He blew her a kiss and then went out to the garage where his bike – a racing-style German bike rather than a Schwinn now – was parked. His heart was still racing in his chest, and he felt a mad urge to take the .30-.30 back into the house and shoot both of his parents and then go down to the slope overlooking the freeway. No more worrying about Dussander. No more bad dreams, no more winos. He would shoot and shoot and shoot, only saving one bullet back for the end.

Then reason came back to him and he rode away towards Dussander's, his reflector-patch revolving up and down just above his knee, his long blond hair streaming back from his brow.

'Holy *Christ*!' Todd nearly screamed.

He was standing in the kitchen door. Dussander was slumped on his elbows, his china cup between them. Large drops of sweat stood out on his forehead. But it was not Dussander Todd was looking at. It was the blood. There seemed to be blood everywhere – it was puddled on the table, on the empty kitchen chair, on the floor.

'Where are you bleeding?' Todd shouted, at last getting

his frozen feet to move again — it seemed to him that he had been standing in the doorway for at least a thousand years. *This is the end*, he was thinking, *this is the absolute end of everything. The balloon is going up high, baby, all the way to the sky, baby, and it's toot-toot-tootsie, goodbye.* All the same, he was careful not to step in any of the blood. 'I thought you said you had a fucking heart attack!'

'It's not my blood,' Dussander muttered.

'What?' Todd stopped. 'What did you say?'

'Go downstairs. You will see what has to be done.'

'What the hell *is* this?' Todd asked. A sudden terrible idea had come into his head.

'Don't waste our time, boy. I think you will not be too surprised at what you find downstairs. I think you have had experience in such matters as the one in my cellar. First-hand experience.'

Todd looked at him, unbelieving, for another moment, and then he plunged down the cellar stairs two by two. His first look in the feeble yellow glow of the basement's only light made him think that Dussander had pushed a bag of garbage down there. Then he saw the protruding legs, and the dirty hands held down at the sides by the cinched belt.

'Holy Christ,' he repeated, but this time the words had no force at all — they emerged in a slight, skeletal whisper.

He pressed the back of his right hand against lips that were as dry as sandpaper. He closed his eyes for a moment . . . and when he opened them again, he felt in control of himself at last.

Todd started moving.

He saw the spade-handle protruding from a shallow hole in the far corner and understood at once what Dussander had being doing when his ticker had seized up. A moment later he became fully aware of the cellar's fetid aroma – a smell like rotting tomatoes. He had smelled it before, but upstairs it was much fainter . . . and, of course, he hadn't been here very often over the last couple of years. Now he understood *exactly* what that smell meant and for several moments he had to struggle with his gorge. A series of choked gagging sounds, muffled by the hand he had clapped over his mouth and nose, came from him.

Little by little he got control of himself again.

He seized the wino's legs and dragged him across to the edge of the hole. He dropped them, skidded sweat from his forehead with the heel of his left hand, and stood absolutely still for a moment, thinking harder than he ever had in his life.

Then he seized the spade and began to deepen the hole. When it was five feet deep, he got out and shoved the derelict's body in with his foot. Todd stood at the edge of the grave, looking down. Tattered bluejeans. Filthy, scab-encrusted hands. It was a stewbum, all right. The irony was almost funny. So funny a person could scream with laughter.

He ran back upstairs.

'How are you?' he asked Dussander.

'I'll be all right. Have you taken care of it?'

'I'm doing it, okay?'

'Be quick. There's still up here.'

'I'd like to find some pigs and feed you to them,' Todd said, and went back down the cellar before Dussander could reply.

He had almost completely covered the wino when he began to think there was something wrong. He stared into the grave, grasping the spade's handle with one hand. The wino's legs stuck partway out of the mound of dirt, as did the tips of his feet — one old shoe, possibly a Hush Puppy, and one filthy athletic sock that might actually have been white around the time that Taft was President.

One Hush Puppy? *One?*

Todd half-ran back around the furnace to the foot of the stairs. He glanced around wildly. A headache was beginning to thud against his temples, dull drillbits trying to work their way out. He spotted the old shoe five feet away, overturned in the shadow of some abandoned shelving. Todd grabbed it, ran back to the grave with it, and threw it in. Then he started to shovel again. He covered the shoe, the legs, everything.

When all the dirt was back in the hole, he slammed the spade down repeatedly to tamp it. Then he grabbed the rake and ran it back and forth, trying to disguise the fact the earth here had been recently turned. Not much use; without good camouflage, a hole that has been recently dug and then filled in always looks like a hole that has been recently dug and then filled in. Still, no one would have any occasion to come down here, would they? He and Dussander would damn well have to hope not.

Todd ran back upstairs. He was starting to pant.

Dussander's elbows had spread wide and his head had sagged down to the table. His eyes were closed, the lids a shiny purple — the colour of asters.

'Dussander!' Todd shouted. There was a hot, juicy taste in his mouth — the taste of fear mixed with adrenalin and pulsing hot blood. 'Don't you *dare* die on me, you old fuck!'

'Keep your voice down,' Dussander said without opening his eyes. 'You'll have everyone on the block over here.'

'Where's your cleaner? Lestoil . . . Top Job . . . something like that. And rags. I need rags.'

'All that is under the sink.'

A lot of the blood had now dried on. Dussander raised his head and watched as Todd crawled across the floor, scrubbing first at the puddle on the linoleum and then at the drips that had straggled down the legs of the chair the wino had been sitting in. The boy was biting compulsively at his lips, champing at them, almost, like a horse at a bit. At last the job was finished. The astringent smell of cleaner filled the room.

'There is a box of old rags under the stairs,' Dussander said. 'Put those bloody ones on the bottom. Don't forget to wash your hands.'

'I don't need your advice. You got me into this.'

'Did I? I must say you took hold well.' For a moment the old mockery was in Dussander's voice, and then a bitter grimace pulled his face into a new shape. 'Hurry.'

Todd took care of the rags, then hurried up the cellar stairs for the last time. He looked nervously down the stairs for a moment, then snapped off the light and closed the door. He went to the sink, rolled up his sleeves, and washed in the hottest water he could stand. He plunged his hands into the suds . . . and came up holding the butcher knife Dussander had used.

'I'd like to cut your throat with this,' Todd said grimly.

'Yes, and then feed me to the pigs. I have no doubt of it.'

Todd rinsed the knife, dried it, and put it away. He did the rest of the dishes quickly, let the water out, and rinsed the sink. He looked at the clock as he dried his hands and saw it was twenty past ten.

He went to the phone in the hallway, picked up the

receiver, and looked at it thoughtfully. The idea that he had forgotten something – something as potentially damning as the wino's shoe – nagged unpleasantly at his mind. What? He didn't know. If not for the headache, he might be able to get it. The triple-damned headache. It wasn't like him to forget things, and it was scary.

He dialled 222 and after a single ring, a voice answered: 'This is Santa Donato MED-Q. Do you have a medical problem?'

'My name is Todd Bowden. I'm at 963 Claremont Lane. I need an ambulance.'

'What's the problem, son?'

'It's my friend, Mr D–' He bit down on his lip so hard that it squirted blood, and for a moment he was lost, drowning in the pulses of pain from his head. *Dussander.* He had almost given this anonymous MED-Q voice Dussander's real name.

'Calm down, son,' the voice said. 'Take it slow and you'll be fine.'

'My friend Mr Denker,' Todd said. 'I think he's had a heart attack.'

'His symptoms?'

Todd began to give them, but the receptionist had heard enough as soon as Todd described the chest pain that had migrated to the left arm. He told Todd the ambulance would arrive in ten to twenty minutes, depending on the traffic. Todd hung up and pressed the heels of his hands against his eyes.

'Did you get it?' Dussander called weakly.

'*Yes!*' Todd screamed. '*Yes, I got it! Yes goddammit yes! Yes yes yes! Just shut up!*'

He pressed his hands even harder against his eyes, creating

first senseless starflashes of light and then a bright field of red. *Get hold of yourself, Todd-baby. Get down, get funky, get cool. Dig it.*

He opened his eyes and picked up the telephone again. Now the hard part. Now it was time to call home.

'Hello?' Monica's soft, cultured voice in his ear. For a moment – just a moment – he saw himself slamming the muzzle of the .30-.30 into her nose and pulling the trigger into the first flow of blood.

'It's Todd, mommy. Let me talk to dad, quick.'

He didn't call her mommy anymore. He knew she would get that signal quicker than anything else, and she did. 'What's the matter? Is something wrong, Todd?'

'Just let me talk to him!'

'But what –'

The phone rattled and clinked. He heard his mother saying something to his father. Todd got ready.

'Todd? What's the problem?'

'It's Mr Denker, daddy. He . . . it's a heart attack, I think. I'm pretty sure it is.'

'Jesus!' His father's voice lagged away for a moment and Todd heard him repeating the information to his wife. Then he was back. 'He's still alive? As far as you can tell?'

'He's alive. Conscious.'

'All right, thank God for that. Call an ambulance.'

'I just did.'

'222?'

'Yes.'

'Good boy. How bad is he, can you tell?'

(not fucking bad enough!)

'I don't know, dad. They said the ambulance would be

here soon, but . . . I'm sorta scared. Can you come over and wait with me?'

'You bet. Give me four minutes.'

Todd could hear his mother saying something else as his father hung up, breaking the connection. Todd replaced the receiver on his end.

Four minutes.

Four minutes to do anything that had been left undone. Four minutes to remember whatever it was that had been forgotten. Or *had* he forgotten anything? Maybe it was just nerves. God, he wished he hadn't had to call his father. But it was the natural thing to do, wasn't it? Sure. Was there some natural thing that he *hadn't* done? Something –?

'Oh, you shit-for-brains!' he suddenly moaned, and bolted back into the kitchen. Dussander's head lay on the table, his eyes half-open, sluggish.

'Dussander!' Todd cried. He shook Dussander roughly, and the old man groaned. 'Wake up! Wake up, you stinking old bastard!'

'What? Is it the ambulance?'

'The letter! My father is coming over, he'll be here in no time. *Where's the fucking letter?*'

'What . . . what letter?'

'You told me to tell them you got an important letter. I said . . .' His heart sank. 'I said it came from overseas . . . from Germany. Christ!' Todd ran his hands through his hair.

'A letter.' Dussander raised his head with slow difficulty. His seamed cheeks were an unhealthy yellowish-white, his lips blue. 'From Willi, I think. Willi Frankel. Dear . . . dear Willi.'

Todd looked at his watch and saw that already two minutes had passed since he had hung up the phone. His father would not, *could* not make it from their house to Dussander's in four minutes, but he could do it damn fast in the Porsche. Fast, that was it. Everything was moving too fast. And there was still something wrong here; he *felt* it. But there was no time to stop and hunt around for the loophole.

'Yes, okay, I was reading it to you, and you got excited and had this heart attack. Good. Where is it?'

Dussander looked at him blankly.

'The letter! Where is it?'

'What letter?' Dussander asked vacantly, and Todd's hands itched to throttle the drunken old monster.

'The one I was reading to you! The one from Willi What's-his-face! Where is it?'

They both looked at the table, as if expecting to see the letter materialize there.

'Upstairs,' Dussander said finally. 'Look in my dresser. The third drawer. There is a small wooden box in the bottom of that drawer. You will have to break it open. I lost the key a long time ago. There are some very old letters from a friend of mine. None signed. None dated. All in German. A page or two will serve for window-fittings, as you would say. If your hurry —'

'Are you *crazy*?' Todd raged. 'I don't understand German! How could I read you a letter written in German, you numb fuck?'

'Why would Willi write me in English?' Dussander countered wearily. 'If you read me the letter in German, *I* would understand it even if *you* did not. Of course your pronunciation would be butchery, but still, I could —'

Dussander was right — right again, and Todd didn't wait to hear more. Even after a heart attack the old man was a step ahead. Todd raced down the hall to the stairs, pausing just long enough by the front door to make sure his father's Porsche wasn't pulling up even now. It wasn't, but Todd's watch told him just how tight things were getting; it had been five minutes now.

He took the stairs two at a time and burst into Dussander's bedroom. He had never been up here before, hadn't even been curious, and for a moment he only looked wildly around at the unfamiliar territory. Then he saw the dresser, a cheap item done in the style his father called Discount Store Modern. He fell on his knees in front of it and yanked at the third drawer. It came halfway out, then jigged sideways in its slot and stuck firmly.

'Goddam you,' he whispered at it. His face was dead pale except for the spots of dark, bloody colour flaring in each cheek and his blue eyes, which looked as dark as Atlantic storm-clouds. 'Goddam you fucking thing come *out*!'

He yanked so hard that the entire dresser tottered forward and almost fell on him before deciding to settle back. The drawer shot all the way out and landed in Todd's lap. Dussander's socks and underwear and handkerchiefs spilled out all around him. He pawed through the stuff that was still in the drawer and came up with a wooden box about nine inches long and three inches deep. He tried to pull up the lid. Nothing happened. It was locked, just as Dussander had said. Nothing was free tonight.

He stuffed the spilled clothes back into the drawer and then rammed the drawer back into its oblong slot. It stuck again. Todd worked to free it, wiggling it back and forth, sweat running freely down his face. At last he was able to slam it shut. He got up with the box. How much time had passed now?

Dussander's bed was the type with posts at the foot and Todd brought the lock side of the box down on one of these posts as hard as he could, grinning at the shock of pain that vibrated in his hands and travelled all the way up to his elbows. He looked at the lock. The lock looked a bit dented, but it was intact. He brought it down on the post again, even harder this time, heedless of the pain. This time a chunk of wood flew off the bedpost, but the lock still didn't give. Todd uttered a little shriek of laughter and took the box to the other end of the bed. He raised it high over his head this time and brought it down with all his strength. This time the lock splintered.

As he flipped the lid up, headlights splashed across Dussander's window.

He pawed wildly through the box. Postcards. A locket. A much-folded picture of a woman wearing frilly black garters and nothing else. An old billfold. Several sets of ID. An empty leather passport folder. At the bottom, letters.

The lights grew brighter, and now he heard the distinctive beat of the Porsche's engine. It grew louder . . . and then cut off.

Todd grabbed three sheets of airmail-type stationery, closely written in German on both sides of each sheet, and ran out of the room again. He had almost gotten to the stairs when he realized he had left the forced box lying on Dussander's bed. He ran back, grabbed it, and opened the third dresser drawer.

It stuck again, this time with a firm shriek of wood against wood.

Out front, he heard the ratchet of the Porsche's emergency brake, the opening of the driver's side door, the slam shut.

Faintly, Todd could hear himself moaning. He put the box in the askew drawer, stood up, and lashed at it with his foot. The drawer closed neatly. He stood blinking at it for a moment and then fled back down the hall. He raced down the stairs. Halfway down them, he heard the rapid rattle of his father's shoes on Dussander's walk. Todd vaulted over the banister, landed lightly, and ran into the kitchen, the airmail pages fluttering from his hand.

A hammering on the door. 'Todd? Todd, it's me!'

And he could hear an ambulance siren in the distance as well. Dussander had drifted away into semi-consciousness again.

'Coming, dad!' Todd shouted.

He put the airmail pages on the table, fanning them a little as if they had been dropped in a hurry, and then he went back down the hall and let his father in.

'Where is he?' Dick Bowden asked, shouldering past Todd.

'In the kitchen.'

'You did everything just right, Todd,' his father said, and then hugged him in a rough, embarrassed way.

'I just hope I remembered everything,' Todd said modestly, and then followed his father down the hall and into the kitchen.

In the rush to get Dussander out of the house, the letter was almost completely ignored. Todd's father picked it up briefly, then put it down when the medics came in with the stretcher. Todd and his father followed the ambulance, and his explanation of what had happened was accepted without question by the doctor attending Dussander's case. 'Mr Denker' was, after all, seventy-nine years old, and his habits were not the best. The doctor also offered Todd a brusque commendation for his quick thinking and action. Todd thanked him wanly and then asked his father if they could go home.

As they rode back, Dick told him again how proud of him he was. Todd barely heard him. He was thinking about his .30–.30 again.

18

That was the same day Morris Heisel broke his back.

Morris had never *intended* to break his back; all he had *intended* to do was nail up the corner of the rain-gutter on the west side of his house. Breaking his back was the furthest thing from his mind, he had had enough grief in his life without that, thank you very much. His first wife had died at the age of twenty-five, and both of their daughters were also dead. His brother was dead, killed in a tragic car accident not far from Disneyland in 1971. Morris himself was nearing sixty, and had a case of arthritis that was worsening early and fast. He also had warts on both hands, warts that seemed to grow back as fast as the doctor could burn them off. He was *also* prone to migraine headaches, and in the last couple of years, that *potzer* Rogan next door had taken to calling him 'Morris the Cat'. Morris had wondered aloud to Lydia, his second wife, how Rogan would like it if Morris took up calling him 'Rogan the haemorrhoid'.

'Quit it, Morris,' Lydia said on these occasions. 'You can't take a joke, you never *could* take a joke, sometimes I wonder how I could marry a man with absolutely *no* sense of humour. We go to Las Vegas,' Lydia had said, addressing the empty kitchen as if an invisible horde of spectators which only she could see was standing there, 'we see Buddy Hackett, and Morris doesn't laugh *once*.'

Besides arthritis, warts, and migraines, Morris also had Lydia, who, God love her, had developed into something of a nag over the last five years or so . . . ever since her hysterectomy. So he had plenty of sorrows and plenty of problems without adding a broken back.

'*Morris!*' Lydia cried, coming to the back door and wiping suds from her hands with a dishtowel. 'Morris, you come down off that ladder right now!'

'What?' He twisted his head so he could see her. He was on the second-highest step of his aluminium stepladder. There was a bright yellow sticker on this step which said: DANGER! BALANCE MAY SHIFT WITHOUT WARNING ABOVE THIS STEP! Morris was wearing his carpenter's apron with the wide pockets, one of the pockets filled with nails and the other filled with heavy-duty staples. The ground under the stepladder's feet was slightly uneven and the ladder rocked a little when he moved. His neck ached with the unlovely prelude to one of his migraines. He was out of temper. '*What?*'

'Come down from there, I said, before you break your back.'

'I'm almost finished.'

'You're rocking on that ladder like you were on a boat, Morris. Come down.'

'I'll come down when I'm done!' he said angrily. 'Leave me alone!'

'You'll break your back,' she reiterated dolefully, and went into the house again.

Ten minutes later, as he was hammering the last nail into the rain-gutter, tipped back nearly to the point of overbalancing, he heard a feline yowl followed by fierce barking.

'What in God's name —?'

He looked around and the stepladder rocked alarmingly. At that same moment, their cat — it was named Lover Boy, *not* Morris — tore around the corner of the garage, its fur bushed out into hackles and its green eyes flaring. The Rogans' collie pup was in hot pursuit, its tongue hanging out and its leash dragging behind it.

Lover Boy, apparently not superstitious, ran under the stepladder. The collie pup followed.

'Look out, look out, you dumb mutt!' Morris shouted.

The ladder rocked. The pup bunted it with the side of its body. The ladder tipped over and Morris tipped with it, uttering a howl of dismay. Nails and staples flew out of his carpenter's apron. He landed half on and half off the concrete driveway, and a gigantic agony flared in his back. He did not so much hear his spine snap as feel it happen. Then the world greyed out for awhile.

When things swam back into focus, he was still lying half on and half off the driveway in a litter of nails and staples. Lydia was kneeling over him, weeping. Rogan from next door was there, too, his face as white as a shroud.

'I told you!' Lydia babbled. 'I told you to come down off that ladder! Now look! Now look at this!'

Morris found he had absolutely no desire to look. A suffocating, throbbing band of pain had cinched itself around his middle like a belt, and that was bad, but there was something much worse: he could feel nothing below that belt of pain — nothing at all.

'Wail later,' he said huskily. 'Call the doctor now.'

'I'll do it,' Rogan said, and ran back to his own house.

'Lydia,' Morris said. He wet his lips.

'What? What, Morris?' She bent over him and a tear splashed on his cheek. It was touching, he supposed, but it had made him flinch, and the flinch had made the pain worse.

'Lydia, I also have one of my migraines.'

'Oh, poor darling! Poor Morris! But I *told* you –'

'I've got the headache because that *potzer* Rogan's dog barked all night and kept me awake. Today the dog chases my cat and knocks over my ladder and I think my back is broken.'

Lydia shrieked. The sound made Morris's head vibrate.

'Lydia,' he said, and wet his lips again.

'What, darling?'

'I have suspected something for many years. Now I am sure.'

'My poor Morris! What?'

'There is no God,' Morris said, and fainted.

They took him to Santa Donato and his doctor told him, at about the same time that he would have ordinarily been sitting down to one of Lydia's wretched suppers, that he would never walk again. By then they had put him in a body cast. Blood and urine samples had been taken. Dr Kemmelman had peered into his eyes and tapped his knees with a little rubber hammer – but no reflexive twitch of the foot answered the taps. And at every turn there was Lydia, the tears streaming from her eyes, as she used up one handkerchief after another. Lydia, a woman who would have been at home married to Job, went everywhere well supplied with little lace snotrags, just in case reason for an extended crying spell should occur. She had called her mother, and her mother would be here soon ('That's nice, Lydia' – although if there was anyone on earth Morris honestly loathed, it was Lydia's mother). She had called the rabbi, he would be here soon, too ('That's nice, Lydia' – although he hadn't set foot inside the synagogue in five years and wasn't sure what the rabbi's name was). She had called his boss, and while he wouldn't be here soon, he sent his greatest sympathies and condolences ('That's nice, Lydia' – although if there was anyone in a class with Lydia's mother, it was that cigar-chewing *putz* Frank Haskell). At last they gave Morris a Valium and took Lydia away. Shortly afterwards, Morris just drifted away – no worries, no migraine, no nothing. If they kept giving him little blue pills like that, went his last thought, he would go on up that stepladder and break his back again.

When he woke up – or regained consciousness, that was more like it – dawn was just breaking, and the hospital was as quiet as Morris supposed it ever got. He felt very calm . . . almost serene. He had no pain; his body felt swaddled and weightless. His bed had been surrounded by some sort of contraption like a squirrel cage – a thing of stainless steel bars, guy wires, and pulleys. His legs were being held up by cables attached to this gadget. His back seemed to be bowed by something beneath, but it was hard to tell – he had only the angle of his vision to judge by.

Others have it worse, he thought. *All over the world, others have it worse. In Israel, the Palestinians kill busloads of farmers who were committing the political crime of going into town to see a movie. The Israelis cope with this injustice by dropping bombs on the Palestinians and killing children along with whatever terrorists may be there. Others have it worse than me . . . which is not to say this is* good, *don't get that idea, but others have it worse.*

He lifted one hand with some effort – there was pain somewhere in his body, but it was very faint – and made a weak fist in front of his eyes. There. Nothing wrong with his hands. Nothing wrong with his arms, either. So he couldn't feel anything below the waist, so what? There were people all over the world paralyzed from the *neck* down. There were people with leprosy. There were people dying of syphilis. Somewhere in the world right now, there might be people walking down the jetway and onto a plane that was going to crash. No, this wasn't good, but there were worse things in the world.

And there had been, once upon a time, *much* worse things in the world.

He raised his left arm. It seemed to float, disembodied, before his eyes – a scrawny old man's arm with the muscles deteriorating. He was in a hospital johnny but it had short sleeves and he could still read the number on the forearm, tattooed there in faded blue ink. A499965214. Worse things, yes, worse things than falling off a suburban stepladder and breaking your back and being taken to a clean and sterile metropolitan hospital and being given a Valium that was guaranteed to bubble your troubles away.

There were the showers, they were worse. His first wife, Heather, had died in one of their filthy showers. There were the trenches that became graves – he could close his eyes and still see the men lined up along the open maw of the trenches, could still hear the volley of rifle fire, could still remember the way they flopped backwards into the earth like badly made puppets. There were the crematoriums, they were worse, too, the crematoriums that filled the air with the steady sweet smell of Jews burning like torches no one could see. The horror-struck faces of old friends and relatives . . . faces that melted away like guttering candles, faces that seemed to melt away *before your very eyes* – thin, thinner, thinnest. Then one day they were gone. Where? Where does a torch-flame go when the cold wind has blown it out? Heaven? Hell? Lights in the darkness, candles in the wind. When Job finally broke down and questioned, God asked him: *Where were you when I made the world?* If Morris Heisel had been Job, he would have responded: *Where were You when my Heather was dying, You potzer, You? Watching the Yankees and the Senators? If You can't pay attention to Your business better than this, get out of my face.*

Yes, there were worse things than breaking your back, he had no doubt of it. But what sort of God would have allowed him to break his back and become paralyzed for life after watching his wife die, and his daughters, and his friends?

No God at all, that was Who.

A tear trickled from the corner of his ear. Outside the hospital room, a bell rang softly. A nurse squeaked by on white crêpe-soled shoes. His door was ajar, and on the far wall of the corridor outside he could read the letters NSIVE CA and guessed that the whole sign must read INTEN-SIVE CARE.

There was movement in the room – a rustle of bedclothes.

Moving very carefully, Morris turned his head to the right, away from the door. He saw a night-table next to him with a pitcher of water on it. There were two call-buttons on the table. Beyond it was another bed, and in the bed was a man who looked even older and sicker than Morris felt.

He was not hooked into a giant exercise-wheel for gerbils like Morris was, but an IV feed stood beside his bed and some sort of monitoring console stood at its foot. The man's skin was sunken and yellow. Lines around his mouth and eyes had driven deep. His hair was yellowish-white, dry and life-less. His thin eyelids had a bruised and shiny look, and in his big nose Morris saw the burst capillaries of the life-long drinker.

Morris looked away . . . and then looked back. As the dawn light grew stronger and the hospital began to wake up, he began to have the strangest feeling that he knew his roommate. Could that be? The man looked to be some-where between seventy-five and eighty, and Morris didn't believe he knew anyone quite that old – except for Lydia's mother, a horror Morris sometimes believed to be older than the Sphinx, whom the woman closely resembled.

Maybe the guy was someone he had known in the past, maybe even before he, Morris, came to America. Maybe. Maybe not. And why all of a sudden did it seem to matter? For that matter, why had all his memories of the camp, of Patin, come flooding back tonight, when he always tried to – and most times succeeded in – keeping those things buried?

He broke out in a sudden rash of gooseflesh, as if he had stepped into some mental haunted house where old bodies were unquiet and old ghosts walked. Could that be, even here and now in this clean hospital, thirty years after those dark times had ended?

He looked away from the old man in the other bed, and soon he had begun to feel sleepy again.

It's a trick of your mind that this other man seems familiar.

Only your mind, amusing you in the best way it can, amusing you the way it used to try to amuse you in –

But he would not think of that. He would not *allow* himself to think of that.

Drifting into sleep, he thought of a boast he had made to Heather (but never to Lydia; it didn't pay to boast to Lydia; she was not like Heather, who would always smile sweetly at his harmless puffing and crowing): *I never forget a face.* Here was his chance to find out if that was still so. If he had really known the man in the other bed at some time or other, perhaps he could remember when . . . and where.

Very close to sleep, drifting back and forth across its threshold, Morris thought: *Perhaps I knew him in the camp.*

That would be ironic indeed – what they called 'a jest of God'.

What God? Morris Heisel asked himself again, and slept.

19

Todd graduated salutatorian of his class, just possibly because of his poor grade on the trig final he had been studying for the night Dussander had his heart attack. It dragged his final grade in the course down to 91, one point below A- average.

A week after graduation, the Bowdens went to visit Mr Denker at Santa Donato General. Todd fidgeted through fifteen minutes of banalities and thank-yous and how-do-you-feels and was grateful for the break when the man in the other bed asked him if he could come over for a minute.

'You'll pardon me,' the other man said apologetically. He was in a huge body cast and was for some reason attached to an overhead system of pulleys and wires. 'My name is Morris Heisel. I broke my back.'

'That's too bad,' Todd said gravely.

'*Oy*, too bad, he says! This boy has the gift of understatement!'

Todd started to apologize, but Heisel raised his hand, smiling a little. His face was pale and tired, the face of any old man in the hospital facing a life full of sweeping changes just ahead – and surely few of them for the better. In that way, Todd thought, he and Dussander were alike.

'No need,' Morris said. 'No need to answer a rude comment. You are a stranger. Does a stranger need to be inflicted with my problems?'

'"No man is an island, separate from the main –"' Todd began, and Morris laughed.

'Donne, he quotes at me! A smart kid! Your friend there, is he very bad off?'

'Well, the doctors say he's doing fine, considering his age. He's seventy-nine.'

'That old!' Morris exclaimed. 'He doesn't talk to me much, you know. But from what he does say, I'd guess he's naturalized. Like me. I'm Polish, you know. Originally, I mean. From Raden.'

'Oh?' Todd said politely.

'Yes. You know what they call an orange manhole cover in Radan?'

'No,' Todd said, smiling.

'Howard Johnson's,' Morris said, and laughed. Todd laughed, too. Dussander glanced over at them, startled by the sound and frowning a little. Then Monica said something and he looked back at her again.

'*Is* your friend naturalized?'

'Oh, yes,' Todd said. 'He's from Germany. Essen. Do you know that town?'

'No,' Morris said, 'but I was only in Germany once. I wonder if he was in the war.'

'I really couldn't say.' Todd's eyes had gone distant.

'No? Well, it doesn't matter. That was a long time ago, the war. In another two years there will be people in this country constitutionally eligible to become President – President! – who weren't even born until after the war was over. To them it must seem there is no difference between the Miracle of Dunkirk and Hannibal taking his elephants over the Alps.'

'Were you in the war?' Todd asked.

'I suppose I was, in a manner of speaking. You're a good boy to visit such an old man . . . two old men, counting me.'

Todd smiled modestly.

'I'm tired now,' Morris said. 'Perhaps I'll sleep.'

'I hope you'll feel better very soon,' Todd said.

Morris nodded, smiled, and closed his eyes. Todd went back to Dussander's bed, where his parents were just getting ready to leave – his dad kept glancing at his watch and exclaiming with bluff heartiness at how late it was getting. But Morris Heisel wasn't asleep, and he didn't sleep – not for a long time.

Two days later, Todd came back to the hospital alone. This time, Morris Heisel, immured in his body-cast, was deeply asleep in the other bed.

'You did well,' Dussander said quietly. 'Did you go back to the house later?'

'Yes. I put the box back and burned the damned letter. I don't think anyone was too interested in that letter, and I was afraid . . . I don't know.' He shrugged, unable to tell Dussander he'd been almost superstitiously afraid about that letter – afraid that maybe someone would wander into the house who could read German, someone who would notice references in the letter that were ten, perhaps twenty years out of date.

'Next time you come, smuggle me in something to drink,' Dussander said. 'I find I don't miss the cigarettes, but –'

'I won't be back again,' Todd said flatly. 'Not ever. It's the end. We're quits.'

'Quits.' Dussander folded his hands on his chest and smiled. It was not a gentle smile . . . but it was perhaps as close as Dussander could come to such a thing. 'I thought that was on the cards. They are going to let me out of this grave-yard next week . . . or so they promise. The doctor says I may have a few years left in my skin yet. I ask him how many, and he just laughs. I suspect that means no more than three, and probably no more than two. Still, I may give him a surprise and see in Orwell's year.'

Todd, who would have frowned suspiciously over such a reference two years ago, now only nodded.

'But between you and me, boy, I have almost given up my hopes of seeing the century turn.'

'I want to ask you about something,' Todd said, looking at Dussander steadily. 'That's why I came in today. I want to ask you about something you said once.'

Todd glanced over his shoulder at the man in the other bed and then drew his chair closer to Dussander's bed. He could smell Dussander's smell, as dry as the Egyptian room in the museum.

'So ask.'

'That wino. You said something about me having experience. First-hand experience. What was that supposed to mean?'

Dussander's smile widened a bit. 'I read the newspapers, boy. Old men always read the newspapers, but not in the same way younger people do. Buzzards are known to gather at the ends of certain airport runways in South America when the crosswinds are treacherous, did you know that? That is how an old man reads the newspaper. A month ago there was a story in the Sunday paper. Not a front page story, no one cares enough about bums and alcoholics to put them on the front page, but it was the lead story in the feature section, IS SOMEONE STALKING SANTA DONATO'S DOWN-AND-OUTS? – that's what it was called. Crude. Yellow journalism. You Americans are famous for it.'

Todd's hands were clenched into fists, hiding the butchered nails. He never read the Sunday papers, he had better things to do with his time. He had of course checked the papers every day for at least a week following each of his little adventures, and none of his stewbums had ever gotten beyond page three. The idea that someone had been making connections behind his back infuriated him.

'The story mentioned several murders, extremely brutal murders. Stabbings, bludgeonings. "Subhuman brutality" was how the writer put it, but you know reporters. The writer of this lamentable piece admitted that there is a high death-rate among these unfortunates, and that Santa Donato has had more than its share of the indigent over the years. In any given year, not all of these men die naturally, or of their

310

own bad habits. There are frequent murders. But in most cases the murderer is usually one of the deceased degenerate's compatriots, the motive no more than an argument over a penny-ante card-game or a bottle of muscatel. The killer is usually happy to confess. He is filled with remorse.

'But these recent killings have not been solved. Even more ominous, to this yellow journalist's mind – or whatever passes for his mind – is the high disappearance rate over the last few years. Of course, he admits again, these men are not much more than modern-day hobos. They come and go. But some of these left without picking up welfare cheques or day-labour cheques from Spell O'Work, which only pays on Fridays. Could some of these have been victims of this yellow journalist's Wino Killer, he asks? Victims who haven't been found? *Pah!*'

Dussander waved his hand in the air as if to dismiss such arrant irresponsibility.

'Only titillation, of course. Give people a comfortable little scare on Sunday morning. He calls up old bogies, threadbare but still useful – the Cleveland Torso Murderer, Zodiac, the mysterious Mr X who killed the Black Dahlia, Springheel Jack. Such drivel. But it makes me think. What does an old man have to do but think when old friends don't come to visit anymore?'

Todd shrugged.

'I thought: "If I wished to help this odious yellow-dog journalist, which I certainly do *not*, I could explain some of the disappearances. Not the corpses found stabbed or bludgeoned, not *them*, God rest their besotted souls, but some of the disappearances. Because at least some of the bums who disappeared are in my cellar."'

'How many down there?' Todd asked in a low voice.

'Five,' Dussander said calmly. 'Counting the one you helped me dispose of, just five.'

'You're really nutso,' Todd said. The skin below his eyes had gone white and shiny. 'At some point you just blew all your fucking wheels.'

'"Blew my wheels." What a charming idiom! Perhaps you're right! But then I said to myself: "This newspaper jackal would love to pin the murders and the disappearances on the same somebody – his hypothetical Wino Killer. But I think maybe that's not what happened at all."

'Then I say to myself: "Do I know anybody who might be doing such things? Somebody who has been under as much strain as I have during the last few years? Someone who has also been listening to old ghosts rattle their chains?" And the answer is yes. I know *you*, boy.'

'I've never killed anyone.'

The image that came was not of the winos; they weren't people, not really people at all. The image that came was of himself crouched behind the dead tree, peering through the telescopic sight of his .30–.30, the crosshairs fixed on the temple of the man with the scuzzy beard, the man driving the Brat pick-up.

'Perhaps not,' Dussander agreed, amicably enough. 'Yet you took hold so well the other night. Your surprise was mostly anger at having been put in such a dangerous position by an old man's infirmity, I think. Am I wrong?'

'No, you're not wrong,' Todd said. 'I was pissed off at you, and I still am. I covered it up for you because you've got something in a safety deposit box that could destroy my life.'

'No. I do not.'

'What? What are you talking about?'

'It was as much a bluff as your "letter left with a friend". You never wrote such a letter, there never was such a friend, and I have never written a single word about our . . . association, shall I call it? Now I lay my cards on the table. You saved my life. Never mind that you acted only to protect yourself; that does not change how speedily and efficiently you acted. I cannot hurt you, boy. I tell you that freely. I have looked death in the face and it frightens me, but not as badly as I thought it would. There is no document. It is as you say: we are quits.'

Todd smiled: a weird upward corkscrewing of the lips. A strange, sardonic light danced and fluttered in his eyes.

'Herr Dussander,' he said, 'if only I could believe that.'

In the evening Todd walked down to the slope overlooking the freeway, climbed down to the dead tree, and sat on it. It was just past twilight. The evening was warm. Car headlights cut through the dusk in long yellow daisy chains.

There is no document.

He hadn't realized how completely irretrievable the entire situation was until the discussion that had followed. Dussander suggested Todd search the house for a safety deposit key, and when he didn't find one, that would prove there was no safety deposit box and hence no document. But a key could be hidden anywhere — it could be put in a Crisco can and then buried, it could be put in a Sucrets tin and slid behind a board that had been loosened and then replaced; he might even have ridden the bus to San Diego and put it behind one of the rocks in the decorative stone wall which surrounds the bears' environmental area. For that matter, Todd went on, Dussander could even have thrown the key away. Why not? He had only needed it once, to put his written document in. If he died, someone else would take it out.

Dussander nodded reluctantly at this, but after a moment's thought he made another suggestion. When he got well enough to go home, he would have the boy call every single bank in Santa Donato. He would tell each bank official he was calling for his grandfather. Poor grandfather, he would say, had grown lamentably senile over the last two years, and now he had misplaced the key to his safety deposit box. Even worse, he could no longer remember which bank the box was in. Could they just check their files for an Arthur Denker, no middle initial? And when Todd drew a blank at every bank in town –

Todd was already shaking his head again. First, a story like that was almost guaranteed to raise suspicions. It was too pat. They would probably suspect a con-game and get in touch with the police. Even if every one of them bought the story, it would do no good. If none of the almost nine dozen banks in Santa Donato had a box in the Denker name, it didn't mean that Dussander hadn't rented one in San Diego, LA, or any town in between.

At last Dussander gave up.

'You have all the answers, boy. All, at least, but one. What would I stand to gain by lying to you? I invented this story to protect myself from you – that is a motive. Now I am trying to uninvent it. What possible gain do you see in that?'

Dussander got laboriously up on one elbow.

'For that matter, why would I need a document at all, at this point? I could destroy your life from this hospital bed, if that was what I wanted. I could open my mouth to the first passing doctor, they are all Jews, they would all know who I am, or at least who I was. But why would I do this? You are a fine student. You have a fine career ahead of you . . . unless you get careless with those winos of yours.'

Todd's face froze. 'I never told you –'

'I know. You never heard of them, you never touched so much as a hair on their scaly, tick-ridden heads, all right, good, fine. I say no more about it. Only tell me, boy: why should I lie about this? We are quits, you say. But I tell you we can only be quits if we can trust each other.'

Now, sitting behind the dead tree on the slope which ran down to the freeway, looking at all the anonymous head-lights disappearing endlessly like slow tracer bullets, he knew well enough what he was afraid of.

Dussander talking about trust. That made him afraid.

The idea that Dussander might be tending a small but perfect flame of hatred deep in his heart, that made him afraid, too.

A hatred of Todd Bowden, who was young, clean-featured, unwrinkled; Todd Bowden, who was an apt pupil with a whole bright life stretching ahead of him.

But what he feared most was Dussander's refusal to use his name.

Todd. What was so hard about that, even for an old Kraut whose teeth were mostly false? *Todd*. One syllable. Easy to say. Put your tongue against the roof of your mouth, drop your teeth a little, replace your tongue, and it was out. Yet Dussander had always called him 'boy'. Only that. Contemptuous. *Anonymous.* Yes, that was it, anonymous. As anonymous as a concentration camp serial number.

Perhaps Dussander *was* telling the truth. No, not just perhaps; *probably.* But there were those fears . . . the worst of them being Dussander's refusal to use his name.

And at the root of it all was his own inability to make a hard and final decision. At the root of it all was a rueful truth: even after four years of visiting Dussander, he still didn't know what went on in the old man's head. Perhaps he wasn't such an apt pupil after all.

Cars and cars and cars. His fingers itched to hold his rifle. How many could he get? Three? Six? An even baker's dozen? And how many miles to Babylon?

He stirred restlessly, uneasily.

Only Dussander's death would tell the final truth, he supposed. Sometime during the next five years, maybe even sooner. Three to five . . . it sounded like a prison sentence. *Todd Bowden, this court hereby sentences you to three to five for associating with a known war criminal. Three to five of bad dreams and cold sweats.*

Sooner or later Dussander would simply drop dead. Then the waiting would begin. The knot in the stomach every time the phone or the doorbell rang.

He wasn't sure he could stand that.

His fingers itched to hold the gun and Todd curled them into fists and drove both fists into his crotch. Sick pain swallowed his belly and he lay for some time afterwards in a writhing ball on the ground, his lips pulled back in a silent shriek. The pain was dreadful, but it blotted out the endless parade of thoughts.

At least for a while.

20

For Morris Heisel, that Sunday was a day of miracles.

The Atlanta Braves, his favourite baseball team, swept a double-header from the high and mighty Cincinnati Reds by scores of 7–1 and 8–0. Lydia, who boasted smugly of always taking care of herself and whose favourite saying was 'An ounce of prevention is worth a pound of cure,' slipped on her friend Janet's wet kitchen floor and sprained her hip. She was at home in bed. It wasn't serious, not at all, and thank God (what God?) for that, but it meant she wouldn't be able to visit him for at least two days, maybe as long as four.

Four days without Lydia! Four days that he wouldn't have to hear about how she had warned him that the stepladder was wobbly and how he was up too high on it in the bargain. Four days when he wouldn't have to listen to her tell him how she'd always said the Rogans' pup was going to cause them grief, always chasing Lover Boy that way. Four days without Lydia asking him if he wasn't glad now that she had kept after him about sending in that insurance application, for if she had not, they would surely be on their way to the poorhouse now. Four days without having Lydia tell him that many people lived perfectly normal lives – almost, anyway – paralyzed from the waist down; why, every museum and gallery in the city had wheelchair ramps as well as stairs, and there were even special buses. After this observation, Lydia would smile bravely and then inevitably burst into tears.

Morris drifted off into a contented late afternoon nap.

When he woke up it was half-past five in the afternoon.

His roommate was asleep. He still hadn't placed Denker, but all the same he felt sure that he had known the man at some time or other. He had begun to ask Denker about himself once or twice, but then something had held him back. That same something kept him from making more than the most banal conversation with the man – the weather, the last earthquake, the next earthquake, and yeah, the *Guide* says Myron Floren is going to come back for a special guest appearance this weekend on the Welk show.

Morris told himself he was holding back because it gave him a mental game to play, and when you were in a body-cast from your shoulders to your hips, mental games can come in handy. If you had a little mental contest going on, you didn't have to spend quite so much time wondering how it was going to be, pissing through a catheter for the rest of your life.

If he came right out and asked Denker, the mental game would probably come to a swift and unsatisfying conclusion. They would narrow their pasts down to some common experience – a train trip, a boat ride, possibly even the camp. Denker might have been in Patin; there had been plenty of German Jews there.

On the other hand, one of the nurses had told him Denker would probably be going home in a week or two. If Morris couldn't figure it out by then, he would mentally declare the game lost and ask the man straight out: *Say, I've had the feeling I know you –*

But there was more to it than just that, he admitted to himself. There was something in his feelings, a nasty sort of undertow, that made him think of that story 'The Monkey's Paw', where every wish had been granted as the result of

318

some evil turn of fate. The old couple who came into possession of the paw wished for a hundred dollars and received
it as a gift of condolence when their only son was killed in
a nasty mill accident. Then the mother had wished for the
son to return to them. They had heard footsteps dragging
up their walk shortly afterwards; then pounding on the door,
a perfect fusillade of blows. The mother, mad with joy, had
gone rushing down the stairs to let in her only child. The
father, mad with quite another emotion, scrabbled through
the darkness for the dried paw, found it at last, and wished
his son dead again. The mother threw the door open a
moment later and found nothing on the stoop but an eddy
of night wind.

In some way Morris felt that perhaps he *did* know where
he and Denker had been acquainted, but that his knowledge was like the son of the old couple in the story —
returned from the grave, but not as he was in his mother's
memory; returned, instead, horribly crushed and mangled
from his fall into the gnashing, whirling machinery. He felt
that his knowledge of Denker might be a subconscious thing,
pounding on the door between that area of his mind and
that of rational understanding and recognition, demanding
admittance . . . and that another part of him was searching
frantically for the monkey's paw, or its psychological equivalent; for the talisman that would wish away the knowledge
forever.

Now he looked at Denker, frowning.

*Denker. Denker. Where have I known you, Denker? Was it
Patin? Is that why I don't want to know? But surely, two survivors
of a common horror do not have to be afraid of each other. Unless,
of course . . .*

He frowned. He felt very close to it, suddenly, but his feet were tingling, breaking his concentration, annoying him. They were tingling in just the way a limb tingles when you've slept on it and it's returning to normal circulation. If it wasn't for the damned body-cast, he could sit up and rub his feet until that tingle went away. He could –

Morris's eyes widened.

For a long time he lay perfectly still, Lydia forgotten, Denker forgotten, Patin forgotten, *everything* forgotten except that tingly feeling in his feet. Yes, *both* feet, but it was stronger in the right one. When you felt that tingle, you said *My foot went to sleep*.

But what you really meant, of course, was *My foot is waking up*.

Morris fumbled for the call-button. He pressed it again and again until the nurse came.

The nurse tried to dismiss it – she had had hopeful patients before. His doctor wasn't in the building, and the nurse didn't want to call him at home. Dr Kemmelman had a vast reputation for evil temper . . . especially when he was called at home. Morris wouldn't let her dismiss it. He was a mild man, but now he was prepared to make more than a fuss; he was prepared to make an uproar if that's what it took. The Braves had taken two. Lydia had sprained her hip. But good things came in threes, everyone knew that.

At last the nurse came back with an intern, a young man named Dr Timpnell whose hair looked as if it had last been cut by a Lawn Boy with very dull blades. Dr Timpnell pulled a Swiss Army knife from the pocket of his white pants, folded out the Phillips screwdriver attachment, and ran it from the toes of Morris's right foot down to the heel. The foot did not curl, but his toes twitched — it was an obvious twitch, too definite to miss. Morris burst into tears.

Timpnell, looking rather dazed, sat beside him on the bed and patted his hand.

'This sort of thing happens from time to time,' he said (possibly from his wealth of practical experience, which stretched back perhaps as far as six months). 'No doctor predicts it, but it *does* happen. And apparently it's happened to you.'

Morris nodded through his tears.

'Obviously, you're not totally paralyzed.' Timpnell was still patting his hand. 'But I wouldn't try to predict if your recovery will be slight, partial, or total. I doubt if Dr Kemmelman will, either. I suspect you'll have to undergo a lot of physical therapy, and not all of it will be pleasant. But it will be more pleasant than . . . you know.'

'Yes,' Morris said through his tears. 'I know. Thank God!' He remembered telling Lydia there was no God and felt his face fill up with hot blood.

'I'll see that Dr Kemmelman is informed,' Timpnell said, giving Morris's hand a final pat and rising.

'Could you call my wife?' Morris asked. Because, doom-crying and hand-wringing aside, he felt *something* for her. Maybe it was even love, an emotion which seemed to have little to do with sometimes feeling like you could wring a person's neck.

'Yes, I'll see that it's done. Nurse, would you —?'

'Of course, doctor,' the nurse said, and Timpnell could barely stifle his grin.

'Thank you,' Morris said, wiping his eyes with a Kleenex from the box on the nightstand. 'Thank you very much.'

Timpnell went out. At some point during the discussion, Mr Denker had awakened. Morris considered apologizing for all the noise, or perhaps for his tears, and then decided no apology was necessary.

'You are to be congratulated, I take it,' Mr Denker said.

'We'll see,' Morris said, but like Timpnell, he was barely able to stifle his grin. 'We'll see.'

'Things have a way of working out,' Denker replied vaguely, and then turned on the TV with the remote control device. It was now quarter to six, and they watched the last of *Hee-Haw*. It was followed by the evening news. Unemployment was worse. Inflation was not so bad. The hostages were still hostages. A new Gallup poll showed that, if the election were to be held right then, there were four Republican candidates who could beat Jimmy Carter. And there had been racial incidents following the murder of a black child in Atlanta (it would be another six months before a grisly pattern of murder began to emerge in the Atlanta murders) – 'A night of violence', the newscaster called it. Closer to home, an unidentified man had been found in an orchard near Highway 46, stabbed and bludgeoned.

Lydia called just before 6.30. Dr Kemmelman had called her and, based on the young intern's report, he had been cautiously optimistic. Lydia was cautiously joyous. She vowed to come in the following day even if it killed her. Morris told her he loved her. Tonight he loved everyone – Lydia, Dr Timpnell with his Lawn Boy haircut, Mr Denker, even the young girl who brought in the supper trays as Morris hung up.

Supper was hamburgers, mashed potatoes, a carrots-and-peas combination, and small dishes of ice cream for dessert. The candy striper who served it was Felice, a shy blonde girl of perhaps twenty. She had her own good news – her boyfriend had landed a job as a computer programmer with IBM and had formally asked her to marry him.

Mr Denker, who exuded a certain courtly charm that all the young ladies responded to, expressed great pleasure. 'Really, how wonderful. You must sit down and tell us all about it. Tell us everything. Omit nothing.'

Felice blushed and smiled and said she couldn't do that. 'We've still got the rest of B wing to do and C wing after that. And look, here it is six-thirty!'

'Then tomorrow night, for sure. We insist – don't we, Mr Heisel?'

'Yes indeed,' Morris murmured, but his mind was a million miles away.

(*you must sit down and tell us all about it*)

Words spoken in that exact-same bantering tone. He had heard them before; of that there could be no doubt. But had Denker been the one to speak them? *Had* he?

(*tell us everything*)

The voice of an urbane man. A cultured man. But there was a threat in the voice. A steel hand in a velvet glove. Yes.

Where?

(*tell us everything. Omit nothing.*)

(*?Patin?*)

Morris Heisel looked at his supper. Mr Denker had already fallen to with a will. The encounter with Felice had left him in the best of spirits – the way he had been after the young boy with the blond hair came to visit him.

'A nice girl,' Denker said, his words muffled by a mouthful of carrots and peas.

'Oh yes –'

(*you must sit down*)

'– Felice, you mean. She's

(*and tell us all about it.*)

'very sweet.'

(*tell us everything. Omit nothing.*)

He looked down at his own supper, suddenly remembering how it got to be in the camps after a while. At first you would have killed for a scrap of meat, no matter how maggoty or green with decay. But after a while, that crazy hunger went away and your belly lay inside your middle like a small grey rock. You felt you would never be hungry again.

Until someone showed you food.

(*'tell us everything, my friend. Omit nothing. You must sit down and tell us AAALLLLL about it.'*)

The main course on Morris's plastic hospital tray was hamburger. Why should it suddenly make him think of lamb? Not mutton, not chops – mutton was often stringy, chops often tough, and a person whose teeth had rotted out like old stumps would perhaps not be overly tempted by mutton or a chop. No, what he thought of was a savoury lamb stew, gravy-rich and full of vegetables. Soft, tasty vegetables. Why think of lamb stew? Why, unless –

The door banged open. It was Lydia, her face rosy with smiles. An aluminium crutch was propped in her armpit and she was walking like Marshall Dillon's friend Chester. '*Morris!*' she trilled. Trailing her and looking just as tremulously happy was Emma Rogan from next door.

Mr Denker, startled, dropped his fork. He cursed softly under his breath and picked it up off the floor with a wince.

'It's so *WONDERFUL!*' Lydia was almost baying with excitement. 'I called Emma and asked her if we could come tonight instead of tomorrow, I had the crutch already, and I said, "Em", I said, "if I can't bear this agony for Morris, what kind of wife am I to him?" Those are my very words, aren't they, Emma?'

Emma Rogan, perhaps remembering that her collie pup had caused at least some of the problem, nodded eagerly.

'So I called the hospital,' Lydia said, shrugging her coat off and settling in for a good long visit, 'and *they* said it was past visiting hours but in my case they would make an exception, except we couldn't stay too long because we might bother Mr Denker. We aren't bothering you, are we, Mr Denker?'

'No, dear lady,' Mr Denker said resignedly.

'Sit down, Emma, take Mr Denker's chair, he's not using it. Here, Morris, stop with the ice cream, you're slobbering it all over yourself, just like a baby. Never mind, we'll have you up and around in no time. I'll feed it to you. Goo-goo, ga-ga. Open wide . . . over the teeth, over the gums . . . look out, stomach, here it comes! . . . No, don't say a word, mommy knows best. Would you look at him, Emma, he hardly has any hair left and I don't wonder, thinking he might never walk again. It's God's mercy. I told him that stepladder was wobbly. I said, "Morris," I said, "Come down off there before —"'

She fed him ice cream and chattered for the next hour and by the time she left, hobbling ostentatiously on the crutch while Emma held her other arm, thoughts of lamb stew and voices echoing up through the years were the last things in Morris Heisel's mind. He was exhausted. To say it had been a busy day was putting it mildly. Morris fell deeply asleep.

He awoke sometime between three and four a.m. with a scream locked behind his lips.

Now he knew. He knew exactly where and exactly when he had been acquainted with the man in the other bed. Except his name had not been Denker *then*. Oh no, not at all.

He had awakened from the most terrible nightmare of his whole life. Someone had given him and Lydia a monkey's paw, and they had wished for money. Then, somehow, a Western Union boy in a Hitler Youth uniform had been in the room with them. He handed Morris a telegram which read: REGRET TO INFORM YOU BOTH DAUGHTERS DEAD STOP PATIN CONCENTRATION CAMP STOP GREATEST REGRETS AT THIS FINAL SOLUTION STOP COMMANDANT'S LETTER FOLLOWS STOP WILL TELL YOU EVERYTHING AND OMIT NOTHING STOP PLEASE ACCEPT OUR CHECK FOR 100 REICH-MARKS ON DEPOSIT YOUR BANK TOMORROW STOP SIGNED ADOLF HITLER CHANCELLOR.

A great wail from Lydia, and although she had never even seen Morris's daughters, she held the monkey's paw high and wished for them to be returned to life. The room went dark. And suddenly, from outside, came the sound of dragging, lurching footfalls.

Morris was down on his hands and knees in a darkness that suddenly stank of smoke and gas and death. He was searching for the paw. One wish left. If he could find the paw he could wish this dreadful dream away. He would spare himself the sight of his daughters, thin as scarecrows, their eyes deep wounded holes, their numbers burning on the scant flesh of their arms.

Hammering on the door, a perfect fusillade of blows.

In the nightmare, his search for the paw became ever

more frenzied, but it bore no fruit. It seemed to go on for years. And then, behind him, the door crashed open. *No*, he thought. *I won't look. I'll close my eyes. Rip them from my head if I have to, but I won't look.*

But he did look. He had to look. In the dream it was as if huge hands had grasped his head and wrenched it around.

It was not his daughters standing in the doorway; it was Denker. A much younger Denker, a Denker who wore a Nazi SS uniform, the cap with its lightning-bolt insignia cocked rakishly to one side. His buttons gleamed heartlessly, his boots were polished to a killing gloss.

Clasped in his arms was a huge and slowly bubbling pot of lamb stew.

And the dream-Denker, smiling his dark, suave smile, said: *You must sit down and tell us all about it — as one friend to another, eh? We have heard that gold has been hidden. That tobacco has been hoarded. That it was not food-poisoning with Schneibel at all but powdered glass in his supper two nights ago. You must not insult our intelligence by pretending you know nothing. You know EVERYTHING. So tell it all. Omit nothing.*

And in the dark, smelling the maddening aroma of the stew, he told them everything. His stomach, which had been a small grey rock, was now a raving tiger. Words spilled helplessly from his lips. They spewed from him in the senseless sermon of a lunatic, truth and falsehood all mixed up together.

Brodin has his mother's wedding ring taped below his scrotum!

('you must sit down')

Laslo and Herman Dorsky have talked about rushing guard tower number three!

('and tell us everything!')

Rachel Tannenbaum's husband has tobacco, he gave the guard who comes on after Zeickert, the one they call Booger-Eater because he is always picking his nose and then putting his fingers in his mouth, Tannenbaum gave some of it to Booger-Eater so he wouldn't take his wife's pearl earrings!

('oh that makes no sense at all you've mixed up two different stories I think but that's all right quite all right we'd rather have you mix up two stories than omit one completely you must omit NOTHING!')

There is a man who has been calling out his dead son's name in order to get double rations!

('tell us his name')

I don't know it but I can point him out to you please yes I can show him to you I will I will I will I

('tell us everything you know')

will I will I will I will I will I will I will I

Until he swam up into consciousness with a scream in his throat like fire.

Trembling uncontrollably, he looked at the sleeping form in the other bed. He found himself staring particularly at the wrinkled, caved-in mouth. Old tiger with no teeth. Ancient and vicious rogue elephant with one tusk gone and the other rooted loose in its socket. Senile monster.

'Oh my *God*,' Morris Heisel whispered. His voice was high and faint, inaudible to anyone but himself. Tears trickled down his cheeks towards his ears. 'Oh dear *God*, the man who murdered my wife and my daughters is sleeping in the same room with me, my *God*, oh dear dear *God*, he is here with me now in this room.'

The tears began to flow faster now – tears of rage and horror, hot, scalding.

He trembled and waited for morning, and morning did not come for an age.

21

The next day, Monday, Todd was up at six o'clock in the morning and poking listlessly at a scrambled egg he had fixed for himself when his father came down still dressed in his monogrammed bathrobe and slippers.

'Mumph,' he said to Todd, going past him to the refrigerator for orange juice.

Todd grunted back without looking up from his book, one of the 87th Squad mysteries. He had been lucky enough to land a summer job with a landscaping outfit that operated out of Sausalito. That would have been much too far to commute ordinarily, even if one of his parents had been willing to loan him a car for the summer (neither was), but his father was working on-site not far from there, and he was able to drop Todd off at a bus stop on his way and pick him up at the same place on his way back. Todd was less than wild about the arrangement; he didn't like riding home from work with his father and absolutely detested riding to work with him in the morning. It was in the mornings that he felt the most naked, when the wall between what he was and what he might be seemed the thinnest. It was worse after a night of bad dreams, but even if no dreams had come in the night, it was bad. One morning he realized with a fright so sudden it was almost terror that he had been seriously considering reaching across his father's briefcase, grabbing the wheel of the Porsche, and sending them corkscrewing into the two express lanes, cutting a swath of destruction through the morning commuters.

'You want another egg, Todd-O?'

'No thanks, dad.' Dick Bowden ate them fried. How could anyone stand to eat a fried egg? On the grill of the Jenn-Aire for two minutes, then over easy. What you got on your plate at the end looked like a giant dead eye with a cataract over it, an eye that would bleed orange when you poked it with your fork.

He pushed his scrambled egg away. He had barely touched it.

Outside, the morning paper slapped the step.

His father finished cooking, turned off the grill, and came to the table. 'Not hungry this morning, Todd-O?'

You call me that one more time and I'm going to stick my knife right up your fucking nose . . . dad-O.

'Not much appetite, I guess.'

Dick grinned affectionately at his son; there was still a tiny dab of shaving cream on the boy's right ear. 'Betty Trask stole your appetite. That's my guess.'

'Yeah, maybe that's it.' He offered a wan smile that vanished as soon as his father went down the stairs from the break-fast nook to get the paper. *Would it wake you up if I told you what a cunt she is, dad-O? How about if I said, 'Oh, by the way, did you know your good friend Ray Trask's daughter is one of the biggest sluts in Santa Donato? She'd kiss her own twat if she was double-jointed, dad-O. That's how much she thinks of it. Just a stinking little slut. Two lines of coke and she's yours for the night. And if you don't happen to have any coke, she's still yours for the night. She'd fuck a dog if she couldn't get a man.' Think that'd wake you up, dad-O? Get you a flying start on the day?*

He pushed the thoughts away viciously, knowing they wouldn't stay gone.

His father came back with the paper. Todd glimpsed the headline: SPY TRIALS CLOSER, STATE DEPARTMENT SOURCE SAYS.

Dick sat down. 'Betty's a fine-looking girl,' he said. 'She reminds me of your mother when I first met her.'

'Is that so?'

'Pretty . . . young . . . fresh.' Dick Bowden's eyes had gone vague. Now they came back, focusing almost anxiously on his son. 'Not that your mother isn't still a fine-looking woman. But at that age a girl has a certain . . . glow, I guess you'd say. It's there for a while, and then it's gone.' He shrugged and opened the paper. '*C'est la vie*, I guess.'

She's a bitch in heat. Maybe that's what makes her glow.

'You're treating her right, aren't you, Todd-O?' His father was making his usual rapid trip through the paper towards the sports pages. 'Not getting too fresh?'

'Everything's cool, dad.'

(*if he doesn't stop pretty soon I'll . . . I'll . . . do . . . something. Scream. Throw his coffee in his face. Something.*)

'Ray thinks you're a fine boy,' Dick said absently. He had at last reached the sports. He became absorbed. There was blessed silence at the breakfast table.

Betty Trask had been all over him the very first time they went out. He had taken her to the local lover's lane after the movie because he knew it would be expected of him; they could swap spits for half an hour or so and have all the right things to tell their respective friends the next day. She could roll her eyes and tell how she had fought off his advances – boys were so tiresome, really, and she never fucked

331

on the first date, she wasn't that kind of girl. Her friends would agree and then all of them would troop into the girls' room and do whatever it was they did in there – put on fresh makeup, smoke Tampax, whatever.

And for a guy . . . well, you had to make out. You had to get at least to second base and try for third. Because there were reputations and reputations. Todd couldn't have cared less about having a stud reputation; he only wanted a reputation for being normal. And if you didn't at least *try*, word got around. People started to wonder if you were all right.

So he took them up on Jane's Hill, kissed them, felt their tits, went a little further than that if they would allow it. And that was it. The girl would stop him, he would put up a little goodnatured argument, and then take her home. No worries about what might be said in the girls' room the next day. No worries that anyone was going to think Todd Bowden was anything but normal. Except –

Except Betty Trask *was* the kind of girl who fucked on the first date. On every date. And in between dates.

The first time had been a month or so before the goddam Nazi's heart attack, and Todd thought he had done pretty well for a virgin . . . perhaps for the same reason a young pitcher will do well if he's tapped to throw the biggest game of the year with no forewarning. There had been no time to worry, to get all strung up about it.

Always before, Todd had been able to sense when a girl had made up her mind that on the next date she would just allow herself to be carried away. He was aware that he was personable and that both his looks and his prospects were good. The kind of boy their cunty mothers regarded as 'a good catch'. And when he sensed that physical capitulation was about to happen, he would start dating some other girl. And whatever it said about his personality, Todd was able to admit to himself that if he ever started dating a truly frigid girl, he would probably be happy to date her for years to come. Maybe even marry her.

But the first time with Betty had gone fairly well – *she* was no virgin, even if he was. She had to help him get his cock into her, but she seemed to take that as a matter of course. And halfway through the act itself she had gurgled up from the blanket they were lying on: 'I just *love* to fuck!' It was the tone of voice another girl might have used to express her love for strawberry whirl ice cream.

Later encounters – there had been five of them (five and a half, he supposed, if you wanted to count last night) – hadn't been so good. They had, in fact, gotten worse at what seemed an exponential rate . . . although he didn't believe even now that Betty had been aware of that (at least not until last night). In fact, quite the opposite. Betty apparently believed she had found the battering-ram of her dreams.

Todd hadn't felt any of the things he was supposed to feel at a time like that. Kissing her lips was like kissing warm but uncooked liver. Having her tongue in his mouth only made him wonder what kind of germs she was carrying, and sometimes he thought he could smell her fillings – an unpleasant metallic odour, like chrome. Her breasts were bags of meat. No more.

Todd had done it twice more with her before Dussander's heart attack. Each time he had more trouble getting erect. In both cases he had finally succeeded by using a fantasy. She was stripped naked in front of all their friends. Crying.

Todd was forcing her to walk up and down between them while he cried out: *Show your tits! Let them see your snatch, you cheap slut! Spread your cheeks! That's right, bend over and SPREAD them!*

Betty's appreciation was not at all surprising. He was a very good lover, not in spite of his problems but because of them. Getting hard was only the first step. Once you achieved erection, you had to have an orgasm. The fourth time they had done it – this was three days after Dussander's heart attack – he had pounded away at her for over ten minutes. Betty Trask thought she had died and gone to heaven; she had three orgasms and was trying for a fourth when Todd recalled an old fantasy . . . what was, in fact, the First Fantasy. The girl on the table, clamped and helpless. The huge dildo. The rubber squeeze-bulb. Only now, desperate and sweaty and almost insane with his desire to come and get this horror over with, the face of the girl on the table became Betty's face. That brought on a joyless, rubbery spasm that he supposed was, technically, at least, an orgasm. A moment later Betty was whispering in his ear, her breath warm and redolent of Juicy Fruit gum: 'Lover, you do me any old time. Just call me.'

Todd had nearly groaned aloud.

The nub of his dilemma was this: Wouldn't his reputation suffer if he broke off with a girl who so obviously wanted to put out for him? Wouldn't people wonder why? Part of him said they would not. He remembered walking down the hall behind two senior boys during his freshman year and hearing one of them tell the other he had broken off with his girlfriend. The other wanted to know why. 'Fucked 'er out,' the first said, and both of them bellowed goatish laughter.

If someone asks me why I dropped her, I'll just say I fucked her out. But what if she says we only did it five times? Is that enough? What? . . . How much? . . . How many? . . . Who'll talk? . . . What'll they say?

So his mind ran on, as restless as a hungry rat in an insoluble maze. He was vaguely aware that he was turning a minor problem into a big problem, and that his very inability to solve the problem had something to say about how shaky he had gotten. But knowing it brought him no fresh ability to change his behaviour, and he sank into a black depression.

College. College was the answer. College offered an excuse to break with Betty that no one could question. But September seemed so far away.

The fifth time it had taken him almost twenty minutes to get hard, but Betty had proclaimed the experience well worth the wait. And then, last night, he hadn't been able to perform at all.

'What are you, anyway?' Betty had asked petulantly. After twenty minutes of manipulating his lax penis, she was dishevelled and out of patience. 'Are you one of those AC/DC guys?'

He very nearly strangled her on the spot. And if he'd had his .30-.30 –

'Well, I'll be a son of a *gun*! Congratulations, son!'

'Huh?' He looked up and out of his black study.

'You made the Southern Cal High School All-Stars!' His father was grinning with pride and pleasure.

'Is that so?' For a moment he hardly knew what his father was talking about; he had to grope for the meaning of the words. 'Say, yeah, Coach Haller mentioned something to me about that at the end of the year. Said he was putting me and Billy DeLyons up. I never expected anything to happen.'

'Well Jesus, you don't seem very excited about it!'

'I'm still trying

(*who gives a ripe fuck?*)

to get used to the idea.' With a huge effort, he managed a grin. 'Can I see the article?'

His father handed the paper across the table to Todd and got to his feet. 'I'm going to wake Monica up. She's got to see this before we leave.'

No, God − I can't face both of them this morning.

'Aw, don't do that. You know she won't be able to get back to sleep if you wake her up. We'll leave it for her on the table.'

'Yes, I suppose we could do that. You're a damned thoughtful boy, Todd.' He clapped Todd on the back, and Todd squeezed his eyes closed. At the same time he shrugged his shoulders in an aw-shucks gesture that made his father laugh. Todd opened his eyes again and looked at the paper.

4 BOYS NAMED TO SOUTHERN CAL ALL-STARS, the headline read. Beneath were pictures of them in their uniforms − the catcher and left-fielder from Fairview High, the jigaboo shortstop from Mountford, and Todd to the far right, grinning openly out at the world from beneath the bill of his baseball cap. He read the story and saw that Billy DeLyons had made the second squad. That, at least, was something to feel happy about. DeLyons could claim he was a Methodist until his tongue fell out, if it made him feel good, but he wasn't fooling Todd. He knew perfectly well what Billy DeLyons was. Maybe he ought to introduce him to Betty Trask, she was another sheeny. He had wondered

about that for a long time, and last night he had decided for sure. The Trasks were passing for white. One look at her nose and that olive complexion – her old man's was even worse – and you knew. That was probably why he hadn't been able to get it up. It was simple: his cock had known the difference before his brain. Who did they think they were kidding, calling themselves Trask?

'Congratulations again, son.'

He looked up and first saw his father's hand stuck out, then his father's foolishly grinning face.

Your buddy Trask is a yid! he heard himself yelling into his father's face. *That's why I was impotent with his slut of a daughter last night! That's the reason!* Then, on the heels of that, the cold voice that sometimes came at moments like this rose up from deep inside him, shutting off the rising flood of irrationality, as if

(*GET HOLD OF YOURSELF RIGHT NOW*)

behind steel gates.

He took his father's hand and shook it. Smiled guilelessly into his father's proud face. Said: 'Jeez, thanks, dad.'

They left that page of the newspaper folded back and a note for Monica, which Dick insisted Todd write and sign: *Your All-Star Son, Todd.*

22

Ed French, aka 'Pucker' French, aka Sneaker Pete and The Ked Man, *also* aka Rubber Ed French, was in the small and lovely seaside town of San Remo for a guidance counsellors' convention. It was a waste of time if ever there had been one – all guidance counsellors could ever agree on was not to agree on anything – and he grew bored with the papers, seminars, and discussion periods after a single day. Halfway through the second day, he discovered he was also bored with San Remo, and that of the adjectives small, lovely, and seaside, the *key* adjective was probably *small*. Gorgeous views and redwood trees aside, San Remo didn't have a movie theatre or a bowling alley, and Ed hadn't wanted to go in the place's only bar – it had a dirt parking lot filled with pick-up trucks, and most of the pick-ups had Reagan stickers on their rusty bumpers and tailgates. He wasn't afraid of being picked on, but he hadn't wanted to spend an evening looking at men in cowboy hats and listening to Loretta Lynn on the jukebox.

So here he was on the third day of a convention which stretched out over an incredible four days; here he was in room 217 of the Holiday Inn, his wife and daughter at home, the TV broken, an unpleasant smell hanging around in the bathroom. There was a swimming pool, but his eczema was so bad this summer that he wouldn't have been caught dead in a bathing suit. From the shins down he looked like a leper. He had an hour before the next workshop (Helping the Vocally Challenged Child – what they meant was doing something for kids who stuttered or who had cleft palates, but we wouldn't want to come right out and *say* that, Christ no, someone might lower our salaries), he had eaten lunch at San Remo's only restaurant, he didn't feel like a nap, and the TV's one station was showing a rerun of *Bewitched*.

So he sat down with the telephone book and began to flip through it aimlessly, hardly aware of what he was doing, wondering distantly if he knew anyone crazy enough about either small, lovely, or seaside to live in San Remo. He supposed this was what all the bored people in all the Holiday

Inns all over the world ended up doing – looking for a forgotten friend or relative to call up on the phone. It was that, *Bewitched*, or the Gideon Bible. And if you did happen to get hold of somebody, what the hell did you say? 'Frank! How the hell are you? And by the way, which was it – small, lovely, or seaside?' Sure. Right. Give that man a cigar and set him on fire.

Yet, as he lay on the bed flipping through the thin San Remo white pages and half-scanning the columns, it seemed to him that he *did* know somebody in San Remo. A book salesman? One of Sondra's nieces or nephews, of which there were marching battalions? A poker buddy from college? The relative of a student? That seemed to ring a bell, but he couldn't fine it down any more tightly.

He kept thumbing, and found he was sleepy after all. He had almost dozed off when it came to him and he sat up, wide awake again.

Lord Peter!

They were rerunning those Wimsey stories on PBS just lately – *Clouds of Witness, Murder Must Advertise, The Nine Tailors*. He and Sondra were hooked. A man named Ian Carmichael played Wimsey, and Sondra was nuts for him. So nuts, in fact, that Ed, who didn't think Carmichael looked like Lord Peter at all, actually became quite irritated.

'Sandy, the shape of his face is all wrong. And he's wearing false teeth, for heaven's sake!'

'Poo,' Sondra had replied airily from the couch where she was curled up. 'You're just jealous. He's so *handsome.*'

'Daddy's jealous, Daddy's jealous,' little Norma sang, prancing around the living room in her duck pyjamas.

'You should have been in bed an hour ago,' Ed told her,

gazing at his daughter with a jaundiced eye. 'And if I keep noticing you're *here*, I'll probably remember that you aren't *there*.'

Little Norma was momentarily abashed. Ed turned back to Sondra.

'I remember back three or four years ago. I had a kid named Todd Bowden, and his grandfather came in for a conference. Now *that* guy looked like Wimsey. A very *old* Wimsey, but the shape of his face was right, and –'

'*Wim*-zee, Wim-zee, *Dim*-zee, *Jim*-zee,' little Norma sang. '*Wim*-zee, *Bim*-zee, doodle-oodle-ooo-doo –'

'Shh, both of you,' Sondra said. 'I think he's the most *beautiful* man.' Irritating woman!

But hadn't Todd Bowden's grandfather retired to San Remo? Sure. Todd had been one of the brightest boys in that year's ninth grade class. Then, all at once, his grades had gone to hell. The old man had come in, told a familiar tale of marital difficulties, and had persuaded Ed to let the situation alone for a while and see if things didn't straighten themselves out. Ed's view was that the old *laissez-faire* bit didn't work – if you told a teenage kid to root, hog, or die, the kid usually died. But the old man had been almost eerily persuasive (it was the resemblance to Wimsey, perhaps), and Ed had agreed to give Todd to the end of the next Flunk Card period. And damned if Todd hadn't pulled through. The old man must have gone right through the whole family and really kicked some ass, Ed thought. He looked like the type who not only could do it, but who might derive a certain dour pleasure from it. Then, just two days ago, he had seen Todd's picture in the paper – he had made the Southern Cal All-Stars in baseball. No mean feat when you considered that about five hundred boys were nominated each spring. He supposed he might never have come up with the grandfather's name if he hadn't seen the picture.

He flickered through the white pages more purposefully now, ran his finger down a column of fine type, and there it was. BOWDEN, VICTOR S. 403 Ridge Lane. Ed dialled the number and it rang several times at the other end. He was just about to hang up when an old man answered. 'Hello?'

'Hello, Mr Bowden. Ed French. From Santa Donato Junior High.'

'Yes?' Politeness, but no more. Certainly no recognition. Well, the old guy was four years further along (weren't they all!) and things undoubtedly slipped his mind from time to time.

'Do you remember me, sir?'

'Should I?' Bowden's voice was cautious, and Ed smiled. The old man forgot things but he didn't want anybody to know if he could help it. His own old man had been that way when his hearing started to go.

'I was your grandson Todd's guidance counsellor at S.D.J.H.S. I called to congratulate you. He sure tore up the pea-patch when he got to high school, didn't he? And now he's All-Conference to top it off. Wow!'

'*Todd!*' the old man said, his voice brightening immediately. 'Yes, he certainly did a fine job, didn't he? Second in his class! And the girl who was ahead of him took the business courses.' A sniff of disdain in the old man's voice. 'My son called and offered to take me to Todd's commencement, but I'm in a wheelchair now. I broke my hip last January. I didn't want to go in a wheelchair. But I have his graduation picture right in the hall, you bet! Todd's made his parents very proud. And me, of course.'

'Yes, I guess we got him over the hump,' Ed said. He was smiling as he said it, but his smile was a trifle puzzled – somehow Todd's grandfather didn't sound the same. But it had been a long time ago, of course.

'Hump? What hump?'

'That little talk we had. When Todd was having problems with his course-work. Back in ninth.'

'I'm not following you,' the old man said slowly. 'I would never presume to speak for Richard's son. It would cause trouble . . . ho-ho, you don't *know* how much trouble it would cause. You've made a mistake, young fellow.'

'But –'

'Some sort of mistake. Got me confused with another student and another grandfather, I imagine.'

Ed was moderately thunderstruck. For one of the few times in his life, he could not think of a single thing to say. If there was confusion, it sure wasn't on *his* part.

'Well,' Bowden said doubtfully, 'it was nice of you to call, Mr –'

Ed found his tongue. 'I'm right here in town, Mr Bowden. It's a convention. Guidance counsellors. I'll be done around ten tomorrow morning, after the final paper is read. Could I come around to . . .' He consulted the phone book again. '. . . to Ridge Lane and see you for a few minutes?'

'What in the world for?'

'Just curiosity, I guess. It's all water over the dam now. But about four years ago, Todd got himself into a real crack with his grades. They were so bad I had to send a letter home with his report-card requesting a conference with a parent, or, ideally, with both of his parents. What I got was his grandfather, a very pleasant man named Victor Bowden.'

'But I've already told you —'

'Yes. I know. Just the same, I talked to *somebody* claiming to be Todd's grandfather. It doesn't matter much now, I suppose, but seeing is believing. I'd only take a few minutes of your time. It's all I *can* take, because I'm expected home by suppertime.'

'Time is all I have,' Bowden said, a bit ruefully. 'I'll be here all day. You're welcome to stop in.'

Ed thanked him, said goodbye, and hung up. He sat on the end of the bed, staring thoughtfully at the telephone. After a while he got up and took a pack of Phillies Cheroots from the sport coat hanging on the back of the desk chair. He ought to go; there was a workshop, and if he wasn't there, he would be missed. He lit his Cheroot with a Holiday Inn match and dropped the burnt stub into a Holiday Inn ashtray. He went to the Holiday Inn window and looked blankly out into the Holiday Inn courtyard.

It doesn't matter much now, he had told Bowden, but it mattered to him. He wasn't used to being sold a bill of goods by one of his kids, and this unexpected news upset him. Technically he supposed it could still turn out to be a case of an old man's senility, but Victor Bowden hadn't sounded as if he was drooling in his beard yet. And, damn it, he didn't sound the *same*.

Had Todd Bowden jobbed him?

He decided it could have been done. Theoretically, at least. Especially by a bright boy like Todd. He could have jobbed *everyone*, not just Ed French. He could have forged his mother or father's name to the Flunk Cards he had been issued during his bad patch. Lots of kids discovered a latent forging ability when they got Flunk Cards. He could have used ink eradicator on his second and third quarter reports, changing the grades up for his parents and then back down again so that his home room teacher wouldn't notice anything weird if he or she glanced at his card. The double application of eradicator would be visible to someone who was really looking, but home room teachers carried an average of sixty students each. They were lucky if they could get the entire roll called before the first bell, let alone spot-checking returned cards for tampering.

As for Todd's final class standing, it would have dipped perhaps no more than three points overall – two bad marking periods out of a total of twelve. His other grades had been lopsidedly good enough to make up most of the difference. And how many parents drop by the school to look at the student records kept by the California Department of Education? Especially the parents of a bright student like Todd Bowden?

Frown lines appeared on Ed French's normally smooth forehead.

It doesn't matter much now. That was nothing but the truth. Todd's high school work had been exemplary; there was no way in the world you could fake a 94 average. The boy was going on to Berkeley, the newspaper article had said, and Ed supposed his folks were damned proud – as they had every right to be. More and more it seemed to Ed that there was a vicious downside to American life, a greased skid of opportunism, cut corners, easy drugs, easy sex, a morality that grew cloudier each year. When your kid got through in standout style, parents had a right to be proud.

It doesn't matter now . . . but who was his frigging grandfather?
That kept sticking into him. Who, indeed? Had Todd
Bowden gone to the local branch office of the Screen Actors'
Guild and hung a notice on the bulletin board? YOUNG
MAN IN GRADES TROUBLE NEEDS OLDER MAN,
PREF. 70–80 YRS, TO GIVE BOFFO PERFORMANCE
AS GRANDFATHER, WILL PAY UNION SCALE? Uh-
uh. No way, Jose. And just what sort of adult would have
fallen in with such a crazy conspiracy, and for what reason?

Ed French, aka Pucker, aka Rubber Ed, just didn't know.
And because it didn't really matter, he stubbed out his Cheroot
and went to his workshop. But his attention kept wandering.

The next day he drove over to Ridge Lane and had a long
talk with Victor Bowden. They discussed grapes; they
discussed the retail grocery business and how the big chain
stores were pushing the little guys out; they discussed the
hostage situation in Iran (that summer *everyone* discussed the
hostage situation in Iran); they discussed the political climate
in southern California. Mr Bowden offered Ed a glass of
wine. Ed accepted with pleasure. He felt that he needed a
glass of wine, even if it was only 10.40 in the morning.
Victor Bowden looked as much like Peter Wimsey as a
machine gun looks like a shillelagh. Victor Bowden had no
trace of the faint accent Ed remembered, and he was quite
fat. The man who had purported to be Todd's grandfather
had been whip-thin.

Before leaving, Ed told him: 'I'd appreciate it if you
wouldn't mention any of this to Mr or Mrs Bowden. There
may be a perfectly reasonable explanation for all of it . . . and
even if there isn't, it's all in the past.'

'Sometimes,' Bowden said, holding his glass of wine up to the sun and admiring its rich dark colour, 'the past don't rest so easy. Why else do people study history?'

Ed smiled uneasily and said nothing.

'But don't you worry. I never meddle in Richard's affairs. And Todd is a good boy. Salutatorian of his class . . . he must be a good boy. Am I right?'

'As rain,' Ed French said heartily, and then asked for another glass of wine.

23

Dussander's sleep was uneasy; he lay in a trench of bad dreams.

They were breaking down the fence. Thousands, perhaps millions of them. They ran out of the jungle and threw themselves against the electrified barbed wire and now it was beginning to lean ominously inward. Some of the strands had given way and now coiled uneasily on the packed earth of the parade ground, squirting blue sparks. And still there was no end to them, no end. The Führer was as mad as Rommel had claimed if he thought now – if he had ever thought – there could be a final solution to this problem. There were billions of them; they filled the universe; and they were all after him.

'Old man. Wake up, old man. Dussander. Wake up, old man, wake up.'

At first he thought this was the voice of the dream.

Spoken in German; it had to be part of the dream. That was why the voice was so terrifying, of course. If he awoke he would escape it, so he swam upwards . . .

The man was sitting by his bed on a chair that had been

turned around backwards – a real man. 'Wake up, old man,' this visitor was saying. He was young – no more than thirty. His eyes were dark and studious behind plain steel-framed glasses. His brown hair was longish, collar-length, and for a confused moment Dussander thought it was the boy in a disguise. But this was not the boy, wearing a rather old-fashioned blue suit much too hot for the California climate. There was a small silver pin on one lapel of the suit. Silver, the metal you used to kill vampires and werewolves. It was a Jewish star.

'Are you speaking to me?' Dussander asked in German.

'Who else? Your roommate is gone.'

'Heisel? Yes. He went home yesterday.'

'Are you awake now?'

'Of course. But you've apparently mistaken me for someone else. My name is Arthur Denker. Perhaps you have the wrong room.'

'My name is Weiskopf. And yours is Kurt Dussander.'

Dussander wanted to lick his lips but didn't. Just possibly this was still all part of the dream – a new phase, no more. *Bring me a wino and a steak-knife, Mr Jewish Star in the Lapel, and I'll blow you away like smoke.*

'I know no Dussander,' he told the young man. 'I don't understand you. Shall I ring for the nurse?'

'You understand,' Weiskopf said. He shifted position slightly and brushed a lock of hair from his forehead. The prosiness of this gesture dispelled Dussander's last hope.

'Heisel,' Weiskopf said, and pointed at the empty bed.

'Heisel, Dussander, Weiskopf . . . none of these names mean anything to me.'

'Heisel fell off a ladder while he was nailing a new gutter

onto the side of his house,' Weiskopf said. 'He broke his back. He may never walk again. Unfortunate. But that was not the only tragedy of his life. He was an inmate of Patin, where he lost his wife and daughters. Patin, which you commanded.'

'I think you are insane,' Dussander said. 'My name is Arthur Denker. I came to this country when my wife died. Before that I was —'

'Spare me your tale,' Weiskopf said, raising a hand. 'He has not forgotten your face. This face.'

Weiskopf flicked a photograph into Dussander's face like a magician doing a trick. It was one of the two the boy had shown him years ago. A young Dussander in a jauntily cocked SS cap, swagger stick held firmly under one arm.

Dussander spoke slowly, in English now, enunciating carefully.

'During the war I was a factory machinist. My job was to oversee the manufacture of drive-columns and power-trains for armoured cars and trucks. Later I helped to build Tiger tanks. My reserve unit was called up during the battle of Berlin and I fought honourably, if briefly. After the war I worked in the Essen Motor Works until —'

'— until it became necessary for you to run away to South America. With your gold that had been melted down from Jewish teeth and your silver melted down from Jewish jewellery and your numbered Swiss bank account. Mr Heisel went home a happy man, you know. Oh, he had had a bad moment when he woke up in the dark and realized with whom he was sharing a room. But he feels better now. He feels that God allowed him the sublime privilege of breaking his back so that he could be instrumental in the capture of one of the greatest butchers of human beings to ever live.'

Dussander spoke slowly, enunciating carefully.

'During the war I was a factory machinist –'

'Oh, why not drop it? Your papers will not stand up to a serious examination. I know it and you know it. You are found out.'

'My job was to oversee the manufacture of –'

'Of corpses! One way or another, you will be in Tel Aviv before Christmas. The authorities are cooperating with us this time, Dussander. The Americans want to make us happy, and you are one of the things that will make us happy.'

'– the manufacture of drive-columns and power-trains for armoured cars and trucks. Later I helped to build Tiger tanks.'

'Why be tiresome? Why drag it out?'

'My reserve unit was called up –'

'Very well then. You'll see me again. Soon.'

Weiskopf rose. He left the room. For a moment his shadow bobbed on the wall and then that was gone, too. Dussander closed his eyes. He wondered if Weiskopf could be telling the truth about American cooperation. Three years ago, when oil was tight in America, he would have believed it. But the stupid Iranian militants had hardened American support for Israel. It was possible. And what did it matter? One way or the other, legal or illegal, Weiskopf and his colleagues would have him. On the subject of Nazis they were intransigent, and on the subject of the camps they were lunatics.

He was trembling all over. But he knew what he must do now.

24

The school records for the pupils who had passed through Santa Donato Junior High were kept in an old, rambling warehouse on the north side. It was not far from the abandoned trainyards. It was dark and echoing and it smelled of wax and polish and 999 Industrial Cleaner − it was also the school department's custodial warehouse.

Ed French got there around four in the afternoon with Norma in tow. A janitor let them in, told Ed what he wanted was on the fourth floor, and showed them to a creeping, clanking warehouse that frightened Norma into an uncharacteristic silence.

She regained herself on the fourth floor, prancing and capering up and down the dim aisles of stacked boxes and files while Ed searched for and eventually found the files containing report-cards from 1975. He pulled the second box and began to leaf through the Bs. BORK. BOSTWICK. BOSWELL. BOWDEN, TODD. He pulled the card, shook his head impatiently over it in the dim light, and took it across to one of the high, dusty windows.

'Don't run around in here, honey,' he called over his shoulder.

'Why, daddy?'

'Because the trolls will get you,' he said, and held Todd's card up to the light.

He saw it at once. This report card, in those files for four years now, had been carefully, almost professionally, doctored.

'Jesus Christ,' Ed French muttered.

'Trolls, trolls, trolls!' Norma sang gleefully, as she continued to dance up and down the aisles.

25

Dussander walked carefully down the hospital corridor. He was still a bit unsteady on his legs. He was wearing his blue bathrobe over his white hospital johnny. It was night now, just after eight o'clock, and the nurses were changing shifts. The next half hour would be confused – he had observed that all the shift changes were confused. It was a time for exchanging notes, gossip, and drinking coffee at the nurses' station, which was just around the corner from the drinking fountain.

What he wanted was just across from the drinking fountain.

He was not noticed in the wide hallway, which at this hour reminded him of a long and echoing train station minutes before a passenger train departs. The walking wounded paraded slowly up and down, some dressed in robes as he was, others holding the backs of their johnnies together. Disconnected music came from half a dozen different transistor radios in half a dozen different rooms. Visitors came and went. A man laughed in one room and another man seemed to be weeping across the hall. A doctor walked by with his nose in a paperback novel.

Dussander went to the fountain, got a drink, wiped his mouth with his cupped hand, and looked at the closed door across the hall. This door was always locked . . . at least, that was the theory. In practice he had observed that it was some-times both unlocked and unattended. Most often during the chaotic half hour when the shifts were changing and the nurses were gathered around the corner. Dussander had observed all of this with the trained and wary eye of a man who has been on the jump for a long, long time. He only wished he could observe the unmarked door for another week or so, looking for dangerous breaks in the pattern – he would only have the one chance. But he didn't have another week. His status as Werewolf in Residence might not become known for another two or three days, but it might happen tomorrow. He did not dare wait. When it came out, he would be watched constantly.

He took another small drink, wiped his mouth again, and looked both ways. Then, casually, with no effort of conceal-ment, he stepped across the hall, turned the knob, and walked into the drug closet. If the woman in charge had happened to already be behind her desk, he was only nearsighted Mr Denker. So sorry, dear lady, I thought it was the WC. Stupid of me.

But the drug closet was empty.

He ran his eye over the top shelf at his left. Nothing but eyedrops and eardrops. Second shelf: laxatives, suppositories. On the third shelf he saw Seconal and Veronal. He slipped a bottle of Seconals into the pocket of his robe. Then he went back to the door and stepped out without looking around, a puzzled smile on his face – that certainly wasn't the WC, was it? *There* it was, right next to the drinking fountain. Stupid me!

He crossed to the door labelled MEN, went inside, and washed his hands. Then he went back down the hall to the semi-private room that was now completely private since the departure of the illustrious Mr Heisel. On the table between the beds was a glass and a plastic pitcher filled with water. Pity there was no bourbon; really, it was a shame. But the pills would float him off just as nicely no matter how they were washed down.

'Morris Heisel, *salud*,' he said with a faint smile, and poured himself a glass of water. After all those years of jumping at shadows, of seeing faces that looked familiar on park benches or in restaurants or bus terminals, he had finally been recognized and turned in by a man he wouldn't have known from Adam. It was *almost* funny. He had barely spared Heisel two glances, Heisel and his broken back from God. On second thoughts, it wasn't *almost* funny; it was *very* funny.

He put three pills in his mouth, swallowed them with water, took three more, then three more. In the room across the hall he could see two old men hunched over a night-table, playing a grumpy game of cribbage. One of them had a hernia, Dussander knew. What was the other? Gallstones? Kidney stones? Tumour? Prostate? The horrors of old age. They were legion.

He refilled his water glass but didn't take any more pills right away. Too many could defeat his purpose. He might throw them up and they would pump the residue out of his stomach, saving him for whatever indignities the Americans and the Israelis could devise. He had no intention of trying to take his life stupidly, like a *hausfrau* on a crying jag. When he began to get drowsy, he would take a few more. That would be fine.

The quavering voice of one of the cribbage players came to him, thin and triumphant: 'A double run of four for ten . . . fifteens for eighteen . . . and the right jack for nineteen. How do you like *those* apples?'

'Don't worry,' the old man with the hernia said confidently. 'I got first count. I'll peg out.'

Peg out, Dussander thought, sleepy now. An apt enough

phrase – but the Americans had a turn for idiom. *I don't give a tin shit, get hip or get out, stick it where the sun don't shine, money talks, nobody walks.* Wonderful idiom.

They thought they had him, but he was going to peg out before their very eyes.

He found himself wishing, of all absurd things, that he could leave a note for the boy. Wishing he could tell him to be very careful. To listen to an old man who had finally overstepped himself. He wished he could tell the boy that in the end he, Dussander, had come to respect him, even if he could never like him, and that talking to him had been better than listening to the run of his own thoughts. But any note, no matter how innocent, might cast suspicion on the boy, and Dussander did not want that. Oh, he would have a bad month or two, waiting for some government agent to show up and question him about a certain document that had been found in a safety deposit box rented to Kurt Dussander, aka Arthur Denker . . . but after a time, the boy would come to believe he had been telling the truth. There was no need for the boy to be touched by any of this, as long as he kept his head.

Dussander reached out with a hand that seemed to stretch for miles, got the glass of water, and took another three pills. He put the glass back, closed his eyes, and settled deeper into his soft, soft pillow. He had never felt so much like sleeping, and his sleep would be long. It would be restful.

Unless there were dreams.

The thought shocked him. *Dreams? Please God, no. Not those dreams. Not for eternity, not with all possibility of awakening gone. Not –*

In sudden terror, he tried to struggle awake. It seemed

that hands were reaching eagerly up out of the bed to grab him, thin hands with hungry fingers.

(!NO!)

His thoughts broke up in a steepening spiral of darkness, and he rode down that spiral as if down a greased slide, down and down, to whatever dreams there are.

His overdose was discovered at 1.35 a.m., and he was pronounced dead fifteen minutes later. The nurse on duty was young and had been susceptible to elderly Mr Denker's slightly ironic courtliness. She burst into tears. She was a Catholic, and she could not understand why such a sweet old man, who had been getting better, would want to do such a thing and damn his immortal soul to hell.

26

On Saturday morning in the Bowden household, nobody got up until at least nine. This morning at 9.30, Todd and his father were reading at the table and Monica, who was a slow waker, served them scrambled eggs, juice, and coffee without speaking, still half in her dreams.

Todd was reading a paperback science fiction novel and Dick was absorbed in *Architectural Digest* when the paper slapped against the door.

'Want me to get it, dad?'

'I will.'

Dick brought it in, started to sip his coffee, and then choked on it as he got a look at the front page.

'Dick, what's wrong?' Monica asked, hurrying towards him.

Dick coughed out coffee that had gone down the wrong

pipe, and while Todd looked at him over the top of his paperback in mild wonder, Monica started to pound him on the back. On the third stroke, her eyes fell to the paper's headline and she stopped in mid-stroke, as if playing statues. Her eyes widened until it seemed they might actually fall onto the table.

'Holy God up in heaven!' Dick Bowden managed in a choked voice.

'Isn't that . . . I can't believe . . .' Monica began, and then stopped. She looked at Todd. 'Oh, honey —'

His father was looking at him, too.

Alarmed now, Todd came around the table. 'What's the matter?'

'Mr Denker,' Dick said — it was all he could manage.

Todd read the headline and understood everything. In dark letters it read: FUGITIVE NAZI COMMITS SUICIDE IN SANTA DONATO HOSPITAL. Below were two photos, side by side. Todd had seen both of them before. One showed Arthur Denker, six years younger and spryer. Todd knew it had been taken by a hippie street photographer, and that the old man had bought it only to make sure it didn't fall into the wrong hands by chance. The other photo showed an SS officer named Kurt Dussander, swagger-stick cocked jauntily (arrogantly, some might have said) under one arm, his cap cocked to one side.

If they had the photograph the hippie had taken, they had been in his house.

Todd skimmed the article, his mind whizzing franti-cally. No mention of the winos. But the bodies would be found, and when they were, it would be a worldwide story. PATIN COMMANDANT NEVER LOST HIS TOUCH,

HORROR IN NAZI'S BASEMENT. HE NEVER STOPPED KILLING.

Todd Bowden swayed on his feet.

Far away, echoing, he heard his mother cry sharply: 'Catch him, Dick! He's fainting!'

The word

(faintingfaintingfainting)

repeated itself over and over. He dimly felt his father's arm grab him, and then for a little while Todd felt nothing, heard nothing at all.

27

Ed French was eating a Danish when he unfolded the paper. He coughed, made a strange gagging sound, and spat dismembered pastry all over the table.

'Eddie!' Sondra French said with some alarm. 'Are you okay?'

'Daddy's chokin', daddy's chokin',' little Norma proclaimed with nervous good humour, and then happily joined her mother in slamming Ed on the back. Ed barely felt the blows. He was still goggling down at the newspaper.

'What's wrong, Eddie?' Sondra asked again.

'Him! Him!' Ed shouted, stabbing his finger down at the paper so hard that his fingernail tore all the way through the A section. 'That man! Lord Peter!'

'What in God's name are you t —'

'That's Todd Bowden's grandfather!'

'What? That war criminal? Eddie, that's *crazy*!'

'But it's *him*,' Ed almost moaned. 'Jesus Christ *Almighty*, that's *him*!'

Sondra French looked at the picture long and fixedly.

'He doesn't look like Peter Wimsey at all,' she said finally.

28

Todd, pale as window-glass, sat on a couch between his mother and father.

Opposite them was a greying, polite police detective named Richler. Todd's father had offered to call the police, but Todd had done it himself, his voice cracking through the registers as it had done when he was fourteen.

He finished his recital. It hadn't taken long. He spoke with a mechanical colourlessness that scared the hell out of Monica. He was almost eighteen, true enough, but he was still a boy in so many ways. This was going to scar him forever.

'I read him . . . oh, I don't know. *Tom Jones. The Mill on the Floss.* That was a boring one. I didn't think we'd ever get through it. Some stories by Hawthorne – I remember he especially liked "The Great Stone Face" and "Young Goodman Brown". We started *The Pickwick Papers*, but he didn't like it. He said Dickens could only be funny when he was being serious, and *Pickwick* was only kittenish. That was his word, kittenish. We got along the best with *Tom Jones.* We both liked that one.'

'And that was four years ago,' Richler said.

'Yes. I kept stopping in to see him when I got the chance, but in high school we were bussed across town . . . and some of the kids got up a scratch ball team . . . there was more homework . . . you know . . . things just came up.'

'You had less time.'

'Less time, that's right. The work in high school was a lot harder . . . making the grades to get into college.'

'But Todd is a very apt pupil,' Monica said almost automatically. 'He graduated salutatorian. We were so proud.'

'I'll bet you were,' Richler said with a warm smile. 'I've got two boys in Fairview, down in the valley, and they're just about able to keep their sports eligibility.' He turned back to Todd. 'You didn't read him any more books after you started high school?'

'No. Once in a while I'd read him the paper. I'd come over and he'd ask me what the headlines were. He was interested in Watergate when that was going on. And he always wanted to know about the stock market, and the print on that page used to drive him batshit – sorry, Mom.'

She patted his hand.

'I don't know why he was interested in the stocks, but he was.'

'He had a few stocks,' Richler said. 'That's how he was getting by. You want to hear a really crazy coincidence? The man who made the investments for him was convicted on a murder charge in the late forties. Dussander had five different sets of ID salted around that house. He was a cagey one, all right.'

'I suppose he kept the stocks in a safe deposit box somewhere,' Todd remarked.

'Pardon me?' Richler raised his eyebrows.

'His stocks,' Todd said. His father, who had also looked puzzled, now nodded at Richler.

'His stock certificates were in a footlocker under his bed,' Richler said, 'along with that photo of him as Denker. Did he have a safety deposit box, son? Did he ever say he did?'

Todd thought, and then shook his head. 'I just thought that was where you kept your stocks. I don't know. This . . . this whole thing has just . . . you know . . . it blows my wheels.' He shook his head in a dazed way that was perfectly real. He really *was* dazed. Yet, little by little, he felt his instincts of self-preservation surfacing. He felt a growing alertness, and the first stirrings of confidence. If Dussander had really taken a safety deposit box in which to store his insurance document, wouldn't he have transferred his stock certificates there? And that photograph?

'We're working with the Israelis on this,' Richler said. 'In a very unofficial way. I'd be grateful if you didn't mention that if you decide to see any press people. They're real professionals. There's a man named Weiskopf who'd like to talk to you tomorrow, Todd. If that's okay by you and your folks.'

'I guess so,' Todd said, but he felt a touch of atavistic dread at the thought of being sniffed over by the same hounds that had chased Dussander for the last third of his life. Dussander had had a healthy respect for them, and Todd knew he would do well to keep that in mind.

'Mr and Mrs Bowden? Do you have any objections to Todd seeing Mr Weiskopf?'

'Not if Todd doesn't,' Dick Bowden said. 'I'd like to be present, though. I've read about these Mossad characters –'

'Weiskopf isn't Mossad. He's what the Israelis call a special operative. In fact, he teaches Yiddish grammar – if you can believe that – and English Literature. Also, he's written two novels.' Richler smiled.

Dick raised a hand, dismissing it. 'Whatever he is, I'm not going to let him badger Todd. From what I've read, these fellows can be a little *too* professional. Maybe he's okay. But

I want you and this Weiskopf to remember that Todd tried to help that old man. He was flying under false colours, but Todd didn't know that.'

'That's okay, dad,' Todd said with a wan smile.

'I just want you to help us all that you can,' Richler said. 'I appreciate your concern, Mr Bowden. I think you're going to find that Weiskopf is a pleasant, low-pressure kind of guy. I've finished my own questions, but I'll break a little ground by telling you what the Israelis are most interested it. Todd was with Dussander when he had the heart attack that landed him in the hospital –'

'He asked me to come over and read him a letter,' Todd said.

'We know.' Richler leaned forward, elbows on his knees, tie swinging out to form a plumb-line to the floor. 'The Israelis want to know about that letter. Dussander was a big fish, but he wasn't the last one in the lake – or so Sam Weiskopf says, and I believe him. They think Dussander might have known about a lot of the other fish. Most of those still alive are probably in South America, but there may be others in a dozen countries . . . including the United States. Did you know they collared a man who had been an *Unterkommandant* at Buchenwald in the lobby of a Tel Aviv hotel?'

'Really!' Monica said, her eyes widening.

'Really,' Richler nodded. 'Two years ago. The point is just that the Israelis think the letter Dussander wanted Todd to read might have been from one of those other fish. Maybe they're right, maybe they're wrong. Either way, they want to know.'

Todd, who had gone back to Dussander's house and

burned the letter, said: 'I'd help you – or this Weiskopf – if I could, Lieutenant Richler, but the letter was in German. It was really tough to read. I felt like a fool. Mr Denker . . . Dussander . . . kept getting more excited and asking me to spell the words he couldn't understand because of my, you know, pronunciation. But I guess he was following all right. I remember once he laughed and said, "Yes, yes, that is what you'd do, isn't it?" Then he said something in German. This was about two or three minutes before he had the heart attack. Something about *Dummkop*. That means stupid in German, I think.'

He was looking at Richler uncertainly, inwardly quite pleased with this lie.

Richler was nodding. 'Yes, we can understand that the letter was in German. The admitting doctor heard the story from you and corroborated it. But the letter *itself*, Todd . . . do you remember what happened to it?'

Here it is, Todd thought. *The crunch.*

'I guess it was still on the table when the ambulance came. When we all left. I couldn't testify to it in court, but –'

'I think there was a letter on the table,' Dick said. 'I picked something up and glanced at it. Airmail stationery, I think, but I didn't notice it was written in German.'

'Then it should still be there,' Richler said. 'That's what we can't figure out.'

'It's not?' Dick said. 'I mean, it wasn't?'

'It wasn't, and it isn't.'

'Maybe somebody broke in,' Monica suggested.

'There would have been no need to *break* in,' Richler said. 'In the confusion of getting him out, the house was never locked. Dussander himself never thought to ask someone to lock up, apparently. His latchkey was still in the pocket of his pants when he died. His house was unlocked from the time the MED-Q attendants wheeled him out until we sealed it this morning at 2.30 a.m.'

'Well, there you are,' Dick said.

'No,' Todd said. 'I see what's bugging Lieutenant Richler.' Oh yes, he saw it very well. You'd have to be blind to miss it. 'Why would a burglar steal nothing but a letter? Especially one written in German? It doesn't listen. Mr Denker didn't have much to steal, but a guy who broke in could find something better than that.'

'You've got it, all right,' Richler said. 'Not bad.'

'Todd used to want to be a detective when he grew up,' Monica said, and ruffled Todd's hair a bit. Since he had gotten big he seemed to object to that, but right now he didn't seem to mind. God, she hated to see him looking so pale. 'I guess he's changed his mind to history these days.'

'History is a good field,' Richler said. 'You can be an investigative historian. Have you ever read Josephine Tey?'

'No, sir.'

'Doesn't matter. I just wish my boys had some ambition greater than seeing the Angels win the pennant this year.'

Todd offered a wan smile and said nothing.

Richler turned serious again. 'Anyway, I'll tell you the theory we're going on. We figure that someone, probably right here in Santa Donato, knew who and what Dussander was.'

'Really?' Dick said.

'Oh yes. Someone who knew the truth. Maybe another fugitive Nazi. I know that sounds like Robert Ludlum stuff, but who would have thought there was even *one* fugitive Nazi in a quiet little suburb like this? And when Dussander was taken to the hospital, we think that Mr X scooted over to the house and got that incriminating letter. And that by now it's so many decomposing ashes floating around in the sewer system.'

'That doesn't make much sense either,' Todd said.

'Why not, Todd?'

'Well, if Mr Denk . . . if *Dussander* had an old buddy from the camps, or just an old Nazi buddy, why did he bother to have me come over and read him that letter? I mean, if you could have heard him correcting me, and stuff . . . at least this old Nazi buddy you're talking about would know how to speak German.'

'A good point. Except maybe this other fellow is in a wheelchair, or blind. For all we know, it might be Bormann himself and he doesn't even dare go out and show his face.'

'Guys that are blind or in wheelchairs aren't that good at scooting out to get letters,' Todd said.

Richler looked admiring again. 'True. But a blind man could steal a letter even if he couldn't read it, though. Or hire it done.'

Todd thought this over, and nodded – but he shrugged at the same time to show how farfetched he thought the idea. Richler had progressed far beyond Robert Ludlum and into the land of Sax Rohmer. But how farfetched the idea was or wasn't didn't matter one fucking little bit, did it? No, what mattered was that Richler was still sniffing around . . . and that sheeny, Weiskopf, was also sniffing around. The letter, the goddam letter! If only he hadn't been forced to make something up on the spur of the moment like that! And suddenly he was thinking of his .30-.30, cased and resting on its shelf in the cool, dark garage. He pulled his mind away from it quickly. The palms of his hands had gone damp.

'*Did* Dussander have any friends that you knew of?' Richler was asking.

'Friends? No. There used to be a cleaning lady, but she moved away and he didn't bother to get another one. In the summer he hired a kid to mow his lawn, but I don't think he'd gotten one this year. The grass is pretty long, isn't it?'

'Yes. We've knocked on a lot of doors, and it doesn't seem as if he'd hired anyone. Did he get phone-calls?'

'Sure,' Todd said off-handedly – here was a gleam of light, a possible escape-hatch that was relatively safe. Dussander's phone had actually rung only half a dozen times or so in all the time Todd had known him – salesmen, a polling organization asking about breakfast foods, the rest wrong numbers. He only had the phone in case he got sick . . . as he finally had, might his soul rot in hell. 'He used to get a call or two every week.'

'Did he speak German on those occasions?' Richler asked quickly. He seemed excited.

'No,' Todd said, suddenly cautious. He didn't like Richler's excitement – there was something wrong about it, something dangerous. He felt sure of it, and suddenly Todd had to work furiously to keep himself from breaking a sweat. 'He didn't talk much at all. I remember that a couple of times he said things like, "The boy who reads to me is here right now. I'll call you back."'

'I'll bet that's it!' Richler said, whacking his palms on his thighs. 'I'd bet two weeks' pay that was the guy!' He closed his notebook with a snap (so far as Todd could see he had done nothing but doodle in it) and stood up. 'I want to thank all three of you for your time. You in particular, Todd. I know all of this has been a hell of a shock to you, but it will be over soon. We're going to turn the house upside down this afternoon – cellar to attic and then back down to the cellar again. We're bringing in all the special teams. We may find some trace of Dussander's phonemate yet.'

'I hope so,' Todd said.

Richler shook hands all around and left. Dick asked Todd if he felt like going out back and hitting the badminton birdie around until lunch. Todd said he didn't feel much like badminton *or* lunch, and went upstairs with his head down and his shoulders slumped. His parents exchanged sympathetic, troubled glances. Todd lay down on his bed, stared at the ceiling, and thought about his .30-.30. He could see it very clearly in his mind's eye. He thought about shoving the blued steel barrel right up Betty Trask's slimy Jewish cooze – just what she needed, a prick that never went soft. *How do you like it, Betty?* he heard himself asking her. *You just tell me if you get enough, okay?* He imagined her screams. And at last a terrible flat smile came to his face. *Sure, just tell me, you bitch . . . okay? Okay? Okay? . . .*

'So what do you think?' Weiskopf asked Richler when Richler picked him up at a luncheonette three blocks from the Bowden home.

'Oh, I think the kid was in on it somehow,' Richler said. 'Somehow, some way, to some degree. But is he cool? If you poured hot water into his mouth I think he'd spit out ice-cubes. I tripped him up a couple of times, but I've got nothing I could use in court. And if I'd gone much further, some smart lawyer might be able to get him off on entrapment a year or two down the road even if something *does* pull together. I mean, he's still a juvenile. Technically, at least. In some ways, I'd guess he hasn't *really* been a juvenile since he was maybe eight. He's creepy, man.' Richler stuck a cigarette in his mouth and laughed – the laugh had a shaky sound. 'I mean, really fuckin' creepy.'

'What slips did he make?'

'The phone calls. That's the main thing. When I slipped him the idea, I could see his eyes light up like a pinball machine.' Richler turned left and wheeled the nondescript Chevy Nova down the freeway entrance ramp. Two hundred yards to their right was the slope and the dead tree where Todd had dry-fired his rifle at the freeway traffic one Saturday morning not long ago.

'He's saying to himself, "This cop is off the wall if he thinks Dussander had a Nazi friend here in town, but if he *does* think that, it takes me off ground-zero." So he says yeah, Dussander got one or two calls a week. Very mysterious. "I can't talk now, Z-5, call later" – that type of thing. But Dussander's been getting a special "quiet phone" rate for the last seven years. Almost no activity at all, and *no* long distance. He wasn't getting a call or two a week.'

'What else?'

'He immediately jumped to the conclusion that the letter had been stolen and nothing else. He knew that was the only thing missing because he was the one who went back and took it.'

Richler jammed his cigarette out in the ashtray.

'We *think* the letter was just a prop. We *think* that Dussander had the heart attack while he was trying to bury that body . . . the freshest body. There was dirt on his shoes and his cuffs, and it was fresh, so that's a pretty fair assumption. That means he called the kid *after* he had the heart attack, not before. He crawls upstairs and phones the kid. The kid flips out – as much as he ever flips out, anyway – and cooks up the letter story on the spur of the moment. It's not great, but not that bad, either . . . considering the circumstances. He goes over there and cleans up Dussander's mess for him. Now the kid is in fucking overdrive. MED-Q's coming, his father is coming, and he needs that letter for stage-dressing. He goes upstairs and breaks open that box –'

'You've got confirmation on that?' Weiskopf asked, lighting a cigarette of his own. It was an unfiltered Player, and to Richler it smelled like horseshit. No wonder the British Empire fell, he thought, if they started smoking cigarettes like that.

'Yes, we've got confirmation right up the ying-yang,' Richler said. 'There are fingerprints on the box which match those in his school records. But his fingerprints are on almost *everything* in the goddam house!'

'Still, if you confront him with all of that, you can rattle him,' Weiskopf said.

'Oh, listen, hey, you don't know this kid. When I said he was cool, I meant it. He'd say Dussander asked him to fetch the box once or twice so he could put something in it or take something out of it.'

'His fingerprints are on the shovel.'

'He'd say he used it to plant a rose-bush in the back yard.' Richler took out his cigarettes but the pack was empty. Weiskopf offered him a Player. Richler took one puff and began coughing. 'They taste as bad as they smell,' he choked.

'Like those hamburgers we had for lunch yesterday,' Weiskopf said, smiling. 'Those Mac-Burgers.'

'Big Macs,' Richler said, and laughed. 'Okay. So cross-cultural pollination doesn't always work.' His smile faded. 'He looks so clean-cut, you know?'

'Yes.'

'This is no jd from Vasco with hair down to his asshole and chains on his motorcycle boots.'

'No.' Weiskopf stared at the traffic all around them and was very glad he wasn't driving. 'He's just a boy. A white boy from a good home. And I find it difficult to believe that –'

'I thought you had them ready to handle rifles and grenades by the time they were eighteen. In Israel.'

'Yes. But he was *fourteen* when all of this started. Why should a fourteen-year-old-boy mix himself up with such a man as Dussander? I have tried and tried to understand that and still I can't.'

'I'd settle for how,' Richler said, and flicked the cigarette out the window. It was giving him a headache.

'Perhaps, if it did happen, it was just luck. A coincidence. There is a word I like very much, Lieutenant Richler – serendipity. I think there is black serendipity as well as white.'

'I don't know what you're talking about,' Richler said gloomily. 'All I know is the kid is creepier than a bug under a rock.'

'What I'm saying is simple. Any other boy would have been more than happy to tell his parents, or the police. To say, "I have recognized a wanted man. He is living at this address. Yes, I am sure." And then let the authorities take over. Or do you feel I am wrong?'

'No, I wouldn't say so. The kid would be in the lime-light for a few days. Most kids would dig that. Picture in the paper, an interview on the evening news, probably a school assembly award for good citizenship.' Richler laughed. 'Hell, the kid would probably get a shot on *Real People*.'

'What's that?'

'Never mind,' Richler said. He had to raise his voice slightly because a ten-wheeler was passing the Nova on either side. Weiskopf looked nervously from one to the other. 'You don't want to know. But you're right about most kids. *Most* kids.'

'But not *this* kid,' Weiskopf said. 'This boy, probably by dumb luck alone, penetrates Dussander's cover. Yet instead of going to his parents or the authorities . . . he goes to Dussander. Why? You say you don't care, but I think you do. I think it haunts you just as it does me.'

'Not blackmail,' Richler said. 'That's for sure. That kid's got everything a kid could want. There was even a dune-buggy in the garage, not to mention an elephant gun on the wall. And even if he wanted to squeeze Dussander just for the thrill of it, Dussander was practically unsqueezable. Except for those few stocks, he didn't have a pot to piss in.'

'How sure are you that the boy doesn't know you've found the bodies?'

'I'm sure. Maybe I'll go back this afternoon and hit him with that. Right now it looks like our best shot.' Richler struck the steering wheel lightly. 'If all of this had come out even one day sooner, I think I would have tried for a search warrant.'

'The clothes the boy was wearing that night?'

'Yeah. If we could have found soil samples on his clothes that matched the dirt in Dussander's cellar, I almost think we could break him. But the clothes he was wearing that night have probably been washed six times since then.'

'What about the other dead winos? The ones your police department has been finding around the city?'

'Those belong to Dan Bozeman. I don't think there's any connection anyhow. Dussander just wasn't that strong . . . and more to the point, he had such a neat little racket already worked out. Promise them a drink and a meal, take them home on the city bus – *the fucking city bus*! – and waste them right in his kitchen.'

Weiskopf said quietly: 'It wasn't *Dussander* I was thinking of.'

'What do you mean by th –' Richler began, and then his mouth snapped suddenly closed. There was a long, unbelieving moment of silence, broken only by the drone of the traffic all around them. Then Richler said softly: 'Hey. Hey, come on now. Give me a fucking br –'

'As an agent of my government, I am only interested in Bowden because of what, if anything, he may know about Dussander's remaining contacts with the Nazi underground. But as a human being, I am becoming more and more interested in the boy himself. I'd like to know what makes him tick. I want to know *why*. And as I try to answer that question to my own satisfaction, I find that more and more I am asking myself *What else*.'

'But –'

'Do you suppose, I ask myself, that the very atrocities in which Dussander took part formed the basis of some attraction between them? That's an unholy idea, I tell myself. The things that happened in those camps still have power enough to make the stomach flutter with nausea. I feel that way myself, although the only close relative I ever had in the camps was my grandfather, and he died when I was three. But maybe for all of us there is something about what the

Germans did that pleases and excites us − something that opens the catacombs of the imagination. Maybe part of our dread and horror comes from a secret knowledge that under the right − or wrong − set of circumstances, we ourselves would be willing to build such places and staff them. Black serendipity. Maybe we know that under the right set of circumstances the things that live in the catacombs would be glad to crawl out. And what do you think they would look like? Like mad führers with forelocks and shoe-polish moustaches, heiling all over the place? Like red devils, or demons, or the dragon that floats on its stinking reptile wings?'

'I don't know,' Richler said.

'I think most of them would look like ordinary accountants,' Weiskopf said. 'Little mind-men with graphs and flow-charts and electronic calculators, all ready to start maximizing the kill ratios so that next time we could perhaps kill twenty or thirty millions instead of only seven or eight or twelve. And some of them might look like Todd Bowden.'

'You're damn near as creepy as he is,' Richler said.

Weiskopf nodded. 'It's a creepy subject. Finding those dead men and animals in Dussander's cellar . . . *that* was creepy, *nu*? Have you ever thought that maybe this boy began with a simple interest in the camps? An interest not much different from the interests of boys who collect coins or stamps or who like to read about Wild West desperados? And that he went to Dussander to get his information straight from the horse's head?'

'Mouth,' Weiskopf muttered. It was almost lost in the roar of another ten-wheeler passing them. BUDWEISER was printed on the side in letters six feet tall. What an amazing country, Weiskopf thought and lit a fresh cigarette. They don't understand how we can live surrounded by half-mad Arabs, but if I lived here for two years I would have a nervous breakdown.'Maybe. And maybe it isn't possible to stand close to murder piled on murder and not be touched by it.'

29

The short guy who entered the squadroom brought stench after him like a wake. He smelled like rotten bananas and Wildroot Cream Oil and cockroach shit and the inside of a city garbage truck at the end of a busy morning. He was dressed in a pair of ageing herringbone pants, a ripped grey institutional shirt, and a faded blue warmup jacket from which most of the zipper hung loose like a string of pygmy teeth. The uppers of his shoes were bound to the lowers with Krazy Glue. A pestiferous hat sat on his head. He looked like death with a hangover.

'Oh Christ, get out of here!' the duty sergeant cried. 'You're not under arrest, Hap! I swear to God! I swear it on my mother's name! Get out of here! I want to breathe again.'

'I want to talk to Lieutenant Bozeman.'

'He died, Hap. It happened yesterday. We're all really fucked up over it. So get out and let us mourn in peace.'

'I want to talk to Lieutenant Bozeman!' Hap said more loudly. His breath drifted fragrantly from his mouth: a juicy, fermenting mixture of pizza, Hall's Mentholyptus lozenges, and sweet red wine.

'He had to go to Siam on a case, Hap. So why don't you just get out of here? Go someplace and eat a lightbulb.'

'I want to talk to Lieutenant Bozeman and I ain't leaving until I do!'

The duty sergeant fled the room. He returned about five minutes later with Bozeman, a thin, slightly stooped man of fifty.

'Take him into your office, okay, Dan?' the duty sergeant begged. 'Won't that be all right?'

'Come on, Hap,' Bozeman said, and a minute later they were in the three-sided stall that was Bozeman's office. Bozeman prudently opened his only window and turned on his fan before sitting down. 'Do something for you, Hap?'

'You still on those murders, Lieutenant Bozeman?'

'The derelicts? Yeah, I guess that's still mine.'

'Well, I know who greased 'em.'

'Is that so, Hap?' Bozeman asked. He was busy lighting his pipe. He rarely smoked the pipe, but neither the fan nor the open window was quite enough to overwhelm Hap's smell. Soon, Bozeman thought, the paint would begin to blister and peel. He sighed.

'You member I tole you Sonny was talking to a guy just a day before they found him all cut up in that pipe? You member me tellin' you that, Lieutenant Bozeman?'

'I remember.' Several of the winos who hung around the Salvation Army and the soup kitchen a few blocks away had told a similar story about two of the murdered derelicts, Charles 'Sonny' Brackett and Peter 'Poley' Smith. They had seen a guy hanging around, a young guy, talking to Sonny and Poley. Nobody knew for sure if Sonny had gone off with the guy, but Hap and two others claimed to have seen Poley Smith walk off with him. They had the idea that the 'guy' was underage and willing to spring for a bottle of musky in exchange for some juice. Several other winos claimed to have seen a 'guy' like that around. The description of this 'guy' was superb, bound to stand up in court, coming as it did from such unimpeachable sources. Young, blond, and white. What else did you need to make a bust?

'Well, last night I was in the park,' Hap said, 'and I just happened to have this old bunch of newspapers –'

'There's a law against vagrancy in this city, Hap.'

'I was just collectin' 'em up,' Hap said righteously. 'It's so awful the way people litter. I was doin' a public surface, Lieutenant. A friggin' public surface. Some of those papers was a week old.'

'Yes, Hap,' Bozeman said. He remembered – vaguely – being quite hungry and looking forward keenly to his lunch. That time seemed long ago now.

'Well, when I woke up, one of those papers had blew onto my face and I was looking right *at* the guy. Gave me a hell of a jump, I can tell you. Look. This is the guy. This guy right here.'

Hap pulled a crumpled, yellowed, water-spotted sheet of newspaper from his warmup jacket and unfolded it. Bozeman leaned forward, now moderately interested. Hap put the paper on his desk so he could read the headline: 4 BOYS NAMED TO SOUTHERN CAL ALL-STARS. Below the head were four photos.

'Which one, Hap?

Hap put a grimy finger on the picture to the far right. 'Him. It says his name is Todd Bowden.'

Bozeman looked from the picture to Hap, wondering how many of Hap's brain-cells were still unfried and in some kind of working order after twenty years of being sautéed in a bubbling sauce of cheap wine seasoned with an occasional shot of sterno.

'How can you be sure, Hap? He's wearing a baseball cap in the picture. I can't tell if he's got blond hair or not.'

'The grin,' Hap said. 'It's the way he's grinnin'. He was grinnin' at Poley in just that same ain't-life-grand way when they walked off together. I couldn't mistake that grin in a million years. That's him, that's the guy.'

Bozeman barely heard this last; he was thinking, and thinking hard. *Todd Bowden.* There was something familiar about that name. Something that bothered him even worse than the thought that a local high school hero might be going around and offing winos. He thought he had heard that name just this morning in conversation. He frowned, trying to remember where.

Hap was gone and Dan Bozeman was still trying to figure it out when Richler and Weiskopf came in . . . and it was the sound of their voices as they got coffee in the squad-room that finally brought it home to him.

'Holy God,' said Lieutenant Bozeman, and got up in a hurry.

30

Both of his parents had offered to cancel their afternoon plans – Monica at the market and Dick golfing with some business people – and stay home with him, but Todd told them he would rather be alone. He thought he would clean his rifle and just sort of think the whole thing over. Try to get it straight in his mind.

'Todd,' Dick said, and suddenly found he had nothing much to say. He supposed if he had been his own father, he would have at this point advised prayer. But the generations had turned, and the Bowdens weren't much into that these days. 'Sometimes these things happen,' he finished lamely, because Todd was still looking at him. 'Try not to brood about it.'

'I'll be all right,' Todd said.

After they were gone, he took some rags and a bottle of Alpaca gun oil out onto the bench beside the roses. He went back into the garage and got the .30-.30. He took it to the bench and broke it down, the dusty-sweet smell of the flowers lingering pleasantly in his nose. He cleaned the gun thoroughly, humming a tune as he did it, sometimes whistling a snatch between his teeth. Then he put the gun together again. He could have done it just as easily in the dark. His mind wandered free. When it came back some five minutes later, he observed that he had loaded the gun. The idea of target shooting didn't much appeal, not today, but he had still loaded it. He told himself he didn't know why.

Sure you do, Todd-baby. The time, so to speak, has come.

And that was when the shiny yellow Saab turned into the driveway. The man who got out was vaguely familiar to Todd, but it wasn't until he slammed the car door and started to walk towards him that Todd saw the sneakers – low-topped Keds, light blue. Talk about Blasts from the Past; here, walking up the Bowden driveway, was Rubber Ed French, the Ked Man.

'Hi, Todd. Long time no see.'

Todd leaned the rifle against the side of the bench and offered his wide and winsome grin. 'Hi, Mr French. What are you doing out here on the wild side of town?'

'Are your folks home?'

'Gee, no. Did you want them for something?'

'No,' Ed French said after a long, thoughtful pause. 'No, I guess not. I guess maybe it would be better if just you and I talked. For starters, anyway. You may be able to offer a perfectly reasonable explanation for all this. Although God knows I doubt it.'

He reached into his hip pocket and brought out a newsclipping. Todd knew what it was even before Rubber Ed passed it to him, and for the second time that day he was looking at the side-by-side pictures of Dussander. The one the street-photographer had taken had been circled in black ink. The meaning was clear enough to Todd; French had recognized Todd's 'grandfather'. And now he wanted to tell everyone in the world all about it. He wanted to midwife the good news. Good old Rubber Ed, with his jive talk and his motherfucking sneakers.

The police would be very interested – but, of course, they already were. He knew that now. The sinking feeling had begun about thirty minutes after Richler left. It was as if he had been riding high in a balloon filled with happy-gas. Then a cold steel arrow had ripped through the balloon's fabric, and now it was sinking steadily.

The phone calls, that was the biggie. Fucking Richler had trotted that out just as slick as warm owlshit. *Sure*, he had said, practically breaking his neck to rush into the trap. *He gets one or two calls a week.* Let them go ranting all over southern California looking for geriatric ex-Nazis. Fine. Except maybe they had gotten a different story from Ma Bell. Todd didn't know if the phone company could tell how much you used your phone for local calls . . . but there had been a look in Richler's eyes . . .

Then there was the letter. He had inadvertently told

Richler that the house hadn't been burgled, and Richler had no doubt gone away thinking that the only way Todd could have known that was if he had been back . . . as he had been, not just once but three times, first to get the letter and twice more looking for anything incriminating. There had been nothing; even the Gestapo uniform was gone, disposed of by Dussander sometime during the last four years.

And then there were the bodies. Richler had never mentioned the bodies.

At first Todd had thought that was good. Let them hunt a little longer while he got his own head – not to mention his story – straight. No fear about the dirt that had gotten on his clothes burying the body; they had all been cleaned later that same night. He ran them through the washer-dryer himself, perfectly aware that Dussander might die and then everything might come out. You can't be too careful, boy, as Dussander himself would have said.

Then, little by little, he had realized it was *not* good. The weather had been warm, and the warm weather always made the cellar smell worse; on his last trip to Dussander's house it had been a rank presence. Surely the police would have been interested in that smell, and would have tracked it to its source. So why had Richler withheld the information? Was he saving it for later? Saving it for a nasty little surprise? And if Richler was into planning nasty little surprises, it could mean that he suspected.

Todd looked up from the clipping and saw that Rubber Ed had half turned away from him. He was looking into the street, although not much was happening out there. Richler could suspect, but suspicion was the best he could do.

Unless there was some sort of concrete evidence binding Todd to the old man.

Exactly the sort of evidence Rubber Ed French could give.

Ridiculous man in a pair of ridiculous sneakers. Such a ridiculous man hardly deserved to live. Todd touched the barrel of the .30–.30.

Yes, Rubber Ed was the link they didn't have. They could *never* prove that Todd had been an accessory to one of Dussander's murders. But with Rubber Ed's testimony they could prove conspiracy. And would even *that* end it? Oh, no. They would get his high school graduation picture next and start showing it to the stewbums down in the Mission district. A long shot, but one Richler could ill afford not to play. If we can't pin one bunch of winos on him, maybe we can get him for the other bunch.

What next? Court next.

His father would get him a wonderful bunch of lawyers, of course. And the lawyers would get him off, of course. Too much circumstantial evidence. He would make too favourable an impression on the jury. But by then his life would be ruined anyway. It would all be dragged through the newspapers, dug up and brought into the light like the half-decayed bodies in Dussander's cellar.

'The man in that picture is the man who came to my office when you were in the ninth grade,' Ed told him abruptly, turning to Todd again. 'He purported to be your grand-father. Now it turns out he was a wanted war criminal.'

'Yes,' Todd said. His face had gone oddly blank. It was the face of a department store dummy. All the healthiness, life, and vivacity had drained from it. What was left was frightening in its vacuous emptiness.

'How did it happen?' Ed asked, and perhaps he intended his question as a thundering accusation, but it came out sounding plaintive and lost and somehow cheated. 'How did this happen, Todd?'

'Oh, one thing just followed another,' Todd said, and picked up the .30–.30. 'That's really how it happened. One thing just . . . followed another.' He pushed the safety catch to the off position with his thumb and pointed the rifle at Rubber Ed. 'As stupid as it sounds, that's just what happened. That's all there was to it.'

'Todd,' Ed said, his eyes widening. He took a step backward. 'Todd, you don't want to . . . please, Todd. We can talk this over. We can disc –'

'You and the fucking kraut can discuss it down in hell,' Todd said, and pulled the trigger.

The sound of the shot rolled away in the hot and windless quiet of the afternoon. Ed French was flung back against his Saab. His hand groped behind him and tore off a windshield wiper. He stared at it foolishly as blood spread on his blue turtleneck, and then he dropped it and looked at Todd.

'Norma,' he whispered.

'Okay,' Todd said. 'Whatever you say, champ.' He shot Rubber Ed again and roughly half of his head disappeared in a spray of blood and bone.

Ed turned drunkenly and began to grope towards the driver's side door, speaking his daughter's name over and over again in a choked and failing voice. Todd shot him again, aiming for the base of the spine, and Ed fell down. His feet drummed briefly on the gravel and then were still.

Sure did die hard for a guidance counsellor, Todd thought, and brief laughter escaped him. At the same moment a burst of pain as sharp as an icepick drove into his brain and he closed his eyes.

When he opened them again, he felt better than he had in months – maybe better than he had felt in years. Everything was fine. Everything was together. The blankness left his face and a kind of wild beauty filled it.

He went back into the garage and got all the shells he had, better than four hundred rounds. He put them in his old knapsack and shouldered it. When he came back out into the sunshine he was smiling excitedly, his eyes dancing – it was the way boys smile on their birthdays, on Christmas, on the Fourth of July. It was a smile that betokened skyrockets, tree-houses, secret signs and secret meeting-places, the aftermath of the triumphal big game when the players are carried into town on the shoulders of the exultant fans. The ecstatic smile of tow-headed boys going off to war in coal-scuttle helmets.

'*I'm king of the world!*' he shouted mightily at the high blue sky, and raised the rifle two-handed over his head for a moment. Then, switching it to his right hand, he started towards that place above the freeway where the land fell away and where the dead tree would give him shelter.

It was five hours later and almost dark before they took him down.

Fall from Innocence

THE BODY

For George McLeod

1

The most important things are the hardest things to say. They are the things you get ashamed of, because words diminish them — words shrink things that seemed limitless when they were in your head to no more than living size when they're brought out. But it's more than that, isn't it? The most important things lie too close to wherever your secret heart is buried, like landmarks to a treasure your enemies would love to steal away. And you may make revelations that cost you dearly only to have people look at you in a funny way, not understanding what you've said at all, or why you thought it was so important that you almost cried while you were saying it. That's the worst, I think. When the secret stays locked within not for want of a teller but for want of an understanding ear.

I was twelve going on thirteen when I first saw a dead human being. It happened in 1960, a long time ago . . . although sometimes it doesn't seem that long to me. Especially on the nights I wake up from those dreams where the hail fell into his open eyes.

2

We had a treehouse in a big elm which overhung a vacant lot in Castle Rock. There's a moving company on that lot today, and the elm is gone. Progress. It was a sort of social club, although it had no name. There were five, maybe six steady guys and some other wet ends who just hung around. We'd let them come up when there was a card game and we needed some fresh blood. The game was usually blackjack and we played for pennies, nickel limit. But you got double money on blackjack and five-card-under . . . *triple* money on six-card-under, although Teddy was the only guy crazy enough to go for that.

The sides of the treehouse were planks scavenged from the shitpile behind Makey Lumber & Building Supply on Carbine Road – they were splintery and full of knotholes we plugged with either toilet paper or paper towels. The roof was a corrugated tin sheet we hawked from the dump, looking over our shoulders all the time we were hustling it out of there, because the dump custodian's dog was supposed to be a real kid-eating monster. We found a screen door out there on the same day. It was flyproof but really rusty – I mean, that rust was *extreme*. No matter what time of day you looked out that screen door, it looked like sunset.

Besides playing cards, the club was a good place to go and smoke cigarettes and look at girly books. There were half a dozen battered tin ashtrays that said CAMELS on the bottom, a lot of centrefolds tacked to the splintery walls, twenty or thirty dog-eared packs of Bike cards (Teddy got them from his uncle, who ran the Castle Rock Stationery Shoppe – when Teddy's unc asked him one day what kind of cards we played, Teddy said we had cribbage tournaments and Teddy's unc thought that was just fine), a set of plastic poker chips, and a pile of ancient *Master Detective* murder magazines to leaf through if there was nothing else shaking. We also built a 12″ x 10″ secret compartment under the floor to hide most of this stuff in on the rare occasions when some kid's father decided it was time to do the We're Really Good Pals routine. When it rained, being in the club was like being inside a Jamaican steel drum . . . but that summer there had been no rain.

It had been the driest and hottest since 1907 – or so the newspapers said, and on that Friday preceding the Labour Day weekend and the start of another school year, even the goldenrod in the fields and the ditches beside the backroads looked parched and poorly. Nobody's garden had done doodly-squat that year, and the big displays of canning stuff in the Castle Rock Red & White were still there, gathering dust. No one had anything to put up that summer, except maybe dandelion wine.

Teddy and Chris and I were up in the club on that Friday morning, glooming to each other about school being so near and playing cards and swapping the same old travelling salesman jokes and Frenchman jokes. How do you know when a Frenchman's been in your back yard? Well, your garbage cans are empty and your dog is pregnant. Teddy would try to look offended, but he was the first one to bring in a joke as soon as he heard it, only switching Frenchman to Polack.

The elm gave good shade, but we already had our shirts off so we wouldn't sweat them up too bad. We were playing three-penny-scat, the dullest card game ever invented, but it was too hot to think about anything more complicated. We'd had a pretty fair scratch ballteam until the middle of August and then a lot of kids just drifted away. Too hot.

I was down to my ride and building spades. I'd started with thirteen, gotten an eight to make twenty-one, and nothing had happened since then. Chris knocked. I took my last draw and got nothing helpful.

'Twenty-nine,' Chris said, laying down diamonds.

'Twenty-two,' Teddy said, looking disgusted.

'Piss up a rope,' I said, and tossed my cards onto the table face-down.

'Gordie's out, ole Gordie just bit the bag and stepped out the door,' Teddy bugled, and then gave out with his patented Teddy Duchamp laugh – *Eeee-eee-eee*, like a rusty nail being slowly hauled out of a rotten board. Well, he was weird; we all knew it. Close to being thirteen like the rest of us, the thick glasses and the hearing aid he wore sometimes made him look like an old man. Kids were always trying to cadge smokes off him on the street, but the bulge in his shirt was just his hearing aid battery.

In spite of the glasses and the flesh-coloured button always screwed into his ear, Teddy couldn't see very well and often misunderstood the things people said to him. In baseball you had to have him play the fences, way beyond Chris in left field and Billy Greer in right. You just hoped no one would hit one that far because Teddy would go grimly after it, see it or not. Every now and then he got bonked a good one, and once he went out cold when he ran full tilt boogie into the fence by the treehouse. He lay there on his back with his eyes showing whites for almost five minutes, and I got scared. Then he woke up and walked around with a bloody nose and a huge purple lump rising on his forehead, trying to claim that the ball was foul.

His eyesight was just naturally bad, but there was nothing natural about what had happened to his ears. Back in those days, when it was cool to get your hair cut so that your ears stuck out like a couple of jug-handles, Teddy had Castle Rock's first Beatle haircut – four years before anyone in America had even heard of the Beatles. He kept his ears covered because they looked like two lumps of warm wax.

One day when he was eight, Teddy's father got pissed at him for breaking a plate. His mother was working at the shoe factory in South Paris when it happened and by the time she found out about it, everything had happened.

Teddy's dad took Teddy over to the big woodstove at the back of the kitchen and shoved the side of Teddy's head down against one of the cast-iron burner plates. He held it down there for about ten seconds. Then he yanked Teddy up by the hair and did the other side. Then he called the Central Maine General Emergency Unit and told them to come get his boy. Then he hung up the phone, went into the closet, got his four-ten, and sat down to watch the daytime stories on TV with the shotgun laid across his knees. When Mrs Burroughs from next door came over to ask if Teddy was all right – she'd heard the screaming – Teddy's dad pointed the shotgun at her. Mrs Burroughs went out of the Duchamp house at roughly the speed of light, locked herself into her own house, and called the police. When the ambulance came, Mr Duchamp let the orderlies in and then went out on the back porch to stand guard while they wheeled Teddy to the old portholed Buick ambulance on a stretcher.

Teddy's dad explained to the orderlies that while the fucking brass hats said the area was clear, there were still Kraut snipers everywhere. One of the orderlies asked Teddy's dad if he thought he could hold on. Teddy's dad smiled tightly and told the orderly he'd hold until hell was a Frigidaire dealership, if that's what it took. The orderly saluted, and Teddy's dad snapped it right back at him. A few minutes after the ambulance left, the state police arrived and relieved Norman Duchamp of duty.

He'd been doing odd things like shooting cats and lighting fires in mailboxes for over a year, and after the atrocity he had visited upon his son, they had a quick hearing and sent him to Togus, which is a special sort of V.A. hospital. Togus is where you have to go if you're a section eight. Teddy's dad had stormed the beach at Normandy, and that's just the way Teddy always put it. Teddy was proud of his old man in spite of what his old man had done to him, and Teddy went with his mom to visit him every week.

He was the dumbest guy we hung around with, I guess, and he was crazy. He'd take the craziest chances you can imagine, and get away with them. His big thing was what he called Truck Dodging. He'd run out in front of them on 196 and sometimes they'd miss him by bare inches. God knew how many heart attacks he'd caused, and he'd be laughing while the windblast from the passing truck rippled his clothes. It scared us because his vision was so lousy. Coke-bottle glasses or not. It seemed like only a matter of time before he misjudged one of those trucks. And you had to be careful what you dared him, because Teddy would do anything on a dare.

'Gordie's out, eeeeee-eee-eee!'

'Screw,' I said, and picked up a *Master Detective* to read while they played it out. I turned to 'He Stomped the Pretty Co-Ed to Death in a Stalled Elevator' and got right into it.

Teddy picked up the cards, gave them one brief look, and said: 'I knock.'

'You four-eyed pile of shit!' Chris cried.

'The pile of shit has a thousand eyes,' Teddy said seriously, and both Chris and I cracked up. Teddy stared at us with a slight frown, as if wondering what had gotten us laughing. That was another thing about the cat – he was always coming out with weird stuff like 'The pile of shit has a thousand eyes', and you could never be sure if he *meant* it to be funny or if it just happened that way. He'd look at the people who were laughing with that slight frown on his face, as if to say *O Lord what is it this time?*

Teddy had a natural thirty – jack, queen, and king of clubs. Chris had only sixteen and went down to his ride.

Teddy was shuffling the cards in his clumsy way and I was just getting to the gooshy part of the murder story, where this deranged sailor from New Orleans was doing the Bristol Stomp all over this college girl from Bryn Mawr because he couldn't stand being in closed-in spaces, when we heard someone coming fast up the ladder nailed to the side of the elm. A fist rapped on the underside of the trapdoor.

'Who goes?' Chris yelled.

'Vern!' He sounded excited and out of breath.

I went to the trapdoor and pulled the bolt. The trapdoor banged up and Vern Tessio, one of the other regulars, pulled himself into the clubhouse. He was sweating buckets and his hair, which he usually kept combed in a perfect imitation of his rock and roll idol, Bobby Rydell, was plastered to his bullet head in chunks and strings.

'Wow, man,' he panted. 'Wait'll you hear this.'

'Hear what?' I asked.

'Lemme get my breath. I ran all the way from my house.'

'*I ran all the way home,*' Teddy wavered in a dreadful Little Anthony falsetto, '*just to say I'm soh-ree –*'

'Fuck your hand, man,' Vern said.

'Drop dead in a shed, Fred,' Teddy returned smartly.

'You ran all the way from your place?' Chris asked unbelievingly. 'Man, you're crazy.' Vern's house was two miles down Grand Street. 'It must be ninety out there.'

'This is worth it,' Vern said. 'Holy Jeezum. You won't

believe this. Sincerely.' He slapped his sweaty forehead to show us how sincere he was.

'Okay, what?' Chris asked.

'Can you guys camp out tonight?' Vern was looking at us earnestly, excitedly. His eyes looked like raisins pushed into dark circles of sweat. 'I mean, if you tell your folks we're gonna tent out in my back field?'

'Yeah, I guess so,' Chris said, picking up his new hand and looking at it. 'But my dad's on a mean streak. Drinkin', y'know.'

'You got to, man,' Vern said. 'Sincerely. You won't *believe* this. Can you, Gordie?'

'Probably.'

I was able to do most stuff like that – in fact, I'd been like the Invisible Boy that whole summer. In April my older brother, Dennis, had been killed in a Jeep accident. That was at Fort Benning, Georgia, where he was in basic. He and another guy were on their way to the PX and an army truck hit them broadside. Dennis was killed instantly and his passenger had been in a coma ever since. Dennis would have been twenty later that week. I'd already picked out a birthday card for him at Dahlie's over in Castle Green.

I cried when I heard, and I cried more at the funeral, and I couldn't believe that Dennis was gone, that anyone that used to knuckle my head or scare me with a rubber spider until I cried or give me a kiss when I fell down and scraped both knees bloody and whisper in my ear, 'Now stop cryin', ya baby!' – that a person who had *touched* me could be dead. It hurt me and it scared me that he could be dead . . . but it seemed to have taken all the heart out of my parents. For me, Dennis was hardly more than an acquaintance. He was eight years older than me if you can dig it, and he had his own friends and classmates. We ate at the same table for a lot of years, and sometimes he was my friend and sometimes my tormentor, but mostly he was, you know, just a guy. When he died he'd been gone for a year except for a couple of furloughs. We didn't even look alike. It took me a long time after that summer to realize that most of the tears I cried were for my mom and dad. Fat lot of good it did them, or me.

'So what are you pissing and moaning about, Vern-O?' Teddy asked.

'I knock,' Chris said.

'*What?*' Teddy screamed, immediately forgetting all about Vern. 'You friggin' liar! You ain't got no pat hand. I didn't deal you no pat hand.'

Chris smirked. 'Make your draw, shitheap.'

Teddy reached for the top card of the pile of Bikes. Chris reached for the Winstons on the ledge behind him. I bent over to pick up my detective magazine.

Vern Tessio said: 'You guys want to go see a dead body?'

Everybody stopped.

3

We'd all heard about it on the radio, of course. The radio, a Philco with a cracked case which had also been scavenged from the dump, played all the time. We kept it tuned to WLAM in Lewiston, which churned out the super-hits and the boss oldies: 'What in the World's Come Over You' by Jack Scott and 'This Time' by Troy Shondell and 'King Creole' by Elvis and 'Only the Lonely' by Roy Orbison. When the news came on we usually switched some mental dial over to Mute. The news was a lot of happy horseshit about Kennedy and Nixon and Quemoy and Matsu and the missile gap and what a shit that Castro was turning out to be after all. But we had all listened to the Ray Brower story a little more closely, because he was a kid our age.

He was from Chamberlain, a town forty miles or so east of Castle Rock. Three days before Vern came busting into the clubhouse after a two-mile run up Grand Street, Ray Brower had gone out with one of his mother's pots to pick blueberries. When dark came and he still wasn't back, the Browers called the county sheriff and a search started – first just around the kid's house and then spreading to the surrounding towns of Motton and Durham and Pownal. Everybody got into the act – cops, deputies, game wardens, volunteers. But three days later the kid was still missing. You could tell, hearing about it on the radio, that they were never going to find that poor sucker alive; eventually the search would just peter away into nothing. He might have gotten smothered in a gravel pit slide or drowned in a brook, and ten years from now some hunter would find his bones. They were already dragging the ponds in Chamberlain, and the Motton Reservoir.

Nothing like that could happen in south-western Maine today; most of the area has become suburbanized, and the bedroom communities surrounding Portland and Lewiston have spread out like the tentacles of a giant squid. The woods are still there, and they get heavier as you work your way west towards the White Mountains, but these days if you can keep your head long enough to walk five miles in one consistent direction, you're certain to cross two-lane blacktop. But in 1960 the whole area between Chamberlain and Castle Rock was undeveloped, and there were places that hadn't even been logged since before World War II. In those days it was still possible to walk into the woods and lose your direction there and die there.

4

Vern Tessio had been under his porch that morning, digging.

We all understood that right away, but maybe I should take just a minute to explain it to you. Teddy Duchamp was only about half-bright, but Vern Tessio would never be spending any of his spare time on Quiz Kids either. Still, his brother Billy was even dumber, as you will see. But first I have to tell you why Vern was digging under the porch.

Four years ago, when he was eight, Vern buried a quart jar of pennies under the long Tessio front porch. Vern called the dark space under the porch his 'cave'. He was playing a pirate sort of game, and the pennies were buried treasure – only if you were playing pirate with Vern, you couldn't call it buried treasure, you had to call it 'booty'. So he buried the jar of pennies deep, filled in the hole, and covered the fresh dirt with some of the old leaves that had drifted under there over the years. He drew a treasure map which he put up in his room with the rest of his junk. He forgot all about it for a month or so. Then, being low on cash for a movie or something, he remembered the pennies and went to get his map. But his mom had been in to clean two or three times since then, and had collected all the old homework papers and candy wrappers and comic magazines and joke books. She burned them in the stove to start the cook-fire one morning, and Vern's treasure map went right up the kitchen chimney.

Or so he figured it.

He tried to find the spot from memory and dug there. No luck. To the right and the left of that spot. Still no luck. He gave up for the day but had tried off and on ever since. Four years, man. Four *years*. Isn't that a pisser? You didn't know whether to laugh or cry.

It had gotten to be sort of an obsession with him. The Tessio front porch ran the length of the house, probably forty feet long and seven feet wide. He had dug through damn near every inch of that area two, maybe three times and no pennies. The *number* of pennies began to grow in his mind. When it first happened he told Chris and me that there had been maybe three dollars' worth. A year later he was up to five and just lately it was running around ten, more or less, depending on how broke he was.

Every so often we tried to tell him what was so clear to us – that Billy had known about the jar and dug it up himself. Vern refused to believe it, although he hated Billy like the Arabs hate the Jews and probably would have cheerfully voted the death penalty on his brother for shoplifting, if the opportunity had ever presented itself. He also refused to ask Billy point blank. Probably he was afraid Billy would laugh and say *Course I got them, you stupid pussy, and there was twenty bucks' worth of pennies in that jar and I spent every fuckin' cent of it*. Instead, Vern went out and dug for the pennies whenever the spirit moved him (and whenever Billy wasn't around). He always crawled out from under the porch with his jeans dirty and his hair leafy and his hands empty. We ragged him about it something wicked, and his nickname was Penny – Penny Tessio. I think he came up to the club with his news as quick as he did not just to get it out but to show us that some good had finally come of his penny-hunt.

He had been up that morning before anybody, ate his cornflakes, and was out in the driveway shooting baskets through the old hoop nailed up on the garage, nothing much to do, no one to play Ghost with or anything, and he decided to have another dig for his pennies. He was under the porch when the screen door slammed up above. He froze, not making a sound. If it was his dad, he would crawl out; if it was Billy, he'd stay put until Billy and his jd friend Charlie Hogan had taken off.

Two pairs of footsteps crossed the porch, and then Charlie Hogan himself said in a trembling, cry-baby voice: 'Jesus Christ, Billy, what are we gonna do?'

Vern said that just hearing Charlie Hogan talk like that – Charlie, who was one of the toughest kids in town – made him prick up his ears. Charlie, after all, hung out with Ace Merrill and Eyeball Chambers, and if you hung out with cats like that, you had to be tough.

'Nuthin',' Billy said. 'That's all we're gonna do. Nuthin'.'

'We gotta do *somethin'*,' Charlie said, and they sat down on the porch close to where Vern was hunkered down. 'Didn't you *see* him?'

Vern took a chance and crept a little closer to the steps, practically slavering. At that point he thought that maybe Billy and Charlie had been really drunked up and had run somebody down. Vern was careful not to crackle any of the old leaves as he moved. If the two of them found out he was under the porch and had overheard them, you could have put what was left of him in a Ken-L-Ration dogfood can.

'It's nuthin' to us,' Billy Tessio said. 'The kid's dead so it's nuthin' to him, neither. Who gives a fuck if they ever find him? I don't.'

'It was that kid they been talkin' about on the radio,' Charlie said. 'It was, sure as shit. Brocker, Brower, Flowers, whatever his name is. Fuckin' train must have hit him.'

'Yeah,' Billy said. Sound of a scratched match. Vern saw it flicked into the gravel driveway and then smelled cigarette smoke. 'It sure did. And you puked.'

No words, but Vern sensed emotional waves of shame radiating off Charlie Hogan.

'Well, the girls didn't see it,' Billy said after a while. 'Lucky break.' From the sound, he clapped Charlie on the back to buck him up. 'They'd blab it from here to Portland. We tore out of there fast, though. You think they knew there was something wrong?'

'No,' Charlie said. 'Marie don't like to go down that Back Harlow Road past the cemetery, anyway. She's afraid of ghosts.' Then again in that scared cry-baby voice: 'Jesus, I wish we'd never boosted no car last night! Just gone to the show like we was gonna!'

Charlie and Billy went with a couple of scags named Marie Daughtery and Beverly Thomas; you never saw such gross-looking broads outside of a carnival show – pimples, moustaches, the whole works. Sometimes the four of them – or maybe six or eight if Fuzzy Brackowicz or Ace Merrill were along with their girls – would boost a car from a Lewiston parking lot and go joyriding out into the country with two or three bottles of Wild Irish Rose wine and a six-pack of ginger ale. They'd take the girls parking somewhere in Castle View or Harlow or Shiloh, drink Purple Jesuses, and make out. Then they'd dump the car somewhere near home. Cheap thrills in the monkeyhouse, as Chris sometimes said. They'd never been caught at it, but Vern kept hoping. He really dug the idea of visiting Billy on Sundays at the reformatory.

'If we told the cops, they'd want to know how we got way the hell out in Harlow,' Billy said. 'We ain't got no car, neither of us. It's better if we just keep our mouths shut. Then they can't touch us.'

'We could make a nonnamus call,' Charlie said.

'They trace those fuckin' calls,' Billy said ominously. 'I seen it on *Highway Patrol*. And *Dragnet*.'

'Yeah, right,' Charlie said miserably. 'Jesus. I wish Ace'd been with us. We could have told the cops we was in his car.'

'Well, he wasn't.'

'Yeah,' Charlie said. He sighed. 'I guess you're right.' A cigarette butt flicked into the driveway. 'We hadda walk up and take a piss by the tracks, didn't we? Couldn't walk the other way, could we? And I got puke on my new Keds.' His voice sank a little. 'Fuckin' kid was laid right out, you know it? Didja see that sonofawhore, Billy?'

'I seen him,' Billy said, and a second cigarette butt joined the first in the driveway. 'Let's go see if Ace is up. I want some juice.'

'We gonna tell him?'

'Charlie, we ain't gonna tell *nobody*. *Nobody never*. You dig me?'

'I dig you,' Charlie said. 'Chrise-Jesus, I wish we never boosted that fuckin' Dodge.'

'Aw, shut the fuck up and come on.'

Two pairs of legs clad in tight, wash-faded pegged jeans, two pairs of feet in black engineer boots with side-buckles, came down the steps. Vern froze on his hands and knees ('My balls crawled up so high I thought they was trine to get back home,' he told us), sure his brother would sense him beneath the porch and drag him out and kill him – he and Charlie Hogan would kick the few brains the good Lord had seen fit to give him right out his jug ears and then stomp him with their engineer boots. But they just kept going and when Vern was sure they were really gone, he had crawled out from under the porch and run here.

5

'You're really lucky,' I said. 'They *would* have killed you.'

Teddy said, 'I know the Back Harlow Road. It comes to a dead end by the river. We used to fish for cossies out there.'

Chris nodded. 'There used to be a bridge, but there was a flood. A long time ago. Now there's just the train-tracks.'

'Could a kid really have gotten all the way from Chamberlain to Harlow?' I asked Chris. 'That's twenty or thirty miles.'

'I think so. He probably happened on the train tracks and followed them the whole way. Maybe he thought they'd take him out, or maybe he thought he could flag down a train if he had to. But that's just a freight run now – GS&WM up to Derry and Brownsville – and not many of those anymore. He'd had to've walked all the way to Castle Rock to get out. After dark a train must have finally come along . . . and el smacko.'

Chris drove his right fist down against his left palm, making a flat noise. Teddy, a veteran of many close calls dodging the pulp-trucks on 196, looked vaguely pleased. I felt a little sick, imagining the kid so far away from home, scared to death but doggedly following the GS&WM tracks, probably walking on the ties because of the night-noises from the overhanging trees and bushes . . . maybe even from the culverts underneath the railroad bed. And here comes the train, and maybe the big headlight on the front hypnotised him until it was too late to jump. Or maybe he was just lying there on the tracks in a hunger-faint when the train came along. Either way, any way, Chris had the straight of it: el smacko had been the final result. The kid was dead.

'So anyway, you want to go see it?' Vern asked. He was squirming around like he had to go to the bathroom he was so excited.

We all looked at him for a long second, no one saying anything. Then Chris tossed his cards down and said, 'Sure! And I bet you anything we get our pictures in the paper!'

'Huh?' Vern said.

'Yeah?' Teddy said, and grinned his crazy truck-dodging grin.

'Look,' Chris said, leaning across the ratty card-table. 'We can find the body and report it! We'll be on the news!'

'I dunno,' Vern said, obviously taken aback. 'Billy will know where I found out. He'll beat the living shit outta me.'

'No he won't,' I said, 'because it'll be *us* guys that find that kid, not Billy and Charlie Hogan in a boosted car. Then they won't have to worry about it anymore. They'll probably pin a medal on you, Penny.'

'Yeah?' Vern grinned, showing his bad teeth. It was a dazed sort of grin, as if the thought of Billy being pleased with anything he did had acted on him like a hard shot to the chin. 'Yeah, you think so?'

Teddy was grinning, too. Then he frowned and said, 'Oh-oh.'

'What?' Vern asked. He was squirming again, afraid that

some really basic objection to the idea had just cropped up in Teddy's mind . . . or what passed for Teddy's mind.

'Our folks,' Teddy said. 'If we find that kid's body over in South Harlow tomorrow, they're gonna know we didn't spend the night campin' out in Vern's back field.'

'Yeah,' Chris said. 'They'll know we went lookin' for that kid.'

'No they won't,' I said. I felt funny – both excited and scared because I knew we could do it and get away with it. The mixture of emotions made me feel heatsick and headachey. I picked up the Bikes to have something to do with my hands and started box-shuffling them. That and how to play cribbage was about all I got for older brother stuff from Dennis. The other kids envied that shuffle, and I guess everyone I knew had asked me to show them how it went . . . everyone except Chris. I guess only Chris knew that showing someone would be like giving away a piece of Dennis, and I just didn't have so much of him that I could afford to pass pieces around.

I said: 'We'll just tell 'em we got bored tenting in Vern's field because we've done it so many times before. So we decided to hike up the tracks and have a campout in the woods. I bet we don't even get hided for it because everybody'll be so excited about what we found.'

'My dad'll hide me anyway,' Chris said. 'He's on a really mean streak this time.' He shook his head sullenly. 'To hell, it's worth a hiding.'

'Okay,' Teddy said, getting up. He was still grinning like crazy, ready to break into his high-pitched, cackling laugh at any second. 'Let's all get together at Vern's house after lunch. What can we tell 'em about supper?'

Chris said, 'You and me and Gordie can say we're eating at Vern's.'

'And I'll tell my mom I'm eating over at Chris's,' Vern said.

That would work unless there was some emergency we couldn't control or unless any of the parents got together. And neither Vern's folks or Chris's had a phone. Back then there were a lot of families which still considered a telephone a luxury, especially families of the shirttail variety. And none of us came from the upper crust.

My dad was retired. Vern's dad worked in the mill and was still driving a 1952 DeSoto. Teddy's mom had a house on Danberry Street and she took in a boarder whenever she could get one. She didn't have one that summer; the FURNISHED ROOM TO LET sign had been up in the parlour window since June. And Chris's dad was always on a 'mean streak', more or less; he was a drunk who got welfare off and on – mostly on – and spent most of his time hanging out in Sukey's Tavern with Junior Merrill, Ace Merrill's old man, and a couple of other local rumpots.

Chris didn't talk much about his dad, but we all knew he hated him like poison. Chris was marked up every two weeks or so, bruises on his cheeks and neck or one eye swelled up and as colourful as a sunset, and once he came into school with a big clumsy bandage on the back of his head. Other times he never got to school at all. His mom would call him in sick because he was too lamed up to come in. Chris was smart, really smart, but he played truant a lot, and Mr Halliburton, the town truant officer, was always showing up at Chris's house, driving his old black Chevrolet with the NO RIDERS sticker in the corner of the windshield. If Chris was being truant and Bertie (as we called him – always behind his back, of course) caught him, he would haul him back to school and see that Chris got detention for a week. But if Bertie found out that Chris was home because his father had beaten the shit out of him, Bertie just went away and didn't say boo to a cuckoo-bird. It never occurred to me to question this set of priorities until about twenty years later.

The year before, Chris had been suspended from school for two weeks. A bunch of milk-money disappeared when it was Chris's turn to be room-monitor and collect it, and because he was a Chambers from those no-account Chamberses, he had to take a walk even though he always swore he never hawked that money. That was the time Mr Chambers put Chris in the hospital for an overnight stay; when his dad heard Chris was suspended, he broke Chris's nose and his right wrist. Chris came from a bad family, all right, and everybody thought he would turn out bad . . . including Chris. His brothers had lived up to the town's expectations admirably. Dave, the eldest, ran away from home when he was seventeen, joined the Navy, and ended up doing a long stretch in Portsmouth for rape and criminal assault. The next-eldest, Richard (his right eye was all funny and jittery, which was why everybody called him Eyeball), had dropped out of high school in the tenth grade, and chummed around with Charlie and Billy Tessio and their jd buddies.

'I think all that'll work,' I told Chris. 'What about John and Marty?' John and Marty DeSpain were two other members of our regular gang.

'They're still away,' Chris said. 'They won't be back until Monday.'

'Oh. That's too bad.'

'So are we set?' Vern asked, still squirming. He didn't want the conversation sidetracked even for a minute.

'I guess we are,' Chris said. 'Who wants to play some more scat?'

No one did. We were too excited to play cards. We climbed down from the treehouse, climbed the fence into the vacant lot, and played three-flies-six-grounders for a while with Vern's old friction-taped baseball, but that was no fun, either. All we could think about was that kid Brower, hit by a train, and how we were going to see him, or what was left of him. Around ten o'clock we all drifted away home to fix it with our parents.

6

I got to my house at quarter to eleven, after stopping at the drugstore to check out the paperbacks. I did that every couple of days to see if there were any new John D MacDonalds. I had a quarter and I figured if there was, I'd take it along. But there were only the old ones, and I'd read most of those half a dozen times.

When I got home the car was gone and I remembered that my mom and some of her hen-party friends had gone to Boston to see a concert. A great old concert-goer, my mother. And why not? Her only kid was dead and she had to do something to take her mind off it. I guess that sounds pretty bitter. And I guess if you'd been there, you'd understand why I felt that way.

Dad was out back, passing a fine spray from the hose over his ruined garden. If you couldn't tell it was a lost cause from his glum face, you sure could by looking at the garden itself. The soil was light, powdery grey. Everything in it was dead except for the corn, which had never grown so much as a single edible ear. Dad said he'd never known how to water a garden; it had to be mother nature or nobody. He'd water too long in one spot and drown the plants. In the next row, plants were dying of thirst. He could never hit a happy medium. But he didn't talk about it often. He'd lost a son in April and a garden in August. And if he didn't want to talk about either one, I guess that was his privilege. It just bugged me that he'd given up talking about everything else, too. That was taking democracy too fucking far.

'Hi, daddy,' I said, standing beside him. I offered him the Rollos I'd bought at the drugstore. 'Want one?'

'Hello, Gordon. No thanks.' He kept flicking the fine spray over the hopeless grey earth.

'Be okay if I camp out in Vern Tessio's back field tonight with some of the guys?'

'What guys?'

'Vern. Teddy Duchamp. Maybe Chris.'

I expected him to start right in on Chris – how Chris was bad company, a rotten apple from the bottom of the barrel, a thief, and an apprentice juvenile delinquent.

But he just sighed and said, 'I suppose it's okay.'

'Great! Thanks!'

I turned to go into the house and check out what was on the boob tube when he stopped me with: 'Those are the only people you want to be with, aren't they, Gordon?'

I looked back at him, braced for an argument, but there was no argument in him that morning. It would have been better if there had been, I think. His shoulders were slumped.

His face, pointed towards the dead garden and not towards me, sagged. There was a certain unnatural sparkle in his eyes that might have been tears.

'Aw, dad, they're okay –'

'Of course they are. A thief and two feebs. Fine company for my son.'

'Vern Tessio isn't feeble,' I said. Teddy was a harder case to argue.

'Twelve years old and still in the fifth grade,' my dad said. 'And that time he slept over. When the Sunday paper came the next morning, he took an hour and a half to read the funnypages.'

That made me mad, because I didn't think he was being fair. He was judging Vern the way he judged all my friends, from having seen them off and on, mostly going in and out of the house. He was wrong about them. And when he called Chris a thief I always saw red, because he didn't know *anything* about Chris. I wanted to tell him that, but if I pissed him off he'd keep me home. And he wasn't really mad anyway, not like he got at the supper-table sometimes, ranting so loud that nobody wanted to eat. Now he just looked sad and tired out and used. He was sixty-three years old, old enough to be my grandfather.

My mom was fifty-five – no spring chicken, either. When she and dad got married they tried to start a family right away and my mom got pregnant and had a miscarriage. She miscarried two more and the doctor told her she'd never be able to carry a baby to term. I got all of this stuff, chapter and verse, whenever one of them was lecturing me, you understand. They wanted me to think I was a special delivery from God and I wasn't appreciating my great good fortune in being conceived when my mother was forty-two and starting to grey. I wasn't appreciating my great good fortune and I wasn't appreciating her tremendous pain and sacrifices, either.

Five years after the doctor said mom would never have a baby she got pregnant with Dennis. She carried him for eight months and then he just sort of fell out, all eight pounds of him – my father used to say that if she had carried Dennis to term, the kid would have weighed fifteen pounds. The doctor said, Well, sometimes nature fools us, but he'll be the only one you'll ever have. Thank God for him and be content. Ten years later she got pregnant with me. She not only carried me to term, the doctor had to use forceps to yank me out. Did you ever hear of such a fucked-up family? I came into the world the child of two Geritol-chuggers, not to go on and on about it, and my only brother was playing league baseball in the big kids' park before I even got out of diapers.

In the case of my mom and dad, one gift from God had been enough. I won't say they treated me badly, and they sure never beat me, but I was a hell of a big surprise and I guess when you get into your forties you're not as partial to surprises as you were in your twenties. After I was born, Mom got that operation her hen-party friends referred to as 'the Band-Aid'. I guess she wanted to make a hundred per cent sure that there wouldn't be any more gifts from God. When I got to college I found out I'd beaten long odds just by not being born retarded . . . although I think my dad had his doubts when he saw my friend Vern taking ten minutes to puzzle out the dialogue in Beetle Bailey.

This business about being ignored: I could never really

pin it down until I did a book report in high school on this novel called *Invisible Man*. When I agreed to do the book for Miss Hardy I thought it was going to be the science fiction story about the guy in bandages and Foster Grants – Claude Rains played him in the movies. When I found out this was a different story I tried to give the book back but Miss Hardy wouldn't let me off the hook. I ended up being real glad. This *Invisible Man* is about a Negro. Nobody ever notices him at all unless he fucks up. People look right through him. When he talks, nobody answers. He's like a black ghost. Once I got into it, I ate that book up like it was a John D MacDonald, because that cat Ralph Ellison was writing about *me*. At the supper table it was Denny how many did you strike out and Denny who asked you to the Sadie Hopkins dance and Denny I want to talk to you man to man about that car we were looking at. I'd say, 'Pass the butter', and Dad would say, Denny, are you sure the army is what you want? I'd say, 'Pass the butter someone, okay?' and Mom would ask Denny if he wanted her to pick him up one of the Pendleton shirts on sale downtown, and I'd end up getting the butter myself. One night when I was nine, just to see what would happen, I said, 'Please pass those goddam spuds.' And my Mom said, Denny, Auntie Grace called today and she asked after you and Gordon.

The night Dennis graduated with honours from Castle Rock High School I played sick and stayed home. I got Stevie Darabont's oldest brother Royce to buy me a bottle of Wild Irish Rose and I drank half of it and puked in my bed in the middle of the night.

In a family situation like that, you're supposed to either hate the older brother or idolize him hopelessly – at least that's what they teach you in college psychology. Bullshit, right? But so far as I can tell, I didn't feel either way about Dennis. We rarely argued and never had a fist-fight. That would have been ridiculous. Can you see a fourteen-year-old boy finding something to beat up his four-year-old brother about? And our folks were always a little too impressed with him to burden him with the care of his kid brother, so he never resented me the way some older kids come to resent their sibs. When Denny took me with him somewhere, it was of his own free will, and those were some of the happiest times I can remember.

'Hey Lachance, who the fuck is that?'

'My kid brother and you better watch your mouth, Davis. He'll beat the crap out of you. Gordie's tough.'

They gather around me for a moment, huge, impossibly tall, just a moment of interest like a patch of sun. They are so big, they are so old.

'Hey kid! This wet end really your big brother?'

I nod shyly.

'He's a real asshole, ain't he, kid?'

I nod again and everybody, Dennis included, roars with laughter. Then Dennis claps his hands together twice, briskly, and says: 'Come on, we gonna have a practice or stand around here like a bunch of pussies?'

They run to their positions, already peppering the ball around the infield.

'Go sit over there on the bench, Gordie. Be quiet. Don't bother anybody.'

I go sit over there on the bench. I am good. I feel impossibly small under the sweet summer clouds. I watch my brother pitch. I don't bother anybody.

But there weren't many times like that.

Sometimes he read me bedtime stories that were better than mom's; mom's stories were about the Gingerbread Man and the Three Little Pigs, okay stuff, but Dennis's were about stuff like Bluebeard and Jack the Ripper. He also had a version of Billy Goat's Gruff where the troll under the bridge ended up the winner. And, as I have already said, he taught me the game of cribbage and how to do a box-shuffle. Not that much, but hey! in this world you take what you can get, am I right?

As I grew older, my feelings of love for Dennis were replaced with an almost clinical awe, the kind of awe so-so Christians feel for God, I guess. And when he died, I was mildly shocked and mildly sad, the way I imagine those same so-so Christians must have felt when *Time* magazine said God was dead. Let me put it this way: I was as sad for Denny's dying as I was when I heard on the radio that Dan Blocker had died. I'd seen them both about as frequently, and Denny never ever got any re-runs.

He was buried in a closed coffin with the American flag on top (they took the flag off the box before they finally stuck it in the ground and folded it – the flag, not the box – into a cocked hat and gave it to my mom). My parents just fell to pieces. Six months hadn't been long enough to put them back together again; I didn't know if they'd *ever* be whole again. Mr and Mrs Dumpty. Denny's room was in suspended animation just one door down from my room, suspended animation or maybe in a time-warp. The ivy-league college pennants were still on the walls, and the senior pictures of the girls he had dated were still tucked into the mirror where he had stood for what seemed like hours at a stretch, combing his hair back into a ducktail like Elvis's. The stack of *Trues* and *Sports Illustrateds* remained on his desk, their dates looking more and more antique as time passed. It's the kind of thing you see in sticky-sentimental movies. But it wasn't sentimental to me; it was terrible. I didn't go into Dennis's room unless I had to because I kept expecting that he would be behind the door, or under the bed, or in the closet. Mostly it was the closet that preyed on my mind, and if my mother sent me in to get Denny's postcard album or his shoebox of photographs so she could look at them, I would imagine that door swinging slowly open while I stood rooted to the spot with horror. I would imagine him pallid and bloody in the darkness, the side of his head walloped in, a grey-veined cake of blood and brains drying on his shirt. I would imagine his arms coming up, his bloody hands hooking into claws, and he would be croaking: *It should have been you, Gordon. It should have been you.*

7

Stud City, by Gordon Lachance. Originally published in *Greenspun Quarterly*, issue 45, Fall, 1970. Used by permission of the author.

March.

Chico stands at the window, arms crossed, elbows on the ledge that divides upper and lower panes, naked, looking out, breath fogging the glass. A draught against his belly. Bottom right pane is gone. Blocked by a piece of cardboard.

'Chico.'

He doesn't turn. She doesn't speak again. He can see a ghost of her in the glass, in his bed, sitting, blankets pulled up in apparent defiance of gravity. Her eye makeup has smeared into deep hollows under her eyes.

Chico shifts his gaze beyond her ghost, out beyond the house. Raining. Patches of snow sloughed away to reveal the bald ground underneath. He sees last year's dead grass, a plastic toy – Billy's – a rusty rake. His brother Johnny's Dodge is up on blocks, the detyred wheels sticking out like stumps. He remembers times he and Johnny worked on it, listening to the superhits and boss oldies from WLAM in Lewiston pour out of Johnny's old transistor radio – a couple of times Johnny would give him a beer. *She gonna run fast, Chico*, Johnny would say. *She gonna eat up everything on this road from Gates Falls to Castle Rock. Wait till we get that Hearst shifter in her!*

But that had been then, and this was now.

Beyond Johnny's Dodge was the highway. Route 14, goes to Portland and New Hampshire south, all the way to Canada north, if you turned left on US 1 at Thomaston.

'Stud city,' Chico says to the glass. He smokes his cigarette.

'What?'

'Nothing, babe.'

'Chico?' Her voice is puzzled. He will have to change the sheets before Dad gets back. She bled.

'What?'

'I love you, Chico.'

'That's right.'

Dirty March. *You're some old whore*, Chico thinks. *Dirty, staggering old baggy-tits March with rain in her face.*

'This room used to be Johnny's,' he says suddenly.

'Who?'

'My brother.'

'Oh. Where is he?'

'In the Army,' Chico says, but Johnny isn't in the Army. He had been working the summer before at Oxford Plains Speedway and a car went out of control and skidded across the infield towards the pit area, where Johnny had been changing the back tyres on a Chevy charger-class stocker. Some guys shouted at him to look out, but Johnny never heard them. One of the guys who shouted was Johnny's brother Chico.

'Aren't you cold?' she asks.

'No. Well, my feet. A little.'

And he thinks suddenly: *Well, my God. Nothing happened to Johnny that isn't going to happen to you too, sooner or later.* He sees it again, though: the skidding, skating Ford Mustang, the knobs of his brother's spine picked out in a series of dimpled shadows against the white of his Haines T-shirt; he had been hunkered down, pulling one of the Chevy's back tyres. There had been time to see rubber flaying off the tyres of the runaway Mustang, to see its hanging muffler scraping up sparks from the infield. It had struck Johnny even as Johnny tried to get to his feet. Then the yellow shout of flame.

Well, Chico thinks, *it could have been slow*, and he thinks of his grandfather. Hospital smells. Pretty young nurses bearing bedpans. A last papery breath. Were there any good ways?

He shivers and wonders about God. He touches the small silver St Christopher's medal that hangs on a chain around his neck. He is not a Catholic and he's surely not a Mexican:

his real name is Edward May and his friends all call him Chico because his hair is black and he greases it back with Brylcreem and he wears boots with pointed toes and Cuban heels. Not Catholic, but he wears this medallion. Maybe if Johnny had been wearing one, the runaway Mustang would have missed him. You never knew.

He smokes and stares out the window and behind him the girl gets out of bed and comes to him quickly, almost mincing, maybe afraid he will turn around and look at her. She puts a warm hand on his back. Her breasts push against his side. Her belly touches his buttock.

'Oh. It *is* cold.'

'It's this place.'

'Do you love me, Chico?'

'You bet!' he says offhandedly, and then, more seriously: 'You were cherry.'

'What does that —'

'You were a virgin.'

The hand reaches higher. One finger traces the skin on the nape of his neck. 'I said, didn't I?'

'Was it hard? Did it hurt?'

She laughs. 'No. But I was scared.'

They watch the rain. A new Oldsmobile goes by on 14, spraying up water.

'Stud City,' Chico says.

'What?'

'That guy. He's going Stud City. In his new stud car.'

She kisses the place her finger has been touching gently and he brushes at her as if she were a fly.

'What's the matter?'

He turns to her. Her eyes flick down to his penis and

then up again hastily. Her arms twitch to cover herself, and then she remembers that they never do stuff like that in the movies and she drops them to her sides again. Her hair is black and her skin is winter white, the colour of cream. Her breasts are firm, her belly perhaps a little too soft. One flaw to remind, Chico thinks, that this isn't the movies.

'Jane?'

'What?' He can feel himself getting ready. Not beginning, but getting ready.

'It's all right,' he said. 'We're friends.' He eyes her deliberately, letting himself reach at her in all sorts of ways. When he looks at her face again, it is flushed. 'Do you mind me looking at you?'

'I . . . no. No, Chico.'

She steps back, closes her eyes, sits on the bed, and leans back, legs spread. He sees all of her. The muscles, the little muscles on the inside of her thighs . . . they're jumping, uncontrolled, and this suddenly excites him more than the taut cones of her breasts or the mild pink pearl of her cunt. Excitement trembles in him, some stupid Bozo on a spring. Love may be as divine as the poets say, he thinks, but sex is Bozo the clown bouncing around on a spring. How could a woman look at an erect penis without going off into mad gales of laughter?

The rain beats against the roof, against the window, against the sodden cardboard patch blocking the glassless lower pane. He presses his hand against his chest, looking for a moment like a stage Roman about to orate. His hand is cold. He drops it to his side.

'Open your eyes. We're friends, I said.'

Obediently, she opens them. She looks at him. Her eyes

appear violet now. The rainwater running down the window makes rippling patterns on her face, her neck, her breasts. Stretched across the bed, her belly has been pulled tight. She is perfect in her moment.

'Oh,' she says. 'Oh Chico, it feels so *funny*.' A shiver goes through her. She has curled her toes involuntarily. He can see the insteps of her feet. Her insteps are pink. 'Chico. Chico.'

He steps towards her. His body is shivering and her eyes widen. She says something, one word, but he can't tell what it is. This isn't the time to ask. He half-kneels before her for just a second, looking at the floor with frowning concentration, touching her legs just above the knees. He measures the tide within himself. Its pull is thoughtless, fantastic. He pauses a little longer.

The only sound is the tinny tick of the alarm clock on the bedtable, standing brassy-legged atop a pile of *Spiderman* comic books. Her breathing flutters faster and faster. His muscles slide smoothly as he dives upward and forward. They begin. It's better this time. Outside, the rain goes on washing away the snow.

A half-hour later Chico shakes her out of a light doze. 'We gotta move,' he says. 'Dad and Virginia will be home pretty quick.'

She looks at her wristwatch and sits up. This time she makes no attempt to shield herself. Her whole tone – her body English – has changed. She has not matured (although she probably believes she has) nor learned anything more complex than tying a shoe, but her tone has changed just the same. He nods and she smiles tentatively at him. He reaches for the cigarettes on the bedtable. As she draws on her panties, he thinks of a line from an old novelty song:

Keep playin' till I shoot through, Blue . . . play your didgeridoo.
'Tie Me Kangaroo Down', by Rolf Harris. He grins. That
was a song Johnny used to sing. It ended, *So we tanned his
hide when he died, Clyde, and that's it hanging on the shed.*

She hooks her bra and begins buttoning her blouse. 'What
are you smiling about, Chico?'

'Nothing,' he says.

'Zip me up?'

He goes to her, still naked, and zips her up. He kisses her
cheek. 'Go on in the bathroom and do your face if you
want,' he says. 'Just don't take too long, okay?'

She goes up the hall gracefully, and Chico watches her,
smoking. She is a tall girl – taller than he – and she has to
duck her head a little going through the bathroom door.
Chico finds his underpants under the bed. He puts them in
the dirty clothes bag hanging just inside the closet door, and
gets another pair from the bureau. He puts them on, and
then, while walking back to the bed, he slips and almost falls
in a patch of wetness the square of cardboard has let in.

'Goddam,' he whispers resentfully.

He looks around at the room, which had been Johnny's
until Johnny died (*why did I tell her he was in the* Army, *for
Christ's sake*? he wonders . . . a little uneasily). Fibreboard
walls, so thin he can hear Dad and Virginia going at it at
night, that don't quite make it all the way to the ceiling. The
floor has a slightly crazy hipshot angle so that the room's
door will only stay open if you block it open – if you forget,
it swings stealthily closed as soon as your back is turned. On
the far wall is a movie poster from *Easy Rider – Two Men
Went Looking for America and Couldn't Find it Anywhere.* The
room had more life when Johnny lived here. Chico doesn't

know how or why; only that it's true. And he knows something else, as well. He knows that sometimes the room spooks him at night. Sometimes he thinks that the closet door will swing open and Johnny will be standing there, his body charred and twisted and blackened, his teeth yellow dentures poking out of wax that has partially melted and re-hardened; and Johnny will be whispering: *Get out of my room, Chico. And if you lay a hand on my Dodge, I'll fuckin' kill you. Got it?*

Got it, bro, Chico thinks.

For a moment he stands still, looking at the rumpled sheet spotted with the girl's blood, and then he spreads the blankets up in one quick gesture. Here. Right here. How do you like that, Virginia? How does that grab your snatch? He puts on his pants, his engineer boots, finds a sweater.

He's dry-combing his hair in front of the mirror when she comes out of the john. She looks classy. Her too-soft stomach doesn't show in the jumper. She looks at the bed, does a couple of things to it, and it comes out looking made instead of just spread up.

'Good,' Chico says.

She laughs a little self-consciously and pushes a lock of hair behind her ear. It is an evocative, poignant gesture.

'Let's go,' he says.

They go out through the hall and the living room. Jane pauses in front of the tinted studio photograph on top of the TV. It shows his father and Virginia, a high-school-age Johnny, a grammar-school-age Chico, and an infant Billy – in the picture, Johnny is holding Billy. All of them have fixed, stoned grins . . . all except Virginia, whose face is its sleepy, indecipherable self. That picture, Chico remembers, was taken less than a month after his Dad married the bitch.

'That your mother and father?'

'It's my father,' Chico said. 'She's my step-mother, Virginia. Come on.'

'Is she still that pretty?' Jane asks, picking up her coat and handing Chico his windbreaker.

'I guess my old man thinks so,' Chico says.

They step out into the shed. It's a damp and draughty place – the wind hoots through the cracks in its slapstick walls. There is a pile of old bald tyres, Johnny's old bike that Chico inherited when he was ten and which he promptly wrecked, a pile of detective magazines, returnable Pepsi bottles, a greasy monolithic engine block, an orange crate full of paperback books, an old paint-by-the-numbers of a horse standing on dusty green grass.

Chico helps her pick her way outside. The rain is falling with disheartening steadiness. Chico's old sedan stands in a driveway puddle, looking downhearted. Even up on blocks and with a red piece of plastic covering the place where the windshield should go, Johnny's Dodge has more class. Chico's car is a Buick. The paint is dull and flowered with spots of rust. The front seat upholstery has been covered with a brown Army Blanket. A large button pinned to the sun visor on the passenger side says: I WANT IT EVERY DAY. There is a rusty starter assembly on the back seat; if it ever stops raining he will clean it, he thinks, and maybe put it into the Dodge. Or maybe not.

The Buick smells musty and his own starter grinds a long time before the Buick starts up.

'Is it your battery?' she asks.

'Just the goddam rain, I guess.' He backs out onto the road, flicking on the windshield wipers and pausing for a

moment to look at the house. It is a completely unap-
petizing aqua colour. The shed sticks off from it at a ragtag,
double-jointed angle, tarpaper and peeled-looking shingles.

The radio comes on with a blare and Chico shuts it off
at once. There is the beginning of a Sunday afternoon
headache behind his forehead. They ride past the Grange
hall and the Volunteer Fire Department and Brownie's Store.
Sally Morrison's T-Bird is parked by Brownie's hi-test pump,
and Chico raises a hand to her as he turns off onto the old
Lewiston road.

'Who's that?'

'Sally Morrison.'

'Pretty lady.' Very neutral.

He feels for his cigarettes. 'She's been married twice and
divorced twice. Now she's the town pump, if you believe
half the talk that goes on in this shitass little town.'

'She looks young.'

'She is.'

'Have you ever –'

He slides his hand up her leg and smiles. 'No,' he says.
'My brother, maybe, but not me. I like Sally, though. She's
got her alimony and her big white Bird, and she doesn't
care what people say about her.'

It starts to seem like a long drive. The Androscoggin, off
to the right, is slaty and sullen. The ice is all out of it now.
Jane has grown quiet and thoughtful. The only sound is the
steady snap of the windshield wipers. When the car rolls
through the dips in the road there is groundfog, waiting for
evening when it will creep out of these pockets and take
over the whole River Road.

They cross into Auburn and Chico drives the cutoff and

swings onto Minot Avenue. The four lanes are nearly deserted, and all the suburban homes look packaged. They see one little boy in a yellow plastic raincoat walking up the sidewalk, carefully stepping in all the puddles.

'Go, man,' Chico says softly.

'What?' Jane asks.

'Nothing, babe. Go back to sleep.'

She laughs a little doubtfully.

Chico turns up Keston Street and into the driveway of one of the packaged houses. He doesn't turn off the ignition.

'Come in and I'll give you cookies,' she says.

He shakes his head. 'I have to get back.'

'I know.' She puts her arms around him and kisses him. 'Thank you for the most wonderful time of my life.'

He smiles suddenly. His face shines. It is nearly magical. 'I'll see you Monday, Janey-Jane. Still friends, right?'

'You know we are,' she says, and kisses him again . . . but when he cups a breast through her jumper, she pulls away. 'Don't. My father might see.'

He lets her go, only a little of the smile left. She gets out of the car quickly and runs through the rain to the back door. A second later she's gone. Chico pauses for a moment to light a cigarette and then he backs out of the driveway. The Buick stalls and the starter seems to grind forever before the engine manages to catch. It is a long ride home.

When he gets there, Dad's station wagon is parked in the driveway. He pulls in beside it and lets the engine die. For a moment he sits inside silently, listening to the rain. It is like being inside a steel drum.

Inside, Billy is watching Carl Stormer and his Country Buckaroos on the TV set. When Chico comes in, Billy jumps up, excited. 'Eddie, hey Eddie, you know what Uncle Pete said? He said him and a whole mess of other guys sank a Kraut sub in the war! Will you take me to the show next Saturday?'

'I don't know,' Chico says, grinning. 'Maybe if you kiss my shoes every night before supper all week.' He pulls Billy's hair. Billy hollers and laughs and kicks him in the shins.

'Cut it out, now,' Sam May says, coming into the room. 'Cut it out you two. You know how your mother feels about the roughhousing.' He has pulled his tie down and unbuttoned the top button of his shirt. He's got a couple – three red hotdogs on a plate. The hotdogs are wrapped in white bread, and Sam May has put the old mustard right to them. 'Where you been, Eddie?'

'At Jane's.'

The toilet flushes in the bathroom. Virginia. Chico wonders briefly if Jane has left any hairs in the sink, or a lipstick, or a bobby pin.

'You should have come with us to see your Uncle Pete and Aunt Ann,' his father says. He eats a frank in three quick bites. 'You're getting to be like a stranger around here, Eddie. I don't like that. Not while we provide the bed and board.'

'Some bed,' Chico says. 'Some board.'

Sam looks up quickly, hurt at first, then angry. When he speaks, Chico sees that his teeth are yellow with French's mustard. He feels vaguely nauseated. 'Your lip. Your goddam lip. You aren't too big yet, snotnose.'

Chico shrugs, peels a slice of Wonder Bread off the loaf standing on the TV tray by his father's chair, and spreads it with ketchup. 'In three months I'm going to be gone anyway.'

'What the hell are you talking about?'

'I'm gonna fix up Johnny's car and go out to California. Look for work.'

'Oh yeah. Right.' He is a big man, big in a shambling way, but Chico thinks now that he got smaller after he married Virginia, and smaller again after Johnny died. And in his mind he hears himself saying to Jane: *My brother, maybe. Not me.* And on the heels of that: *Play your didgeridoo, Blue.* 'You ain't never going to get that car as far as Castle Rock, let alone Canada.'

'You don't think so? Just watch my fucking dust.'

For a moment his father only looks at him and then he throws the frank he has been holding. It hits Chico in the chest, spraying mustard on his sweater and on the chair.

'Say that word again and I'll break your nose for you, smartass.'

Chico picks up the frank and looks at it. Cheap red frank, smeared with French's mustard. Spread a little sunshine. He throws it back at his father. Sam gets up, his face the colour of an old brick, the vein in the middle of his forehead pulsing. His thigh connects with the TV tray and it overturns. Billy stands in the kitchen doorway watching them. He's gotten himself a plate of franks and beans and the plate has tipped and bean-juice runs onto the floor. Billy's eyes are wide, his mouth trembling. On the TV, Carl Stormer and his Country Buckaroos are tearing through *Long Black Veil* at a breakneck pace.

'You raise them up best you can and they spit on you,' his father says thickly. 'Ayuh. That's how it goes.' He gropes blindly on the seat of his chair and comes up with the half-eaten hotdog. He holds it in his fist like a severed phallus. Incredibly, he begins to eat it . . . at the same time, Chico

424

sees that he has begun to cry. 'Ayuh, they spit on you, that's just how it goes.'

'Well, why in the hell did you have to marry *her*?' he bursts out, and then has to bite down on the rest of it: *If you hadn't married her, Johnny would still be alive.*

'That's none of your goddam business!' Sam May roars through his tears. 'That's my business!'

'Oh?' Chico shouts back. 'Is that so? I only have to live with her! Me and Billy, we have to live with her! Watch her grind you down! And you don't even know –'

'What?' his father says, and his voice is suddenly low and ominous. The chunk of hotdog left in his closed fist is like a bloody chunk of bone. 'What don't I know?'

'You don't know shit from Shinola,' he says, appalled at what has almost come out of his mouth.

'You want to stop it now,' his father says. 'Or I'll beat the hell out of you, Chico.' He only calls him this when he is very angry indeed.

Chico turns and sees that Virginia is standing at the other side of the room, adjusting her skirt minutely, looking at him with her large, calm, brown eyes. Her eyes are beautiful; the rest of her is not so beautiful, so self-renewing, but those eyes will carry her for years yet, Chico thinks, and he feels the sick hate come back – *So we tanned his hide when he died, Clyde, and that's it hanging on the shed.*

'She's got you pussywhipped and you don't have the guts to do anything about it!'

All of this shouting has finally become too much for Billy – he gives a great wail of terror, drops his plate of franks and beans, and covers his face with his hands. Bean-juice splatters his Sunday shoes and sprays across the rug.

Sam takes a single step forward and then stops when Chico makes a curt beckoning gesture, as if to say: *Yeah, come on, let's get down to it, what took you so fuckin long?* They stand like statues until Virginia speaks – her voice is low, as calm as her brown eyes.

'Have you had a girl in your room, Ed? You know how your father and I feel about that.' Almost as an afterthought: 'She left a handkerchief.'

He stares at her, savagely unable to express the way he feels, the way she is dirty, the way she shoots unerringly at the back, the way she clips in behind you and cuts at your hamstrings.

You could hurt me if you wanted to, the calm brown eyes say. *I know you know what was going on before he died. But that's the only way you can hurt me, isn't it, Chico? And only then if your father believed you. And if he believed you, it would kill him.*

His father lunges at the new gambit like a bear. 'Have you been screwing in my house, you little bastard?'

'Watch your language, please, Sam,' Virginia says calmly.

'Is that why you didn't want to come with us? So you could scr – so you could –'

'*Say it!*' Chico weeps. 'Don't let her do it to you! Say it! Say what you mean!'

'Get out,' he says dully. 'Don't you come back until you can apologize to your mother and me.'

'Don't you dare!' he cries. 'Don't you dare call that bitch my mother! I'll kill you!'

'Stop it, Eddie!' Billy screams. The words are muffled, blurred, through his hands, which still cover his face. 'Stop yelling at daddy! Stop it, *please*!'

Virginia doesn't move from the doorway. Her calm eyes remain on Chico.

Sam blunders back a step and the back of his knees strike the edge of his easy-chair. He sits down in it heavily and averts his face against a hairy forearm. 'I can't even look at you when you got words like that in your mouth, Eddie. You are making me feel so bad.'

'*She* makes you feel bad! Why won't you admit it?'

He does not reply. Still not looking at Chico, he fumbles another frank wrapped in bread from the plate on the TV tray. He fumbles for the mustard. Billy goes on crying. Carl Stormer and his Country Buckaroos are singing a truck-driving song. 'My rig is old, but that don't mean she's slow,' Carl tells all his western Maine viewers.

'The boy doesn't know what he's saying, Sam,' Virginia says gently. 'It's hard, at his age. It's hard to grow up.'

She's whipped him. That's the end, all right.

He turns and heads for the door which leads first into the shed and then outdoors. As he opens it he looks back at Virginia, and she gazes at him tranquilly when he speaks her name.

'What is it, Ed?'

'The sheets are bloody.' He pauses. 'I broke her in.'

He thinks something has stirred in her eyes, but that is probably only his wish. 'Please go now, Ed. You're scaring Billy.'

He leaves. The Buick doesn't want to start and he has almost resigned himself to walking in the rain when the engine finally catches. He lights a cigarette and backs out onto 14, slamming the clutch back in and racing the mill when it starts to jerk and splutter. The generator light blinks balefully at him twice, and then the car settles into a rugged idle. At last he is on his way, creeping up the road towards Gates Falls.

He spares Johnny's Dodge one last look.

Johnny could have had steady work at Gates Mills & Weaving, but only on the night shift. Nightwork didn't bother him, he had told Chico, and the pay was better than at the Plains, but their father worked days, and working nights at the mill would have meant Johnny would have been home with her, home alone or with Chico in the next room . . . and the walls were thin. *I can't stop and she won't let me try*, Johnny said. *Yeah, I know what it would do to him. But she's . . . she just won't stop and it's like I can't stop . . . she's always at me, you know what I mean, you've seen her, Billy's too young to understand, but you've seen her . . .*

Yes. He had seen her. And Johnny had gone to work at the Plains, telling their father it was because he could get parts for the Dodge on the cheap. And that's how it happened that he had been changing a tyre when the Mustang came skidding and skating across the infield with its muffler dragging up sparks; that was how his stepmother had killed his brother, so just keep playing until I shoot through, Blue, 'cause we goin Stud City right here in this shitheap Buick, and he remembers how the rubber smelled, and how the knobs of Johnny's spine cast small crescent shadows on the bright white of his tee-shirt, he remembers seeing Johnny get halfway up from the squat he had been working in when the Mustang hit him, squashing him between it and the Chevy, and there had been a hollow bang as the Chevy came down off its jacks, and then the bright yellow flare of flame, the rich smell of gasoline –

Chico strikes the brakes with both feet, bringing the sedan to a crunching, juddering halt on the sodden shoulder. He leans widely across the seat, throws open the passenger door, and sprays yellow puke onto the mud and snow. The sight of it makes him puke again, and the thought of it makes him dry-heave one more time. The car almost stalls, but he catches it in time. The generator light winks out reluctantly when he guns the engine. He sits, letting the shakes work their way out of him. A car goes by fast, a new Ford, white, throwing up great dirty fans of water and slush.

'Stud City,' Chico says. 'In his new stud car. Funky.'

He tastes puke on his lips and in his throat and coating his sinuses. He doesn't want a cigarette. Danny Carter will let him sleep over. Tomorrow will be time enough for further decisions. He pulls back into Route 14 and gets rolling.

8

Pretty fucking melodramatic, right?

The world has seen one or two better stories, I know that – one or two hundred thousand better ones, more like it. It ought to have THIS IS A PRODUCE OF AN UNDERGRADUATE CREATIVE WRITING WORK-SHOP stamped on every page . . . because that's just what it was, at least up to a certain point. It seems both painfully derivative and painfully sophomoric to me now; style by Hemingway (except we've got the whole thing in the present tense for some reason – how too fucking trendy), theme by Faulkner. Could anything be more *serious*? More *lit'ry*?

But even its pretensions can't hide the fact that it's an extremely sexual story written by an extremely inexperienced young man (at the time I wrote *Stud City*, I had been to bed with two girls and had ejaculated prematurely all over one of them – not much like Chico in the foregoing tale, I guess). Its attitude towards women goes beyond hostility and to a point which verges on actual ugliness – two of the women in *Stud City* are sluts, and the third is a simple receptacle who says things like 'I love you, Chico,' and 'Come in, I'll give you cookies.' Chico, on the other hand, is a macho cigarette-smoking working-class hero who could have stepped whole and breathing from the grooves of a Bruce Springsteen record – although Springsteen was yet to be heard from when I published the story in the college literary magazine (where it ran between a poem called *Images of Me* and an essay on student parietals written entirely in the lower case). It is the work of a young man every bit as insecure as he was inexperienced.

And yet it was the first story I ever wrote that felt like *my* story – the first one that really felt *whole*, after five years of trying. The first one that might still be able to stand up, even with its props taken away. Ugly but alive. Even now when I read it, stifling a smile at its pseudo-toughness and its pretensions, I can see the true face of Gordon Lachance lurking just behind the lines of print, a Gordon Lachance younger than the one living and writing now, one certainly more idealistic than the best-selling novelist who is more apt to have his paperback contracts reviewed than his books, but not so young as the one who went with his friends that day to see the body of a dead kid named Ray Brower. A Gordon Lachance halfway along in the process of losing the shine.

No, it's not a very good story – its author was too busy listening to other voices to listen as closely as he should have to the one coming from inside. But it was the first time I had ever really used the places I knew and the things I felt in a piece of fiction, and there was a kind of dreadful exhilaration in seeing things that had bothered me for years come out in a new form, *a form over which I had imposed control*. It had been years since that childhood idea of Denny being in the closet of his spookily preserved room had occurred to me; I would have honestly believed I had forgotten it. Yet there it is in *Stud City*, only slightly changed . . . but *controlled*.

I've resisted the urge to change it a lot more, to rewrite it, to juice it up – and that urge was fairly strong, because I find the story quite embarrassing now. But there are still things in it I like, things that would be cheapened by changes made by this later Lachance, who has the first threads of grey in his hair. Things, like that image of the shadows on Johnny's white tee-shirt or that of the rain-ripples on Jane's naked body, that seem better than they have any right to be.

Also, it was the first story I never showed to my mother and father. There was too much Denny in it. Too much Castle Rock. And most of all, too much 1960. You always know the truth, because when you cut yourself or someone else with it, you bleed.

9

My room was on the second floor, and it must have been at least ninety degrees up there. It would be a hundred and ten by afternoon, even with all the windows open. I was really glad I wasn't sleeping there that night, and the thought of where we were going made me excited all over again. I made two blankets into a bedroll and tied it with my old belt. I collected all my money, which was sixty-eight cents. Then I was ready to go.

I went down the back stairs to avoid meeting my Dad in front of the house, but I hadn't needed to worry; he was still out in the garden with the hose, making useless rainbows in the air and looking through them.

I walked down Summer Street and cut through a vacant lot to Carbine – where the offices of the Castle *Call* stand today. I was headed up Carbine towards the clubhouse when a car pulled over to the kerb and Chris got out. He had his old Boy Scout pack in one hand and two blankets rolled up and tied with clothesrope in the other.

'Thanks, mister,' he said, and trotted over to join me as the car pulled away. His Boy Scout canteen was slung around his neck and under one arm so that it finally ended up banging on his hip. His eyes were sparkling.

'Gordie! You wanna see something?'

'Sure, I guess so. What?'

'Come on down here first.' He pointed at the narrow space between the Blue Point Diner and the Castle Rock Drug Store.

'What is it, Chris?'

'Come on, I said!'

He ran down the alley and after a brief moment (that's all it took me to cast aside my better judgment) I ran after him. The two buildings were set slightly towards each other rather than running parallel, and so the alley narrowed as it went back. We waded through trashy drifts of old newspapers and stepped over cruel, sparkly nests of broken beer and soda bottles. Chris cut behind the Blue Point and put his bedroll down. There were eight or nine garbage cans lined up here and the stench was incredible.

'Phew! Chris! Come on, gimme a break!'

432

'Gimme your arm,' Chris said, by rote.

'No, sincerely, I'm gonna throw u —'

The words broke off in my mouth and I forgot all about the smelly garbage cans. Chris had unslung his pack and opened it and reached inside. Now he was holding out a huge pistol with dark wood grips.

'You wanna be the Lone Ranger or the Cisco Kid?' Chris asked, grinning.

'Walking, talking Jesus! Where'd you get that?'

'Hawked it out of my dad's bureau. It's a .45.'

'Yeah, I can see that,' I said, although it could have been a .38 or a .357 for all I knew — in spite of all the John D MacDonalds and Ed McBains I'd read, the only pistol I'd ever seen up close was the one Constable Bannerman carried . . . and although all the kids asked him to take it out of its holster, Banner never would. 'Man, your dad's gonna hide you when he finds out. You said he was on a mean streak *anyway*.'

His eyes just went on dancing. 'That's *it*, man. He ain't gonna find out *nothing*. Him and these other rummies are all laid up down in Harrison with six or eight bottles of wine. They won't be back for a week. Fucking rummies.' His lips curled. He was the only guy in our gang who would never take a drink, even to show he had, you know, big balls. He said he wasn't going to grow up to be a fucking tosspot like his old man. And he told me once privately — this was after the DeSpain twins showed up with a six-pack they'd hawked from their old man and everybody teased Chris because he wouldn't take a beer or even a swallow — that he was *scared* to drink. He said his father never got his nose all the way out of the bottle anymore, that his older brother had been drunk out of his tits when he raped that girl, and that Eyeball was always guzzling purple Jesuses with Ace Merrill and Charlie Hogan and Billy Tessio. What, he asked me, did I think his chances of letting go of the bottle would be once he picked it up? Maybe you think that's funny, a twelve-year-old worrying that he might be an incipient alcoholic, but it wasn't funny to Chris. Not at all. He'd thought about the possibility a lot. He'd had occasion to.

'You got shells for it?'

'Nine of them — all that was left in the box. He'll think he used 'em himself, shooting at cans while he was drunk.'

'Is it loaded?'

'*No!* Chrissake, what do you think I *am*?'

I finally took the gun. I liked the heavy way it sat there in my hand. I could see myself as Steve Carella of the 87th precinct, going after that guy The Heckler or maybe covering Myer Myer or Kling while they broke into a desperate junkie's sleazy apartment. I sighted on one of the smelly trashcans and squeezed the trigger.

KA-BLAM!

The gun bucked in my hand. Fire licked from the end. It felt as if my wrist had just been broken. My heart vaulted nimbly into the back of my mouth and crouched there, trembling. A big hole appeared in the corrugated metal surface of the trash can — it was the work of an evil conjuror.

'Jesus!' I screamed.

Chris was cackling wildly — in real amusement or hysterical terror I couldn't tell. 'You did it, you did it! *Gordie did it!*' he bugled. '*Hey, Gordon Lachance is shooting up Castle Rock!*'

'*Shut up! Let's get out of here!*' I screamed, and grabbed him by the shirt.

As we ran, the back door of the Blue Point jerked open and Francine Tupper stepped out in her white rayon waitress's uniform. 'Who did that? Who's letting off cherry-bombs back here?'

We ran like hell, cutting behind the drug store and the hardware store and the Emporium Galorium, which sold antiques and junk and dime books. We climbed a fence, spiking our palms with splinters, and finally came out on Curran Street. I threw the .45 at Chris as we ran; he was killing himself laughing but caught it and somehow managed to stuff it back into his knapsack and close one of the snaps. Once around the corner of Curran and back on Carbine Street, we slowed to a walk so we wouldn't look suspicious, running in the heat. Chris was still giggling.

'Man, you shoulda seen your face. Oh man, that was priceless. That was really fine. My fucking-A.' He shook his head and slapped his leg and howled.

'You knew it was loaded, didn't you? You wet! I'm gonna be in trouble. That Tupper babe saw me.'

'Shit, she thought it was a firecracker. Besides, ole Thunderjugs Tupper can't see past the end of her own nose, you know that. Thinks wearing glasses would spoil her *pretty face.*' He put one palm against the small of his back and bumped his hips and got laughing again.

'Well, I don't care. That was a mean trick, Chris. Really.'

'Come on, Gordie.' He put a hand on my shoulder. 'I didn't know it was loaded, honest to God, I swear on my mother's name. I just took it out of my dad's bureau. He always unloads it. He must have been really drunk when he put it away the last time.'

'You really didn't load it?'

'No sir.'

'You swear it on your mother's name even if she goes to hell for you telling a lie?'

'I swear.' He crossed himself and spat, his face as open and repentant as any choirboy's. But when we turned into the vacant lot where our treehouse was and we saw Vern and Teddy sitting on their bedrolls waiting for us, he started to laugh again. He told them the whole story and after everybody had had their yucks, Teddy asked him what Chris thought they needed a pistol for.

'Nothin',' Chris said. 'Except we might see a bear. Something like that. Besides, it's spooky sleeping out at night in the woods.'

Everybody nodded at that. Chris was the biggest, toughest guy in our gang, and he could always get away with saying things like that. Teddy, on the other hand, would have gotten his ass ragged off if he even hinted he was afraid of the dark.

'Did you set your tent up in the field?' Teddy asked Vern.

'Yeah. And I put two turned-on flashlights in it so it'll look like we're there after dark.'

'Hot shit!' I said, and clapped Vern on the back. For him, that was real thinking. He grinned and blushed.

'So let's *go*,' Teddy said. 'Come on, it's almost twelve already!'

Chris got up and we gathered around him.

'We'll walk across Beeman's field and behind that furniture place by Sonny's Texaco,' he said. 'Then we'll get on the railroad tracks down by the dump and just walk across the trestle into Harlow.'

'How far do you think it's gonna be?' Teddy asked.

Chris shrugged. 'Harlow's big. We're gonna be walking at least twenty miles. That sound right to you, Gordie?'

'Yeah. It might even be thirty.'

'Even if it's thirty we ought to be there by tomorrow afternoon, if no one goes pussy.'

'No pussies here,' Teddy said at once.

We all looked at each other for a second.

'*Miaoww*,' Vern said, and we all laughed.

'Come on, you guys,' Chris said, and shouldered his pack. We walked out of the vacant lot together, Chris slightly in the lead.

10

By the time we got across Beeman's field and had struggled up the cindery embankment to the Great Southern and Western Maine tracks, we had all taken our shirts off and tied them around our waists. We were sweating like pigs. At the top of the embankment we looked down the tracks, towards where we'd have to go.

I'll never forget that moment, no matter how old I get. I was the only one with a watch – a cheap Timex I'd gotten as a premium for selling Cloverine Brand Salve the year before. Its hands stood at straight up noon, and the sun beat down on the dry, shadeless vista before us with savage heat. You could feel it working to get in under your skull and fry your brains.

Behind us was Castle Rock spread out on the long hill that was known as Castle View, surrounding its green and shady common. Further down Castle River you could see the stacks of the woollen mill spewing smoke into a sky the colour of gunmetal and spewing waste into the water. The Jolly Furniture Barn was on our left. And straight ahead of us the railroad tracks, bright and heliographing in the sun. They paralleled the Castle River, which was on our left. To our right was a lot of overgrown scrubland (there's a motorcycle track there today – they have scrambles every Sunday afternoon at two p.m.). An old abandoned water tower stood on the horizon, rusty and somehow scary.

We stood there for that one noontime moment and then Chris said impatiently, 'Come on, let's get going.'

We walked beside the tracks in the cinders, kicking up little puffs of blackish dust at every step. Our socks and sneakers were soon gritty with it. Vern started singing 'Roll Me Over in the Clover' but soon quit it, which was a break for our ears. Only Teddy and Chris had brought canteens, and we were all hitting them pretty hard.

'We could fill all the canteens again at the dump faucet,' I said. 'My dad told me that's a safe well. It's a hundred and ninety feet deep.'

'Okay,' Chris said, being the tough platoon leader. 'That'll be a good place to take five, anyway.'

'What about food?' Teddy asked suddenly. 'I bet nobody thought to bring something to eat. I know I didn't.'

Chris stopped. 'Shit! I didn't, either. Gordie?'

I shook my head, wondering how I could have been so dumb.

'Vern?'

'Zip,' Vern said. 'Sorry.'

'Well, let's see how much money we got,' I said. I untied my shirt, spread it on the cinders, and dropped my own sixty-eight cents onto it. The coins glittered feverishly in the sunlight. Chris had a tattered dollar and two pennies. Teddy had two quarters and two nickels. Vern had exactly seven cents.

'Two-thirty-seven,' I said. 'Not bad. There's a store at the end of that little road that goes to the dump. Somebody'll have to walk down there and get some hamburger and some tonics while the others rest.'

'Who?' Vern asked.

'We'll match for it when we get to the dump. Come on.'

I slid all the money into my pants pocket and was just tying my shirt around my waist again when Chris hollered: '*Train!*'

I put my hand out on one of the rails to feel it, even though I could already hear it. The rail was thrumming crazily; for a moment it was like holding the train in my hand.

'*Paratroops over the side!*' Vern bawled, and leapt halfway down the embankment in one crazy, clownish stride. Vern was nuts for playing paratroops anyplace the ground was soft – a gravel pit, a haymow, an embankment like this one. Chris jumped after him. The train was really loud now, probably headed straight up our side of the river towards Lewiston. Instead of jumping, Teddy turned in the direction of which it was coming. His thick glasses glittered in the sun. His long hair flopped untidily over his brow in sweat-soaked stringers.

'Go on, Teddy,' I said.

'No, huh-uh, I'm gonna dodge it.' He looked at me, his magnified eyes frantic with excitement. 'A train-dodge, dig it? What's trucks after a fuckin' train-dodge?'

'You're crazy, man. You want to get killed?'

'Just like the beaches at Normandy!' Teddy yelled, and strode out into the middle of the tracks. He stood on one of the cross-ties, lightly balanced.

I stood stunned for a moment, unable to believe stupidity of such width and breadth. Then I grabbed him, dragged him fighting and protesting to the embankment, and pushed him over. I jumped after him and Teddy caught me a good one in the guts while I was still in the air. The wind whooshed out of me, but I was still able to hit him in the sternum with my knee and knock him flat on his back before he could get all the way up. I landed, gasping and sprawling, and Teddy grabbed me around the neck. We went rolling all the way to the bottom of the embankment, hitting and clawing at each other while Chris and Vern stared at us, stupidly surprised.

'You little son of a bitch!' Teddy was screaming at me. 'You fucker! Don't you throw your weight around on me! I'll kill you, you dipshit!'

I was getting my breath back now, and I made it to my feet. I backed away as Teddy advanced, holding my open hands up to slap away his punches, half laughing and half scared. Teddy was no one to fool around with when he went into one of his screaming fits. He'd take on a big kid in that state, and after the big kid broke both of his arms, he'd bite.

'Teddy, you can dodge anything you want after we see what we're going to see but'

whack on the shoulder as one wildly-swinging fist got past me

'until then no one's supposed to *see* us, you'

440

whack on the side of the face, and then we might have had a real fight if Chris and Vern

'stupid wet end!'

hadn't grabbed us and kept us apart. Above us, the train roared by in a thunder of diesel exhaust and the great heavy clacking of boxcar wheels. A few cinders bounced down the embankment and the argument was over . . . at least until we could hear ourselves talk again.

It was only a short freight, and when the caboose had trailed by, Teddy said: 'I'm gonna kill him. At least give him a fat lip.' He struggled against Chris, but Chris only grabbed him tighter.

'Calm down, Teddy,' Chris said quietly, and he kept saying it until Teddy stopped struggling and just stood there, his glasses hanging askew and his hearing-aid cord dangling limply against his chest on its way down to the battery, which he had shoved into the pocket of his jeans.

When he was completely still, Chris turned to me and said: 'What the hell are you fighting with him about, Gordon?'

'He wanted to dodge the train. I figured the engineer would see him and report it. They might send a cop out.'

'Ahhh, he'd be too busy makin' chocolate in his drawers,' Teddy said, but he didn't seem angry anymore. The storm had passed.

'Gordie was just trying to do the right thing,' Vern said. 'Come on, peace.'

'Peace, you guys,' Chris agreed.

'Yeah, okay,' I said, and held out my hand, palm up. 'Peace, Teddy?'

'I coulda dodged it,' he said to me. 'You know that, Gordie?'

'Yeah,' I said, although the thought turned me cold inside. 'I know it.'

'Okay. Peace, then.'

'Skin it, man,' Chris ordered, and let go of Teddy.

Teddy slapped his hand down on mine hard enough to sting and then turned it over. I slapped his.

'Fucking pussy Lachance,' Teddy said.

'Meeiowww,' I said.

'Come on, you guys,' Vern said. 'Let's go, okay?'

'Go anywhere you want, but don't go here,' Chris said solemnly, and Vern drew back as if to hit him.

11

We got to the dump around one-thirty, and Vern led the way down the embankment with a *Paratroops over the side!* We went to the bottom in big jumps and leaped over the brackish trickle of water oozing listlessly out of the culvert which pocked out of the cinders. Beyond this small boggy area was the sandy, trash-littered verge of the dump.

There was a six-foot security fence surrounding it. Every twenty feet weather-faded signs were posted. They said:

CASTLE ROCK DUMP
HOURS 4–8 PM
CLOSED MONDAYS
TRESPASSING STRICTLY FORBIDDEN

We climbed to the top of the fence, swung over, and jumped down. Teddy and Vern led the way towards the well, which you tapped with an old-fashioned pump – the kind from which you had to call the water with elbow-grease. There was a Crisco can filled with water next to the pump handle, and the great sin was to forget to leave it filled for the next guy to come along. The iron handle stuck off at an angle, looking like a one-winged bird that was trying to fly. It had once been green, but almost all of the paint had been rubbed off by the thousands of hands that had worked that handle since 1940.

The dump is one of my strongest memories of Castle Rock. It always reminds me of the surrealist painters when I think of it – those fellows who were always painting pictures of clockfaces lying limply in the crotches of trees or Victorian living rooms standing in the middle of the Sahara or steam engines coming out of fireplaces. To my child's eye, *nothing* in the Castle Rock Dump looked as if it really belonged there.

We had entered from the back. If you came from the front, a wide dirt road came in through the gate, broadened out into a semicircular area that had been bulldozed as flat as a dirt landing-strip, and then ended abruptly at the edge of the dumping-pit. The pump (Teddy and Vern were currently standing there and squabbling about who was going to prime it) was at the back of this great pit. It was maybe eighty feet deep and filled with all the American things that get empty, wear out, or just don't work anymore. There was so much stuff that my eyes hurt just looking at it – or maybe it was your brain that actually hurt, because it could never quite decide what your eye should stop on. Then your eye *would* stop, or be stopped, by something that seemed as out of place as those limp clock-faces or the living room in the desert. A brass bedstead leaning drunkenly in the sun. A little girl's dolly looking amazedly between her thighs as she gave birth to stuffing. An overturned Studebaker automobile with its chrome bullet nose glittering in the sun like some Buck

Rogers missile. One of those giant water bottles they have in office buildings, transformed by the summer sun into a hot, blazing sapphire.

There was plenty of wildlife there, too, although it wasn't the kind you see in the Walt Disney nature films or at those tame zoos where you can pet the animals. Plump rats, woodchucks grown sleek and lumbering on such rich chow as rotting hamburger and maggoty vegetables, seagulls by the thousands, and stalking among the gulls like thoughtful, introspective ministers, an occasional huge crow. It was also the place where the town's stray dogs came for a meal when they couldn't find any trashcans to knock over or any deer to run. They were a miserable, ugly-tempered, mongrel lot; slat-sided and grinning bitterly, they would attack each other over a flyblown piece of bologna or a pile of chicken guts fuming in the sun.

But these dogs never attacked Milo Pressman, the dumpkeeper, because Milo was never without Chopper at his heel. Chopper was — at least until Camber's dog Cujo went rabid twenty years later — the most feared and least seen dog in Castle Rock. He was the meanest dog for forty miles around (or so we heard), and ugly enough to stop a striking clock. The kids whispered legends about Chopper's meanness. Some said he was half German Shepherd, some said he was mostly Boxer, and a kid from Castle View with the unfortunate name of Harry Horr claimed that Chopper was a Doberman Pinscher whose vocal cords had been surgically removed so you couldn't hear him when he was on the attack. There were other kids who claimed Chopper was a maniacal Irish Wolfhound and Milo Pressman fed him a special mixture of Gaines Meal and chicken blood. These same kids claimed that Milo didn't dare take Chopper out of his shack unless the dog was hooded like a hunting falcon.

The most common story was that Pressman had trained Chopper not just to sic but to sic specific *parts* of the human anatomy. Thus an unfortunate kid who had illegally scaled the dump fence to pick for illicit treasures might hear Milo Pressman cry: 'Chopper! Sic! Hand!' And Chopper would grab that hand and hold on, ripping skin and tendons, powdering bones between his slavering jaws, until Milo told him to quit. It was rumoured that Chopper could take an ear, an eye, a foot, or a leg . . . and that a second offender who was surprised by Milo and the ever-loyal Chopper would hear the dread cry: 'Chopper! Sic! Pecker!' And that kid would be a soprano for the rest of his life. Milo himself was more commonly seen and thus more commonly regarded. He was just a half-bright working joe who supplemented his small town salary by fixing things people threw away and selling them around town.

There was no sign of either Milo or Chopper today.

Chris and I watched Vern prime the pump while Teddy worked the handle frantically. At last he was rewarded with a flood of clear water. A moment later both of them had their heads under the trough, Teddy still pumping away a mile a minute.

'Teddy's crazy,' I said softly.

'Oh yeah,' Chris said matter-of-factly. 'He won't live to be twice the age he is now, I bet. His dad burnin' his ears like that. That's what did it. He's crazy to dodge trucks the way he does. He can't see worth a shit, glasses or no glasses.'

'You remember that time in the tree?'

'Yeah.'

The year before, Teddy and Chris had been climbing the big pine tree behind my house. They were almost to the top and Chris said they couldn't go any further because all of the branches up there were rotten. Teddy got that crazy stubborn look on his face and said fuck that, he had pine tar all over his hands and he was gonna go up until he could touch the top. Nothing Chris said could talk him out of it. So up he went, and he actually made it — he only weighed seventy-five pounds or so, remember. He stood there, clutching the top of the pine in one tar-gummy hand, shouting that he was king of the world or some stupid thing like that, and then there was a sickening, rotted crack as the branch he was standing on gave way and he plummeted. What happened next was one of those things that makes you sure there must be a God. Chris reached out, purely on reflex, and what he caught was a fistful of Teddy Duchamp's hair. And although his wrist swelled up fat and he was unable to use his right hand very well for almost two weeks, Chris held him until Teddy, screaming and cursing, got his foot on a live branch thick enough to support his weight. Except for Chris's blind grab, he would have turned and crashed and smashed all the way to the foot of the tree, a hundred and twenty feet below. When they got down, Chris was grey-faced and almost puking with the fear reaction. And Teddy wanted to fight him for pulling his hair. They would have gone at it, too, if I hadn't been there to make peace.

'I dream about that every now and then,' Chris said, and looked at me with strangely defenceless eyes. 'Except in this dream I have, I always miss him. I just get a couple of hairs and Teddy screams and down he goes. Weird, huh?'

'Weird,' I agreed, and for just one moment we looked in

each other's eyes and saw some of the true things that made us friends. Then we looked away again and watched Teddy and Vern throwing water at each other, screaming and laughing and calling each other pussies.

'Yeah, but you didn't miss him,' I said. 'Chris Chambers never misses, am I right?'

'Not even when the ladies leave the seat down,' he said. He winked at me, formed an O with his thumb and forefinger, and spat a neat white bullet through it.

'Eat me raw, Chambers,' I said.

'Through a Flavour Straw,' he said, and we grinned at each other.

Vern yelled: '*Come on and get your water before it runs back down the pipe!*'

'Race you,' Chris said.

'In this heat? You're off your gourd.'

'Come on,' he said, still grinning. 'On my go.'

'Okay.'

'*Go!*'

We raced, our sneakers digging up the hard, sunbaked dirt, our torsos leaning out ahead of our flying bluejeaned legs, our fists doubled. It was a dead heat, with both Vern on Chris's side and Teddy on mine holding up their middle fingers at the same moment. We collapsed laughing in the still, smoky odour of the place, and Chris tossed Vern his canteen. When it was full, Chris and I went to the pump and first Chris pumped for me and then I pumped for him, the shockingly cold water sluicing off the soot and the heat all in a flash, sending our suddenly freezing scalps four months ahead into January. Then I refilled the lard can and we all walked over to sit down in the shade of the dump's only tree, a stunted ash forty feet from Milo Pressman's tarpaper shack. The tree was hunched slightly to the west, as if what it really wanted to do was pick up its roots the way an old lady would pick up her skirts and just get the hell out of the dump.

'The most!' Chris said, laughing, tossing his tangled hair back from his brow.

'A blast,' I said, nodding, still laughing myself.

'This is really a good time,' Vern said simply, and he didn't just mean being off-limits inside the dump, or fudging our folks, or going on a hike up the railroad tracks into Harlow; he meant those things but it seems to me now that there was more, and that we all knew it. Everything was there and around us. We knew exactly who we were and exactly where we were going. It was grand.

We sat under the tree for a while, shooting the shit like we always did – who had the best ballteam (still the Yankees with Mantle and Maris, of course), what was the best car ('55 Thunderbird, with Teddy holding out stubbornly for the '58 Corvette), who was the toughest guy in Castle Rock who wasn't in our gang (we all agreed it was Jamie Gallant, who gave Mrs Ewing the finger and then sauntered out of her class with his hands in his pockets while she shouted at him), the best TV show (either *The Untouchables* or *Peter Gunn* – both Robert Stack as Eliot Ness and Craig Stevens as Gunn were cool), all that stuff.

It was Teddy who first noticed that the shade of the ash tree was getting longer and asked me what time it was. I looked at my watch and was surprised to see it was quarter past two.

'Hey, man,' Vern said. 'Somebody's got to go for provisions. Dump opens at four. I don't want to still be here when Milo and Chopper make the scene.'

Even Teddy agreed. He wasn't afraid of Milo, who had a pot belly and was at least forty, but every kid in Castle Rock squeezed his balls between his legs when Chopper's name was mentioned.

'Okay,' I said. 'Odd man goes?'

'That's you, Gordie,' Chris said, smiling. 'Odd as a cod.'

'So's your mother,' I said, and gave them each a coin. 'Flip.'

Four coins glittered up into the sun. Four hands snatched them from the air. Four flat smacks on four grimy wrists. We uncovered. Two heads and two tails. We flipped again and this time all four of us had tails.

'Oh Jesus, that's a goocher,' Vern said, not telling us anything we didn't know. Four heads, or a moon, was supposed to be extraordinarily good luck. Four tails was a goocher, and that meant very bad luck.

'Fuck that shit,' Chris said. 'It doesn't mean anything. Go again.'

'No, man,' Vern said earnestly. 'A goocher, that's really bad. You remember when Clint Bracken and those guys got wiped out on Sirois Hill in Durham? Billy tole me they was flippin' for beers and they came up a goocher just before they got into the car. And bang! they all get fuckin' totalled. I don't like that. Sincerely.'

'Nobody believes that crap about moons and goochers,' Teddy said impatiently. 'It's baby stuff, Vern. You gonna flip or not?'

Vern flipped, but with obvious reluctance. This time he, Chris and Teddy all had tails. I was showing Thomas Jefferson on a nickel. And I was suddenly scared. It was as if a shadow had crossed some inner sun. They still had a goocher, the three of them, as if dumb fate had pointed at them a second time. Abruptly I thought of Chris saying: *I just get a couple of hairs and Teddy screams and down he goes. Weird, huh?*

Three tails, one head.

Then Teddy was laughing his crazy, cackling laugh and pointing at me and the feeling was gone.

'I heard that only fairies laugh like that,' I said, and gave him the finger.

'Eeee-eeee-eeee, Gordie,' Teddy laughed. 'Go get the provisions, you fuckin' morphadite.'

I wasn't really sorry to be going. I was rested up and didn't mind going down the road to the Florida Market.

'Don't call me any of your mother's pet names,' I said to Teddy.

'Eeee-eee-eeee, what a fuckin' wet you are, Lachance.'

'Go on, Gordie,' Chris said. 'We'll wait over by the tracks.'

'You guys better not go without me,' I said.

Vern laughed. 'Goin' without you'd be like goin' with Schlitz instead of Budweiser's, Gordie.'

'Ah, shut up.'

They chanted together: 'I don't shut up, I *grow* up. And when I look at you I *throw* up.'

'Then your mother goes around the corner and licks it up,' I said, and hauled ass out of there, giving them the finger over my shoulder as I went. I never had any friends later on like the ones I had when I was twelve. Jesus, did you?

12

Different strokes for different folks, they say now, and that's cool. So if I say *summer* to you, you get one set of private, personal images that are all the way different from mine. That's cool. But for me, *summer* is always going to mean running down the road to the Florida Market with change jingling in my pockets, the temperature in the gay nineties, my feet dressed in Keds. The word conjures an image of the GS&WM railroad tracks running into a perspective-point in the distance, burnished so white under the sun that when you closed your eyes you could still see them there in the dark, only blue instead of white.

But there was more to that summer than our trip across the river to look for Ray Brower, although that looms the largest. Sounds of The Fleetwoods singing 'Come Softly Darling' and Robin Luke singing 'Susie Darlin'' and Little Anthony popping the vocal on 'I Ran All the Way Home'. Were they all hits in that summer of 1960? Yes and no. Mostly yes. In the long purple evenings when rock and roll from WLAM blurred into night baseball from WCCU, time shifted. I think it was all 1960 and that the summer went on for a space of years, held magically intact in a web of sounds: the sweet hum of crickets, the machine-gun roar of playing-cards riffling against the spokes of some kid's bicycle as he pedalled home for a late supper of cold cuts and iced tea, the flat Texas voice of Buddy Knox singing 'Come along and be my party doll, and I'll make love to you, to you,' and the baseball announcer's voice mingling with the song and with the smell of freshly cut grass: 'Count's three and two now. Whitey Ford leans over . . . shakes off the sign . . . now he's got it . . . Ford pauses . . . pitches . . . *and there it goes! Williams got all of that one! Kiss it goodbye! RED SOX LEAD, THREE TO ONE!'* Was Ted Williams still playing for the Red Sox in 1960? Absolutely not. But he *was*. I remember that he was very clearly. Baseball had become important to me in the last couple of years, ever since I'd had to face the knowledge that baseball players were as much flesh and blood as I was. The knowledge came when Roy Campanella's car overturned and the papers screamed mortal news from the front pages: his career was done, he was going to sit in a wheelchair for the rest of his life. How that came back to me, with that same sickening mortal thud, when I sat down to this typewriter one morning two years ago, turned on the radio, and heard that Thurman Munson had died while trying to land his airplane.

There were movies to go see at the Gem, which has long since been torn down; science fiction movies like *Gog* with Richard Egan and westerns with Audie Murphy (Teddy saw every movie Audie Murphy made at least three times; he believed Murphy was almost a god) and war movies with John Wayne. There were games and endless bolted meals, lawns to mow, places to run to, walls to pitch pennies against, people to clap you on the back. And now I sit here trying to look through an IBM keyboard and see that time, trying to recall the best and worst of that green and brown summer, and I can almost feel the skinny, scabbed boy still buried in this advancing body and hear those sounds. But the apotheosis of the memory and the time is Gordon Lachance running down the road to the Florida Market with change in his pockets and sweat running down his back.

I asked for three pounds of hamburger and got some hamburger rolls, four bottles of Coke and a two-cent churchkey to open them with. The owner, a man named George Dusset, got the meat and then leaned by his cash register, one hammy hand planted on the counter by the big bottle of hardcooked eggs, a toothpick in his mouth, his huge beer belly rounding his white T-shirt like a sail filled with a good wind. He stood right there as I shopped, making sure I didn't try to hawk anything. He didn't say a word until he was weighing up the hamburger.

'I know you. You're Denny Lachance's brother. Ain't you?' The toothpick journeyed from one corner of his mouth to the other, as if on ball bearings. He reached behind the cash register, picked up a bottle of S'OK cream soda, and chugged it.

'Yes, sir. But Denny, he —'

'Yeah, I know. That's a sad thing, kid. The Bible says: "In the midst of life, we are in death." Did you know that . . . Yuh. I lost a brother in Korea. You look just like Denny, people ever tell you that? Yuh. Spitting image.'

'Yes, sir, sometimes,' I said glumly.

'I remember the year he was All Conference. Halfback, he played. Yuh. Could he run? Father God and Sonny Jesus! You're probably too young to remember.' He was looking over my head, out through the screen door and into the blasting heat, as if he were having a beautiful vision of my brother.

'I remember. Uh, Mr Dusset?'

'What, kid?' His eyes were still misty with memory; the toothpick trembled a little between his lips.

'Your thumb is on that scales.'

'*What?*' He looked down, astounded, to where the ball of his thumb was pressed firmly on the white enamel. If I hadn't moved away from him a little bit when he started talking about Dennis, the ground meat would have hidden it. 'Why, so it is. Yuh. I guess I just got thinkin' about your brother, God love him.' George Dusset signed a cross on himself. When he took his thumb off the scales, the needle sprang back six ounces. He patted a little more meat on top and then did the package up with white butcher's paper.

'Okay,' he said past the toothpick. 'Let's see what we got here. Three pounds of hamburg, that's a dollar forty-four. Hamburg rolls, that's twenty-seven. Four tonics, forty cents. One churchkey, two pence. Come to . . .' He added it up on the bag he was going to put the stuff in. 'Two-twenty-nine.'

'Thirteen,' I said.

He looked up at me very slowly, frowning. 'Huh?'

'Two-thirteen. You added it wrong.'

'Kid, are you —'

'You added it wrong,' I said. 'First you put your thumb on the scales and then you overcharged on the groceries, Mr Dusset. I was gonna throw some Hostess Twinkies on top of that order but now I guess I won't.' I spanged two dollars and thirteen cents down on the Schlitz placemat in front of him.

He looked at the money, then at me. The frown was now tremendous, the lines on his face as deep as fissures. 'What are you, kid?' he said in a low voice that was ominously confidential. 'Are you some kind of smartass?'

'No, sir,' I said. 'But you ain't gonna jap me and get away with it. What would your mother say if she knew you was japping little kids?'

He thrust our stuff into the paper bag with quick stiff movements, making the Coke bottles clink together. He thrust the bag at me roughly, not caring if I dropped it and broke the tonics or not. His swarthy face was flushed and dull, the frown now frozen in place. 'Okay, kid. Here you go. Now what you do is you get the Christ out of my store. I see you in here again and I going to throw you out, me. Yuh. Smartass little sonofawhore.'

'I won't come in again,' I said, walking over to the screen door and pushing it open. The hot afternoon buzzed somnolently along its appointed course outside, sounding green and brown and full of silent light. 'Neither will none of my friends. I guess I got fifty or so.'

'Your brother wasn't no smartass!' George Dusset yelled.

'*Fuck you!*' I yelled, and ran like hell down the road.

I heard the screen door bang open like a gunshot and his bull roar came after me: '*If you ever come in here again I'll fat your lip for you, you little punk!*'

I ran until I was over the first hill, scared and laughing to myself, my heart beating out a triphammer pulse in my chest. Then I slowed to a fast walk, looking back over my shoulder every now and then to make sure he wasn't going to take after me in his car, or anything.

He didn't, and pretty soon I got to the dump gate. I put the bag inside my shirt, climbed the gate, and monkeyed down the other side. I was halfway across the dump area when I saw something I didn't like – Milo Pressman's portholed '56 Buick was parked behind his tarpaper shack. If Milo saw me, I was going to be in a world of hurt. As yet there was no sign of either him or the infamous Chopper, but all at once the chain-link fence at the back of the dump seemed very far away. I found myself wishing I'd gone around the outside, but I was now too far into the dump to want to turn around and go back. If Milo saw me climbing the dump fence, I'd probably be in dutch when I got home, but that didn't scare me as much as Milo yelling for Chopper to sic would.

Scary violin music started to play in my head. I kept putting one foot in front of the other, trying to look casual, trying to look as if I belonged here with a paper grocery sack poking out of my shirt, heading for the fence between the dump and the railroad tracks.

I was about fifty feet from the fence and just beginning to think that everything was going to be all right after all when I heard Milo shout. 'Hey! Hey, you! Kid! Get away f'm that fence! Get outta here!'

The smart thing to have done would have been to just agree with the guy and go around, but then I was so keyed up that instead of doing the smart thing I just broke for the fence with a wild yell, my sneakers kicking up dust. Vern, Teddy, and Chris came out of the underbrush on the other side of the fence and stared anxiously through the chain-link.

'*You come back here!*' Milo bawled. '*Come back here or I'll sic my dawg on you, goddammit!*'

I did not exactly find that to be the voice of sanity and conciliation, and I ran even faster for the fence, my arms pumping, the brown grocery bag crackling against my skin. Teddy started to laugh his idiotic chortling laugh, *eee-eee-eeee* into the air like some reed instrument being played by a lunatic.

'Go, Gordie! Go!' Vern screamed.

And Milo yelled: 'Sic 'im, Chopper! Go get 'im, boy!'

I threw the bag over the fence and Vern elbowed Teddy out of the way to catch it. Behind me I could hear Chopper coming, shaking the earth, blurting fire out of one distended nostril and ice out of the other, dripping sulphur from his champing jaws. I threw myself halfway up the fence with one leap, screaming. I made it to the top in no more than three seconds and simply leaped – I never thought about it, never even looked down to see what I might land on. What I *almost* landed on was Teddy, who was doubled over and laughing like crazy. His glasses had fallen off and tears were streaming out of his eyes. I missed him by inches and hit the clay-gravel embankment just to his left. At the same instant, Chopper hit the chain-link fence behind me and let out a howl of mingled pain and disappointment. I turned around, holding one skinned knee, and got my first look at the famous Chopper – and my first lesson in the vast differences between myth and reality.

Instead of some huge hellhound with red, savage eyes and teeth jutting out of his mouth like straight-pipes from a hotrod, I was looking at a medium-sized mongrel dog that was a perfectly common black and white. He was yapping and jumping fruitlessly, going up on his back legs to paw the fence.

Teddy was now strutting up and down in front of the fence, twiddling his glasses in one hand, and inciting Chopper to even greater rage.

'Kiss my ass, Choppie!' Teddy invited, spittle flying from his lips. 'Kiss my ass! Bite shit!'

He bumped his fanny against the chain-link fence and Chopper did his level best to take Teddy up on his invitation. He got nothing for his pains but a good healthy nose-bump. He began to bark crazily, foam flying from his snout. Teddy kept bumping his rump against the fence and Chopper kept lunging at it, always missing, doing nothing but racking out his nose, which was now bleeding. Teddy kept exhorting him, calling him by the somehow grisly diminutive 'Choppie', and Chris and Vern were lying weakly on the embankment, laughing so hard that they could now do little more than wheeze.

And here came Milo Pressman, dressed in sweat-stained fatigues and a New York Giants baseball cap, his mouth drawn down in distracted anger.

'Here, here!' he was yelling. 'You boys stop a-teasing that dawg! You hear me? *Stop it right now!*'

'Bite it, Choppie!' Teddy yelled, strutting up and down on our side of the fence like a mad Prussian reviewing his troops. 'Come on and sic me! Sic me!'

Chopper went nuts. I mean it sincerely. He ran around in a big circle, yelping and barking and foaming, rear feet spewing up tough little dry clods. He went around about three times, getting his courage up, I guess, and then he lauched himself straight at the security fence. He must have been going thirty miles an hour when he hit it, I kid you not – his doggy lips were stretched back from his teeth and his ears were flying in the slipstream. The whole fence made a low, musical sound as the chain-link was not just driven back against the posts but sort of *stretched* back. It was like a zither note – *yimmmmmmm*. A strangled yawp came out of Chopper's mouth, both eyes came up blank, and he did a totally amazing reverse snap-roll, landing on his back with a solid thump that sent dust puffing up around him. He just lay there for a moment and then he crawled off with his tongue hanging crookedly from the left side of his mouth.

At this, Milo himself went almost berserk with rage. His complexion darkened to a scary plum colour – even his scalp was purple under the short hedgehog bristles of his flattop haircut. Sitting stunned in the dirt, both knees of my jeans torn out, my heart still thudding from the nearness of my escape, I thought that Milo looked like a human version of Chopper.

'I know you!' Milo raved. 'You're Teddy Duchamp! I know *all* of you! Sonny, I'll beat your ass, teasing my dawg like that!'

'Like to see you try!' Teddy raved right back. 'Let's see you climb over this fence and get me, fat-ass!'

'*WHAT? WHAT DID YOU CALL ME?*'

'*FAT-ASS!*' Teddy screamed happily. '*LARD-BUCKET! TUBBAGUTS! COME ON! COME ON!*' He was jumping up and down, fists clenched, sweat flying from his hair. '*TEACH YOU TO SIC YOUR STUPID DOG ON PEOPLE! COME ON! LIKE TO SEE YOU TRY!*'

'You little tin-weasel peckerwood loony's son! I'll see your mother gets an invitation to go down and talk to the judge in court about what you done to my dawg!'

'What did you call me?' Teddy asked hoarsely. He had stopped jumping up and down. His eyes had gone huge and glassy, and his skin was the colour of lead.

Milo had called Teddy a lot of things, but he was able to go back and get the one that had struck home with no trouble at all — since then I have noticed again and again what a genius people have for that . . . for finding the LOONY button down inside and not just pressing it but hammering on the fucker.

'Your dad was a loony,' he said, grinning. 'Loony up in Togus, that's what. Crazier'n a shithouse rat. Crazier'n a buck with tickwood fever. Nuttier'n a long-tailed cat in a room fulla rockin' chairs. Loony. No wonder you're actin' the way you are, with a loony for a f –'

'*YOUR MOTHER BLOWS DEAD RATS!*' Teddy screamed. '*AND IF YOU CALL MY DAD A LOONY AGAIN. I'LL FUCKING KILL YOU. YOU COCK-SUCKER!*'

'Loony,' Milo said smugly. He'd found the button, all right. 'Loony's kid, loony's kid, your father's got toys in the attic, kid, tough break.'

Vern and Chris had been getting over their laughing fit, perhaps getting ready to appreciate the seriousness of the situation and call Teddy off, but when Teddy told Milo that his mother blew dead rats, they went back into hysterics again, lying there on the bank, rolling from side to side, their feet kicking, holding their bellies. 'No more,' Chris said weakly. 'No more, please, no more, I swear to God I'm gonna *bust!*'

Chopper was walking around in a large, dazed figure-eight behind Milo. He looked like the losing fighter about ten seconds after the ref has ended the match and awarded the winner a TKO. Meanwhile, Teddy and Milo continued their discussion of Teddy's father, standing nose to nose, with the wire fence Milo was too old and too fat to climb between them.

'Don't you say nothing else about my dad! My dad stormed the beaches at Normandy, you fucking wet end!'

'Yeah, well, where is he now, you ugly little four-eyed turd? He's up to Togus, ain't he? He's up to Togus because *HE WENT FUCKING SECTION EIGHT!*'

'Okay, that's it,' Teddy said. 'That's it, that's the end, I'm gonna kill you.' He threw himself at the fence and started up.

'You come on and try it, you slimy little bastard.' Milo stood back, grinning and waiting.

'No!' I shouted. I got to my feet, grabbed Teddy by the loose seat of his jeans, and pulled him off the fence. We both staggered back and fell over, him on top. He squashed my balls pretty good and I groaned. Nothing hurts like having your balls squashed, you know it? But I kept my arms locked around Teddy's middle.

'Lemme up!' Teddy sobbed, writhing in my arms. 'Lemme up, Gordie! Nobody ranks out my old man. *LEMME UP GODDAMMIT LEMME UP!*'

'That's just what he wants!' I shouted in his ear. 'He wants to get you over there and beat the piss out of you and then take you to the cops!'

'Huh?' Teddy craned around to look at me, his face dazed.

'Never mind your smartmouth, kid,' Milo said, advancing to the fence again with his hands curled into ham-sized fists. 'Let 'im fight his own battles.'

'Sure,' I said. 'You only outweigh him by five hundred pounds.'

'I know you, too,' Milo said ominously. 'Your name's Lachance.' He pointed to where Vern and Chris were finally picking themselves up, still breathing fast from laughing so hard. 'And those guys are Chris Chambers and one of those stupid Tessio kids. All your fathers are going to get calls from me, except for the loony up to Togus. You'll go to the 'formatory, every one of you. Juvenile delinquents!'

He stood flat on his feet, big freckled hands held out like a guy who wanted to play One Potato Two Potato, breathing hard, eyes narrow, waiting for us to cry or say we were sorry or maybe give him Teddy so he could feed Teddy to Chopper.

Chris made an O out of his thumb and index finger and spat neatly through it.

Vern hummed and looked to the sky.

Teddy said: 'Come on, Gordie. Let's get away from this asshole before I puke.'

'Oh, you're gonna get it, you foulmouthed little whore-master. Wait'll I get you to the constable.'

'We heard what you said about his father,' I told him. 'We're all witnesses. And you sicced that dog on me. That's against the law.'

Milo looked a trifle uneasy. 'You was trespassin'.'

'The hell I was. The dump's public property.'

'You climbed the fence?'

'Sure I did, after you sicced your dog on me,' I said, hoping that Milo wouldn't recall that I'd also climbed the gate to get in. 'What'd you think I was gonna do? Stand there and let 'im rip me to pieces? Come on, you guys. Let's go. It stinks around here.'

''Formatory,' Milo promised hoarsely, his voice shaking. ''Formatory for you wiseguys.'

'Can't wait to tell the cops how you called a war vet a fuckin' loony,' Chris called back over his shoulder as we moved away. 'What did *you* do in the war, Mr Pressman?'

'*NONE OF YOUR DAMN BUSINESS!*' Milo shrieked. '*YOU HURT MY DAWG!*'

'Put it on your t.s. slip and send it to the chaplain,' Vern muttered, and then we were climbing the railroad embankment again.

'Come back here!' Milo shouted, but his voice was fainter now and he seemed to be losing interest.

Teddy shot him the finger as we walked away. I looked back over my shoulder when we got to the top of the embankment. Milo was standing there behind the security fence, a big man in a baseball cap with his dog sitting beside him. His fingers were hooked through the small chain-link diamonds as he shouted at us, and all at once I felt sorry for him – he looked like the biggest third-grader in the world, locked inside the playground by mistake, yelling for someone to let him out. He kept yelling for a while and then he either gave up or we got out of range. No more was seen or heard of Milo Pressman and Chopper that day.

13

There was some discussion – in righteous tones that were actually kind of forced-sounding – about how we had shown that creepy Milo Pressman we weren't just another bunch of pussies. I told how the guy at the Florida Market had tried to jap us, and then we fell into a gloomy silence, thinking it over.

For my part, I was thinking that maybe there was some-thing to that stupid goocher business after all. Things couldn't have turned out much worse – in fact, I thought, it might be better to just keep going and spare my folks the pain of having one son in the Castle View Cemetery and one in South Windham Boys' Correctional. I had no doubt that Milo would go to the cops as soon as the importance of the dump having been closed at the time of the incident filtered into his thick skull. When that happened, he would realize that I really *had* been trespassing, public property or not. Probably that gave him every right in the world to sic his stupid dog on me. And while Chopper wasn't the hell-hound he was cracked up to be, he sure would have ripped the sitdown out of my jeans if I hadn't won the race to the fence. All of it put a big dark crimp in the day. And there was another gloomy idea rolling around inside my head – the idea that this was no lark after all, and maybe we deserved our bad luck. Maybe it was even God warning us to go home. What were we doing, anyway, going to look at some kid that had gotten himself all mashed up by a freight train?

But we were doing it, and none of us wanted to stop.

We had almost reached the trestle which carried the tracks across the river when Teddy burst into tears. It was as if a great inner tidal wave had broken through a carefully constructed set of mental dykes. No bullshit – it was that sudden and that fierce. The sobs doubled him over like punches and he sort of collapsed into a heap, his hands going from his stomach to the mutilated gobs of flesh that were the remains of his ears. He went on crying in hard, violent bursts. None of us knew what the fuck to do. It wasn't crying like when you got hit by a line drive while you were playing shortstop or smashed on the head playing tackle football on the common or when you fell off your bike. There was nothing physically wrong with him. We walked away a little and watched him, our hands in our pockets.

'Hey, man . . .' Vern said in a very thin voice. Chris and I looked at Vern hopefully. 'Hey, man' was always a good start. But Vern couldn't follow it up.

Teddy leaned forward onto the crossties and put a hand over his eyes. Now he looked like he was doing the Allah bit – 'Salami, salami, baloney,' as Popeye says. Except it wasn't funny.

At last, when the force of his crying had trailed off a little, it was Chris who went to him. He was the toughest guy in our gang (maybe even tougher than Jamie Gallant, I thought privately), but he was also the guy who made the best peace. He had a way about it. I'd seen him sit down on the kerb next to a little kid with a scraped knee, a kid he didn't even fucking *know*, and get him talking about something – the Shrine Circus that was coming to town or Huckleberry Hound on TV – until the kid forgot he was supposed to be hurt. Chris was good at it. He was tough enough to be good at it.

'Listen, Teddy, what do you care what a fat old pile of shit like him said about your father? Huh? I mean, sincerely! That don't change nothing, does it? What a fat old pile of shit like him says? Huh? Huh? Does it?'

Teddy shook his head violently. It changed nothing. But to hear it spoken of in bright daylight, something must have gone over and over in his mind while he was lying awake in bed and looking at the moon offcentre in one windowpane, something he must have thought about in his slow and broken way until it seemed almost holy, trying to make sense out of it, and then to have it brought home to him that everybody else had merely dismissed his dad as a loony . . . that had rocked him. But it changed nothing. Nothing.

'He still stormed the beaches at Normandy, right?' Chris said. He picked up one of Teddy's sweaty, grimy hands and patted it.

Teddy nodded fiercely, crying. Snot was running out of his nose.

'Do you think that pile of shit was at Normandy?'

Teddy shook his head violently. '*Nuh-Nuh-No!*'

'Do you think that guy knows you?'

'Nuh-No! No, b-b-but –'

'Or your father? He one of your father's buddies?'

'*NO!*' Angry, horrified. The thought. Teddy's chest heaved and more sobs came out of it. He had pushed his hair away from his ears and I could see the round brown plastic button of the hearing aid set in the middle of the right one. The shape of the hearing aid made more sense than the shape of his ear, if you get what I mean.

Chris said calmly: 'Talk is cheap.'

Teddy nodded, still not looking up.

'And whatever's between you and your old man, talk can't change that.'

Teddy's head shook without definition, unsure if this was true. Someone had redefined his pain, and redefined it in shockingly common terms. That would

(*loony*)

have to be examined

(*fucking section eight*)

later. In depth. On long sleepless nights.

Chris rocked him. 'He was rankin' you, man,' he said in soothing cadences that were almost a lullaby. 'He was just tryin' to rank you over that friggin' fence, you know it? No strain, man. No fuckin' strain. He don't know nothing about your old man. He don't know nothin' but stuff he heard from those rumdums down at the Mellow Tiger. He's just dogshit, man. Right, Teddy? Huh? Right?'

Teddy's crying was down to sniffles. He wiped his eyes, leaving two sooty rings around them, and sat up.

'I'm okay,' he said, and the sound of his own voice seemed to convince him. 'Yeah, I'm okay.' He stood up and put his glasses back on – dressing his naked face, it seemed to me.

He laughed thinly and swiped his bare arm across the snot on his upper lip. 'Fuckin' crybaby, right?'

'No, man,' Vern said uncomfortably. 'If anyone was rankin' out my dad –'

'Then you got to kill 'em!' Teddy said briskly, almost arrogantly. 'Kill their asses. Right, Chris?'

'Right,' Chris said amiably, and clapped Teddy on the back.

'Right, Gordie?'

'Absolutely,' I said, wondering how Teddy could care so much for his dad when his dad had practically killed him, and how I couldn't seem to give much of a shit one way or the other about my own dad, when so far as I could remember, he had never laid a hand on me since I was three and got some bleach from under the sink and started to eat it.

We walked another two hundred yards down the tracks and Teddy said in a quieter voice: 'Hey, if I spoiled your good time, I'm sorry. I guess that was pretty stupid shit back there at that fence.'

'I ain't sure I want it to be no good time,' Vern said suddenly.

Chris looked at him. 'You sayin' you want to go back, man?'

'No, huh-uh!' Vern's face knotted in thought. 'But goin' to see a dead kid . . . it shouldn't be a party, maybe. I mean, if you can dig it. I mean . . .' He looked at us rather wildly. 'I mean, I could be a little scared. If you get me.'

Nobody said anything and Vern plunged on:

'I mean, sometimes I get nightmares. Like . . . aw, you guys remember the time Danny Naughton left that pile of old funnybooks, the ones with the vampires and people getting cut up and all that shit? Jeezum-crow, I'd wake up in the middle of the night dreamin' about some guy hangin' in a house with his face all green or somethin', you know, like that, and it seems like there's somethin' under the bed and if I dangled a hand over the side, that thing might, you know, grab me . . .'

We all began to nod. We knew about the night-sweats. I would have laughed then, though, if you had told me that one day not too many years from then I'd parley a simple case of the night-sweats into about a million dollars.

'And I don't dare say anything because my friggin' *brother* . . . well, you know Billy . . . he'd broadcast it . . .' He shrugged miserably. 'So I'm ascared to look at that kid 'cause if he's, you know, if he's really *bad* . . .'

I swallowed and glanced at Chris. He was looking gravely at Vern and nodding for him to go on.

'If he's really *bad*,' Vern resumed, 'I'll have nightmares about *him* and wake up thinkin' it's *him* under my bed, all cut up in a pool of blood like he just came out of one of those Saladmaster gadgets they show on TV, just eyeballs and hair, but *movin'* somehow, if you can dig that, *movin'* somehow, you know, and gettin' ready to *grab* –'

'Jesus Christ,' Teddy said thickly. 'What a fuckin' bedtime story.'

'Well I can't *help* it,' Vern said, his voice defensive. 'But I feel like we *hafta* see him, even if there are bad dreams. You know? Like we *hafta*. But . . . but maybe it shouldn't be no good time.'

'Yeah,' Chris said softly. 'Maybe it shouldn't.'

Vern said pleadingly: 'You won't tell none of the other guys, will you? I don't mean about the nightmares, every-body has those – I mean about wakin' up and thinkin' there might be somethin' under the bed. I'm too fuckin' old for the boogeyman.'

We all said we wouldn't tell, and a glum silence fell over us again. It was only quarter to three, but it felt much later. It was too hot and too much had happened. We weren't even over into Harlow yet. We were going to have to pick them up and lay them down if we were going to make some real miles before dark.

We passed the railroad junction and a signal on a tall, rusty pole and all of us paused to chuck cinders at the steel flag on top, but nobody hit it. And around three-thirty we came to the Castle River and the GS&WM trestle which crossed it.

14

The river was better than a hundred yards across at that point in 1960; I've been back to look at it since then, and found it had narrowed up quite a bit during the years between. They're always fooling with the river, trying to make it work better for the mills, and they've put in so many dams that it's pretty well tamed. But in those days there were only three dams on the whole length of the river as it ran across all of New Hampshire and half of Maine. The Castle was still pretty free back then, and every third spring it would overflow its banks and cover Route 136 in either Harlow or Danvers Junction or both.

Now, at the end of the driest summer western Maine had seen since the depression, it was still broad. From where we stood on the Castle Rock side, the bulking forest on the Harlow side looked like a different country altogether. The pines and spruces over there were bluish in the heat-haze of the afternoon. The rails went across the water fifty feet up, supported by an underpinning of tarred wooden support posts and crisscrossing beams. The water was so shallow you could look down and see the tops of the cement plugs which had been planted ten feet deep in the riverbed to hold up the trestle.

The trestle itself was pretty chintzy – the rails ran over a long, narrow wooden platform of six-by-fours. There was a four-inch gap between each pair of these beams where you could look all the way down into the water. On the sides, there was no more than eighteen inches between the rail and the edge of the trestle. If a train came it was maybe enough room to avoid getting plastered . . . but the wind generated by a highballing freight would surely sweep you off to fall to a certain death against the rocks just below the surface of the shallow running water.

Looking at the trestle, we all felt fear start to crawl around in our bellies . . . and mixing uneasily with the fear was the excitement of a boss dare, a really big one, something you could brag on for weeks after you got home . . . *if* you got home. That queer light was creeping back into Teddy's eyes and I thought he wasn't seeing the GS&WM train trestle at all but a long sandy beach, a thousand LSTs aground in the foaming waves, ten thousand GIs charging up the sand, combat boots digging. They were leaping rolls of barbed wire! Tossing grenades at pillboxes! Overrunning machine-gun nests!

We were standing beside the tracks where the cinders sloped away towards the river's cut – the place where the embankment stopped and the trestle began. Looking down, I could see where the slope started to get steep. The cinders gave way to straggly, tough-looking bushes and slabs of grey rock. Further down there were a few stunted firs with exposed roots writhing their way out of fissures in the plates of rock; they seemed to be looking down at their own miserable reflections in the running water.

At this point, the Castle River actually looked fairly clean; at Castle Rock it was just entering Maine's textile-mill belt. But there were no fish jumping out there, although the river was clear enough to see the bottom – you had to go another ten miles upstream and towards New Hampshire before you could see any fish in the Castle. There were no fish, and along the edges of the river you could see dirty collars of foam around some of the rocks – the foam was the colour of old ivory. The river's smell was not particularly pleasant, either; it smelled like a laundry hamper full of mildewy towels. Dragonflies stitched at the surface of the water and laid their eggs with impunity. There were no trout to eat them. Hell, there weren't even any shiners.

'Man,' Chris said softly.

'Come on,' Teddy said in that brisk, arrogant way. 'Let's go.' He was already edging his way out, walking on the six-by-fours between the shining rails.

'Say,' Vern said uneasily, 'any of you guys know when the next train's due?'

We all shrugged.

I said: 'There's the Route 136 bridge . . .'

'Hey, come on, gimme a break!' Teddy cried. 'That means walkin' five miles down the river on this side and then five miles back up on the other side . . . it'll take us until dark! If we use the trestle, we can get to the same place in *ten minutes*!'

'But if a train comes, there's nowheres to go,' Vern said.

He wasn't looking at Teddy. He was looking down at the fast, bland river.

'Fuck there isn't!' Teddy said indignantly. He swung over the edge and held one of the wooden supports between the rails. He hadn't gone out very far – his sneakers were almost touching the ground – but the thought of doing that same thing above the middle of the river with a fifty-foot drop beneath and a train bellowing by just over my head, a train that would probably be dropping some nice hot sparks into my hair and down the back of my neck . . . none of that actually made me feel like Queen for a Day.

'See how easy it is?' Teddy said. He dropped to the embankment, dusted his hands, and climbed back up beside us.

'You tellin' me you're gonna hang on that way if it's a two hundred car freight?' Chris asked. 'Just sorta hang there by your hands for five or ten minutes?'

'You chicken?' Teddy shouted.

'No, just askin' what you'd do,' Chris said, grinning. 'Peace, man.'

'Go around if you want to!' Teddy brayed. 'Who gives a fuck? I'll wait for you! I'll take a *nap*!'

'One train already went by,' I said reluctantly. 'And there probably isn't any more than one, two trains a day that go through Harlow. Look at this.' I kicked the weeds growing up through the railroad ties with one sneaker. There were no weeds growing between the tracks which ran between Castle Rock and Lewiston.

'There. See?' Teddy was triumphant.

'But still, there's a *chance*,' I added.

'Yeah,' Chris said. He was looking only at me, his eyes sparkling. 'Dare you, Lachance.'

'Dares go first.'

'Okay,' Chris said. He widened his gaze to take in Teddy and Vern. 'Any pussies here?'

'*NO!*' Teddy shouted.

Vern cleared his throat, croaked, cleared it again, and said 'no' in a very small voice. He smiled a weak, sick smile.

'Okay,' Chris said . . . but we hesitated for a moment, even Teddy, looking warily up and down the tracks. I knelt down and took one of the steel rails firmly in my hand, never minding that it was almost hot enough to blister the skin. The rail was mute.

'Okay,' I said, and as I said it some guy pole-vaulted in my stomach. He dug his pole all the way into my balls, it felt like, and ended up sitting astride my heart.

We went out onto the trestle single-file: Chris first, then Teddy, then Vern, and me playing tail-end Charlie because I was the one who said dares go first. We walked on the platform crossties between the rails, and you had to look at your feet whether you were scared of heights or not. A misstep and you would go down to your crotch, probably with a broken ankle to pay.

The embankment dropped away beneath me, and every step further out seemed to seal our decision more firmly . . . and to make it feel more suicidally stupid. I stopped to look up when I saw the rocks giving way to water far beneath me. Chris and Teddy were a long way ahead, almost out over the middle, and Vern was tottering slowly along behind them, peering studiously down at his feet. He looked like an old lady trying out stilts with his head poked downward, his back hunched, his arms held out for balance. I looked back over my shoulder. Too far, man, I had to keep going now, and not only because a train might come. If I went back, I'd be a pussy for life.

So I got walking again. After looking down at that endless series of crossties for a while, with a glimpse of running water between each pair, I started to feel dizzy and disoriented. Each time I brought my foot down, part of my brain assured me it was going to plunge through into space, even though I could see it was not.

I became acutely aware of all the noises inside me and outside me, like some crazy orchestra tuning up to play. The steady thump of my heart, the bloodbeat in my ears like a drum being played with brushes, the creak of sinews like the strings of a violin that has been tuned radically upward, the steady hiss of the river, the hot hum of a locust digging into tight bark, the monotonous cry of a chickadee, and somewhere, far away, a barking dog. Chopper, maybe. The mildewy smell of the Castle River was strong in my nose. The long muscles in my thighs were trembling. I kept thinking how much safer it would be (probably faster, as well) if I just got down on my hands and knees and scuttered along that way. But I wouldn't do that – none of us would. If the Saturday matinee movies down to the Gem had taught us anything, it was that Only Losers Crawl. It was one of the central tenets of the Gospel According to Hollywood. Good guys walk firmly upright, and if your sinews are creaking like overtuned violin strings because of the adrenalin rush going on in your body, and if the long muscles in your thighs are trembling for the same reason, why, so be it.

I had to stop in the middle of the trestle and look up at the sky for a while. That dizzy feeling had been getting worse. I saw phantom crossties – they seemed to float right in front of my nose. Then they faded out and I began to feel okay again. I looked ahead and saw I had almost caught up with Vern, who was slowpoking along worse than ever. Chris and Teddy were almost all the way across.

And although I've since written seven books about people who can do such exotic things as read minds and precognit the future, that was when I had my first and last psychic flash. I'm sure that's what it was; how else to explain it? I squatted and made a fist around the rail on my left. It thrummed in my hand. It was thrumming so hard that it was like gripping a bundle of deadly metallic snakes.

You've heard it said 'His bowels turned to water'? I know what that phrase means – *exactly* what it means. It may be the most accurate cliché ever coined. I've been scared since, badly scared, but I've never been as scared as I was in that moment, holding that hot live rail. It seemed that for a moment all my works below throat level just went limp and lay there in an internal faint. A thin stream of urine ran listlessly down the inside of one thigh. My mouth opened. I didn't open it, it opened by itself, the jaw dropping like a trapdoor from which the hingepins had suddenly been moved. My tongue was plastered suffocatingly against the roof of my mouth. All my muscles were locked. That was the worst. My works were limp but my muscles were in a kind of dreadful lockbolt and I couldn't move at all. It was only for a moment, but in the subjective timestream, it seemed forever.

All sensory input became intensified, as if some power-surge had occurred in the electrical flow of my brain, cranking everything up from a hundred and ten volts to two-twenty. I could hear a plane passing in the sky somewhere near and had time to wish I was on it, just sitting in a window seat with a Coke in my hand and gazing idly down at the shining line of a river whose name I did not know. I could see every little splinter and gouge in the tarred crosstie I was squatting on. And out of the corner of my eye I could see the rail itself with my hand still clutched around it, glittering insanely. The vibration from that rail sank so deeply into my hand that when I took it away it still vibrated, the nerve-endings kicking each other over again and again, tingling the way a hand or a foot tingles when it has been asleep and is starting to wake up. I could taste my saliva, suddenly all electric and sour and thickened to curds along my gums. And worst, somehow most horrible of all, I couldn't *hear* the train yet, could not know if it was rushing at me from ahead or behind, or how close it was. It was invisible. It was unannounced, except for that shaking rail in my hand. There was only that to advertise its imminent arrival. An image of Ray Brower, dreadfully mangled and thrown into a ditch somewhere like a ripped-open laundry bag, reeled before my eyes. We would join him, or at least Vern and I would, or at least I would. We had invited ourselves to our own funerals.

The last thought broke the paralysis and I shot to my feet. I probably would have looked like a jack-in-the-box to anyone watching, but to myself I felt like a boy in underwater slow motion, shooting up not through five feet of air but rather up through five hundred feet of water, moving slowly, moving with a dreadful languidness as the water parted grudgingly.

But at last I did break the surface.

I screamed: '*TRAIN!*'

The last of the paralysis fell from me and I began to run. Vern's head jerked back over his shoulder. The surprise that distorted his face was almost comically exaggerated, written as large as the letters in a Dick and Jane primer. He saw me break into my clumsy, shambling run, dancing from one horribly high crosstie to the next, and knew I wasn't joking. He began to run himself.

Far ahead, I could see Chris stepping off the ties and onto the solid safe embankment and I hated him with a sudden bright green hate as juicy and as bitter as the sap in an April leaf. He was safe. *That* fucker was *safe*. I watched him drop to his knees and grab a rail.

My left foot almost slipped into the yaw beneath me. I flailed with my arms, my eyes as hot as ball bearings in some runaway piece of machinery, got my balance, and ran on. Now I was right behind Vern. We were past the halfway point and for the first time I heard the train. It was coming from behind us, coming from the Castle Rock side of the river. It was a low rumbling noise that began to rise slightly and sort itself into the diesel thrum of the engine and the higher, more sinister sound of big grooved wheels turning heavily on the rails.

'*Awwwwwwww, shit!*' Vern screamed.

'Run, you pussy!' I yelled, and thumped him on the back.

'I can't! I'll fall!'

'*Run faster!*'

'*AWWWWWWWWWWWW-SHIT!*'

But he ran faster, a shambling scarecrow with a bare, sunburnt back, the collar of his shirt swinging and dangling below his butt. I could see the sweat standing out on his peeling shoulderblades, standing out in perfect little beads. I could see the fine down on the nape of his neck. His muscles clenched and loosened, clenched and loosened, clenched and loosened. His spine stood out in a series of knobs, each knob casting its own crescent-shaped shadow – I could see that these knobs grew closer together as they approached his neck. He was still holding his bedroll and I was still holding mine. Vern's feet thudded on the crossties. He almost missed one, lunged forward with his arms out, and I whacked him on the back again to keep him going.

'*Gordeeee I can't AWWWWWWWWWWW-SHE-EEEEYIT*—'

'*RUN FASTER, DICKFACE!*' I bellowed and was I *enjoying* this?

Yeah – in some peculiar, self-destructive way that I have experienced since only when completely and utterly drunk, I was. I was driving Vern Tessio like a drover getting a particularly fine cow to market. And maybe he was enjoying his own fear in that same way, bawling like that self-same cow, hollering and sweating, his ribcage rising and falling like the bellows of a blacksmith on a speed-trip, clumsily keeping his footing, lurching ahead.

The train was very loud now, its engine deepening to a steady rumble. Its whistle sounded as it crossed the junction point where we had paused to chuck cinders at the rail-flag. I had finally gotten my hellhound, like it or not. I kept waiting for the trestle to start shaking under my feet. When that happened, it would be right behind us.

'*GO FASTER, VERN! FAAASTER!*'

'Oh Gawd Gordie oh Gawd Gordie oh Gawd AWWWWWWW-SHEEEEEEEYIT!'

The freight's electric horn suddenly spanked the air into a hundred pieces with one long loud blast, making everything you ever saw in a movie or a comic book or one of your own daydreams fly apart, letting you know what both the heroes and the cowards really heard when death flew at them:

WHHHHHHHHONNNNNNK!

WHHHHHHHHHHHONNNNNNNNNK!

And then Chris was below us and to the right, and Teddy was behind him, his glasses flashing back arcs of sunlight, and they were both mouthing a single word and the word was *jump*! but the train had sucked all the blood out of the word, leaving only its shape in their mouths. The trestle began to shake as the train charged across it. We jumped.

Vern landed full-length in the dust and the cinders and I landed right beside him, almost on top of him. I never did see that train, nor do I know if its engineer saw us – when I mentioned the possibility that he hadn't seen us to Chris a couple of years later, he said: 'They don't blow the electric horn like that just for chucks, Gordie.' But he *could* have; he could have been blowing it just for the hell of it. I suppose. Right then, such fine points didn't much matter. I clapped my hands over my ears and dug my face into the hot dirt as the freight went by, metal squalling against metal, the air buffeting us. I had no urge to look at it. It was a long freight but I never looked at all. Before it had passed completely, I felt a warm hand on my neck and knew it was Chris's.

When it was gone – when I was *sure* it was gone – I raised my head like a soldier coming out of his foxhole at the end of a day-long artillery barrage. Vern was still plastered into the dirt, shivering. Chris was sitting cross-legged between us, one hand on Vern's sweaty neck, the other still on mine.

When Vern finally sat up, shaking all over and licking his

lips compulsively, Chris said, 'What you guys think if we drink those Cokes? Could anybody use one besides me?'

We all thought we could use one.

15

About a quarter of a mile along on the Harlow side, the GS&WM tracks plunged directly into the woods. The heavily wooded land sloped down to a marshy area. It was full of mosquitoes almost as big as fighter-planes, but it was cool . . . blessedly cool.

We sat down in the shade to drink our Cokes. Vern and I threw our shirts over our shoulders to keep the bugs off, but Chris and Teddy just sat naked to the waist, looking as cool and collected as two Eskimos in an icehouse. We hadn't been there five minutes when Vern had to go off into the bushes and take a squat, which led to a good deal of joking and elbowing when he got back.

'Train scare you much, Vern?'

'No,' Vern said. 'I was gonna squat when we got across, anyway. I *hadda* take a squat, you know?'

'*Verrrrrrrn?*' Chris and Teddy chorused.

'Come on, you guys, I *did*. Sincerely.'

'Then you won't mind if we examine the seat of your Jockeys for Hershey-squirts, willya?' Teddy asked, and Vern laughed, finally understanding that he was getting ribbed.

'Go screw.'

Chris turned to me. 'That train scare you, Gordie?'

'Nope,' I said, and sipped my Coke.

'Not much, you sucker.' He punched my arm.

'Sincerely! I wasn't scared at all.'

'Yeah? You wasn't scared?' Teddy was looking me over carefully.

'No. I was fuckin' *petrified*.'

This slew all of them, even Vern, and we laughed long and hard. Then we just laid back, not goofing anymore, just drinking our Cokes and being quiet. My body felt warm, exercised, at peace with itself. Nothing in it was working crossgrain to anything else. I was alive and glad to be. Everything seemed to stand out with a special clearness, and although I never could have said that out loud I didn't think it mattered – maybe that sense of clearness was something I wanted just for myself.

I think I began to understand a little bit that day what makes men become daredevils. I paid twenty dollars to watch Evel Knievel attempt his jump over the Snake River Canyon a couple of years ago and my wife was horrified. She told me that if I'd been born a Roman I would have been right there in the Coliseum, munching grapes and watching as the lions disembowelled the Christians. She was wrong, although it was hard for me to explain why (and, really, I think *she* thought I was just jiving her). I didn't cough up that twenty to watch the man die on coast-to-coast closed-circuit TV, although I was quite sure that was exactly what was going to happen. I went because of the shadows that are always somewhere behind our eyes, because of what Bruce Springsteen calls the darkness on the edge of town in one of his songs, and at one time or another I think everyone wants to dare that darkness in spite of the jalopy bodies that some joker of a God gave us human beings. No . . . not in *spite* of our jalopy bodies but *because* of them.

'Hey, tell that story,' Chris said suddenly, sitting up.

'What story?' I asked, although I guess I knew.

I always felt uncomfortable when the talk turned to my stories, although all of them seemed to like them – wanting to tell stories, even wanting to write them down . . . that was just peculiar enough to be boss, like wanting to grow up to be a sewer inspector or a Grand Prix mechanic. Richie Jenner, a kid who hung around with us until his family moved to Nebraska in 1959, was the first one to find out that I wanted to be a writer when I grew up, that I wanted to do that for my full-time job. We were up in my room, just fooling around, and he found a bunch of handwritten pages under the comic books in a carton in my closet. What's *this*? Richie asks. Nothin', I say, and try to grab them back. Richie held the pages up out of reach . . . I must admit that I didn't try very *hard* to get them back. I wanted him to read them and at the same time I didn't – an uneasy mix of pride and shyness that has never changed in me very much when someone asks to look. The act of writing itself is done in secret, like masturbation – oh, I have one friend who has done things like write stories in the display windows of bookshops and department stores, but this is a man who is nearly crazy with courage, the kind of man you'd like to have with you if you just happened to fall down with a heart attack in a city where no one knew you. For me, it always wants to be sex and always falls short – it's always that adolescent handjob in the bathroom with the door locked.

Richie sat right there on the end of my bed for most of the afternoon reading his way through the stuff I had been doing, most of it influenced by the same sort of comic books as the ones that had given Vern nightmares. And when he was done, Richie looked at me in a strange new way that made me feel very peculiar, as if he had been forced to reappraise my whole personality. He said, You're pretty good at this. Why don't you show these to Chris? I said no, I wanted it to be a secret, and Richie said: Why . . . It ain't pussy. You ain't no queer. I mean, it ain't *poetry*.

Still, I made him promise not to tell anybody about my stories and of course he did and it turned out most of them liked to read the stuff I wrote, which was mostly about getting buried alive or some crook coming back from the dead and slaughtering the jury that had condemned him in Twelve Interesting Ways or a maniac that went crazy and chopped a lot of people into veal cutlets before the hero, Curt Cannon, 'cut the subhuman, screeching madman to pieces with round after round from his smoking .45 automatic.'

In my stories, they were always rounds. *Never* bullets.

For a change of pace, there were the Le Dio stories. Le Dio was a town in France, and during 1942, a grim squad of tired American dog-faces were trying to re-take it from the Nazis (this was two years before I discovered that the Allies didn't land in France until 1944). They went on trying to re-take it, fighting their way from street to street, through about forty stories which I wrote between the ages of nine and fourteen. Teddy was absolutely made for the Le Dio stories, and I think I wrote the last dozen or so just for him – by then I was heartily sick of Le Dio and writing things like *Mon Dieu* and *Cherchez le Boche!* and *Fermez la porte!* In Le Dio, French peasants were always hissing to GI dogfaces to *Fermez la porte!* But Teddy would hunch over the pages, his eyes big, his brow beaded with sweat, his face twisting. There were times when I could almost hear air-cooled

Brownings and whistling 88s going off in his skull. The way he clamoured for more Le Dio stories was both pleasing and frightening.

Nowadays writing is my work and the pleasure has diminished a little, and more and more often that guilty, masturbatory pleasure has become associated in my head with the coldly clinical images of artificial insemination: I come according to the rules and regs laid down in my publishing contract. And although no one is ever going to call me the Thomas Wolfe of my generation, I rarely feel like a cheat: I get it off as hard as I can every fucking time. Doing less would, in an odd way, be like going faggot – or what that meant to us back then. What scares me is how often it hurts these days. Back then I was sometimes disgusted by how damned *good* it felt to write. These days I sometimes look at this typewriter and wonder when it's going to run out of good words. I don't want that to happen. I guess I can bear the pain as long as I don't run out of good words, you know?

'What's this story?' Vern asked uneasily. 'It ain't a horror story, is it, Gordie? I don't think I want to hear no horror stories. I'm not up for that, man.'

'No, it ain't a horror,' Chris said. 'It's really funny. Gross, but funny. Go on, Gordie. Hammer that fucker to us.'

'Is it about Le Dio?' Teddy asked.

'No, it ain't about Le Dio, you fuckin' psycho,' Chris said, and rabbit-punched him. 'It's about this pie-eatin' contest.'

'Hey, I didn't even write it down yet,' I said.

'Yeah, but tell it.'

'You guys want to hear it?'

'Sure,' Teddy said. 'Boss.'

'Well, it's about this made-up town, Gretna, I call it. Gretna, Maine.'

'*Gretna?*' Vern said, grinning. 'What kind of name is that? There ain't no *Gretna* in Maine.'

'Shut up, fool,' Chris said. 'He just toldja it was made-up, didn't he?'

'Yeah, but *Gretna*, that sounds pretty stupid –'

'Lots of *real* towns sound stupid,' Chris said. 'I mean, what about *Alfred*, Maine? Or *Saco*, Maine? Or Jerusalem's Lot? Or Castle-fuckin'-Rock? There ain't no castle here. *Most* town names are stupid. You just don't think so because you're used to 'em. Right, Gordie?'

'Sure,' I said, but privately I thought Vern was right – Gretna was a pretty stupid name for a town. I just hadn't been able to think of another one. 'So anyway, they're having their annual Pioneer Days, just like in Castle Rock –'

'Yeah, Pioneer Days, that's a fuckin' *blast*,' Vern said earnestly. 'I put my whole family in that jail on wheels they have, even fuckin' Billy. It was only for half an hour and it cost me my whole allowance but it was worth it just to know where that sonofawhore was –'

'Will you shut up and let him tell it?' Teddy hollered.

Vern blinked. 'Sure. Yeah. Okay.'

'Go on, Gordie,' Chris said.

'It's not really much –'

'Naw, we don't expect much from a wet end like you,' Teddy said, 'but tell it anyway.'

I cleared my throat. 'So anyway. It's Pioneer Days, and on the last night they have these three big events. There's an egg-roll for the little kids and a sack-race for kids that are like eight or nine, and then there's the pie-eating contest.

And the main guy of the story is this fat kid nobody likes named Davie Hogan.'

'Like Charlie Hogan's brother if he had one,' Vern said, and then shrank back as Chris rabbit-punched him again.

'This kid, he's our age, but he's fat. He weighs like one-eighty and he's always gettin' beat up and ranked out. And all the kids, instead of calling him Davie, they call him Lard Ass Hogan and rank him out whenever they get the chance.'

They nodded respectfully, showing the proper sympathy for Lard Ass, although if such a guy ever showed up in Castle Rock, we all would have been out teasing him and ranking him to the dogs and back.

'So he decided to take revenge because he's, like, fed up, you know? He's only in the pie-eating contest, but that's like the final event during Pioneer Days and everyone really digs it. The prize is five bucks —'

'So he wins it and gives the finger to everybody!' Teddy said. 'Boss!'

'No, it's better than that,' Chris said. 'Just shut up and listen.'

'Lard Ass figures to himself, five bucks, what's that? If anybody remembers anything at all in two weeks, it'll just be that fuckin' pig Hogan out-ate everybody, well, it figures, let's go over his house and rank the shit out of him, only now we'll call him Pie Ass instead of Lard Ass.'

They nodded some more, agreeing that Davie Hogan was a thinking cat. I began to warm to my own story.

'But everybody expects him to enter the contest, you know. Even his mom and dad. Hey, they practically got that five bucks spent for him already.'

'Yeah, right,' Chris said.

'So he's thinkin' about it and hating the whole thing, because being fat isn't really his fault. See, he'd got these weird fuckin' glands, somethin', and –'

'My cousin's like that!' Vern said excitedly. 'Sincerely! She weighs close to three hundred pounds! Supposed to be her Hyboid Gland or something like that. I dunno about her Hyboid Gland, but what a fuckin' blimp, no shit, she looks like a fuckin' Thanksgiving turkey, and this one time –'

'Will you shut the fuck *up*, Vern?' Chris cried violently. 'For the last time! Honest to God!' He had finished his Coke and now he turned the hourglass-shaped green bottle upside down and brandished it over Vern's head.

'Yeah, right, I'm sorry. Go on, Gordie. It's a swell story.'

I smiled. I didn't really mind Vern's interruptions, but of course I couldn't tell Chris that; he was the self-appointed Guardian of Art.

'So he's turnin' it over in his mind, you know, the whole week before the contest. At school kids keep comin' up to him and sayin' Hey Lard Ass, how many pies ya gonna eat? Ya gonna eat ten? Twenty? Fuckin' *eighty*? And Lard Ass, *he* says, How should I know. I don't even know what *kind* they are. And see, there's quite a bit of interest in the contest because the champ is this grownup whose name is, uh, Bill Traynor, I guess. And this guy Traynor, he ain't even fat. In fact, he's a real stringbean. But he can eat pies like a whiz, and the year before he ate six pies in five minutes.'

'*Whole* pies?' Teddy asked, awe-struck.

'Right you are. And Lard Ass, he's the youngest guy to ever be in the contest.'

'Go, Lard Ass!' Teddy cried excitedly. 'Scoff up those fuckin' pies!'

'Tell 'em about the other guys in it,' Chris said.

'Okay. Besides Lard Ass Hogan and Bill Traynor, there was Calvin Spier, the fattest guy in town – he ran the jewellery store –'

'Gretna Jewels,' Vern said, and snickered. Chris gave him a black look.

'And then there's this guy who's a disc jockey at a radio station up in Lewiston, he ain't exactly fat but he's sorta chubby, you know. And the last guy was Hubert Gretna the Third, who was the principal of Lard Ass Hogan's school.'

'He was eatin' against his own *principal?*' Teddy asked.

Chris clutched his knees and rocked back and forth joyfully. 'Ain't that *great?* Go on, Gordie!'

I had them now. They were all leaning forward. I felt an intoxicating sense of power. I tossed my empty Coke bottle into the woods and scrunched around a little bit to get comfortable. I remember hearing the chickadee again, off in the woods, farther away now, lifting its monotonous, endless call into the sky: *dee-dee-dee-dee* . . .

'So he gets this idea,' I said. 'The greatest revenge idea a kid ever had. The big night comes – the end of Pioneer Days. The pie-eating contest comes just before the fireworks. The Main Street of Gretna has been closed off so people can walk around in it, and there's this big platform set up right in the street. There's bunting hanging down and a big crowd in front. There's also a photographer from the paper, to get a picture of the winner with blueberries all over his face, because it turned out to be bluebcrry pies that year. Also, I almost forgot to tell you this, they had to eat the pies with their hands tied behind their backs. So, dig it, they come up onto the platform . . .'

16

From *The Revenge of Lard Ass Hogan*, by Gordon Lachance, originally published in *Cavalier* magazine, March, 1975. Used by permission.

They came up onto the platform one by one and stood behind a long trestle table covered with a linen cloth. The table was stacked high with pies and stood at the edge of the platform. Above it were looped necklaces of bare 100-watt bulbs, moths and night-fliers banging softly against them and haloing them. Above the platform, bathed in spotlights, was a long sign which read: THE GREAT GRETNA PIE-EAT OF 1960! To either side of this sign hung battered loudspeakers, supplied by Chuck Day of the Great Day Appliance Shop. Bill Travis, the reigning champion, was Chuck's cousin.

As each contestant came up, his hands bound behind him and his shirtfront open, like Sidney Carton on his way to the guillotine. Mayor Charbonneau would announce his name over Chuck's PA system and tie a large white bib around his neck. Calvin Spier received token applause only; in spite of his belly, which was the size of a twenty-gallon waterbarrel, he was considered an underdog second only to the Hogan kid (most considered Lard Ass a comer, but too young and inexperienced to do much this year).

After Spier, Bob Cormier was introduced. Cormier was a disc jockey who did a popular afternoon programme at WLAM in Lewiston. He got a bigger hand, accompanied by a few screams from the teenaged girls in the audience. The girls thought he was 'cute'. John Wiggins, principal of Gretna Elementary School, followed Cormier. He received a hearty cheer from the older section of the audience – and a few scattered boos from fractious members of his student body. Wiggins managed to beam paternally and frown sternly down on the audience at the same time.

Next, Mayor Charbonneau introduced Lard Ass.

'A new participant in the annual Great Gretna Pie-Eat, but one we expect great things from in the future . . . *young master David Hogan!*' Lard Ass got a big round of applause as Mayor Charbonneau tied on his bib, and as it was dying away, a rehearsed Greek chorus just beyond the reach of the 100-watt bulbs cried out in wicked unison: '*Go-get-'em-Lard Ass!*'

There were muffled shrieks of laughter, running footsteps, a few shadows that no one could (or would) identify, some nervous laughter, some judicial frowns (the largest from Hizzoner Charbonneau, the most visible figure of authority). Lard Ass himself appeared to not even notice. The small smile greasing his thick lips and creasing his thick chops did not change as the Mayor, still frowning largely, tied his bib around his neck and told him not to pay any attention to fools in the audience (as if the Mayor had even the faintest inkling of what monstrous fools Lard Ass Hogan had suffered and would continue to suffer as he rumbled through life like a Nazi Tiger Tank). The Mayor's breath was warm and smelled of beer.

The last contestant to mount the bunting-decorated stage drew the loudest and most sustained applause; this was the legendary Bill Travis, six feet five inches tall, gangling, voracious. Travis was a mechanic at the local Amoco station down by the railyard, a likeable fellow if there ever was one.

It was common knowledge around town that there was

more involved in the Great Gretna Pie-Eat than a mere five dollars – at least, for Bill Travis there was. There were two reasons for this. First, people always came by the station to congratulate Bill after he won the contest, and most everyone who came to congratulate stayed to get his gas-tank filled. And the two garage-bays were sometimes booked up for a solid month after the contest. Folks would come in to get a muffler replaced or their wheel-bearings greased, and would sit in the theatre chairs ranged along one wall (Jerry Maling, who owned the Amoco, had salvaged them from the old Gem Theatre when it was torn down in 1957), drinking Cokes and Moxies from out of the machine and gassing with Bill about the contest as he changed sparkplugs or rolled around on a crawlie-wheelie under someone's International Harvester pickup, looking for holes in the exhaust system. Bill always seemed willing to talk, which was one of the reasons he was so well-liked in Gretna.

There was some dispute around town as to whether Jerry Maling gave Bill a flat bonus for the extra business his yearly feat (or yearly eat, if you prefer) brought in, or if he got an out-and-out raise. Whatever way it was, there could be no doubt that Travis did much better than most small-town wrench jokeys. He had a nice-looking two-storey ranch out on the Sabbatus Road, and certain snide people referred to it as 'the house that pies built'. That was probably an exaggeration, but Bill had it coming another way . . . which brings us to the second reason there was more in it for Travis than just five dollars.

The pie-eat was a hot wagering event in Gretna. Perhaps most people only came to laugh, but a goodly minority also came to lay their money down. Contestants were observed and discussed by these betters as ardently as thoroughbreds are observed and discussed by racing touts. The wagerers accosted contestants' friends, relatives, even mere acquaintances. They pried out any and all details concerning the contestants' eating habits. There was always a lot of discussion about that year's official pie – apple was considered a 'heavy' pie, apricot a 'light' one (although a contestant had to resign himself to a day or two of the trots after downing three or four apricot pies). That year's official pie, blueberry, was considered a happy medium. Betters, of course, were particularly interested in their man's stomach for blueberry dishes. How did he do on blueberry buckle? Did he favour blueberry jam over strawberry preserve? Had he been known to sprinkle blueberries on his breakfast cereal, or was he strictly a bananas-and-cream sort of fellow?

There were other questions of some moment. Was he a fast eater who slowed down or a slow eater who started to speed up as things got serious or just a good steady all-around trencher-man? How many hot dogs could he put away while watching a Babe Ruth League game down at the St Dom's baseball field? Was he much of a beer-drinker, and, if so, how many bottles did he usually put away in the course of an evening? Was he a belcher? It was believed that a good belcher was a bit tougher to beat over the long haul.

All of this and other information was sifted, the odds laid, the bets made. How much money actually changed hands during the week or so following pie-night I have no way of knowing, but if you held a gun to my head and forced me to guess, I'd put it at close to a thousand dollars – that probably sounds like a pretty paltry figure, but it was a lot of money to be passing around in such a small town fifteen years ago.

And because the contest was honest and a strict time-limit of ten minutes was observed, no one objected to a competitor betting on himself, and Bill Travis did so every year. Talk was, as he nodded, smiling, to his audience on that summer night in 1960, that he had bet a substantial amount on himself again, and that the best he had been able to do this year was one-for-five odds. If you're not the betting type, let me explain it this way: he'd have to put two hundred and fifty dollars at risk to win fifty. Not a good deal at all, but it was the price of success – and as he stood there, soaking up the applause and smiling easy, he didn't look too worried about it.

'And the defending cham*peen*,' Mayor Charbonneau trumpeted, 'Gretna's own *Bill Travis*!'

'Hoo, Bill!'

'How many you goin' through tonight, Bill?'

'You goin' for ten, Billy-boy?'

'I got a two-spot on you, Bill! Don't let me down, boy!'

'Save me one of those pies, Trav!'

Nodding and smiling with all proper modesty, Bill Travis allowed the Mayor to tie his bib around his neck. Then he sat down at the far right end of the table, near the place where Mayor Charbonneau would stand during the contest. From right to left, then, the eaters were Bill Travis, David 'Lard Ass' Hogan, Bob Cormier, principal John Wiggins, and Calvin Spier holding down the stool on the far left.

Mayor Charbonneau introduced Sylvia Dodge, who was even more of a contest figure than Bill Travis himself. She had been President of the Gretna Ladies' Auxiliary for years beyond telling (since the First Manassas, according to some town wits), and it was she who oversaw the baking of each year's pies, strictly subjecting each to her own rigorous quality control, which included a weigh-in ceremony on Mr Bancichek's butcher's scales down at the Freedom Market – this to make sure that each pie weighed within an ounce of the others.

Sylvia smiled regally down at the crowd, her blue hair twinkling under the hot glow of the light-bulbs. She made a short speech about how glad she was that so much of the town had turned out to celebrate their hardy pioneer forebears, the people who made this country great, for it *was* great, not only on the grassroots level where Mayor Charbonneau would be leading the local Republicans to the hallowed seats of town government again in November, but on the national level where the team of Nixon and Lodge would take the torch of freedom from Our Great and Beloved General and hold it high for –

Calvin Spier's belly rumbled noisily – *Goinnnngg*! There was laughter and even some applause. Sylvia Dodge, who knew perfectly well that Calvin was both a Democrat and a Catholic (either would have been forgivable alone, but the two combined, never), managed to blush, smile, and look furious all at the same time. She cleared her throat and wound up with a ringing exhortation to every boy and girl in the audience, telling them to always hold the red, white, and blue high, both in their hands and in their hearts, and to remember that smoking was a dirty, evil habit which made you cough. The boys and girls in the audience, most of whom would be wearing peace medallions and smoking not Camels but marijuana in another eight years, shuffled their feet and waited for the action to begin.

'Less talk, more eatin'!' someone in the back row called,

and there was another burst of applause – it was heartier this time.

Mayor Charbonneau handed Sylvia a stopwatch and a silver police whistle, which she would blow at the end of the ten minutes of all-out pie-eating. Mayor Charbonneau would then step forward and hold up the hand of the winner.

'Are you *ready*??' Hizzoner's voice rolled triumphantly through the Great Day PA and off down Main Street.

The five pie-eaters declared they were ready.

'Are you *SET*??' Hizzoner enquired further.

The eaters growled that they were indeed set. Downstreet, a boy set off a rattling skein of firecrackers.

Mayor Charbonneau raised one pudgy hand and then dropped it. '*GO!!!*'

Five heads dropped into five pie-plates. The sound was like five large feet stamping firmly into mud. Wet chomping noises rose on the mild night air and then were blotted out as the betters and partisans in the crowd began to cheer on their favourites. And no more than the first pie had been demolished before most people realised that a possible upset was in the making.

Lard Ass Hogan, a seven-to-one underdog because of his age and inexperience, was eating like a boy possessed. His jaws machine-gunned up crust (the contest rules required that only the top crust of the pie be eaten, not the bottom), and when that had disappeared, a huge sucking sound issued from between his lips. It was like the sound of an industrial vacuum cleaner going to work. Moments later his whole head disappeared into the pie-plate. He raised it fifteen seconds later to indicate he was done. His cheeks and fore-head were smeared with blueberry juice, and he looked like an extra in a minstrel show. He was done – done before the legendary Bill Travis had finished *half* of *his* first pie.

Startled applause went up as the Mayor examined Lard Ass's pie-plate and pronounced it clean enough. He whipped a second pie into place before the pace-maker. Lard Ass had gobbled a regulation-size pie in just forty-two seconds. It was a contest record.

He went at the second pie even more furiously yet, his head bobbing and smooching in the soft blueberry filling, and Bill Travis threw him a worried glance as he called for his second blueberry pie. As he told friends later, he felt he was in a real contest for the first time since 1957, when George Gamache gobbled three pies in four minutes and then fainted dead away. He had to wonder, he said, if he was up against a boy or a demon. He thought of the money he had riding on this and redoubled his efforts.

But if Travis had redoubled, Lard Ass had trebled. Blueberries flew from his second pie-dish, staining the table-cloth around him like a Jackson Pollock painting. There were blueberries in his hair, blueberries in his bib, blueberries standing out on his forehead as if, in an agony of concen-tration, he had actually begun to *sweat* blueberries.

'*Done!*' he cried, lifting his head from his second pie dish before Bill Travis had even consumed the crust on his new pie.

'Better slow down, boy,' Hizzoner murmured. Charbonneau himself had ten dollars riding on Bill Travis. 'You got to pace yourself if you want to hold out.'

It was as if Lard Ass hadn't heard. He tore into his third pie with lunatic speed, jaws moving with lightning rapidity. And then –

But I must interrupt for a moment to tell you that there was an empty bottle in the medicine cabinet at Lard Ass Hogan's house. Earlier, that bottle had been three-quarters full of pearl-yellow castor oil, perhaps the most noxious fluid that the good Lord, in His infinite wisdom, ever allowed upon or beneath the face of the earth. Lard Ass had emptied that bottle himself, drinking every last drop and then licking the rim, his mouth twisting, his belly gagging sourly, his brain filled with thoughts of sweet revenge.

And as he rapidly worked his way through his third pie (Calvin Spier, dead last as predicted, had not yet finished his first), Lard Ass began to deliberately torture himself with grisly fantasies. He was not eatin' pies at all; he was eating cowflops. He was eating great big gobs of greasy grimy gopher-guts. He was eating diced-up woodchuck intestines with blueberry sauce poured over them. *Rancid* blueberry sauce.

He finished his third pie and called for his fourth, now one full pie ahead of the legendary Bill Travis. The fickle crowd, sensing a new and unexpected champ in the making, began to cheer him on lustily.

But Lard Ass had no hope or intention of winning. He could not have continued at the pace he was currently setting if his own mother's life had been the prize. And besides, winning for him was losing; revenge was the only blue ribbon he sought. His belly groaning with castor oil, his throat opening and closing sickly, he finished his fourth pie and called for his fifth, the Ultimate Pie – Blueberries Become Electra, so to speak. He dropped his head into the dish, breaking the crust, and snuffled blueberries up his nose. Blueberries went down his shirt. The contents of his stomach seemed to suddenly gain weight. He chewed up pastry crust and swallowed it. He inhaled blueberries.

And suddenly the moment of revenge was at hand. His stomach, loaded beyond endurance, revolted. It clenched like a strong hand encased in a slick rubber glove. His throat opened.

Lard Ass raised his head.

He grinned at Bill Travis with blue teeth.

Puke rumbled up his throat like a six-ton Peterbilt shooting through a tunnel.

It roared out of his mouth in a huge blue-and-yellow glurt, warm and gaily steaming. It covered Bill Travis, who only had time to utter one nonsense syllable – '*Goog!*' was what it sounded like. Women in the audience screamed. Calvin Spier, who had watched this unannounced event with a numb and surprised expression on his face, leaned conversationally over the table as if to explain to the gaping audience just what was happening, and puked on the head of Marguerite Charbonneau, the Mayor's wife. She screamed and backed away, pawing futilely at her hair, which was now covered with a mixture of crushed berries, baked beans, and partially digested frankfurters (the latter two had been Cal Spier's dinner). She turned to her good friend Maria Lavin and threw up on the front of Maria's buckskin jacket.

In rapid succession, like a replay of the firecrackers:

Bill Travis blew a great – and seemingly supercharged – jet of vomit out over the first two rows of spectators, his stunned face proclaiming to one and all, *Man, I just can't believe I'm doing this*;

Chuck Day, who had received a generous portion of Bill Travis's surprise gift, threw up on his Hush Puppies and then blinked at them wonderingly, knowing full well that stuff would *never* come off suede;

John Wiggins, principal of Gretna Elementary, opened his blue-lined mouth and said reprovingly: 'Really, this has . . . *YURRRK!*' As befitted a man of his breeding and position, he did it in his own pie-plate;

Hizzoner Charbonneau, who found himself suddenly presiding over what must have seemed more like a stomach-flu hospital ward than a pie-eating contest, opened his mouth to call the whole thing off and upchucked all over the microphone.

'*Jesus save us!*' moaned Sylvia Dodge, and then her outraged supper − fried clams, cole slaw, butter-and-sugar corn (two ears' worth), and a generous helping of Muriel Harrington's Bosco chocolate cake − bolted out the emergency exit and landed with a large wet splash on the back of the Mayor's Robert Hall suitcoat.

Lard Ass Hogan, now at the absolute apogee of his young life, beamed happily out over the audience. Puke was everywhere. People staggered around in drunken circles, holding their throats and making weak cawing noises. Somebody's pet Pekinese ran past the stage, yapping crazily, and a man wearing jeans and a Western-style silk shirt threw up on it, nearly drowning it. Mrs Brockway, the Methodist minister's wife, made a long, basso belching noise which was followed by a gusher of degenerated roast beef and mashed potatoes and apple cobbler. The cobbler looked as if it might have been quite good when it first went down. Jerry Maling, who had come to see his pet mechanic walk away with all the marbles again, decided to get the righteous fuck out of this madhouse. He got about fifteen yards before tripping over a kid's little red wagon and realizing he had landed in a puddle of warm bile, Jerry tossed his cookies in his own lap and told folks later he only thanked Providence he had been wearing his coveralls. And Miss Norman, who taught Latin and English Fundamentals at the Gretna Consolidated High School, vomited into her own purse in an agony of propriety.

Lard Ass Hogan watched it all, his large face calm and beaming, his stomach suddenly sweet and steady with a warm balm it might never know again – that balm was a feeling of utter and complete satisfaction. He stood up, took the slightly tacky microphone from the trembling hand of Mayor Charbonneau, and said . . .

17

"'I declare this contest a draw.' Then he puts the mike down, walks off the back of the platform, and goes straight home. His mother's there, on account of she couldn't get a babysitter for Lard Ass's little sister, who was only two. And as soon as he comes in, all covered with puke and pie drool, still wearin' his bib, she says, "Davie, did you win?" But he doesn't say a fuckin' word, you know. Just goes upstairs to his room, locks the door, and lays down on his bed.'

I downed the last swallow in Chris's Coke and tossed it into the woods.

'Yeah, that's cool, then what happened?' Teddy asked eagerly.

'I don't know.'

'What do you mean, you don't *know*?' Teddy asked.

'It means it's the end. When you don't know what happens next, that's the end.'

'*Whaaaat?*' Vern cried. There was an upset, suspicious look on his face, like he thought maybe he'd just gotten rooked playing penny-up Bingo at the Topsham Fair. 'What's all this happy crappy? How'd it come *out?*'

'You have to use your imagination,' Chris said patiently.

'No, I ain't!' Vern said angrily. '*He's* supposed to use *his* imagination! He made up the fuckin' story!'

'Yeah, what happened to the cat?' Teddy persisted. 'Come on, Gordie, tell us.'

'I think his dad was at the Pie-Eat and when he came home he beat the living crap out of Lard Ass.'

'Yeah, right,' Chris said. 'I bet that's just what happened.'

'And,' I said, 'the kids went right on calling him Lard Ass. Except that maybe some of them started calling him Puke-Yer-Guts, too.'

'That ending sucks,' Teddy said sadly.

'That's why I didn't want to tell it.'

'You could have made it so he shot his father and ran away and joined the Texas Rangers,' Teddy said. 'How about that?'

Chris and I exchanged a glance. Chris raised one shoulder in a barely perceptible shrug.

'I guess so,' I said.

'Hey, you got any new Le Dio stories, Gordie?'

'Not just now. Maybe I'll think of some.' I didn't want to upset Teddy, but I wasn't very interested in checking out what was happening in Le Dio, either. 'Sorry you didn't go for this one better.'

'Nah, it was good,' Teddy said. 'Right up to the end, it was good. All that pukin' was really cool.'

'Yeah, that was cool, really gross,' Vern agreed. 'But Teddy's right about the ending. It was sort of a gyp.'

'Yeah,' I said, and sighed.

Chris stood up. 'Let's do some walking,' he said. It was still bright daylight, the sky a hot, steely blue, but our shadows had begun to trail out long. I remember that as a kid, September days always seemed to end much too soon, catching me by surprise – it was as if something inside my heart expected it to always be June, with daylight lingering in the sky until almost nine-thirty. 'What time is it, Gordie?'

I looked at my watch and was astonished to see it was after five.

'Yeah, let's go,' Teddy said. 'But let's make camp before dark so we can see to get wood and stuff. I'm gettin' hungry, too.'

'Six-thirty,' Chris promised. 'Okay with you guys?'

It was. We started to walk again, using the cinders beside the tracks now. Soon the river was so far behind us we couldn't even hear its sound. Mosquitoes hummed and I slapped one off my neck. Vern and Teddy were walking up ahead, working out some sort of complicated comic book trade. Chris was beside me, hands in his pockets, shirt slapping against his knees and thighs like an apron.

'I got some Winstons,' he said. 'Hawked 'em off my old man's dresser. One apiece. For after supper.'

'Yeah? That's boss.'

'That's when a cigarette tastes best,' Chris said. 'After supper.'

'Right.'

We walked in silence for a while.

'That's a really fine story,' Chris said suddenly. 'They're just a little too dumb to understand.'

'No, it's not that hot. It's a mumbler.'

'That's what you always say. Don't give me that bullshit you don't believe. Are you gonna write it down? The story?'

'Probably. But not for a while. I can't write 'em down right after I tell 'em. It'll keep.'

'What Vern said? About the ending being a gyp?'

'Yeah?'

Chris laughed. '*Life's* a gyp, you know it? I mean, look at us.'

'Nah, we have a great time.'

'Sure,' Chris said. 'All the fuckin' time, you wet.'

I laughed. Chris did, too.

'They come outta you just like bubbles out of soda-pop,' he said after a while.

'What does?' But I thought I knew what he meant.

'The stories. That really bugs me, man. It's like you could tell a million stories and still only get the ones on top. You'll be a great writer someday, Gordie.'

'No, I don't think so.'

'Yeah, you will. Maybe you'll even write about us guys if you ever get hard up for material.'

'Have to be pretty fuckin' hard up.' I gave him the elbow.

There was another period of silence and then he asked suddenly: 'You ready for school?'

I shrugged. Who ever was? You got a little excited thinking about going back, seeing your friends; you were curious about your new teachers and what they would be like – pretty young things just out of teachers' college that you could rag or some old topkick that had been there since the Alamo. In a funny way you could even get excited about the long droning classes, because as the summer vacation neared its end you sometimes got bored enough to believe you could learn something. But summer boredom was nothing like the school boredom that always set in by the end of the second week, and by the beginning of the third week you got down to the *real* business: Could you hit Stinky Fiske in the back of the head with your art-gum while the teacher was putting The Principal Exports of South America on the board? How many good loud squeaks could you get off on the varnished surface of your desk if your hands were real sweaty? Who could cut the loudest farts in the locker room while changing up for phys ed? How many girls could you get to play Who Goosed the Moose during lunch hour? Higher learning, baby.

'Junior High,' Chris said. 'And you know what, Gordie? By next June, we'll all be quits.'

'What are you talking about? Why would *that* happen?'

'It's not gonna be like grammar school, that's why. You'll be in the college course. Me and Teddy and Vern, we'll all be in the shop courses, playing pocket-pool with the rest of the retards, making ashtrays and birdhouses. Vern might even have to go into Remedial. You'll meet a lot of new guys. Smart guys. That's just the way it works, Gordie. That's how they got it set up.'

'Meet a lot of pussies is what you mean,' I said.

He gripped my arm. 'No, man. Don't say that. Don't even *think* that. They'll get your stories. Not like Vern and Teddy.'

'Fuck the stories. I'm not going in with a lot of pussies. No sir.'

'If you don't, then you're an asshole.'

'What's asshole about wanting to be with your friends?'

He looked at me thoughtfully, as if deciding whether or not to tell me something. We had slowed down; Vern and Teddy had pulled almost half a mile ahead. The sun, lower now, came at us through the overlacing trees in broken, dusty shafts, turning everything gold – but it was a tawdry gold, dimestore gold, if you can dig that. The tracks stretched ahead of us in the gloom that was just starting to gather – they seemed almost to twinkle. Star-pricks of light stood out on them here and there, as if some nutty rich guy masquerading as a common labourer had decided to embed a diamond in the steel every sixty yards or so. It was still hot. The sweat rolled off us, slicking our bodies.

'It's asshole if your friends can drag you down,' Chris said finally. 'I know about you and your folks. They don't give a shit about you. Your big brother was the one they cared about. Like my dad, when Frank got thrown into the stockade in Portsmouth. That was when he started always bein' mad at us other kids and hitting us all the time. Your dad doesn't beat on you, but maybe that's even worse. He's got you asleep. You could tell him you were enrolling in the fuckin' shop division and you know what he'd do? He'd turn to the next page in his paper and say, Well, that's nice, Gordon, go ask your mother what's for dinner. And don't try to tell me different. I've met him.'

I didn't try to tell him different. It's scary to find out that someone else, even a friend, knows just how things are with you.

'You're just a kid, Gordie –'

'Gee, thanks, Dad.'

'I wish to fuck I was your father!' he said angrily. 'You wouldn't go around talking about taking those stupid shop courses if I was! It's like God gave you something, all those stories you can make up, and He said, This is what we got for you, kid. Try not to lose it. But kids lose *everything* unless somebody looks out for them and if your folks are too fucked up to do it then maybe I ought to.'

His face looked like he was expecting me to take a swing at him; it was set and unhappy in the green-gold late afternoon light. He had broken the cardinal rule for kids in those days. You could say anything about another kid, you could rank him to the dogs and back, but you didn't say a bad word *ever* about his mom and dad. That was the Fabled Automatic, the same way not inviting your Catholic friends home to dinner on Friday unless you'd checked first to make sure you weren't having meat was the Fabled Automatic. If a kid ranked out your Mom and Dad, you had to feed him a knuckle sandwich.

'Those stories you tell, they're no good to anybody but you, Gordie. If you go along with us just because you don't want the gang to break up, you'll wind up just another grunt, making Cs to get on the teams. You'll get to High and take the same fuckin' shop courses and throw erasers and pull your meat along with the rest of the grunts. Get detentions. Fuckin' *suspensions*. And after a while all you'll care about is gettin' a car so you can take some skag to the hops or down to the fuckin' Twin Bridges Tavern. Then you'll knock her up and spend the rest of your life in the mill or some fuckin' shoeshop in Auburn or maybe even up to Hillcrest pluckin' chickens. And that pie story will never get written down. *Nothin'll* get written down. 'Cause you'll just be another wiseguy with shit for brains.'

Chris Chambers was twelve when he said all that to me. But while he was saying it his face crumpled and folded into something older, oldest, ageless. He spoke tonelessly, colourlessly, but nevertheless, what he said struck terror into my bowels. It was as if he had lived that whole life already, that life where they tell you to step right up and spin the

Wheel of Fortune, and it spins so pretty and the guy steps on a pedal and it comes up double zeros, house number, everybody loses. They give you a free pass and then turn on the rain machine, pretty funny, huh, a joke even Vern Tessio could appreciate.

He grabbed my naked arm and his fingers closed tight. They dug grooves in my flesh. They ground at the bones. His eyes were hooded and dead – so dead, man, that he might have just fallen out of his own coffin.

'I know what people think of my family in this town. I know what they think of me and what they expect. Nobody even *asked* me if I took the milk-money that time. I just got a three-day vacation.'

'*Did* you take it?' I asked. I had never asked him before, and if you had told me I ever would, I would have called you crazy. The words came out in a little dry bullet.

'Yeah,' he said. 'Yeah, I took it.' He was silent for a moment, looking ahead at Teddy and Vern. 'You knew I took it, Teddy knew, *everybody* knew. Even Vern knew, I think.'

I started to deny it, and then closed my mouth. He was right. No matter what I might have said to my mother and father about how a person was supposed to be innocent until proved guilty, I had known.

'Then maybe I was sorry and tried to give it back,' Chris said.

I stared at him, my eyes widening. 'You tried to give it *back*?'

'*Maybe*, I said. Just *maybe*. And maybe I took it to old lady Simons and told her, and maybe the money was all there and I got a three-day vacation *anyway*, because the money never showed up. And maybe the next week old lady Simons had this brand-new skirt on when she came to school.'

I stared at Chris, speechless with horror. He smiled at me, but it was a crimped, terrible smile that never touched his eyes.

'Just *maybe*,' he said, but I remembered the new skirt – a light brown paisley, sort of full. I remembered thinking that it made old lady Simons look younger, almost pretty.

'Chris, how much was that milk-money?'

'Almost seven bucks.'

'Christ,' I whispered.

'So I just say that *I* stole the milk-money but then old lady Simons stole it from *me*. Just suppose. Then suppose I told that story. Me, Chris Chambers. Kid brother of Frank Chambers and Eyeball Chambers. You think anybody would have believed it?'

'No way,' I whispered. 'Jesus, Chris!'

He smiled his wintry, awful smile. 'And do you think that bitch would have dared try something like that if it had been one of those dootchbags from up on The View that had taken the money?'

'No,' I said.

'Yeah. If it had been one of them, Simons would have said, 'kay, 'kay, we'll forget it this time, but we're gonna spank your wrist real hard and if you ever do it again we'll have to spank *both* wrists. But *me* . . . well, maybe she had her eye on that skirt for a long time. Anyway, she saw her chance and she took it. I was the stupid one for even trying to give that money back. But I never thought . . . I never thought that a *teacher* . . . oh who gives a fuck, anyway? Why am I even talkin' about it?'

He swiped an arm angrily across his eyes and I realized he was almost crying.

'Chris,' I said, 'why don't you go into the college courses? You're smart enough.'

'They decide all of that in the office. And in their smart little conferences. The teachers, they sit around in this big circle-jerk and all they say is Yeah, Yeah, Right, Right. All they give a fuck about is whether you behaved yourself in grammar school and what the town thinks of your family. All they're deciding is whether or not you'll contaminate all those precious college-course dootchbags. But maybe I'll try to work myself up. I don't know if I could do it, but I might try. Because I want to get out of Castle Rock and go to college and never see my old man or any of my brothers again. I want to go someplace where nobody knows me and I don't have any black marks against me before I start. But I don't know if I can do it.'

'Why not?'

'People. People drag you down.'

'Who?' I asked, thinking he must mean the teachers, or adult monsters like Miss Simons, who had wanted a new skirt, or maybe his brother Eyeball who hung around with Ace and Billy and Charlie and the rest, or maybe his own Mom and Dad.

But he said: 'Your friends drag you down, Gordie. Don't you know that?' He pointed at Vern and Teddy, who were standing and waiting for us to catch up. They were laughing about something; in fact, Vern was just about busting a gut. 'Your friends do. They're like drowning guys that are holding on to your legs. You can't save them. You can only drown with them.'

'Come on, you fuckin' slowpokes!' Vern shouted, still laughing.

'Yeah, comin'!' Chris called, and before I could say anything else, he began to run. I ran, too, but he caught up to them before I could catch up to him.

18

We went another mile and then decided to camp for the night. There was still some daylight left, but nobody really wanted to use it. We were pooped from the scene at the dump and from our scare on the train trestle, but it was more than that. We were in Harlow now, in the woods. Somewhere up ahead was a dead kid, probably mangled and covered with flies. Maggots, too, by this time. Nobody wanted to get too close to him with the night coming on. I had read somewhere – in an Algernon Blackwood story, I think – that a guy's ghost hangs out around his dead body until that body is given a decent Christian burial, and there was no way I wanted to wake up in the night and confront the glowing, disembodied ghost of Ray Brower, moaning and gibbering and floating among the dark and rustling pines. By stopping here we figured there had to be at least ten miles between us and him, and of course all four of us knew there were no such things as ghosts, but ten miles seemed just about far enough in case what everybody knew was wrong.

Vern, Chris, and Teddy gathered wood and got a modest little campfire going on a bed of cinders. Chris scraped a bare patch all around the fire – the woods were powder-dry, and he didn't want to take any chances. While they were doing that I sharpened some sticks and made what my brother Denny used to call 'Pioneer Drumsticks' – lumps of hamburger pushed into the ends of green branches. The three of them laughed and bickered over their woodcraft (which was almost nil; there was a Castle Rock Boy Scout troop, but most of the kids who hung around our vacant lot considered it to be an organization made up mostly of pussies), arguing about whether it was better to cook over flames or over coals (a moot point; we were too hungry to wait for coals), whether dried moss would work as kindling, what they would do if they used up all the matches before they got the fire to stay lit. Teddy claimed he could make a fire by rubbing two sticks together. Chris claimed he was so full of shit he squeaked. They didn't have to try; Vern got the small pile of twigs and dry moss to catch from the second match. The day was perfectly still and there was no wind to puff out the light. We all took turns feeding the thin flames until they began to grow stouter on wrist-thick chunks of wood fetched from an old deadfall some thirty yards into the forest.

When the flames began to die back a little bit, I stuck the sticks holding the Pioneer Drumsticks firmly into the ground at an angle over the fire. We sat around watching them as they shimmered and dripped and finally began to brown. Our stomachs made pre-dinner conversation.

Unable to wait until they were really cooked, we each took one of them, stuck it in a roll, and yanked the hot stick out of the centre. They were charred outside, raw inside, and totally delicious. We wolfed them down and wiped the grease from our mouths with our bare arms. Chris opened his pack and took out a tin Band-Aids box (the pistol was way at the bottom of his pack, and because he hadn't told Vern and Teddy, I guessed it was to be our secret). He opened it and gave each of us a battered Winston. We lit them with flaming twigs from the fire and then leaned back, men of the world, watching the cigarette smoke drift away into the soft twilight. None of us inhaled because we might cough and that would mean a day or two of ragging from the others. And it was pleasant enough just to drag and blow, hawking into the fire to hear the sizzle (that was the summer I learned how you can pick out someone who is just learning to smoke: if you're new at it you spit a lot). We were feeling good. We smoked the Winstons down to the filters, then tossed them into the fire.

'Nothin' like a smoke after a meal,' Teddy said.

'Fucking-A,' Vern agreed.

Crickets had started to hum in the green gloom. I looked up at the lane of sky visible through the railroad cut and saw that the blue was now bruising towards purple. Seeing that outrider of twilight made me feel sad and calm at the same time, brave but not really brave, comfortably lonely.

We tramped down a flat place in the underbrush beside the embankment and laid out our bedrolls. Then, for an hour or so, we fed the fire and talked, the kind of talk you can never quite remember once you get past fifteen and discover girls. We talked about who was the best dragger in Castle Rock, if Boston could maybe stay out of the cellar this year, and about the summer just past. Teddy told about the time he had been at White's Beach in Brunswick and some kid had hit his head while diving off the float and almost drowned. We discussed at some length the relative merits of the teachers we had had. We agreed that Mr Brooks was the biggest pussy in Castle Rock Elementary – he would just about cry if you sassed him back. On the other hand, there was Mrs Cote (pronounced Cody) – she was just about the meanest bitch God had ever set down on the earth. Vern said he'd heard she hit a kid so hard two years ago that the kid almost went blind. I looked at Chris, wondering if he would say anything about Miss Simons, but he didn't say anything at all, and he didn't see me looking at him – he was looking at Vern and nodding soberly at Vern's story.

We didn't talk about Ray Brower as the dark drew down, but I was thinking about him. There's something horrible and fascinating about the way dark comes to the woods, its coming unsoftened by headlights or streetlights or house-lights or neon. It comes with no mothers' voices, calling for their kids to leave off and come on in now, to herald it. If you're used to the town, the coming of the dark in the woods seems more like a natural disaster than a natural phenomenon; it rises like the Castle River rises in the spring.

And as I thought about the body of Ray Brower in this light – or lack of it – what I felt was not queasiness or fear that he would suddenly appear before us, a green and gibbering banshee whose purpose was to drive us back the way we had come before we could disturb his – *its* – peace, but a sudden and unexpected wash of pity that he should be so alone and so defenceless in the dark that was now coming over our side of the earth. If something wanted to eat on him, it would. His mother wasn't here to stop that from happening, and neither was his father, nor Jesus Christ in the company of all the saints. He was dead and he was all alone, flung off the railroad tracks and into the ditch, and I realized that if I didn't stop thinking about it I was going to cry.

So I told a Le Dio story, made up on the spot and not

very good, and when it ended as most of my Le Dio stories did, with one lone American dogface coughing out a dying declaration of patriotism and love for the girl back home into the sad and wise face of the platoon sergeant, it was not the white, scared face of some pfc from Castle Rock or White River Junction I saw in my mind's eye but the face of a much younger boy, already dead, his eyes closed, his features troubled, a rill of blood running from the left corner of his mouth to his jawline. And in back of him, instead of the shattered shops and churches of my Le Dio dreamscape, I saw only dark forest and the cindered railway bed bulking against the starry sky like a prehistoric burial mound.

19

I came awake in the middle of the night, disorientated, wondering why it was so chilly in my bedroom and who had left the windows open. Denny, maybe. I had been dreaming of Denny, something about body-surfing at Harrison State Park. But it had been four years ago that we had done that.

This wasn't my room: this was someplace else. Somebody was holding me in a mighty bearhug. Somebody else was pressed against my back, and a shadowy third was crouched beside me, head cocked in a listening attitude.

'What the fuck?' I asked in honest puzzlement.

A long drawn-out groan in answer. It sounded like Vern.

That brought things into focus, and I remembered where I was . . . but what was everybody doing awake in the middle of the night? Or had I only been asleep for seconds? No, that couldn't be, because a thin sliver of moon was floating dead centre in an inky sky.

'Don't let it get me,' Vern gibbered. 'I swear I'll be a good boy, I won't do nothin' bad, I'll put the ring up before I take a piss, I'll . . . I'll . . .' With some astonishment I realized that I was listening to a prayer – or at least the Vern Tessio equivalent of a prayer.

I sat bolt upright, scared. 'Chris?'

'Shut up, Vern,' Chris said. He was the one crouching and listening. 'It's nothing.'

'Oh yes it is,' Teddy said ominously. 'It's something.'

'*What* is?' I asked. I was still sleepy and disorientated, unstrung from my place in space and time. It scared me that I had come in late on whatever had developed – too late to defend myself properly, maybe.

Then, as if to answer my question, a long and hollow scream rose languidly from the woods – it was the sort of scream you might expect from a woman dying in extreme agony and extreme fear.

'Oh-dear-to-Jesus!' Vern whimpered, his voice high and filled with tears. He reapplied the bearhug that had wakened me, making it hard for me to breathe and adding to my own terror. I threw him loose with an effort but he scrambled right back beside me like a puppy which can't think of anyplace else to go.

'It's that Brower kid,' Teddy whispered hoarsely. 'His ghost's out walkin' in the woods.'

'Oh God!' Vern screamed, apparently not crazy about that idea at all. 'I promise I won't hawk no more dirty books out of Dahlie's Market! I promise I won't give my carrots to the dog no more I . . . I . . . I . . .' He floundered there, wanting to bribe God with everything but unable to think of anything really good in the extremity of his fear. '*I won't smoke no more unfiltered cigarettes! I won't say no bad swears! I won't put my Bazooka in the offerin' plate! I won't –'*

'Shut up, Vern,' Chris said, and beneath his usual author-itative toughness I could hear the hollow boom of awe. I wondered if his arms and back and belly were as stiff with gooseflesh as my own were, and if the hair on the nape of his neck was trying to stand up in hackles, as mine was.

Vern's voice dropped to a whisper as he continued to expand the reforms he planned to institute if God would only let him live through this night.

'It's a bird, isn't it?' I asked Chris.

'No. At least, I don't think so. I think it's a wildcat. My dad says they scream bloody murder when they're getting ready to mate. Sounds like a woman, doesn't it?'

'Yeah,' I said. My voice hitched in the middle of the word and two ice-cubes broke off in the gap.

'But no woman could scream that loud,' Chris said . . . and then added helplessly: 'Could she, Gordie?'

'It's his ghost,' Teddy whispered again. His eyeglasses reflected the moonlight in weak, somehow dreamy smears. 'I'm gonna go look for it.'

I don't think he was serious, but we took no chances. When he started to get up, Chris and I hauled him back down. Perhaps we were too rough with him, but our muscles had been turned to cables with fear.

'Let me up, fuckheads!' Teddy hissed, struggling. 'If I say I wanna go look for it, then I'm gonna go look for it! I wanna see it! I wanna see the ghost! I wanna see it –'

The wild, sobbing cry rose into the night again, cutting the air like a knife with a crystal blade, freezing us with our hands on Teddy – if he'd been a flag, we would have looked like that picture of the Marines claiming Iwo Jima. The scream climbed with a crazy ease through octave after octave, finally reaching a glassy, freezing edge. It hung there for a moment and then whirled back down again, disappearing into an impossible bass register that buzzed like a monstrous honeybee. This was followed by a burst of what sounded like mad laughter . . . and then there was silence again.

'Jesus H Baldheaded Christ,' Teddy whispered, and he talked no more of going into the woods to see what was making that screaming noise. All four of us huddled up together and I thought of running. I doubt if I was the only one. If we had been tenting in Vern's field – where our folks *thought* we were – we probably *would* have run. But Castle Rock was too far, and the thought of trying to run across that trestle in the dark made my blood freeze. Running deeper into Harlow and closer to the corpse of Ray Brower was equally unthinkable. We were stuck. If there was a ha'ant out there in the woods – what my dad called a Goosalum – and it wanted us, it would probably get us.

Chris proposed we keep a guard and everyone was agreeable to that. We flipped for watches and Vern got the first one. I got the last. Vern sat up cross-legged by the husk of the campfire while the rest of us lay down again. We huddled together like sheep.

I was positive that sleep would be impossible, but I did sleep – a light, uneasy sleep that skimmed through unconsciousness like a sub with its periscope up. My half-sleeping dreams were populated with wild cries that might have been real or might have only been products of my imagination. I saw – or thought I saw – something white and shapeless steal through the trees like a grotesquely ambulatory bedsheet.

At last I slipped into something I knew was a dream. Chris and I were swimming at White's Beach, a gravel-pit in Brunswick that had been turned into a miniature lake when the gravel-diggers struck water. It was where Teddy had seen the kid hit his head and almost drown.

In my dream we were out over our heads, stroking lazily along, with a hot July sun blazing down. From behind us, on the float, came cries and shouts and yells of laughter as kids climbed and dived or climbed and were pushed. I could hear the empty kerosene drums that held the float up clanging and booming together – a sound not unlike that of church-bells, which are so solemn and emptily profound. On the sand-and-gravel beach, oiled bodies lay face down on blankets, little kids with buckets squatted on the verge of the water or sat happily flipping muck into their hair with plastic shovels, and teenagers clustered in grinning groups, watching the young girls promenade endlessly back and forth in pairs and trios, never alone, the secret places of their bodies wrapped in Jantzen tank suits. People walked up the hot sand on the balls of their feet, wincing, to the snackbar. They came back with chips, Devil Dogs, Red Ball Popsicles.

Mrs Cote drifted past us on an inflatable rubber raft. She was lying on her back, dressed in her typical September-to-June school uniform: a grey two-piece suit with a thick sweater instead of a blouse under the jacket, a flower pinned over one almost nonexistent breast, thick support hose the colour of Canada Mints on her legs. Her black old lady's high-heeled shoes were trailing in the water, making small V's. Her hair was blue-rinsed, like my mother's, and done up in those tight, medicinal-smelling clockspring curls. Her glasses flashed brutally in the sun.

'Watch your steps, boys,' she said. 'Watch your steps or I'll hit you hard enough to strike you blind. I can do that; I have been given that power by the school board. Now, Mr Chambers, "Mending Wall", if you please. By rote.'

'I tried to give the money back,' Chris said. 'Old lady Simons said okay, but she *took* it! Do you hear me? She *took* it! Now what are you going to do about it? Are you going to whack *her* blind?'

'"Mending Wall," Mr Chambers, if you please. By *rote*.'

Chris threw me a despairing glance, as if to say *Didn't I tell you it would be this way?*, and then began to tread water. He began. '"Something there is that doesn't love a wall, that sends the frozen groundswell under it –"' And then his head went under, his reciting mouth filling with water.

He popped back up, crying: 'Help me, Gordie! Help me!'

Then he was dragged under again. Looking into the clear water I could see two bloated, naked corpses holding his ankles. One was Vern and the other was Teddy, and their open eyes were as blank and pupilless as the eyes of Greek statues. Their small pre-pubescent penises floated limply up from their distended bellies like albino strands of kelp. Chris's head broke water again. He held one hand up limply to me and voiced a screaming, womanish cry that rose and rose, ululating in the hot sunny summer air. I looked wildly towards the beach but nobody had heard. The lifeguard, his bronzed, athletic body lolling attractively on the seat at the top of his whitewashed cruciform wooden tower, just went on smiling down at a girl in a red bathing suit. Chris's scream turned into a bubbling waterchoked gurgle as the corpses pulled him under again. And as they dragged him down to black water I could see his rippling, distorted eyes turned up to me in pleading agony; I could see his white starfish hands held helplessly up to the sun-burnished roof of the water. But instead of diving down and trying to save him, I stroked madly for the shore, or at least to a place where the water would not be over my head. Before I could get there – before I could even get close – I felt a soft, rotted, implacable hand wrap itself around my calf and begin to pull. A scream built up in my chest . . . but before I could utter it, the dream washed away into a grainy facsimile of reality. It was Teddy with his hand on my leg. He was shaking me awake. It was my watch.

Still half in the dreams, almost talking in my sleep, I asked him thickly: 'You alive, Teddy?'

'No. I'm dead and you're a black nigger,' he said crossly. It dispelled the last of the dream. I sat up by the campfire and Teddy lay down.

20

The others slept heavily through the rest of the night. I was in and out, dozing, waking, dozing again. The night was far from silent; I heard the triumphant screech-squawk of a pouncing owl, the tiny cry of some small animal perhaps about to be eaten, a larger something blundering wildly through the undergrowth. Under all of this, a steady tone, were the crickets. There were no more screams. I dozed and woke, woke and dozed, and I suppose if I had been discovered standing such a slipshod watch in Le Dio, I probably would have been court-martialled and shot.

I snapped more solidly out of my last doze and became aware that something was different. It took a moment or two to figure it out: although the moon was down, I could see my hands resting on my jeans. My watch said quarter to five. It was dawn.

I stood, hearing my spine crackle, walked two dozen feet away from the lumped-together bodies of my friends, and pissed into a clump of sumac. I was starting to shake the night-willies; I could feel them sliding away. It was a fine feeling.

I scrambled up the cinders to the railroad tracks and sat on one of the rails, idly chucking cinders between my feet, in no hurry to wake the others. At that precise moment the new day felt too good to share.

Morning came on apace. The noise of the crickets began to drop, and the shadows under the trees and bushes evaporated like puddles after a shower. The air had that peculiar lack of taste that presages the latest hot day in a famous series of hot days. Birds that had maybe cowered all night just as we had done now began to twitter self-importantly. A wren landed on top of the deadfall from which we had taken our firewood, preened itself, and then flew off.

I don't know how long I sat there on that rail, watching the purple steal out of the sky as noiselessly as it had stolen in the evening before. Long enough for my butt to start complaining, anyway. I was about to get up when I looked to my right and saw a deer standing in the railroad bed not ten yards from me.

My heart went up into my throat so high that I think I could have put my hand in my mouth and touched it. My stomach and genitals filled with a hot, dry excitement. I didn't move. I couldn't have moved if I wanted to. Her eyes weren't brown but a dark, dusty black – the kind of velvet you see backgrounding jewellery displays. Her small ears were scuffed suede. She looked serenely at me, head slightly lowered in what I took for curiosity, seeing a kid with his hair in a sleep-scarecrow of whirls and many-tined cowlicks, wearing jeans with cuffs and a brown khaki shirt with the elbows mended and the collar turned up in the hoody tradition of the day. What I was seeing was some sort of gift, something given with a carelessness that was appalling.

We looked at each other for a long time . . . I *think* it was a long time. Then she turned and walked off to the other side of the tracks, white bobtail flipping insouciantly. She found grass and began to crop. I couldn't believe it. She had begun to *crop*. She didn't look back at me and didn't need to; I was frozen solid.

Then the rail started to thrum under my ass and bare seconds later the doe's head came up, cocked back towards Castle Rock. She stood there, her branch-black nose working on the air, coaxing it a little. Then she was gone in three gangling leaps, vanishing into the woods with no sound but one rotted branch, which broke with a sound like a track ref's starter-gun.

I sat there, looking mesmerized at the spot where she had been, until the actual sound of the freight came up through the stillness. Then I skidded back down the bank to where the others were sleeping.

The freight's slow, loud passage woke them up, yawning and scratching. There was some funny, nervous talk about 'the case of the screaming ghost', as Chris called it, but not as much as you might imagine. In daylight it seemed more foolish than interesting – almost embarrassing. Best forgotten.

It was on the tip of my tongue to tell them about the deer, but I ended up not doing it. That was one thing I kept to myself. I've never spoken or written of it until just now, today. And I have to tell you that it seems a lesser thing written down, damn near inconsequential. But for me it was the best part of that trip, the cleanest part, and it was a moment I found myself returning to, almost helplessly, when there was trouble in my life – my first day in the bush in Viet Nam, and this fellow walked into the clearing where we were with his hand over his nose and when he took his hand away there was no nose there because it had been shot off; the time the doctor told us our youngest son might be hydrocephalic (he turned out just to have an oversized head, thank God); the long, crazy weeks before my mother died. I would find my thoughts turning back to that morning, the scuffed suede of her ears, the white flash of her tail. But five hundred million Red Chinese don't give a shit, right? The most important things are the hardest to say, because words diminish them. It's hard to make strangers care about the good things in your life.

21

The tracks now bent south-west and ran through tangles of second-growth fir and heavy underbrush. We got a breakfast of late blackberries from some of these bushes, but berries never fill you up; your stomach just gives them a thirty-minute option and then begins growling again. We went back to the tracks – it was about eight o'clock by then – and took five. Our mouths were a dark purple and our naked torsos were scratched from the blackberry brambles. Vern wished glumly aloud for a couple of fried eggs with bacon on the side.

That was the last day of the heat, and I think it was the worst of all. The early scud of clouds melted away and by nine o'clock the sky was a pale steel colour that made you feel hotter just looking at it. The sweat rolled and ran from our chests and backs, leaving clean streaks through the accumulated soot and grime. Mosquitoes and black-flies whirled and dipped around our heads in aggravating clouds. Knowing that we had eight, maybe ten miles to go didn't make us feel any better. Yet the fascination of the thing drew us on and kept us walking faster than we had any business doing, in that heat. We were all crazy to see that kid's body – I can't put it any more simply or honestly than that. Whether it was harmless or whether it turned out to have the power to murder sleep with a hundred mangled dreams, we wanted to see it. I think that we had come to believe we *deserved* to see it.

It was about nine-thirty when Teddy and Chris spotted water up ahead – they shouted to Vern and me. We ran over to where they were standing. Chris was laughing, delighted. 'Look there! Beavers did that!' He pointed.

It was the work of beavers, all right. A large-bore culvert ran under the railroad embankment a little way ahead, and the beavers had sealed the right end with one of their neat and industrious little dams – sticks and branches cemented together with leaves, twigs, and dried mud. Beavers are busy little fuckers, all right. Behind the dam was a clear and shining pool of water, brilliantly mirroring the sunlight. Beaver houses humped up and out of the water in several places – they looked like wooden igloos. A small creek trickled into the far end of the pool, and the trees which bordered it were gnawed a clean bone-white to a height of almost three feet in places.

'Railroad'll clean this shit out pretty soon,' Chris said.

'Why?' Vern asked.

'They can't have a pool here,' Chris said, 'it'd undercut their previous railroad line. That's why they put that culvert in there to start with. They'll shoot them some beavers and scare off the rest and then knock out their dam. Then this'll go back to being a bog, like it probably was before.'

'I think that eats the meat,' Teddy said.

Chris shrugged. 'Who cares about beavers? Not the Great Western and Southern Maine, that's for sure.'

'You think it's deep enough to swim in?' Vern asked, looking hungrily at the water.

'One way to find out,' Teddy said.

'Who goes first?' I asked.

'Me!' Chris said. He went running down the bank, kicking off his sneakers and untying his shirt from around his waist with a jerk. He pushed his pants and undershorts down with a single shove of his thumbs. He balanced, first on one leg and them on the other, to get his socks. Then he made a shallow dive. He came up shaking his head to get his wet hair out of his eyes. 'It's fuckin' *great!*' he shouted.

'How deep?' Teddy called back. He had never learned to swim.

Chris stood up in the water and his shoulders broke the surface. I saw something on one of them – a blackish-greyish something. I decided it was a piece of mud and dismissed it. If I had looked more closely I could have saved myself a lot of nightmares later on. 'Come on in, you chickens!'

He turned and thrashed off across the pool in a clumsy breast-stroke, turned over, and thrashed back. By then we were all getting undressed. Vern was in next, then me.

Hitting the water was fantastic – clean and cool. I swam across to Chris, loving the silky feel of having nothing on but water. I stood up and we grinned into each other's faces.

'Boss!' We said it at exactly the same instant.

'Fuckin' jerkoff,' he said, splashed water in my face, and swam off the other way.

We goofed off in the water for almost half an hour before we realized that the pond was full of bloodsuckers. We dived, swam under water, ducked each other. We never knew a thing. Then Vern swam into the shallower part, went under, and stood on his hands. When his legs broke water in a shaky but triumphant V, I saw that they were covered with blackish-grey lumps, just like the one I had seen on Chris's shoulder. They were slugs – big ones.

Chris's mouth dropped open, and I felt all the blood in my body go as cold as dry ice. Teddy screamed, his face going pale. Then all three of us were thrashing for the bank, going just as fast as we could. I know more about fresh-water slugs now than I did then, but the fact that they are mostly harmless has done nothing to allay the almost insane horror of them I've had ever since that day in the beaver-pool. They carry a local anaesthetic and an anticoagulant in their alien saliva, which means that the host never feels a thing when they attach themselves. If you don't happen to see them they'll go on feeding until their swelled, loathsome bodies fall off you, sated, or until they actually burst.

We pulled ourselves up on the bank and Teddy went into a hysterical paroxysm as he looked down at himself. He was screaming as he picked the leeches off his naked body.

Vern broke the water and looked at us, puzzled. 'What the hell's wrong with hi –'

'*Leeches!*' Teddy screamed, pulling two of them off his trembling thighs and throwing them just as far as he could. 'Dirty motherfuckin' *bloodsuckers!*' His voice broke shrilly on the last word.

'*OhGodOhGodOhGod!*' Vern cried. He paddled across the pool and stumbled out.

I was still cold; the heat of the day had been suspended. I kept telling myself to catch hold. Not to get screaming. Not to be a pussy. I picked half a dozen off my arms and several more off my chest.

Chris turned his back to me. 'Gordie? Are there any more? Take 'em off if there are, please, Gordie!' There *were* more, five or six, running down his back like grotesque black buttons. I pulled their soft, boneless bodies off him.

I brushed even more off my legs, then got Chris to do my back.

I was starting to relax a little . . . and that was when I looked down at myself and saw the granddaddy of them all clinging to my testicles, its body swelled to four times its normal size. Its blackish-grey skin had gone a bruised purplish-red. That was when I began to lose control. Not outside, at least not in any big way, but inside, where it counts.

I brushed its slick, glutinous body with the back of my hand. It held on. I tried to do it again and couldn't bring myself to actually touch it. I turned to Chris, tried to speak, couldn't. I pointed instead. His cheeks, already ashy, went whiter still.

'I can't get it off,' I said through numb lips. 'You . . . can you . . .'

But he backed away, shaking his head, his mouth twisted.

'I can't, Gordie,' he said, unable to take his eyes away. 'I'm sorry but I can't. No. Oh. No.' He turned away, bowed with one hand pressed to his midsection like the butler in a musical comedy, and was sick in a stand of juniper bushes.

You got to hold onto yourself, I thought, looking at the leech that hung off me like a crazy beard. Its body was still visibly swelling. *You got to hold onto yourself and get him. Be tough. It's the last one. The. Last. One.*

I reached down again and picked it off and it burst between my fingers. My own blood ran across my palm and inner wrist in a warm flood. I began to cry.

Still crying, I walked back to my clothes and put them on. I wanted to stop crying, but I just didn't seem able to turn off the waterworks. Then the shakes set in, making it worse. Vern ran up to me, still naked.

'They off, Gordie? They off me? They off me?'

He twirled in front of me like an insane dancer on a carnival stage.

'They off? Huh? Huh? They off me, Gordie?'

His eyes kept going past me, as wide and white as the eyes of a plaster horse on a merry-go-round.

I nodded that they were and just kept on crying. It seemed that crying was going to be my new career. I tucked my shirt in and then buttoned it all the way to the neck. I put on my socks and my sneakers. Little by little the tears began to slow down. Finally there was nothing left but a few hitches and moans, and then they stopped, too.

Chris walked over to me, wiping his mouth with a handful of elm leaves. His eyes were wide and mute and apologetic.

When we were all dressed we just stood there looking at each other for a moment, and then we began to climb the railroad embankment. I looked back once at the burst leech lying on top of the tramped-down bushes where we had danced and screamed and groaned them off. It looked deflated . . . but still ominous.

Fourteen years later I sold my first novel and made my first trip to New York. 'It's going to be a three-day celebration,' my new editor told me over the phone. 'People slinging bullshit will be summarily shot.' But of course it was three days of unmitigated bullshit. I went away thinking the publishing house believed me to be the reincarnation of Thomas Wolfe; they saw me off with perhaps other things in mind – paperback sales in the millions, for instance.

While I was there I wanted to do all the standard out-of-towner things – see a stage show at Radio City Music Hall, go to the top of the Empire State Building (fuck the World Trade Center; the building King Kong climbed in 1933 is always gonna be the tallest one in the world for me), visit Times Square by night. Keith, my editor, seemed more than pleased to show his city off. The last touristy thing we did was to take a ride on the Staten Island Ferry, and while leaning on the rail I happened to look down and see scores of used condoms floating on the mild swells. And I had a moment of almost total recall – or perhaps it was an actual incidence of time-travel. Either way, for one second I was literally *in* the past, pausing halfway up that embankment and looking back at the burst leech: dead, deflated . . . but still ominous.

Keith must have seen something in my face because he said: 'Not very pretty, are they?'

I only shook my head, wanting to tell him not to apologize, wanting to tell him that you didn't have to come to the Apple and ride the ferry to see used rubbers, wanting to say: *The only reason anyone writes stories is so they can understand the past and get ready for some future mortality; that's why all the verbs in stories have -ed endings, Keith my good man, even the ones that sell millions of paperbacks. The only two useful artforms are religion and stories.*

I was pretty drunk that night, as you may have guessed.

What I did tell him was: 'I was thinking of something else, that's all.' The most important things are the hardest things to say.

22

We walked further down the tracks – I don't know just how far – and I was starting to think: *Well, okay, I'm going to be able to handle it, it's all over anyway, just a bunch of leeches, what the fuck;* I was still thinking it when waves of whiteness suddenly began to come over my sight and I fell down.

I must have fallen hard, but landing on the crossties was like plunging into a warm and puffy feather bed. Someone turned me over. The touch of hands was faint and unimportant. Their faces were disembodied balloons looking down at me from miles up. They looked the way the ref's face must look to a fighter who has been punched silly and is currently taking a ten-second rest on the canvas. Their words came in gentle oscillations, fading in and out.

'. . . him?'

'. . . be all . . .'

'. . . if you think the sun . . .'

'Gordie, are you . . .'

Then I must have said something that didn't make much sense because they began to look *really* worried.

'We better take him back, man,' Teddy said, and then the whiteness came over everything again.

When it cleared, I seemed to be all right. Chris was squatting next to me, saying: 'Can you hear me, Gordie? You there, man?'

'Yes,' I said, and sat up. A swarm of black dots exploded in front of my eyes, and then went away. I waited to see if they'd come back, and when they didn't, I stood up.

'You scared the cheesly old shit outta me, Gordie,' he said. 'You want a drink of water?'

'Yeah.'

He gave me his canteen, half-full of water, and I let three warm gulps roll down my throat.

'Why'd you faint, Gordie?' Vern asked anxiously.

'Made a bad mistake and looked at your face,' I said.

'Eeee-eee-eeeee!' Teddy cackled. 'Fuckin' Gordie! You wet!'

'You really okay?' Vern persisted.

'Yeah. Sure. It was . . . bad there for a minute. Thinking about those suckers.'

They nodded soberly. We took five in the shade and then went on walking, me and Vern on one side of the tracks again, Chris and Teddy on the other. We figured we must be getting close.

23

We weren't as close as we thought, and if we'd had the brains to spend two minutes looking at a roadmap, we would have seen why. We knew that Ray Brower's corpse had to be near the Back Harlow Road, which dead-ends on the bank of the Royal River. Another trestle carries the GS&WM tracks across the Royal. So this is the way we figured: Once we got close to the Royal, we'd be getting close to the Back Harlow Road, where Billy and Charlie had been parked when they saw the boy. And since the Royal was only ten miles from the Castle River, we figured we had it made in the shade.

But that was ten miles as the crow flies, and the tracks didn't move on a straight line between the Castle and the Royal. Instead, they made a very shallow loop to avoid a hilly, crumbling region called The Bluffs. Anyway, we could have seen that loop quite clearly if we had looked on a map, and figured out that instead of ten miles, we had about sixteen to walk.

Chris began to suspect the truth when noon had come and gone and the Royal still wasn't in sight. We stopped while he climbed a high pine tree and took a look around. He came down and gave us a simple enough report: it was going to be at least four in the afternoon before we got to the Royal, and we would only make it by then if we humped right along.

'Ah, *shit!*' Teddy cried. 'So what're we gonna do now?'

We looked into each other's tired, sweaty faces. We were hungry and out of temper. The big adventure had turned into a long slog – dirty and sometimes scary. We would have been missed back home by now, too, and if Milo Pressman hadn't already called the cops on us, the engineer of the train crossing the trestle might have done it. We had been planning to hitchhike back to Castle Rock, but four o'clock was just three hours from dark, and *nobody* gives four kids on a back country road a lift after dark.

I tried to summon up the cool image of my deer, crop-ping at green morning grass, but even that seemed dusty and no good, no better than a stuffed trophy over the mantle in some guy's hunting lodge, the eyes sprayed to give them that phony lifelike shine.

Finally Chris said: 'It's still closer going ahead. Let's go.'

He turned and started to walk along the tracks in his dusty sneakers, head down, his shadow only a puddle at his feet. After a minute or so the rest of us followed him, strung out in Indian file.

24

In the years between then and the writing of this memoir, I've thought remarkably little about those two days in September, at least consciously. The associations the memories bring to the surface are as unpleasant as week-old rivercorpses brought to the surface by cannonfire. As a result, I never really questioned our decision to walk down the tracks. Put another way, I've wondered sometimes about *what* we had decided to do but never about how we did it.

But now a much simpler scenario comes to mind. I'm confident that if the idea *had* come up it would have been shot down – walking down the tracks would have seemed neater, *bosser*, as we said then. But if the idea had come up and *hadn't* been shot down in flames, none of the things which occurred later would have happened. Maybe Chris and Teddy and Vern would even be alive today. No, they didn't die in the woods or on the railroad tracks; nobody dies in this story except some bloodsuckers and Ray Brower, and if you want to be completely fair about it, he was dead before it even started. But it *is* true that, of the four of us who flipped coins to see who would go down to the Florida Market to get supplies, only the one who actually went is still alive. The Ancient Mariner at thirty-four, with you, Gentle Reader, in the role of wedding guest (at this point shouldn't you flip to the jacket photo to see if my eye holdeth you in its spell?) . . . If you sense a certain flipness on my part, you're right – but maybe I have cause. At an age when all four of us would be considered too young and immature to be President, three of us are dead. And if small events really do echo up larger and larger through time, yes, maybe if we had done the simple thing and simply hitched into Harlow, they would still be alive today.

We could have hooked a ride all the way up Route 7 to the Shiloh Church, which stood at the intersection of the highway and the Back Harlow Road (at least until 1967, when it was levelled by a fire attributed to a tramp's smouldering cigarette butt). With reasonable luck we could have been beating the bushes in the area where Billy and Charlie parked with their skag girlfriends before sundown of the previous day.

But the idea wouldn't have lived. It wouldn't have been shot down with tightly buttressed arguments and debating society rhetoric, but with grunts and scowls and farts and raised middle fingers. The verbal part of the discussion would have been carried forward with such trenchant and sparkling contributions as 'Fuck no', 'That sucks', and that old reliable standby, 'Did your mother ever have any kids that lived?'

Unspoken – maybe it was too fundamental to be spoken – was the idea that this was a *big* thing. It wasn't screwing around with firecrackers or trying to look through the knothole in the back of the girls' privy at Harrison State Park. This was something on a par with getting laid for the first time, or going into the Army, or buying your first bottle of legal liquor – just bopping into that state store, if you can dig it, selecting a bottle of good Scotch, showing the clerk your draft card and drivers' licence, then walking out with a grin on your face and that brown bag in your hand, member of a club with just a few more rights and privileges than our old treehouse with the tin roof.

There's a high ritual to all fundamental events, the rites of passage, the magic corridor where the change happens. Buying the condoms. Standing before the minister. Raising your hand and taking the oath. Or, if you please, walking down the railroad tracks to meet a fellow your own age halfway, the same as I'd walk halfway up Grand Street to meet Chris if he was coming over to my house, or the way Teddy would walk halfway down Gates Street to meet me if I was going to his. It seemed right to do it this way, because the rite of passage *is* a magic corridor and so we always provide an aisle – it's what you walk down when you get married, what they carry you down when you get buried. Our corridor was those twin rails, and we walked between them, just bopping along towards whatever this was supposed to mean. You don't hitchhike your way to a thing like that, maybe. And maybe we thought it was also right that it should have turned out to be harder than we had expected. Events surrounding our hike had turned it into what we had suspected it was all along: serious business.

What we *didn't* know as we walked around The Bluffs was that Billy Tessio, Charlie Hogan, Jack Mudgett, Norman 'Fuzzy' Brackowicz, Vince Desjardins, Chris's older brother

Eyeball, and Ace Merrill himself were all on their way to take a look at the body themselves – in a weird kind of way, Ray Brower had become famous, and our secret had turned into a regular roadshow. They were piling into Ace's chopped and channelled '52 Ford and Vince's pink '54 Studebaker even as we started on the last leg of our trip.

Billy and Charlie had managed to keep their enormous secret for just about twenty-four hours. Then Charlie spilled it to Ace while they were shooting pool, and Billy had spilled it to Jack Mudgett while they were fishing for steelies from the Boom Road bridge. Both Ace and Jack had sworn solemnly on their mothers' names to keep the secret, and that was how everybody in their gang knew about it by noon. Guess you could tell what those assholes thought about their mothers.

They all congregated down at the pool hall, and Fuzzy Brackowicz advanced a theory (which you have heard before, Gentle Reader) that they could all become heroes – not to mention instant radio and TV personalities – by 'discovering' the body. All they had to do, Fuzzy maintained, was to take two cars with a lot of fishing gear in the trunks. After they found the body, their story would be a hundred per cent. We was just plannin' to take a few pickerel out of the Royal River, officer. Heh-heh-heh. Look what we found.

They were burning up the road from Castle Rock to the Back Harlow area just as we started to finally get close.

25

Clouds began to build in the sky around two o'clock, but at first none of us took them seriously. It hadn't rained since the early days of July, so why should it rain now? But they kept building to the south of us, up and up and up, thunderheads in great pillars as purple as bruises, and they began to move slowly our way. I looked at them closely, checking for that membrane beneath that means it's already raining twenty miles away, or fifty. But there was no rain yet. The clouds were still just building.

Vern got a blister on his heel and we stopped and rested while he packed the back of his left sneaker with moss stripped from the bark of an old oak tree.

'Is it gonna rain, Gordie?' Teddy asked.

'I think so.'

'Pisser!' he said, and sighed. 'The pisser good end to a pisser good day.'

I laughed and he tipped me a wink.

We started to walk again, a little more slowly now out of respect for Vern's hurt foot. And in the hour between two and three, the quality of the day's light began to change, and we knew for sure that rain was coming. It was just as hot as ever, and even more humid, but we knew. And the birds did. They seemed to appear from nowhere and swoop across the sky, chattering and crying shrilly to each other. And the light. From a steady, beating brightness it seemed to evolve into something filtered, almost pearly. Our shadows, which had begun to grow long again, also grew fuzzy and ill-defined. The sun had begun to sail in and out through the thickening decks of clouds, and the southern sky had gone a copper shade. We watched the thunderheads lumber closer, fascinated by their size and their mute threat. Every now and then it seemed that a giant flashbulb had gone off inside one of them, turning their purplish, bruised colour momentarily to a light grey. I saw a jagged fork of lightning lick down from the underside of the closest. It was bright enough to print a blue tattoo on my retinas. It was followed by a long, shaking blast of thunder.

We did a little bitching about how we were going to get caught out in the rain, but only because it was the expected thing – of course we were all looking forward to it. It would be cold and refreshing . . . and leech-free.

At a little past three-thirty, we saw running water through a break in the trees.

'That's it!' Chris yelled jubilantly. 'That's the Royal!'

We began to walk faster, taking our second wind. The storm was getting close now. The air began to stir, and it seemed that the temperature dropped ten degrees in a space of seconds. I looked down and saw that my shadow had disappeared entirely.

We were walking in pairs again, each two watching a side of the railroad embankment. My mouth was dry, throbbing with a sickish tension. The sun sailed behind another cloud-bank and this time it didn't come back out. For a moment the bank's edges were embroidered with gold, like a cloud in an Old Testament Bible illustration, and then the wine-coloured, dragging belly of the thunderhead blotted out all traces of the sun. The day became gloomy – the clouds were rapidly eating up the last of the blue. We could smell the river so clearly that we might have been horses – or perhaps it was the smell of rain impending in the air as well. There was an ocean above us, held in by a thin sac that might rupture and let down a flood at any second.

I kept trying to look into the underbrush, but my eyes were continually drawn back to that turbulent, racing sky;

in its deepening colours you could read whatever doom you liked: water, fire, wind, hail. The cool breeze became more insistent, hissing in the firs. A sudden impossible bolt of lightning flashed down, seemingly from directly overhead, making me cry out and clap my hands to my eyes. God had taken my picture, a little kid with his shirt tied around his waist, duckbumps on his bare chest and cinders on his cheeks. I heard the rending fall of some big tree not sixty yards away. The crack of thunder which followed made me cringe. I wanted to be at home reading a good book in a safe place . . . like down in the potato cellar.

'Jeezis!' Vern screamed in a high, fainting voice. 'Oh my Jeezis Chrise, lookit *that*!'

I looked in the direction Vern was pointing and saw a blue-white fireball bowling its way up the lefthand rail of the GS&WM tracks, crackling and hissing for all the world like a scalded cat. It hurried past us as we turned to watch it go, dumbfounded, aware for the first time that such things could exist. Twenty feet beyond us it made a sudden – *pop!!* – and just disappeared, leaving a greasy smell of ozone behind.

'What am I *doin'* here, anyway?' Teddy muttered.

'What a pisser!' Chris exclaimed happily, his face upturned. 'This is gonna be a pisser like you wouldn't *believe*!' But I was with Teddy. Looking up at that sky gave me a dismaying sense of vertigo. It was more like looking into some deeply mysterious marbled gorge. Another lightning-bolt crashed down, making us duck. This time the ozone smell was hotter, more urgent. The following clap of thunder came with no perceptible pause at all.

My ears were still ringing from it when Vern began to

screech triumphantly: '*THERE! THERE HE IS! RIGHT THERE! I SEE HIM!*'

I can see Vern right this minute, if I want to – all I have to do is sit back for a minute and close my eyes. He's standing there on the lefthand rail like an explorer on the prow of his ship, one hand shielding his eyes from the silver stroke of lightning that has just come down, the other extended and pointing.

We ran up beside him and looked. I was thinking to myself: Vern's imagination just ran away with him, that's all. The suckers, the heat, now this storm . . . his eyes are dealing wild cards, that's all. But that wasn't what it was, although there was a split second when I wanted it to be. In that split second I knew I never wanted to see a corpse, not even a runover woodchuck.

In the place where we were standing, early spring rains had washed part of the embankment away, leaving a gravelly, uncertain four-foot drop-off. The railroad maintenance crews had either not yet gotten around to it in their yellow diesel-operated repair carts, or it had happened so recently it hadn't yet been reported. At the bottom of this washout was a marshy, mucky tangle of undergrowth that smelled bad. And sticking out of a wild clockspring of blackberry brambles was a single pale white hand.

Did any of us breathe? I didn't.

The breeze was now a wind – harsh and jerky, coming at us from no particular direction, jumping and whirling, slapping at our sweaty skins and open pores. I hardly noticed. I think part of my mind was waiting for Teddy to cry out *Paratroops over the side!*, and I thought if he did that I might just go crazy. It would have been better to see the whole body, all at once, but instead there was only that limp outstretched hand, horribly white, the fingers limply splayed, like the hand of a drowned boy. It told us the truth of the whole matter. It explained every graveyard in the world. The image of that hand came back to me every time I heard or read of an atrocity. Somewhere, attached to that hand, was the rest of Ray Brower.

Lightning flickered and stroked. Thunder ripped in behind each stroke as if a drag race had started over our heads.

'Sheeeee . . .' Chris said, the sound not quite a cuss word, not quite the country version of *shit* as it is pronounced around a slender stem of timothy grass when the baler breaks down – instead it was a long, tuneless syllable without meaning; a sigh that had just happened to pass through the vocal cords.

Vern was licking his lips in a compulsive sort of way, as if he had tasted some obscure new delicacy, a Howard Johnson's 29th Flavour, Tibetan Sausage Rolls, Interstellar Escargot, something so weird that it excited and revolted him at the same time.

Teddy only stood and looked. The wind whipped his greasy, clotted hair first away from his ears and then back over them. His face was a total blank. I could tell you I saw something there, and perhaps I did, in hindsight . . . but not then.

There were black ants trundling back and forth across the hand.

A great whispering noise began to rise in the woods on either side of the tracks, as if the forest had just noticed we were there and was commenting on it. The rain had started.

Dime-sized drops fell on my head and arms. They struck

the embankment, turning the fill dark for a moment – and then the colour changed back again as the greedy dry ground sucked the moisture up.

Those big drops fell for maybe five seconds and then they stopped. I looked at Chris and he blinked back at me.

Then the storm came all at once, as if a shower chain had been pulled in the sky. The whispering sound changed to loud contention. It was as if we were being rebuked for our discovery, and it was frightening. Nobody tells you about the pathetic fallacy until you're in college . . . and even then I noticed that nobody but the total dorks completely believed it *was* a fallacy.

Chris jumped over the side of the washout, his hair already soaked and clinging to his head. I followed. Vern and Teddy came close behind, but Chris and I were first to reach the body of Ray Brower. He was face down. Chris looked into my eyes, his face set and stern – an adult's face. I nodded slightly, as if he had spoken aloud.

I think he was down here and relatively intact instead of up there between the rails and completely mangled because he was trying to get out of the way when the train hit him, knocking him head over heels. He had landed with his head pointed towards the tracks, arms over his head like a diver about to execute. He had landed in this boggy cup of land that was becoming a small swamp. His hair was a dark reddish colour. The moisture in the air had made it curl slightly at the ends. There was blood in it, but not a great deal, not a gross-out amount. The ants were grosser. He was wearing a solid colour dark green tee-shirt and bluejeans. His feet were bare, and a few feet behind him, caught in tall blackberry brambles, I saw a pair of filthy low-topped Keds. For a moment I was puzzled – why was he here and his tennies there . . . Then I realized, and the realization was like a dirty punch below the belt. My wife, my kids, my friends – they all think that having an imagination like mine must be quite nice; aside from making all this dough, I can have a little mind-movie whenever things get dull. Mostly they're right. But every now and then it turns around and bites the shit out of you with these long teeth, teeth that have been filed to points like the teeth of a cannibal. You see things you'd just as soon not see, things that keep you awake until first light. I saw one of those things now, saw it with absolute clarity and certainty. He had been knocked spang out of his Keds. The train had knocked him out of his Keds just as it had knocked the life out of his body.

That finally rammed it all the way home for me. The kid was dead. The kid wasn't sick, the kid wasn't sleeping. The kid wasn't going to get up in the morning anymore or get the runs from eating too many apples or catch poison ivy or wear out the eraser on the end of his Ticonderoga No 2 during a hard math test. The kid was dead; stone dead. The kid was never going to go out bottling with his friends in the spring, gunnysack over his shoulder to pick up the returnables the retreating snow uncovered. The kid wasn't going to wake up at two o'clock a.m. on the morning of 1 November this year, run to the bathroom, and vomit up a big glurt of cheap Halloween candy. The kid wasn't going to pull a single girl's braid in home room. The kid wasn't going to give a bloody nose, or get one. The kid was *can't, don't, won't, never, shouldn't, wouldn't, couldn't.* He was the side of the battery where the terminal says NEG. The fuse you have to put a penny in. The wastebasket by the teacher's desk, which always smells of wood-shavings from the sharpener and dead orange-peels from lunch. The haunted house outside of town where the windows are crashed out, the NO TRESPASSING signs whipped away across the fields, the attic full of bats, the cellar full of worms. The kid was dead, mister, ma'am, young sir, little miss. I could go on all day and never get it right about the distance between his bare feet on the ground and his dirty Keds hanging in the bushes. It was thirty-plus inches, it was a googol of light-years. The kid was disconnected from his Keds beyond all hope of reconciliation. He was dead.

We turned him face up into the pouring rain, the lightning, the steady crack of thunder.

There were ants and bugs all over his face and neck. They ran briskly in and out of the round collar of his tee-shirt. His eyes were open, but terrifyingly out of sync – one was rolled back so far that we could see only a tiny arc of pupil; the other stared straight up into the storm. There was a dried froth of blood above his mouth and on his chin – from a bloody nose, I thought – and the right side of his face was lacerated and darkly bruised. Still, I thought, he didn't really look bad. I had once walked into a door my brother Dennis was shoving open, came off with bruises even worse than this kid's, *plus* the bloody nose, and still had two helpings of everything for supper after it happened.

Teddy and Vern stood behind us and if there had been any sight at all left in that one upward-staring eye, I suppose we would have looked to Ray Brower like pallbearers in a horror movie.

A beetle came out of his mouth, trekked across his fuzz-less cheek, stepped onto a nettle, and was gone.

'D'joo see that?' Teddy asked in a high, strange, fainting voice. 'I bet he's fuckin' *fulla* bugs! I bet his *brains*'re –'

'Shut up, Teddy,' Chris said, and Teddy did, looking relieved. Lightning forked blue across the sky, making the boy's single eye light up. You could almost believe he was glad to be found, and found by boys his own age. His torso had swelled up and there was a faint gassy odour about him, like the smell of old farts.

I turned away, sure I was going to be sick, but my stomach was dry, hard, steady. I suddenly rammed two fingers down my throat, trying to *make* myself heave, needing to do it, as if I could sick it up and get rid of it. But my stomach only hitched a little and then was steady again.

The roaring downpour and the accompanying thunder had completely covered the sound of cars approaching along the Back Harlow Road, which lay bare yards beyond this boggy tangle. It likewise covered the crackle-crunch of the underbrush as they blundered through it from the dead end where they had parked.

And the first we knew of them was Ace Merrill's voice raised above the tumult of the storm, saying: 'Well what the fuck do you know about this?'

26

We all jumped like we had been goosed and Vern cried out – he admitted later that he thought, for just a second, that the voice had come from the dead boy.

On the far side of the boggy patch, where the woods

took up again, masking the butt end of the road, Ace Merrill and Eyeball Chambers stood together, half-obscured by a pouring grey curtain of rain. They were both wearing red nylon high school jackets, the kind you can buy in the office if you're a regular student, the same kind they give away free to varsity sports players. Their da haircuts had been plastered back against their skulls and a mixture of rainwater and Vitalis ran down their cheeks like ersatz tears.

'Sumbitch!' Eyeball said. 'That's my little brother!'

Chris was staring at Eyeball with his mouth open. His shirt, wet, limp and dark, was still tied around his skinny middle. His pack, stained a darker green by the rain, was hanging against his naked shoulderblades.

'You get away, Rich,' he said in a trembling voice. 'We found him. We got dibs.'

'Fuck your dibs. We're gonna report 'im.'

'No you're not,' I said. I was suddenly furious with them, turning up this way at the last minute. If we'd thought about it, we'd have known something just like this was going to happen . . . but this was one time, somehow, that the older, bigger kids weren't going to steal it – to take something they wanted as if by divine right, as if their easy way was the right way, the only way. They had come in *cars* – I think that was what made me angriest. They had come in *cars*. 'There's four of us, Eyeball. You just try.'

'Oh, we'll *try*, don't worry,' Eyeball said, and the trees shook behind him and Ace, Charlie Hogan and Vern's brother Billy stepped through them, cursing and wiping water out of their eyes. I felt a lead ball drop into my belly. It grew bigger as Jack Mudgett and Fuzzy Brackowicz stepped out behind Charlie and Billy.

'Here we all are,' Ace said, grinning. 'So you just –'

'*VERN!!* Billy Tessio cried in a terrible, accusing, my-justice-cometh-and-that-right-early voice. He made a pair of dripping fists. 'You little sonofawhore! You was under the porch! Cock-*knocker*!'

Vern flinched.

Charlie Hogan waxed positively lyrical: 'You little keyhole-peeping cunt-licking *bungwipe!* I ought to beat the living shit out of you!'

'Yeah? Well, try it!' Teddy brayed suddenly. His eyes were crazily alight behind his rainspotted glasses. 'Come on, fightcha for 'im! Come on! Come on, big men!'

Billy and Charlie didn't need a second invitation. They started forward together and Vern flinched again – no doubt visualizing the ghosts of Beatings Past and Beatings Yet To Come. He flinched . . . but hung tough. He was with his friends, and we had been through a lot, and we hadn't got here in a couple of *cars*.

But Ace held Billy and Charlie back, simply by touching each of them on the shoulder.

'Now listen, you guys,' Ace said. He spoke patiently, just as if we weren't all standing in a roaring rainstorm. 'There's more of us than there are of you. We're bigger. We'll give you one chance to just blow away. I don't give a fuck where. Just make like a tree and leave.'

Chris's brother giggled and Fuzzy clapped Ace on the back in appreciation of his great wit. The Sid Caesar of the jd set.

''Cause *we're* takin' him.' Ace smiled gently, and you could imagine him smiling that same gentle smile just before breaking his cue over the head of some uneducated punk

547

who had made the terrible mistake of lipping off while Ace was lining up a shot. 'If you go, we'll take him. If you stay, we'll beat the piss outta you and still take him. Besides,' he added, trying to gild the thuggery with a little righteousness, 'Charlie and Billy found him, so it's their dibs anyway.'

'They was chicken!' Teddy shot back. 'Vern told us about it! They was fuckin' chicken right outta their fuckin' minds!' He screwed his face up into a terrified, snivelling parody of Charlie Hogan. ' "I wish we never boosted that car! I wish we never went on no Back Harlow Road to whack off a piece! Oh Billee, what are we gonna do? Oh Billee, I think I just made a pile in my Fruit of the Looms! Oh Billee —" '

'That's it,' Charlie said, starting forward again. His face was knotted with rage and sullen embarrassment. 'Kid, whatever your name is, get ready to reach down your fuckin' throat the next time you need to pick your nose.'

I looked wildly down at Ray Brower. He stared calmly up into the rain with his one eye, below us but above it all. The thunder was still booming steadily, but the rain had begun to slack off.

'What do you say, Gordie?' Ace asked. He was holding Charlie lightly by the arm, the way an accomplished trainer would restrain a vicious dog. 'You must have at least some of your brother's sense. Tell these guys to back off. I'll let Charlie beat up the foureyes el punko a little bit and then we all go about our business. What do you say?'

He was wrong to mention Denny. I had wanted to reason with him, to point out what Ace knew perfectly well, that we had every right to take Billy and Charlie's dibs since Vern had heard them giving said dibs away. I wanted to tell him how Vern and I had almost gotten run down by a freight

train on the trestle which spans the Castle River. About Milo
Pressman and his fearless – if stupid – sidekick, Chopper the
Wonder-Dog. About the bloodsuckers, too. I guess all I really
wanted to tell him was come on, Ace, fair is fair. You know
that. But he had to bring Denny into it, and what I heard
coming out of my mouth instead of sweet reason was my
own death warrant: 'Suck my fat one, you cheap dimestore
hood.'

Ace's mouth formed a perfect O of surprise – the expression was so unexpectedly prissy that under other circumstances
it would have been a laff riot, so to speak. All of the others –
on both sides of the bog – stared at me, dumbfounded.

Then Teddy screamed gleefully: 'That's telling 'im, Gordie!
Oh boy! Too cool!'

I stood numbly, unable to believe it. It was like some
crazed understudy had shot onstage at the critical moment
and declaimed lines that weren't even in the play. Telling a
guy to suck was as bad as you could get without resorting
to his mother. Out of the corner of my eye I saw that Chris
had unshouldered his knapsack and was digging into it frantically, but I didn't get it – not then, anyway.

'Okay,' Ace said softly. 'Let's take 'em. Don't hurt nobody
but the Lachance kid. I'm gonna break both his fuckin' arms.'

I went dead cold. I didn't piss myself the way I had on
the railroad trestle, but it must have been because I had
nothing inside to let out. He meant it, you see; the years
between then and now have changed my mind about a lot
of things, but not about that. When Ace said he was going
to break both of my arms, he absolutely meant it.

They started to walk towards us through the slackening
rain. Jackie Mudgett took a DeMano switchknife out of his

pocket and hit the chrome. Six inches of steel flicked out, dove-grey in the afternoon half-light. Vern and Teddy dropped suddenly into fighting crouches on either side of me. Teddy did so eagerly, Vern with a desperate, cornered grimace on his face.

The big kids advanced in a line, their feet splashing through the bog, which was now one big sludgy puddle because of the storm. The body of Ray Brower lay at our feet like a waterlogged barrel. I got ready to fight ... and that was when Chris fired the pistol he had hawked out of his old man's dresser.

KA-BLAM!

God, what a wonderful sound that was! Charlie Hogan jumped right up into the air. Ace Merrill, who had been staring straight at me, now jerked around and looked at Chris. His mouth made that O again. Eyeball looked absolutely astounded.

'Hey, Chris, that's Daddy's,' he said. 'You're gonna get the tar whaled out of you –'

'That's nothing to what you'll get,' Chris said. His face was horribly pale, and all the life in him seemed to have been sucked upward, into his eyes. They blazed out of his face. 'Gordie was right, you're nothing but a bunch of cheap hoods. Charlie and Billy didn't want their fuckin' dibs and you all know it. We wouldn't have walked way to fuck out here if they said they did. They just went someplace and puked the story up and let Ace Merrill do their thinkin' for them.' His voice rose to a scream. '*But you ain't gonna get him, do you hear me?*'

'Now listen,' Ace said. 'You better put that down before you take your foot off with it. You ain't got the sack to shoot a woodchuck.' He began to walk forward again, smiling his gentle smile as he came. 'You're just a sawed-off pint-sized pissy-assed little runt and I'm gonna make you *eat* that fuckin' gun.'

'Ace, if you don't stand still I'm going to shoot you. I swear to God.'

'You'll go to *jayyy-ail*,' Ace crooned, not even hesitating. He was still smiling. The others watched him with horrified fascination . . . much the same way as Teddy and Vern and I were looking at Chris. Ace Merrill was the hardest case for miles around and I didn't think Chris could bluff him down. And what did that leave? Ace didn't think a twelve-year-old punk would actually shoot him. I thought he was wrong; I thought Chris would shoot Ace before he let Ace take his father's pistol away from him. In those few seconds I was sure there was going to be bad trouble, the worst I'd ever known. Killing trouble, maybe. And all of it over who got dibs on a dead body.

Chris said softly, with great regret: 'Where do you want it, Ace? Arm or leg? I can't pick. You pick for me.'

And Ace stopped.

27

His face sagged, and I saw sudden terror on it. It was Chris's tone rather than his actual words, I think; the real regret that things were going to go from bad to worse. If it was a bluff, it's still the best I've ever seen. The other big kids were totally convinced; their faces were squinched up as if someone had just touched a match to a cherry bomb with a short fuse.

Ace slowly got control of himself. The muscles in his face tightened again, his lips pressed together, and he looked at Chris the way you'd look at a man who has made a serious business proposition – to merge with your company, or handle your line of credit, or shoot your balls off. It was a waiting, almost curious expression, one that made you know that the terror was either gone or tightly lidded. Ace had recomputed the odds on not getting shot and had decided that they weren't as much in his favour as he had thought. But he was still dangerous – maybe more than before. Since then I've thought it was the rawest piece of brinkmanship I've ever seen. Neither of them was bluffing; they both meant business.

'All right,' Ace said softly, speaking to Chris. 'But I know how you're going to come out of this, motherfuck.'

'No you don't,' Chris said.

'You little prick!' Eyeball said loudly. 'You're gonna wind up in traction for this!'

'Bite my bag,' Chris told him.

With an inarticulate sound of rage Eyeball started forward and Chris put a bullet into the water about ten feet in front of him. It kicked up a splash. Eyeball jumped back, cursing.

'Okay, now what?' Ace asked.

'Now you guys get into your cars and bomb on back to Castle Rock. After that I don't care. But you ain't getting him.' He touched Ray Brower lightly, almost reverently, with the toe of one sopping sneaker. 'You dig me?'

'But we'll get *you*,' Ace said. He was starting to smile again. 'Don't you know that?'

'We'll get you hard,' Ace said, smiling. 'We'll hurt you. I can't believe you don't *know* that. We'll put you all in the fuckin' hospital with fuckin' ruptures. Sincerely.'

'Oh, why don't you go home and fuck your mother some more? I hear she loves the way you do it.'

Ace's smile froze. 'I'll kill you for that. Nobody ranks my mother.'

'I heard your mother fucks for bucks,' Chris informed him, and as Ace began to pale, as his complexion began to approach Chris's own ghastly whiteness, he added: 'In fact, I heard she throws blowjobs for jukebox nickels. I heard –'

Then the storm came back, viciously, all at once. Only this time it was hail instead of rain. Instead of whispering or talking, the woods now seemed alive with hokey B-movie jungle drums – it was the sound of big ice hailstones bonking off treetrunks. Stinging pebbles began to hit my shoulders – it felt as if some sentient, malevolent force was throwing them. Worse than that, they began to strike Ray Brower's upturned face with an awful splatting sound that reminded us of him again, of his terrible and unending patience.

Vern caved in first, with a wailing scream. He fled up the embankment in huge, gangling strides. Teddy held out a minute longer, then ran after Vern, his hands held up over his head. On their side, Vince Desjardins floundered back under some nearby trees and Fuzzy Brackowicz joined him. But the others stood pat, and Ace began to grin again.

'Stick with me, Gordie,' Chris said in a low, shaky voice. 'Stick with me, man.'

'I'm right here.'

'Go on, now,' Chris said to Ace, and he was able, by some

magic, to get the shakiness out of his voice. He sounded as if he was instructing a stupid infant.

'We'll get you,' Ace said. 'We're not going to forget it, if that's what you're thinking. This is big time, baby.'

'That's fine. You just go on and do your getting another day.'

'We'll fuckin' ambush you, Chambers. We'll —'

'*Get out!*' Chris screamed, and levelled the gun. Ace stepped back.

He looked at Chris a moment longer, nodded, then turned around. 'Come on,' he said to the others. He looked back over his shoulder at Chris and me once more. 'Be seeing you.'

They went back into the screen of trees between the bog and the road. Chris and I stood perfectly still in spite of the hail that was wetting us, reddening our skins, and piling up all around us like summer snow. We stood and listened and above the crazy calypso sound of the hail hitting the treetrunks we heard two cars start up.

'Stay right here,' Chris told me, and he started across the bog.

'Chris!' I said, panicky.

'I got to. Stay here.'

It seemed he was gone a very long time. I became convinced that either Ace or Eyeball had lurked behind and grabbed him. I stood my ground with nobody but Ray Brower for company and waited for somebody — anybody — to come back. After a while, Chris did.

'We did it,' he said. 'They're gone.'

'You sure?'

'Yeah. Both cars.' He held his hands up over his head,

locked together with the gun between them, and shook the double fist in a wry championship gesture. Then he dropped them and smiled at me. I think it was the saddest, scaredest smile I ever saw. ' "Suck my fat one" – whoever told you you had a fat one, Lachance?'

'Biggest one in four counties,' I said. I was shaking all over.

We looked at each other warmly for a second, and then, maybe embarrassed by what we were seeing, looked down together. A nasty thrill of fear shot through me, and the sudden *splash/splash* as Chris shifted his feet let me know that he had seen, too. Ray Brower's eyes had gone wide and white, starey and pupilless, like the eyes that look out at you from Grecian statuary. It only took a second to understand what had happened, but understanding didn't lessen the horror. His eyes had filled up with round white hailstones. Now they were melting and the water ran down his cheeks as if he were weeping for his own grotesque position – a tatty prize to be fought over by two bunches of stupid hick kids. His clothes were also white with hail. He seemed to be lying in his own shroud.

'Oh, Gordie, hey,' Chris said shakily. 'Say-hey, man. What a creepshow for him.'

'I don't think he knows –'

'Maybe that *was* his ghost we heard. Maybe he knew this was gonna happen. What a fuckin' creepshow, I'm sincere.'

Branches crackled behind us. I whirled, sure they had flanked us, but Chris went back to contemplating the body after one short, almost casual glance. It was Vern and Teddy, their jeans soaked black and plastered to their legs, both of them grinning like dogs that have been sucking eggs.

'What are we gonna do, man?' Chris asked, and I felt a weird chill steal through me. Maybe he was talking to me, maybe he was . . . but he was still looking down at the body.

'We're gonna take him back, ain't we?' Teddy asked, puzzled. 'We're gonna be heroes. Ain't that right?' He looked from Chris to me and back to Chris again.

Chris looked up as if startled out of a dream. His lip curled. He took big steps towards Teddy, planted both hands on Teddy's chest, and pushed him roughly backwards. Teddy stumbled, pinwheeled his arms for balance, then sat down with a soggy splash. He blinked up at Chris like a surprised muskrat. Vern was looking warily at Chris, as if he feared madness. Perhaps that wasn't far from the mark.

'You keep your trap shut,' Chris said to Teddy. 'Paratroops over the side my ass. You lousy rubber chicken.'

'It was the *hail*!' Teddy cried out, angry and ashamed. 'It wasn't those guys, Chris! I'm ascared of *storms*! I can't help it! I would have taken all of 'em on at once, I swear on my mother's name! But I'm ascared of *storms*! Shit! I can't help it!' He began to cry again, sitting there in the water.

'What about you?' Chris asked, turning to Vern. 'Are you ascared of storms too?'

Vern shook his head vacuously, still astounded by Chris's rage. 'Hey, man, I thought we was all runnin'.'

'You must be a mind-reader then, because you ran first.'

Vern swallowed twice and said nothing.

Chris stared at him, his eyes sullen and wild. Then he turned to me. 'Going to build him a litter, Gordie.'

'If you say so, Chris.'

'Sure! Like in Scouts.' His voice had begun to climb into

strange, reedy levels. 'Just like in the fuckin' Scouts. A litter – poles and shirts. Like in the handbook. Right, Gordie?'

'Yeah. If you want. But what if those guys –'

'*Fuck those guys!*' he screamed. '*You're all a bunch of chickens! Fuck off, creeps!*'

'Chris, they could call the sheriff. To get back at us.'

'*He's ours and we're gonna take him OUT!*'

'Those guys would say anything to get us in dutch,' I told him. My words sounded thin, stupid, sick with the flu. 'Say anything and then lie each other up. You know how people can get other people in trouble telling lies, man. Like with the milk-mo –'

'*I DON'T CARE!*' he screamed, and lunged at me with his fists up. But one of his feet struck Ray Brower's ribcage with a soggy thump, making the body rock. He tripped and fell full-length and I waited for him to get up and maybe punch me in the mouth but instead he lay where he had fallen, head pointing towards the embankment, arms stretched out over his head like a diver about to execute, in the exact posture Ray Brower had been in when we found him. I looked wildly at Chris's feet to make sure his sneakers were still on. Then he began to cry and scream, his body bucking in the muddy water, splashing it around, fists drumming up and down in it, head twisting from side to side. Teddy and Vern were staring at him, agog, because nobody had ever seen Chris Chambers cry. After a moment or two I walked back to the embankment, climbed it, and sat down on one of the rails. Chris and Vern followed me. And we sat there in the rain, not talking, looking like those three Monkeys of Virtue they sell in dimestores and those sleazy gift-shops that always look like they are tottering on the edge of bankruptcy.

28

It was twenty minutes before Chris climbed the embankment to sit down beside us. The clouds had begun to break. Spears of sun came down through the rips. The bushes seemed to have gone three shades darker green in the last forty-five minutes. He was mud all the way up one side and down the other. His hair was standing up in muddy spikes. The only clean parts of him were the whitewashed circles around his eyes.

'You're right, Gordie,' he said. 'Nobody gets last dibs. Goocher all around, huh?'

I nodded. Five minutes passed. No one said anything. And I happened to have a thought . . . just in case they *did* call Bannerman. I went back down the embankment and over to where Chris had been standing. I got down on my knees and began to comb carefully through the water and marsh-grass with my fingers.

'What you doing?' Teddy asked, joining me.

'It's to your left, I think,' Chris said, and pointed.

I looked there and after a minute or two I found both shell casings. They winked in the fresh sunlight. I gave them to Chris. He nodded and stuffed them into a pocket of his jeans.

'Now we go,' Chris said.

'Hey, come *on!*' Teddy yelled, in real agony. 'I wanna *take* 'im!'

'Listen, dummy,' Chris said, 'if we take him back we could all wind up in the reformatory. It's like Gordie says. Those guys could make up any story they wanted to. What if they said *we* killed him, huh? How would you like that?'

'I don't give a damn,' Teddy said sulkily. Then he looked at us with absurd hope. 'Besides, we might only get a couple of months or so. As excessories. I mean, we're only twelve fuckin' years old, they ain't gonna put us in Shawshank.'

Chris said softly: 'You can't get in the army if you got a record, Teddy.'

I was pretty sure that was nothing but a bald-faced lie – but somehow this didn't seem the time to say so. Teddy just looked at Chris for a long time, his mouth trembling. Finally he managed to squeak out: 'No shit?'

'Ask Gordie.'

He looked at me hopefully.

'He's right,' I said, feeling like a great big turd. 'He's right, Teddy. First thing they do when you volunteer is to check your name through R&I.'

'Holy *God*!'

'We're gonna shag ass back to the trestle,' Chris said. 'Then we'll get off the tracks and come into Castle Rock from the other direction. If people ask where we were, we'll say we went campin' up on Brickyard Hill and got lost.'

'Milo Pressman knows better,' I said. 'That creep at the Florida Market does, too.'

'Well, we'll say Milo scared us and that's when we decided to go up on the Brickyard.'

I nodded. That might work. If Vern and Teddy could remember to stick to it.

'What about if our folks get together?' Vern asked.

'You worry about it if you want,' Chris said. 'My dad'll still be juiced up.'

'Come on, then,' Vern said, eyeing the screen of trees between us and the Back Harlow Road. He looked like he expected Bannerman, along with a brace of bloodhounds, to come crashing through at any moment. 'Let's get while the gettin's good.'

We were all on our feet now, ready to go. The birds were singing like crazy, pleased with the rain and the shine and the worms and just about everything in the world, I guess. We all turned around, as if pulled on strings, and looked back at Ray Brower.

He was lying there, alone again. His arms had flopped out when we turned him over and now he was sort of spreadeagled, as if to welcome the sunshine. For a moment it seemed all right, a more natural deathscene than any ever constructed for a viewing-room audience by a mortician. Then you saw the bruise, the caked blood on the chin and under the nose, and the way the corpse was beginning to bloat. You saw that the bluebottles had come out with the sun and that they were circling the body, buzzing indolently. You remembered that gassy smell, sickish but dry, like farts in a closed room. He was a boy our age, he was dead, and I rejected the idea that anything about it could be natural; I pushed it away with horror.

'Okay,' Chris said, and he meant to be brisk but his voice came out of his throat like a handful of dry bristles from an old whiskbroom. 'Double time.'

We started to almost-trot back the way we had come. We didn't talk. I don't know about the others, but I was too busy thinking to talk. There were things that bothered me about the body of Ray Brower – they bothered me then and they bother me now.

A bad bruise on the side of his face, a scalp laceration, a bloody nose. No more – at least, no more visible. People walk away from bar-fights in worse condition and go right on drinking. Yet the train *must* have hit him; why else would his sneakers be off his feet that way? And how come the engineer hadn't seen him? Could it be that the train had hit him hard enough to toss him but not to kill him? I thought that, under just the right combination of circumstances, that could have happened. Had the train hit him a hefty, teeth-rattling sideswipe as he tried to get out of the way? Hit him and knocked him in a flying, backwards somersault over that caved-in banking? Had he perhaps lain awake and trembling in the dark for hours, not just lost now but disorientated as well, cut off from the world? Maybe he had died of fear. A bird with crushed tailfeathers once died in my cupped hands in just that way. Its body trembled and vibrated lightly, its beak opened and closed, its dark, bright eyes stared up at me. Then the vibration quit, the beak froze half-open, and the black eyes became lacklustre and uncaring. It could have been that way with Ray Brower. He could have died because he was simply too frightened to go on living.

But there was another thing, and that bothered me most of all, I think. He had started off to go berrying. I seemed to remember the news reports saying he'd been carrying a tin pail. When we got back I went to the library and looked it up in the newspapers just to be sure, and I was right. He'd been berrying, and he'd had a pail. But we hadn't found it. We found him, and we found his sneakers. He must have thrown it away somewhere between Chamberlain and the boggy patch of ground in Harlow where he died. He perhaps clutched it even tighter at first, as though it linked him to home and safety. But as his fear grew, and with it that sense of being utterly alone, with no chance of rescue except for whatever he could do by himself, as the real cold terror set it, he maybe threw it away into the woods on one side of the tracks or the other, hardly even noticing it was gone.

I've thought of going back and looking for it — how does that strike you for morbid? I've thought of driving to the end of the Back Harlow Road in my almost new Ford van and getting out of it some bright summer morning, all by myself, my wife and children far off in another world where, if you turn a switch, lights come on in the dark. I've thought about how it would be. Pulling my pack out of the back and resting it on the customized van's rear bumper while I carefully remove my shirt and tie it around my waist. Rubbing my chest and shoulders with Muskol insect repellent and then crashing through the woods to where that boggy place was, the place where we found him. Would the grass grow up yellow there, in the shape of his body? Of course not, there would be no sign, but still you wonder, and you realize what a thin film there is between your rational man costume — the writer with leather elbow-patches on his corduroy jacket — and the capering, Gorgon myths of childhood. Then climbing the embankment, now overgrown with weeds, and walking slowly beside the rusted tracks and rotted ties towards Chamberlain.

Stupid fantasy. An expedition looking for a fourteen-year-old blueberry pail, which was probably cast deep into the woods or ploughed under by a bulldozer readying a half-acre plot for a tract house or so deeply overgrown by weeds and brambles it had become invisible. But I feel sure it is still there, somewhere along the old discontinued GS&WM line, and at times the urge to go and look is almost a frenzy.

It usually comes early in the morning, when my wife is showering and the kids are watching *Batman* and *Scooby-Doo* on channel 38 out of Boston, and I am feeling the most like the pre-adolescent Gordon Lachance that once strode the earth, walking and talking and occasionally crawling on his belly like a reptile. That boy was *me*, I think. And the thought which follows, chilling me like a dash of cold water, is: *Which boy do you mean?*

Sipping a cup of tea, looking at sun slanting through the kitchen windows, hearing the TV from one end of the house and the shower from the other, feeling the pulse behind my eyes that means I got through one beer too many the night before, I feel sure I could find it. I would see clear metal winking through rust, the bright summer sun reflecting it back to my eyes. I would go down the side of the embankment, push aside the grasses that had grown up and twined toughly around its handle, and then I would . . . what? Why, simply pull it out of time. I would turn it over and over in my hands, wondering at the feel of it, marvelling at the knowledge that the last person to touch it had been long years in his grave. Suppose there was a note in it? *Help me, I'm lost.* Of course there wouldn't be – boys don't go out to pick blueberries with paper and pencil – but just suppose. I imagine the awe I'd feel would be as dark as an eclipse. Still, it's mostly just the idea of holding that pail in my two hands, I guess – as much a symbol of my living as his dying, proof that I really do know which boy it was – which boy of the five of us. Holding it. Reading every year in its cake of rust and the fading of its bright shine. Feeling it, trying to understand the suns that shone on it, the rains that fell on it, and the snows that covered it. And to wonder where

I was when each thing happened to it in its lonely place, where I was, what I was doing, who I was loving, how I was getting along, where I was. I'd hold it, read it, feel it . . . and look at my own face in whatever reflection might be left. Can you dig it?

29

We got back to Castle Rock a little past five o'clock on Sunday morning, the day before Labour Day. We had walked all night. Nobody complained, although we all had blisters and were all ravenously hungry. My head was throbbing with a killer headache, and my legs felt twisted and burning with fatigue. Twice we had to scramble down the embankment to get out of the way of freights. One of them was going our way, but moving far too fast to hop. It was seeping daylight when we got to the trestle spanning the Castle again. Chris looked at it, looked at the river, looked back at us.

'Fuck it. I'm walkin' across. If I get hit by a train I won't have to watch out for fuckin' Ace Merrill.'

We all walked across it – plodded might be the better verb. No train came. When we got to the dump we climbed the fence (no Milo and no Chopper, not this early, and not on a Sunday morning) and went directly to the pump. Vern primed it and we all took turns sticking our heads under the icy flow, slapping the water over our bodies, drinking until we could hold no more. Then we had to put our shirts on again because the morning seemed chilly. We walked – limped – back into town and stood for a moment on the sidewalk in front of the vacant lot. We looked at our treehouse so we wouldn't have to look at each other.

'Well,' Teddy said at last, 'seeya in school on Wednesday. I think I'm gonna sleep until then.'

'Me too,' Vern said. 'I'm too pooped to pop.'

Chris whistled tunelessly through his teeth and said nothing.

'Hey, man,' Teddy said awkwardly. 'No hard feelin's, okay?'

'No,' Chris said, and suddenly his sombre, tired face broke into a sweet and sunny grin. 'We did it, didn't we? We did the bastard.'

'Yeah,' Vern said. 'Your fuckin' A. Now Billy's gonna do *me*.'

'So what?' Chris said. 'Richie's gonna tool up on me and Ace is probably gonna tool up on Gordie and somebody else'll tool up on Teddy. But we *did* it.'

'That's right,' Vern said. But he still sounded unhappy.

Chris looked at me. 'We did it, didn't we?' he asked softly. 'It was worth it, wasn't it?'

'Sure it was,' I said.

'Fuck this,' Teddy said in his dry I'm-losing-interest way. 'You guys sound like fuckin' *Meet the Press*. Gimme some skin, man. I'm gonna toot home and see if Mom's got me on the Ten Most Wanted list.'

We all laughed, Teddy gave us his surprised Oh-Lord-what-now look, and we gave him skin. Then he and Vern started off in their direction and I should have gone in mine . . . but I hesitated for a second.

'Walk with you,' Chris offered.

'Sure, okay.'

We walked a block or so without talking. Castle Rock was awesomely quiet in the day's first light, and I felt an almost holy tiredness-is-slipping-away sort of feeling. We were awake and the whole world was asleep and I almost expected to turn the corner and see my deer standing at the far end of Carbine Street, where the GS&WM tracks pass through the mill's loading yard.

Finally Chris spoke. 'They'll tell,' he said.

'You bet they will. But not today or tomorrow, if that's what you're worried about. It'll be a long time before they tell, I think. Years, maybe.'

He looked at me, surprised.

'They're scared, Chris. Teddy especially, that they won't take him in the army. But Vern's scared, too. They'll lose some sleep over it, and there's gonna be times this fall when it's right on the tips of their tongues to tell somebody, but I don't think they will. And then . . . you know what? It sounds fucking crazy, but . . . I think they'll almost forget it ever happened.'

He was nodding slowly. 'I didn't think of it just like that. You see through people, Gordie.'

'Man, I wish I did.'

'You do, though.'

We walked another block in silence.

'I'm never gonna get out of this town,' Chris said, and sighed. 'When you come back from college on summer vacation, you'll be able to look me and Vern and Teddy up down at Sukey's after the seven-to-three shift's over. If you want to. Except you'll probably never want to.' He laughed a creepy laugh.

'Quit jerking yourself off,' I said, trying to sound tougher than I felt — I was thinking about being out there in the woods, about Chris saying: *And maybe I took it to old lady*

Simons and told her, and maybe I got a three-day vacation anyway, because the money never showed up . . . and maybe the next week old lady Simons had this brand-new skirt on when she came to school . . . The look. The look in his eyes.

'No jerk-off, daddy-O,' Chris said.

I rubbed my first finger against my thumb. 'This is the world's smallest violin playing "My Heart Pumps Purple Piss for You".'

'He was *ours*,' Chris said, his eyes dark in the morning light.

We had reached the corner of my street and we stopped there. It was quarter past six. Back towards town we could see the Sunday *Telegram* truck pulling up in front of Teddy's uncle's stationery shop. A man in bluejeans and a tee-shirt threw off a bundle of papers. They bounced upside down on the sidewalk, showing the colour funnies (always Dick Tracey and Blondie on the first page). Then the truck drove on, its driver intent on delivering the outside world to the rest of the whistlestops up the line – Otisfield, Norway-South Paris, Waterford, Stoneham. I wanted to say something more to Chris and didn't know how to.

'Gimme some skin, man,' he said, sounding tired.

'Chris –'

'Skin.'

I gave him some skin. 'I'll see you.'

He grinned – that same sweet, sunny grin. 'Not if I see you first, fuckface.'

He walked off, still laughing, moving easily and gracefully, as though he didn't hurt like me and have blisters like me and like he wasn't lumped and bumped with mosquito and chigger and blackfly bites like me. As if he didn't have a care in the world, as if he was going to some real boss place instead of just home to a three-room house (shack would have been closer to the truth) with no indoor plumbing and broken windows covered with plastic and a brother who was probably laying for him in the front yard. Even if I'd known the right thing to say, I probably couldn't have said it. Speech destroys the functions of love, I think – that's a hell of a thing for a writer to say, I guess, but I believe it to be true. If you speak to tell a deer you mean it no harm, it glides away with a single flip of its tail. The word is the harm. Love isn't what these asshole poets like McKuen want you to think it is. Love has teeth; they bite; the wounds never close. No word, no combination of words, can close those lovebites. It's the other way around, that's the joke. If those wounds dry up, the words die with them. Take it from me. I've made my life from the words, and I know that is so.

30

The back door was locked so I fished the spare key out from under the mat and let myself in. The kitchen was empty, silent, suicidally clean. I could hear the hum the fluorescent bars over the sink made when I turned on the switch. It had been literally years since I had been up before my mother; I couldn't even remember the last time such a thing had happened.

I took off my shirt and put it in the plastic clothesbasket behind the washing machine. I got a clean rag from under the sink and sponged off with it – face, neck, pits, belly. Then I unzipped my pants and scrubbed my crotch – my testicles in particular – until my skin began to hurt. It seemed I couldn't get clean enough down there, although the red weal left by the bloodsucker was rapidly fading. I still have a tiny crescent-shaped scar there. My wife once asked about it and I told her a lie before I was even aware I meant to do so.

When I was done with the rag, I threw it away. It was filthy.

I got out a dozen eggs and scrambled six of them together. When they were semi-solid in the pan, I added a side dish of crushed pineapple and half a quart of milk. I was just sitting down to eat when my mother came in, her grey hair tied in a knot behind her head. She was wearing a faded pink bathrobe and smoking a Camel.

'Gordon, where have you been?'

'Camping,' I said, and began to eat. 'We started off in Vern's field and then went up the Brickyard Hill. Vern's mom said she would call you. Didn't she?'

'She probably talked to your father,' she said, and glided past me to the sink. She looked like a pink ghost. The fluorescent bars were less than kind to her face; they made her complexion look almost yellow. She sighed . . . almost sobbed. 'I miss Dennis most in the mornings,' she said. 'I always look in his room and it's always empty, Gordon. Always.'

'Yeah, that's a bitch,' I said.

'He always slept with his window open and the blankets . . . Gordon? Did you say something?'

'Nothing important, Mom.'

'. . . and the blankets pulled up to his chin,' she finished. Then she just stared out the window, her back to me. I went on eating. I was trembling all over.

31

The story never did get out.

Oh, I don't mean that Ray Brower's body was never found; it was. But neither our gang not their gang got the credit. In the end, Ace must have decided that an anonymous phonecall was the safest course, because that's how the location of the corpse was reported. What I mean was that none of our parents ever found out what we'd been up to that Labour Day weekend.

Chris's dad was still drinking, just as Chris had said he would be. His mom had gone off to Lewiston to stay with her sister, the way she almost always did when Mr Chambers was on a bender. She went and left Eyeball in charge of the younger kids. Eyeball had fulfilled his responsibility by going off with Ace and his jd buddies, leaving nine-year-old Sheldon, five-year-old Emery, and two-year-old Deborah to sink or swim on their own.

Teddy's mom got worried the second night and called Vern's mom. Vern's mom, who was also never going to do the gameshow circuit, said we were still out in Vern's tent. She knew because she could look right out the kitchen window and see a light on in there. Teddy's mom said she sure hoped no one was smoking cigarettes in there and Vern's mom said it looked like a flashlight to her, and besides, she was sure that none of Vern's or Billy's friends smoked.

My dad asked me some vague questions, looked mildly troubled at my evasive answers, said we'd go fishing together sometime, and that was the end of it. If the parents had gotten together in the week or two afterwards, everything would have fallen down . . . but they never did.

Milo Pressman never spoke up, either. My guess is that he thought twice about it being our word against his, and how we would all swear that he sicced Chopper on me.

So the story never came out – but that wasn't the end of it.

32

One day near the end of the month, while I was walking home from school, a black 1952 Ford cut into the kerb in front of me. There was no mistaking that car. Gangster white-walls and spinner hubcaps, highrise chrome bumpers and lucite deathknob with a rose embedded in it clamped to the steering wheel. Painted on the back deck was a deuce and a one-eyed jack. Beneath them, in Roman Gothic script, were the words WILD CARD.

The doors flew open; Ace Merrill and Fuzzy Brackowicz stepped out.

'Cheap hood, right?' Ace said, smiling his gentle smile. 'My mother loves the way I do it to her, right?'

'We're gonna rack you, baby,' Fuzzy said.

I dropped my schoolbooks on the sidewalk and ran. I was busting my buns but they caught me before I even made the end of the block. Ace hit me with a flying tackle and I went full-length on the paving. My chin hit the cement and I didn't see stars; I saw whole constellations, whole nebulae. I was already crying when they picked me up, not so much from my elbows and knees, both pairs scraped and bleeding, or even from fear – it was vast, impotent rage that made me cry. Chris was right. He had been ours.

I twisted and turned and almost squiggled free. Then

Fuzzy hoicked his knee into my crotch. The pain was amazing, incredible, nonpareil; it widened the horizons of pain from plain old wide screen to VistaVision. I began to scream. Screaming seemed to be my best chance.

Ace punched me twice in the face, long and looping haymaker blows. The first one closed my left eye; it would be four days before I was really able to see out of that eye again. The second broke my nose with a crunch that sounded the way crispy cereal sounds inside your head when you chew. Then old Mrs Chalmers came out on her porch with her cane clutched in one arthritis-twisted hand and a Herbert Tareyton jutting from one corner of her mouth. She began to bellow at them:

'Hi! Hi there, you boys! You stop that! Let 'im alone! Let 'im up! Bullies! Bullies! *Two on one! Police! Poleeeece!*'

'Don't let me see you around, dipshit,' Ace said, smiling, and they let go of me and backed off. I sat up and then leaned over, cupping my wounded balls, sickly sure I was going to throw up and then die. I was still crying, too. But when Fuzzy started to walk around me, the sight of his pegged jeans-leg snugged down over the top of his motor-cycle boot brought all the fury back. I grabbed him and bit his calf through his jeans. I bit him just as hard as I could. Fuzzy began to do a little screaming of his own. He also began hopping around on one leg, and, incredibly, he was calling me a dirty fighter. I was watching him hop around and that was when Ace stamped down on my left hand, breaking the first two fingers. I heard them break. They didn't sound like crispy cereal. They sounded like pretzels. Then Ace and Fuzzy were going back to Ace's '52, Ace sauntering with his hands in his back pockets, Fuzzy hopping on one leg and throwing curses back over his shoulder at me. I curled up on the sidewalk, crying. Aunt Evvie Chalmers came down her walk, thudding her cane angrily as she came. She asked me if I needed the doctor. I sat up and managed to stop most of the crying. I told her I didn't.

'Bullshit,' she bellowed – Aunt Evvie was deaf and bellowed everything. 'I saw where that bully got you. Boy, your sweetmeats are going to swell up to the size of Mason jars.'

She took me into her house, gave me a wet rag for my nose – it had begun to resemble a summer squash by then – and gave me a big cup of medicinal-tasting coffee that was somehow calming. She kept bellowing at me that she should call the doctor and I kept telling her not to. Finally she gave up and I walked home. Very slowly, I walked home. My balls weren't the size of Mason jars yet, but they were on their way.

My mom and dad got a look at me and wigged right out – I was sort of surprised that they noticed anything at all, to tell the truth. Who were the boys? Could I pick them out of a line-up? That from my father, who never missed *Naked City* and *The Untouchables*. I said I didn't think I could pick the boys out of a line-up. I said I was tired. Actually I think I was in shock – in shock and more than a little drunk from Aunt Evvie's coffee, which must have been at least sixty per cent VSOP brandy. I said I thought they were from some other town, or from 'up the city' – a phrase everyone understood to mean Lewiston-Auburn.

They took me to Dr Clarkson in the station wagon – Dr Clarkson, who is still alive today, was even then old enough to have quite possibly been on armchair-to-armchair terms with God. He set my nose and my fingers and gave my mother a prescription for painkiller. Then he got them out of the examining room on some pretext or other and came over to me, shuffling, head forward, like Boris Karloff approaching Igor.

'Who did it, Gordon?'

'I don't know, Dr Cla –'

'You're lying.'

'No, sir. Huh-uh.'

His sallow cheeks began to glow with colour. 'Why should you protect the cretins who did this? Do you think they will respect you? They will laugh and call you stupid-fool! "Oh," they'll say, "there goes the stupid fool we beat up for kicks the other day. Ha-ha! Hoo-hoo! Har-de-har-har-har!"'

'I didn't know them. Really.'

I could see his hands itching to shake me, but of course he couldn't do that. So he sent me out to my parents, shaking his white head and muttering about juvenile delinquents. He would no doubt tell his old friend God all about it that night over their cigars and sherry.

I didn't care if Ace and Fuzzy and the rest of those assholes respected me or thought I was stupid or never thought about me at all. But there was Chris to think of. His brother Eyeball had broken his arm in two places and had left his face looking like a Canadian sunrise. They had to set the elbow-break with a steel pin. Mrs McGinn from down the road saw Chris staggering along the soft shoulder, bleeding from both ears and reading a Richie Rich comic book. She took him to the CMG Emergency Room where Chris told the doctor he had fallen down the cellar stairs in the dark.

'Right,' the doctor said, every bit as disgusted with Chris

as Dr Clarkson had been with me, and then he went to call Sheriff Bannerman.

While he did that from his office, Chris went slowly down the hall, holding the temporary sling against his chest so the arm wouldn't swing and grate the broken bones together, and used a nickel in the pay phone to call home – he told me later it was the first collect call he had ever made and he was scared to death that Mrs McGinn wouldn't accept the charges – but she did.

'Chris, are you all right?' she asked.

'Yes, thank you,' Chris said.

'I'm sorry I couldn't stay with you, Chris, but I had pies in the –'

'That's all right, Missus McGinn,' Chris said. 'Can you see the Buick in our dooryard?' The Buick was the car Chris's mother drove. It was ten years old and when the engine got hot it smelled like frying Hush Puppies.

'It's there,' she said cautiously. Best not to mix in too much with the Chamberses. Poor white trash; shanty Irish.

'Would you go over and tell Mamma to go downstairs and take the lightbulb out of the socket in the cellar?'

'Chris, I really, my pies –'

'Tell her,' Chris said implacably, 'to do it right away. Unless she maybe wants my brother to go to jail.'

Vern and Teddy took their lumps, too, although not as bad as either Chris or I. Billy was laying for Vern when Vern got home. He took after him with a stovelength and hit him hard enough to knock him unconscious after only four or five good licks. Vern was no more than stunned, but Billy got scared he might have killed him and stopped. Three of them caught Teddy walking home from the vacant lot one afternoon. They punched him out and broke his glasses. He fought them, but they wouldn't fight him when they realized he was groping after them like a blindman in the dark.

We hung out together at school looking like the remains of a Korean assault force. Nobody knew exactly what had happened, but everybody understood that we'd had a pretty serious run-in with the big kids and comported ourselves like men. A few stories went around. All of them were wildly wrong.

When the casts came off and the bruises healed, Vern and Teddy just drifted away. They had discovered a whole new group of contemporaries that they could lord it over. Most of them were real wets – scabby, scrubby little fifth-grade assholes – but Vern and Teddy kept bringing them to the treehouse, ordering them around, strutting like Nazi generals.

Chris and I began to drop by there less and less frequently, and after a while the place was theirs by default. I remember going up one time in the spring of 1961 and noticing that the place smelled like a shootoff in a haymow. I never went there again that I can recall. Teddy and Vern slowly became just two more faces in the halls or in 3.30 detention. We nodded and said hi. That was all. It happens. Friends come in and out of your life like busboys in a restaurant, did you ever notice that? But when I think of that dream, the corpses under the water pulling implacably at my legs, it seems right that it should be that way. Some people drown, that's all. It's not fair, but it happens. Some people drown.

33

Vern Tessio was killed in a housefire that swept a Lewiston apartment building in 1966 – in Brooklyn and the Bronx, they call that sort of apartment building a slum tenement, I believe. The Fire Department said it started around two in the morning, and the entire building was nothing but cinders in the cellar-hole by dawn. There had been a large drunken party; Vern was there. Someone fell asleep in one of the bedrooms with a live cigarette going. Vern himself, maybe, drifting off, dreaming of his pennies. They identified him and the four others who died by their teeth.

Teddy went in a squalid car crash. There used to be a saying when I was growing up: 'If you go out alone you're a hero. Take somebody else with you and you're dogpiss.' Teddy, who had wanted nothing but the service since the time he was old enough to want anything, was turned down by the Air Force and classified 4-F by the draft. Anyone who had seen his glasses and his hearing aid knew it was going to happen – anyone but Teddy. In his junior year at high school he got a three-day vacation from school for calling the guidance counsellor a lying sack of shit. The g.c. had observed Teddy coming in every so often – like every day – and checking over his career-board for new service literature. He told Teddy that maybe he should think about another career, and that was when Teddy blew his stack.

He was held back a year for repeated absences, tardies, and the attendant flunked courses . . . but he *did* graduate. He had an ancient Chevrolet Bel Aire, and he used to hang around the places where Ace and Fuzzy and the rest had hung around before him: the pool hall, the dance hall, Sukey's Tavern, which is closed now, and the Mellow Tiger, which isn't. He eventually got a job with the Castle Rock Public Works Department, filling up holes with hotpatch.

The crash happened over in Harlow. Teddy's Bel Aire was

full of his friends (two of them had been part of that group he and Vern took to bossing around way back in 1960), and they were all passing around a couple of joints and a couple of bottles of Popov. They hit a utility pole and sheared it off and the Chevrolet rolled six times. One girl came out technically still alive. She lay for six months in what the nurses and orderlies at Central Maine General call the C&T Ward – Cabbages and Turnips. Then some merciful phantom pulled the plug on her respirator. Teddy Duchamp was posthumously awarded the Dogpiss of the Year Award.

Chris enrolled in the college courses in his second year of junior high – he and I both knew that if he waited any longer it would be too late; he would never catch up. Everyone jawed at him about it: his parents, who thought he was putting on airs, his friends, most of whom dismissed him as a pussy, the guidance counsellor, who didn't believe he could do the work, and most of all the teachers, who didn't approve of this duck-tailed, leather-jacketed, engineer-booted apparition who had materialized without warning in their classrooms. You could see that the sight of those boots and that many-zippered jacket offended them in connection with such high-minded subjects as algebra, Latin, and earth science; such attire was meant for the shop courses only. Chris sat among the well-dressed, vivacious boys and girls from the middle-class families in Castle View and Brickyard Hill like some silent, brooding Grendel that might turn on them at any moment, produce a horrible roaring like the sound of dual glasspack mufflers, and gobble them up, penny loafers, Peter Pan collars, button-down paisley shirts and all.

He almost quit a dozen times that year. His father in

particular hounded him, accusing Chris of thinking he was better than his old man, accusing Chris of wanting 'to go up there to the college so you can turn me into a bankrupt.' He once broke a Rhinegold bottle over the back of Chris's head and Chris wound up in the CMG Emergency Room again, where it took four stitches to close his scalp. His old friends, most of whom were now majoring in Smoking Area, catcalled him on the streets. The guidance counsellor huckstered him to take at least *some* shop courses so he wouldn't flunk the whole slate. Worst of all, of course, was just this: he'd been fucking off for the entire first seven years of his public education, and now the bill had come due with a vengeance.

We studied together almost every night, sometimes for as long as six hours at a stretch. I always came away from those sessions exhausted, and sometimes I came away frightened as well – frightened by his incredulous rage at just how murderously high that bill was. Before he could even begin to understand Introductory Algebra, he had to relearn the fractions that he and Teddy and Vern had played pocket pool through in the fifth grade. Before he could even begin to understand *Pater noster qui est in caelis,* he had to be told what nouns and prepositions and objects were. On the inside of his English grammar, neatly lettered, were the words FUCK GERUNDS. His compositional ideas were good and not badly organized, but his grammar was bad and he approached the whole business of punctuation as if with a shotgun. He wore out his copy of Warriner's and bought another in a Portland bookstore – it was the first hardcover book he actually owned, and it became a queer sort of Bible to him.

But by our junior year in high school, he had been accepted. Neither of us made top honours, but I came out seventh and Chris stood nineteenth. We were both accepted at the University of Maine, but I went to the Orono campus while Chris enrolled at the Portland campus. Pre-law, can you believe that? More Latin.

We both dated through high school, but no girl ever came between us. Does that sound like we went faggot? It would have to most of our old friends, Vern and Teddy included. But it was only survival. We were clinging to each other in deep water. I've explained about Chris, I think; my reasons for clinging to him were less definable. His desire to get away from Castle Rock and out of the mill's shadow seemed to me to be my best part, and I could not just leave him to sink or swim on his own. If he had drowned, that part of me would have drowned with him, I think.

Near the end of the spring semester in 1968, the year when we all grew our hair long and cut classes to go to teach-ins about the war in Viet Nam, Chris went into a Chicken Delight to get a three-piece Snack Bucket. Just ahead of him, two men started arguing about which one had been first in line. One of them pulled a knife. Chris, who had always been the best of us at making peace, stepped between them and was stabbed in the throat. The man with the knife had spent time in four different institutions; he had been released from Shawshank Penitentiary only the week before. Chris died almost instantly.

I was out of school when I read about it in the paper – Chris had been finishing his second year of graduate studies. Me, I had been married a year and a half and was teaching high school English. My wife was pregnant and I was trying to write a book. When I read the news item – STUDENT FATALLY STABBED IN PORTLAND RESTAURANT – I told my wife I was going out for a milkshake. I drove out of town, parked, and cried for him. Cried for damn near half an hour, I guess. I couldn't have done that in front of my wife, much as I love her. It would have been pussy.

34

Me?

'I'm a writer now, like I said. A lot of the critics think what I write is shit. A lot of the time I think they are right . . . but it still freaks me out to put those words, 'Freelance Writer', down in the *Occupation* blank of the forms you have to fill out at credit desks and in doctors' offices. My story sounds so much like a fairytale that it's fucking absurd.

I sold the book and it was made into a movie and the movie got good reviews and it was a smash hit besides. This all had happened by the time I was twenty-six. The second book was made into a movie as well, as was the third. I told you – it's fucking absurd. Meantime, my wife doesn't seem to mind having me around the house and we have three kids now. They all seem perfect to me, and most of the time I'm happy.

But the writing isn't so easy or as much fun as it used to be. The phone rings a lot. Sometimes I get headaches, bad ones, and then I have to go into a dim room and lie down until they go away. The doctor says they aren't true migraines; he called them 'stressaches' and told me to slow down. I worry about myself sometimes. What a stupid habit that is . . . and yet I can't quite seem to stop it. And I wonder if there is really any point in what I'm doing, or what I'm supposed to make of a world where a man can get rich playing 'let's pretend'.

But it's funny how I saw Ace Merrill again. My friends are dead but Ace is alive. I saw him pulling out of the mill parking lot just after the three o'clock whistle the last time I took my kids down home to see my dad.

The '52 Ford had become a '77 Ford station wagon. A faded bumper-sticker said REAGAN/BUSH 1980. His hair was mowed into a crewcut and he'd gotten fat. The sharp, handsome features I remembered were now buried in an avalanche of flesh. I had left the kids with dad long enough to go downtown and get the paper. I was standing on the corner of Main and Carbine and he glanced at me as I waited to cross. There was no sign of recognition on the face of this thirty-two-year-old man who had broken my nose in another dimension of time.

I watched him wheel the Ford wagon into the dirt parking lot beside the Mellow Tiger, get out, hitch at his pants, and walk inside. I could imagine the brief wedge of country-western as he opened the door, the brief sour whiff of Knick and Gansett on draught, the welcoming shouts of the other regulars as he closed the door and placed his large ass on the same stool which had probably held him up for at least three hours every day of his life – except Sundays – since he was twenty-one.

I thought: *So that's what Ace is now.*

I looked to the left, and beyond the mill I could see the Castle River, not so wide now but a little cleaner, still flowing under the bridge between Castle Rock and Harlow. The trestle upstream is gone now, but the river is still around. So am I.

A Winter's Tale

THE BREATHING METHOD

For Peter and Susan Straub

1: The Club

I dressed a bit more speedily than normal on that snowy, windy, bitter night – I admit it. It was 23 December, 197–, and I suspect that there were other members of the club who did the same. Taxis are notoriously hard to come by in New York on stormy nights, so I called for a radio-cab. I did this at five-thirty for an eight o'clock pick-up – my wife raised an eyebrow but said nothing. I was under the awning of the apartment building on East 58th Street, where Ellen and I had lived since 1946, by quarter to eight, and when the taxi was five minutes late, I found myself pacing up and down impatiently.

The taxi arrived at 8.10 and I got in, too glad to be out of the wind to be as angry with the driver as he probably deserved. That wind, part of a cold front that had swept down from Canada the day before, meant business. It whistled and whined around the cab's window, occasionally drowning out the salsa on the driver's radio and rocking the big Checker on its springs. Many of the stores were open but the side-walks were nearly bare of last-minute shoppers. Those that were abroad looked uncomfortable or actually pained.

It had been flurrying off and on all day, and now the snow began again, coming first in thin membranes, then twisting into cyclone shapes ahead of us in the street. Coming home that night, I would think of the combination of snow, a taxi, and New York City with considerably greater unease . . . but I did not of course know that then.

At the corner of 3rd and Fortieth, a large tinsel Christmas bell went floating through the intersection like a spirit.

'Bad night,' the cabbie said. 'They'll have an extra two dozen in the morgue tomorrow. Wino Popsicles. Plus a few bag-lady Popsicles.'

'I suppose.'

The cabbie ruminated. 'Well, good riddance,' he said finally. 'Less welfare, right?'

'Your Christmas spirit,' I said, 'is stunning in its width and depth.'

The cabbie ruminated. 'You one of those bleeding-heart liberals?' he asked finally.

'I refuse to answer on the grounds that my answer might tend to incriminate me,' I said. The cabbie gave a why-do-I-always-get-the-wisenheimers snort . . . but he shut up.

He let me out at 2nd and Thirty-Fifth, and I walked halfway down the block to the club, bent over against the whistling wind, holding my hat on my head with one gloved hand. In almost no time at all the life-force seemed to have been driven deep into my body, a flickering blue flame about the size of the pilot-light in a gas oven. At seventy-three, a man feels the cold quicker and deeper. That man should be home in front of a fireplace . . . or at least in front of an electric heater. At seventy-three, hot blood isn't even really a memory; it's more of an academic concept.

The latest flurry was letting up, but snow as dry as sand still beat into my face. I was glad to see that the steps leading up to the door of 249 had been sanded – that was Stevens's work, of course – Stevens knew the base alchemy of old age well enough: not lead into gold but bones into glass.

When I think about such things, I believe that God probably thinks a great deal like Groucho Marx.

Then Stevens was there, holding the door open, and a
moment later I was inside. Down the mahogany-panelled
hallway, through double doors standing three-quarters of the
way open on their recessed tracks, into the library *cum* reading-
room *cum* bar. It was a dark room in which occasional pools
of light gleamed – reading-lamps. A richer, more textured
light glowed across the oak parquet floor, and I could hear
the steady snap of birch logs in the huge fireplace. The heat
radiated all the way across the room – surely there is no
welcome for a man or a woman that can equal a fire on the
hearth. A paper rustled – dry, slightly impatient. That would
be Johanssen, with his *Wall Street Journal*. After ten years, it
was possible to recognize his presence simply by the way he
read his stocks. Amusing . . . and in a quiet way, amazing.

Stevens helped me off with my overcoat, murmuring that
it was a dirty night; WCBS was now forecasting heavy snow
before morning.

I agreed that it was indeed a dirty night and looked back
into that big, high-ceilinged room again. A dirty night, a
roaring fire . . . and a ghost story. Did I say that at seventy-
three hot blood is a thing of the past? Perhaps so. But I felt
something warm in my chest at the thought . . . something
that hadn't been caused by the fire of Stevens's reliable, digni-
fied welcome.

I think it was because it was McCarron's turn to tell the
tale.

I had been coming to the brownstone which stands at 249
East 35th Street for ten years – coming at intervals that were

almost – but not quite – regular. In my own mind I think of it as a 'gentleman's club', that amusing pre-Gloria Steinem antiquity. But even now I am not sure that's what it really is, or how it came to be in the first place.

On the night Emlyn McCarron told his story – the story of the Breathing Method – there were perhaps thirteen club-members in all, although only six of us had come out on that howling, bitter night. I can remember years when there might have been as few as eight full-time members, and others when there were at least twenty, and perhaps more.

I suppose Stevens might know how it all came to be – one thing I *am* sure of is that Stevens has been there from the first, no matter how long that may be . . . and I believe Stevens to be older than he looks. Much, *much* older. He has a faint Brooklyn accent, but in spite of that he is as brutally correct and as cuttingly punctilious as a third-gener-ation English butler. His reserve is part of his often maddening charm, and Stevens's small smile is a locked and latched door. I have never seen any club records – if he keeps them. I have never gotten a receipt of dues – there are no dues. I have never been called by the club secretary – there is no secretary, and at 249 East 35th, there are no phones. There is no box of white marbles and black balls. And the club – if it *is* a club – has never had a name.

I first came to the club (as I must continue to call it) as the guest of George Waterhouse. Waterhouse headed the law firm for which I had worked since 1951. My progress upward in the firm – one of New York's three biggest – had been steady but extremely slow; I was a slogger, a mule for work, something of a centrepuncher . . . but I had no real flair or genius. I had seen men who had begun at the same time I had, promoted in giant steps while I only continued to pace – and I saw it with no real surprise.

Waterhouse and I had exchanged pleasantries, attended the obligatory dinner put on by the firm each October, and had little more congress until the fall of 196–, when he dropped by my office one day in early November.

This in itself was unusual enough, and it had me thinking black thoughts (dismissal) that were counterbalanced by giddy ones (an unexpected promotion). It was a puzzling visit. Waterhouse leaned in the doorway, his Phi Beta Kappa key gleaming mellowly on his vest, and talked in amiable generalities – none of what he said seemed to have any real substance or importance. I kept expecting him to finish the pleasantries and get down to cases: 'Now about this Casey brief,' or 'We've been asked to research the Mayor's appointment of Salkowitz to –' But it seemed there *were* no cases. He glanced at his watch, said he had enjoyed our talk and that he had to be going.

I was still blinking, bewildered, when he turned back and said casually: 'There's a place where I go most Thursday nights – a sort of club. Old duffers, mostly, but some of them are good company. They keep a really excellent cellar, if you've a palate. Every now and then someone tells a good story, as well. Why not come down some night, David? As my guest.'

I stammered some reply – even now I'm not sure what it was. I was bewildered by the offer. It had a spur-of-the-moment sound, but there was nothing spur-of-the-moment about his eyes, blue Anglo-Saxon ice under the bushy white whorls of his eyebrows. And if I don't remember exactly how I replied, it was because I felt suddenly sure that this offer – vague and puzzling as it was – had been exactly the specific I had kept expecting him to get down to.

Ellen's reaction that evening was one of amused exasperation. I had been with Waterhouse, Carden, Lawton, Frasier, and Effingham for something like twenty years, and it was clear enough that I could not expect to rise much above the mid-level position I now held; it was her idea that this was the firm's cost-efficient substitute for a gold watch.

'Old men telling war stories and playing poker,' she said. 'A night of that and you're supposed to be happy in the Research Library until they pension you off, I suppose . . . oh, I put two Becks' on ice for you.' And she kissed me warmly. I suppose she had seen something on my face – God knows she's good at reading me after all the years we've spent together.

Nothing happened over a course of weeks. When my mind turned to Waterhouse's odd offer – certainly odd coming from a man with whom I met less than a dozen times a year, and who I only saw socially at perhaps three parties a year, including the company party in October – I supposed that I had been mistaken about the expression in his eyes, that he really had made the offer casually, and had forgotten it. Or regretted it – ouch! And then he approached me one late afternoon, a man of nearly seventy who was still broad-shouldered and athletic looking. I was shrugging on my topcoat with my briefcase between my feet. He said: 'If you'd still like to have a drink at the club, why not come tonight?'

'Well . . . I . . .'

'Good.' He slapped a slip of paper into my hand. 'Here's the address.'

He was waiting for me at the foot of the steps that evening, and Stevens held the door for us. The wine was as excellent as Waterhouse had promised. He made no attempt whatsoever to 'introduce me around' – I took that for snobbery but later recanted the idea – but two or three of them introduced themselves to me. One of those who did so was Emlyn McCarron, even then in his early seventies. He held out his hand and I clasped it briefly. His skin was dry, leathery, tough; almost turtlelike. He asked me if I played bridge. I said I did not.

'God damned good thing,' he said. 'That god damned game has done more in this century to kill intelligent after-dinner conversation than anything else I can think of.' And with that pronouncement he walked away into the murk of the library, where shelves of books went up apparently to infinity.

I looked around for Waterhouse, but he had disappeared. Feeling a little uncomfortable and a lot out of place, I wandered over to the fireplace. It was, as I believe I have already mentioned, a huge thing – it seemed particularly huge in New York, where apartment-dwellers such as myself have trouble imagining such a benevolence big enough to do anything more than pop corn or toast bread. The fireplace at 249 East 35th was big enough to broil an ox whole. There was no mantle; instead a brawny stone arch curved over it. This arch was broken in the centre by a keystone which jutted out slightly. It was just on the level of my eyes, and although the light was dim, I could read the legend engraved on that stone with no trouble: *IT IS THE TALE, NOT HE WHO TELLS IT*.

'Here you go, David,' Waterhouse said from my elbow,

and I jumped. He hadn't deserted me after all; had only trudged off into some uncharted locale to bring back drinks. 'Bombay martini's yours, isn't it?'

'Yes. Thank you, Mr Waterhouse –'

'George,' he said. 'Here it's just George.'

'George, then,' I said, although it seemed slightly mad to be using his first name. 'What is all of –'

'Cheers,' he said.

We drank. The martini was perfect. I said so instead of finishing my question.

'Stevens tends the bar. He makes fine drinks. He likes to say it's a small but vital skill.'

The martini took the edge off my feelings of disorientation and awkwardness (the edge, but the feelings themselves remained – I had spent nearly half an hour gazing into my closet and wondering what to wear; I had finally settled on dark brown slacks and a rough tweed jacket that almost matched them, hoping I would not be wandering into a group of men either turned out in tuxedos or wearing bluejeans and L.L. Bean's lumberjack shirts . . . it seemed that I hadn't gone too far wrong on the matter of dress, anyway). A new place and a new situation makes one crucially aware of every social act, no matter how small, and at that moment, drink in hand and the obligatory small toast made, I wanted very much to be sure that I hadn't overlooked any of the amenities.

'Is there a guest book I ought to sign?' I asked. 'Something like that?'

He looked mildly surprised. 'We don't have anything like that,' he said. 'At least, I don't *think* we do.' He glanced around the dim, quiet room. Johanssen rattled his *Wall Street Journal*.

I saw Stevens pass in a doorway at the far end of the room, ghostly in his white messjacket. George put his drink on an endtable and tossed a fresh log onto the fire. Sparks corkscrewed up the black throat of the chimney.

'What does that mean?' I asked, pointing to the inscription on the keystone. 'Any idea?'

Waterhouse read it carefully, as if for the first time. *IT IS THE TALE, NOT HE WHO TELLS IT.*

'I suppose I have an idea,' he said. 'You may, too, if you should come back. Yes, I should say you may have an idea or two. In time. Enjoy yourself, David.'

He walked away. And, although it may seem odd, having been left to sink or swim in such an unfamiliar situation, I *did* enjoy myself. For one thing, I have always loved books, and there was a trove of interesting ones to examine here. I walked slowly along the shelves, examining the spines as best I could in the faint light, pulling one out now and then, and pausing once to look out a narrow window at the 2nd Avenue intersection up the street. I stood there and watched through the frost-rimmed glass as the traffic light at the intersection cycled from red to green to amber and back to red again, and quite suddenly I felt the queerest – and yet very welcome – sense of peace come to me. It did not flood in; instead it seemed to almost steal in. *Oh yes*, I can hear you saying, *that makes great sense: watching a stop-and-go light gives* everyone *a sense of peace.*

All right; it made *no* sense. I grant you that. But the feeling was there, just the same. It made me think for the first time in years of the winter nights in the Wisconsin farmhouse where I grew up: lying in bed in a draughty upstairs room and marking the contrast between the whistle of the January wind outside, drifting snow as dry as sand along miles of snowfence, and the warmth my body created under the two quilts.

There were some law books, but they were pretty damn strange: *Twenty Cases of Dismemberment and Their Outcomes under British Law* is one title I remember. *Pet Cases* was another. I opened that one and sure enough, it was a scholarly legal tome dealing with the law's treatment (American law, this time) of cases which bore in some important respect upon pets – everything from housecats that had inherited great sums of money to an ocelot that had broken its chain and seriously injured a postman.

There was a set of Dickens, a set of Defoe, a nearly endless set of Trollope; and there was also a set of novels – eleven of them – by a man named Edward Gray Seville. They were bound in handsome green leather, and the name of the firm gold-stamped on the spine was Stedham & Son. I had never heard of Seville nor of his publishers. The copyright date of the first Seville – *These Were Our Brothers* – was 1911. The date of the last, *Breakers*, was 1935.

Two shelves down from the set of Seville novels was a large folio volume which contained careful step by step plans for Erector Set enthusiasts. Next to it was another folio volume which featured famous scenes from famous movies. Each of these pictures filled one whole page, and opposite each, filling the facing pages, were free-verse poems either about the scenes with which they were paired or inspired by them. Not a very remarkable concept, but the poets who were represented *were* remarkable – Robert Frost, Marianne Moore, William Carlos Williams, Wallace Stevens, Louis Zukofsky, and Erica Jong, to mention just a few. Halfway through the book I found a poem by Archibald MacLeish set next to that famous photograph of Marilyn Monroe standing on the subway grating and trying to hold her skirt down. The poem was titled 'The Toll' and it began:

> The shape of the skirt is
> — we would say —
> the shape of a bell
> The legs are the clapper —

And some such more. Not a terrible poem, but certainly not MacLeish's best or anywhere near the top drawer. I felt I could hold such an opinion because I had read a good deal of Archibald MacLeish over the years. I could not, however, recall this poem about Marilyn Monroe (which it is; the poem announces it even when divorced from the picture — at the end MacLeish writes: *My legs clap my name:/Marilyn*, ma belle). I have looked for it since then and haven't been able to find it . . . which means nothing, of course. Poems are not like novels or legal opinions; they are more like blown leaves and any omnibus volume titled The Complete So-and-So must certainly be a lie. Poems have a way of getting lost under sofas — it is one of their charms, and one of the reasons they endure. But —

At some point Stevens came by with a second martini (by then I had settled into a chair of my own with a volume of Ezra Pound). It was as perfect as the first. As I sipped it I saw two of those present, George Gregson and Harry Stein (Harry was six years dead on the night Emlyn McCarron told us the story of the Breathing Method), leave the room by a peculiar door less than three feet high. It was an Alice Down the Rabbit-Hole door if ever there was one. They left it open, and shortly after their odd exit from the library I heard the muted click of billiard balls.

Stevens passed by and asked if I would like another martini. I declined with real regret. He nodded. 'Very good, sir.' His face never changed, and yet I had an obscure feeling that I had somehow pleased him.

Laughter startled me from my book sometime later. Someone had thrown a packet of chemical powder into the fire and turned the flames momentarily parti-coloured. I thought of my boyhood again . . . but not in any wistful, sloppily romantic-nostalgic way. I feel a great need to emphasize that, God knows why. I thought of times when I had done just such a thing as a kid, but the memory was a strong one, pleasant, untinged with regret.

I saw that most of the others had drawn chairs up around the hearth in a semi-circle. Stevens had produced a heaping, smoking platter of marvellous hot sausages. Harry Stein returned through the down-the-rabbit-hole door, introducing himself hurriedly but pleasantly to me. Gregson remained in the billiard room, practising shots, by the sound.

After a moment's hesitation I joined the others. A story was told — not a pleasant one. It was Norman Stett who told it, and while it is not my purpose to recount it here, perhaps you'll understand what I mean about its quality if I tell you that it was about a man who drowned in a telephone booth.

When Stett — who is also dead now — finished, someone said, 'You should have saved it for Christmas, Norman.' There was laughter, which I of course did not understand. At least, not then.

Waterhouse himself spoke up then, and such a Waterhouse

I never would have dreamed of in a thousand years of dreaming. A graduate of Yale, a Phi Beta Kappa, silver-haired, three-piece-suited head of a law firm so large it was more enterprise than company – *this* Waterhouse told a story that had to do with a teacher who had gotten stuck in a privy. The privy stood behind the one-room schoolhouse in which she had taught, and the day she got her caboose jammed into one of the privy's two holes also happened to be the day the privy was scheduled to be taken away as Anniston County's contribution to the Life As It Was in New England exhibition being held at the Prudential Center in Boston. The teacher hadn't made a sound during all the time it took to load the privy onto the back of a flatbed truck and to spike it down; she was struck dumb with embarrassment and horror, Waterhouse said. And then the privy door blew off into the passing lane of Route 128 in Somerville during rush hour –

But draw a curtain over that, and over any other stories which might have followed it; they are not my stories tonight. At some point Stevens produced a bottle of brandy that was more than just good; it was damned near exquisite. It was passed around and Johanssen raised a toast – *the* toast, one might almost say: The tale, not he who tells it.

We drank to that.

Not long after, men began slipping away. It wasn't late; not yet midnight, anyway; but I've noticed that when your fifties give way to your sixties, late begins coming earlier and earlier. I saw Waterhouse slipping his arms into the overcoat Stevens was holding open for him, and decided that must be my cue. I thought it strange that Waterhouse would slip away without so much as a word to me (which certainly seemed to be what he was doing; if I had come back from shelving the Pound book forty seconds later, he would have been gone), but no stranger than most of the other things that had gone on that evening.

I stepped out just behind him, and Waterhouse glanced around, as if surprised to see me . . . and almost as if he had been startled out of a light doze. 'Share a taxi?' he asked, as though we had just met by chance on this deserted, windy street.

'Thank you,' I said. I meant thanks for a great deal more than his offer to share a cab, and I believe that was unmistakable in my tone, but he nodded as if that was all I had meant. A taxi with its for-hire light lit was cruising slowly down the street – fellows like George Waterhouse seem to luck onto cabs even on those miserably cold or snowy New York nights when you would swear there isn't a cab to be had on the entire island of Manhattan – and he flagged it.

Inside, safely warm, the taxi-meter charting our journey in measured clicks, I told him how much I had enjoyed his story. I couldn't remember laughing so hard or so spontaneously since I was eighteen, I told him, which was not flattery but only the simple truth.

'Oh? How kind of you to say.' His voice was chillingly polite. I subsided, feeling a dull flush in my cheeks. One does not always need to hear a slam to know that the door has been closed.

When the taxi drew up to the kerb in front of my building, I thanked him again, and this time he showed a trifle more warmth. 'It was good of you to come on such short notice,' he said. 'Come again, if you like. Don't wait for an invitation; we don't stand much on ceremony at two-four-nine.

Thursdays are best for stories, but the club is there every night.'

Am I then to assume membership?

The question was on my lips. I meant to ask it; it seemed *necessary* to ask it. I was only mulling it over, listening to it in my head (in my tiresome lawyer's way) to hear if I had got the phrasing right – perhaps that was a little too blunt – when Waterhouse told the cabbie to drive on. The next moment the taxi was rolling on towards Madison. I stood there on the sidewalk for a moment, the hem of my topcoat whipping around my shins, thinking: *He knew I was going to ask that question – he knew it, and he purposely had the driver go on before I could.* Then I told myself that was utterly absurd – paranoid, even. And it was. But it was also true. I could scoff all I liked; none of the scoffing changed that essential certainty.

I walked slowly to the door of my building and went inside.

Ellen was sixty per cent asleep when I sat down on the bed to take off my shoes. She rolled over and made a fuzzy interrogative sound deep in her throat. I told her to go back to sleep.

She made the muzzy sound again. This time it approximated English: 'Howwuzzit?'

For a moment I hesitated, my shirt half-unbuttoned. And I thought with one moment's utter clarity: *If I tell her, I will never see the other side of that door again.*

'It was all right,' I said. 'Old men telling war stories.'

'I told you so.'

'But it wasn't bad. I might go back again. It might do me some good with the firm.'

'"The firm",' she mocked lightly. 'What an old buzzard you are, my love.'

'It takes one to know one,' I said, but she had already fallen asleep again. I undressed, showered, towelled, put on my pyjamas . . . and then, instead of going to bed as I should have done (it was edging past one by that time), I put on my robe and had another bottle of Beck's. I sat at the kitchen table, drinking it slowly, looking out the window and up the cold canyon of Madison Avenue, thinking. My head was a trifle buzzy from my evening's intake of alcohol – for me an unexpectedly large intake. But the feeling was not at all unpleasant, and I had no sense of an impending hangover.

The thought which had come to me when Ellen asked me about my evening was as ridiculous as the one I'd entertained about George Waterhouse as the cab drew away from me – what in God's name could be wrong with telling my wife about a perfectly harmless evening at my boss's stuffy men's club . . . and even if something *were* wrong with telling her, who would know that I had? No, it was every bit as ridiculous and paranoid as those earlier musings . . . and, my heart told me, every bit as true.

I met George Waterhouse the next day in the hallway between Accounts and the Reading Library. Met him . . . Passed him would be more accurate. He nodded my way and went on without speaking . . . as he had done for years.

My stomach muscles ached all day long. That was the only thing that completely convinced me the evening had been real.

★   ★   ★

Three weeks passed. Four . . . five. No second invitation came from Waterhouse. Somehow I just hadn't been right; hadn't fitted. Or so I told myself. It was a depressing, disappointing thought. I supposed it would begin to fade and lose its sting, as all disappointments eventually do. But I thought of that evening at the oddest moments – the isolated pools of library lamplight, so still and tranquil and somehow civilized; Waterhouse's absurd and hilarious tale of the schoolteacher stuck in the privy; the rich smell of leather in the narrow stacks. Most of all I thought of standing by that narrow window and watching the frost crystals change from green to amber to red. I thought of that sense of peace I had felt.

During that same five-week period I went to the library and checked out four volumes of Archibald MacLeish's poetry (I had three others myself, and had already checked through them); one of these volumes purported to be The Complete Poems of. I reacquainted myself with some old favourites, including my favourite MacLeish poem, 'Epistle to Be Left in Earth.' But I found no poem called 'The Toll' in any of the volumes.

On that same trip to the New York Public Library, I checked the card catalogue for works of fiction by a man named Edward Gray Seville. A mystery novel by a woman named Ruth Seville was the closest I came.

Come again, if you like; don't wait for an invitation . . .

I was waiting for an invitation anyway, of course; my mother taught me donkey's years ago not to automatically believe people who tell you glibly to 'drop by anytime' or that 'the door is always open'. I didn't feel I needed an engraved card delivered to my apartment door by a footman in livery bearing a gilt plate, I don't mean that, but I did want *something*, even if it was only a casual remark: 'Coming by some night, David? Hope we didn't bore you.' That kind of thing.

But when even that didn't come, I began to think more seriously about going back anyway – after all, sometimes people really *did* want you to drop in anytime; I supposed that, at some places, the door always *was* open; and that mothers weren't always right.

. . . don't wait for an invitation . . .

Anyway, that's how it happened that, on 10 December of that year, I found myself putting on my rough tweed coat and dark brown pants again and looking for my darkish red tie. I was rather more aware of my heartbeat than usual that night, I remember.

'George Waterhouse finally broke down and asked you back?' Ellen asked. 'Back into the sty with the rest of the male chauvinist oinkers?'

'That's right,' I said, thinking it must be the first time in at least a dozen years that I had told her a lie . . . and then I remembered that, after the first meeting, I had answered her questions about what it had been like with a lie. Old men telling war stories, I had said.

'Well, maybe there really *will* be a promotion in it,' she said . . . though without much hope. To her credit, she said it without much bitterness, either.

'Stranger things have happened,' I said, and kissed her goodbye.

'Oink-oink,' she said as I went out the door.

The taxi ride that night seemed very long. It was cold, still, and starry. The cab was a Checker and I felt somehow very small in it, like a child seeing the city for the first time.

It was excitement I was feeling as the cab pulled up in front of the brownstone – something as simple and yet complete as that. But such simple excitement seems to be one of life's qualities that slips away almost unnoticed, and its rediscovery as one grows older is always something of a surprise, like finding a black hair or two in one's comb years after one had last found such a thing.

I paid the driver, got out, and walked towards the four steps leading to the door. As I mounted them, my excitement curdled into plain apprehension (a feeling the old are much more familiar with). What exactly was I doing here?

The door was of thick panelled oak, and to my eye it looked as stout as the door of a castle keep. There was no doorbell that I could see, no knocker, no closed circuit TV camera mounted unobtrusively in the shadow of a deep eave, and, of course, no Waterhouse waiting to take me in. I stopped at the foot of the steps and looked around. Thirty-Fifth Street suddenly seemed darker, colder, more threatening. The brownstones all looked somehow secret, as if hiding mysteries best not investigated. Their windows looked like eyes.

Somewhere, behind one of those windows, there may be a man or woman contemplating murder, I thought. A shudder worked up my spine. *Contemplating it . . . or doing it.*

Then, suddenly, the door was open and Stevens was there.

I felt an intense surge of relief. I am not an overly imaginative man, I think – at least not under ordinary circumstances – but this last thought had had all the eerie clarity of prophecy. I might have babbled aloud if I hadn't glanced at Stevens's eyes first. His eyes did not know me. His eyes did not know me at all.

Then there was another instance of that eerie, prophetic clarity; I saw the rest of my evening in perfect detail. Three hours in a quiet bar. Three martinis (perhaps four) to dull the embarrassment of having been fool enough to go where I wasn't wanted. The humiliation my mother's advice had been intended to avoid – that which comes with knowing one has overstepped.

I saw myself going home a little tipsy, but not in a good way. I saw myself merely sitting through the cab ride rather than experiencing it through that childlike lens of excitement and anticipation. I heard myself saying to Ellen, *It wears thin after a while . . . Waterhouse told the same story about winning a consignment of T-bone steaks for the 3rd Battalion in a poker game . . . and they play Hearts for a dollar a point, can you believe it? . . . go back? . . . I suppose I might, but I doubt it.* And that would be the end of it. Except, I suppose, for my own humiliation.

I saw all of this in the nothing of Stevens's eyes. Then the eyes warmed. He smiled slightly and said: 'Mr Adley! Come in. I'll take your coat.'

I mounted the steps and Stevens closed the door firmly behind me. How different a door can feel when you are on the warm side of it! He took my coat and was gone with it. I stood in the hall for a moment, looking at my own reflection in the pier glass, a man of sixty-three whose face was rapidly becoming too gaunt to look middle-aged. And yet the reflection pleased me.

I slipped into the library.

Johanssen was there, reading his *Wall Street Journal.* In another island of light, Emlyn McCarron sat over a chessboard opposite Peter Andrews. McCarron was and is a cadaverous man, possessed of a narrow, bladelike nose; Andrews was huge, slope-shouldered, and choleric. A vast ginger-coloured beard sprayed over his vest. Face to face over the inlaid board with its carved pieces of ivory and ebony, they looked like Indian totems: eagle and bear.

Waterhouse was there, frowning over that day's *Times*. He glanced up, nodded at me without surprise, and disappeared into the paper again.

Stevens brought me a Bombay martini, unasked.

I took it into the stacks and found that puzzling, enticing set of green volumes again. I began reading the works of Edward Gray Seville that night. I started at the beginning, with *These Were Our Brothers*. Since then I have read them all, and believe them to be eleven of the finest novels of our century.

Near the end of the evening there was a story – just one – and Stevens brought brandy around. When the tale was told, people began to rise, preparing to leave. Stevens spoke from the double doorway which communicated with the hallway. His voice was low and pleasant, but carrying:

'Who will bring us a tale for Christmas, then?'

People stopped what they were doing and glanced around. There was some low, goodnatured talk and a burst of laughter.

Stevens, smiling but serious, clapped his hands together twice, like a grammar school teacher calling an unruly class to order. 'Come, gentlemen – who'll bring the tale?'

Peter Andrews, he of the sloped shoulders and gingery beard, cleared his throat. 'I have something I've been thinking about. I don't know if it's quite right; that is, if it's –'

'That will be fine,' Stevens interrupted, and there was

more laughter. Andrews had his back slapped good naturedly. Cold draughts swirled up the hallway as men slipped out.

Then Stevens was there, as if by benign magic, holding my coat for me. 'Good evening, Mr Adley. Always a pleasure.'

'Do you really meet on Christmas night?' I asked, buttoning my coat. I was a little disappointed that I was going to miss Andrews's story, but we had made firm plans to drive to Schenectady and keep the holiday with Ellen's sister.

Stevens managed to look both shocked and amused at the same time. 'In no case,' he said. 'Christmas is a night a man should spend with his family. That night, if no other. Don't you agree, sir?'

'I certainly do.'

'We always meet on the Thursday before Christmas. In fact, that is the one night of the year when we're assured a large turnout.'

He hadn't used the word *members*, I noticed – just happenstance or neat avoidance?

'Many tales have been spun out in the main room, Mr Adley, tales of every sort, from the comic to the tragic to the ironic to the sentimental. But on the Thursday before Christmas, it's always a tale of the uncanny. It's always been that way, at least as far back as I can remember.'

That at least explained the comment I had heard on my first visit, the one to the effect that Norman Stett should have saved his story for Christmas. Other questions hovered on my lips, but I saw a reflected caution in Stevens's eyes. Do you catch my drift? It was not a warning that he would not answer my questions; it was, rather, a warning that I should not even ask them.

'Was there something else, Mr Adley?'

We were alone in the hall now. All the others had left. And suddenly the hallway seemed darker, Stevens's long face paler, his lips redder. A knot exploded in the fireplace and a red glow washed momentarily across the polished parquet floor. I thought I heard, from somewhere in those as-yet-unexplored rooms beyond, a kind of slithery bump. I did not like the sound. Not at all.

'No,' I said in a voice that was not quite steady. 'I think not.'

'Goodnight, then,' Stevens said, and I crossed the threshold. I heard the heavy door close behind me. I heard the lock turn. And then I was walking towards the lights of 2nd Avenue, not looking back over my shoulder, somehow afraid to look back, as if I might see some frightful fiend matching me stride for stride, or glimpse some secret better kept than known. I reached the corner, saw an empty cab, and flagged it.

'More war stories?' Ellen asked me that night. She was in bed with Philip Marlowe, the only lover she has ever taken.

'There was a war story or two,' I said, hanging up my overcoat. 'Mostly I sat and read a book.'

'When you weren't oinking.'

'Yes, that's right. When I wasn't oinking.'

'Listen to this: "*The first time I ever laid eyes on Terry Lennox he was drunk in a Rolls-Royce Silver Wraith outside the terrace of the Dancers,*"' Ellen read. '"*He had a young-looking face but his hair was bone white. You could tell by his eyes that he was plastered to the hairline, but otherwise he looked like any other nice young guy in a dinner jacket who had been spending too much*

money in a place that exists for that purpose and for no other.'
Nice, huh? It's –'

'*The Long Goodbye,*' I said, taking off my shoes. 'You read me that same passage once every three years. It's part of your life-cycle.'

She wrinkled her nose at me. 'Oink-oink.'

'Thank you,' I said.

She went back to her book. I went out into the kitchen to get a bottle of Beck's. When I came back, she had laid *The Long Goodbye* open on the counterpane and was looking at me closely. 'David, are you going to join this club?'

'I suppose I might . . . if I'm asked.' I felt uncomfortable. I had perhaps told her another lie. If there was such a thing as membership at 249 East 35th, I already was a member.

'I'm glad,' she said. 'You've needed something for a long time now. I don't think you even know it, but you have. I've got the Relief Committee and the Commission on Women's Rights and the Theatre Society. But you've needed something. Some people to grow old with, I think.'

I went to the bed and sat beside her and picked up *The Long Goodbye*. It was a bright, new-minted paperback. I could remember buying the original hardback edition as a birthday present for Ellen. In 1953. 'Are we old?' I asked her.

'I suspect we are,' she said, and smiled brilliantly at me.

I put the book down and touched her breast. 'Too old for this?'

She turned the covers back with ladylike decorum . . . and then, giggling, kicked them onto the floor with her feet. 'Beat me, daddy,' Ellen said, 'eight to the bar.'

'Oink, oink,' I said, and then we were both laughing.

★　　★　　★

The Thursday before Christmas came. That evening was much the same as the others, with two notable exceptions. There were more people there, perhaps as many as eighteen. And there was a sharp, indefinable sense of excitement in the air. Johanssen took only a cursory glance at his *Journal* and then joined McCarron, Hugh Beagleman, and myself. We sat near the windows, talking of this and that, and finally fell into a passionate – and often hilarious – discussion of pre-war automobiles.

There was, now that I think of it, a third difference as well – Stevens had concocted a delicious eggnog punch. It was smooth, but it was also hot with rum and spices. It was served from an incredible Waterford bowl that looked like an ice-sculpture, and the animated hum of the conversation grew ever higher as the level of the punch grew lower.

I looked over in the corner by the tiny door leading to the billiard room and was astounded to see Waterhouse and Norman Stett flipping baseball cards into what looked like a genuine beaver tophat. They were laughing uproariously.

Groups formed and re-formed. The hour grew late . . . and then, at the time when people usually began slipping out through the front door, I saw Peter Andrews seated in front of the fire with an unmarked packet, about the size of a seed envelope, in one hand. He tossed it into the flames without opening it, and a moment later the fire began to dance with every colour of the spectrum – and some, I would have sworn, from outside it – before turning yellow again. Chairs were dragged around. Over Andrews's shoulder I could see the keystone with its etched homily: *IT IS THE TALE, NOT HE WHO TELLS IT*.

Stevens passed unobtrusively among us, taking punch glasses

and replacing them with snifters of brandy. There were murmurs of 'Merry Christmas' and 'Top of the season, Stevens,' and for the first time I saw money change hands – a ten dollar bill was unobtrusively tendered here, a bill that looked like a fifty there, one which I clearly saw was a hundred from another chair.

'Thank you, Mr McCarron . . . Mr Johanssen . . . Mr Beagleman . . .' A quiet, well-bred murmur.

I have lived in New York long enough to know that the Christmas season is a carnival of tips; something for the butcher, the baker, the candlestick-maker – not to mention the doorman, the super, and the cleaning lady who comes in Tuesdays and Fridays. I've never met anyone of my own class who regarded this as anything but a necessary nuisance . . . but I felt none of that grudging spirit on that night. The money was given willingly, even eagerly . . . and suddenly, for no reason (it was the way thoughts often seemed to come when one was at 249), I thought of the boy calling up to Scrooge on the still, cold air of a London Christmas morning: 'Wot? The goose that's as big as me?' And Scrooge, nearly crazed with joy, giggling '*A good* boy! An *excellent* boy!'

I found my own wallet. In the back of this, behind the pictures of Ellen I keep, there has always been a fifty dollar bill which I keep for emergencies. When Stevens gave me my brandy, I slipped it into his hand with never a qualm . . . although I was not a rich man.

'Happy Christmas, Stevens,' I said.

'Thank you, sir. And the same to you.'

He finished passing out the brandies and collecting his honorariums and retired. I glanced around once, at the midpoint of Peter Andrews's story, and saw him standing by the double doors, a dim manlike shadow, still and silent.

'I'm a lawyer now, as most of you know,' Andrews said after sipping at his glass, clearing his throat, and then sipping again. 'I've had offices on Park Avenue for the last twenty-two years. But before that, I was a legal assistant in a firm of lawyers which did business in Washington, DC. One night in July I was required to stay late in order to finish indexing case citations in a brief which hasn't anything at all to do with this story. But then a man came in — a man who was at that time one of the most widely known Senators on the Hill, a man who later almost became President. His shirt was matted with blood and his eyes were bulging from their sockets.

'"I've got to talk to Joe," he said. Joe, you understand, was Joseph Woods, the head of my firm, one of the most influential private-sector lawyers in Washington, and this Senator's close personal friend.

'"He went home hours ago," I said. I was terribly frightened, I can tell you — he looked like a man who had just walked away from a dreadful car accident, or perhaps from a knife-fight. And somehow seeing his face which I had seen in newspaper photos and on *Meet the Press* — seeing it streaked with gore, one cheek twitching spasmodically below one wild eye . . . all of that made my fright worse. "I can call him if you —" I was already fumbling with the phone, mad with eagerness to turn this unexpected responsibility over to someone else. Looking behind him, I could see the caked and bloody footprints he had left on the carpet.

'"I've got to talk to Joe right now," he reiterated as if he hadn't heard me. '"There's something in the trunk of my car . . . something I found out at the Virginia place. I've shot it and stabbed it and I can't kill it. It's not human, and I can't kill it."

'He began to giggle . . . and then to laugh . . . and finally to scream. And he was still screaming when I finally got Mr Woods on the phone and told him to come, for God's sake, to come as fast as he could . . .'

It is not my purpose to tell Peter Andrews's story, either. As a matter of fact, I am not sure I would dare to tell it. Suffice it to say that it was a tale so gruesome that I dreamed of it for weeks afterwards, and Ellen once looked at me over the breakfast table and asked me why I had suddenly cried out 'His head! His head is still speaking in the earth!' in the middle of the night.

'I suppose it was a dream,' I said. 'One of those you can't remember afterwards.'

But my eyes dropped immediately to my coffee cup, and I think that Ellen knew the lie that time.

One day in August of the following year, I was buzzed as I worked in the Readers' Library. It was George Waterhouse. He asked me if I could step up to his office. When I got there I saw that Robert Carden was also there, and Henry Effingham. For one moment I was positive I was about to be accused of some really dreadful act of stupidity or malfeasance.

Then Carden stepped around to me and said: 'George believes the time has come to make you a junior partner, David. The rest of us agree.'

'It's going to be a little bit like being the world's oldest JayCee,' Effingham said with a grin, 'but it's the channel you have to go through, David. With any luck, we can make you a full partner by Christmas.'

There were no bad dreams that night. Ellen and I went out to dinner, drank too much, went on to a jazz place where we hadn't been in nearly six years, and listened to that amazing blue-eyed black man, Dexter Gordon, blow his horn until almost two in the morning. We woke up the next morning with fluttery stomachs and achey heads, both of us still unable to completely believe what had happened. One of them was that my salary had just climbed by eight thousand dollars a year long after our expectations of such a staggering income jump had fallen by the wayside.

The firm sent me to Copenhagen for six weeks that fall, and I returned to discover that John Hanrahan, one of the regular attendees at 249, had died of cancer. A collection was taken up for his wife, who had been left in unpleasant circumstances. I was pressed into service to total the amount – which was given entirely in cash – and convert it to a cashier's check. It came to almost ten thousand dollars. I turned the check over to Stevens and I suppose he mailed it.

It just so happened that Arlene Hanrahan was a member of Ellen's Theatre Society, and Ellen told me some time later that Arlene had received an anonymous check for ten thousand four hundred dollars. Written on the check stub was the brief and unilluminating message 'Friends of your late husband John'.

'Isn't that the most amazing thing you ever heard in your *life*?' Ellen asked me.

'No,' I said, 'but it's right up there in the top ten. Are there any more strawberries, Ellen?'

*   *   *

The years went by. I discovered a warren of rooms upstairs at 249 – a writing room, a bedroom where guests sometimes stayed overnight (although after that slithery bump I had heard – or imagined I had heard – I believe I personally would rather have registered at a good hotel), a small but well-equipped gymnasium, and a sauna bath. There was also a long, narrow room which ran the length of the building and contained two bowling alleys.

In those same years I re-read the novels of Edward Gray Seville, and discovered an absolutely stunning poet – the equal of Ezra Pound and Wallace Stevens, perhaps – named Norbert Rosen. According to the back flap on one of the three volumes of his work in the stacks, he had been born in 1924 and killed at Anzio. All three volumes of his work had been published by Stedham & Son, New York and Boston.

I remember going back to the New York Public Library on a bright spring afternoon during one of those years (of which year I am no longer sure) and requesting twenty years' worth of Literary Market Place. The LMP is an annual publication the size of a large city's Yellow Pages, and the reference room librarian was quite put out with me, I'm afraid. But I persisted, and went through each volume carefully. And although LMP is supposed to list every publisher, great and small, in the United States (in addition to agents, editors, and book club staffs), I found no listing for Stedham & Son. A year later – or perhaps it was two years later – I fell into conversation with an antiquarian book dealer and asked him about the imprint. He said he had never heard of it.

I thought of asking Stevens – saw that warning light in his eyes – and dropped the question unasked.

⋆   ⋆   ⋆

And, over those years, there were stories.

Tales, to use Stevens's word. Funny tales, tales of love found and love lost, tales of unease. Yes, and even a few war stories, although none of the sort Ellen had likely been thinking of when she made the suggestion.

I remember Gerard Tozeman's story the most clearly – the tale of an American base of operations which took a direct hit from German artillery four months before the end of World War I, killing everyone present except for Tozeman himself.

Lathrop Carruthers, the American general who everyone had by then decided must be utterly insane (he had been responsible for better than eighteen *thousand* casualties by then – lives and limbs spent as casually as you or I might spend a quarter in a jukebox), was standing at a map of the front lines when the shell struck. He had been explaining yet another mad flanking operation at that moment – an operation which would have succeeded only on the level of all the others Carruthers had hatched: it would be wonderfully successful at making new widows.

And when the dust cleared, Gerard Tozeman, dazed and deaf, bleeding from his nose, his ears, and the corners of both eyes, his testicles already swelling from the force of the concussion, had come upon Carruthers's body while looking for a way out of the abbatoir that had been the staff HQ only minutes before. He looked at the general's body . . . and then began to scream and laugh. The sounds went unheard by his own shellshocked ears, but they served to notify the medicos that someone was still alive in that strew of matchwood.

Carruthers had not been mutilated by the blast . . . at

least, Tozeman said, it hadn't been what the soldiers of that long-ago war had come to think of as mutilation – men whose arms had been blown off, men with no feet, no eyes; men whose lungs had been shrivelled by gas. No, he said, it was nothing like that. The man's mother would have known him at once. But the map . . .

. . . the map before which Carruthers had been standing with his butcher's pointer when the shell struck . . .

It had somehow *been driven into his face*. Tozeman had found himself staring into a hideous, tattooed deathmask. Here was the stony shore of Brittany on the bony ridge of Lathrop Carruthers's brow. Here was the Rhine flowing like a blue scar down his left cheek. Here were some of the finest wine-growing provinces in the world bumped and ridged over his chin. Here was the Saar drawn around his throat like a hangman's noose . . . and printed across one bulging eyeball was the word VERSAILLES.

That was our Christmas story in the year 197–.

I remember many others, but they do not belong here. Properly speaking, Tozeman's doesn't, either . . . but it was the first 'Christmas tale' I heard at 249, and I could not resist telling it. And then, on the Thursday after Thanksgiving of this year, when Stevens clapped his hands together for attention and asked who would favour us with a Christmas tale, Emlyn McCarron growled: 'I suppose I've got something that bears telling. Tell it now or tell it never; God'll shut me up for good soon enough.'

In the years I had been coming to 249, I had never heard McCarron tell a story. And perhaps that's why I called the taxi so early, and why, when Stevens passed out eggnog to the six of us who had ventured out on that bellowing, frigid night, I felt so keenly excited. Nor was I the only one; I saw that same excitement on a good many other faces.

McCarron, old and dry and leathery, sat in the huge chair by the fire with the packet of powder in his gnarled hands. He tossed it in, and we watched the flames shift colours madly before returning to yellow again. Stevens passed among us with brandy, and we passed him his Christmas honorariums. Once, during that yearly ceremony, I heard the clink of change passing from the hand of the giver to the hand of the receiver; on another occasion, I had seen a one thousand dollar bill for a moment in the firelight. On both occasions the murmur of Stevens's voice had been exactly the same: low, considerate, and entirely correct. Ten years, more or less, had passed since I had first come to 249 with George Waterhouse, and while much had changed in the world outside, nothing had changed in here, and Stevens seemed not to have aged a month, or even a single day.

He moved back into the shadows, and for a moment there was a silence so perfect that we could hear the faint whistle of boiling sap escaping from the burning logs on the hearth. Emlyn McCarron was looking into the fire and we all followed his gaze. The flames seemed particularly wild that night. I felt almost hypnotized by the sight of the fire – as, I suppose, the cavemen who birthed us were once hypnotized by it as the wind walked and talked outside their cold northern caves.

At last, still looking into the fire, bent slightly forward so that his forearms rested on his thighs and his clasped hands hung in a knot between his knees, McCarron began to speak.

2: The Breathing Method

I am nearly eighty now, which means that I was born with the century. All my life I have been associated with a building which stands almost directly across from Madison Square Garden; this building, which looks like a great grey prison – something out of *A Tale of Two Cities* – is actually a hospital, as most of you know. It is Harriet White Memorial Hospital. The Harriet White after whom it was named was my father's first wife, and she got her practical experience in nursing when there were still actual sheep grazing on the Sheep's Meadow in Central Park. A statue of the lady herself (who would have been my stepmother, had she still been alive when I was born) stands on a pedestal in a pavilion before the building, and if any of you have seen it, you may have wondered how a woman with such a stern and uncompromising face could have found such a gentle occupation. The motto chiselled into the statue's base, once you get rid of the Latin folderol, is even less comforting: *There is no comfort without pain; thus we define salvation through suffering.* Cato, if you please . . . or if you don't please!

I was born inside that grey stone building on 20 March, 1900. I returned there as an intern in the year 1926. Twenty-six is old to be just starting out in the world of medicine, but I had done a more practical internship in France, at the end of World War I, trying to pack ruptured guts back into stomachs that had been blown wide open and dealing on the black market for morphine which was often tinctured and sometimes dangerous.

As with the generation of physicians following World War II, we were a bedrock-practical lot of sawbones, and the records of the major medical schools show a remarkably small number of washouts in the years 1919 to 1928. We were older, more experienced, steadier. Were we also wiser? I don't know . . . but we were certainly more cynical. There was none of this nonsense you read about in the popular medical novels, stuff about fainting or vomiting at one's first autopsy. Not after Belleau Wood, where mamma rats sometimes raised whole litters of ratlings in the gas-exploded intestines of the soldiers left to rot in no-man's land. We had gotten all our puking and passing out behind us.

The Harriet White Memorial Hospital also figured largely in something that happened to me nine years after I had interned there — and this is the story I want to tell you gentlemen tonight. It is not a tale to be told at Christmas, you would say (although its final scene was played out on Christmas Eve), and yet, while it is certainly horrible, it also seems to express to me all the amazing power of our cursed, doomed species. In it I see the wonder of our will . . . and also its horrible, tenebrous power.

Birth itself, gentlemen, is a horrid thing to many; it is the fashion now that fathers should be present at the birth of their children, and while this fashion has served to inflict many men with a guilt which I feel they may not deserve (it is a guilt which some women use knowingly and with an almost prescient cruelty), it seems by and large to be a healthful, salubrious thing. Yet I have seen men leave the delivery room white and tottering and I have seen them swoon like girls, overcome by the cries and the blood. I remember one father who held up just fine . . . only to begin screaming hysterically as his perfectly healthy son pushed its way into the world. The infant's eyes were open, it gave the impression of looking around . . . and then its eyes settled on the father.

Birth is wonderful, gentlemen, but I have never found it beautiful — not by any stretch of the imagination. I believe it is too brutal to be beautiful. A woman's womb is like an engine. With conception, that engine is turned on. At first it barely idles . . . but as the creative cycle nears the climax of birth, that engine revs up and up and up. Its idling whisper becomes a steady running hum, and then a rumble, and finally a bellowing, frightening roar. Once that silent engine has been turned on, every mother-to-be understands that her life is in check. Either she will bring the baby forth and the engine will shut down again, or that engine will pound louder and harder and faster until it explodes, killing her in blood and pain.

This is a story of birth, gentlemen, on the eve of that birth we have celebrated for almost two thousand years.

I began practising medicine in 1929 — a bad year to begin anything. My grandfather was able to loan me a small sum of money, so I was luckier than many of my colleagues, but I still had to survive over the next four years mostly on my wits.

By 1935, things had improved a bit. I had developed a bedrock of steady patients and was getting quite a few out-patient referrals from White Memorial. In April of that year I saw a new patient, a young woman whom I will call Sandra Stansfield — that name is close enough to what her name really was. This was a young woman, white, who stated her age to be twenty-eight. After examining her, I guessed her true age to be between three and five years younger than that. She was blonde, slender, and tall for that time – about five feet eight inches. She was quite beautiful, but in an austere way that was almost forbidding. Her features were clear and regular, her eyes intelligent . . . and her mouth every bit as determined as the stone mouth of Harriet White on the statue in the pavilion across from Madison Square Garden. The name she put on her form was not Sandra Stansfield but Jane Smith. My examination subsequently showed her to be about two months gone in pregnancy. She wore no wedding ring.

After the preliminary exam – but before the results of the pregnancy test were in, my nurse, Ella Davidson, said: 'That girl yesterday? Jane Smith? If that isn't an assumed name, I never heard one.'

I agreed. Still, I rather admired her. She had not engaged in the usual shilly-shallying, toe-scuffing, blushing, tearful behaviour. She had been straightforward and businesslike. Even her alias had seemed more a matter of business than of shame. There had been no attempt to provide verisimilitude by creating a 'Betty Rucklehouse' or whomping up a 'Ternina DeVille'. *You require a name for your form*, she seemed to be saying, *because that is the law. So here is a name; but rather than trusting to the professional ethics of a man I don't know, I'll trust in myself. If you don't mind.*

Ella sniffed and passed a few remarks – 'modern girls' and 'bold as brass' – but she was a good woman, and I don't think she said those things except for the sake of form. She knew as well as I did that, whatever my new patient might be, she was no little trollop with hard eyes and round heels. No; 'Jane Smith' was merely an extremely serious, extremely determined young woman – if either of those things can be described by such a milquetoast adverb as 'merely'. It was an unpleasant situation (it used to be called 'getting in a scrape', as you gentlemen may remember; nowadays it seems that many young women use a scrape to get out of the scrape), and she meant to go through it with whatever grace and dignity she could manage.

A week after her initial appointment, she came in again. That was a peach of a day – one of the first real days of spring. The air was mild, the sky a soft, milky shade of blue, and there was a smell on the breeze – a warm, indefinable smell that seems to be nature's signal that she is entering her own birth cycle again. The sort of day when you wish you were miles from any responsibility, sitting opposite a lovely woman of your own – at Coney Island, maybe, or on the Palisades across the Hudson with a picnic hamper on a checkered cloth and the lady in question wearing a great white cartwheel hat and a sleeveless gown as pretty as the day.

'Jane Smith's' dress had sleeves, but it was still almost as pretty as the day; a smart white linen with brown edging. She wore brown pumps, white gloves, and a cloche hat that was slightly out of fashion – it was the first sign I saw that she was a far from rich woman.

'You're pregnant,' I said. 'I don't believe you doubted it much, did you?'

If there are to be tears, I thought, they will come now.

'No,' she said with perfect composure. There was no more a sign of tears in her eyes than there were rainclouds on the horizon that day. 'I'm very regular as a rule.'

There was a pause between us.

'When may I expect to deliver?' she asked then, with an

almost soundless sigh. It was the sound a man or woman might make before bending over to pick up a heavy load.

'It will be a Christmas baby,' I said. '10 December is the date I'll give you, but it could be two weeks on either side of that.'

'All right.' She hesitated briefly, and then plunged ahead. 'Will you attend me? Even though I'm not married?'

'Yes,' I said. 'On one condition.'

She frowned, and in that moment her face was more like the face of Harriet White, my father's first wife, than ever. One would not think that the frown of a woman perhaps only twenty-three could be particularly formidable, but this one was. She was ready to leave, and the fact that she would have to go through this entire embarrassing process again with another doctor was not going to deter her.

'And what might that be?' she asked with perfect, colour-less courtesy.

Now it was I who felt an urge to drop my eyes from her steady hazel ones, but I held her gaze. 'I insist upon knowing your real name. We can continue to do business on a cash basis if that is how you prefer it, and I can continue to have Mrs Davidson issue you receipts in the name of Jane Smith. But if we are going to travel through the next seven months or so together, I would like to be able to address you by the name to which you answer in all the rest of your life.'

I finished this absurdly stiff little speech and watched her think it through. I was somehow quite sure she was going to stand up, thank me for my time, and leave forever. I was going to feel disappointed if that happened. I liked her. Even more, I liked the straightforward way she was handling a problem which would have reduced ninety women out of a hundred to inept and undignified liars, terrified by the living clock within and so deeply ashamed of their situation that to make any reasonable plan for coping with it became impossible.

I suppose many young people today would find such a state of mind ludicrous, ugly, even hard to believe. People have become so eager to demonstrate their broad-mindedness that a pregnant woman who has no wedding ring is apt to be treated with twice the solicitude of one who does. You gentlemen will well remember when rectitude and hypocrisy were combined to make a situation that was viciously difficult for a woman who had gotten herself 'in a scrape'. In those days, a married pregnant woman was a radiant woman, sure of her position and proud of fulfilling what she considered to be the function God put her on earth for. An unmarried pregnant woman was a trollop in the eyes of the world and apt to be a trollop in her own eyes as well. They were, to use Ella Davidson's word, 'easy', and in that world and that time, easiness was not quickly forgiven. Such women crept away to have their babies in other towns or cities. Some took pills or jumped from buildings. Others went to butcher abortionists with dirty hands or tried to do the job themselves; in my time as a physician I have seen four women die of blood-loss before my eyes as the result of punctured wombs – in one case the puncturing was done by the jagged neck of a Dr Pepper bottle that had been tied to the handle of a whisk-broom. It *is* hard to believe now that such things happened, but they did, gentlemen. They did. It was, quite simply, the worst situation a healthy young woman could find herself in.

'All right,' she said at last. 'That's fair enough. My name

is Sandra Stansfield.' And she held her hand out. Rather amazed, I took it and shook it. I'm rather glad Ella Davidson didn't see me do that. She would have made no comment, but the coffee would have been bitter for the next week.

She smiled – at my own expression of bemusement, I imagine – and looked at me frankly. 'I hope we can be friends, Dr McCarron. I need a friend just now. I'm quite frightened.'

'I can understand that, and I'll try to be your friend if I can, Miss Stansfield. Is there anything I can do for you now?'

She opened her handbag and took out a dime-store pad and a pen. She opened the pad, poised the pen, and looked up at me. For one horrified instant I believed she was going to ask me for the name and address of an abortionist. Then she said: 'I'd like to know the best things to eat. For the baby, I mean.'

I laughed out loud. She looked at me with some amazement.

'Forgive me – it's just that you seem so businesslike.'

'I suppose,' she said. 'This baby is part of my business now, isn't it, Dr McCarron?'

'Yes. Of course it is. And I have a folder which I give to all my pregnant patients. It deals with diet and weight and drinking and smoking and lots of other things. Please don't laugh when you look at it. You'll hurt my feelings if you do, because I wrote it myself.'

And so I had – although it was really more of a pamphlet than a folder, and in time became my book, *A Practical Guide to Pregnancy and Delivery*. I was quite interested in obstetrics and gynaecology in those days – still am – although it was not a thing to specialize in back then unless you had plenty of uptown connections. Even if you did, it might take ten or fifteen years to establish a strong practice. Having hung out my shingle at a rather too-ripe age as a result of the war, I didn't feel I had the time to spare. I contented myself with the knowledge that I would see a great many happy expectant mothers and deliver a great many babies in the course of my general practice. And so I did; at last count I had delivered well over two thousand babies – enough to fill two hundred classrooms.

I kept up with the literature on having babies more smartly than I did on that applying to any other area of general practice. And because my opinions were strong, enthusiastic ones, I wrote my own pamphlet rather than just passing along the stale chestnuts so often foisted on young mothers then. I won't run through the whole catalogue of these chestnuts – we'd be here all night – but I'll mention a couple.

Expectant mothers were urged to stay off their feet as much as possible, and on no account were they to walk any sustained distance lest a miscarriage or 'birth damage' result. Now giving birth is an extremely strenuous piece of work, and such advice is like telling a football player to prepare for the big game by sitting around as much as possible so he won't tire himself out! Another sterling piece of advice, given by a good many doctors, was that moderately over-weight mothers-to-be take up smoking . . . *smoking!* The rationale was perfectly expressed by an advertising slogan of the day: 'Have a Lucky instead of a sweet.' People who have the idea that when we entered the twentieth century we also entered an age of medical light and reason have no idea of how utterly crazy medicine could sometimes be. Perhaps it's just as well; their hair would turn white.

I gave Miss Stansfield my folder and she looked through it with complete attention for perhaps five minutes. I asked her permission to smoke my pipe and she gave it absently, without looking up. When she did look up at last, there was a small smile on her lips. 'Are you a radical, Dr McCarron?' she asked.

'Why do you say that? Because I advise that the expectant mother should walk her round of errands instead of riding in a smoky, jolting subway car?'

'"Pre-natal vitamins," whatever they are . . . swimming recommended . . . and breathing exercises! What breathing exercises?'

'That comes later on, and no – I'm not a radical. Far from it. What I am is five minutes overdue on my next patient.'

'Oh! I'm sorry.' She got to her feet quickly, tucking the thick folder into her purse.

'No need.'

She shrugged into her light coat, looking at me with those direct hazel eyes as she did so. 'No,' she said. 'Not a radical at all. I suspect you're actually quite . . . comfortable? Is that the word I want?'

'I hope it will serve,' I said. 'It's a word I like. If you speak to Mrs Davidson, she'll give you an appointment schedule. I'll want to see you again early next month.'

'Your Mrs Davidson doesn't approve of me.'

'Oh, I'm sure that's not true at all.' But I've never been a particularly good liar, and the warmth between us suddenly slipped away. I did not accompany her to the door of my consulting room. 'Miss Stansfield?'

She turned towards me, coolly enquiring.

'Do you intend to keep the baby?'

She considered me briefly and then smiled – a secret smile which I am convinced only pregnant women know. 'Oh yes,' she said, and let herself out.

By the end of that day I had treated identical twins for identical cases of poison ivy, lanced a boil, removed a hook of metal from a sheet-welder's eye, and had referred one of my oldest patients to White Memorial for what was surely cancer. I had forgotten all about Sandra Stansfield by then. Ella Davidson recalled her to my mind by saying:

'Perhaps she's not a chippie after all.'

I looked up from my last patient's folder. I had been looking at it, feeling that useless disgust most doctors feel when they know they have been rendered completely helpless, and thinking I ought to have a rubber stamp made up for such files – only instead of saying ACCOUNT RECEIVABLE or PAID IN FULL or PATIENT MOVED, it would simply say DEATH-WARRANT. Perhaps with a skull and crossbones above, like those on bottles of poison.

'Pardon me?'

'Your Miss Jane Smith. She did a most peculiar thing after her appointment this morning.' The set of Mrs Davidson's head and mouth made it clear that this was the sort of peculiar thing of which she approved.

'And what was that?'

'When I gave her her appointment card, she asked me to tot up her expenses. *All* of her expenses. Delivery and hospital stay included.'

That *was* a peculiar thing, all right. This was 1935, remember, and Miss Stansfield gave every impression of being a woman on her own. Was she well off, even comfortably off? I didn't think so. Her dress, shoes, and gloves had all been smart, but she had worn no jewellery — not even costume jewellery. And then there was her hat, that decidedly out-of-date cloche.

'Did you do it?' I asked.

Mrs Davidson looked at me as though I might have lost my senses. '*Did I? Of course* I did! And she paid the entire amount. In cash.'

The last, which apparently had surprised Mrs Davidson the most (in an extremely pleasant way, of course), surprised me not at all. One thing which the Jane Smiths of the world can't do is write cheques.

'Took a bank-book out of her purse, opened it, and counted the money right out onto my desk,' Mrs Davidson was continuing. 'Then she put her receipt in where the cash had been, put the bank-book into her purse again, and said good day. Not half bad, when you think of the way we've had to chase some of these so-called "respectable" people to make them pay their bills!'

I felt chagrined for some reason. I was not happy with the Stansfield woman for having done such a thing, with Mrs Davidson for being so pleased and complacent with the arrangement, and with myself, for some reason I couldn't define then and can't now. Something about it made me feel small.

'But she couldn't very well pay for a hospital stay now, could she?' I asked — it was a ridiculously small thing to seize on, but it was all I could find at that moment on which to express my pique and half-amused frustration. 'After all, none of us know how long she'll have to remain there. Or are you reading the crystal now, Ella?'

'I told her that very thing, and she asked what the average

stay was following an uncomplicated birth. I told her three days. Wasn't that right, Dr McCarron?'

I had to admit it was.

'She said that she would pay for three days, then, and if it was longer, she would pay the difference, and if –'

'– if it was shorter, we could issue her a refund,' I finished wearily. I thought: *Damn the woman, anyway!* – and then I laughed. She had guts. One couldn't deny that. All kinds of guts.

Mrs Davidson allowed herself a smile . . . and if I am ever tempted, now that I am in my dotage, to believe I know all there is to know about one of my fellow creatures, I try to remember that smile. Before that day I would have staked my life that I would never see Mrs Davidson, one of the most 'proper' women I have ever known, smile fondly as she thought about a girl who was pregnant out of wedlock.

'Guts? I don't know, Doctor. But she knows her own mind, that one. She certainly does.'

A month passed, and Miss Stansfield showed up promptly for her appointment, simply appearing out of that wide, amazing flow of humanity that was New York then and is New York now. She wore a fresh-looking blue dress to which she managed to communicate a feeling of originality, of one-of-a-kind-ness, despite the fact that it had been quite obviously picked from a rack of dozens just like it. Her pumps did not match it; they were the same brown ones in which I had seen her last time.

I checked her over carefully and found her normal in every way. I told her so and she was pleased. 'I found the pre-natal vitamins, Dr McCarron.'

'Did you? That's good.'

Her eyes sparkled impishly. 'The druggist advised me against them.'

'God save me from pestle-pounders,' I said, and she giggled against the heel of her palm – it was a childlike gesture, winning in its unselfconsciousness. 'I never met a druggist that wasn't a frustrated doctor. And a Republican. Pre-natal vitamins are new, so they're regarded with suspicion. Did you take his advice?'

'No, I took yours. You're my doctor.'

'Thank you.'

'Not at all.' She looked at me straightforwardly, not giggling now. 'Dr McCarron, when will I begin to show?'

'Not until August, I should guess. September, if you choose garments which are . . . uh, voluminous.'

'Thank you.' She picked up her purse but did not rise immediately to go. I thought that she wanted to talk . . . and didn't know where or how to begin.

'You're a working woman, I take it?'

She nodded. 'Yes. I work.'

'Might I ask where? If you'd rather I didn't –'

She laughed – a brittle, humourless laugh, as different from that giggle as day is from dark. 'In a department store. Where else does an unmarried woman work in the city? I sell perfume to fat ladies who rinse their hair and then have it done up in tiny finger-waves.'

'How long will you continue?'

'Until my delicate condition is noticed. I suppose then I'll be asked to leave, lest I upset any of the fat ladies. The shock of being waited on by a pregnant woman with no wedding-band might cause their hair to straighten.'

Quite suddenly her eyes were bright with tears. Her lips began to tremble, and I groped for a handkerchief. But the tears didn't fall – not so much as a single one. Her eyes brimmed for a moment and then she blinked them back. Her lips tightened . . . and then smoothed out. She simply decided she was not going to lose control of her emotions . . . and she did not. It was a remarkable thing to watch.

'I'm sorry,' she said. 'You've been very kind to me. I won't repay your kindness with what would be a very common story.'

She rose to go, and I rose with her.

'I'm not a bad listener,' I said, 'and I have some time. My next patient cancelled.'

'No,' she said. 'Thank you, but no.'

'All right,' I said. 'But there's something else.'

'Yes?'

'It's not my policy to make my patients – *any* of my patients – pay for services in advance of those services being rendered. I hope if you . . . that is, if you feel you'd like to . . . or have to . . .' I fumbled my way into silence.

'I've been in New York four years, Dr McCarron, and I'm thrifty by nature. After August – or September – I'll have to live on what's in my savings account until I can go back to work again. It's not a great amount and sometimes, during the nights, mostly, I become frightened.'

She looked at me steadily with those wonderful hazel eyes.

'It seemed better to me – safer – to pay for the baby first. Ahead of everything. Because that is where the baby is in my thoughts, and because, later on, the temptation to spend that money might become very great.'

'All right,' I said. 'But please remember that I see it as having been paid before accounts. If you need it, say so.'

'And bring out the dragon in Mrs Davidson again?' The impish light was back in her eyes. 'I don't think so. And now, Doctor –'

'You intend to work as long as possible? Absolutely as long as possible?'

'Yes. I have to. Why?'

'I think I'm going to frighten you a little before you go,' I said.

Her eyes widened slightly. 'Don't do that,' she said. 'I'm frightened enough already.'

'Which is exactly why I'm going to do it. Sit down again, Miss Stansfield.' And when she only stood there, I added: 'Please.'

She sat. Reluctantly.

'You're in a unique and unenviable position,' I told her, leaning back against the examination table. 'You are dealing with the situation with remarkable grace.'

She began to speak, and I held up my hand to silence her.

'That's good. I salute you for it. But I would hate to see you hurt your baby in any way out of concern for your own financial security. I had a patient who, in spite of my strenuous advice to the contrary, continued packing herself into a girdle month after month, strapping it tighter and tighter as her pregnancy progressed. She was a vain, stupid, tiresome woman, and I don't believe she really wanted the baby anyway. I don't subscribe to many of these theories of the subconscious which everyone seems to discuss over the Mah-Jong boards these days, but if I did, I would say that she – or some part of her – was trying to kill the baby.'

'And did she?' Her face was very still.

'No, not at all. But the baby was born retarded. It's very possible that the baby would have been born retarded anyway, and I'm not saying otherwise – we know next to nothing about what causes such things. But she *may* have caused it.'

'I take your point,' she said in a low voice. 'You don't want me to . . . to pack myself in so I can work another month or six weeks. I'll admit the thought had crossed my mind. So . . . thank you for the fright.'

This time I walked her to the door. I would have liked to ask her just how much – or how little – she had left in that savings book, and just how close to the edge she was. It was a question she would not answer; I knew that well enough. So I merely bade her goodbye and made a joke about her vitamins. She left. I found myself thinking about her at odd moments over the next month, and –

Johanssen interrupted McCarron's story at this point. They were old friends, and I suppose that gave him the right to ask the question that had surely crossed all our minds.

'Did you love her, Emlyn? Is that what all this is about, this stuff about her eyes and smile and how you "thought of her at odd moments"?'

I thought that McCarron might be annoyed at this interruption, but he was not. 'You have a right to ask the question,' he said, and paused, looking into the fire. It seemed that he might almost have fallen into a doze. Then a dry knot of wood exploded, sending sparks up the chimney in a swirl, and McCarron looked around, first at Johanssen and then at the rest of us.

'No. I didn't love her. The things I've said about her sound like the things a man who is falling in love would notice – her eyes, her dresses, her laugh.' He lit his pipe with a special boltlike pipe-lighter that he carried, drawing the flame until there was a bed of coals there. Then he snapped the bolt shut, dropped it into the pocket of his jacket, and blew out a plume of smoke that shifted slowly around his head in an aromatic membrane.

'I admired her. That was the long and short of it. And my admiration grew with each of her visits. I suppose some of you sense this as a story of love crossed by circumstance. Nothing could be further from the truth. Her story came out a bit at a time over the next half-year or so, and when you gentlemen hear it, I think you'll agree that it was every bit as common as she herself said it was. She had been drawn to the city like a thousand other girls; she had come from a small town . . .

. . . in Iowa or Nebraska. Or possibly it was Minnesota – I don't really remember anymore. She had done a lot of high school dramatics and community theatre in her small town – good reviews in the local weekly written by a drama critic with an English degree from Cow and Sileage Junior College – and she came to New York to try a career in acting.

She was practical even about that – as practical as an impractical ambition will allow one to be, anyway. She came to New York, she told me, because she didn't believe the unstated thesis of the movie magazines – that any girl who came to Hollywood could become a star, that she might be sipping a soda in Schwab's Drug Store one day and playing opposite Gable or MacMurray the next. She came to New York, she said, because she thought it might be easier to get her foot in the door there . . . and, I think, because the legitimate theatre interested her more than the talkies.

She got a job selling perfume in one of the big department stores and enrolled in acting classes. She was smart and terribly determined, this girl – her will was pure steel, through and through – but she was as human as anyone else. She was lonely, too. Lonely in a way that perhaps only single girls fresh from small midwestern towns know. Homesickness is not always a vague, nostalgic, almost beautiful emotion, although that is somehow the way we always seem to picture it in our mind. It can be a terribly keen blade, not just a sickness in metaphor but in fact as well. It can change the way one looks at the world; the faces one sees in the street look not just indifferent but ugly . . . perhaps even malignant. Homesickness is a real sickness – the ache of the uprooted plant.

Miss Stansfield, admirable as she may have been, determined as she may have been, was not immune to it. And the rest follows so naturally it needs no telling. There was a young man in her acting classes. The two of them went out several times. She did not love him, but she needed a friend. By the time she discovered he was not that and never would be, there had been two incidents. Sexual incidents. She discovered she was pregnant. She told the young man, who told her he would stand by her and 'do the decent thing'. A week later he was gone from his lodgings, leaving no forwarding address. That was when she came to me.

During her fourth month, I introduced Miss Stansfield to the Breathing Method – what is today called the Lamaze

Method. In those days, you understand, Monsieur Lamaze was yet to be heard from.

'In those days' — the phrase has cropped up again and again, I notice. I apologize for it but am unable to help it — so much of what I have told you and will tell you happened as it did because it happened 'in those days'.

So . . . 'in those days', over forty-five years ago, a visit to the delivery rooms in any large American hospital would have sounded to you like a visit to a madhouse. Women weeping wildly, women screaming that they wished they were dead, women screaming that they could not bear such agony, women screaming for Christ to forgive them their sins, women screaming out strings of curses and gutter-words their husbands and fathers never would have believed they knew. All of this was quite the accepted thing, in spite of the fact that most of the world's women give birth in almost complete silence, aside from the grunting sounds of strain that we would associate with any piece of hard physical labour.

Doctors were responsible for some of this hysteria, I'm sorry to say. The stories the pregnant woman heard from friends and relatives who had already been through the birthing process also contributed to it. Believe me: if you are told that some experience is going to hurt, it *will* hurt. Most pain is in the mind, and when a woman absorbs the idea that the act of giving birth is excruciatingly painful — when she gets this information from her mother, her sisters, her married friends, *and* her physician — that woman has been mentally prepared to feel great agony.

Even after only six years' practice, I had become used to seeing women who were trying to cope with a twofold problem: not just the fact that they were pregnant and must plan for the new arrival, but also the fact – what most of them *saw* as a fact, anyway – *that they had entered the valley of the shadow of death.* Many were actually trying to put their affairs in coherent order so that if they *should* die, their husbands would be able to carry on without them.

This is neither the time nor place for a lesson on obstetrics, but you should know that for a long time before 'those days', the act of giving birth *was* extremely dangerous in the Western countries. A revolution in medical procedure, beginning around 1900, had made the process much safer, but an absurdly small number of doctors bothered to tell their expectant mothers that. God knows why. But in light of this, is it any wonder that most delivery rooms sounded like Ward Nine in Bellevue? Here are these poor women, their time come round at last, experiencing a process which has, because of the almost Victorian decorum of the times, been described to them only in the vaguest of terms; here are these women experiencing that engine of birth finally running at full power. They were seized with an awe and wonder which they immediately interpreted as insupportable pain, and most of them felt that they would very shortly die a dog's death.

In the course of my reading on the subject of pregnancy, I discovered the principle of the silent birth and the idea of the Breathing Method. Screaming wastes energy which would be better used to expel the baby, it causes the women to hyperventilate, and hyperventilation puts the body on an emergency basis – adrenals running full blast, respiration and pulse-rate up – that is really unnecessary. The Breathing Method was supposed to help the mother focus her attention on the job at hand and to cope with pain by utilizing the body's own resources.

It was used widely at that time in India and Africa; in America, the Shoshone, Kiowa, and Micmac Indians all used it; the Eskimos have always used it; but, as you may guess, most Western doctors had little interest in it. One of my colleagues – an intelligent man – returned the typescript of my pregnancy pamphlet to me in the fall of 1931 with a red line drawn through the entire section on the Breathing Method. In the margin he had scribbled that if he wanted to know about 'nigger superstitions', he would stop by a newsstand and buy an issue of *Weird Tales!*

Well, I didn't cut the section from the pamphlet as he had suggested, but I had mixed results with the method – that was the best one could say. There were women who used it with great success. There were others who seemed to grasp the idea perfectly in principle but who lost their discipline completely as soon as their contractions became deep and heavy. In most of those cases I found that the entire idea had been subverted and undermined by well-meaning friends and relatives who had never heard of such a thing and thus could not believe it would actually work.

The method was based on the idea that, while no two labours are ever the same in their specifics, all are pretty much alike in general. There are four stages: contractive labour, mid-labour, birth, and the expulsion of the afterbirth. Contractions are a complete hardening of the abdominal and pelvic-area muscles, and the expectant mother often finds them beginning in the sixth month. Many women pregnant for the first time expect something rather nasty, like bowel cramps, but I'm told it's much cleaner – a strongly physical sensation, which may deepen into a pain like a charley horse. A woman employing the Breathing Method began to breathe in a series of short, measured inhales and exhales when she felt a contraction coming on. Each breath was expelled in a puff, as if one were blowing a trumpet Dizzy Gillespie fashion.

During mid-labour, when more painful contractions begin coming every fifteen minutes or so, the woman switched to long inhales followed by long exhales – it's the way a marathon runner breathes when he's starting his final kick. The harder the contraction, the longer the inhale–exhale. In my pamphlet, I called this stage 'riding the waves'.

The final stage we need concern ourselves with here I called 'locomotive', and Lamaze instructors today frequently call it the 'choo-choo' stage of breathing. Final labour is accompanied by pains which are most frequently described as deep and glassy. They are accompanied by an irresistible urge on the mother's part to push . . . to expel the baby. This is the point, gentlemen, at which that wonderful, frightening engine reaches its absolute crescendo. The cervix is fully dilated. The baby has begun its short journey down the birth canal, and if you were to look directly between the mother's legs, you would be apt to see the baby's fontanelle pulsing only inches from the open air. The mother using the Breathing Method now begins to take and let out short, sharp breaths between her lips, not filling her lungs, not hyperventilating, but almost panting in a perfectly controlled fashion. It really is the sound children make when they are imitating a steam-driven locomotive.

All of this has a salutary effect on the body – the mother's oxygen is kept high without putting her systems on an emergency basis, and she herself remains aware and alert, able to ask and answer questions, able to take instructions. But of course the *mental* results of the Breathing Method were even more important. The mother felt she was actively participating in the birth of her child – that she was in some part guiding the process. She felt on top of the experience . . . and on top of the pain.

You can understand that the whole process was utterly dependent on the patient's state of mind. The Breathing Method was uniquely vulnerable, uniquely delicate, and if I had a good many failures, I'd explain them this way – what a patient can be convinced of by her doctor she may be unconvinced of by relatives who raise their hands in horror when told of such a heathenish practice.

From this aspect, at least, Miss Stansfield was the ideal patient. She had neither friends nor relatives to talk her out of her belief in the Breathing Method (although, in all fairness, I must add that I doubt anyone ever talked her out of *anything* once she had made up her mind on the subject) once she came to believe in it. And she *did* come to believe in it.

'It's a little like self-hypnosis, isn't it?' she asked me the first time we really discussed it.

I agreed, delighted. 'Exactly! But you mustn't let that make you think it's a trick, or that it will let you down when the going gets tough.'

'I don't think that at all. I'm very grateful to you. I'll practise assiduously, Dr McCarron.' She was the sort of woman the Breathing Method was invented for, and when she told me she would practise, she spoke nothing but the truth. I have never seen anyone embrace an idea with such enthusiasm . . . but, of course, the Breathing Method was uniquely suited to her temperament. There are docile men and women in this world by the millions, and some of them are damn fine people. But there are others whose hands ache to hold the throttles of their own lives, and Miss Stansfield was one of those.

When I say she embraced the Breathing Method totally, I mean it . . . and I think the story of her final day at the department store where she sold perfumes and cosmetics proves the point.

The end of her gainful employment finally came late in August. Miss Stansfield was a slim young woman in fine physical condition, and this was, of course, her first child. Any doctor will tell you that such a woman is apt not to 'show' for five, perhaps even six months . . . and then, one day and all at once, *everything* will show.

She came in for her monthly checkup on the first of September, laughed ruefully, and told me she had discovered the Breathing Method had another use.

'What's that?' I asked her.

'It's even better than counting to ten when you're mad as hell at someone,' she said. Those hazel eyes were dancing. 'Although people look at you as if you might be a lunatic when you start puffing and blowing.'

She told me the tale readily enough. She had gone to work as usual on the previous Monday, and all I can think is that the curiously abrupt transition from a slim young woman to an obviously pregnant young woman – and the transition really can be almost as sudden as day to dark in the tropics – had happened over the weekend. Or maybe her supervisor finally decided that her suspicions were no longer just suspicions.

'I'll want to see you in the office on your break,' this woman, a Mrs Kelly, said coldly. She had previously been quite friendly to Miss Stansfield. She had shown her pictures of her two children, both in high school, and they had exchanged recipes at one point. Mrs Kelly was always asking her if she had met 'a nice boy' yet. That kindliness and friendliness was gone now. And when she stepped into Mrs Kelly's office on her break, Miss Stansfield told me, she knew what to expect.

'You're in trouble,' this previously kind woman said curtly.

'Yes,' Miss Stansfield said. 'It's called that by some people.'

Mrs Kelly's cheeks had gone the colour of old brick. 'Don't you be smart with me, young woman,' she said. 'From the looks of your belly, you've been too smart by half already.'

I could see the two of them in my mind's eye as she told me the story – Miss Stansfield, her direct hazel eyes fixed on Mrs Kelly, perfectly composed, refusing to drop her eyes, or weep, or exhibit shame in any other way. I believe she had a much more practical conception of the trouble she was in than her supervisor did, with her two almost grown children and her respectable husband, who owned his own barber-shop and voted Republican.

'I must say you show remarkably little shame at the way you've deceived me!' Mrs Kelly burst out bitterly.

'I have never deceived you. No mention of my pregnancy has been made until today.' She looked at Mrs Kelly almost curiously. 'How can you say I have deceived you?'

'I took you home!' Mrs Kelly cried. 'I had you to dinner . . . with my *sons*.' She looked at Miss Stansfield with utter loathing.

This is when Miss Stansfield began to grow angry. Angrier,

she told me, than she had ever been in her life. She had not been unaware of the sort of reaction she could expect when the secret came out, but as any one of you gentlemen will attest, the difference between academic theory and practical application can sometimes be shockingly huge.

Clutching her hands firmly together in her lap, Miss Stansfield said: 'If you are suggesting I made or ever would make any attempt to seduce your sons, that's the dirtiest, filthiest thing I've ever heard in my life.'

Mrs Kelly's head rocked back as if she had been slapped. That bricky colour drained from her cheeks, leaving only two small spots of hectic colour. The two women looked grimly at each other across a desk littered with perfume samples in a room that smelled vaguely of flowers. It was a moment, Miss Stansfield said, that seemed much longer than it actually could have been.

Then Mrs Kelly yanked open one of her drawers and brought out a buff-coloured cheque. A bright pink severance slip was attached to it. Showing her teeth, actually seeming to bite off each word, she said, 'With hundreds of decent girls looking for work in this city, I hardly think we need a strumpet such as yourself in our employ, dear.'

She told me it was that final, contemptuous 'dear' that brought all her anger to a sudden head. A moment later Mrs Kelly's jaw dropped and her eyes widened as Miss Stansfield, her hands locked together as tightly as links in a steel chain, so tightly she left bruises on herself (they were fading but still perfectly visible when I saw her on 1 September), began to 'locomotive' between her clenched teeth.

It wasn't a funny story, perhaps, but I burst out laughing at the image and Miss Stansfield joined me. Mrs Davidson looked in – to make sure we hadn't gotten into the nitrous oxide, perhaps – and then left again.

'It was all I could think to *do*,' Miss Stansfield said, still laughing and wiping her streaming eyes with her handkerchief. 'Because at that moment, I saw myself reaching out and simply sweeping those sample bottles of perfume – every one of them – off her desk and onto the floor, which was uncarpeted concrete. I didn't just *think* it, I *saw* it! I saw them crashing to the floor and filling the room with such a God-awful mixed stench that the fumigators would have to come.

'I was going to do it; nothing was going to stop me doing it. Then I began to Breathe, and everything was all right. I was able to take the cheque, and the pink slip, and get up, and get out. I wasn't able to thank her, of course – I was still being a locomotive!'

We laughed again, and then she sobered.

'It's all passed off now, and I am even able to feel a little sorry for her – or does that sound like a terribly stiff-necked thing to say?'

'Not at all. I think it's an admirable way to be able to feel.'

'May I show you something I bought with my severance pay, Dr McCarron?'

'Yes, if you like.'

She opened her purse and took out a small flat box. 'I bought it at a pawnshop,' she said. 'For two dollars. And it's the only time during this whole nightmare that I've felt ashamed and dirty. Isn't that strange?'

She opened the box and laid it on my desk so I could look inside. I wasn't surprised at what I saw. It was a plain gold wedding ring.

'I'll do what's necessary,' she said. 'I am staying in what

Mrs Kelly would undoubtedly call "a respectable boarding house". My landlady has been kind and friendly . . . but Mrs Kelly was kind and friendly, too. I think she may ask me to leave at any time now, and I suspect that if I say anything about the rent-balance due me, or the damage deposit I paid when I moved in, she'll laugh in my face.'

'My dear young woman, that would be quite illegal. There are courts and lawyers to help you answer such –'

'The courts are men's clubs,' she said steadily, 'and not apt to go out of their way to befriend a woman in my position. Perhaps I could get my money back, perhaps not. Either way, the expense and the trouble and the . . . the unpleasantness . . . hardly seem worth the forty-seven dollars or so. I had no business mentioning it to you in the first place. It hasn't happened yet, and maybe it won't. But in any case, I intend to be practical from now on.'

She raised her head, and her eyes flashed at mine.

'I've got my eye on a place down in the Village – just in case. It's on the third floor, but it's clean, and it's five dollars a month cheaper than where I'm staying now.' She picked the ring out of the box. 'I wore this when the landlady showed me the room.'

She put it on the third finger of her left hand with a small moue of disgust of which I believe she was unaware. 'There. Now I'm Mrs Stansfield. My husband was a truck-driver who was killed on the Pittsburgh–New York run. Very sad. But I am no longer a little roundheels strumpet, and my child is no longer a bastard.'

She looked up at me, and the tears were in her eyes again. As I watched, one of them overspilled and rolled down her cheek.

'Please,' I said, distressed, and reached across the desk to take her hand. It was very, very cold. 'Don't, my dear.'

She turned her hand – it was the left – over in my hand and looked at the ring. She smiled, and that smile was as bitter as gall and vinegar, gentlemen. Another tear fell – just that one.

'When I hear cynics say that the days of magic and miracles are all behind us, Dr McCarron, I'll know they're deluded, won't I? When you can buy a ring in a pawnshop for a dollar and a half and that ring will instantly erase both bastardy and licentiousness, what else would you call that but magic? Cheap magic.'

'Miss Stansfield . . . Sandra, if I may . . . if you need help, if there's anything I can do –'

She drew her hand away from me – if I had taken her right hand instead of her left, perhaps she would not have done. I did not love her, I've told you, but in that moment I could have loved her; I was on the verge of falling in love with her. Perhaps, if I'd taken her right hand instead of the one with that lying ring on it, and if she had allowed me to hold her hand only a little longer, until my own warmed it, perhaps then I should have.

'You're a good, kind man, and you've done a great deal for me and my baby . . . and your Breathing Method is a much better kind of magic than this awful ring. After all, it kept me from being jailed on charges of wilful destruction, didn't it?'

She left soon after that, and I went to the window to watch her move off down the street towards Madison Avenue. God, I admired her just then! She looked so slight, so young, and so obviously pregnant – but there was still nothing timid or tentative about her. She did not scutter up the street; she walked as if she had every right to her place on the sidewalk.

She left my view and I turned back to my desk. As I did so, the framed photograph which hung on the wall next to my diploma caught my eye, and a terrible shudder worked through me. My skin – all of it, even the skin on my forehead and the backs of my hands – crawled up into cold knots of gooseflesh. The most suffocating fear of my entire life fell on me like a horrible shroud, and I found myself gasping for breath. It was a precognitive interlude, gentlemen. I do not take part in arguments about whether or not such things can occur; I know they can, because it has happened to me. Just that once, on that hot early September afternoon. I pray to God I never have another.

The photograph had been taken by my mother on the day I finished medical school. It showed me standing in front of White Memorial, hands behind my back, grinning like a kid who's just gotten a full-day pass to the rides at Palisades Park. To my left the statue of Harriet White can be seen, and although the photograph cuts her off at about mid-shin, the pedestal and that queerly heartless inscription – *There is no comfort without pain; thus we define salvation through suffering* – could be clearly seen. It was at the foot of the statue of my grandfather's first wife, directly below that inscription, that Sandra Stansfield died not quite four months later in a senseless accident that occurred just as she arrived at the hospital to deliver her child.

She exhibited some anxiety that fall that I would not be there to attend her during her labour – that I would be away for the Christmas holidays or not on call. She was partly afraid that she would be delivered by some doctor who would ignore her wish to use the Breathing Method and who would instead give her gas or a spinal block.

I assured her as best I could. I had no reason to leave the city, no family to visit over the holidays. My mother had died two years before, and there was no one else except a maiden aunt in California . . . and the train didn't agree with me, I told Miss Stansfield.

'Are you ever lonely?' she asked.

'Sometimes. Usually I keep too busy. Now, take this.' I jotted my home telephone number on a card and gave it to her. 'If you get the answering service when your labour begins, call me here.'

'Oh, no, I couldn't —'

'Do you want to use the Breathing Method, or do you want to get some sawbones who'll think you're mad and give you a capful of ether as soon as you start to "locomotive"?'

She smiled a little. 'All right. I'm convinced.'

But as the autumn progressed and the butchers on 3rd Avenue began advertising the per-pound price of their 'young and succulent Toms', it became clear that her mind was still not at rest. She had indeed been asked to leave the place where she had been living when I first met her, and had moved to the Village. But that, at least, had turned out quite well for her. She had even found work of a sort. A blind woman with a fairly comfortable income had hired her to come in twice a week, do some light housework, and then to read to her from the works of Jean Stratton-Porter and Pearl Buck. She had taken on that blooming, rosy look that most healthy women come to have during the final trimester of their pregnancies. But there was a shadow on her face. I would speak to her and she would be slow to answer . . . and once, when she didn't answer at all, I looked up from the notes I was making and saw her looking at the framed photograph next to my diploma with a strange, dreamy expression in her eyes. I felt a recurrence of that chill . . . and her response, which had nothing to do with my question, hardly made me feel easier.

'I have a feeling, Dr McCarron, sometimes quite a strong feeling, that I am doomed.'

Silly, melodramatic word! And yet, gentlemen, the response that rose to my own lips was this: *Yes; I feel that, too.* I bit it off, of course; a doctor who would say such a thing should immediately put his instruments and medical books up for sale and investigate his future in the plumbing or carpentry business.

I told her that she was not the first pregnant woman to have such feelings, and would not be the last. I told her that the feeling was indeed so common that doctors knew it by the tongue-in-cheek name of The Valley of the Shadow Syndrome. I've already mentioned it tonight, I believe.

Miss Stansfield nodded with perfect seriousness, and I remember how young she looked that day, and how large her belly seemed. 'I know about that,' she said. 'I've felt it. But it's quite separate from this other feeling. This other feeling is like . . . like something looming up. I can't describe it any better than that. It's silly, but I can't shake it.'

'You must try,' I said. 'It isn't good for the –'

But she had drifted away from me. She was looking at the photograph again.

'Who is that?'

'Emlyn McCarron,' I said, trying to make a joke. It sounded extraordinarily feeble. 'Back before the Civil War, when he was quite young.'

'No, I recognized you, of course,' she said. 'The woman. Who is the woman?'

'Her name is Harriet White,' I said, and thought: *And hers will be the first face you see when you arrive to deliver your child.* The chill came back – that dreadful drifting formless chill. *Her stone face.*

'And what does it say there at the base of the statue?' she asked, her eyes still dreamy, almost trancelike.

'I don't know,' I lied. 'My conversational Latin is not that good.'

That night I had the worst dream of my entire life – I woke up from it in utter terror, and if I had been married, I suppose I would have frightened my poor wife to death.

In the dream I opened the door to my consulting room and found Sandra Stansfield in there. She was wearing the brown pumps, the smart white linen dress with the brown edging, and the slightly out-of-date cloche hat. But the hat was between her breasts, because she was carrying her head in her arms. The white linen was stained and streaked with gore. Blood jetted from her neck and splattered the ceiling.

And then her eyes fluttered open – those wonderful hazel eyes – and they fixed on mine.

'Doomed,' the speaking head told me. 'Doomed. I'm doomed. There's no salvation without suffering. It's cheap magic, but it's all we have.'

That's when I woke up screaming.

★   ★   ★

Her due date of 10 December came and went. I examined her on 17 December and suggested that, while the baby would almost certainly be born in 1935, I no longer expected the child to put in his or her appearance until after Christmas. Miss Stansfield accepted this with good grace. She seemed to have thrown off the shadow that had hung over her that fall. Mrs Gibbs, the blind woman who had hired her to read aloud and do light housework, was impressed with her – impressed enough to tell her friends about the brave young widow who, in spite of her recent bereavement and delicate condition, was facing her own future with such determined good cheer. Several of the blind woman's friends had expressed an interest in employing her following the birth of her child.

'I'll take them up on it, too,' she told me. 'For the baby. But only until I'm on my feet again, and able to find something steady. Sometimes I think the worst part of this – of everything that's happened – is that it's changed the way I look at people. Sometimes I think to myself, "How can you sleep at night, knowing that you've deceived that dear old thing?" and then I think, "If she knew, she'd show you the door, just like all the others." Either way, it's a lie, and I feel the weight of it on my heart sometimes.'

Before she left that day, she took a small, gaily wrapped package from her purse and slid it shyly across the desk to me. 'Merry Christmas, Dr McCarron.'

'You shouldn't have,' I said, sliding open a drawer and taking out a package of my own. 'But since I did, too –'

She looked at me for a moment, surprised . . . and then we laughed together. She had gotten me a silver tie-clasp with the medical symbol on it. I had gotten her an album in which to keep photographs of her baby. I still have the tie-clasp. What happened to the album, I cannot say.

I saw her to the door, and as we reached it, she turned to me, put her hands on my shoulders, stood on tiptoe, and kissed me on the mouth. Her lips were cool and firm. It was not a passionate kiss, gentlemen, but neither was it the sort of kiss you might expect from a sister or an aunt.

'Thank you again, Dr McCarron,' she said a little breathlessly. The colour was high in her cheeks and her hazel eyes glowed lustrously. 'Thank you for so much.'

I laughed – a little uneasily. 'You speak as if we'll never meet again, Sandra.' It was, I believe, the second and last time I ever used her Christian name.

'Oh, we'll meet again,' she said. 'I don't doubt it a bit.'

And she was right – although neither of us could have foreseen the dreadful cricumstances of that last meeting.

Sandra Stansfield's labour began on Christmas Eve, at just past six p.m. By that time, the snow which had fallen all that day had changed to sleet. And by the time Miss Stansfield entered mid-labour, not quite two hours later, the city streets were a dangerous glaze of ice.

Mrs Gibbs, the blind woman, had a large and spacious first-floor apartment, and at 6.30 p.m. Miss Stansfield worked her way carefully downstairs, knocked at her door, was admitted, and asked if she might use the telephone to call a cab.

'Is it the baby, dear?' Mrs Gibbs asked, fluttering already.

'Yes. The labour's only begun, but I can't chance the weather. It will take a cab a long time.'

She made that call and then called me. At that time, 6.40,

the pains were coming at intervals of about twenty-five minutes. She repeated to me that she had begun everything early because of the foul weather. 'I'd rather not have my child in the back of a Yellow,' she said. She sounded extraordinarily calm.

The cab was late and Miss Stansfield's labour was progressing more rapidly than I would have predicted – but as I have said, no two labours are alike in their specifics. The driver, seeing that his fare was about to have a baby, helped her down the slick steps, constantly adjuring her to 'be careful, lady'. Miss Stansfield only nodded, preoccupied with her deep inhale-exhales as a fresh contraction seized her. Sleet ticked off streetlights and the roofs of cars; it melted in large, magnifying drops on the taxi's yellow dome-light. Miss Gibbs told me later that the young cab driver was more nervous than her 'poor, dear Sandra', and that was probably a contributing cause to the accident.

Another was almost certainly the Breathing Method itself.

The driver threaded his hack through the slippery streets, working his way slowly past the fender-benders and inching through the clogged intersections, slowly closing on the hospital. He was not seriously injured in the accident, and I talked to him in the hospital. He said the sound of the steady deep breathing coming from the back seat made him nervous; he kept looking in the rear view mirror to see if she was 'dine or sumpin''. He said he would have felt less nervous if she had let out a few healthy bellows, the way a woman in labour was supposed to do. He asked her once or twice if she was feeling all right and she only nodded, continuing to 'ride the waves' in deep inhales and exhales.

Two or three blocks from the hospital, she must have felt

the onset of labour's final stage. An hour had passed since she had entered the cab – the traffic was that snarled – but this was still an extraordinarily fast labour for a woman having her first baby. The driver noticed the change in the way she was breathing. 'She started pantin' like a dog on a hot day, Doc,' he told me. She had begun to 'locomotive'.

At almost the same time the cabbie saw a hole open up in the crawling cross-traffic and shot through it. The way to White Memorial was now open. It was less than three blocks ahead. 'I could see the statue of that broad,' he said. Eager to be rid of his panting, pregnant passenger, he stepped down on the gas again and the cab leaped forward, wheels spinning over the ice with little or no traction.

I had walked to the hospital, and my arrival coincided with the cab's arrival only because I had underestimated just how bad driving conditions had become. I believed I would find her upstairs, a legally admitted patient with all her papers signed, her prep completed, working her way steadily through her mid-labour. I was mounting the steps when I saw the sudden sharp convergence of two sets of headlights reflected from the patch of ice where the janitors hadn't yet spread cinders. I turned just in time to see it happen.

An ambulance was nosing its way out of the Emergency Wing rampway as Miss Stansfield's cab came across the Square and towards the hospital. The cab was simply going too fast to stop. The cabbie panicked and stamped down on the brake-pedal rather than pumping it. The cab slid, then began to turn broadside. The pulsing dome-light of the ambulance threw moving stripes and blotches of blood-coloured light over the scene, and, freakishly, one of these illuminated the face of Sandra Stansfield. For that one moment it was the face in my dream, the same bloody, open-eyed face that I had seen on her severed head.

I cried out her name, took two steps down, slipped, and fell sprawling. I cracked my elbow a paralyzing blow but somehow managed to hold on to my black bag. I saw the rest of what happened from where I lay, head ringing, elbow smarting.

The ambulance braked, and it also began to fishtail. Its rear end struck the base of the statue. The loading doors flew open. A stretcher, mercifully empty, shot out like a tongue and then crashed upside down in the street with its wheels spinning. A young woman on the sidewalk screamed as the two vehicles approached each other and tried to run. Her feet went out from under her after two strides and she fell on her stomach. Her purse flew out of her hand and shot down the icy sidewalk like a weight in a pinball bowling game.

The cab swung all the way around, now travelling backwards, and I could see the cabbie clearly. He was spinning his wheel madly, like a kid in a Dodgem Car. The ambulance rebounded from Mrs White's statue at an angle . . . and smashed broadside into the cab. The taxi spun around once in a tight circle and was slammed against the base of the statue with fearful force. Its yellow light, the letters ON RADIO CALL still flashing, exploded like a bomb. The left side of the cab crumpled like tissue-paper. A moment later I saw that it was not just the left side; the cab had struck an angle of the pedestal hard enough to tear it in two. Glass sprayed onto the slick ice like diamonds. And my patient was thrown through the rear right-side window of the dismembered cab like a rag-doll.

I was on my feet again without even knowing it. I raced down the icy steps, slipped again, caught at the railing, and kept on. I was only aware of Miss Stansfield lying in the uncertain shadow cast by that hideous statue of Harriet White, some twenty feet from where the ambulance had come to rest on its side, flasher still strobing the night with red. There was something terribly wrong with that figure, but I honestly don't believe I knew what it was until my foot struck something with a heavy enough thud to almost send me sprawling again. The thing I'd kicked skittered away – like the young woman's purse, it slid rather than rolled. It skittered away and it was only the fall of hair – bloodstreaked but still recognizably blonde, speckled with bits of glass – that made me realize what it was. She had been decapitated in the accident. What I had kicked into the frozen gutter was her head.

Moving in total numb shock, now I reached her body and turned it over. I think I tried to scream as soon as I had done it, as soon as I saw. If I did, no sound came out; I could not make a sound. The woman was still breathing, you see, gentlemen. Her chest was heaving up and down in quick, light, shallow breaths. Ice pattered down on her open coat and her blood-drenched dress. And I could hear a high, thin whistling noise. It waxed and waned like a teakettle which can't quite reach the boil. It was air being pulled into her severed windpipe and then exhaled again; the little screams of air through the crude reed of the vocal chords which no longer had a mouth to shape their sounds.

I wanted to run but I had no strength; I fell on my knees beside her on the ice, one hand cupped to my mouth. A moment later I was aware of fresh blood seeping through the lower part of her dress – and of movement there. I became suddenly, frenziedly convinced that there was still a chance to save the baby.

'Cheap magic!' I roared into the sleet, and I believe that as I yanked her dress up to her waist I began laughing. I believe I was mad. Her body was warm. I remember that. I remember the way it heaved with her breathing. One of the ambulance attendants came up, weaving like a drunk, one hand clapped to the side of his head. Blood trickled through his fingers.

'Cheap magic!' I screamed again, still laughing, still groping. My hands had found her fully dilated.

The attendant stared down at Sandra Stansfield's headless body with wide eyes. I don't know if he realized the corpse was still somehow breathing or not. Perhaps he thought it was merely a thing of the nerves – a kind of final reflex action. If he did think such a thing, he could not have been driving an ambulance long. Chickens may walk around for a while with their heads cut off, but people only twitch once or twice . . . if that.

'Stop staring at her and get me a blanket,' I snapped at him.

He wandered away, but not back towards the ambulance. He was pointed more or less towards Times Square. He simply walked off into the sleety night. I have no idea what became of him. I turned back to the dead woman who was somehow not dead, hesitated a moment, and then stripped off my overcoat. Then I lifted her hips so I could get it under her. Still I heard that whistle of breath as her head-less body did 'locomotive' breathing. I sometimes hear it still, gentlemen. In my dreams.

Please understand that all of this had happened in an

extremely short time – it seemed longer to me, but only because my perceptions had been heightened to a feverish pitch. People were only beginning to run out of the hospital to see what had happened, and behind me a woman shrieked as she saw the severed head lying by the edge of the street.

I yanked open my black bag, thanking God I hadn't lost it in my fall, and pulled out a short scalpel. I opened it, cut through her underwear, and pulled it off. Now the ambulance driver approached – he came to within fifteen feet of us and then stopped dead. I glanced over at him, still wanting that blanket. I wasn't going to get it from him, I saw; he was staring down at the breathing body, his eyes widening until it seemed they must slip from their orbits and simply dangle from their optic nerves like grotesque seeing yo-yos. Then he dropped to his knees and raised his clasped hands. He meant to pray, I am quite sure of that. The attendant might not have known he was seeing an impossibility, but this fellow did. The next moment he had fainted dead away.

I had packed forceps in my bag that night; I don't know why. I hadn't used such things in three years, not since I had seen a doctor I will not name punch through a newborn's temple and into the child's brain with one of those infernal gadgets. The child died instantly. The corpse was 'lost' and what went on the death certificate was *stillborn*. But, for whatever reason, I had them.

Miss Stansfield's body tightened down, her belly clenching, turning from flesh to stone. And the baby crowned. I saw the crown for just a moment, bloody and membranous and pulsing. *Pulsing*. It was alive, at least then. Definitely alive.

Stone became flesh again. The crown slipped back out of sight. And a voice behind me said: 'What can I do, Doctor?'

It was a middle-aged nurse, the sort of woman who is so often the backbone of our profession. Her face was as pale as milk, and while there was terror and a kind of superstitious awe on her face as she looked down at that weirdly breathing body, there was none of that dazed shock which would have made her difficult and dangerous to work with.

'You can get me a blanket, stat,' I said curtly. 'We've still got a chance, I think.' Behind her I saw perhaps two dozen people from the hospital standing on the steps, not wanting to come any closer. How much or how little did they see? I have no way of knowing for sure. All I know is that I was avoided for days afterwards (and forever by some of them), and no one, including this nurse, ever spoke to me of it.

She now turned and started back towards the hospital.

'Nurse!' I called. 'No time for that. Get one from the ambulance. This baby is coming *now*.'

She changed course, slipping and sliding through the slush in her white crêpe-soled shoes. I turned back to Miss Stansfield.

Rather than slowing down, the locomotive breathing had actually begun to speed up . . . and then her body turned hard again, locked and straining. The baby crowned again. I waited for it to slip back but it did not; it simply kept coming. There was no need for the forceps after all. The baby all but *flew* into my hands. I saw the sleet ticking off its naked, bloody body – for it *was* a boy, his sex unmistakable. I saw steam rising from it as the black, icy night snatched away the last of its mother's heat. Its blood-grimed fists waved feebly; it uttered a thin, wailing cry.

'*Nurse!*' I bawled, '*move your ass, you bitch!*' It was perhaps inexcusable language, but for a moment I felt I was back in France, that in a few moments the shells would begin to whistle overhead with a sound like that remorselessly ticking sleet; the machine-guns would begin their hellish stutter; the Germans would begin to materialize out of the murk, running and slipping and cursing and dying in the mud and smoke. *Cheap magic*, I thought, seeing the bodies twist and turn and fall. *But you're right, Sandra, it's all we have.* It was the closest I have ever come to losing my mind, gentlemen.

'NURSE, FOR GOD'S SAKE!'

The baby wailed again – such a tiny, lost sound! – and then it wailed no more. The steam rising from its skin had thinned to ribbons. I put my mouth against its face, smelling blood and the bland, damp aroma of placenta. I breathed into its mouth and heard the jerky susurrus of its breathing resume. Then the nurse was there, the blanket in her arms. I held out my hand for it.

She started to give it to me, and then held it back. 'Doctor, what . . . what if it's a monster? Some kind of monster?'

'Give me that blanket,' I said. 'Give it to me now, Sarge, before I kick your fucking asshole right up your fucking shoulderblades.'

'Yes, doctor,' she said with perfect calmness (we must bless the women, gentlemen, who so often understand simply by not trying to), and gave me the blanket. I wrapped the child and gave it to her.

'If you drop him, Sarge, you'll be eating those stripes.'

'Yes, doctor.'

'It's cheap fucking magic, Sarge, but it's all God left us with.'

'Yes, doctor.'

I watched her half-walk, half-run back to the hospital with the child and watched the crowd on the steps part for her. Then I rose to my feet and backed away from the body. Its breathing, like the baby's, hitched and caught . . . stopped . . . hitched again . . . stopped . . .

I began to back away from it. My foot struck something. I turned. It was her head. And obeying some directive from outside of me, I dropped to one knee and turned the head over. The eyes were open – those direct hazel eyes that had always been full of such life and such determination. They were full of determination still. Gentlemen, *she was seeing me*.

Her teeth were clenched, her lips slightly parted. I heard the breath slipping rapidly back and forth between those lips and through those teeth as she 'locomotived'. Her eyes moved; they rolled slightly to the left in their sockets so as to see me better. Her lips parted. They mouthed four words: *Thank you, Doctor McCarron*. And I *heard* them, gentlemen, but not from her mouth. They came from twenty feet away. From her vocal cords. And because her tongue and lips and teeth, all of which we use to shape our words, were here, they came out only in unformed modulations of sound. But there were seven of them, seven distinct sounds, just as there are seven syllables in that phrase, *Thank you, Doctor McCarron*.

'You're welcome, Miss Stansfield,' I said. 'It's a boy.'

Her lips moved again, and from behind me, thin, ghostly, came the sound *hoyyyyyy* –

Her eyes lost their focus and their determination. They seemed now to look at something beyond me, perhaps in that black, sleety sky. Then they closed. She began to loco-motive again . . . and then she simply stopped. Whatever had happened was now over. The nurse had seen some of it, the ambulance driver had perhaps seen some of it before he fainted. But it was over now, over for sure. There was only the remains of an ugly accident out here . . . and a new baby in there.

I looked up at the statue of Harriet White and there she still stood, looking stonily away towards the Garden across the way, as if nothing of any particular note had happened, as if such determination in a world as hard and as senseless as this one meant nothing . . . or worse still, that it was perhaps the only thing which meant *anything*, the only thing that made any difference at all.

As I recall, I knelt there in the slush before her severed head and began to weep. As I recall, I was still weeping when an intern and two nurses helped me to my feet and inside.

McCarron's pipe had gone out.

He relit it with his bolt-lighter while we sat in perfect, breathless silence. Outside, the wind howled and moaned. He snapped his lighter closed and looked up. He seemed mildly surprised to find us still there.

'That's all,' he said. 'That's the end! What are you waiting for? Chariots of fire?' He snorted, then seemed to debate for a moment. 'I paid her burial expenses out of my own pocket. She had no one else, you see.' He smiled a little. 'Well . . . there was Ella Davidson, my nurse. She insisted on chipping in twenty-five dollars, which she could ill afford. But when Davidson insisted on a thing –' He shrugged, and then laughed a little.

'You're quite sure it wasn't a reflex?' I heard myself demanding suddenly. 'Are you *quite* sure –'

'Quite sure,' McCarron said imperturbably. 'The first contraction, perhaps. But the completion of her labour was not a matter of seconds but of minutes. And I sometimes think she might have held on even longer, if it had been necessary. Thank God it was not.'

'What about the baby?' Johanssen asked.

McCarron puffed at his pipe. 'Adopted,' he said. 'And you'll understand that, even in those days, adoption records were kept as secret as possible.'

'Yes, but what about the baby?' Johanssen asked again, and McCarron laughed in a cross way.

'You never let go of a thing, do you?' he asked Johanssen.

Johanssen shook his head. 'Some people have learned it to their sorrow. What about the baby?'

'Well, if you've come with me this far perhaps you'll also understand that I had a certain vested interest in knowing how it all came out for that child. Or I felt that I did. There was a young man and his wife – their name was not Harrison, but that is close enough. They lived in Maine. They could have no children of their own. They adopted the child and named him . . . well, John's good enough, isn't it? John will do you fellows, won't it?'

He puffed at his pipe but it had gone out again. I was faintly aware of Stevens hovering behind me, and knew that somewhere our coats would be at the ready. Soon we would slip back into them . . . and back into our lives. As McCarron had said, the tales were done for another year.

'The child I delivered that night is now head of the English Department at one of the two or three most respected private colleges in the country,' McCarron said. 'He's not forty-five yet. A young man. It's early for him, but the day may well come when he will be President of that school. I shouldn't doubt it a bit. He is handsome, intelligent, and charming.

'Once, on a pretext, I was able to dine with him in the private faculty club. We were four that evening. I said little and so was able to watch him. He has his mother's determination, gentlemen . . .

'. . . and his mother's hazel eyes.'

3: The Club

Stevens saw us out as he always did, holding coats, wishing men the happiest of happy Christmases, thanking them for their generosity. I contrived to be the last, and Stevens looked at me with no surprise when I said:

'I have a question I'd like to ask, if you don't mind.'

He smiled a little. 'I suppose you should,' he said. 'Christmas is a fine time for questions.'

Somewhere down the hallway to our left – a hall I had never been down – a grandfather clock ticked sonorously, the sound of the age passing away. I could smell old leather and oiled wood and, much more faintly than either of these, the smell of Stevens's aftershave.

'But I should warn you,' Stevens added as the wind rose in a gust outside, 'it's better not to ask too much. Not if you want to keep coming here.'

'People have been closed out for asking too much?' *Closed out* was not really the phrase I wanted, but it was as close as I could come.

'No,' Stevens said, his voice as low and polite as ever. 'They simply choose to stay away.'

I returned his gaze, feeling a chill prickle its way up my

back – it was as if a large, cold, invisible hand had been laid on my spine. I found myself remembering that strangely liquid thump I had heard upstairs one night and wondered (as I had more than once before) exactly how many rooms there really *were* here.

'If you still have a question, Mr Adley, perhaps you'd better ask it. The evening's almost over –'

'And you have a long train-ride ahead of you?' I asked, but Stevens only looked at me impassively. 'All right,' I said. 'There are books in this library that I can't find anywhere else – not in the New York Public Library, not in the catalogues of any of the antiquarian book-dealers I've checked with, and certainly not in *Books in Print*. The billiard table in the Small Room is a Nord. I'd never heard of such a brand, and so I called the International Trademark Commission. They have two Nords – one makes cross-country skis and the other makes wooden kitchen accessories. There's a Seafront jukebox in the Long Room. The ITC has a See*burg* listed, but no Sea*front*.'

'What is your question, Mr Adley?'

His voice was as mild as ever, but there was something terrible in his eyes suddenly . . . no; if I am to be truthful, it was not just in his eyes; the terror I felt had infused the atmosphere all around me. The steady tock-tock from down the lefthand hall was no longer the pendulum of a grand-father clock; it was the tapping foot of the executioner as he watches the condemned led to the scaffold. The smells of oil and leather turned bitter and menacing, and when the wind rose in another wild whoop, I felt momentarily sure that the front door would blow open, revealing not 35th Street but an insane Clark Ashton Smith landscape where the bitter shapes of twisted trees stood silhouetted on a sterile horizon below which double suns were setting in a gruesome red glare.

Oh, he knew what I had meant to ask; I saw it in his grey eyes.

Where do all these things come from? I had meant to ask. Oh, I know well enough where you come from, Stevens; that accent isn't Dimension X, it's pure Brooklyn. But where do you go? What has put that timeless look in your eyes and stamped it on your face? And, Stevens —

— where are we RIGHT THIS SECOND?

But he was waiting for my question.

I opened my mouth. And the question that came out was: 'Are there many more rooms upstairs?'

'Oh, yes, sir,' he said, his eyes never leaving mine. 'A great many. A man could become lost. In fact, men *have* become lost. Sometimes it seems to me that they go on for miles. Rooms and corridors.'

'And entrances and exits?'

His eyebrows went up slightly. 'Oh yes. Entrances and exits.'

He waited, but I had asked enough, I thought — I had come to the very edge of something that would, perhaps, drive me mad.

'Thank you, Stevens.'

'Of course, sir.' He held out my coat and I slipped into it.

'There will be more tales?'

'Here, sir, there are *always* more tales.'

That evening was some time ago, and my memory has not improved between then and now (when a man reaches my age, the opposite is much more likely to be true), but I remember with perfect clarity the stab of fear that went through me when Stevens swung the oaken door wide – the cold certainty that I would see that alien landscape, cracked and hellish in the bloody light of those double suns, which might set and bring on an unspeakable darkness of an hour's duration, or ten hours, or ten thousand years. I cannot explain it, but I tell you that world *exists* – I am as sure of that as Emlyn McCarron was sure that the severed head of Sandra Stansfield went on breathing. I thought for that one timeless second that the door would open and Stevens would thrust me out into that world and I would then hear that door slam shut behind me . . . forever.

Instead, I saw 35th Street and a radio-cab standing at the curb, exhaling plumes of exhaust. I felt an utter, almost debilitating relief.

'Yes, always more tales,' Stevens repeated. 'Goodnight, sir.'

Always more tales.

Indeed there have been. And, one day soon, perhaps I'll tell you another.

AFTERWORD

'Although 'Where do you get your ideas?' has always been the question I'm most frequently asked (it's number one with a bullet, you might say), the runner-up is undoubtedly this one: 'Is horror *all* you write?' When I say it isn't, it's hard to tell if the questioner seems relieved or disappointed.

Just before the publication of *Carrie*, my first novel, I got a letter from my editor, Bill Thompson, suggesting it was time to start thinking about what we were going to do for an encore (it may strike you as a bit strange, this thinking about the next book before the first was even out, but because the pre-publication schedule for a novel is almost as long as the post-production schedule on a film, we had been living with *Carrie* for a long time at that point – nearly a year). I promptly sent Bill the manuscripts of two novels, one called *Blaze* and one called *Second Coming*. The former had been written immediately after *Carrie*, during the six-month period when the first draft of *Carrie* was sitting in a desk drawer, mellowing; the latter was written during the year or so when *Carrie* inched, tortoiselike, closer and closer to publication.

Blaze was a melodrama about a huge, almost retarded criminal who kidnaps a baby, planning to ransom it back to the child's rich parents . . . and then falls in love with the child instead. *Second Coming* was a melodrama about vampires taking over a small town in Maine. Both were literary imitations of a sort, *Second Coming* of *Dracula*, *Blaze* of Steinbeck's *Of Mice and Men*.

I think Bill must have been flabbergasted when these two manuscripts arrived in a single big package (some of the pages of *Blaze* had been typed on the reverse sides of milkbills, and the *Second Coming* manuscript reeked of beer because someone had spilled a pitcher of Black Label on it during a New Year's Eve party three months before) – like a woman who wishes for a bouquet of flowers and discovers her husband has gone out and bought her a hothouse. The two manuscripts together totalled about five hundred and fifty single-spaced pages.

He read them both over the next couple of weeks – scratch an editor and find a saint – and I went down to New York from Maine to celebrate the publication of *Carrie* (April, 1974, friends and neighbours – Lennon was alive, Nixon was still hanging in there as President, and this kid had yet to see the first grey hair in his beard) and to talk about which of the two books should be next . . . or if neither of them should be next.

I was in the city for a couple of days, and we talked around the question three or four times. The final decision was made on a street-corner – Park Avenue and 44th Street, in fact. Bill and I were standing there waiting for the light, watching the cabs roll into that funky tunnel or whatever it is – the one that seems to burrow straight through the Pan Am Building. And Bill said, 'I think it should be *Second Coming.*'

Well, that was the one I liked better myself – but there was something so oddly reluctant in his voice that I looked at him sharply and asked him what the matter was. 'It's just that if you do a book about vampires as the follow-up to a book about a girl who can move things by mind-power, you're going to get typed,' he said.

'Typed?' I asked, honestly bewildered. I could see no similarities to speak of between vampires and telekinesis. 'As *what*?'

'As a horror-writer,' he said, more reluctantly still.

'Oh,' I said, vastly relieved. 'Is *that* all!'

'Give it a few years,' he said, 'and see if you still think it's "all".'

'Bill,' I said, amused, 'no one can make a living writing just horror stories in America. Lovecraft starved in Providence. Bloch gave it up for suspense novels and *Unknown*-type spoofs. *The Exorcist* was a one-shot. You'll see.'

The light changed. Bill clapped me on the shoulder. 'I think you're going to be very successful,' he said, 'but I don't think you know shit from Shinola.'

He was closer to the truth than I was. It turned out that it *was* possible to make a living writing horror stories in America. *Second Coming*, eventually retitled *'Salem's Lot*, did very well. By the time it was published, I was living in Colorado with my family and writing a novel about a haunted hotel. On a trip into New York, I sat up with Bill half the night in a bar called Jasper's of the Rock-Ola; you had to kind of lift him up to see what the selections were, and told him the plot. By the end, his elbows were planted on either side of his bourbon and his head was in his hands, like a man with a monster migraine.

'You don't like it,' I said.

'I like it a lot,' he said hollowly.

'Then what's wrong?'

'*First* the telekinetic girl, *then* the vampires, *now* the haunted hotel and the telepathic kid. You're gonna get typed.'

This time I thought about it a little more seriously – and then I thought about all the people who *had* been typed as horror writers, and who had given me such great pleasure over the years – Lovecraft, Clark Ashton Smith, Frank Belknap Long, Fritz Leiber, Robert Bloch, Richard Matheson, and Shirley Jackson (yes, even she was typed as a spook writer). And I decided there in Jasper's with the cat asleep on the juke and my editor sitting beside me with his head in his hands, that I could be in worse company. I could, for example, be an 'important' writer like Joseph Heller and publish a novel every seven years or so, or a 'brilliant' writer like John Gardner and write obscure books for bright academics who eat macrobiotic foods and drive old Saabs with faded but still legible GENE McCARTHY FOR PRESIDENT stickers on the rear bumpers.

'That's okay, Bill,' I said, 'I'll be a horror writer if that's what people want. That's just fine.'

We never had the discussion again. Bill's still editing and I'm still writing horror stories, and neither of us is in analysis. It's a good deal.

So I got typed and I don't much mind – after all, I write true to type . . . at least, *most* of the time. But is horror *all* I write? If you've read the foregoing stories, you *know* it's not . . . but elements of horror can be found in all of the tales, not just in *The Breathing Method* – that business with the slugs in *The Body* is pretty gruesome, as is much of the dream imagery in *Apt Pupil*. Sooner or later, my mind always seems to turn back in that direction, God knows why.

Each one of these longish stories was written immediately after completing a novel – it's as if I've always finished the big job with just enough gas left in the tank to blow off one good-sized novella. *The Body*, the oldest story here, was written direct after *'Salem's Lot*; *Apt Pupil* was written in a two-week period following the completion of *The Shining* (and following *Apt Pupil* I wrote nothing for three months – I was pooped); *Rita Hayworth and Shawshank Redemption* was written after finishing *The Dead Zone*; and *The Breathing Method*, the most recently written of these stories, immediately following *Firestarter*.*

None of them has been published previous to this book; none has even been submitted for publication. Why? Because each of them comes out to 25,000 to 35,000 words – not exactly, maybe, but that's close enough to be in the ballpark. I've got to tell you: 25,000 to 35,000 words are numbers apt to make even the most stout-hearted writer of fiction shake and shiver in his boots. There is no hard-and-fast definition of what either a novel or a short story is – at least not in terms of word-count – nor should there be. But when a writer approaches the 20,000-word mark, he knows he is edging out of the country of the short story. Likewise, when he passes the 40,000-word mark, he is edging into the country of the novel. The borders of the country between these two more orderly regions are ill-defined, but at some point the writer wakes up with alarm and realizes that he's come or is coming to a really terrible place, an anarchy-ridden literary banana republic called the 'novella' (or, rather too cutesy for my taste, the 'novelette').

---

*Something else about them, which I just realized: each one was written in a different house – three of those in Maine and one in Boulder, Colorado.

Now, artistically speaking, there's nothing at all wrong with the novella. Of course, there's nothing wrong with circus freaks, either, except that you rarely see them outside of the circus. The point is that there are great novellas, but they traditionally only sell to the 'genre markets' (that's the polite term; the impolite but more accurate one is 'ghetto markets'). You can sell a good mystery novella to *Ellery Queen's Mystery Magazine* or *Mike Shayne's Mystery Magazine*, a good science fiction novella to *Amazing* or *Analog*, maybe even to *Omni* or *The Magazine of Fantasy and Science Fiction*. Ironically, there are also markets for good horror novellas: the aforementioned *F&SF* is one; *The Twilight Zone* is another and there are various anthologies of original creepy fiction, such as the *Shadows* series published by Doubleday and edited by Charles L. Grant.

But for novellas which can, on measure, only be described with the word 'mainstream' (a word almost as depressing as 'genre') . . . boy, as far as marketability goes, you in a heap o' trouble. You look at your 25,000-to-35,000-word manuscript dismally, twist the cap off a beer, and in your head you seem to hear a heavily accented and rather greasy voice saying: '*Buenos dias, señor*! How was your flight on Revolución Airways? You like to eeet pretty-good fine I theenk, *si*? Welcome to Novella, *señor*! You going to like heet here preety-good-fine, I theenk! Have a cheap cigar! Have some feelthy peectures! Put your feet up, *señor*, I theenk your story is going to be here a long, *long* time . . . *qué pasa*? Ah-ha-hah-hah-hah!'

Depressing.

Once upon a time (he mourned) there really *was* a market for such tales – there were magical magazines such as *The Saturday Evening Post*, *Collier's*, and *The American Mercury*. Fiction – fiction both short and long – was a staple of these and others. And, if the story was too long for a single issue, it was serialized in three parts, or five, or nine. The poisonous idea of 'condensing' or 'excerpting' novels was as yet unknown (both *Playboy* and *Cosmopolitan* have honed this particular obscenity to a noxious science: you can now read an entire novel in twenty minutes!), the tale was given the space it demanded, and I doubt if I'm the only one who can remember waiting for the mailman all day long because the new *Post* was due and a new short story by Ray Bradbury had been promised, or perhaps because the final episode of the latest Clarence Buddington Kelland serial was due.

(My anxiety made me a particularly easy mark. When the postman finally did show up, walking briskly with his leather bag over his shoulder, dressed in his summer-issue shorts and wearing his summer-issue sun helmet, I'd meet him at the end of the walk, dancing from one foot to the other as if I badly needed to go to the bathroom; my heart in my throat. Grinning rather cruelly, he'd hand me an electric bill. Nothing but that. Heart plummets into my shoes. Finally he relents and gives me the *Post* after all: grinning Eisenhower on the cover, painted by Norman Rockwell; an article on Sophia Loren by Pete Martin; 'I Say He's a Wonderful Guy', by Pat Nixon, concerning – yeah, you guessed it – her husband Richard; and, of course, stories. Long ones, short ones, and the last chapter of the Kelland serial. Praise God!)

And this didn't happen just once in a while; this happened *every fucking week*! The day that the *Post* came, I guess I was the happiest kid on the whole eastern seaboard.

There are still magazines that publish long fiction – *Atlantic Monthly* and *The New Yorker* are two which have been particularly sympathetic to the publication problems of a writer who has delivered (we won't say 'gotten'; that's too close to 'misbegotten') a 30,000-word novella. But neither of these magazines has been particularly receptive to my stuff, which is fairly plain, not very literary, and sometimes (although it hurts like hell to admit it) downright clumsy.

To some degree or other, I would guess that those very qualities – unadmirable though they may be – have been responsible for the success of my novels. Most of them have been plain fiction for plain folks, the literary equivalent of a Big Mac and a large fries from McDonald's. I am able to recognize elegant prose and to respond to it, but have found it difficult or impossible to write it myself (most of my idols as a maturing writer were muscular novelists with prose styles which ranged from the horrible to the nonexistent: cats like Theodore Dreiser and Frank Norris). Subtract elegance from the novelist's craft and one finds himself left with only one strong leg to stand on, and that leg is good weight. As a result, I've tried as hard as I can, always, to give good weight. Put another way, if you find out you can't run like a thoroughbred, you can still pull your brains out (A voice rises from the balcony: '*What* brains, King?' Ha-ha, very funny, fella, you can leave now).

The result of all this is that, when it came to the novellas you've just read, I found myself in a puzzling position. I had gotten to a place with my novels where people were saying King could publish his laundry list if he wanted to (and there are critics who claim that's exactly what I've been doing for the last eight years or so), but I couldn't publish these tales because they were too long to be short and too short to be really long. If you see what I mean.

'*Si, señor*, I see! Take off your shoes! Have some cheap rum! Soon thee Medicore Revolución Steel Band iss gonna come along and play some bad calypso! You like eet preety-good-fine, I theenk! And you got time, *señor*! You got time because I theenk your story ees gonna –'

– be here a long time, yeah, yeah, great, why don't you go somewhere and overthrow a puppet imperialist democracy?

So I finally decided to see if Viking, my hardcover publisher, and New American Library, my paperback publisher, would want to do a book with stories in it about an off-beat prison-break, an old man and a young boy locked up in a gruesome relationship based on mutual parasitism, a quartet of country boys on a journey of discovery, and an off-the-wall horror story about a young woman determined to give birth to her child no matter what (or maybe the story is actually about that odd Club that isn't a Club). The publishers said okay. And that is how I managed to break these four long stories out of the banana republic of the novella.

I hope you liked them preety-good-fine, *muchachos* and *muchachas*.

Oh, one thing about type-casting before I call it a day.

Was talking to my editor – not Bill Thompson, this is my *new* editor, real nice guy named Alan Williams, smart, witty, able, but usually on jury duty somewhere deep in the bowels of New Jersey – about a year ago.

'Loved *Cujo*,' Alan says (the editorial work on that novel, a real shaggy-dog story, had just been completed). 'Have you thought about what you're going to do next?'

Déjà vu sets in. I have had this conversation before.

'Well, yeah,' I say. 'I *have* given it some thought —'

'Lay it on me.'

'What would you think about a book of four novellas? Most or all of them just sort of ordinary stories? What would you think about that?'

'Novellas,' Alan says. He is being a good sport, but his voice says some of the joy may have just gone out of his day; his voice says he feels he has just won two tickets to some dubious little banana republic on Revolución Airways. 'Long stories, you mean.'

'Yeah, that's right,' I say. 'And we'll call the book something like "Different Seasons", just so people will get the idea that it's not about vampires or haunted hotels or anything like that.'

'Is the *next* one going to be about vampires?' Alan asks hopefully.

'No, I don't think so. What do you think, Alan?'

'A haunted hotel, maybe?'

'No, I did that one, already. *Different Seasons*, Alan. It's got a nice ring to it, don't you think?'

'It's got a great ring, Steve,' Alan says, and sighs. It is the sigh of a good sport who has just taken his seat in third class on Revolución Airways' newest plane — a Lockheed Tri-Star — and has seen the first cockroach trundling busily over the top of the seat ahead of him.

'I hoped you'd like it,' I say.

'I don't suppose,' Alan says, 'we could have a horror story in it? Just one? A sort of . . . *similar* season?'

I smile a little — just a little — thinking of Sandra Stansfield and Dr McCarron's Breathing Method. 'I can probably whomp something up.'

'Great! And about the new novel –'

'How about a haunted car?' I say.

'My *man*!' Alan cries. I have the feeling that I'm sending him back to his editorial meeting – or possibly to jury duty in East Rahway – a happy man. I'm happy, too – I *love* my haunted car, and I think it's going to make a lot of people nervous about crossing busy streets after dark.

But I've been in love with each of these stories, too, and part of me always will be in love with them, I guess. I hope that you liked them, Reader; that they did for you what any good story should do – make you forget the real stuff weighing on your mind for a little while and take you away to a place you've never been. It's the most amiable sort of magic I know.

Okay. Gotta split. Until we see each other again, keep your head together, read some good books, be useful, and don't take any shit from anybody.

Love and good wishes,

Stephen King
January 4th, 1982
Bangor, Maine